BELLE ISLE TO 8 MILE:
AN INSIDER'S GUIDE TO DETROIT
SECOND EDITION

Editors:
Andy Linn, Emily Linn, and Rob Linn

Authors:
Ryan Healy, Andy Linn, Emily Linn, and Rob Linn

Contributing Authors:
Cassie Basler, Rachel Harkai, Lisa Kim, Greg Lenhoff,
Alison Piech Linn, Jennifer Quartararo, and Rachel Reed

Contributors:
Sara Aldridge, D'Marco Ansari, Justin Ames, Maia Asshaq,
Matt Beuckelaere, Achille Bianchi, Amy Elliott Bragg,
Margaret Cassetto, John Drain, Anna Hipsman-Springer,
Emily Kostrzewa, Matthew Lewis, Diane Linn, Thom Linn,
Steph Manor, Zach Massad, Matt McIntyre, Aaron Mondry,
Glen Morren, John Notarianni, Kit Parks, Matthew Piper, Jim
Sechelski, Nicole Rupersburg, Molly Schoen, and
Angela Wisniewski

Project Manager: Andy Linn
Cover Design: Emily Linn
Illustrations: Courtney Jentzen and Emily Linn
Design and Layout: Andrea Farhat and Angela Fortino
Map Design: Rob Linn
Copy Editing: Dan Austin and Diane Linn

Published by City Bird, LLC

ISBN: 978-0-578-42269-5
Second Edition

Written, researched, designed, illustrated, edited, and printed in Detroit, Michigan.

If you discover errors, corrections, or possible additions, please drop us a line: belleisleto8mile@gmail.com.

Belle Isle to 8 Mile: An Insider's Guide to Detroit is available for purchase by institutions and retailers. For information, send inquiries to: wholesale@citybirddetroit.com.

This book is dedicated to our parents, Thom and Diane Linn—for their endless support and love, and for always believing in Detroit—and to our favorite city kid, Arthur Linn Beuckelaere, for inspiring us with his boundless curiosity and enthusiasm.

We're grateful to Matt Beuckelaere, Alison Piech Linn, and Steph Manor for their incredible kindness, support, and patience.

This project would not have been possible without those who generously supported the first edition of the book, including the Awesome News Taskforce Detroit, Detroit SOUP, The Next Big Thing presented by Model D, and our Kickstarter backers.

CONTENTS

WELCOME
TO DETROIT

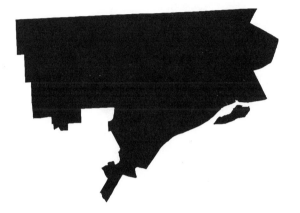

NUMBER	NEIGHBORHOOD	6	NEW CENTER AREA
1	DOWNTOWN	7	EAST RIVERFRONT
2	MIDTOWN	8	UPPER EAST SIDE
3	EASTERN MARKET	9	AVENUE OF FASHION AREA
4	CORKTOWN	10	FAR WEST SIDE
5	SOUTHWEST	11	HAMTRAMCK & HIGHLAND PARK

MILES

0   1.25   2.5   5

WELCOME TO DETROIT

Whether traveling from across the globe or across 8 Mile Road, visitors to Detroit should come expecting an authentic, resilient city with a rich history and an exciting present. With a past as French as New Orleans', a musical heritage as significant as Nashville's, and a hardscrabble working-class legacy that has earned it the nickname "The Motor City," Detroit offers an unparalleled glimpse at American history through a beauty that can be difficult to capture. Detroit's troubles have been well-documented, but it has nothing left to hide, and a new chapter of its story has begun. In this resurgent city of neighborhoods, each community offers a different angle on the same prism: blue-collar epicureanism, raw art, bootstrap entrepreneurship, moxie-filled residents, and historic architecture. Whether in town for an instant or indefinitely, visitors and residents should look forward to an effusive welcome and numerous opportunities for immersion, inquiry, indulgence, inebriation, and introspection in a city that never misses an opportunity for celebration or inspiration.

HISTORY

1701 to World War II - Founded as a French city in 1701—when New Orleans was just a twinkle in Louis XIV's eye—Detroit embarked on what would become a proud, dynamic history several generations before the United States became a country. Built in the heart of Miami, Huron, and Ottawa tribal territories, city founder Antoine de La Mothe Cadillac named his settlement for the Detroit River—le détroit du Lac Érié—or, the strait of Lake Erie—and helped establish the city's ribbon farms. These long, narrow farms stretched several miles from the river and gave rise to a burgeoning agricultural center. After the Erie Canal opened in 1825, the city quickly became a center of Great Lakes transportation, shipbuilding, and manufacturing, and began its meteoric rise. Between 1820 and 1920, Detroit's population more than doubled nearly every decade, from 1,422 to 993,678 over a century. In 1896, a young Henry Ford built his first automobile, forever altering the city's future. Ford was soon joined by automotive luminaries such as William Durant, James Packard, Louis Chevrolet, Walter Chrysler, David Dunbar Buick, and the Dodge brothers, and Detroit quickly emerged as the world's center of automobile manufacturing. Attracted by middle-class

salaries and bountiful single-family homes, thousands of residents moved to the city each month until the dawn of World War II.

Post-World War II - Despite a proud, dynamic history for its first 250 years, Detroit is perhaps most associated with its most recent historical chapter. Although it served as the "Arsenal of Democracy" and manufactured materiel during the war, the end of World War II marked the beginning of a long, challenging time for the city. New manufacturing strategies and postwar trends in single-family housing, coupled with plant closures, ill-advised government policy, suburban sprawl, redlining, highway construction, urban renewal, racism, white flight, contagious abandonment, unemployment, and crime created a perfect storm that perpetuated rapid population loss. Despite promising developments Downtown, and tenacious positive action by neighborhood residents and community groups, the city lost a crippling 1,135,791 residents—60% of its population— between 1950 and 2010.

Today - In recent years, the city has developed a renewed energy. In the core neighborhoods especially, new bars, restaurants, shops, and cultural attractions are opening alongside their steadfast, older counterparts. While outlying neighborhoods have traditionally been the most challenged by the city's problems, many are emerging with newfound vitality, as communities discover new, innovative approaches to reactivating vacant spaces and dealing with abandonment. These incremental, positive developments have spurred a change in public perception.

Further Reading - Those looking to learn more about the history, culture, and evolution of Detroit should check out one or more of the following books. Many of these titles are written by local authors and scholars—including Dan Austin, Amy Elliott Bragg, John Carlisle, John Gallagher, and Bill McGraw—who have played an important role in a recent surge of interest in the city's history.

- *313: Life in the Motor City* - John Carlisle
- *A Detroit Anthology* - Anna Clark
- *American Odyssey* - Robert E. Conot
- *Arc of Justice* - Kevin Boyle
- *Before Motown* - Lars Bjorn and Jim Gallert
- *The Buildings of Detroit* - W. Hawkins Ferry

- *Detroit 1967: Origins, Impacts, Legacies* - Joel Stone
- *The Detroit Almanac* - Peter Gavrilovich and Bill McGraw
- *Forgotten Landmarks of Detroit* - Dan Austin
- *Greetings from Detroit: Historic Postcards from the Motor City* - Dan Austin
- *Grit, Noise, and Revolution* - David Carson
- *Hard Stuff* - Coleman Young and Lonnie Wheeler
- *Hidden History of Detroit* - Amy Elliott Bragg
- *How To Live In Detroit Without Being A Jackass* - Aaron Foley
- *Lafayette Park Detroit* - Charles Waldheim
- *The Origins of the Urban Crisis* - Thomas J. Sugrue
- *Reimagining Detroit* - John Gallagher
- *The Unreal Estate Guide to Detroit* - Andrew Herscher

PLANNING YOUR VISIT

Pure Michigan Detroit Welcome Center - For visitors stopping in Detroit before heading elsewhere in Michigan, the Pure Michigan Detroit Welcome Center offers a host of information about Detroit and other Michigan cities, including lodging, travel, and touring pamphlets. 2835 Bagley Ave., (313) 962-2360.

Events - The 1980 Republican National Convention slogan still rings true: "Detroit loves a good party." From the nation's largest local music festival to the nation's second-oldest Thanksgiving Day parade, Detroiters love having a good time and sharing their city with visitors. Detroit has many parties, parades, festivals, and traditions of its own, as well as outstanding celebrations for all of the national holidays. The events section of this book offers more than 75 notable events, and some of the larger events—such as America's Thanksgiving Day Parade in late November, and the Movement Electronic Music Festival in late May—that tend to take over the city.

News, Information, and Events Listings - Before visiting the city, visitors can better tailor a trip to Detroit by keeping up with local news, learning about the city's history and architecture, and getting up to speed on the many events, concerts, festivals, and lectures that make Detroit such a lively city. In addition to the events listings and

history sections of this book, the following sites offer information to help tell Detroit's story and put it in context:

- *Crain's Detroit Business* - www.crainsdetroit.com
- *Curbed Detroit* - www.detroit.curbed.com
- *Detroit 1701* - www.detroit1701.org
- *Detroit Free Press* - www.freep.com
- *Detroit News* - www.detroitnews.com
- *Detroit Urbex* - www.detroiturbex.com
- *Detroit Yes* - www.detroityes.com
- *Eater Detroit* - www.detroit.eater.com
- *Historic Detroit* - www.historicdetroit.org
- *Hour Detroit* - www.hourdetroit.com
- *Metro Times* - www.metrotimes.com
- *Model D Media* - www.modeldmedia.com
- *Night Train to Detroit* - www.nighttraintodetroit.com
- *WDET 101.9 FM (public radio)* - www.wdetfm.org

GETTING HERE

Air - Detroit Metro Airport is 20 miles outside of downtown; travelers' options include taxis, Uber/Lyft, car services, car rental, or personal arrangements. The SMART FAST service offers express service to and from downtown Detroit multiple times each hour.

Bus - Detroit is served by Megabus and Greyhound. Megabus has stops at the Rosa Parks Transit Center *(360 Michigan Ave.)* and Wayne State University *(Cass Ave. and W. Forest Ave.).* The Greyhound terminal is located downtown at the Howard Street Station *(1001 Howard St.).*

Car - If driving in, freeways are usually the fastest option: I-94 from the east/west, I-75 from the north/south, I-96 from the west side of Michigan, and from Canada, either the Ambassador Bridge via I-96, or the centrally located Detroit-Windsor Tunnel. The tunnel is usually the speedier option, but travelers can check ahead for travel times online. *www.dwtunnel.com.*

Rail - Train service into Detroit is restricted to eastbound travelers on Amtrak's Wolverine Line, though Amtrak offers service from Toledo by bus. The Amtrak station in Detroit is conveniently located in New Center. *11 W. Baltimore Ave.*

LODGING

234 Winder Street Inn - Guests at 234 Winder Street Inn stay in this elegant 1872 Second Empire home in the heart of the Brush Park historic district. Visitors can enjoy a marble fireplace, antique hardwood furniture, chandeliers, and homemade breakfasts—features that help make 234 Winder an excellent value. Suite options include an expansive 1,800-square-foot loft. *234 Winder St., www.234winderstinn.com, (313) 831-4091.*

Aloft Detroit at the David Whitney - This 19-story 1915 Neo-Renaissance masterpiece was beautifully rehabilitated in 2014 into the local outpost of Aloft Hotels. The four-story retail atrium, with its imposing columns, glowing lights, and glass ceiling, is among the most beautiful interior spaces in the city. Upstairs, the 136 guest rooms offer bright, colorful decor and striking views of Capitol Park. *One Park Ave., www.davidwhitneybuilding.com, (313) 237-1700.*

Detroit Foundation Hotel - Neoclassical architecture and contemporary design beautifully collide at this 100-room boutique hotel. Throughout this former central fire station and department headquarters, many once-pragmatic original design elements are dramatic in a new context. The story-and-a-half main floor that originally accommodated fire trucks, now creates an airy, ravishing restaurant and cocktail bar. The rooms are cozy, luxe, and refined, especially those with southern or eastern views. *250 W Larned St., www.detroitfoundationhotel.com, (313) 800-5500.*

Detroit Marriott at the Renaissance Center - A 73-story hotel on Detroit's riverfront, the Marriott offers comfortable rooms at competitive prices. The nearly 1,300 rooms feature 37-inch flat-screen televisions, Wi-Fi, and floor-to-ceiling windows for jaw-dropping views of the city. There are two restaurants and a fitness center available, and leisure travelers can use the People Mover to tour downtown conveniently. *400 Renaissance Center, (313) 568-8000.*

DoubleTree Suites by Hilton Hotel Detroit Downtown - Fort Shelby - In the heart of Detroit's downtown, the Fort Shelby provides refined and comfortable accommodations for visiting professionals. Rooms feature HDTVs, ergonomic chairs and desks, high-speed-internet access, and include complimentary shuttle and gym access. Prices are higher than local competitors, but its conference capacities make it ideal for business patrons. The hotel is housed in a beautifully restored Classical Revival structure, originally constructed in two phases in 1916 and 1920. *525 W. Lafayette Blvd., (313) 963-5600.*

El Moore Lodge - The brainchild of owners Tom and Peggy Brennan, this sustainably-renovated 19th-century apartment building is a local model of environmental design. The 11 handsome rooms use occupancy-controlled LED lighting, geothermal heating and cooling, integrated recycling programs, and solar photovoltaic power generation to minimize environmental impact. The four stunning rooftop "urban cabins" offer unique skyline views through sweeping windows, and from private rooftop decks, while the four main-floor park-view rooms boast sightlines with lush, native landscaping. *624 W Alexandrine St., www.elmoore.com/lodge, (313) 924-4374.*

Honor & Folly - A small design-focused inn, Honor & Folly is a Corktown treasure. Located on Michigan Avenue above Slows Bar B Q, owner Meghan McEwen's cozy, light-filled bed and breakfast is decorated with charming antiques and Detroit- and Midwest-made goods—many of which are also for sale. There are just two rooms available, and weekends especially book up early, so plan ahead. Not just for out-of-towners, the space can also be rented out for an afternoon or evening for events. *2132 Michigan Ave., www.honorandfolly.com.*

Hostel Detroit - A hostel in a simple art-infused two-story building in North Corktown, Hostel Detroit provides affordable private and shared accommodations for travelers. In addition to offering an hour-long orientation aimed at educating visitors about the city, its history, and options for their stay, the hostel also has bikes for rent. Online reservation only; no walk-ins accepted. *2700 Vermont St., www.hosteldetroit.com, (313) 451-0333.*

The Inn on Ferry Street - Providing refined, comfortable lodging across a range of room types, the Inn on Ferry Street spans four separate late 19th-century Victorian homes and two carriage houses in Detroit's East Ferry Historic District (see separate entry). Each of the rooms—40 in all—offers unique, distinct design schemes, and boasts elegant hardwood furnishings and decor. Full personal and business amenities including breakfast, in-room cable and Wi-Fi, and a complimentary shuttle service for greater downtown. Prices are best suited to business travelers and vary by room. *84 E. Ferry St., www.innonferrystreet.com, (313) 871-6000.*

Rivertown Inn & Suites - Located two blocks north of the RiverWalk, Rivertown Inn & Suites is an upmarket motel suitable for Detroit's pleasure or budget business travelers. Rooms are kept clean, and feature amenities like HBO and Wi-Fi, as well as available room service from its in-house restaurant, the Clique (see separate entry). Car rental and free on-site parking available. *1316 E. Jefferson, www.therivertowninn.com, (313) 568-3000.*

Shinola Hotel - In 2018, this 1925 T.B. Rayl & Co. hardware store was reborn as an elegant 130-room boutique hotel. In addition to luxe rooms with postcard views, the smart hotel features a sun-dappled conservatory barroom, a grand wood-walled library, a cozy fireplace-anchored living room, and a number of contemporary boutiques, restaurants, and bars onsite. *1400 Woodward Ave., www.shinolahotel.com.*

Siren Hotel - After a stunning renovation of the slender Wurlitzer Building, a 1926 Renaissance Revival masterpiece, the building was reborn as one of Detroit's most stylish boutique hotels. In addition to 106 sleek, vintage-style rooms with flat-screen televisions, custom Italian linens, intricate terrazzo tile bathrooms, and hand-loomed blankets, the hotel offers a rooftop deck and a number of trendy onsite shops and restaurants. *1509 Broadway St., www.thesirenhotel.com, (313) 277-4736.*

Trumbull & Porter Hotel - This 1960s Holiday Inn motel underwent a dramatic renovation to become a 144-room, design-forward, boutique hotel in the middle of the Corktown bustle. The streamlined architecture of the original mid-century modern building alongside the original letterpress art and luxurious linens make for a stunning combination. The award-winning Red Dunn Kitchen restaurant, a manicured courtyard, and 24-hour fitness center round out the hotel's offerings. *1331 Trumbull Ave., www.trumbullandporterhotel.com, (313) 496-1400.*

The Westin Book Cadillac Detroit - Immaculately (and miraculously) restored in 2008, the 453-room Book Cadillac offers a range of comfortable, stately rooms for downtown guests. The

historic Italian Renaissance-style building flawlessly melds comfort and elegance, complete with 42-inch flat-screen televisions, spacious bathrooms, and cloud-like beds. In addition to appropriate business amenities and a swimming pool, there are five bars and restaurants in the building. *1114 Washington Blvd., www.bookcadillacwestin.com, (313) 442-1600.*

GETTING AROUND

Orientation - In the wake of the great fire of 1805, Judge Augustus B. Woodward implemented his Woodward Plan. Inspired by Pierre Charles L'Enfant's plan for Washington, D.C., the Woodward Plan established a hexagonal street grid centered on Grand Circus Park and Campus Martius Park. Though the plan was abandoned after only 11 years and was never fully realized, Woodward's diagonal grid remains intact throughout Downtown and in the city's radial arterial streets. Often following the path of earlier Native American trails, these six arterial streets begin at or near Campus Martius and run far into the suburbs. From downtown Detroit, Woodward runs north, Grand River northwest, Michigan Avenue west, Fort Street west-southwest, Jefferson Avenue east-northeast, and Gratiot northeast. Even beyond downtown and the arterials, the map offers clues about local history. In these outlying areas, the city has two street orientations: shoreline and grid. Early on, property lines ran parallel or perpendicular to the Detroit River, and roads did the same. Streets like Brush, Beaubien, Bagley, Kercheval, Rosa Parks, and Trumbull follow this pattern. Later, as development shifted increasingly far from the waterfront after World War I, the city began a square-mile grid system. On the orderly northwest side, Ford Road extends straight west from Michigan Avenue in Campus Martius Park, and acts as the street grid's mile zero. Heading north, these parallel one-mile-grid thoroughfares are Warren Avenue (1 Mile), Joy Road (2 Mile), Plymouth Road (3 Mile), Schoolcraft Street (4 Mile), Fenkell Avenue (5 Mile), McNichols Road (6 Mile), 7 Mile Road, and 8 Mile Road. On the ground, the meeting point of these two grids often appears haphazard, with wide bends and sharp angels. These junctures, however, offer a quiet clue about when the area was developed.

Navigating Detroit - With myriad sudden one-ways, dead ends, and diagonal thoroughfares, finding your way around Detroit can be trickier than Richard Nixon. Smartphone-less visitors can observe a few rules to avoid getting lost or stuck in traffic.

- The city, split along Woodward Avenue, is essentially divided into east and west halves. Woodward Avenue is the dividing line for all east streets and west streets. Streets perpendicular to Woodward are numbered like different streets on their east and west sides—numbers increase as you drive away from Woodward. Streets parallel to Woodward are numbered heading north, so numbers increase as you drive or ride away from the river. (Grand Boulevard and Outer Drive both follow horseshoe patterns, and don't follow these rules).

- When lost in Detroit, look for the city's southern stars—the light atop the Renaissance Center and the unusual red globe atop the Penobscot Building—they are usually visible across the city. Drive towards them, and you will eventually get downtown. Drive away from them to get to the suburbs. If they are to your left, you're heading west. If they are to your right, you're heading east.

- When on freeways, pay attention to the time of day: Rush hours vary depending on where you're headed—into the city in the morning, out of the city in the afternoon.

Buses - Detroit Department of Transportation (DDOT) buses can take you around Detroit, Hamtramck, Highland Park, and a few suburban destinations. This system dovetails with SMART, a regional bus agency servicing a few major routes in the city, as well as suburbs in Wayne, Oakland, and Macomb counties. Neither bus gives change, so have surplus silver on hand. *www.smartbus.org*

Car Rentals - Though less common in the city itself, rental agencies are easy to find at the main entry points. For a local car rental, Enterprise has offices in the lower east side, Downtown, and New Center.

Zipcar - An international car-sharing business, Zipcar allows members to rent a car for a short time, usually a day at most. Zipcars are available in Midtown, but are available only to members, so plan accordingly.

Parking - Though parking is free in most areas, free on-street parking is a rare commodity in greater downtown. Each district is different, though meters are generally enforced until 10pm, Monday through Saturday. Detroit's parking enforcement officers are on the ball, so err

DETROIT
INTRODUCTION

on the side of paying too much over too little. Detroit uses a pay-by-plate zoned metering system, allowing visitors to pay via on-street kiosks or the ParkDetroit mobile app. Once parked, visitors may move their car within the same zone without penalty and can purchase more time through the app, remotely.

Taxis and Ride Shares - Detroit is served by several traditional taxi companies, the largest of which is Checker Cab. As a general rule, the city is more of a "call for a cab" place than a "hail a cab" place. Major on-demand ride-sharing apps like Uber and Lyft are also prevalent in Detroit, and can normally be found city-wide throughout the day (and night) using either company's proprietary app. As experienced riders know, look out for "surge pricing" at major gatherings and events, as both companies charge based on demand.

Cycling - Though called the Motor City, Detroit is a cycling paradise. The city is flat, and its surface streets are rarely congested. Cyclists can stow their bike on an outside rack aboard many DDOT buses, all SMART buses, or the inside rack aboard the QLINE, all of which are free. In recent years, the city added protected bike lanes to many thoroughfares, and has seen the continued expansion of its exquisite dedicated greenways, especially the Dequindre Cut (north/south) and the RiverWalk (west/east). Traditional hourly and daily bicycle rentals are available from Wheelhouse Detroit on the waterfront.

MoGo - Detroit's immensely popular bikeshare system, MoGo, offers 430 bikes across a network of 44 stations, conveniently located throughout the core of the city. Visitors can check out cruiser-style rides with a credit card for unlimited 30-minute trips within a 24-hour period, returning the bike to any station in the network between rides. Longer trips are available for an additional charge.

Detroit People Mover - Detroit's elevated rail system offers a cheap way to get around Downtown quickly, with a truly unique view along the way. The People Mover can get you from the Renaissance Center to Grand Circus Park, or one of the other 11 stops, for 75 cents in a matter of minutes. Riding the complete track takes 14 minutes, and it's highly recommended as a scenic diversion, especially with kids: the views from the 45' track are unmatched. *www.thepeoplemover.com.*

QLINE - Running along the Woodward Avenue, Detroit's modern 3.3-mile streetcar system runs from the waterfront to the North End, connecting Downtown, Midtown, and New Center. The train stops at 12 stations, including stops near the Detroit People Mover and Amtrak station. Tickets can be purchased at stops, onboard the train, and with the convenient QLINE app, which also allows users to (somewhat accurately) track the train's location.

Scooters - The city is served by several dockless scooter-share systems, including Bird, Lime, and Spin. Each company offers several hundred of these motorized, battery-powered scooters, which can travel up to 15 miles per hour. Using each company's app, visitors can pay $1 with a credit card to unlock a scooter, and once finished, pay a small additional amount for each minute used (normally about 15 cents). Scooters can be found throughout the city, especially as they organically spread out over the course of a day, but they are dramatically more prevalent in the greater downtown area.

Walking - Walking is a good way to get around short distances, and neighborhoods at the heart of the city are closer together than they might seem. For example, Downtown to New Center is three-and-a-half miles, about an hour's worth of walking, a similar distance as Midtown to Southwest.

Spirit of Detroit, pg. 108

TOURS

Though Detroit is served by a considerable number of tour operators, a few stand out for their knowledgeable tour leaders and unique modes of travel:

Antique Touring Co. - For some, Detroit history is seen best from a piece of Detroit history. Antique Detroit Touring Co. offers tours of Detroit from a 1930 Ford Model A Phaeton. Each history-rich tour is individually scheduled to fit your needs. *www.antiquetouring.com.*

Backseat Detroit - Local expert Joe Krause leads tours with a unique you-drive format, allowing visitors to take the wheel in their own cars. The content and duration of each tour is tailored to your interests and availability. Krause's tours are unique for the contextual storytelling he uses to connect local landmarks to a broader historical narrative. Walking tours also available. *www.backseatdetroit.com.*

Detroit Experience Factory - A highly regarded local non-profit organization serving as a welcome mat for the city, Detroit Experience Factory offers a number of renowned tours. It holds free, public afternoon walking tours of Detroit's downtown and notable buildings weekly on Saturdays, various insiders' bus tours of city's core on select Saturdays, and a "practically free" bar tour of the greater downtown's watering holes. Private tours available. *www.detroitexperiencefactory.org.*

Detroit Segway - This Segway outfit offers a host of specialized tours of the city, including Eastern Market, Belle Isle, and the Riverfront. The comprehensive The Whole Shebang Tour takes you through highlights of Eastern Market, Downtown, and Brush Park, sharing the history and significance of the city's landmarks along the way. Tours leave from Eastern Market and must be booked in advance. *www.detroitsegway.com.*

Diamond Jack's River Tours - These waterborne tours offer narrated sightseeing tours along the Detroit river from a beautifully maintained vintage 1955 ferry. Tours run Thursday through Sunday all summer, leaving from Rivard Plaza along the Detroit RiverWalk. *www.diamondjack.com.*

Oneita Cab Driver - For an impassioned insider's tour packed with personality, sage opinions, humor, and endearing quirkiness, give Oneita a call. A writer and author, Oneita knows Detroit inside and out, and offers a one-of-a-kind ride around the city. *(313) 282-5428.*

Preservation Detroit Tours - Detroit's renowned historic preservation society offers expert tours of local architectural marvels, historic sites, public art, and cemeteries. The expert guides share encyclopedic knowledge and often capitalize on unique relationships to offer rare behind-the-scenes tours. The group offers walking and biking tours, such as the especially renowned Yamasaki architecture and Downtown theater walking tours. Some tours require advance tickets. *www.preservationdetroit.org.*

Soaring Sports - This company provides patrons the opportunity to view Detroit from a breathtaking new vantage point—from a hot air balloon hundreds of feet in the air. Note that the gondola allows for only a few people at a time, and rides must be booked in advance. *www.soaringsports.com.*

Show Me Detroit Tours - This popular tour operator offers daily guided private van tours, highlighting the city's landmarks and cultural centers in greater downtown. Tours run for two hours and must be booked in advance. Custom tours available. *www.showmedetroittours.com.*

Urb Appeal Tours - With incredibly knowledgeable guides, these tours cover historic Detroit buildings, artwork, and urban development trends, all delivered with a sense of humor. Tours are scheduled, and must be booked in advance. *www.urbappealtours.com.*

Wheelhouse Detroit - This beloved bike shop offers wonderful two-wheeled tours spring through fall, on Saturdays and Sundays. The friendly staff hosts a variety of tour options, with varying ride lengths, difficulties, and tour themes, which can range from automotive history to architecture to public art. For a modest additional fee, customers can rent a bike for the tour. *www.wheelhousedetroit.com.*

GETTING IT STRAIT

Talking like a Detroiter - Those looking to talk like locals should begin with the city's street names and the unusual pronunciations Detroiters use. Some of the most unique street name pronunciations in Detroit/**Deh**troit/Dee-troit include: Gratiot/Gra**sh**-it; Schoenherr/**Shay-ner**; Livernois/Liver**noy**/Liver**noyz**; Larned/Lar-**ned**; Cadieux/Ca**djew**; Moross/Mor**aw**ss; Kercheval/Kerche**vull**; Fenkell/Fink-**el**; Charlevoix/**Shar-le-voy**; Chene/**Shane**; Beaubien/**Bo-be-in**; Vernor/

Ve**rner**; Freud/**Frood**; Goethe/Go**ath**-ee; Lahser/Lah**surr** (also La**sh**er, which will be the same road if you hear it). People who live in or are from Detroit are called De**h**troiters. When visiting Hamtramck/Hamtram**ick** remember these: Dequindre/Dequind**er**; Jos Campau/**Joseph Com-poe**; Conant/**Cone**-it. Residents of Hamtramck are technically called *Hamtramckans*, but don't be surprised if this sounds strange to them, or you, and if you never actually need to say it.

ABOUT THIS BOOK

Belle Isle to 8 Mile is organized geographically to encourage immersive exploration of Detroit's many neighborhoods. The book begins with Downtown, and each successive chapter covers increasingly outlying areas before closing with a brief chapter covering a few suburban highlights. For the purpose of this guide, we have included the two small municipalities completely surrounded by the city—Hamtramck and Highland Park—as a combined chapter. The back of the book includes an extensive events listing and an index of included sites. The bulk of the book, however, is the series of 12 area-specific chapters, each of which is broken into seven sections, listed below. Many businesses that defy ready classification—such as bakeries that serve coffee and could be listed as a shop or a cafe—are placed in the category that seems to most represent their raison d'être.

Throughout the book, we have flagged select entries with a star. This symbol denotes destinations that are exceptional or particularly unique, and essential for first-time visitors. To further guide your exploration of the city, in chapter 13 of this book, we've also listed our top picks for various categories, from burgers to a nice night out, as well as some favorite annual events.

The sections are:

- **Introduction** - A brief history of the area, including descriptions of the people, neighborhoods, architecture, and highlights that make it an engaging place to visit.

- **Bars & Restaurants** - The bars, restaurants, cafes, diners, eateries, doughnut shops, and food trucks that make the area unique. Some bakeries that focus on cafe goods are included in this section.

- **Shopping & Services -** Perhaps the most wide-ranging section of the book, Shopping & Services covers commercial amenities from boutiques to spas, and architectural salvage to bike shops.

- **Cultural Attractions -** From basement museums to upscale galleries to one of the nation's finest art museums, the range of these places highlights the city's diverse creativity.

- **Entertainment & Recreation -** A section devoted to the places where Detroiters unwind, Entertainment & Recreation covers casinos, parks, bowling alleys, gyms, concert venues, sports teams, and theaters.

- **Sites -** These monuments, curiosities, historic places, architectural masterpieces, historic districts, and cemeteries are the city's finest, most notable attractions, that, although worth seeing, are a feast for only the eyes and are generally non-interactive.

- **Points of Interest -** A catchall category for minor attractions, such as urban gardens, ghost signs, record labels, miscellaneous graves, murals, curious commercial art, statues, movie scenes, and stars' homes that a tour guide might point out, but for which he or she wouldn't stop the bus. These entries are typically brief.

Be a Contributor - We love to hear from residents and travelers. If you encounter something that has changed or something that belongs in a future update of the book, drop us a line *(belleisleto8mile@gmail.com)*, and we'll work to incorporate the change in future editions.

CHAPTER 1
DOWNTOWN

The historic, bustling heart of the city, Downtown is the commercial, entertainment, dining, and public art center of the region, making it the essential starting point of any visit to the city. The area's concentration and mix of elegant eateries, popular bars, historic architecture, and rich entertainment offerings is unparalleled in the region. Downtown, as we define it, is the area bordered by I-375, I-75, M-10, and the Detroit River.

As the oldest section of the city, Downtown's 1.16 square miles are awash with municipal history, with reminders of the city's future-shaping past around every corner. Perhaps like no other area of Detroit, Downtown has undergone a continuous—and ongoing—evolution. Downtown's development began with the city's first structure, Antoine de la Mothe Cadillac's Fort Pontchartrain du Detroit, at what is now the corner of Larned Street and Griswold Street. When the city incorporated in 1806, the small heart of downtown comprised the extent of the city and its 1,650 residents. By 1849, Detroit's burgeoning population led city leaders to annex all of what is now Downtown Detroit. In the antebellum period, Downtown became a transportation hub, and began its swift population growth and a consequent wave of commercial development. In 1886, the Edison Illuminating Co. began making Downtown Detroit one of the nation's first electrified cities, and the city's network of so-called moonlight towers (street lights) and rapidly growing collection of Gilded Age architecture led many to refer to Downtown Detroit as the "Paris of the West." The frantic pace of downtown development accelerated through the first decades of the 20th century, peaking in the late 1920s, when Detroit issued an inflation-adjusted $2.5 billion in building permits in 1926, including 27 for buildings more than 20 stories—the most of any U.S. city. During the Great Depression and Second World War, Downtown development was largely stagnant before a revival in the postwar years. During the 1950s and 1960s, Downtown development became increasingly automobile-oriented in an era marked by demolition, freeway development, parking structure construction, and car-centric new buildings such as One Woodward Avenue and Cobo Center. Since that period, development has evolved with mayoral administrations, from marquee civic and commercial projects, such as Joe Louis Arena and the Renaissance Center in the 1970s and 1980s, to a preference for catalytic entertainment and recreation development, such as MGM Grand Casino, Campus Martius, the Detroit RiverWalk, and Comerica Park in the 1990s and 2000s.

As a commercial area with a relatively small population of nearly 6,500, Downtown is comprised more of commercial districts than of traditional neighborhoods. These districts—including Bricktown, Campus Martius, Capitol Park, Financial District, Foxtown, Grand Circus Park, Greektown, Harmonie Park, and the International Waterfront—draw their identities from their common use or shared anchor. Although each district is distinct, with a unique aesthetic, history, and future, their proximity encourages collective exploration. Together, these areas offer the city's grandest collection of architecture on its distinctive street grid—Judge Woodward's signature baroque, hub-and-spoke arterial street system. Keen-eyed architecture observers will spot beautiful examples of many styles among Downtown's eight historic districts, including Art Deco, Art Moderne, Arts and Crafts, Beaux-Arts, Chicago School, Classical Revival, Gothic Revival, International, Italian Renaissance, Modern, Mid-Century Modern, Neo-classical, Neo-Georgian, Tudor Revival and Victorian.

In recent years, Downtown has welcomed levels of development and investment not seen in a century. In 2010, nearly a third of Downtown's buildings were vacant, though by the close of 2018, construction cranes outnumbered abandoned buildings in the area. Led by famed investor Dan Gilbert, the area's revival has brought new residents, businesses, art, jobs, and development to a Downtown now rarely described by the media as anything but "burgeoning." These changes have stoked concerns about equity and displacement, sparking a critical citywide dialogue as government officials and residents grapple with gentrification—a somewhat unfamiliar issue in recent history.

No trip to Detroit is complete without a visit to Downtown. The area's matchless roster of entertainment offerings, fine eateries, party bars, recreational spaces, and stunning architecture creates a diverse, lively destination not to be missed. Although every corner of Downtown offers unique experiences, a few are worth cancelling a flight for. Visitors looking to take in live music, theater, or opera should head for Foxtown and Grand Circus Park which, together, anchor Detroit's theater district—the nation's second largest with more than 25,000 seats. Those in search of gourmet cuisine that is nearby and near-perfection should look no further than the International Waterfront and Financial District areas, where the numerous delicious options include tiny chef-driven concepts, and a subterranean steakhouse originally founded 75 years ago. All of Downtown is a sports fan's paradise, being home to—or neighboring—all three of the city's major stadiums and a glut of sports bars. Architecture admirers should look no further than Harmonie Park, Grand Circus Park, and the Financial District, which together showcase inspired examples of nearly every architectural style since the Civil War.

BARS & RESTAURANTS

7 Greens Detroit Salad Co. - Lettuce tell you about 7 Greens. Established in 2014, this popular Downtown lunch spot is a homegrown destination for the best fashion-your-own salads in the city. The friendly staff at this bright green, modern farm-to-fork restaurant offer their signature salads, bowls, or wraps with tasty homemade, gluten free dressings and sauces. From arugula to zesty vegan kimchi, 7 Greens has it all, with standout lunchtime selections including the healthy Yoga Girl salad and the zesty Spicy Buddha Bowl. If you're looking for something a little less green, other menu options include made-from-scratch smoothies, parfaits, granola, and sweets. Feeling withered from lunchtime hunger and in a rush? Don't worry, this spot offers fresh-forward online ordering for quick pickups. May we suggest a picnic in nearby Campus Martius park? (See separate entry.) *1222 Library St., www.7greens.com, (313) 964-9005.*

24grille - Located on the ground floor of historic Book-Cadillac, and paying homage to the year that the stunning hotel opened, 24grille offers diners an exquisite experience, from the haute cuisine interpretations of classic American dishes highlighting seasonal, regional flavors, to the chichi champagne room (one of the only champagne rooms in the state). Although the menu rarely disappoints, the Thai-fried shrimp and mango salad, poutine with pulled pork, truffled mac and cheese, and risotto croquettes stand out. Hand-blown glass baubles, tempered glass panels, exposed structural elements, and a floating "fireplace" give 24grille an edgy sophistication, yet it is still decidedly unstuffy, with a wide selection of Michigan craft beers and an affordable happy hour Monday through Friday. Next time you find yourself sporting a Twisted Sister shirt and craving some confit l'orange, fear not—24grille has no dress code. *204 Michigan Ave., (313) 964-3821.*

AK Takeaway - Opened in 2018, this Downtown favorite, a take-out oriented satellite location of the popular suburban **Anita's Kitchen,** offers Mediterranean-inspired fare in a Scandinavian-inspired space. The stark white interior is both cleaner and brighter than some operating rooms, and, aside from some decorative pottery, puts the emphasis on the food. Owner Jennifer Wegrzyn's menu centers on fresh Lebanese fare with a contemporary American flair, emphasizing vegetarian, vegan, halal, antibiotic-free, and gluten-free options. The salad-heavy menu offers seven grain bowls with falafel, tabbouleh, or mujadara; pitas with kafta, shawarma, gyro, or falafel; and salads topped with quinoa and fattoush, among others. Breakfast gets similar treatment, with a host of egg-and-potato-based bowls and sandwiches available. Wash it all down with coffee, mint ice tea, kombucha, or La Croix. A cozy dining room and al fresco patio are available, through most guests opt for carryout to eat in one of the nearby parks. *150 W. Jefferson Ave., www.aktakeaway.com, (313) 771-3030.*

Albena - Named for his grandmother, Chef Garrett Lipar opened this much-anticipated restaurant in 2018. Nominated twice for the James Beard Rising Star Chef of the Year and lauded with critical acclaim at his previous restaurants, at Albena, Lipar focuses on hyper-seasonal modern Great Lakes cuisine in an intimate setting. The tasting-menu dinner, which the restaurant describes as "a minimalist approach to progressive dining" takes place in an open kitchen within a private area of the hotel that is simultaneously modern and rustic. Expect up to 12 plates served at a brisk pace, with stunning, minimalist presentation, exceptional quality, and exquisite flavors. Offering some of the city's finest, most innovative cuisine, Albena promises surprise—and an absolutely memorable experience. As there are only eight seats and three seatings per night, advance reservations, which can be booked online for about $130, are required. While the menu is prix fixe, vegetarians can be accommodated. *1509 Broadway St. (enter from the alley), www.albenadetroit.com.*

★**American Coney Island -** An authentic Detroit institution—and one of the world's first two coney island restaurants—American Coney Island has been a mecca for the city's coney fans since 1917. With its metallic ceiling, white-and-black-checkered floor, dinette tables and staff in paper soda-jerk hats, the restaurant's retro diner atmosphere is an integral part of its position as a cherished city tradition. Though American offers a full menu—including Greek salads, tuna salad sandwiches, gyro platters and baklava—the real draw are the coney dogs. The coneys begin with a warm, steamed bun, with a specially seasoned natural-skin casing Dearborn Sausage wiener, the restaurant's signature spicy chili sauce, and are topped with a line of mustard and sweet Vidalia onions. For a classic Detroit experience, sit in the flatiron-like acute corner, and watch traffic and bustle pass as you scarf down tradition. Check out the bitter rival next door, Lafayette Coney Island (see separate entry), and pick your favorite. Small menu of beer available. Open 24/365. *114 W. Lafayette Blvd., www.americanconeyisland.com, (313) 961-7758.*

Anchor Bar - The crinkled, yellowing photos of long-gone journalists set the scene at this Downtown watering hole. Nestled between the headquarters of The Detroit News, Detroit Free Press, the WDIV studios, and city hall, The Anchor Bar is Detroit's de-facto muckraker drinking spot. In the old days, beat reporters would stop in for a beer and a shot on their way to cover the City Council. More recently, much of the Pulitzer Prize-winning reporting that led to Mayor Kwame Kilpatrick's resignation was unfurled in booth three. Although the bar recently changed hands after being owned by the same family for nearly 60 years, the new owners promise to honor its storied history by maintaining its classic menu and funky old-school charm. *450 W. Fort St., (313) 964-9127.*

Andiamo Detroit Riverfront - Andiamo and the Riverfront are a perfect pair. With excellent views of the river and superb cuisine, this location of the small regional chain is the definitive Andiamo experience. White-coated waiters observe classical restaurant-service techniques, setting and resetting your table with each course. Located just off the Renaissance Centers' Winter Garden, the dining rooms of Andiamo are open and large, yet feel intimate. A full menu of Italian favorites is beautifully presented—from simple pasta dishes to elegant entrees, including some dishes prepared with a healthier approach. Try the gnocchi or the veal marsala and be sure to dine on the waterfront patio when weather permits. Those looking for a more casual fare should check out sister location **Presto Gourmet Deli** next door. Offering tasty and affordable weekday breakfast and lunch service, the carryout-oriented spot is known throughout the RenCen for its enticing full-pasta lunch, black bean burgers with special habanero sauce, juicy sirloin burgers on pretzel buns, and some of the best cookies around. *400 Renaissance Center, www.andiamoitalia.com/ detroit, (313) 567-9892 (Presto), (313) 567-6700 (Andiamo).*

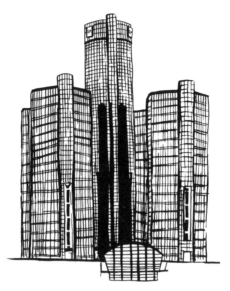

Renaissance Center, pg. 107

★ **Apparatus Room** - Once a Detroit Fire Department engine house, the Apparatus Room is the jaw-dropping crown jewel of the Foundation Hotel. An enchanting adaptive re-use of the 1929 building, the space is steeped in rich historic elements, including gargantuan wooden engine doors that line the exterior, subway tile that stretches up the walls, and distressed original tin ceilings. These timeless elements are tempered with contemporary flourishes such as a flowing wood bar and cascading blown-glass light fixtures that combine to bring an uncommon warmth to the space. It would be easy for a space this rich in character and beauty to upstage the fare, but Michelin-starred chef Thomas Lents has ensured that this doesn't happen. The exceptional up-scale à la carte menu of New American fare is offered throughout the day and is seasonal, but stand-outs include inventive, flavorful vegetable preparations like curried cauliflower, sweet potato gnocchi, vegetable risotto, and a complex carrot salad—as well as perfect, succulent steak and chicken. The establishment also features a comprehensive wine, beer, and craft cocktail program, which complements the menu, or stands on its own. Limited, reservation-only seating is also available at the unparalleled **Apparatus Room Chef's Table** on the mezzanine level—an all-inclusive prix-fixe experience that runs about $175 per chair. *250 W. Larned St., www.detroitfoundationhotel.com/apparatus-room, (313) 915-4422.*

ASHE Supply Co. Flagship Cafe - This gorgeous third-wave Downtown coffee shop churns out *solid* cups of coffee. The hip, graphic space is beautifully designed and contemporary. Filled with dark tones, from the curvaceous reclaimed-wood-bar, to the series of lengthy wood and metal tables that line the sunny windows, the space is bright, modern, and inviting. In addition to being a full-service coffee shop, ASHE Supply Co. roasts their own beans, and offers a range of perfected varieties. Alongside a full slate of espresso drinks and pour-overs, the shop offers siphoned coffee, an uncommon theatrical brewing method that isn't offered elsewhere in Detroit. To satiate your hunger, the shop purveys a range of treats from local spots, including Avalon, Sister Pie and Detroit Institute of Bagels. Describing themselves as a "roaster and clothier," in addition to the delicious coffee, you can find the shop's original designs on tees and other lifestyle clothing. ASHE Supply Co. also operates a second location (see separate entry) in the east side's Rivertown Warehouse District. *1555 Broadway St., www.ashesupplyco.com, (313) 672-2070.*

Astoria Bakery - Opened in 1971, this beloved old-timey bakery in Greektown has been a local favorite for more than 40 years. Inside, under the gorgeous tin ceiling and antique hanging lights, patrons pick their pleasure from the seemingly endless bakery counter and sit at the cozy cafe tables. The bakery offers 120 decadent homemade European sweets, chocolates, cakes, and pies, as well as more than 20 varieties of ice cream, and house-roasted coffee and cappuccino. Though the cafe setting can be a relaxing respite from the bustle of the neighborhood, Astoria can box any of its baked delights and offers cones for the road. The bakery is open until midnight on weekdays and 1am on weekends to best serve the sometimes revelrous Greektown crowds. *541 Monroe St., www.astoriapastryshop.com, (313) 963-9603.*

Avalon Downtown Cafe and Bakery - Night owls and early birds alike will find plenty to crow about at the Downtown outpost of Avalon International Breads. It turns out that Detroit's most beloved bakery is pretty good at breakfast, lunch, and dinner, too. The schoolhouse chairs, chalkboard menu, reclaimed wood walls, and mismatched salvaged-letter signs evoke a sense of charming eclecticism, yet the menu is solidly traditional, albeit with clear contemporary, elevated, healthy influences. Amidst a strong roster, a few menu items stand out. Outstanding options include the brioche French toast, mushroom toast, green goddess cobb (greens, chicken breast, smoked bacon, shaved fennel and red onion, sliced avocado, pea shoots, and green goddess dressing) and deluxe pizza (charred tomato sauce, cider house bacon, pepperoni, sausage, roasted mushrooms, mozzarella, shaved red onions, and herbs). Wash it all down with something from the full-service coffee bar or thoughtfully curated beer list. Large patio available. See index for other Avalon locations, each with their own speciality. *1049 Woodward Ave., www.avalonbreads.net/avalon-cafe-and-bakery-downtown-detroit, (313) 285-8006.*

Bad Luck Bar - Detroit's most elite and exclusive secret craft cocktail speakeasy—ironically located in what was, until recently, an actual beer-out-of-the-cooler blind pig speakeasy—is a must-visit for discerning (and prosperous) cocktalians. Stroll down the seemingly desolate alley off of Capitol Park and look for the grey door with the snake and neon Eye of Providence. Inside, you'll be led into the sophisticated and atmospheric space featuring geometric inlaid walls, minimalist hexagonal chandeliers, an illuminated quartz bar, and a majestic, towering library of liquor. The seasonal one-drink-per-page cocktail menu reads like a deck of tarot cards, and the lavish, experimental cocktails feature obscure liquors, pioneering techniques, and unusual, house-made ingredients. Look for curiosities like hot-branded citrus peels, smoking bell jars, flaming cocktails, lavender popping candy, cereal-infused cream, and Campari dust. While drinks start at $18, they range up to $90 for The Admiral (an exceedingly rare pour of rum, served your way, lucky for you). For guests looking for a more economical experience, we suggest ordering a classic off-menu, which will be exceptional, and run $10-14. All patrons are treated to a complimentary punch aperitif once seated. *1218 Griswold St., in the alley, www.badluckbar.com, (313) 657-9177.*

The Baltimore Bar & Grill - To call the Baltimore pretty might be a stretch, but what the dimly lit Downtown dive lacks in aesthetic appeal, it makes up for with a surprisingly healthy booze selection and tasty grease-heavy bar food that's worth writing home about. In the larger front room, the joint serves breakfast, lunch, and dinner and offers a billiards table. On weekends, the otherwise quiet, speakeasy-style back room hosts dance-friendly DJs and serves free-flowing shots that bring shoulder-to-shoulder crowds. While the Baltimore claims to cook the best burger in town, and it's a solid choice, we suggest its grilled cheese or patty melt, which are both tasty enough to compete with the best out of your grandma's kitchen. *1234 Randolph St., (313) 964-2728.*

Bangkok Crossing - Got the shakes for some larb? Renowned for its speed, outstanding service, and tasty food, this unassuming Thai spot is popular among residents who need to grab some Gang Gai on the go. Although Bangkok Crossing specializes in mild Thai dishes, try some of the more authentic options, like the Pad Ma Kher or Pad Prik Khing after digging into the complimentary shrimp chips and soup. While there is always ample seating in this spare, utilitarian restaurant, Bangkok Crossing offers lightning-fast carryout. Although the vegetarian and vegan selection is minimal, the staff and cooks are very accommodating. *620 Woodward Ave., www.bangkokcrossingthaifood.com, (313) 961-3861.*

BESA - This chef-driven concept found a winning formula with a see-and-be-scene crowd, catalog-worthy interior design, and a deft contemporary menu. The ground-floor Vinton Building space is a striking progressive landmark, with marble tile floors, black leather banquettes, piped gold pendant lights, and sweeping views of the downtown bustle. The basement kitchen slings elegant, inventive dishes that draw upon ingredients like chili thread, oyster mayo, salmon confit, bacon emulsion, and "exploration of onion." Look for smartly plated, contemporary dishes, including the rice flour and coconut udon, with charred squid; the sea scallops, with masa polenta, braised bacon, and gochujang-white chocolate broth; and a lobster tail ceviche, with citrus and popped sorghum that'll leave you weak in the knees. Those looking for lighter fare should look no further than the barroom raw bar with its distinctive oysters and crudos. The curated cocktail program checks all the boxes, but save room for the 200-bottle, globe-trotting wine list. *600 Woodward Ave., www.besadetroit.com, (313) 315-3000.*

Briggs - Whether you're looking to watch the big fight, the big game, or the season finale of RuPaul's Drag Race, this LGBTQ-friendly sportsbar in the heart of Downtown has got you covered. Featuring an extensive beer list and wide range of spirits, Briggs also offers classic sports bar fare like burgers, nachos, and potato skins. With a television in view from just about every vantage point of Briggs' lower level, you won't even need instant replay. Conversely, if you're looking to peel yourself away from the TV, head upstairs during the summer months to Briggs' rooftop patio where, on Fridays and Saturdays, you can dance to the sweet sounds of local DJs spinning records with stunning views of the Downtown skyline as a backdrop. *519 E Jefferson Ave., www.briggsdetroit.com, (313) 656-4820.*

Brome Modern Eatery - Showcasing an utter dedication to the burger craft, Chef Zane Makky puts the best things between sliced bread since sliced bread. With organic, grass-fed beef as his canvas, Chef Makky draws from a diverse stable of ingredients—think corn salsa, aged white cheddar, cherry pepper relish, beef bacon, avocado— to create eight exquisite hamburgers. The masterpiece, undoubtedly, is the deluxe, with its beef bacon, aged white cheddar, red onion, tomato, romaine, and dijonnaise on brioche. A buttermilk fried chicken sandwich, fresh salads, fries, tots, and more than ten milkshakes and concretes round out the menu. These delights are all served in a space best defined as au casurant, with exposed brick covered with hundreds of houseplants, contemporary murals, Edison pendants, Scandinavian-style furniture, and customers wearing everything from French cuffs to cutoffs. Occupying the attached pedestrian skywalk, **Balance Bar** offers a full roster of organic juices, smoothies, and mocktails, including the pina kale-ata—kale, pineapple, avocado, granny smith, spinach, kiwi, and coconut water. *607 Shelby St., www.bromemoderneatery.com, (313) 403-1200.*

Buhl Bar - Flanked by the majestic Guardian Building, the Buhl Bar is a refined, iconic establishment that revives the business happy-hour tradition of Detroit's heyday. The bar exudes old-school class, with a clean, dark setting highlighted by the large wood bar that makes it a natural habitat for Financial District movers and shakers—and those who want to feel like one. In addition to beer and wine, the Buhl offers a delightful spirit and craft cocktail menu overseen by the Detroit Optimist Society, parent company of The Sugar House (see separate entry). The bar also features a selection of aperitifs, including meats, cheeses, and bar mixes that complement the drinks, atmosphere, and clientele. An ideal setting to make an impression, make a deal with your next business partner, persuade the opposition with stiff drinks, or just get gussied up and join the in crowd. *535 Griswold St., (313) 963-6118.*

★ **Cafe D'Mongo's Speakeasy** - A great place to see and be seen, D'Mongo's is an essential stop during a stay in Detroit. The destination has become famous for being a quirky bar and soul food joint that feels like a combination of an antique store and your grandmother's living room. The emerald green walls are clad with photos of famous jazzmen and infamous mobsters, gold-painted accents, classic advertisements, old-timey photos, musical instruments, and "gold" records signed by regulars. The comfy, tufted gold velvet furniture is a sight for sore thighs that contributes to the homespun DIY glamour of the atmosphere. The bar is full of character, as well as characters, and none is more charming than the personable proprietor, Larry Mongo, a tall drink of water who loves greeting customers with a tall glass of whisky or a tall tale. At the bar, guests can get a full line of cocktails—including Larry's signature Vernor's and Canadian Club "Detroit Brown"—and bottled beer. Come early and catch the popular, albeit limited, soul food menu, featuring ribs and barbecued chicken, black-eyed peas, cornbread, and mac and cheese. An extremely varied docket of live music is common. *1439 Griswold St., www.cafedmongos.com.*

Calexico - With six locations in New York City and one in Bahrain, this wildly popular Cal-Mex establishment found its seventh location in Detroit in 2016 and hasn't looked back. Situated in the heart of Downtown, this casual eatery is a sprawling, contemporary, wood-filled maze that features one of the most coveted streetside patio spaces on lower Woodward Avenue. Fresh and mellow West Coast flavors (by way of the East Coast) run throughout the menu, which is filled with staples like carne asada, chipotle pork, and shrimp in tacos, burritos, enchiladas, fajitas, and just about anything else that is more tasty with fillings. Fresh Baja tofu and black bean options abound for vegetarians, and the guacamole is a bright, flavorful way to start off your meal and accompany an unavoidable margarita. Though it's often packed, the restaurant is large enough to accomodate groups with the proper planning, but it's a good idea to try and avoid peak hours if you want a more intimate seating—or a better view on the patio. *1040 Woodward Ave., www.calexico.net, (313) 262-6361.*

★**Candy Bar -** With pastel pink walls and plush booths, an enormous 670-piece glass chandelier, cast white palm trees, stunning pink marble bar, and a giant disco ball for good measure, the cozy Candy Bar exudes the limitless cool of golden age Hollywood. Hidden behind a curtain on the first floor of the Wes Andersonian Siren Hotel, the unusual, enticing appearance of the bar was inspired by legendary old Hollywood haunt Perino's. Not content to rely on looks alone, the lounge offers a menu of exceptional craft cocktails, several of which flirt with the namesake of the bar, such as the signature Bubble Rum, and our favorite, the Supertrain, an unusual but tasty pairing of rye, chartreuse, pistachio, and pineapple. However, the skilled hands behind the bar are more than capable of making more restrained classics. The bar also offers a limited selection of beers and wines. Drinks with a different kind of kick are available at the adjacent **Populace Coffee**, also inside the hotel. Endlessly charming, laid back vibes prevail at this outpost of the revered Bay City roastery. A full slate of coffee drinks and local baked goods are available, including their ever-popular almond milk iced coffees. *1509 Broadway St., www.thesirenhotel.com, www.populace.coffee, (313) 277-4736.*

Caucus Club - Located in the Penobscot Building, this classic Detroit destination which originally opened in 1952, has been reimagined for the late aughts. At its heart, it's the same charming supper club where Barbra Streisand got her start in 1961, but the space has been retooled, refitted, and sleekly tightened in all the right places. The updates have created a new level of elegance—but with more than a nod to the iconic restaurant's storied history, storied stage and all. From the legendary "Bullshot" cocktail (an original variation on the Bloody Mary) to all the wheeling and dealing of automotive America, the Caucus Club's legacy has been redefined for the next generation of hopefuls and power brokers. True to form, the menu includes a range of steaks dry aged in-house, crowd pleasing prime ribs, iconic table-side Caesar salads, and an opulent raw bar featuring snow crab, shrimp, and oysters, which combine for truly decadent dinners. Other epicurean standouts include lobster bisque, burrata caprese, and fresh Michigan perch. Power lunches and a proper cocktail hour(s) have also returned to the club, making this sumptuous, modern bar well worth a visit, for business or pleasure. Reservations encouraged, valet available. *150 W. Congress St., www.caucusclubdetroit.com, (313) 965-4970.*

Penobscot Building, pg. 106

Central Kitchen + Bar - Few names offer such truth in advertising. Named for the long lost Detroit Central Farmer's Market, the restaurant is in the center of Downtown, just a few steps from the literal point of origin for the city's street grid. Despite the fashionable interior—think reclaimed industrial lighting, vintage tin ceiling, midcentury bentwood chairs, and exposed concrete—the restaurant has an approachable, everyman atmosphere. In the summer, tanks and ties appear in equal number. The menu is similarly upscale, but accessible. Strong options abound, including chicken wings with truffle, parmesan, and blue cheese; soba noodle salad with bean sprouts, cilantro, and crispy shiitakes; and fish tacos with catfish, chayote slaw, and queso cotija. On weekends, the menu brunches above its weight class, with elevated fare including huevos rancheros, pork belly hash, and brioche French toast. Behind the bar, expect a wine list thicker than some phonebooks, a thoughtful selection of beers, and an expert cocktail program. *660 Woodward Ave., www.centraldetroit.com, (313) 963-9000.*

Checker Bar - In the heart of the Financial District is a perfect burger 'n' beer dive bar. Founded in 1955 and still family owned and operated, Checker Bar has earned a reputation for its hearty, generous, and perfectly juicy burgers. The place takes pride in using fresh ingredients, also offering vegetarian-friendly nosh like the sassy Eat Your Broccoli Salad and the delightfully weird Deviled Eggs 4 Ways. Best of all, this shotgun-style bar and eatery, decked out with a Coolidge-era tin ceiling, Reagan-era wood paneling, and tables fit for any chess fan, is open until 2am every day. For a more active experience, check out the Pop + Offworld bar arcade upstairs (see separate entry). *124 Cadillac Sq., www.checkerbar.com, (313) 961-9249.*

ChickP - A fresh mediterranean concept centered around the versatile legume, ChickP offers a wholesome, flavorful menu of extremely vegetarian-friendly wraps, bowls, and salads. Primarily open for lunch, favorites include the Hottie—an exceptional falafel wrap, and the Turkey Delight—which appeases the bird nerds. The curated menu is small, but well executed, with delicious, crisp vegetables, exceptional falafel, and some of the city's best hummus. With a small, pleasant contemporary dining area, patrons can choose to stay or take-away. A pint-sized sister location, **Chickpea in the D** is located nearby at 2 John R St, in a delightful blink-and-you'll-miss-it carryout-only lunch window. This location, which is the original, combines a similar menu with a bevy of smoothies, but we suggest sticking with the food. *110 Clifford St., www.chickpdetroit.com, (313) 970-7618.*

CK Mediterranean Grille & Catering - Located on the ground level of the Compuware Building, CK Mediterranean Grille is a concept born out of the popular suburban restaurant **Mr. Kabob**. Known for its fresh, healthy Mediterranean food, the family behind Mr.

Kabob launched a small chain of Café Kabob (CK) Mediterranean Grilles in 2008 and continues to be a leader in providing fast, fresh, healthy food in a casual environment. The stylish cafeteria setting of the Detroit location is buzzing with workers from the many nearby corporate offices throughout the week and is easily one of the best spots downtown to get a flavorful, homemade, healthy Mediterranean meal on the go. *119 Monroe St., www.ckgrille.com, (313) 496-6666.*

Clementina - Popping up seasonally between April and November in Capitol Park, Clementina serves up Latin-inspired food and drinks in a gorgeously decked-out outdoor space. The bright colors, hanging plants, and plentiful seating make for an inviting patio space that conjures Miami Beach vibes. The shipping container bar has frozen cocktails, cervezas, tequila, and non-alcoholic beverages, as well as dessert, like their black coconut and activated charcoal soft serve. The adjacent stationary food truck offers modern takes on street food dishes developed by Ryan Prentiss, the chef at the neighboring steakhouse Prime + Proper (see separate entry). The delicious al pastor tacos, nachos with adobo chicken, and citrus herb guacamole are crowd-pleasing favorites, and are good places to start. The menu includes vegetarian options. Open for lunch and dinner. *150 State St., www.clementinadetroit.com, (313) 636-3200.*

COLORS - With rich, innovative flavors and an ethical business design, this worker-owned eatery is not only a destination for quality cuisine but is also beneficial to the well-being of the city it serves. Located in the basement of the historically German **Harmonie Club**, patrons dine at long, communal tables or sit at small bistro tables in the reserved, white-walled setting highlighted by hardwood floors and antique lighting. Serving lunch and dinner out of the open kitchen, the eatery offers a limited but varied vegetarian-friendly menu of refined food at reasonable prices. Though everything is made with quality, locally sourced ingredients, favorites include the Moroccan Meatballs (made with succulent lamb), perfectly prepared Sweet Potato Wontons, the flavorful Portabella Club, and burgers with uncommon add-ons like fried egg and bacon jelly. While the caliber of the food should be inspiration enough to visit COLORS, a foundation of the establishment is that every employee has a share in the company, collaborating with and training each other to bring each meal to the table, so that you can satisfy not only your stomach but also your conscience. *311 E. Grand River Ave., www.colors-detroit.com, (313) 962-5020.*

Cornerstone Barrel House - An upscale speakeasy for a rapidly evolving downtown, Cornerstone lives up to what its name implies: A restaurant founded on a curation of whiskeys and ready preparation of walk-in pub grub. Situated on the buzzing corner of John R and Woodward, Cornerstone lets patrons take in views of the street life from a lush, brick-walled, oaken interior, and dine on a menu featuring choice favorites like fish and chips with cod battered in flakes of Better Made Salt & Vinegar chips. Patrons should dine at the long bar while they quaff a microbrew or glass of small-batch bourbon, or nosh on Cornerstone's menu of modernized takes on classic meat and potatoes. If you hear bass pumping from the basement, it's not your imagination, it's **Whiskey Disco** downstairs. Descend the concrete stairs, past the "CAR FUL" sign, to find the undulating colored lights of the (literally) underground dance club. Look for music that shifts personality on an almost nightly basis, from vintage funk to hip-hop to EDM. *1456 Woodward Ave., www.cornerstonedetroit.com, (313) 338-3238.*

Dessert Oasis Coffee Roasters - A veritable grounds zero for the city's growing artisanal coffee scene, Dessert Oasis has a well-earned reputation for importing, roasting, and brewing some of the city's finest coffee. A gallery atmosphere prevails at this quiet cafe, in thanks to jazz music in the air, stark white walls, an array of local art, sweeping front windows, and a minimalist, refined industrial aesthetic. Owner Nathan Hamood uses a range of beans—including Burundi Kinyovu, Ethiopia Adado, and Rwanda Ejo Heza—to brew a full slate of traditional coffee and espresso drinks, as well as house-speciality flavored options, like the honey cinnamon latte, lavender latte, and rose latte. The matcha latte especially, with its rich, deep, beautiful flavor, is not to be missed. The baked-good options play a fine supporting cast, including the house-made quiches, cookies, and baklava, as well as nearly two dozen cheesecakes, available by the slice. Check social media to learn about the diverse live shows. *1220 Griswold St., www.docr.coffee, (313) 338-3515.*

Detroit Beer Company - Any restaurant with "beer" in its name is doing something right, but "The Brewery on Broadway" goes all the way with a full menu of food and house-brewed beers and an inviting atmosphere. Inside, guests are treated to a bi-level space with high ceilings and a warm, rich atmosphere highlighted by dark woodwork, exposed brick, and the focal point of the space, the visible fermentation tanks. The establishment offers an eclectic menu that goes far beyond usual pub fare, with a wide selection of brick-oven pizzas, jambalaya, fish tacos, shepherd's pie, and bread-bowl soups. However, as the name would suggest, beer is the main event, with more than two-dozen house brews on tap. We're especially fans of the Detroit Dwarf beer, in homage to one of our favorite Detroit legends and neighborhood parades, the Marche du Nain Rouge (see separate entry)! Don't miss the awesome patio, and don't forget to pick up some beer to go on your way out. *1529 Broadway St., www.detroitbeerco.com, (313) 962-1529.*

The Detroit Club Grille - Detroit's oldest private social club, and once one of the nation's most exclusive, **The Detroit Club** has counted Hazen Pingree, Edsel Ford, and Walter P. Chrysler among its membership. Following a period of decline, the club was purchased in 2013, and after a lengthy renovation, some spaces within were opened to the public for the first time. Today, non-members are permitted to admire the interior of the stunning, four-story Romanesque Revival clubhouse, which dates to 1891, as well as to dine in the 64-seat Grille restaurant, which features French-inspired American fare and personalized service befitting a club of such illustrious pedigree. Appetizer highlights include shareable bone marrow and bao buns, while exceptionally executed entrees like the pork loin persillade, eight-ounce filet mignon, and wild mushroom risotto are sure to delight. Elevate your dining experience with a selection from the restaurant's extensive wine list, or an elegant and inventive cocktail. After your meal, take a self-guided tour to soak in the grandeur of the historic interior, especially the exquisite second floor ballroom, which features ornamental woodwork, a soaring ceiling with antique chandeliers, and a stunning original fireplace fit for Versailles. According to rumors, The Grille will be open to non-members only until membership rolls are filled, so don't dilly dally. *712 Cass Ave., www.thedetroitclub.com, (313) 338-3222.*

Detroiter Bar - The bar that the city was named for—or was it the other way around? Our grandfathers probably drank here, and the bar hasn't changed much since. With its tin ceiling, old-timey patio lights, creaking wood floor, and worn bar, this neighborhood sports dive seems to ooze history. At the same time, the bar is no stranger to some modern amenities, including a multiplicity of TVs and a contemporary beer selection. The Detroiter offers regular bar fare along with some novel additions inspired by its Greektown neighbors, including saganaki, flaming sausage, and gyros. The bar is usually quiet but gets rowdy on game nights. *655 Beaubien St., (313) 963-3355.*

Detroit Seafood Market - This spacious, elegantly designed restaurant and full bar in Harmonie Park, just minutes away from stadiums and theaters, gives customers satisfying, succulent, balanced meals and a wide-range of seafood choices, including swordfish, flounder, snapper, and crab cakes in a comfortable, warm setting. Macaroni and cheese enthusiasts should try the restaurant's popular Lobster Mac 'n' Cheese for a decadent take on a homemade classic. Check out the generous Sunday brunch buffet. Reservations recommended. *1435 Randolph St., www.thedetroitseafoodmarket.com, (313) 962-4180.*

Detroit Water Ice Factory - Harnessing a uniquely Detroit spin on a luscious delicacy imported from the East Coast, celebrated Free Press columnist Mitch Albom developed this charitable water ice enterprise to fund local nonprofit S.A.Y. Detroit. A relative of Italian ice, water ice is a creamy, smooth, sweet treat made of whipped ice and fruit, with a texture and consistency between a snow cone and a slushie. With its floor-to-ceiling subway tile, polished pendant lights, colorful neon lights and hand-lettered chalkboard menus, the shop offers a bright, clean, contemporary, and inviting vibe that puts the emphasis on the water ice. On the menu, look for a range of Detroit-themed flavors, including Corktown Cotton Candy, Zetterberry, Woodward Watermelon, Motown Mint, Riverfront Root Beer, and Stafford's Strawberry Lemonade. Don't leave without trying a Motown Twist, water ice blended with soft serve ice cream, or one of the seasonal varieties, such as pumpkin. *1014 Woodward Ave., www.detroitwaterice.com, (313) 888-9106.*

Dilla's Delights - Opened in 2016 by the uncle of the late and legendary hip-hop producer J Dilla, this donut shop has been a labor of love for Uncle Herm, who has been making donuts his entire adult life. As the story goes, it was Uncle Herm who inspired the name of Dilla's definitive album, Donuts. The walls pay tribute to Dilla, as well as local sports heroes and historic Detroit. There's a turntable with vinyl spinning, but don't think about changing tracks—the house rule is once a record is on, it plays it all the way through. The delectable delights are made with organic flour and high quality ingredients. Highlights among the Detroit-inspired D-lites include Brewster's Banana Pudding Cake and D-Lime-Nut Glaze, which are both crowd favorites. When the weather turns cooler, look for unusual, but tasty savory flavors like potato leek and broccoli cheddar. Coffee and tea are available, as are yummy vegan options. *242 John R St., www.dillasdelights.com, (313) 346-3771.*

Dime Store - Consider the prime location in a historic building, airy contemporary decor, and friendly staff as red herrings: the real belle of this ball is the food. Located off the lobby of the historic Dime Building, now known as Chrysler House, the chic yet unpretentious interior is centered around a bustling open kitchen that complements the industrial concrete floor, salvaged school chairs, and Mercury dime murals that define the space. From within that open kitchen, Executive Chef Josh Taylor churns out a striking take on American brunch and lunch fare that raises culinary standards, including a resplendent smoked salmon eggs Benedict, duck leg confit potato hash with Korean barbecue glaze, and charred fennel and endive salad with kale, Michigan cherries, and aged blue cheese. This spot's morning bar options don't disappoint either, so if you're an early bird, it's a great place to wet your beak. *719 Griswold St., Suite 180, www.eatdimestore.com, (313) 962-9106.*

Downtown Food Trucks - Whether you're looking for a bite to eat during a busy lunch hour, before the big game, or after a night on the town, Downtown has one of the biggest—and most varied—food truck scenes in the city, especially during the week when hungry office workers are seeking sustenance. Hours and locations vary by truck, but Cadillac Square is a good bet from April through October. Most of these trucks can also be spotted in Eastern Market on market days, as well as city-wide at events and gatherings. Southwest Detroit has its own unique taco truck scene (see separate entry). While there are other Downtown food trucks, read on for a few of our favorites, and be sure to visit each food truck's website for their daily schedule:

- **Beignets 2 Go** - When in Detroit, enjoy dessert first! Oui Oui! This New Orleans classic is brought to life (and to your mouth), freshly fried and covered in powdered, sugary goodness. Along with other contemporary options like cronets, you can savor these beignets with chicory coffee or cafe au laits. *www.beignets2go.com.*

- **El Guapo** - On the forefront of the city's food truck scene, this vanguard features Mexican-fusion creations. Though the entire menu is worth exploration, our favorites are the pork belly confit burrito, sweet potato burrito, Ned Nederlander burrito, and Korean Beef tacos. Equipped with veggie options—including fried tofu—as well as Faygo, there's something for everyone in this mobile sensation. *www.elguapogrill.com.*

- **Hero Or Villain** - This punnily named and brightly colored food truck Juggernaut serves up tasty and filling sandwiches named after—you guessed it—your favorite comic book foils, like the Sinister, a trois-fromage grilled cheese that is decidedly not malevolent. Featuring fresh ingredients and delicious options for vegetarians and vegans, this food truck has a certain Mystique with patrons, so be sure to get your subs or they will be gone in a Flash. *www.heroorvillaindeli.com.*

- **Mac Shack** - The cheesiest, richest and best mac and cheese served from a truck in all of Detroit, this spot is known for its decadent takes on its namesake dish, such as the Cluck Like a Buffalo (spicy chicken, green onions, blue cheese, and buffalo sauce) as well as delicious, basically sinful fries, served up with plenty of bacon and other delectable toppings. *www.macshackmichigan.com.*

- **Nosh Pit** - Named best food truck in the city by Hour Detroit in 2018, the Nosh Pit serves up wholesome, delicious, and locally sourced vegetarian and vegan sandwiches like the Denise (lentil-based sloppy joe topped with Better Made chips) and soul-warming soups year-round. See separate entry for their brick-and-mortar Hamtramck restaurant. *www.noshpitdetroit.com.*

- **Yum Village** - Specializing in Afro-Caribbean cuisine, Yum Village puts a delicious spin on the traditional food truck concept with jerk and curry chicken staples and tasty lamb shank, as well as vegetarian and vegan dishes like akara (black eyed pea fritters) and red beans and rice. Look for their forthcoming dine-in location in New Center. *www.yumvillage.com.*

Drive Table Tennis Social Club - Prepare to guard your cocktail from errant serves. Equal parts table tennis hall, cocktail bar, and casual restaurant, this young entrant in an increasingly crowded downtown dining scene sets itself apart with its dedication to ping pong, a delicious take on casual pub food, and an expansive full bar. The sleek and vibrant 4,000-square-foot space features bright murals, posters of celebrities playing table tennis, and five surplus Olympic table tennis tables. On the menu, look for innovative takes on American pub fare, including burgers, pizza, appetizers, and a focus on gourmet all-beef hot dogs, such as the Hawaiian Tiki Dog— a quarter pound beef dog wrapped in bacon and topped with pineapples, red onions, and teriyaki sauce. Behind the contemporary bar, expect a thoughtful collection signature craft cocktails, a thorough wine list, and a wide selection of domestic, imported, and local beers. *645 Griswold St., Suite 144, www.drive-detroit.com, 313-962-1830.*

Drought - While the experience of walking into this minimal, space-age juice shop feels cleansing on its own, it's also highly recommended that you leave with a bottle. While color is sparse in this crisp all-white establishment, it radiates from the glass-doored refrigerator case, which is stocked with the brilliant shades of fresh juice, ranging in hue from deep pink to bright green. Four sisters worked together to build the company from the ground up, and the quality of their efforts is evident in each signature, square glass bottle. Drought's juices are cold-pressed, meaning that the tremendous pressure exerted by their press extracts the natural fruit sugars, vitamins, trace minerals, enzymes, and other vital elements. Cold-pressing also allows the juice to be bottled without preservatives, while maintaining a five-day shelf life. Whenever we're feeling run down, the Immunity Potion, filled with lemon, ginger, cayenne, and turmeric, is our go-to; and you can't help but feel healthier after downing a bottle of the gorgeous Green #1, which is a detoxifying mix of chard, apple, kale, and lemon. *719 Griswold St. #110, www.droughtjuice.com, (313) 888-9950.*

Eatóri Market - From its perch at the foot of the Malcomson Building on Capitol Park, Chef Zak Yatim seamlessly mashes a front cocktail bar and restaurant concept and rear curated grocery into a single, gorgeous space. With its buffalo check tile floors, atmospheric mirrors, intricate woodwork, milk-glass lighting, and preponderance of diverse, stylish patrons, the space is sophisticated, modern, and handsome. In the sunny front room, start with a draft from an epicurean stable of craft beers from the likes of Great Lakes, Odd Side, Old Nation, and Short's, or one of a half dozen thoughtful cocktails, including the Violet 75, with creme de violette, champagne, Bombay Sapphire, and lemon. On the diverse menu, Yatim offers contemporary fare with an international flair: Steamed mussels with leeks and a garlic Chardonnay cream; a bistro-style burger made with a blend of ribeye, short rib, and truffle aioli; and a Moroccan bowl with eggplant, tomato, peppers, couscous, chickpeas, and herbs. In the rear of the space, look for a curated grocery selection that emphasizes grass-fed, organic, and imported options. *1215 Griswold St., www.eatorimarket.com, (313) 395-3030.*

Elwood Bar & Grill - Named for its original location at Elizabeth Street and Woodward Avenue (El and Wood), the Elwood Bar & Grill was opened in 1926 and designed by noted Art Deco architect Charles Noble. In 1997, this small architectural treasure—and the nearby Gem and Century Theatres (see separate entry)—were moved several blocks by owner Chuck Forbes to make way for the Tigers' new home, Comerica Park. At the time of the move, the entire structure was authentically restored to its original splendor, the highlight of which is the glistening white enameled-steel exterior. During games, the place is packed with sports fans sipping on 16-ounce beers. "Off" hours provide a quieter atmosphere at which time the honest, reasonably priced burger-coney-fries menu is yours to savor. *300 E. Adams St., www.elwoodgrill.com, (313) 962-2337.*

Fishbone's Rhythm Kitchen Cafe - A lively Louisiana-themed, gas-lit restaurant in a restored, timbered 19th-century manufacturing building, Fishbone's has been a center of Cajun and Creole cuisine in the city since 1989. The restaurant has a bright, loft-like interior littered with a collection of tchotchkes and exposed brick walls, contemporary woodwork, and a variety of seating options at spacious hardwood tables. Though the menu offers a mix of Japanese, American, and Louisianian options, the sushi and Cajun items seem more distinguished than the other American fare. Undecided visitors should try the crawfish etoufee, snapper beausoleil, lobster po' boy, or Italian muffuletta, all of which are tasty. *400 Monroe St., www.fishbonesusa.com, (313) 965-4600.*

Flood's Bar and Grille - This refined bar occupies the first floor of the historic Detroit Cornice and Slate Building. Regulars mingle either at the impressive central island bar, on the dance floor (with a smaller bar itself), or while dining in view of one of the many flat-screen televisions. Ambient highlights include an exposed brick interior, the scarlet-painted industrial ductwork, and architectural holdovers like outsize wood molding—but most importantly, a focused and refined selection of music: live jazz, soul, contemporary R&B, and dance-oriented DJs. The menu at Flood's is upmarket pub food, with a preference toward refined Southern and soul. Cover charges and minimums apply for live music events and an unimposing dress code applies on all nights. *731 St. Antoine St., www.floodsdetroit.com, (313) 963-1090.*

Foran's Grand Trunk Pub - Want to try a Michigan beer? Or 40? Grand Trunk boasts an impressive beer menu, with 14 taps dedicated exclusively to Michigan brews and more than 30 other locally brewed bottles. Though converted to a bar in 1935, this beautiful 1879 building was originally a jeweler's shop and the Grand Trunk Railway ticket office, and Foran's preserves many of these gorgeous historic features, including 25-foot vaulted ceilings, a hardwood bar, intricate woodwork, and massive chandeliers. Try a bite from the delicious, locally sourced menu of pub-centric comfort food including fish 'n' chips, Jameson meatloaf, shepherd's pie, and the stellar McGee sandwich—shaved turkey, roasted red pepper, avocado, romaine, Monterey jack, and mayo on sourdough. *612 Woodward Ave., www.grandtrunkpub.com, (313) 961-3043.*

Golden Fleece Restaurant - As one of the last mainstays of Greek cuisine in Greektown, the Golden Fleece has a colorful history dating back to 1971, when it was opened by the Dionysopoulos family. An old-timey establishment with a light, unassuming air, guests sit at blue-and-white checked tablecloths under a trellis of charmingly synthetic greenery (you might wonder how that greenery avoids going up in flames at each and every "OPA!" but somehow it survives). Though the casual place offers a full menu of classic, tasty favorites— from house-made spanakopita to shish kebabs and saganaki—the tender lamb gyros are the stars, with meat carved to order right off the spit spinning prominently in the front of the restaurant. To round out the menu, Golden Fleece offers a wide selection of Greek beer and wine, as well as a chilled Ouzo machine, serving up the anise-flavored liqueur. Open until 3am, The Fleece can keep every demographic of the Greektown set satisfied—from family diners to post-bar frenziers. During the summer, check out **Exodus**, the lush rooftop bar, which can be magical and serene, but can devolve, especially on weekends. *525 Monroe St., (313) 962-7093.*

Go! Sy Thai Downtown - The equally hip, but smaller Downtown cousin to Midtown's Go! Sy Thai (see separate entry for more details.) *1226 Griswold St., www.gosythai.com, (313) 638-1467.*

The Greek - Nestled on a bustling block, The Greek is one of Greektown's newest eateries, serving upscale and contemporary Greek food in a sleek yet comfortable setting. Authentic favorites like saganaki, gyros, and spanakopita (spinach and feta pie) are offered alongside Greco-American fusion options like grilled Greek wings and "GRK" nachos. Or opt for a classic burger or crispy chicken sandwich. No matter your taste, The Greek has you covered, and with extra generous portions to boot. Stop on in for the full bar (including spiked hot chocolate, perfect for chilly nights) and a bite to eat before hitting the Greektown party scene. Opa! *535 Monroe St., (313) 962-4687.*

Greenwich Time Pub - Red-yellow-and-chestnut-stained glass windows cast a warm glow on the ample wooden seating and freshly whitewashed walls of the Greenwich Time Pub, named for the owner's wife's fondness of London. Clocks behind the bar display the time for cities all over the world and antique pictures of Detroit and London decorate the walls. The wrap-around bar snakes around the beer tap to the hot grill, where cooks serve up the best fresh burgers for the price—big, juicy cheeseburgers run under $7. If the bar seating isn't for you, follow the winding, weathered wooden staircase up to a lunchtime dining and private banquet area surrounded by tall windows. There, take one of the popular window seats and enjoy the view that's been a Downtown favorite since 1952. *130 Cadillac Sq., (313) 961-7885.*

Ham Shop Cafe - As the name would suggest, the Ham Shop Cafe specializes in serving up a plethora of delicious dishes centered around thick, juicy cuts of the eponymous meat delivered fresh from Dearborn Ham. From ham-sprinkled split-pea soup to the ham-heavy Hungryman breakfast of bacon, ham, sausage, eggs, and spuds, there's plenty to keep pork lovers happy. However, the Ham Shop Cafe also features deli sandwiches (though many feature ham, there is some variety), soul food specials, such as broasted chicken, and a variety of affordable vegetarian breakfast and lunch deals. Carryout is a primary component of the spot, but there are plenty of tables inviting visitors to dine in for breakfast or lunch and enjoy the nice view of Greektown's main drag. *330 Monroe St., www.hamshopcafe.com, (313) 965-0088.*

Harbor House - A relative newcomer to the neighborhood, Harbor House is the Downtown iteration of a classic mainstay of the eastern suburbs. In a low-key but refined setting punctuated by finished woodwork and exposed brick, guests sit at one of the many round tables or the stunning 50-foot bar. Though the menu covers wide, meat-centric territory, the foci are steaks, ribs, and—above all—seafood. Popular favorites include the lobster macaroni and cheese and the crab legs, though those looking for a reason to loosen their belt might prefer the all-you-can-eat concept that's also available.

Sports fans should be sure to check out the inexpensive brunch before Lions games. *440 Clinton St., www.harborhousemi.com, (313) 967-9900.*

Hot Taco - With its sleek, modern design, the taqueria with the dirty name is a lunchtime and late night—they're open until 2am—post-bar favorite. Behind the stainless steel counter, the formidable crew slings Baja-style Mexican fare. While it offers a plethora of burritos, its tacos, which are mostly $3 each or three for $6, are our weapons of choice. Three favorites are the tilapia, veggie, and marinated chicken tacos (a house specialty), which are all especially tasty, and go well with one of the many imported sodas. *2233 Park Ave., www.hottacodetroit.com, (313) 963-4545.*

The Hudson Cafe - For breakfast, brunch, and brinner in Downtown Detroit, hit up the Hudson Cafe. Located in the central business district across from the former site of the storied J. L. Hudson department store, Hudson Cafe offers modern twists on classic breakfast and lunch items from classically French-trained Chef Tom Teknos in a bright, airy space with soaring ceilings and a contemporary vibe. Everything is made from scratch, including the house-made buttery biscuits, corned beef hash, buttermilk fried chicken, and the signature red velvet pancakes with cream cheese drizzle. Enjoy your hearty breakfast with some fresh-squeezed orange juice, or if you're in a hurry, step right up to the coffee bar in the lobby where you can grab a specialty coffee drink to go. You can also make a selection from the Hudson's homemade baked goods display, order an express breakfast sandwich, or pick up carryout orders from the cafe bar. Because of its focus on breakfast foods, the place closes at 3pm on weekdays and 4pm on weekends. *1241 Woodward Ave., www.hudson-cafe.com, (313) 237-1000.*

Jacoby's German Biergarten - One of the oldest establishments in Detroit, Jacoby's has been serving authentic German food and beer since 1904. The stunning old-world two-story tavern is decked out with historic woodwork, antique light fixtures, exposed brick, and character at every turn. In addition to a rotating selection of drafts, the classic night spot offers a mind-boggling 100—and often more—varieties of bottled beer that complement the extensive menu of American pub fare and German favorites like spaetzle, potato pancakes, sausage, and a variety of schnitzels. On weekdays, Jacoby's is popular with lawyers, politicians, and other nine-to-fivers working Downtown, while on nights and weekends the destination favorite draws an eclectic mix of sports fans and music lovers of many stripes.

Though the bar changed hands in 2016, the new owners have retained Jacoby's historic charm, while treating its kitchen and bathrooms to a few necessary upgrades. *624 Brush St., www.jacobysdetroit.com, (313) 962-7067.*

Joe Muer Seafood - Close your eyes and envision (after reading this first) a timelessly perfect anniversary date spot. The table topped with pressed white linen, the glass of garnet-red wine, the plate of plump scallops, a view of your honey in front of you—and glittering waters behind you. You'll find that and more at this iconic—even legendary—Detroit restaurant. This most recent incarnation of Joe Muer Seafood—located on the third floor of the Renaissance Center with sweeping vistas of the Detroit River—is every bit as decadent as the original (which shuttered in 1991), right down to architect Ron Rea's dramatic modern design. It is a classic American seafood and steakhouse with heavy French influence, so expect lots of succulent dishes stuffed with crab and smothered in meuniére sauce. Don't forget to pair your entree with a bottle of wine—there are hundreds of options of all vintages to choose from. The prices reflect the haute cuisine, so be sure you plan on a splurge during your visit, and be sure to dress to the nines—sports attire is allowed on game days only. *400 Renaissance Center, www.joemuerseafood.com, (313) 567-6837.*

The Keep - Need a place to keep all your secrets? Look no further than this dark, cavernous, mysterious watering hole, seemingly hidden amidst the rapid redevelopment of Downtown. With no-nonsense bartenders who will attend to your every liquor-fueled wish, this on-again-off-again-bar offers a true speakeasy vibe. Enjoy the antique-filled first-floor cocktail parlor, or venture below into the expansive brick-walled basement lounge with romantic votives burning bright. The elevated standards on the cocktail list echo Prohibition days, with absinthe and overproof varieties gracing the hefty, but approachable pages. Sassy and more, the bar is equal parts sour and sweet, with rotating specials to please even the most astute cocktailian, or tastemaker. In the warmer months, keep your cool on the patio with a draft cocktail or beer, and enjoy the splendor of Cadillac Square during happy hour. *140 Cadillac Sq., (313) 223-2626.*

La Casa - Set across from a quiet park, the flagship location for this local collection of cigar lounges offers visitors a mellow, relaxing alternative to the urban grind. Housed in the former Harmonie Studios building, made of orange brick with subtly beautiful tile work, La Casa has three distinct facets dedicated to giving aficionados a posh, laid-back experience: a retail cigar shop, a lounge and martini bar, and a paid membership VIP space. Both initiates and beginners can enjoy La Casa's shop—the walk-in humidor housing more than 100 varieties of stogies is staffed by salespeople knowledgeable in cigar manufacture, taste, aroma, and differentiation, and sells high-end cigar paraphernalia like cutters, lighters, cases, chemicals for home humidors, and offers $5 shoe shines in an antique wooden chair. Smokers can light up at the separate lounge—a classy, moodily lit den with red and black leather sofas, flat-screen TVs, ornate original wooden molding, a dark wood bar with a brass rail, and crimson and white wall decoration reminiscent of a finely marbled steak. The vibe is unapologetically comfy, drawing patrons for after-work cocktails from its practically exhaustive bar—a selection of high-end Scotches, bourbons, vodkas, and go-to import lagers are points of emphasis. First-timers will see a fair share of suits worn by a chatty crowd of regulars, but no uniform is required. Live music is offered gratis twice weekly. Upstairs is the club—a leather and wood seclusion spot with Wi-Fi, flat screens, conference space, and personal humidors. True connoisseurs may take advantage of La Casa's roll-to-order service—offering choice Central American tobacco rolled expertly by expat Cubans. *1502 Randolph St., www.lacasacigars.com, (313) 285-8332.*

★**Lafayette Coney Island** - With its original cash register, photo-clad white tile walls, retro all-chrome fixtures, mint green accents, and charmingly gruff staff in paper garrison caps, the shotgun-style diner has been a coney cathedral since 1917. This small, always-packed counter joint features limited table seating, which makes it an eavesdropper's paradise and beautifully reminiscent of pre-war diners. Along with next-door archrival American Coney Island, Lafayette is one of two originators of the coney island dog and is perhaps generally favored by purists. The backbone of the restaurant's limited menu is its coveted coney concoctions: naturally cased Dearborn Sausage franks wrapped in gooey, steamed buns, smothered in its distinctive, flavorful, beefy chili topped with minced Spanish onions and mustard. This tubesteakhouse is firmly carnivore country, though—fries and pies round out the vegetarian portion of the 15-item menu. Open 24 hours a day, seven days a week. *118 W. Lafayette Blvd., (313) 964-8198.*

La Lanterna - Opened in 1956 by Edoardo Barbieri, this popular, parkside Italian spot saw its fortunes turn with its city, and it was shuttered by the end of the 1970s. While things could have ended there, there's an unusual twist. After being closed for four decades, the classic spot was resuscitated by grandson Eddie—and just across the park from its original location. While the interior is contemporary and simple, the menu takes its cues from the restaurant's mythic origins, with a well-executed menu of traditional northern Italian dishes. Patrons will find a full selection of pastas, with sauces made from scratch that highlight rich, bold flavors, as well as classic complements—but the focus is on exceedingly thin and delicious neapolitan brick-oven pizzas. Pie-lites include the simple Fiorentina, a white number with garlic and arugula, and the spicy, red, sausage-garnished Lanterna. The full wine, beer, and craft cocktail list round out the menu at this unassuming neighborhood spot, making it a destination for Downtown diners, and a revived anchor for rapidly evolving Capitol Park. *1224 Griswold St., www.daedoardo.net/lalanterna, (313) 962-8821.*

La Pecora Nera - If you've never had the urge to Scrooge McDuck garlic and herb aioli, you haven't sat at these tables. This Italian deli is a 16-seat affair with stark white walls, subway tile counters, butcher block tables, and chalkboard menus. Like the atmosphere, the food is a contemporary spin on classic deli: Genoa salami, mortadella, spicy capicola, Sy Ginsberg corned beef, fresh mozzarella, extra virgin olive oil, the aforementioned aioli, and the like appear in generous portions and various combinations on fresh, delicate, Italian rolls. Wrapped and tied with a string bow, all of the sandwiches taste and look like gifts from the chef, though the Italiano—with its ham, turkey, salami, mortadella, capicola, provolone, fresh vegetables, and Italian dressing—is a standout. For early birds, La Pecora Nera does better than a worm: A number of breakfast sandwiches, including the Italian breakfast Reuben are available. Wash it all down with a pour-over coffee or an Italian-style gelato. Peruse the curated selection of fine and imported groceries on your way out. *1514 Washington Blvd., www.lapecoraneradetroit.com, (313) 315-3040.*

Loco's Tex-Mex Grille - As you might expect, the most authentic Mexican food in the city isn't found in Greektown at Loco, but it's a solid late-night coney-alternative. Loco's boasts huge portions and stays open 'til 2am on weekdays and 4am on weekends—and it's within stumbling distance of many of Downtown's attractions and bars, to boot! It has a pleasant, lively, spacious dining room, and offer a generous menu of traditional Mexican fare and a selection of Mexican beers and margaritas. Check out the $1 Taco Tuesdays! *454 E. Lafayette St., www.locobarandgrill.net, (313) 965-3737.*

London Chop House - After a storied 53-year existence, the London Chop house closed in 1991 before a celebrated reopening in 2012 in the same basement location that reigned over the Detroit restaurant scene for decades. This elegant, recently re-established Detroit tradition looks and feels much the same as when the founders ran the place, and features the same, circular red leather booths, iron-and-hardwood tables, mirrored oak bar, dark woodwork, and even the old phone number. This mignon minster is a verified sanctuary of sirloin and is not the place for a quick meal. Rather it is an exquisite, dignified destination for rare Scotch and generous portions of aged steaks and rich food fit for the auto barons. The menu boasts delectable takes on American cuisine, with an emphasis on traditional techniques, and the finest, freshest ingredients, with everything made from scratch, in-house. Though every item on the succinct lunch and dinner menus is exceptional, the steak tartare, veal chop Oscar, seared Ahi tuna, New York strip, and baby arugula and roasted beet salad stand out. The well-appointed bar offers an unparalleled selection of fine liquors and a thoughtful beer list. The restaurant also offers a separate cigar bar and small stage, with quiet live music. Limited vegetarian offerings. *155 W. Congress St., www.thelondonchophouse.com, (313) 962-0277.*

Lovers Only - Finally, a burger worth the weight. With its pastel schoolhouse chairs, Wes Anderson-like color palette, cheeky cowboy wallpaper, parquet flooring, globe lights and sweeping windows, the striking space has a distinctly mid-century modern feel. Owner Eli Boyer's menu offers a curated stable of elevated nostalgic favorites, including the bologna sandwich, the all-beef Chicago dog, cold fried chicken sandwich, and delectable hand-cut fries, but it's difficult not to pity folks who order them. Only fools and first-timers don't get a burger. Featuring the signature patty—locally butchered Michigan beef, griddle cooked to rosy perfection—and adding dijonaise, twice-cooked onions, Wisconsin cheddar, onions and relish, the Burlington burger shouldn't be missed. Wash the sins down with one of the eclectic drink options, including basil lemonade, wine, Vernors, craft beers, or one of several signature cocktails. Vegetarians will enjoy the Impossible Burgers. *34 W. Grand River Ave., www.loversonlydetroit.com, (313) 986-1174.*

Luci & Ethel's Diner - For those looking for a respite from an oversaturation of post-bar coney fever—and incredible people-watching—breakfast and well-rounded American fare are served all day (and many nights) at this greasy spoon. With decor installed during the Eisenhower administration and 24-hour service on the weekends, this is a perfect spot for an old-fashioned omelet, breakfast sandwich, low-tech burger, or grilled cheese. Throw in bottomless coffee and wall-to-wall windows that pour in sunlight (or moonlight), and this is quite the Downtown oasis. Though the style is retro, they do have the modern amenity of wireless internet. *400 Bagley St., (313) 962-2300.*

Lumen - One of the city's most architecturally impressive stand-alone restaurants has a menu to match. The stunning, contemporary space features modern geometry, marble tables, leather booths, expansive wall-to-wall windows, and a cantilevered roof that, together, give the restaurant an open, bright, and decidedly mid-century atmosphere. With two large patios, and an open air rooftop dining room, the restaurant connects seamlessly with the adjoining Beacon Park (see separate entry). Chef Gabby Milton's concise menu is similarly memorable. The items most likely to challenge your licking-the-plate-clean inhibitions are the everything bagel wings, pretzels with El Rojo beer cheese, garden and grains salad, pei mussels, and steak and frites. Those looking for lighter fare will enjoy pan-seared salmon, Asian salad, and rustic tomato. On the drink menu, look for extensive draft beer offerings from Griffin Claw Brewing, as well as a range of domestic and imported bottles, a curated wine program, and comprehensive cocktail options. *1903 Grand River Ave., www.lumendetroit.com, (313) 626-5005.*

Lunchtime Global - Located in the stately and historic First National Building, the asynchronously modern Lunchtime Global—with floor-to-ceiling views of Cadillac Square—offers a rotating menu of eight tasty soups made fresh each morning. Other lunch specials are wrapped and ready in the cold case for customers craving affordable items, like the $3 pesto pasta salad, but the main event here—and the real gem—is the soup selection, with a wide-variety of crowd-pleasers like broccoli cheese, split pea, dill pickle, and chicken chili made with locally sourced ingredients. Though meatatarians will be more than satisfied, there's also a well-rounded stable of vegan and vegetarian options, too. If you're on the go, enter directly off of Congress Street. However, if you have some time on your hands, take a stroll through the skylit Woodward Avenue lobby of this elegant historic building and meander through the marble interior. Be sure to check online for the latest list of soups and specials, and try to visit before noon to ensure the daily special hasn't run out! *660 Woodward Ave., www.lunchtimeglobal.com, (313) 963-4871.*

Maru Sushi - Modern Japanese cuisine meets the Motor City in this Downtown outpost of this upscale Michigan micro-chain. Housed in the mid-century modern wing of the Federal Reserve building, this elegant restaurant presents an industrial yet inviting aesthetic, with soaring ceilings, sleek details, and gleaming terrazzo floors. A former revolving door has been transformed into a refined alcove and half-round booth; it's our favorite seat in the house. Service is efficient at this bustling hotspot—all the better for savoring the generous range of unique nigiri, sashimi, unduly prodigious sushi rolls (they're big!)—as well as the delectable shareable plates. Standout menu items include the Firecracker Shrimp, the spicy edamame with Sriracha salt, the Blue Mango and Beach Party rolls, and an unparalleled vegetarian sushi selection—our favorite being the Boogie Veggie. The bar and cocktail list is also expansive, with a healthy selection of Japanese beers and sakes, to help wash down your meal. Don't miss the express lunch menu, which is lauded for its great deals, as well as the daily happy-hour specials for the after-work crowd. A reservation is usually simple to snag and good idea for weekend nights. *160 W. Fort St., www.marusushi.com, (313) 315-3100.*

Monroe St. Steakhouse - A staple of its Greektown neighborhood, this steakhouse is a popular and well-recommended sanctuary for carnivorous diners in need of filling, attentively prepared eats. The masthead offerings at Monroe St. are all Chairman's Reserve cuts—USDA Choice or higher—cooked to order, counterweighted with select seafood, barbecue, and pasta entrees. The subdued atmosphere creates an inviting experience—Monroe St. is well lit and cozy, with exposed brick, a teak ceiling, and numerous symbols of Detroit pride. Service is knowledgeable and attentive without being overzealous, and the Greektown digs mean casual dress works and spontaneous revelers are welcome. Full bar. *561 Monroe St., www.monroeststeakhouse.com, (313) 961-3636.*

Nick's Gaslight - Formerly the home of a four-star restaurant, Nick's Gaslight was a burned-out shell as recently as 1984, when the current owners rebuilt the bar (their previous restaurant, now a People Mover stop, fell to eminent domain). Inside, not much appears to have changed since then (one notable exception: a poster-size photograph of Janet Jackson's infamous Superbowl "wardrobe malfunction"). Today, the bar draws an eclectic mix of Polish union workers, Greek suburbanites, and curious Downtown partygoers. This is perhaps the only bar in Detroit that hosts live Greek music (the first Saturday of the month all winter long), and where you can still get treated to a rousing rendition of "Who Stole The Kishka" by a Polish union boss during the afternoon. *441 Grand River Ave., (313) 963-9191.*

Niki's Pizza - With its waxed-mustachioed mascot, Niki's has been a Detroit-style pizza institution since 1980. Located near the Greektown People Mover stop, this Downtown classic greets customers with a warm, loft-aesthetic of exposed brick, oak structural beams, and hardwood floors—all remnants of the building's historical use as a warehouse. The extensive menu offers a number of variations on the square, Detroit-style deep-dish pizza that the establishment is known for, including several less common Greek toppings, like lamb and feta, though the most popular varieties remain the standards. In addition, patrons are treated to a bevy of traditional Greek dishes like saganaki, moussaka, lamb kebabs, and spanakopita. In the summer months, diners can enjoy the street-side patio, which is the ideal environment for the beer-and-pizza experience. Don't miss half-price pizza on Wednesdays. *735 Beaubien St., www.nikispizza.com, (313) 961-4303.*

The Old Shillelagh - Nestled in Greektown's nightlife center rather than the historically Irish Corktown, The Old Shillelagh is the Downtown mega-pub for Detroiters whose Irish roots go as deep as the volume of Guinness and Jameson they can slug. With three floors (including a rooftop deck) and an outdoor bar that's open for game days, the Old Shillelagh knows how to pack 'em in. And, with a St. Patty's Day following that's 10,000 drinkers strong, you can bet those towers of plastic cups behind the bar aren't just for show. During the day, the wood-and-brick interior accurately evokes the nostalgia of an authentic neighborhood Irish Pub, but on weekends, before ballgames, or during any Downtown drinking holiday, you'll likely be too cramped (and "spirited") to notice. *349 Monroe St., www.oldshillelagh.com, (313) 964-0007.*

Orchid Thai - The power-lunch establishment for the Thai connoisseur, this efficient restaurant has a wide variety of delicious cuisine and generous portions. With cream-colored walls and Spartan Thai decor, the bright yet unassuming space places more emphasis on flavor than ambiance. Though Orchid Thai offers well-balanced takes on classic favorites, such as Pad Thai, the most popular dishes are the spiciest curries, tangy noodles, and fried rice dishes, all of which are offered with beef, chicken, shrimp, and tofu options. Truly vegetarian-friendly, the accommodating staff is happy to hold the fish sauce or substitute tofu. This joint is serious about spice—so be careful how you order. ¡Thai, caramba! In the summer months, get carryout and head for Campus Martius up the block. *115 Monroe St., (313) 962-0225.*

Parc - This locally lauded restaurant sits smack dab in the middle of Campus Martius Park (see separate entry)—close to Woodward Fountain—which offers the majestic opulence of a Parisian square—fountain-misted patio seating included. The restaurant boasts contemporary concept-cuisine centered in the French and Mediterranean traditions, with a heavy twist of refined but hearty Midwestern fare, epitomized by their signature prime dry-aged beef selections. The sleek space features elegant decor with modern finishes and floor-to-ceiling windows on three sides, which highlight the bustle and beauty of the surroundings. Parc's happy hour specials rank high among offerings Downtown, while the elegantly plated dinner dishes can be nothing short of a regal adventure. Favorites include the charred burrata, tuna tartare, and whole grilled trout, while the crisp salads also delight. With sensuous dessert options, including an exceptional *affogato* (an Italian coffee dessert) and a decadent hazelnut brownie sundae, the final course shouldn't be missed, either. Parc also offers a full bar, but it is best known for its wine selection, which makes it a perfect romantic escape for a glass of bubbly after ice skating in the park. Reservations recommended. *800 Woodward Ave., www.parcdetroit.com, (313) 922-7272.*

Parks & Rec Diner - Ever hear the one about the charming brunch diner with amiable staff and delectable takes on contemporary American breakfast standards at reasonable prices? The yolk's brunchline is a real knee-slapper. On the ground floor of the historic Grand Army of the Republic Building (see separate entry), this popular diner sports a pleasant, vaguely Parisian atmosphere with park bench seating, retro lunch counter, chess board table tops, blond wood accents, and spearmint-colored walls. The menu is a tour de force of contemporary takes on brunch staples, all made with fresh, ambrosial ingredients and sumptuous presentation. Though the biscuits and gravy (airy buttermilk biscuits with zesty sausage gravy and a poached egg) are a must-order, other outstanding options abound, including brioche French toast, oatmeal brulée, and a smoked leek strata. Wash your brunch down with the locally roasted coffee or something off the curated cocktail menu; we won't judge. *1942 Grand River Ave., www.parksandrecdiner.com, (313) 446-8370.*

Pegasus Taverna - Open since the 1980s, Pegasus is a stronghold of old Greektown and a reminder of a time when the neighborhood was not just a late-night destination, but an epicenter of Greek culture and food. With an animated neon sign depicting the flapping wings of the mythical flying creature from which the restaurant takes its name, Pegasus offers guests always-packed table, booth, and U-shaped bar seating in a refined Grecian garden setting. With a comprehensive menu of delicious, authentic, and generously portioned Greek cuisine churned out of the gigantic open kitchen, lucky diners can choose from favorites like spanikopita, moussaka, lemon rice soup, pastitsio (blasphemously best described as Greek lasagna), lamb in dozens of preparations, and essential, crowd-pleasing saganaki. In keeping with Greektown hours, the restaurant is open until 3am on weeknights and 4am on weekends. If you're looking for delights to take home, check out the deli counter, where you can purchase cheeses, sweets, and pastries for later. And, honey, don't forget the baklava! *558 Monroe St., www.pegasustavernas.com, (313) 964-6800.*

Pizza Papalis - Founded in Detroit in 1986, Pizza Papalis has perfected the famous Chicago-style round-deep-dish-sauce-on-top pie, producing distinctive pies with rich, buttery, flakey crust, a two-inch-thick pile of dough, cheese, sauce, and toppings, and slightly spicy yet tangy sauce. The Greektown Taverna location keeps things fresh with a large Italian menu and an even larger open-seating area with towering brick archways, tall wooden booths, and a full-service bar flanked by flat-screens. Picky eaters can find options from chicken fingers to salads (and yes, even thin-crust pizza). But because the Spinach Special pizza is so popular that it gets shipped half-frozen to fans across the country, why bother ordering anything else? Stop by for affordable lunch specials that are anything but "junior size," or look online for the latest coupon deals on large pies—perfect for sharing with family and friends! *553 Monroe St., www.pizzapapalis.com, (313) 961-8020.*

★ **Pop + Offworld -** Remember that time you went to Detroit's original bar-arcade, slammed craft drafts, pounded pizza, and played the finest in vintage video entertainment until last call and didn't have a good time? Neither do we. A must for both retro video game fans and the nostalgically curious, this gem is packed with nearly 35 quarter-activated arcade and pinball cabinets from the classic to the obscure—from essential heavy hitters like *Ms. Pac-Man* and *Street Fighter II*, to rarer classics like *Dragon's Lair*. Don't see your favorite? Come back tomorrow—games are swapped out frequently, so there's always a new surprise waiting for you. But the games aren't the only attraction at this destination 80s-tinged dive aesthetically seasoned with a hint of Pee-wee's Playhouse and a dash of Miami Vice. The thin-crust, deliciously greasy pizza is far better than it needs to be or you would expect, with innovative and delectable pies such as the Tater Tot-topped Gordo or Indian-inspired Coco Curry, as well as crowd-pleasing classics. Look for live entertainment or DJs on most weekend nights. Some people say Pop + Offworld can be a little hard to find. Player hint: it's on the second floor of Checker Bar (see separate entry). See you there! We call Chun-Li. *128 Cadillac Sq., www.poppizzabar.com, (313) 961-9249.*

Press Room - Part 21st century automat, part fast casual pizza operation, part bodega, and part upscale coffee house, Press Room is difficult to define but easy to love. Despite a name inspired by its location at the base of the Detroit News Building, the space eschews the congested, frantic, utilitarian vibe of newsrooms. Inside, look for a bright, open industrial space dominated by the kind of windows air traffic controllers dream of, clusters of milk globe lights, and a large Italian pizza oven. The restaurant's four main components: An Intelligentsia coffee lounge, a large outdoor patio, a convenience store, and a restaurant. At the restaurant-ordering terminals, you can pay for coffee, convenience items, and restaurant orders, all without human interaction. While the menu offers up a diverse selection of burgers, soup, salads, seasonal sandwiches, and pizzas, the poached pear and gorgonzola pizza, with its Neapolitan-style crust, poached pears, balsamic onions, and gorgonzola spread is a speciality. *615 W. Lafayette Blvd., www.pressroomdetroit.com, (313) 373-8670.*

Prime + Proper - Billing itself as "a modern interpretation of the American steakhouse," this newcomer to Capitol Park opened its doors in 2017, with great fanfare. Housed in a beautifully restored 1912 building, the well-designed, opulent interior features stunning modern fixtures and finishes, horseshoe booths, and an original marble staircase. On the meticulous menu, look for exceptional steak, seafood, and sides; sumptuous desserts; and an expansive wine list, all of which are sure to impress even the most astute gourmet. A proper occasion can be marked with true fine dining and service at Prime + Proper, especially if you're willing to part with a little coin. Featuring an in-house butcher, you can peer through glass windows into the Himalayan-rock-salt-lined dry-aging vault, and see the finest cuts of American beef and Japanese Wagyu. Dessert is truly lauded—especially the peanut butter "pavé." If you're looking to get a drink and a smaller meal, check out the bar menu with more casual offerings, including duck wings and a burger. There is no stated dress code, but you're going to want to look respectable. *1145 Griswold St., www.primeandproperdetroit.com, (313) 636-3100.*

Punch Bowl Social - With its heady cocktail of bar games, pub food, and, well, cocktails, this millenial playground micro-chain, with 13 locations nationally, has become a downtown favorite. Like any good punch recipe, the aesthetic is an alluring miscellany, incorporating elements like antler chandeliers, cut-log tables, mid-century couches, and tin ceilings, all tied together by exposed brickwork and sweeping windows. Across its 24,000 square feet, Punch Bowl Social checks all the enticing lido deck amusement boxes, with seven bowling lanes, ping pong tables, two private karaoke rooms, a vintage-style arcade, pool tables, foosball tables, shuffleboard, cornhole, and three bars. The menu is equally tempting. On the drink menu, look for an impressive assortment of domestic, craft, and imported beers in cans and on tap, alongside a rigorous cocktail list, boozy milkshakes, and perhaps unsurprisingly, punch bowls. The food offerings might be best described as elevated bachelor comfort food, with options like a grass-fed sloppy joe, spaghetti and meatballs, lobster bacon fries, and monkey bread French toast during brunch. *1331 Broadway St., www.punchbowlsocial.com, (313) 749-9738.*

★**Queens Bar** - One of two distinct Detroit watering holes named for New York City boroughs— the other being Midtown's legendary Bronx Bar (see separate entry)—Queens is an Art Moderne gem. Acting as a refuge from the brodeo that can sometimes overtake downtown, this modern Detroit classic is unassuming and sophisticated. Lovingly restored by owner Paul Howard, the gorgeous bar, with its massive windows and curvy, sleek, historic styling, calls to mind the classic Edward Hopper painting *Nighthawks*. While the inside is stunning in its time warping simplicity, the patio is one of downtown's best, with a frontrow view of a bustling and rapidly evolving slice of the city. The bar offers a full complement of draft and bottled beer, wine, and spirits, as well as a solid menu of bar fare. As an unusual bonus, the bar features Detroit's most lavish and labyrinthian subterranean restrooms. Don't miss capping your evening off at this downtown gem. *35 E. Grand River Ave., (313) 285-8019.*

Ready Player One - One can hope that this is the start of a veritable bar-arcade district, what with this being the fourth arcade bar in about as many blocks. After all, the only thing better than video games and beer is more video games and beer. Compactly but comfortably pressed into a garden level space, the main event at this vintage video game haven is coin-operated games, and, like Street Fighter's Dhalsim, it brings the heat. In addition to all the essential classics, Ready Player

One boasts a slew of rare cult favorites, including Michael Jackson's Moonwalker, Mario Brothers, Sunset Riders, and the mythical two-screen, six-player X-Men cabinet (see their website to confirm current offerings). While the emphasis is on classic games, the joint offers a full bar with eight rotating taps and a comprehensive food menu that can satisfy most palates, with a range of pub grub and snacks, including dips, hot sandwiches, burgers, and pizzas. Being on the fringes of Greektown, the place can lean towards a partying crowd—and fill to capacity—on weekend nights, so, whether or not that's your scene, plan accordingly. Food and drink purchases come with free game tokens, but you can supplement with your own quarters. *407 E Fort St., www.rpodetroit.com, (313) 395-3300.*

Red Smoke - Since bursting onto Detroit's packed barbecue stage in 2010, Red Smoke has been winning accolades and devotees for its contemporary industrial atmosphere, attentive staff, and exemplary wood-smoked barbecue fare. The updated 120-year-old building features a full mezzanine, exposed brick, a massive pig chandelier, and 30-foot ceilings. Don't be fooled, though—owners Michael and Tasso Teftsis' team are as gifted in the kitchen as they are with architecture. While offering a full menu with yummy takes on all the usual suspects—Amish chicken, pulled pork, and ribs—its specialties are the ultra-tender brisket and the delicious green beans with fried leeks. Both would medal in any Detroit barbecue Olympics. Red Smoke has a bevy of appetizers, such as the fried pickles, jalapeño cornbread skillet, and catfish bites that shouldn't be overlooked, despite the linebacker-size entree portions. *573 Monroe St., www.redsmokebarbeque.com, (313) 962-2100.*

★**Republic -** It's fitting that they keep this culinary treasure in a castle. With a home shrouded in local history, a luxurious interior, and a seasonal haute cuisine menu, Republic is a perennial critic favorite. The atmosphere strikes a balance between being relaxed and au courant, thanks to tall ceilings, Edison-bulb fixtures, contemporary art, and oversized windows that seamlessly depart from the carefully restored historic exterior of the Grand Army of the Republic building (see separate entry). Though changing frequently, the highly seasonal, meat-centric menu embraces a nose-to-tail butchering philosophy and an emphasis on local ingredients with each iteration. If in season and available, the sarvecchio ramp tagliatelle, bone marrow fritters, smoked pastrami salmon with pea tendrils, and duck mousse are nonpareil and not to be missed. This emphasis on fine ingredients and scratch cooking extends behind the bar. Look for craft cocktails that showcase handmade syrups and infused spirits alongside a stable of local beers, domestic and imported wines, and 130 whiskeys. *1942 Grand River Ave., www.republictaverndetroit.com, (313) 446-8360.*

Roast - Roast is one of Detroit's most high-profile restaurants and with good reason. Situated on the bottom floor of the beautiful Westin Book Cadillac, a historic hotel that was a beacon of luxury during the earlier days of Detroit's prominence and home to more celebrity stories than *People* magazine, Roast is quite possibly the building's star attraction today. With celebrated chef Michael Symon (of *Iron Chef* and *The Chew* fame) behind it, Roast is a celebration of all things meat—right down to the "roast beast" cooking on a spit in full view of the dining room (but vegetarians are also welcome, and in fact, the vegetarian-friendly dishes are some of the best things on the menu—try the macaroni and cheese). From beef cheek pierogi to roasted marrow served on sawed bone, Roast consistently impresses. With an exceptional wine selection, classically inspired craft cocktails and an extensive craft beer list, Roast is known nearly as well for its bar as it is for its food and atmosphere. Its happy hour is the best in town. *1128 Washington Blvd., www.roastdetroit.com, (313) 961-2500.*

Roasting Plant - With its Jetsons-style brewing technology, modern interior, and a coffee bean selection as geographically diverse as the Summer Olympics, Roasting Plant, a micro-chain with a few locations around the Midwest and East Coast, offers those in need of caffeine a memorable, freshly ground response to the daily grind. The mesmerizing "Javabot" brewing system hurls beans through pneumatic tubes hung from the ceiling, contributing to a sleek tech-startup atmosphere, complete with I-beam accents, boutique glassware, and flat screen menus. The shop's menu is a seasonal, epicurean selection of beans from around the globe, featuring a mix of one-off nano batches and enduring Roasting Plant standards, including the Bali Blue Moon—with its bold complexion and earthy, nutty, flavor—and Jamaica Blue Mountain Peaberry—known for a rich, creamy feel and sweet, custard-like bouquet. *660 Woodward Ave., www.roastingplant.com, (313) 782-4291.*

★ **The Royce -** An absolutely stunning bi-level bar and wine shop, The Royce marries superior selection with an aesthetic that draws on art-deco elegance and industrial authenticity. Spanning the first two floors of the historic Kales building, guests are greeted by a beautiful 12-seat marble bar, copious subway tile, and a soaring walnut wine library complete with a rolling ladder. Drift past the two-tops and climb to the mezzanine to find a cozy and sophisticated lounge that's perfect for larger parties and affords a birds-eye view of the bar. Visitors can draw from the exceptional international organic and biodynamic wine list, or opt for a cocktail. For those looking to explore, we suggest trying a wine flight to sample multiple varietals. To complement these options, The Royce also offers a diverse menu of fine cheeses, charcuterie, and small plates that pair well with their drink menu. Patrons can peruse the impressive array of more than 300 wines displayed on their shelves, and bottles can be purchased for at-home or on-site consumption. For the latter, there is a $10 corkage fee, which can still make picking your own bottle a more economical option if you're looking for more than a quick tipple. Don't miss free wine tastings on Wednesday evenings. *76 W. Adams Ave., www.theroycedetroit.com, (313) 481-2160.*

Rusted Crow - The only full-service restaurant and tasting-room of Dearborn-based distillery **Rusted Crow Spirits**, Detroit's Rusted crow boasts a wild, inventive interior that is a steampunk dream-scape constructed from eye-catching industrial treasures, architectural salvage, beer barrels, steamer trunks, meandering black iron, and Edison bulbs. The timber-rich industrial refuge features a generous menu of creative American fare, including customer favorites like portobello fries, brussel sprout salad, and an inventive grilled brie sandwich with brussel sprouts, peanut butter vinaigrette, and a fig-bacon marmalade. While dining under the watchful eye of 19th-century American innovators depicted in mural form, wash down your meal with one of the 17 beers on tap, or a selection from the craft cocktail menu. Each of the artful, seasonal speciality cocktails highlights the house-line of quality, locally-distilled spirits, including Davy Jones Rum, Ginstache Gin, Detroit Steam Vodka, and others. As an added bonus, the elusive bottles of Rusted Crow Spirits are also available for retail purchase. *78 W. Adams Ave., www.rustedcrowdetroit.com, (313) 782-4751.*

SavannahBlue - Sleek yet vibrant, upscale but down-to-earth, southern with a Detroit twist—SavannahBlue is a happy mélange of tradition and innovation. It's Northern soul food. How else to explain the delicious Georgian hummus, made with black-eyed peas and served with garlicky flatbread? Or the perfectly cooked salmon with an inventive chimichurri sauce? Other dishes stick closer to the classics but are incredible just the same, like the lightly breaded catfish, reminiscent of a New Orleans po' boy. Pair it with your choice of sides, like mac and cheese (the way it's meant to be: crispy on the outside, indulgently creamy on the inside) or collard greens—and don't forget to use the honey-kissed cornbread that comes with your meal to soak up the pot liquor. All you need now is a tart-with-a-hint-of-sweet cocktail like SavannahBlue's Blacker the Berry to keep the good times rolling. *1431 Times Sq., www.savannahbluedetroit.com, (313) 926-0783.*

Shinola Hotel Bars and Restaurants - One of the most hotly anticipated hotel developments in Detroit in the last decade, the Shinola Hotel is opulence for the modern era, with green-friendly design, and an accessible and cozy interior. True to its mission to be a "living room for Detroit," the hotel offers multiple outstanding restaurants and bars for all to enjoy, from haute cuisine to approachable diner fare. **Brakeman** is an unpretentious beer hall with a rotating selection of drafts from the Midwest, as well as pub games like table tennis and shuffleboard. The Detroit outpost of the popular New York cocktail lounge of the same name, **Evening Bar** is a gorgeously embellished bar that emphasizes spirits from artisanal distillers, seasonal ingredients, and craft in its exceptional, boozy concoctions. On the casual side, **Penny Red's** offers American classics, like perfectly spiced buttermilk-brined fried chicken and honey-dipped biscuits, that will fill you up and warm your soul. With a menu developed by James Beard Award-winning chef Andrew Carmellini, **San Morello** is a Southern Italian restaurant that spotlights local ingredients and features homemade pastas, wood-fired cuisine, and pizzas. *1424 Woodward Ave. www.shinolahotel.com.*

Sid Gold's Request Room - This outpost of the New York City piano cabaret mainstay brings its famed glamour and energy, but adds an unmistakable Detroit flair. Beyond its alley entrance, the bar is broken up into two rooms, a front lounge area and a rear barroom for the renowned live piano karaoke. Though opened in 2018, the bar has a vintage vibe reminiscent of an upscale basement bar, thanks in part to the decidedly mid-century influence. The entertainment options vary, though generally begin with cabaret shows, including burlesque, and conclude with guests singing favorite tunes—from pop to soul, and punk to classic rock—along with a live pianist. The sophisticated bar program ought to be a draw all on its own. Look for beer, wine, and a mixture of traditional cocktails alongside music-inspired concoctions like the Velvet Underground (velvet falernum, bourbon, and lime). *1515 Broadway St., www.sidgolds.com.*

The Skip - For those nights when you just want to have a delicious frozen alcoholic slushie in an alley, this delightful biergarten-style bar is tucked away on the side of The Belt (see separate entry). Located in an alcove that was once occupied by dumpsters and trash ("skip" is British slang for dumpster!), the space has been completely transformed, and today it is hip, lush, and fun, with festive lighting, reclaimed wood tables, and an enormous mural by renowned artist Shepard Fairey. Frozen drinks are the signature of this watering hole, and we particularly love the zippy frozen Irish Coffee, made with Intelligentsia cold brew. You'll also find a mix of traditional cocktails, like a gin and tonic, next to more innovative originals like the Little Pigeon, which combines tequila, grapefruit sherbet, soda, and bitters. Come on Thursday nights for Savage Bliss, where DJ Frankie Banks plays a mix of dub, reggae, tropical funk, and hip hop. Though a summer mainstay, The Skip is open year-round. *Located in The Belt, at Grand River Ave., www.theskipdetroit.com.*

Small Plates - With a street-style decor courtesy of local artist Antonio "Shades" Agee and Motor City Denim, Small Plates lays claim to being the first restaurant of its kind in the country with a federally trademarked name and concept. Evolving the tradition of Spanish tapas and Italian antipasti, Small Plates serves a true melting pot of American fare with a particular Detroit flair, highlighting dishes inspired by cuisines prominent in the city, including Mediterranean and Southern. Standouts include fried green tomatoes, chicken and waffles, duck wraps, lotus tuna, and pretzel sliders. Wine and cocktails are recommended, as the bar has just a select few Michigan and local craft beers on draft and you can easily enjoy a round seated at the charming bistro tables. *1521 Broadway St., www.smallplates.com, (313) 963-0702.*

★**Standby** - Look for the gas lamp in the alley and enter to find this James Beard-nominated bar and restaurant, which offers a discerning menu, and arguably the city's best cocktail program. The interior of Standby is a dim, seductive, contemporary space with a low-slung, wood-rich bar alcove and a dramatic dining room lined with blue upholstered banquettes and enormous, bold artworks. The menu is solidly New American, with some elevated diner classics. Though things are seasonal, look for highlights like the flavorful Delhi Chicken, the exquisite and incarnadine lamb ribs, or the popular Tunisian Fried Cauliflower. However, Standby is revered as much for its cocktails as it is for its food. Offering a full bar with a rotating selection of masterful signature creations, you'll find complex, technical cocktails sitting alongside variations on approachable classics. Seasonal standouts include Huarache Nights (a well-balanced gin and coconut delight), Dog Days Negroni (a riff on the classic), and an Amaro submenu with highlights like the Lucano Highball (with celery bitters and soda). Of course, you could always opt for a nip from the Break Even Bottle, a rotating one-ounce pour of a top-shelf spirit sold at cost. *225 Gratiot Ave., www.standbydetroit.com, (313) 736-5533.*

Sweetwater Tavern - Tucked inside a beautiful, quaint, 1941 brick building, Sweetwater Tavern is an upscale bar and restaurant catering to the city's young urban professionals. Beyond its impressive liquor selection and small but well-curated beer list, Sweetwater is a sacred site for wing worshipers, selling 600 pounds a day. Sweetwater's wings are brought in fresh from Eastern Market each morning, marinated for 24 hours, drenched in a delicious spice blend, and fried as you order. Known for its distinctive, tangy, mildly spicy flavor and crispy exterior, these outstanding wings are served with celery and bleu cheese. Not a one-trick pony, the menu also offers succulent breaded catfish and perfect reuben sandwiches. Sweetwater keeps the kitchen open until 2am and offers a free shuttle to the stadiums, making it a great pregame option. Don't stop here on the way to the hospital—the place is usually packed, and the service is on the slow side. *400 E. Congress St., www.sweetwatertavern.net, (313) 962-2210.*

Tommy's Detroit Bar & Grill - The view of the Joe should tell you lots—this Downtown bar has always catered heavily to Detroit sports fans, particularly those who bleed red and white in winter. Tommy's is a comfy, welcoming place to get a quick lunch of house-drenched wings or cheap, fresh burgers cooked deliciously well-done, as well as a spot to take in a game from one of five flat screens while tipping back a few. Tommy's also offers a slice of history: Its red brick building, originating in 1840, still features hidden underground rooms, from the building's role in the Underground Railroad. The rich, woody interior is warm and cozy, and made to resemble the inside sling of a schooner's hull. A game room with pool, darts, and video poker, and a small street-side patio round things out. *624 Third Ave., www.tommysdetroit.com, (313) 965-2269.*

Townhouse - Bright and airy enough to make a greenhouse jealous, Townhouse's all-glass atrium and retractable ceiling make for one of the city's most distinctive dining rooms. The unapologetically au courant interior, with its modernist furniture, constellation of Edison pendants, fashionable patrons, and wrap-around terraced patio, is at once lively, contemporary, and easy on the eyes. Your mouth won't have much to complain about, either. Executive Chef Michael Barrera is renowned for his approach to American bistro-style cuisine: A menu of rich, flavorful, international-inflected comfort food, alongside a full sushi program. Look

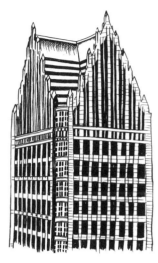

Ally Detroit Center, pg. 96

for diverse offerings, such as steak tartare, bibimbap, tuna nigiri, truffle fries, and trout almondine. With its perfect sear and sharp presentation, the Salmon vs. Everything, is— almost—too pretty to eat, though your nose and the luxurious creme fraiche potatoes will convince you otherwise. On the liquid side of the menu, look for an extensive beer, wine, and cocktail list with highlights such as the El Drake and Stiggins Tropical Daiquiri. *500 Woodward Ave., www.eatattownhouse.com, (313) 723-1000.*

The Town Pump Tavern - A contemporary, laid-back spot in an airy, handsome space, the Town Pump has been a Downtown destination since 1996. Located in the Park Avenue House, an old-school apartment hotel, the bar offers a modern reflection of the historic building, with a forest worth of contemporary wood paneling, antique brass lights, and a tin ceiling. With its convenient location steps from the stadiums, the bar is popular with rowdy sports fans celebrating Tigers triumphs and drowning sorrows after Lions losses. The bar offers 18 drafts alongside a roster of international and domestic bottles, and a menu of hearty pub fare. Though the belles of the ball on the menu are the cheese-laden, hand-tossed pizzas, the tavern also offers tasty sandwiches, salads, sides, and hamburgers, including the popular Atlantic cod po' boy. Local DJs spin on weekends and attract large crowds to this late-night watering hole. *100 W. Montcalm St., www.thetownpumptavern.com, (313) 961-1929.*

Urban Bean Co. - Located in one of Downtown's most peculiar (and small) commercial spaces, this compact coffee shop is perched at the corner of Griswold Street and Grand River Avenue. With two floors of floor-to-ceiling windows, it can offer guests an uncommon bird's eye view of the action below. Downstairs you'll find a respectable menu of tea, locally roasted coffee, and espresso drinks, including some more creative options, like the Pure Evil Latte (a mix of espresso, amaretto, cherry, and milk) along with snacks from local favorite, Avalon International Breads (see separate entry). While the first floor offers just a handful of bar stools, the second floor is a splendid, full-on 1970s throwback, with orange vinyl-covered seats, wood paneling, and an elaborate turntable set-up. While it's a stylish and relaxing (albeit bustling) environment most mornings, look for electronic guest DJs, including the regular Tuesday Techno event. *200 E. Grand River Ave., www.urbanbeanco.com, (313) 496-1010.*

Vertical Detroit - If you like your wine fine, then Vertical is the place to dine. Housed on the first floor and garden levels of the historic Ashley building—a Flatiron-style masterpiece in Harmonie Park—enter through the lush lobby, and step down into the cavernous wine cellar of this fine dining establishment, where the party—and happy hour specials—are very literally in the back. The sensuous, cozy subterranean interior is punctuated with subdued velvet touches and refined industrial finishes, and it feels like a world away. The small-plates fare is well-executed and well-loved. From "The Beginning" to the "The End," the menu is artfully plated, with highlights that include the Sambuca Mussels, a delightful compressed watermelon salad, Wolverine Lamb (served over risotto), and the ever-important Creme Brulee. As you might expect, the wine steals the show, with by-the-glass options and adventurous bottles expertly collected from far and wide by owners and lifelong wine lovers James and Remy Lutfy. Reservations and proper attire encouraged. *1538 Centre St., www.verticaldetroit.com, 313-732-WINE.*

Vicente's Cuban Cuisine - A little piece of Havana in Detroit, Vicente's Cuban Cuisine is renowned for its signature Cuban food and handsome, contemporary space. It serves authentic Spanish-style tapas ranging in Latin influences from traditional Cuban flavors to Spanish and South American styles developed by well-traveled Chilean chef Roberto Caceres. Its extensive menu also includes popular paellas, pressed sandwiches on genuine Cuban bread made with lard, and a variety of Spanish wines, flavored mojitos, and sangria. The refined dining room features elegant tables with bud vases, a bright color palette, wood floors, an open ceiling, and a sweeping hardwood dance floor. On weekend nights, the dance floor supplants the food as the primary attraction, with free salsa lessons, salsa dancing, live bands, and DJs. Vicente's is the full-on Latin supper club experience in Detroit's Central Business District, perfect for business lunches as much as date nights. *1250 Library St., www.vicente.us, (313) 962-8800.*

WaLa - With an impressive roster of hearty, flavorful sandwiches, and a name stemming from its location at Washington and Lafayette, WaLa has become a destination for hungry Detroiters in the market for an outstanding sandwich or ballad-worthy salad since opening in 2012. With contemporary prints adorning the walls, all-chrome chairs, and a street-corner patio, this unassuming space gives off a lively, character-full ambiance to match the food. The menu offers tasty takes on sandwich staples with fresh, local ingredients—including breads from On the Rise Bakery (see separate entry). The shrimp po' boy, mile-high Italian, and Lizzy—panko breaded tilapia and slaw—are standouts. *1010 Washington Blvd., www.waladetroit.com, (313) 963-5450.*

The Well - It's a safe bet that most patrons going to The Well are too busy chatting over basement-priced drinks and spotting a game from The Well's flat-screens or big screen to pay mind to the decoration, but The Well is no slouch for environs. This mellow-lit joint features exposed brick, a long hardwood bar, wood tables and chairs, and a monogrammed glass entrance. There's no need to be bored simply conversing with regulars, but those who want to can enjoy the game room in the rear. Patio seating available. *1228 Randolph St., www.thewellbars.com/detroit, (313) 964-0776.*

The Whiskey Parlor - Look for the glowing red Chinese lanterns on the second floor and head up the stairs—your curiosity will be rewarded. A pre-Prohibition-style cocktail bar that evokes a mystical library, with a twist of refined man-cave comfort, this hidden gem is a must-visit for connoisseurs of whiskey. Overlooking Woodward Avenue, the wood-rich, atmospheric space is both classical and mysterious, with antique maps, books, and photos adorning the walls, and striking globes suspended from a soaring cut-through in the ceiling. The cocktailian bartenders are versatile, with encyclopedic knowledge of their craft, and the bar offers a full range of spirits, beers, and wines, but the focus here is whiskey. With more than 150 varieties lining the shelves, the bar offers an almost godly selection, including bourbons, scotches, and ryes, as well as Tennessee,

American, Canadian, Irish, and world whiskeys. Accordingly, the historically grounded cocktail menu leans almost exclusively towards the namesake spirit. Naturally, our favorite is The Detroit, a boulevardier variation that adds ginger liqueur and black pepper to push the classic in a new direction. A limited menu is available (think charcuterie). Look for live jazz on Thursdays and Saturdays. *608 Woodward Ave., www.whiskyparlor.com, (313) 961-3043.*

Wolfgang Puck Steak - Inside MGM Grand Casino (see separate entry) is this upscale steak and seafood eatery designed by famed chef and restaurateur Wolfgang Puck. Because it's in a casino, no expense was spared on the comfortable and opulent interior—from the lustrous horseshoe bar, to the contemporary furniture, swanky spherical chandeliers suspended from the 20-foot ceiling, and warm wood-paneled earth tones of the walls and floors. The food emphasizes control of preparation and quality of ingredients— choose from a number of excellent cuts of steak, all prepared over hardwood and charcoal and served with a variety of silky house-made sauces. Diners looking for lighter fare are also in luck, with options ranging from succulent pan-roasted branzino to a juicy half-chicken with morel mushrooms. Top it off with a hand-crafted cocktail featuring premium spirits, or a bottle of wine from their gorgeous—and well-stocked—wine cellar. First-timers to a casino should be prepared for highly attentive, professional service. Open for dinner only. *1777 Third Ave., www.mgmgranddetroit.com/restaurants, (877) 888-2121.*

★**Wright & Company -** One of the hottest restaurant tickets in Detroit, and with good reason, this upscale, second-story small plates spot boasts stunning interior decor, elegant heritage architecture, and a meticulously curated, rave-worthy menu. The cuisine mixes thoughtful crowd-pleasers and genuine innovation, which earned Chef Marc Djozlija a nod as a James Beard Award Finalist. Co-owner Dave Kwiatkowski, of Sugar House fame (see separate entry), oversees the drink menu, which includes an extensive list of international beers, wines, and liquors among exceptional seasonal cocktails. Visitors dine windowside with stunning Downtown views, or at luxurious red leather banquettes in a dining room with impressive set pieces of antique chandeliers, sweeping metallic fans, and the bar's centerpiece, an enormous dramatic painting of schooners roiled in a storm. The kitchen exhibits craftsmanship and dedication on par with the best of Detroit and every dish is executed in artful detail in a marriage of presentation and flavor. Highlights include a juicy and tender roasted pork tenderloin, flavorful, pillow-like Parisian Gnocchi, an elevated pork belly slider, and resplendent roasted cauliflower. Use the entrance around the corner on John R Street, and take the elevator to the second floor. *1500 Woodward Ave., www.wrightdetroit.com, (313) 962-7711.*

SHOPPING & SERVICES

Bird Bee - A hip online apparel shop, turned pop-up, turned brick-and-mortar, Bird Bee features a beautiful and contemporary white-washed interior with industrial finishes, geometric touches, and a little inspirational neon for good measure. Located in the rapidly evolving Capitol Park, the shop is a youthful and inviting space that describes its target market as "the expressive and edgy soul," and offers shoppers a Midwest-meets-West Coast aesthetic. Following these guidelines, the shop is an archetypal women's lifestyle boutique, offering on-trend clothing for adventurous, modern Bohemians and young professionals—though sizing favors the slender and petite. In addition, offerings include vintage-inspired accessories, a well-curated shoe tree, select home goods (including delightful candles), and all the essentials you'll need for your bar cart. The compact space employs creative, stylish merchandising, with display sets that effortlessly piece together indie favorites like Free People and more. *1228 Griswold St., www.shopbirdbee.com, 313.315.3070.*

Bon Bon Bon Downtown - Just north of Bon-gress and a few steps away from Campus Martius, this pint-sized chocolate shop is the downtown outpost of the wildly popular Hamtramck chocolatier Bon Bon Bon. The inspired bons are sold in cut-to-order cardboard sleeves. See main Bon Bon Bon entry for more information. *719 Griswold St., www.bonbonbon.com, (313) 316-1430.*

The Broadway - Offering brand name fashions at firesale prices, The Broadway has been a dapper Downtown destination for more than a generation. Fellas looking to look sharp will find a large showroom of fully tailored high-end Moschino and Versace suits for $200–$15,000. The shop carries a number of designer shirts by Luchiano Visconti, Pelle Pelle leather jackets, and the latest in men's sportswear from lines such as Sean Jean. Ladies will appreciate the small—but growing—selection of women's designer jeans and casual tops. Gentlemen will find the perfect finishing touch to any outfit from The Broadway's selection of men's shoes, ties, and cufflinks. *1247 Broadway St., www.shopthebroadway.com, (313) 963-2171.*

City Bark - The sleek white walls and industrial cement floors at this fetching pet boutique put a visual emphasis on the vibrant, colorful array of goods—toys, accessories, and food, petcetra—that ring the room. Walking in, customers are greeted by an expansive selection of leashes and collars, from the demure to the de rigeur. Options include solid colors, plaids, paisleys, polka dots, map prints, and local offerings from the likes of Carhartt and the Detroit Tigers. Further in, owner Jamie Judson has a waggish display of toys, including squeaker whiskey bottles, stuffed plush donuts, rubber kongs, and fleece lobsters. After those re-tail appetizers, guests will find a full selection of wholesome food options, including those from Acana, Blue Buffalo, and Orijen. If you've made use of the store's dog-friendly policy, you'll have no trouble finding the treat bar, offering bulk displays of gorilla chews, salmon skins, elk antlers, water buffalo horns, beef no-hides, and droolicious dog-friendly cookies. *1222 Griswold St., www.citydetroitbark.com, (313) 881-2275.*

City Slicker Shoes - A formal footwear destination since 1977, City Slicker Shoes is the world's largest supplier of men's alligator and crocodile footwear. With rows upon rows of exotic-skin shoes—think ostrich, pony, gator, croc, fox, sting ray, eel, lizard, and goat—in every color and hue under the rainbow, the store has a bright, vibrant atmosphere. Wayne Pittman, the manager, has a passion for helping customers select from among the shop's diverse selection of Mauri, Pajar, Mezian, and Lacoste shoes, as well as helping visitors create custom kicks. Don't miss the photos of famous customers, including Michael Jackson, who have visited over the years. *300 Monroe St., www.cityslickershoes.com, (313) 963-1963.*

Detroit Bikes - Bicycling has seen explosive growth in Detroit over the past decade, but one company unique amid this revival is Detroit Bikes. The startup manufactures chromoly steel bike frames and conducts final assembly for its A, B, C, and Cortello commuters at its factory on the west side of Detroit. This makes the company singular in the region—and almost throughout the country—as the vast majority of bicycles in America are imported. As Detroit cycling has proliferated, so has Detroit Bikes; the company's stylish and durable rides are available in bike shops throughout Michigan. The aesthetic is a mix of modern urban and Prohibition era—the curvy bikes feature classic styling, retro fenders, iconic nameplates, and come in solid, matte colors. The company's Downtown flagship store has a stunning, vintage feel, with a soaring, open ceiling, deep red patterned wallpaper, vintage wood display cases, a gramophone, and other antiques. In the shop, look for limited-edition models, like the Slow Roll A-Type, or the technicolor Faygo B-Type. Cost-conscious riders can shop the Assembly Line, a range of reduced-cost self-assembly bikes available in three styles. Tours of the factory are available for $15, including transportation between locales, and start at the flagship store. *1216 Griswold St., www.detroitbikes.com, (313) 502-5883.*

Détroit Is the New Black - An online shop, turned pop-up, turned flagship Woodward storefront, Détroit Is the New Black is more than just an *it* "T-shirt" and slogan for the city—it's an on-trend lifestyle and fashion brand. The brainchild of Roslyn Karamoko, the label celebrates the city's French history and fashionable future—all with a mind for simplicity and city pride. The shop features original high-design and focused capsule collections of the signature apparel, alongside up-and-coming local designers and renowned cultural touchstones like Anna Sui (born in Detroit!). The striking Downtown storefront features a minimal, contemporary aesthetic, with strong contrast that guides the eye and further elevates the collection, highlighting the original pieces and the Détroit flair. *1426 Woodward Ave., www.detroitisthenewblack.com, (313) 818-3498.*

Djenne Beads & Art - If the beautifully handcrafted African textiles hanging in the window do not draw you in from the streets of Greektown, the rich aromas of Egyptian perfumes will. Djenne Beads founder and glass craftsman Mahamadou Sumareh specializes in authentic imported African artifacts, clothing, jewelry, fabric, baskets, drums, and body oils. Visit him at the International Building, and you might get a crash course in the history of African trade beads. Whether you're a collector of ancient African glass beads, a jewelry lover with a flair for custom-made pieces, or a craft enthusiast looking for a unique gift, Djenne Beads has you covered. *1045 Beaubien St., (313) 965-6620.*

Downtown Clothiers - In recent years, new higher-end national accessory and apparel retail chains have joined a stable of longtime independant area clothiers to create an emerging fashion center downtown. These newcomers have concentrated in a dense, vibrant three-block stretch of Woodward, between State Street and Park

Avenue. Though most of these national outlets are available in luxury malls, their neighbors, architecture, and local flair—many feature art or displays by area artists or merchants—make their Woodward outposts a unique and worthwhile shopping experience. Working north from State Street, national outlets include Under Armour, Nike, Moosejaw, Madewell, Bonobos, Warby Parker, Lululemon, and John Varvatos. The sleek three-story **Under Armour Brand House** offers a full range of the company's renowned athletic wear for men, women, and youths, as well as shoes and Detroit-specific clothing. Up the block, the wildly popular, bi-level **Nike Community Store** offers many discounts on its extensive inventory of men's and women's shoes and athletic wear. Farther north, backpacking and mountaineering outfitter **Moosejaw** carries a curated selection of outdoor gear alongside durable outerwear and Detroit-focused tees. J.Crew ladies' imprint **Madewell** takes a boutique approach, offering their signature, stylish apparel and accessories alongside select pieces from local designers and artists. Across the street, **Bonobos** has planted a guideshop, offering shoppers the chance to feel fabric, meet with a stylist, or try something on, before purchasing online. At the corner, online eyeglass mainstay **Warby Parker** offers optometrist services, fittings, and adjustments for its stylish, vintage-inspired glasses ordered in-store or online. Next door, activewear boutique **Lululemon** offers a curated selection of their high-end leggings, jackets, and other high-performance apparel. Farther up, Detroit-born designer **John Varvatos** hosts a bi-level retail experience, with crystal chandeliers and leather chairs alongside his signature men's couture casual wear, vintage guitars, and records. *1201-1500 Woodward Ave.*

DuMouchelle's Art Galleries - A creaky walk through this glittering treasure trove is truly an eyeful. Open to the public, the two-story gallery is wall-to-wall, floor-to-ceiling antique furniture, jewelry, rugs, paintings, tapestries, books, fine china, silverware, sculptures, and other dazzling decorative objects for your petite maison or mansion. Visit during the monthly auction to be hypnotized by one of the droll auctioneers and raise your paddle for a deal on a carousel horse, Civil War-era bayonet, or marquise diamond ring. The detritus from suburban estate liquidations occasionally brings to light a Warhol, Picasso, or fabulous taxidermy lot and auction previews are conducted at the gallery for one full week prior to the sale. Wondering whether your uncle's collection of antique snuff bottles is worth anything? DuMouchelle's offers free verbal appraisals on

Wednesdays and Saturdays from 1pm to 4pm. With complimentary entry, valet parking, coffee, tea, and the occasional platter of snacks, there is no reason not to stop in for an auction during the third weekend of every month. Beware: It's easy to get caught up in the excitement, so when the gavel drops, you may find yourself the unwitting owner of a rare Steinway piano or wildebeest mount. *409 E. Jefferson Ave., www.dumouchelle.com, (313) 963-6255.*

Emerson's Haberdashery - With a canine mascot that bears more than a passing resemblance to Tintin's Snowy—but a little more dapper—Emerson's Haberdashery is a destination men's clothier a cut above the rest. Owner Charley Marcuse, who became legendary in baseball circles as the "Singing Hot Dog Vendor," doesn't just know how to belt out a tune—he knows how to pair a belt with a finely tailored suit. Always dressed to the nines, Marcuse has built a reputation as one of Detroit's most well-attired gentlemen, and he brings this incredible depth of experience and knowledge to his shop. Able to cater to the experienced, as well as the newcomer, Charley himself will guide customers through the selection process, and help them select a pre-made ensemble, or help assemble a custom-made scene-stealer. From full suits to accessories, fine hats, and flair, Emerson's is a beautiful, thoughtful, and essential stop for well-dressed gentlemen—or gentlemen who would like to be. Located on the second floor of the elegant and historic Archdiocese building. *1234 Washington Blvd., www.emersons.clothing, (313) 444-3565.*

Hot Sam's - Open since 1921, Hot Sam's is a choice Downtown locale for classic men's professional and casual wear. Catering to the office set, the Detroit staple offers a diverse selection of suits, hats, khakis, polos, ties, fedoras, button-ups, and other items that belong in any self-respecting man's wardrobe. The store's selection of fitted items is friendly for any body type, as Hot Sam's offers a wide-variety of big and tall items. Customers can also take advantage of comprehensive tailoring services and free alterations on the store's antique belt-driven sewing machine. *127 Monroe St., www.hotsams.net, (313) 961-6779.*

House of Pure Vin - Step into this sleek, downtown oasis for wine lovers (and the wine curious) and you'll find an impressive and well-curated bounty of more than 1,300 bottles of natural, kosher, Michigan-grown, and international varietals to choose from! House of Pure Vin prides itself on budget-friendly wine and champagne that doesn't compromise quality and fits every palette. The knowledgeable staff is happy to discuss tasting notes while you sip and sample the latest selections. Owner Regina Gaines knows that selecting the right wine is essential for every occasion, and her team has partnered with Claudia Tyagi, one of only three Master Sommeliers in Michigan, to craft this fabulous collection. The award-winning space defines contemporary luxury by combining a refined sense of harmonious minimalism and intricate details. The ample, modern cellar allows you to browse a vast, bottle-filled corridor, while a recessed tasting room regularly hosts private events, an ever popular Jazz Brunch, and regular well-paired wine tastings. This glass is way more than half full! *1433 Woodward Ave., www.houseofpurevin.com, (313) 638-2501.*

NoJo Kicks - "What is art?" begs the eternal question. NoJo Kicks, a rare and collectible sneaker boutique seems to suggest "Why not shoes?" This is not your average shoe store; this is a shoe gallery offering more than a million dollars' worth of Yeezys, Nikes, Adidas, and Deadstock Jordans in hard-to-find styles and colors, elevating erstwhile footwear into a legitimate status symbol. For readers who are not in-the-know sneakerheads, NoJo Kicks offers a chance to browse among collectible kicks with price tags in the thousands of dollars, as well as upscale modern jackets and skateboard gear. Customers can count themselves in good company—NoJo faithful include Lil' Wayne, T.I., Lil' Jon and scores of professional athletes. Don't miss the autographed photos of Jay-Z, Michael Jordan, Kanye West, and others, as well as the Keymaster arcade game, which offers players a chance to win a pair of rare kicks for just the price of a play. *1220 Library St., www.nojokicks.com, (313) 656-4402.*

Paramita Sound - Naming a record store for the Sanskrit word for perfection sets a high bar, but this crate-digger's haven may just clear it. Situated at the foot of the Siren Hotel, the space is inviting and modern, with sweeping windows overlooking the bustle of Broadway Street. Owner Andrey Douthard's contemporary shop stands apart with its thoughtfully curated catalog of new vinyl records, featuring options ranging from independent releases by local acts like Protomartyr and Tunde Olaniran, to reissues of lesser-known African artists such as Hailu Mergia and the Walias, and Chief Commander Ebenezer Obey, though used vinyl is also available. The space also offers a sophisticated bar program, with an imaginative selection of spirits and cocktails. *1515 Broadway St., www.paramitasound.com.*

PenzDetroiT - Don't let the "Z" in the name fool you—PenzDetroiT is serious about fine writing instruments, quality paper, and premium luggage. The owner, Alex Lebarre, is a self-proclaimed collector who can recommend the perfect writing utensil and notepad for your budget. Connoisseurs will find limited edition fountain pens for hundreds to thousands of dollars, and the rest of us can get fine writing utensils for about 15 bucks. Best of all, Alex is happy to let visitors take a pen out for a test-scribble. *333 W. Fort St., www.penzdetroit.com, (313) 961-7474.*

Pure Detroit Downtown - What began as a small T-shirt company and shop in 1998 has grown into a thriving Detroit business and a beloved local brand. Though its flagship store is in New Center (see separate entry), Pure Detroit operates several other stores, including three Downtown. While there are smaller locations in Cobo Hall and the GM Renaissance Center, the brand's grandest presence in the area is in the iconic Guardian Building. This location, especially, offers an elegant shopping experience in a contemporary space with glass walls that allow full view of the building's incredible lobby. While at all Pure Detroit locations, visitors will find the brand's signature designs on tees, totes, sweatshirts, magnets, undies, and pet leashes, as well as Detroit gifts such as Sanders treats, delicious McClure's pickles, and Faygo pop, the Guardian location offers the largest

Guardian Building, pg. 102

selection of books and artwork among them. Pure Detroit has become a destination for visitors and locals alike looking to stock up on some Detroit swag. *www.puredetroit.com; Cobo: 1 Washington Blvd.; GM Renaissance Center: 100 Renaissance Center, (313) 259-5100; Guardian: 500 Griswold St., (313) 963-1440.*

Shinola Downtown - The compact Downtown satellite location of the Midtown flagship store, Shinola Downtown offers a curated selection of the company's luxury watches, leather goods, accessories, and other items. See separate Shinola Detroit entry for more information. *1424 Woodward Ave., www.shinola.com, 313-356-3118.*

Simmons & Clark Jewelers - This is where Detroiters buy fine jewelry—Simmons & Clark has been a good friend to those looking to buy a girl's best friend since 1925. The façade features a beautifully restored black Vitrolite tiles and tall, open storefront windows. Visitors will notice Simmons' respect for the past and pride in old-school quality service as they admire the glass case of black-and-white photographs and newspaper clippings detailing the store's history and browse the selection with owner Michael Simmons. The shop stocks an array of pieces in gold, silver, stainless steel, and platinum in classical and contemporary styles, with special attention to wedding, engagement, anniversary, and religious jewelry. Free validated parking in the Detroit Opera House garage. *1535 Broadway St., www.simmonsandclark.com, (313) 963-2284.*

Spectacles - A Harmonie Park staple for more than a generation, Spectacles is a destination for contemporary apparel and accessories and a focused selection of books and local hip-hop, R&B, and electronic albums. Owner Zana Smith is a knowledgeable, bespectacled woman who's hip to the current and historical goings-on in Detroit's music and fashion scenes. Smith keeps her contemporary, loft-like boutique stocked with her signature Detroit Soul shirts, modern jewelry, vintage military caps, aviators, camouflage outerwear, Schott jackets, books including Butch Jones' autobiography, and a diverse, constantly changing selection of albums from artists like rapper Phat Kat and soulstress Monica Blaire. This boutique becomes a lively venue every Friday, when local DJs spin until close. *230 E. Grand River Ave., www.spectaclesdetroit.com, (313) 963-6886.*

Threads & Legs - From tip to toe, this Downtown boutique has all the finishing touches a woman can want, especially if she's looking to make a bold stride into the world of independent fashion. Though Threads and Legs offers a selection of women's clothing, lingerie, accessories, and jewelry, the focus of the shop is the namesake range of statement hosiery, playful stockings, fashion forward socks, refined fishnets, and classic thigh-highs. The signature offerings exude just the right amount of sass, and will ensure that the wearer stands out. The colorful storefront's selection is well-organized and offers plenty of fashion inspiration, with a slew of diva-worth designs and delightful accoutrements. You won't miss a step! *660 Woodward Ave., (248) 217-0058.*

Vault of Midnight - Belying its name, and breaking with the basement-like aesthetic that sometimes plagues comic shops, Vault of Midnight is bright and airy, with a fun, comic-inspired feel, and features massive windows that overlook the increasingly bustling Library Street. The kid brother to the popular Ann Arbor and Grand Rapids locations, at 2,000 square feet this shop is still nerd nirvana. While the store neatly crams an impressive spectrum of new and vintage comics into the relatively compact space, it also offers a full array of Manga, graphic novels, collectables, toys, and board games. So, if you're a nerd, rest assured, if Catan is more your jam than Spider-Man, you'll still be a fan. And, if you aren't sure what to pick up off the sleek white shelving, with the central, wrap-around counter, the uncommonly friendly and knowledgeable staff is always just a quick wave away. The store also offers a popular subscription program where customers get a discount when they subscribe to an ongoing series. *1226 Library St, www.vaultofmidnight.com, (313) 481-2165.*

CULTURAL ATTRACTIONS

The Carr Center - With a mission to preserve, present, promote, and develop the African and African-American cultural arts traditions, The Carr Center was founded by the Arts League of Michigan in 2009 and has been providing inspiring experiences such as jazz concerts and theater performances to Detroiters for nearly a decade. The Carr Center utilizes a network of venues throughout the city as well as in the surrounding metro area to connect the arts to broader audiences. Focusing on performing arts, visual arts, and education, the center hosts several renowned Artists in Residence, as well as an exciting program of events and exhibitions every season. Find their upcoming shows and ticketing information on their website. *Various venues, www.thecarrcenter.org, (313) 681-5554.*

David Klein Gallery - Establishing his gallery in suburban Birmingham in 1990, and becoming one of the top blue-chip galleries in Michigan, David Klein opened his second gallery in downtown Detroit in 2015, aiming to draw a new audience of young art collectors living in the city. While the Birmingham-based branch deals with aftermarket and Post-war American Art, the Detroit location focuses on contemporary painting, sculpture, and photography by emerging, mid-career, and established artists. Located just south of Grand Circus Park (see separate entry), the

4,000-square-foot space was formerly a department store and bookstore. The striking original black-and-white tile floor make for a dramatic entrance leading to a pristine white cube setting with soaring ceilings. New exhibitions are installed every six weeks with a robust program of supporting events that include talks and performances. *1520 Washington Blvd., www.dkgallery.com, (313) 818-3416.*

★ **Detroit Opera House / Michigan Opera Theatre -** The magnificent C. Howard Crane masterpiece now known as the Detroit Opera House debuted as the Capitol Theatre in 1922 and was one of the five largest theaters in the world when it was completed. The entertainment palace hosted jazz legends like Louis Armstrong and Duke Ellington before taking a turn as the home of the Detroit Symphony Orchestra, but it ultimately devolved into an illicit movie house. Though the building fell into disrepair and closed in 1985, it was purchased by **Michigan Opera Theatre** in 1988, and the organization completed an extensive historic restoration of the structure. The stunning beauty of the building is belied by the relatively reserved exterior—inside, patrons are treated to an opulent architectural feast of ornate details and elegant crystal chandeliers that wrap the stately 2,700-seat auditorium, which offers main floor, balcony, and private box seating. Since the grand opening of the Detroit Opera House in 1996, Michigan Opera Theatre has programmed the storied venue. The company stages four operas annually during the season, hosts dance companies from around the world, and offers elaborate shows and productions ranging from Broadway to comedy. A highlight of the activities also includes one of Detroit's best dress-up parties: BravoBravo, an annual benefit to support the Opera House. Dedicated to education and enrichment, dress-rehearsal seating is available on the cheap for pre-paid groups of students and seniors. *1526 Broadway St., www.michiganopera.org, (313) 237-7464.*

Isaac Agree Downtown Synagogue - Founded in 1921, the Isaac Agree Downtown Synagogue moved into its current, four-story historic home in the early 1960s—you can't miss the rainbow-colored windows along the long sides of the flatiron-shaped building. Its principal mission was to address the unmet needs of the Jewish community, for those who worked downtown or were visiting the city, by providing a traditional, Conservative presence in the heart of Detroit. The institution is currently the only synagogue in the city of Detroit, and over the past several years, it has seen a revival through committed young and old members alike. In addition to the expected Shabbat services, Torah studies, and high holiday services, the synagogue has become a community hub and gathering place, hosting neighborhood events such as book clubs, concerts, film nights, and renowned, well-attended dance parties to which all are welcome. *1457 Griswold St., www.downtownsynagogue.org, (313) 962-4047.*

★**Library Street Collective** - A reimagination of the Long-Sharp/ Curis Gallery that opened with a splash in 2011, the Library Street Collective has established itself as a destination to view exquisite works by prominent, cutting-edge names in modern and contemporary art in regular group and solo exhibitions. The gallery is elegantly utilitarian—the exhibition space is divided into two separate, cavernous white-boxed spaces punctuated by stark industrial columns. The aesthetic of the spaces suits the contemporary art emphasized at the gallery, which (under the two names it has held, both abbreviated as LSC) has shown work by dynamic international names including Jason Revok, Swoon, Shepard Fairey, Sam Friedman, Nina Chanel Abney, Roy Lichtenstein, and Andy Warhol, as well as prominent local names including Charles McGee, Beverly Fishman, and Tiff Massey. Exhibitions are often paired with educational components, such as talks, films, or artist demonstrations and LSC also leads public art efforts throughout the city, including the Z Lot and The Belt (see separate entry). *1260 Library St., www.lscgallery.com, (313) 600-7443.*

Muccioli Studio Gallery - Located on the ground floor of the historic Alexander Chapoton House, which was completed in 1885, this gallery space is home to the work of two artists: Anna Muccioli and her son Nate Muccioli. The late Anna Muccioli was an acclaimed artist in the 1960s and 1970s who practiced in a variety of media, including paintings, mixed media collages, and sculptures. She left a substantial body of work, which is housed and displayed here, at the gallery. Her son, Nate Muccioli is an accomplished metalsmith and jewelry maker who specializes in the lost-wax technique. He creates and repairs custom and antique jewelry in the on-site studio. Don't miss the abstract mural by Anna Muccioli on the south side of the building. Visitors should call ahead to make an appointment. *511 Beaubien St., (313) 962-4700.*

Rose and Robert Skillman Branch, Detroit Public Library -
Built in 1932, the DPL's beautiful, two-story Neoclassical Downtown
branch houses an important public archive (the National Automotive
History Collection), a circulating collection of popular materials,
an Internet cafe, and an auditorium. Clad in limestone, bronze, and
copper, with a grand rotunda and marble floors, the Skillman Branch
is a stirring, well-preserved example of monumental 20th-century
library architecture. It's also a busy branch, boasting the second
largest children's room in the DPL system after the Main Library.
The century-old National Automotive History Collection, actually
a distinct entity within the library, houses more than 600,000
items of particular interest to automotive enthusiasts, journalists,
and historians, and includes photographs, service manuals,
periodicals, advertising literature, and much more. *121 Gratiot Ave.,
www.detroitpubliclibrary.org/branch/skillman, (313) 481-1850.*

ENTERTAINMENT & RECREATION

Beacon Park - Opened in 2017, this 1.2-acre quadrilateral park
has developed a reputation as a vibrant urban plaza, known for
its cutting edge appearance and eclectic programming. The park's
contemporary design is at once eye-catching, thoughtful, and simple.
The focal point is a large circular central lawn, encircled by a walking
path and buttressed by the elegant Lumen restaurant (see separate
entry) on one side and an open stage on the other. Little pockets
of trees, seating, and meandering patio walkways are interspersed
along the periphery. This open design facilitates the flexibility that
has brought the park accolades. In addition to the frequent, ad hoc
strolls, sunbathing, people watching, and chess matches natural to any
well-used greenspace, the park often hosts several events a day. At
various times, the park plays host to food-truck rallies, interactive light
installations, concerts, night markets, fitness bootcamps, movie nights,
and holiday celebrations. Visit the website to plan ahead, or just play
park roulette.*1901 Grand River Ave., www.downtowndetroitparks.com,
(313) 962-0101.*

★**Campus Martius Park -** Known as "Detroit's Gathering Place,"
Campus Martius Park is an award-winning park steeped in local
history. The park was originally conceived by Judge Augustus B.
Woodward as the starting point for Detroit's street system, following
the Fire of 1805. Under Woodward's plan, Campus Martius—"military

ground" in Latin—serves as the hub of the city's arterial streets, and the point of origin for the region's mile roads. As automotive traffic increased in the city, the park was demolished, but was redeveloped and reopened in 2004. Today, Campus Martius is a vibrant, beautiful urban plaza, complete with fountains, sculptures, a bar and cafe (Parc, see separate entry), a games pavilion, two stages, and even a seasonal 7,200-square-foot ice-skating rink, with capacity for 200 skaters. Along with neighboring Cadillac Square, the park is home to a variety of events, including the Meridian Winter Blast in January, movie screenings and a beach in summer, shopping pop-ups and food trucks through most of the year, and the Christmas tree lighting in November. The southern end of the park is anchored by the 60-foot-tall bronze and granite **Michigan Soldiers' and Sailors' Monument**, dedicated to the memory of Michigan's fallen soldiers and sailors. Erected in 1872, this stunning memorial is topped by an 11-foot bronze female warrior with a raised sword. The periphery of the octagonal granite base includes four bronze female figures symbolizing victory, history, emancipation, and union, and four male figures depicting an infantryman, a sailor, a cavalryman, and an artilleryman. Between the figures, visitors will find smaller bronze bas-relief plaques honoring President Abraham Lincoln, General William Tecumseh Sherman, General Ulysses S. Grant, and David Admiral Farragut. *800 Woodward Ave., www.campusmartiuspark.org, (313) 962-0101.*

City Theatre - A compact and intimate seated theatre that rose up from the ashes of Second City's fleeting flirtations with a Detroit location—which produced several notable alumni, including Keegan-Michael Key—the humble City Theatre opened in 2004. Today, the contemporary, 430-seat performance space produces and presents plays, musicals, concerts, and comedy performances on an intermittent basis. Physically connected to the **Hockeytown Cafe**—itself a relic of a bygone era when the city's Red Wings team dominated professional hockey—food and beverages from the full-service restaurant are available to event attendees, with a menu that checks all the American comfort-food boxes, as well as an impressive collection of Red Wings memorabilia... and motorcycles. *2301 Woodward Ave., www.olympiaentertainment.com/city-theatre-1.*

★**Cliff Bell's -** Named for founder John Clifford Bell, Cliff Bell's is a fully restored 1930s Art Deco nightclub, featuring beautiful murals and woodwork, live music, and elegant cocktails. After a storied history, the bar was abandoned in 1956. In 2006, it underwent a thoughtful and thorough restoration by owners Paul Howard, Scott Lowell, and Carolyn Howard, and today the space looks just as it did after Prohibition, with floor-to-ceiling Art Deco woodwork, period murals, ornate backlit bar, original mosaics, antique mirrors, and bartenders in sleeve garters. The food complements the atmosphere, and is as inspired as the space. The menu, with its subtle French and Italian influences, melds traditional and contemporary, and it features shareable appetizers (try the lobster mac and cheese!) and sophisticated entrees like scallops, steaks, and pastas. Those looking for a three-martini (rather than a three-course) meal won't be disappointed by the well-appointed liquor selection and highly regarded wine and beer list. However, surpassing the ambiance and the flavors is the music. The bar hosts one of the city's finest rosters of live jazz, with shows almost every night, many of which don't have a cover. Though the schedule favors traditional and big band music that's appropriate for the setting, look for a variety of musical acts on the stage. Also look for regular WSU student jam sessions, where the city's up-and-coming talent gets experimental, as well as the **Open City** small-business panels that are hosted at the venue. *2030 Park Ave., www.cliffbells.com, (313) 961-2543.*

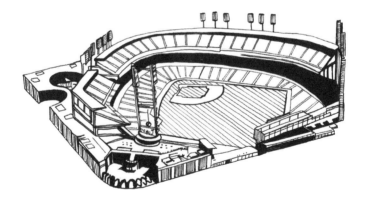

★**Comerica Park / Detroit Tigers** - Historically a titan in Major League Baseball's American League Central Division, the **Detroit Tigers** are one of the nation's most popular and successful baseball clubs. Founded in 1894, Detroit is the oldest single-name, single-city team in the American League, and one of the league's charter members. The team has had 12 MVPs, 40 Gold Glove recipients, four Triple Crowns, 11 American League pennants, and four World Series victories. All of this success has made them a beloved fixture in city culture—Detroit has been the only American League team to draw more than one million fans each year since 1964. The Tigers currently play in Comerica Park. Opened in 2000, the park is still a young stadium, but is packed with nostalgia for Tigers of yore. Along the lower concourse are museum-style chronological displays full of artifacts from the Detroit Tigers' 115-year history, as well as statues of key figures in the team's past, from the legendary Ty Cobb to beloved broadcaster Ernie Harwell. The stadium features large fountains, fireworks displays, a 6,000 square foot scoreboard, a Ferris wheel, and a merry-go-round. Our favorite seats are in Sections 138–143 by third base, although seats in Sections 321–345 offer the best views of Downtown. *2100 Woodward Ave., detroit.tigers.mlb.com, (313) 944-4141.*

Deluxx Fluxx - An otherworldly destination bar, venue, and artcade, Deluxx Fluxx has few parallels in our solar system. Originally an art installation by street artist Bast and the duo known as Faile, versions of Deluxx Fluxx made appearances in several world capitals before landing permanently in Detroit. Look for the neon X's above a door on the North side of the Belt Alley, and descend to discover this subterranean speakeasy. Inside, guests will find an alien landscape from the illustrated and geometric wheatpastes that adorn the walls, to the transfixing undulating square and linear neon lighting, to the radiant floor-to-ceiling blacklight reactive artwork that fills one of the side rooms. On the main stage, in addition to killer karaoke, look for some of the city's best booking for indie-pop, rock, and other independent acts. However, the most buzzed about component of Deluxx Fluxx is the artcade that fills the compact third room. Comprised entirely of custom, bar-exclusive free-play arcade games reminiscent of '80s-and '90s-era machines (but on acid), expect a one-of-a-kind locally referential experience. Join a boxing fight between a ballet dancer and Robocop; spray graffiti tags in Michigan Central Station; make ilicit drops on the Detroit River; or dodge birds in Eastern Market—no matter your choice, these games are the perfect cap on a visit to this bizarre and delightful experience. *1274 Library St., www.deluxxfluxx.com.*

Detroit Athletic Club - Housed in one of the many Detroit buildings designed by famed architect Albert Kahn, this private club has maintained a tradition of regional class and ambassadorship for more than a century. Members—numbering more than 4,000—take advantage of this preeminent athletic club for activities like boxing, fencing, squash, and swimming; socialize at one of the DAC's eateries (including separate kitchens for both the men's and women's locker rooms); and share a collective history that has seen visits from presidents and royalty and members including iconic Detroiters such as Ty Cobb. Facilities include swimming pools, ballrooms, squash and basketball courts, full service exercise rooms, guest rooms, and a venue for a distinguished league of underground bowlers. In addition, the club is home to a considerable collection of fine art, including two pieces by Frederic Remington. On game days, the rooftop bar—and the roof of the parking deck—offer better sightlines than some seats in the stadium. The club is private and open to only members and their guests. *241 Madison St., www.thedac.com, (313) 442-1017.*

Detroit Princess Riverboat - Quietly parked along the city's scenic riverfront, the Detroit Princess could easily be mistaken for a vestige of Mark Twain's time but was originally a Gulf of Mexico-area riverboat casino that came to Detroit via the St. Lawrence Seaway since it was too large to travel up the Mississippi. With a full commercial kitchen and four decks available for guests, the Princess has become a sought-after ticket for floating dinner with concerts or theater, as well as a rental for private parties. Cruise tickets may be purchased in advance online. *201 Civic Center Dr., www.detroitprincess.com, (877) 338-2628.*

★**Detroit RiverWalk Downtown** - The RiverWalk is a wildly popular, scenic riverside promenade that connects dozens of plazas, parks, and public art installations from Rosa Parks Boulevard, through Downtown, to Mt. Elliott Park, near Belle Isle. While Downtown visitors can access the RiverWalk on foot or bicycle from Hart Plaza, or any street that runs south from Jefferson Avenue, it's recommended that four-wheeled visitors approach from Cullen Plaza, on the western edge of the East Riverfront. See the separate Detroit RiverWalk East Riverfront entry for more details about this must-see amenity, which offers stunning views of major Detroit landmarks, Downtown, and Canada. Cullen Plaza: *110 Mt Elliott St. www.detroitriverfront.org.*

The Fillmore Detroit - Located in the heart of the entertainment district, The Fillmore Detroit—previously the **State Theatre**—and the attached 12-story-tall Francis Palms Building were completed in 1925 and designed by legendary architect C. Howard Crane. The highlight of the ornate terra cotta-sheathed Renaissance Revival complex is the breathtaking six-story theater and lobby dotted with

Beaux-Arts ornamentation. Though the theater originally had seating for nearly 3,000 patrons, today, under the management of Live Nation, the venue can accommodate 2,200 concertgoers between the main floor, mezzanine, and balcony. Because of the flexibility of the space—it can be adjusted to allow for either terraced cabaret seating or a hardwood dance floor—entertainment at the venue is widely varied, often highlighting national popular acts, as well as the Detroit Music Awards, which are held annually at the venue every April. The adjoining State Bar & Grill, which has a classy sports bar atmosphere and a full menu of pub food, has its own entrance and is open independent of the venue's schedule. *2115 Woodward Ave., www.thefillmoredetroit.com, (313) 961-5451.*

Ford Field / Detroit Lions - Lions loyalty epitomizes the dedication of Detroiters. Almost all Lions fans remember the team's electrifying former running back, Barry Sanders, one of only three players in NFL history to rush for more than 2,000 yards in a season. Most are also strong enough to forget many of the Lions' most infamous seasons. Though the team has had only one playoff victory in the past half-century, many pundits believe the Lions' better days are near on the horizon. Ford Field, an indoor stadium located Downtown, has been home to the **Detroit Lions** since August 2002. It seats 65,000 for football games and more than 80,000 for other events. In 2006, it hosted Super Bowl XL, features the annual MAC championship game, and also offers the annual Quick Lane Bowl. Ford Field pioneered hosting basketball events in large-capacity arenas in 2003 when MSU played Kentucky in an NCAA men's basketball game, and was later home to the 2009 NCAA Men's Final Four. The stadium occasionally hosts concerts and other large-draw events. Look for unique concession stands featuring favorite dishes from local restaurants like Mercury Burger Bar, Russell Street Deli, Slows To Go, Pegasus, La Shish, and many more. *2000 Brush St., www.detroitlions.com, (313) 262-2012.*

★ **Fox Theatre** - The anchor of the surrounding Foxtown district, the Fox Theatre is as resplendent as it is historic. The theater, which was restored in 1988, is the largest surviving Fox Theatre and is one of the most opulent remaining 1920s movie palaces in the United States. You needn't look far to find it—the enormous winged foxes and Art Deco sign light up Woodward Avenue for blocks. The interior is an extravagant amalgamation of Burmese, Chinese, Indian, and Persian motifs in lavish gold and vivid colors that provide a stunning backdrop for any live performance or event. The first movie theater in the world constructed with built-in sound equipment for "talkies," and one of the few that retains its original custom organ, the Fox continues to be the crown jewel of Detroit's entertainment district. Live shows range from the Rockettes to Bob Dylan, Sigur Rós to the family-friendly Sesame Street Live. *2211 Woodward Ave., www.olympiaentertainment.com, (313) 471-3200.*

Gem and Century Theatres - The Gem and Century Theatres are two separate theatres housed in the same elegant brick building with carved-stone ornamentation. Originally simply the Century Theatre, a cabaret-style venue established in 1903, the complex grew during a Spanish Revival–themed renovation in 1928 to include a new, smaller theater known under six names before its ultimate rechristening as the Gem. In 1997, the entire facility was trucked on wheels to its current location 1,847 feet away from its original site (a record for a building its size) to make way for Comerica Park. Both venues currently offer live theater, though Century typically offers comedies, while the Gem runs dramas. The Century offers rowed seating, but the Gem is composed of seated tables, permitting patrons to bring bar drinks inside. The interior of the complex exudes staid elegance in an atmosphere of incandescent warmth, and there is a garden patio outside. Dressing the part is appreciated but not required. The Gem and Century are available for weddings and other events. *333 Madison St., www.gemcolonyevents.com, (313) 963-8000.*

Greektown Casino - Centrally located in the center of Greektown, this neon-clad casino offers gamblers a contemporary, classically styled atmosphere, with casino-opulence reminiscent of Las Vegas. Easily accessible by car, People Mover, or foot, this 24/7 destination offers three restaurants, a bar, a 400-room hotel, and 2,700 slot and video games and 62 table game tables across its 100,000-square-foot gaming floor. This casino is easily the best for nonsmokers, offering 12 nonsmoking tables in its elegant poker room, which also boasts TVs, complimentary snacks, and attentive bar service. Greektown also offers rotating minimum bets on common table games like baccarat, blackjack, three-card poker, craps, roulette, as well as less common offerings such as Pai Gow Poker, and Mississippi Stud. Those looking to enjoy a weekend downtown or to try their luck in the morning can stay in the casino's luxurious **Greektown Casino-Hotel** and stay fed at one the casino's many dining options, including **Noodle Art**, a colorful Japanese ramen shop, or **Prism**, which features upscale steak and seafood. Bring your ID, as you have to be 21 or older to enter. *555 E. Lafayette Ave., www.greektowncasino.com, (888) 771-4386.*

Hart Plaza - In a city in which buildings and spaces often reflect a curiously sci-fi aesthetic, Hart Plaza—a popular Downtown gathering place that hosts the city's largest outdoor festivals—looks like it might be the landing pad for the mothership. Designed by internationally noted artist, landscape architect, and designer Isamu Noguchi and built in 1976, the plaza, named for U.S. Senator Philip Hart, is an expansive 14-acre public square along the riverfront that hosts the Movement electronic music festival, the African World Festival, and the Motor City Pride Festival, among many other major events. While it boasts several singular subterranean spaces, including an amphitheater and dance floor, aboveground, the concrete landscape plays host to an abundance of public art, including the 120-foot stainless steel *Pylon* (1973) by Noguchi, the at once representational and abstract *Transcending* (2001) by David Barr and Sergio De Giusti, and monuments to the Underground Railroad (see separate entry) and city-founder Antoine de la Mothe Cadillac. The most renowned installation in the plaza is the Noguchi-designed **Horace E. Dodge and Son Memorial Fountain**, erected in 1978 with a $1 million gift from Dodge's widow, Anna Thompson. The stainless-steel fountain is composed of two angled arms extending up 30 feet over a black granite pool and topped by a ring with 300 water jets that spray down into the pool. While Hart Plaza is best known for hosting jam-packed events, it's a lovely spot during quieter moments, too, affording a commanding view of Downtown and Windsor across the river, plenty of space to roam, and easy access to the River Walk. *1 Washington Blvd.*

Leland City Club - This edgy little dungeon club is a good destination if you're dressed to the nines in fishnets and have a slight fetish for electrical tape. Existing in the underbelly of the Leland Hotel at Bagley Street and Grand River Avenue, most night City Club is a dark after-hours spot that pumps industrial music onto a huge dance floor filled with members of the rivet-clad industrial scene. The club has been open since 1983 and formerly was the Leland's Grand Ballroom, which hosted parties for the city's elite in its heyday in the 1920s. This supposedly haunted nightclub hosts many MEMF events and other raucous after-parties. If you need a little party fuel, visit Luci & Ethel's diner upstairs for some bacon and pancakes (see separate entry). *400 Bagley St., www.lelandcityclub.net, (313) 962-2300.*

MGM Grand Detroit - The first of the city's three casinos, the MGM Grand offers the city's gamblers a taste of authentic Las Vegas gaming, and deals a healthy hand of Vegas-style opulence. The casino has a massive, 100,000-square-foot, glittering gaming floor, clad in flashing lights, contemporary decor and luxurious furnishings. With 24 table games across 115 tables and more than 4,000 slot and video machines, the casino has the most diverse offerings of the city's casinos, including all of the de rigueur table game offerings—baccarat, Spanish 21, Texas Hold'Em—as well as less common games—Mississippi Stud Poker, Two-Way Monte, Pai Gow Poker, and Double Exposure Blackjack—at values beginning at $1. The gaming experience is complemented by the plentiful bar service, numerous complimentary pop and coffee bars, video poker bar, and a five-restaurant food court. If you'd like to make a weekend of it, try the attached luxury hotel, spa, **Roasted Bean** cafe, and upscale dining options such as Wolfgang Puck Steak (see separate entry), **Palette Dining Studio** (an elevated buffet), or **TAP**, known for its down-to-earth options like pizza, wings, and burgers. Don't forget your ID—the casino is only for the 21+ crowd. Although MGM allows smoking, non-smoking gamers can enjoy the smoke-free slot room. Good luck! *1777 Third Ave., www.mgmgranddetroit.com, (888) 646-3387.*

Music Hall Center for the Performing Arts - Since Matilda Dodge Wilson opened the Music Hall's doors in 1928, the intimate Downtown venue has been a significant player in Detroit's performing arts sector. Originally named the Wilson Theatre, it was designed in the Art Deco style and the Madison Street facade is flush with decorative orange and tan brick as well as Pewabic tile and stone accents. The Music Hall is the only Detroit venue built for the primary purpose of presenting live performances. Though the theater has served as the home of the Detroit Symphony Orchestra, Michigan Opera Theatre, and a Cinerama screen in the past, today, the hall provides accessible music, theater, dance, and performances from travelling and local acts. **The Jazz Cafe**, a modern addition, offers an intimate bar and performance space for the everyday music lover with an ongoing series that highlights many of Detroit's great native artists from such as Luis Resto and Kimmie Horne. *349 Madison St., www.musichall.org, (313) 887-8500.*

Saint Andrew's Hall / The Shelter - Built in 1907 as the mammoth clubhouse for the St. Andrews Scottish Society of Detroit, Saint Andrew's Hall has served as a popular venue for rock, punk, hip hop, and EDM acts since 1982. The classical brick building recently received a facelift, and it is home to three venues—the Main Ballroom, a wood-floored, balcony-lined 1,000-person space with a 35-foot bar; The Shelter, a subterranean 400-seat venue with cabaret seating and a small stage; and The Society Room, a small, intimate space with hardwood floors, chic communal tables, and gorgeous historic windows where you can grab a drink before, during, or after your

show. While all three venues offer full bars with several dozen liquors and more than 80 domestic and imported beers, The Shelter also offers a limited food menu and is typically open during shows in the other two spaces. Together, many renowned acts have taken the stage at the three venues, including Eminem, Iggy Pop, Bob Dylan, Paul Simon, and Nirvana. *431 E. Congress St., www.saintandrewsdetroit.com, (313) 961-8961.*

Senate Theatre / Detroit Theater Organ Society - Best known for its historical one-of-a-kind instrument, the Senate Theatre boasts an original 1928 Wurlitzer console and organ of 2,300 pipes, specially commissioned by the Fisher brothers for their eponymous theater and relocated to its current home by the (now) Detroit Theater Organ Society (DTOS) in 1964. The massive, ornate console is still decked in its original Mayan-themed makeup with resplendent gold paint, but the organ's voice is what brings members and visitors. Only Wurlitzer parts are used to keep the instrument's rich, mellow sounds filling the theater. For analog aficionados, the organ and its set of 34 instrument voicings are entirely air-driven, powered offstage by a 25-horsepower motor. A gilded age theater, the Senate opened in 1926, and features an enormous vertical marquee and a beautifully restored lobby with lush gold and burgundy trim and antique furniture, as well as a 19th century wood melodeon. The theater was originally used by DTOS as a venue for club organists to play and gather, but is now an all-purpose venue featuring monthly and semi-monthly film screenings, live music, and event rental, including weddings, with a capacity of 800. *6424 Michigan Ave., www.dtos.org, (313) 894-0850.*

SITES

Ally Detroit Center - The work of celebrated post-modernist architects John Burgee and Philip Johnson, Ally Detroit Center, formerly known as **One Detroit Center** and **Comerica Tower**, was constructed between 1991 and 1993. Michigan's second tallest building after the Renaissance Center a few blocks away, the 619-foot, 43-story skyscraper is noted for its juxtaposition of postmodern architectural design with Flemish- inspired neo-gothic accents, which simultaneously contrast with and complement the city's historic skyline. Originally intended to be one of two towers, Two Detroit Center, which was to be directly east of the current structure, was never built. *500 Woodward Ave.*

The Book Brothers' Washington Boulevard - Successful sibling entrepreneurs the Book brothers—James Burgess, Herbert, and Frank—wanted to make Washington Boulevard an elegant commercial district, hoping to create a "Fifth Avenue of the West." While their vision included other structures, including the **Book Building** (1917) and **Industrial Bank Building** (1928), the pinnacles of their impressive efforts are two buildings, the **Book-Cadillac**, which, at the time of its completion in 1924, was the largest and tallest hotel in the world, and the 38-story **Book Tower**, which was the tallest building in the city when it was completed in 1926. Designed by Louis Kamper, the Neo-Renaissance Book-Cadillac had 1,136 rooms across 29 floors, and featured Corinthian pilasters, a marble staircase, and grand chandeliers in the elegant Venetian-style lobby and ornate Florentine-style ballroom. The exquisite facade features statues of important figures in Detroit history, including Antoine de la Mothe Cadillac. After an extended vacancy, the hotel was beautifully restored and has served as the Westin Book Cadillac since 2008. As for the Book Tower, Louis Kamper's elegant Italian Renaissance-style design features intricate Corinthian columns, crests, florets, caryatids, and a cartouche by sculptor Corrado Parducci, all of which are reminiscent of the Academic Classicism style. Unlike the beloved Book-Cadillac, the Book Tower's design has been derided by critics as clumsily garish, with many impracticalities, such as the lack of an interior

evacuation route—necessitating the nation's tallest fire escape—but the building's architectural ornamentation remains unusual and awe-inspiring, sometimes referred to as "cake decoration." Formerly one of the world's tallest empty buildings, the Book Tower is part of a $313 million renovation, which, in tandem with the renovation of the Book Building, will create 180,000 square feet of office and retail space, 95 residential units, and a hotel. Together with the lesser works that line the grand thoroughfare, these stunning landmarks make the boulevard unified in its splendor, and a treat for architecture fans. *1114 Washington Blvd. (Book Cadillac) and 1265 Washington Blvd. (Book Tower).*

Capitol Park - "Do you think there's a dead body in there?" Actually, yes. The State of Michigan's first governor—and the youngest governor in United States history, is interred in the base of a Capitol Park statue commemorating his life. Stevens T. Mason became territorial governor in 1834—at the age of 22—and shepherded Michigan to its 1837 statehood, lobbying successfully for the Upper Peninsula. A state financial crisis drove Mason from power, and he died in 1842. A curious relic of the Woodward Plan of 1805, Capitol Park itself is an old-world urban gathering place paved with bricks and tightly bordered on all sides by 17 historic buildings, most of which are beautifully restored. Historically, Capitol Park was the last stop on the Underground Railroad—escaped slaves, bound for Canada, stayed at Seymour Finney's barn-turned-tavern, though the structure has long since been demolished. During the 1990s, the space was known as an epicenter of Detroit's electronic music scene and a destination for late-night raves. Today, what was once a grassless plaza is now a bustling green space filled with a diverse crowd (and plenty of pooches, thanks to a mini dog park) and lined on all sides by restaurants, cafes, and seasonal pop-up shops housed in beautiful, tiny glass greenhouses. *Bordered by State St., Griswold St., and Shelby St.*

Central United Methodist Church - A Methodist congregation that has served as a wellspring of social justice and progressivism for almost two centuries, Central United Methodist has earned the title of "the Conscience of a City." Though the congregation has had several homes since it was founded in 1822, its current house of worship was completed in 1867. The elaborate gray limestone building is designed in a mix of Tudor and Gothic styles and features a series of spires and gables that cap resplendent stonework and old-world details. Inside, an enormous 70-rank pipe organ, 30-foot-tall white oak reredos, ascendant mural of the apostles, and beautiful stained glass windows add to the stature of the nave, which frames its altar between ornate banners of "Peace" and "Justice." Central United's reputation for causes of human dignity is exemplified from the outcry over an 1830 execution that took place in front of the church. Parishioners immediately launched efforts to ban execution in Michigan, making it the first English-speaking democracy to do so. The church leads events such as rallies and marches, including the annual MLK day march, and has held concerts for social activist performers such as Janis Ian. The church is also home to a peace center and art gallery, **Swords Into Plowshares**, which hosts rotating exhibits and offers limited hours. *23 E. Adams St., www.centralumchurch.com, (313) 965-5422.*

Cobo Center - Though most well-known for hosting the world-famous North American International Auto Show, Cobo Center hosts scores of conventions and events each year and has played an important role in the city's history. Named for former Mayor Albert Cobo, the hall was built in 1960 at the west end of Downtown, along the river. Designed by noted architect Gino Rossetti, Cobo retains many of its original design elements—such as the geometric facade and utilitarian aesthetic—despite considerable remodeling and expansion projects through the years. Most recently, the convention center has seen the expansion of the magnificent Grand Riverview Ballroom and the addition of an impressive glass atrium overlooking the Detroit River. Today, this modern facility boasts 725,000 square feet of exhibit space—625,000 of it contiguous, besting the equivalent of 10 football fields. Inside, the center has a 12-foot bronze statue of Joe Louis and displays one of the gloves the boxer wore when he beat Max Schmeling in a rematch symbolic of the fight against Nazism, the glove now bronzed for posterity. In 2018, Cobo also unveiled a mammoth, colorful mural by Detroit artist Hubert Massey, "Crossroads of Innovation," which represents the region and is a nod to Diego Rivera's "Detroit Industry" fresco cycle at the Detroit Institute of Arts. The center is popular among local historians both because it was built on the same ground that Antoine de la Mothe Cadillac landed upon in 1701, and because Cobo witnessed Martin Luther King Jr. address a crowd of 25,000 Civil Rights activists at the end of the Detroit Freedom Walk in 1963, where he began to articulate his "I Have A Dream" speech. Aside from Dr. King, Cobo has hosted many notable speakers, including

DOWNTOWN
SITES

every sitting U.S. president since Dwight D. Eisenhower, who gave the keynote address at the center's inaugural convention. *1 Washington Blvd., www.cobocenter.com, (313) 877-8777.*

Daniel Burnham Architecture - As Burnham once said, "Make no little plans; they have no magic to stir men's blood." Though he's not a Detroiter (nobody's perfect), Daniel Burnham is regarded as one of the greatest American architects. With a laundry list of achievements—including being a co-author of the city-shaping Chicago Plan of 1909, a founder of the Chicago School of architecture, the chief coordinating architect of the "White City" at the 1893 Columbian Exposition, and the architect of New York's Flatiron Building—Burnham has been called a father of the skyscraper and one of the most influential minds behind early 20th century architecture. During his career, Burnham designed four buildings in Detroit. One, the **Majestic Building**, which was built in 1896 and demolished in 1961, has been lost, but fortunately, three remain. In 1909, the architect completed his first structure in Detroit, the **Ford Building** (no, not that Ford—the Edward Ford Plate Glass Co.) At 18 stories, the structure, a shining example of the refined elegance of the Chicago School, towered over the burgeoning city and was hailed by the *Free Press* as Detroit's "first real skyscraper." In 1912, Burnham completed a more ornate Neoclassical masterpiece dubbed the **Dime Building**, for the bank that once occupied its floors. Connected to the Ford Building with a secret underground tunnel, the 23-story Dime, now known as **Chrysler House**, is similarly a trademark Burnham, clad in white terra cotta. With a stunning renovation completed in 2014, the true masterpiece of Burnham's remaining buildings in Detroit is the **David Whitney Building**. A sentinel standing guard over Grand Circus Park, the reserved exterior of the 19-story building belies the breathtaking Beaux Arts interior which features a dramatic skylight-covered, four-story atrium lobby decked throughout in terracotta and marble. Architecture fans should definitely peek inside. *615 Griswold St., (Ford Building), 719 Griswold St (Dime Building), and 1553 Woodward Ave. (David Whitney Building).*

Fort Street Presbyterian Church - Constructed in the years leading up to the Civil War, this impressive sanctuary has come to define the street from which it drew its name. Built in a Decorated Gothic style, its design elements include a 265-foot spire and intricate flourishes—ornamental finials, flying buttresses, carved limestone faces, and patinaed copper elements intended to recall foliage. The church's interior is a nuanced balance of majestic scale and delicate detail—the soaring sanctuary seats 1,200 parishioners on its main floor and crescent balcony and boasts an organ with more than 3,200 pipes, but this awe-inspiring scale is matched in aesthetic power by subtle refinements like tile work by Pewabic Pottery founder Mary Chase Stratton, 13th century style Grisaille stained glass windows, and a Caen stone baptismal font with Mexican onyx pillars. *631 W. Fort St., www.fortstreet.org, (313) 961-4533.*

Grand Army of the Republic Building - Towering over the corner of Grand River Avenue and Cass Avenue, the turrets and battlements of Detroit's castle make it look like an ancient fort built to defend the city from Ohioan invaders. However, the historic, imposing, and distinctive building, designed by architect Julius Hess in the Richardsonian Romanesque style (read: castle style), opened in 1900 as a place for local Civil War veterans to congregate—the design was selected because the stone fortress was said to look as strong as the republic the boys in blue had fought to preserve. Unfortunately, by 1934, most of the gray-bearded veterans had died and the ground floor retail tenants could no longer cover operating costs for the building. The city converted it into a public space and operated it as the GAR Recreation Center until it was closed in 1982 because of budget constraints and lack of use. In 2014, local company Mindfield Creative completed a restoration of this unusual historic gem. Today, it houses their headquarters, as well as restaurants Republic and Parks and Rec (see separate entries). *1942 Grand River Ave.*

Grand Circus Park - A five-acre semicircular green space anchored by the iconic buildings that surround it, Grand Circus Park, which is bisected by Woodward Avenue, connects the city's theater and financial districts. Though planned as a component of Judge Augustus B. Woodward's radial street plan following the city's catastrophic 1805 fire, the park wasn't established until 1850. In a compact but bucolic setting, the grounds include antique statuary and fountains, the most notable of which is the **Hazen S. Pingree Monument**. Pingree, now considered one of the greatest mayors in United States history, was simultaneously Mayor of Detroit (elected 1889) and Governor of Michigan (elected 1896) until he was forced to resign his mayoral post by the Michigan Supreme Court as it was deemed unacceptable to hold both posts simultaneously. The noted King Edward VII lookalike fought privatized monopolies, advocated

for public transit, encouraged urban farming through his "Potato Patch Plan," exposed corruption, expanded public welfare programs, and created public works projects for the unemployed. Beloved by his constituents, his monument declares that he is "The Idol of the People." Across Woodward Avenue sits the **William Cotter Maybury Monument** that was built by the city's business leaders to honor Pingree's conservative rival and mayoral successor—though Maybury's statue doesn't say "Idol" on it. The park is also home to the **Russell A. Alger Memorial Fountain**, named for a major lumber baron (and later a Michigan governor and Senator) who settled in Detroit after the Civil War, and the **Millennium Bell** (created by artists Chris Turner and Matt Blake), which was commissioned by the city in 2000 and is rung every New Year. With its storied landmarks and historic urban surroundings, Grand Circus Park is a fabulous place to enjoy a carryout lunch or take a late-night stroll—with a loved one or your favorite pooch, thanks to the location's dog park. *1601 Woodward Ave.*

★**Guardian Building** - Known as Detroit's Cathedral of Finance, the lavish, incredibly beautiful facade of the Guardian Building boasts the city's most intricate ornamentation, a theme continued on the opulent interior. Opened in 1929, this Wirt Rowland masterpiece emerged during the height of Art Deco architecture and used the finest materials to create the city's grandest example of the style. The 36-story main structure is topped by two spires, one of which extends four stories, reaching 632 feet. The ornate orange-tan brick facade features stunning pink granite banding, Mankato stone, vibrantly glazed Pewabic tile mosaics, and terra cotta details around entrances, which augment the building's signature Aztec theme. The interior of the structure continues the motif, with a three-story lobby clad in Pewabic and Rockwood tile that features a multi-story mural of Michigan's people and enterprises with gold leaf detail by Anthony Eugenio. The lobby features Italian Travertine marble columns, Belgian marble bases, and red Numidian marble details. *500 Griswold St.*

Joe Louis Arena - Though now vacant, the well-worn Joe Louis Arena—known simply as "the Joe"—was a utilitarian but beloved home to the Detroit Red Wings from 1979-2017. The area holds the distinction of being homebase for the team during one of its most productive periods. Between 1990 and 2017, the Wings made the playoffs a record-setting 25 consecutive times and won four Stanley

Cups, with championships in 1997, 1998, 2002, and 2008. Having been built hastily—to keep the Wings from running to suburban Pontiac in 1979—the Joe is somewhat architecturally indistinct. However, the arena does feature highly unusual and curiously dangerous two-story concrete entry stairs, and connections to other buildings—and the People Mover elevated train—by bizarre pedestrian tubes that give it a monolithic, neo-futurist appearance. The Joe is scheduled for demolition in 2019, so its days are numbered, but until the dust settles, the great history and memories live on. *600 Civic Center Dr.*

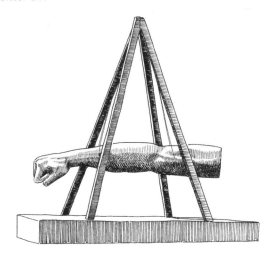

Joe Louis Fist Sculpture - In addition to being one of the greatest heavyweight boxers of all time, with a 140-month, 27-fight championship reign, the Brown Bomber crossed color lines and became an American hero when he defeated Nazi symbol Max Schmeling in 1938. This 24-foot-long bronze fist was commissioned by Sports Illustrated Magazine to honor the Detroit native who became a national icon. Designed by Robert Graham, the sculpture was completed in 1986 and is suspended from a steel harness looming over the intersection of Jefferson Avenue and Woodward Avenue, just north of Hart Plaza. *E. Jefferson Ave. and Woodward Ave.*

Lafayette Greens - Built in 2011 on the site of the Lafayette Building, a singular but neglected 1925 C. Howard Crane designed high-rise demolished in 2009, Lafayette Greens is a Downtown demonstration garden owned and maintained by non-profit **Greening of Detroit**. With fruit trees, a children's garden, and 35 raised beds overflowing

with a multitude of flowers, vegetables, and fruit, this half-acre urban oasis is a masterful burst of color, fragrance, biodiversity, and geometry in the heart of the business district. The garden is open to the public during the week and makes for a perfect spot to eat lunch, read a book, or stroll among the greenery. *142 W. Lafayette Ave., (313) 227-5555.*

Mariners' Church of Detroit - At the foot of Randolph Street lies the oldest stone church in Michigan and the state's only church incorporated by legislative act. Mariners' Church, a national historic site, has served as a non-diocesan parish for sailors since it was founded in 1842. The church is a nautical temple—the Gothic Revival structure sports an insignia of an anchor on its bell tower, there is a nautical compass rose window, and marine-themed stained glass windows overlook its sanctuary. Inside the building, marine artifacts such as anchors, bells, and a collection of paintings from local 19th century artist Robert Hopkin cement the church's maritime legacy. The church building was physically relocated to its current location in the 1950s—a move that revealed a secret basement chamber, evidence of the church's role in the Underground Railroad. In 1975, the church was immortalized in Gordon Lightfoot's "Wreck of the Edmund Fitzgerald," which tells of how the Mariners' bell "chimed 'til it rang 29 times" for each man who perished. To this day, the church holds an annual memorial service every November for all brave seafarers, with Lightfoot himself having performed the song at the 10-year remembrance of the Fitzgerald sinking. Mariners' has been used prominently by other music icons—it hosted the 1980 wedding of punk's high couple of cool, Patti and the late Fred "Sonic" Smith. *170 E. Jefferson Ave., www.marinerschurchofdetroit.org, (313) 259-2206.*

Michigan Theatre Parking Garage - Once one of the world's most exquisite entertainment venues, today it is the world's most exquisite, heartbreaking, and curious parking facility. Built on the site of Henry Ford's original workshop, the building was completed in 1926. With a capacity of 4,050, the jaw-dropping theater, which featured 10-foot chandeliers and a gilded four-story lobby, was described by the *Detroit Free Press* as "beyond the dreams of loveliness; entering, you pass into another world." However, the theater's popularity began to wane. It became a rock venue, and eventually closed in 1976. Though plans eventually surfaced to demolish the structure, they were halted when engineers discovered that such action would destabilize the attached office building next door. Consequently, the majestic interior space was gutted and retrofitted with a 160 car parking structure built within the shell. Many remnants of the glorious Renaissance-style structure remain intact, and hint at its past greatness. Consequently, the facility has become a popular legal urban exploration site, explorable from the safety of your car—as long as you pay for parking. *220 Bagley St.*

Old Wayne County Building - Designed by Detroiter John Scott, this five-story Roman Baroque style edifice features elements of Beaux Arts Classicism that was popular at the time of its completion in 1902. The incredibly ornate pink granite and sandstone facade features numerous sculptures by Edward Wagner and John Massey Rhind, including two stunning bronze allegorical works depicting female figures driving chariots representing Victory and Progress, and four smaller female statues representing Law, Commerce, Agriculture, and Mechanics. The elegant structure is dominated by a sweeping flight of stairs, a portico of Corinthian columns, an ornate balustrade above the third floor, and a dome-topped tower and spire that stands at 247 feet tall. Although Wayne County no longer occupies the building, the name remains. *600 Randolph St.*

One Woodward Avenue - Designed by Minoru Yamasaki, a preeminent architect of the 20th Century and a master practitioner of New Formalism, this 32-story, 430-foot-tall high-rise was completed in 1963. As Yamasaki's first skyscraper, the building introduces elements such as a pre-cast concrete exterior, narrow windows, Gothic arches, decorative tracery, and sculptural gardens that would become the architect's signature motifs. For this reason, the building has been called the forerunner to the architect's iconic World Trade Center in New York. One Woodward Avenue was commissioned by the Michigan Consolidated Gas Company and features a delicate lattice of narrow, 12-inch-wide windows set in a mixture of pre-cast concrete

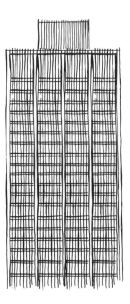

and marble chips, which gives the building a stark brilliance. This minimalist motif, which begins on the second floor, is offset by the incredible gravity-defying glass lobby and loggia, upon which the building seems to float effortlessly. The uppermost floors, which are inset and conceal the building's mechanical systems, are illuminated at night with seasonally appropriate colors. Don't miss the graceful sculpture *Passo di Danza* (Step of the Dance) that was created by Italian sculptor Giacomo Manzù. *1 Woodward Ave.*

Penobscot Building - The 47-story Penobscot Building and its iconic red orb have dominated the city's skyline since its construction in 1928. Detroit's tallest building until the completion of the Renaissance Center in 1977, the opulent Art Deco masterpiece soars 566 feet into the air and is the Indiana limestone-clad anchor of the Financial District. Designed by noted local architect Wirt C. Rowland, the limestone and granite structure features intricate architectural relief sculptures by Corrado Parducci. The building's name and ornamentation were chosen by the original owner and lumber baron, Simon Murphy, who chose the Penobscot Tribe of his home state of Maine as the inspiration for the building's name and elaborate carved Native American motifs. *645 Griswold St.*

People Mover Station Art - Opened in 1987, the **Detroit People Mover** is a 2.9 mile automated monorail system that circles Downtown. Though the system averages only 7,083 riders a day, and its utility as a mode of transportation is sometimes debated—it runs one way in a loop and the subsequent phases that would have connected the system to the city's residents were never built—it is superbly clean and well-maintained and serves as a colorful (climate controlled) top-down tour of Downtown. The People Mover stations themselves are a special visual treat. From 1984 to 1987, 15 artists were commissioned to install large-scale decorative works in each of the 13 stations, resulting in a wide variety of colors, textures, and visually immersive sites for riders. Complimentary tours for groups of 10 to 30 are available by appointment during the week from May to October. Although all of the stations are visually engaging, favorites include the Times Square and Cadillac Center stations, with three elaborate mosaic works made from locally legendary Pewabic tile; the Cobo Center Station with its *Cavalcade of Cars*, a celebration of the Big Three in Venetian glass mosaic; *Siberian Ram* by *Spirit of Detroit* sculptor Marshall Fredericks at the Renaissance Center Station; the eponymous Las Vegas flair of neon for the Greektown Station; *The*

Blue Nile, a Noah's Ark-themed mural in a traditional African style by celebrated local artist Charles McGee at the Broadway Station; and *Catching Up* in the Grand Circus Park Station, a bronze statue of a man reading the paper that often causes passersby to double take. *The stations dot Downtown, but a convenient place to pick up the train is the Times Square Station at Grand River Ave. and Park Pl., www.thepeoplemover.com, (313) 224-2160.*

Renaissance Center - A massive, unmistakable complex of seven buildings along the river that forever changed Detroit's skyline, this city within a city was originally built by Ford Motor Co. between 1977 and 1981 as an urban renewal project. It is currently owned by General Motors and serves as the company's world headquarters. The central, cylindrical, 73-story tower is home to the Detroit Marriott (see separate entry) hotel and is the tallest all-hotel tower in the Western hemisphere. Designed by John Portman with a Modernist's emphasis on glass and a Brutalist's penchant for concrete, the complex aroused the ire of urbanists in the years after its construction for being essentially walled off from the rest of Detroit, as well as being difficult to navigate. A $500 million renovation by GM mitigated these concerns with the addition of a lighted glass walkway and two glass atria, one opening to Jefferson Avenue and the other, the soaring Wintergarden, connecting the complex to the River Walk. With the circular design, new walkway, atria, and all that glass and concrete (including towering columns, unexpected alcoves, and numerous pod-like balconies), it's a strange, spectacular, self-contained world that still feels futuristic. Complimentary tours of the architectural icon are available twice daily, Monday to Friday at 12pm and 2pm and depart from the Pure Detroit store (see separate entry) in the building. *1 Renaissance Center, www.gmrencen.com, (313) 568-5624.*

Second Baptist Church of Detroit - Founded in 1837, the historic Second Baptist Church is the oldest African-American congregation in the Midwest. This large red brick house of worship stretches across nearly a whole block of Monroe Street, lining the sidewalk with panes of turquoise, blue, and yellow stained glass windows and large oak doors. But the real marvels of this church are hidden in the walls of historic sepia-toned photographs, newspaper clippings, murals, and church archives that document visits from Frederick Douglass and Dr. Martin Luther King Jr. The attached bookstore conducts tours of the church, which detail the history of Detroit's African-American community through the church's history as the

last stop before Canada on the Underground Railroad and a center for Civil Rights leadership. Historic tours run for a $5 suggested donation on Wednesday, Friday, and Saturday at 10am, 11:30am, and 1:30pm. Call to schedule a special appointment. Visitors also enjoy free parking at the casino lot near Fishbone's restaurant. *441 Monroe St., www.secondbaptistdetroit.org, (313) 961-0352.*

★ **Spirit of Detroit** - Located at the foot of the **Coleman A. Young Municipal Center**, the *Spirit of Detroit* is a 26-foot-tall oxidized green bronze statue of a man holding a gilded bronze family in one hand and a sun in the other. Though never named by the sculptor, residents have taken to calling it the *Spirit of Detroit* thanks to a quote on a wall to its rear from 2 Corinthians: "Now the Lord is that Spirit: and where the Spirit of the Lord is, there is liberty." The sculpture was crafted in Oslo, Norway, where sculptor Marshall Fredericks waived his fee for the project and absorbed some of the costs personally. The statue is the largest cast bronze statue created since the Renaissance. *The Spirit* instantly became emblematic for the city, and, in recent years, has donned oversized sports jerseys to support Detroit teams playing in respective championships. *2 Woodward Ave.*

Z Lot and The Belt - Detroit is a city known for its vibrant public art, and together, this 10-story Downtown car park and adjacent alley are among the largest, most dense, diverse, and colorful outdoor art sites in the city. The **Z Lot** is named for the Z-shaped parcel it occupies. To decorate the contemporary car park, 27 local, national, and international artists were commissioned by project collaborators Library Street Collective and Bedrock Detroit to create 130-foot wide murals to decorate the interior walls of the 500,000-square-foot garage. The best way to view the "collection" is to take the elevator straight up to the tenth floor, soak in the view, and leisurely make your way down, stopping to admire work from the likes of Dabs Myla, Sam Friedman, Tristan Eaton, How and Nosm, and Lucy McLauchlan, among many others. Created to activate a derelict alley, **The Belt** was brought to life by the same team. The alley is a rich, textured pedestrian walkway that is inviting, visually stimulating, and seemingly primed for Instagram. With overhead string lighting, the alley features work by Shepard Fairey, Nina Chanel Abney, FAILE, Cleon Peterson, Tiff Massey, and a dozen others. The Belt is also home to rotating outdoor exhibitions of large-scale paintings, as part of **Public Matter**, and is home to The Skip,

Standby, and The Library Street Collective (see separate entries). And yes, if you need to stash your ride, the Z Lot is a functioning parking garage. *Z Lot: 1234 Library St.; The Belt: connects Grand River and Gratiot, between Library and Broadway, www.thebelt.org.*

POINTS OF INTEREST

#WhatLiftsYou Mural - Joining a growing international network, Detroit now has it's very own "wings" mural (and we don't mean the hockey team). The Woodward #WhatLiftsYou mural by international street artist and social media phenomenon Kelsey Montague offers a graceful photo-op, made for Instagram-worthy moments. *1550 Woodward Ave.*

Abraham Lincoln Statue - First designed as a way of promoting a freeway stretching from the Atlantic to the Pacific, to be named after President Lincoln, this statue sits comfortably in front of the Skillman Branch of the Detroit Public Library, the inscription reading, "Let Man Be Free." *121 Gratiot Ave.*

Bagley Memorial Fountain - Modeled after a ciborium in St. Mark's Basilica in Venice by architect Henry Hobson Richardson, this 21-foot-tall fountain—which was the city's first drinking fountain—seems to have found a permanent home in **Cadillac Square**, having endured a couple of moves since its dedication in 1887. *Cadillac Sq. and Bates St.*

Beverly Fishman Mural - This intensely bright and enormously large mural by Beverly Fishman leaps off the Brutalist stylings of the Detroit City Club Apartments. *1431 Washington Blvd.*

Birthplace of Kiwanis - The international service organization was born in this building in 1914, when businessmen Allen S. Browne and Joseph G. Prance came up with idea of banding like-minded individuals and businesses together. *Griswold St. and Grand River Ave.*

Black Bottom and Paradise Valley - In the early 20th century, these neighborhoods with a shared boundary jointly served as the epicenter of African-American culture, commerce, and life. Black Bottom, which was developed earlier, began at Gratiot Avenue and extended as far south as the Detroit River between Brush Street and the Dequindre Cut and served primarily as a housing center for the city's African-American population. **Paradise Valley** extended north from Gratiot Avenue, along the same corridor and was a dense district full of cultural amenities and scores of renowned African-American–owned businesses. The two neighborhoods developed in response to discriminatory housing policies in the prewar period and were tragically and systematically erased under the banner of postwar urban renewal programs. *Gratiot Ave. and Brush St.*

Blue Cross Blue Shield Campus Art - The Downtown campus of the health insurance giant contains a number of important sculptures including *Dancing Hands* by Robert Sestok, *Urban Stele* by Sergio De Giusti, and *The Procession (A Family)* by John Nick Pappas, the last being one of the largest bronze statuary ensembles in the United States. *600 E. Lafayette St.*

Broderick Tower - A 1928 project designed by Louis Kamper, the Broderick Tower is a distinctively simple towering 35-story example of the Chicago-School of architecture. In 1997, local artist Robert Wyland painted *Whale Tower*, a 108-foot mural of three humpback whales on the eastern wall of the then-abandoned building which was beautifully redeveloped for apartments in 2012. *10 Witherell St.*

Bunnie Reiss Mural - Painted by L.A. artist Bunnie Reiss in 2018, these colorful geometric shapes stretch across the backside of the Downtown Synagogue. *1457 Griswold St.*

Cadillac Tower Record Labels - This iconic skyscraper was home to two Detroit soul record labels. **Invictus Records** was founded in 1969, when the Motown songwriting team Holland- Dozier-Holland, responsible for many of that label's biggest hits, left the pop giant and started their own imprint. Parliament's first record, "Osmium," was an Invictus release. One year later, in 1970, R&B singer Gino Washington launched his own label, **ATAC International Records**, which released a string of locally popular tracks. *65 Cadillac Sq.*

Christopher Columbus - This larger-than-life bust of the famous explorer, sculpted by Italian artist Augusto Rivalta in 1910, gazes out atop an ornate travertine pedestal. *E. Jefferson Ave. and Randolph St.*

Church of Scientology - After an extensive renovation, the former Raymond James Building was reborn as the Detroit Church of Scientology in 2018. Stop inside to learn about thetans and dianetics, or have your electrodermal activity measured. The onsite cafe is rumored to have good muffins. *1 Griswold St.*

Circles, Dots, Lines, and Shapes Mural - This rhythmic, colorfully chaotic mural by Hense graces the side of the Madison Building downtown, with zig-zagging patterns and curvaceous flourishes, as well as the namesake shapes. *1555 Broadway St.*

Detroit Police Museum and Gift Shop - Located inside of the Detroit Public Safety Building, this free exhibit features curiosities ranging from Jimmy Hoffa's fingerprints and huge 1950s era body armor to traffic "stop-go" signs from the early 1900s. *1301 Third Ave.*

Detroit Skybridge - Part pedestrian bridge of yore, part sculpture and installation, this Phillip K. Smith III intervention connects two of Detroit's most iconic Downtown buildings, One Woodward and the Guardian Building. At night, the 100-foot-long 16th-floor skybridge becomes a floating bar of colored lights hovering over the streets of Downtown Detroit. *500 Griswold St.*

Emily's Across the Street - In the 1970s and 1980s, when the city's morale was at an all-time low, dynamic and charismatic Detroit super-booster Emily Gail worked to shift the paradigm through her beloved, legendary shop in this space, where she encouraged everyone to "Say Nice Things About Detroit." *161 W. Congress St.*

Father Gomidas Armenian Memorial - This striking figure depicts the Armenian priest and composer who was imprisoned by Turkish forces in 1915 and, after being released, died a broken man in Paris. The statue, by Canadian sculptor Arto Tchakmakchian, was funded by local Armenian groups as way of commemorating the genocide of 1.5 million Armenians at the hands of the Turkish government between 1915 and 1923. *W. Jefferson Ave. and Woodward Ave.*

Finney Barn Site Historic Marker - A barn owned by Detroit abolitionist Seymour Finney once sat on this site and acted as an important passenger depot along the Underground Railroad, often as a last stop for escaping slaves as they made their way across the river into Canada. *State St. and Griswold St.*

First National Building - Opened in 1930, this Albert Kahn designed skyscraper uses a unique "Z" shape to expose most of the offices inside to natural light. The ground floor was featured in 2011 George Clooney film *The Ides of March*. *660 Woodward Ave.*

Garrick Theatre Site - Although the Garrick Theatre is gone, it was on this site that Harry Houdini performed for the final time before dying a few days later in Detroit's Grace Hospital. *1120 Griswold St.*

Gateway to Freedom International Memorial to the Underground Railroad - A masterpiece by sculptor Ed Dwight, the memorial includes two larger-than-life-size granite and bronze sculptures across the Detroit River from one another. The profoundly moving U.S. sculpture depicts a family of escaped Canada-bound slaves. The Canadian sculpture depicts the family's arrival. *Detroit RiverWalk at Hart Plaza.*

General Alexander Macomb Monument - This dashing figure, crated by sculptor Adolph Alexander Weinman in 1908, commemorates the accomplishments of a man who earned his fame during the War of 1812 and whose family once owned Belle Isle, Grosse Ile, and most of what we now know as Macomb County. *Washington Blvd. and Michigan Ave.*

General Thaddeus Kosciuszko Statue - A gift from the people of Krakow, Poland, to the city on the occasion of the American Bicentennial in 1976, this huge statue of the Polish and American Revolutionary hero sits confidently on his horse watching the procession of cars and pedestrians down Michigan Avenue. *Michigan Ave. and Third Ave.*

George Washington Statue - Presented to the city in 1966 by the Masons of Michigan, this Donald DeLue bronze statue depicts Washington in the regalia of the Freemason Order. *170 E. Jefferson Ave.*

The Hand of God, Memorial to Frank Murphy - This towering sculpture, designed by Cranbrook artist Carl Milles, was dedicated to famous Detroit politician and eventual U.S. Supreme Court Justice Frank Murphy. The piece consists of a newly created man standing on the fingers of a huge hand, both sitting somewhat precariously atop a 26-foot-tall granite shaft. *St. Antoine St. and Gratiot Ave.*

Harmonie Park - This beautiful little park is home to a handful of sculptures, including *The Entrance* by John Piet, and *Hard Edge Soft Edge* by Hanna Stiebel, both of which were installed in the mid-1970s. *Randolph St. and Centre St.*

Henry Ford Workshop Site - The small workshop, which sat behind his modest home, where Henry Ford built his first car was demolished to make room for the Michigan Theater. You can, however, see a reconstruction of the building at Greenfield Village in Dearborn (see separate entry). *58 Bagley St.*

HENSE Mural - This huge multicolored mural by Atlanta artist HENSE fills the entire southern wall of Downtown's Madison Building, and was completed in 2014. *1555 Broadway St.*

How and Nosm Mural - Standing opposite Shepard Fairey's "Peace and Justice Lotus" mural, this 184-foot-tall mural by New York-based twins How and Nosm, features an uneasy totem in red, pink, black, and white. *Visible from the southwest corner of Farmer St. and State St.*

Kern's Clock - Built in 1929 to advertise the Kern's Department Store, this oversize clock has been a handy point of reference for Detroiters ever since: Meet me at the Kern's Clock! *Woodward Ave. and State St.*

Old Plum Street - In a space now entirely occupied by the MGM Grand Casino, Plum Street was once Detroit's hangout for hippies in the late 1960s. At its peak, 43 shops graced the district. *Plum St. between Fourth St. and Fifth St.*

Old St. Mary's Church - Founded in 1834, this church is the third oldest parish in the city. The edifice of the massive, striking church combines elements of Pisan Romanesque and Venetian Renaissance. Inside, it is spacious and grand, with enormous stained glass windows, beautifully detailed Stations of the Cross, an altar bathed in cool blue colors, and an elegantly intricate apse above the transept. One of the three Sunday liturgies is still held in Latin. *646 Monroe St.*

One Man Army Mural - Spanish artist Aryz painted this enormous mural, which features a hardworking man as the namesake "one man army," repeated along a building. The beautifully rendered work contrasts with the surrounding cityscape. *25 E. Grand River.*

Plum Street Greenhouse - A production-focused greenhouse and site for many educational farming programs located, surprisingly, in between a handful of skyscrapers. *2228 Third Ave.*

Saints Peter and Paul Jesuit Church - Despite the relatively plain exterior, this Catholic church, completed in 1848, is the oldest standing church of any denomination in the city. The architectural highlight of the structure is the subdued and refined interior with stately columns and an incredible vaulted ceiling. *438 St. Antoine St.*

Site of 1805 Fire - In 1805, ashes from the pipe of local baker John Harvey inadvertently set fire to a barn located at this site. The flames spread quickly and destroyed the largely wooden city. In response to the city's destruction, Judge Augustus Woodward proposed reinventing the city with the "Woodward Plan" of radial spokes fanning out from the city's center—the essence of which remains today. *W. Jefferson Ave. and Wayne St.*

Shepard Fairey Mural - Street artist Shepard Fairey, best known as the designer of the 2008 Obama "Hope" poster, created this massive 184-foot-tall mural on the back side of One Campus Martius. The mural, painted in red, black, and cream, features images of stars, lotus leaves, peace signs, and Andre the Giant. *Visible from the southwest corner of Farmer St. and State St.*

St. Aloysius Church - Part of the tight Washington Boulevard streetwall, this church is curiously sandwiched between commercial structures. Completed in 1930, the broad planes of limestone on the exterior are dotted with ornately carved flourishes. Though the interior is relatively aesthetically reserved, the three-story atrium and unusual tiered seating make it one of Downtown's great spaces. *1209 Washington Blvd.*

Stearns Telephone Plaque - On September 22, 1887, a Bell telephone, the first in the city, was installed in the drugstore run on this site by Frederick Stearns, connecting the store to the Stearns laboratory half a mile away. *511 Woodward Ave.*

St. John's Church - Built in 1859, this ornate Victorian Gothic style Episcopalian church boasts a limestone facade with sandstone trim and beautiful buttresses. The single bell tower stands 105 feet tall, overlooking the intricate, decorative gargoyles that dot the roof. Check out the Michigan historic marker facing Woodward. *50 E. Fisher Fwy.*

Theodore J. Levin U.S. Courthouse Seventh Floor - Dubbed "the Million Dollar Courtroom" at the time of its construction, this beautiful space, which was originally located in another building finished in 1897 and then disassembled and rebuilt inside of this 1934 building, contains more than 30 kinds of marble, East Indian Mahogany, and unique sculptural work. *231 W. Lafayette Blvd.*

Unity Mural - This towering 11-story mural, designed by seminal Detroit artist Charles McGee, features a kinetic composition of black and white figures leaping off the northern face of the 28 Grand building in Capitol Park. *28 W. Grand River Ave.*

Untitled Charles McGee Mural - A striking study in color and form, this colorful but faded Charles McGee mural is a visual reminder of the city's recent past and civic beautification projects from the 1970s. *234 W. Larned St.*

Waiting Sculpture by Kaws - These 17-foot-tall bronze figures, designed by renowned New York artist KAWS, received a mixed reaction when they were installed near Campus Martius Park in 2018. The sculptor draws from the iconography of Mickey Mouse in ways that some find compelling and others find disturbing. *One Campus Martius.*

Waterfront Ziggurat - Though ziggurats are technically square, this curious, secluded conical spiral pyramid has earned the nickname anyway and is a popular choice for a quiet late night date or hang out by the water. *Detroit RiverWalk and Steve Yzerman Dr.*

Wish Tree for Detroit - Slightly relocated from its original location to make room for the Rosa Parks Transit Center, this "living sculpture," which was donoated by Yoko Ono and dedicated in 2000, consists of a gingko tree, a granite rock, and a bronze plaque inviting visitors to "Whisper your wish/ to the bark of the tree." *Grand River Ave. and Park Pl.*

Woodward Windows - The many vacant storefronts on this quiet stretch of Woodward Avenue have been reinvented as a public display platform for artists who have filled the storefronts with installations that often reflect on their settings with commentary, observation, and humor. *Woodward Ave. between Park Ave. and Gratiot Ave.*

Wurlitzer Building - Abandoned for decades, but now home to the Siren Hotel, this beautifully restored 14-story Renaissance Revival building was originally completed in 1926. Designed by Robert Finn, the unusually skinny building is a favorite among architecture buffs for its ornate styling and stunning details. *1509 Broadway St.*

CHAPTER 2
MIDTOWN

Come tour museums, visit galleries, admire architecture, catch movies, browse boutiques, enjoy eateries, and hunt for antiques in the bustling commercial, cultural, and geographic heart of the city. Every trip to Detroit should include a visit to Midtown, home to regional assets such as the Detroit Institute of Arts, Museum of Contemporary Art Detroit, Detroit Main Library, Detroit Symphony Orchestra, Detroit Historical Museum, Michigan Science Center, and the Charles H. Wright Museum of African American History. Become one of the two million annual visitors who explore the city's most popular cultural amenities, most diverse architecture, and some of the its densest shopping and dining districts.

As defined for this guide, Midtown spans 2.9 square miles, is bounded by I-94, I-75, M-10, and Grand River Avenue, and encompasses a number of neighborhoods, including Art Center, Brush Park, Cass Corridor, Cultural Center, Jeffries, Medical Center, Sugar Hill, the Wayne State University Campus, and Woodbridge. Collectively, these distinct communities showcase an array of physical forms and styles and are home to the city's most diverse group of residents.

As one of the oldest sections of the city—annexed between 1815 and 1875—Midtown was initially built piecemeal, before the city's automotive renaissance. The neighborhood first developed as a mix of stately mansions and retail along Woodward Avenue, gradually expanding east toward John R Street and west toward Cass Avenue as development pushed north. Over time, the eastern portion of Midtown became home to a large tract of Paradise Valley—a renowned, vibrant, early African-American neighborhood, as well as one of the city's first Jewish enclaves, surrounding the old Temple Beth-El. Although Midtown fell victim to repeated waves of urban renewal—which spurred widespread demolition of the earliest structures and these historic communities—the area remains one of the city's oldest, since most existing buildings date between 1875 and 1931. Before the advent of more spacious worker housing fueled by Ford's $5 days, Midtown's proximity to one of the city's first streetcar lines and nearby factory work led to the development of the area's signature elegant brick mid-rise apartment buildings for neighborhood workers.

Home to nearly a quarter of the city's historic districts, the elegant apartment buildings, remaining stately homes, historic churches, and impressive Wayne State University campus architecture collectively create one of the city's finest, most diverse collections of historic

buildings. Architectural historians will notice beautiful examples of the Art Deco, Modern, Italianate, Romanesque revival, Neo-Byzantine, Beaux-Arts, Neo-Renaissance, International, French Châteauesque, Queen Anne, Shingle, Second Empire, American Foursquare, Craftsman, Tudor Revival, and Italian Renaissance styles. The district offers a beautiful urban fabric to match; parts of Midtown feature elegant parks, tree-lined streets, and a tight street-wall, creating a lively, walkable environment.

Today, Midtown's neighborhoods continue their long traditions of constant evolution. Drawn by the central location, proximity to Wayne State University and the Cultural Center, as well as beautiful architecture, Midtown has attracted scores of young and creative newcomers, who've joined existing residents in opening new businesses and redeveloping large swaths of the area. Today, Midtown is home to more than 20,000 inhabitants, with many areas growing rapidly. Between those drawn to the architecture and culture, and the students, researchers, faculty, and medical professionals moving to be near the educational institutions and hospitals, the neighborhood is becoming younger and increasingly diverse, with many residents hailing from other parts of the region and country.

While nearly every corner of Midtown offers something to visitors, a few areas offer the greatest concentration of destinations. Those looking to enjoy unparalleled cultural and recreational amenities and fine architecture should spend a day along the greater Woodward Avenue corridor, which is home to big-league cultural institutions including the Charles H. Wright Museum of African American History, the Detroit Institute of Arts, and the Museum of Contemporary Art Detroit. Shopping-minded visitors should head for the burgeoning Cass/Canfield retail district, home to a hip, growing collection of boutiques, restaurants, and other businesses along Cass Avenue, Canfield Street, and Willis Street. Many of these independently owned enterprises continue a long local tradition of cultivating and supporting artists, authors, and makers. If looking to soak in some of Detroit's finest bar culture, visitors should start with the Cass Corridor neighborhood, where some of the city's most character-rich dives meet some of its most alluring new watering holes. Together, these diverse destinations offer a unique glimpse into the city's cultural past and present, and should be atop most travel itineraries.

BARS & RESTAURANTS

★ **8° Plato** - It's no hoptical illusion, with a name that references the ratio of water to fermentable sugar in beer, this second location of the popular Ferndale institution is a must for beer lovers. A combination destination bottle shop and craft beer bar, the interior evokes a historic-corner-store atmosphere with myriad reclaimed architectural elements rescued from lost architectural gems, including shelving from the storied Cass Technical High School. Hands down the city's finest selection of beers, ciders, and meads, patrons can peruse hundreds of obscure and delicious bottled and canned libations to take home, or fill growlers. Guests can also post up at the bar if they want to get slap hoppy with the convivial, beer-loving regulars who enjoy friendly conversation as much as the 16 rotating taps. If you require a little guidance, the Plato staff is uncommonly friendly and knowledgeable, and able to offer tasting notes or suggestions on every selection. Look out for friendly canines who bring their owners in for a pint on their way home from Canine to Five next door. Buy a six-pack, or make a mix-six, to score a 10%-off discount on your take-home selections. *3409 Cass Ave., www.8degreesplato.com/detroit, (313) 888-9972.*

2941 Mediterranean Street Food - Part of a Middle Eastern micro-chain—the family-owned business has five stores in as many southeast Michigan communities—2941 Mediterranean Street Food is named for the latitude and longitude of its namesake region. Though, here in metro Detroit, the roster of Middle Eastern eateries is pretty crowded, this carryout-friendly shop distinguishes itself from the rest of the pack by offering visitors a warm and contemporary aesthetic, a full bar, and a simple and innovative fast-casual concept with a focus on build-your-own options. Belly up to the bar and select a protein (falafel and Tandoori Chicken, among others), your food-to-mouth delivery method (chiefly a bowl or samoon pocket sandwich), and your combination of sauces, torshi (fillings), and salad (more fillings). We always opt for the samoon pocket, as the fresh-baked bread alone is otherworldly, and worth the trip. A word to the wise: with seemingly limitless options and variations, the menu here can be a little trickier to follow than you'd expect, but be patient—it's worth it! *4219 Woodward Ave., www.2941streetfood.com (313) 338-3574.*

Alley Taco - The sassy, hip, and tasty Alley Taco is the salvation of taco fans who find themselves outside of the taco paradise that is Southwest Detroit. With a simple, but constantly evolving build-your-own menu, choose your own vessel: quesadilla suzi, giant burrito, bowl-rito, triple taco, crispy tacos, mexi-melt, torta, or nachos—and load up with your choice of fillings and toppings. The portions are admittedly huge and guaranteed to satiate, but that's fine by us—the only thing better than Mexican food is more Mexican food. When it comes to the aforementioned fillings and toppings, we rarely stray from the Pollo, a flame grilled, smoked chicken dynamo, or curry cauliflower, a vegetarian favorite. Alley Taco offers a snappy, contemporary dine-in setting, as well as carryout and delivery. Open late. *418 W. Willis, www.alleytaco.biz, (313) 818-0067.*

★ **Avalon International Breads -** Founded by Ann Perrault and Jackie Victor in 1997, Avalon was an early anchor of retail development in the Cass Corridor and remains a beloved, wildly popular Detroit institution to this day. Customers pack the cafe tables inside and out—and often line up out the door for the incredible baked goods and treats. If you're able to snag a seat and sit there long enough, you'll probably see everyone you know in Detroit! The bakery serves up hearty, flavorful, freshly baked, organic bread, a broad selection of sweet and savory treats (including a bevy of yummy vegan options), a full menu of coffee drinks, and a great selection of packaged local and regional coffees, teas, chocolates, and jams. At lunchtime, check out the coolers for prepared sandwiches (the Garden Works is essential) and salads, or get a made-to-order hot sandwich at the counter. Sealing the deal on the experience is the lively and colorful, character-rich space highlighted by the whimsical hand-drawn signs that feature friendly anthropomorphic baked goods offering up the monthly specials. In addition to using organic flour and other ingredients, Avalon donates generously to the community, so you'll have no problem adhering to its motto—"Eat Well. Do good."—when you buy the bread with cred. Don't leave without a sea salt chocolate chip cookie! *422 W. Willis St., www.avalonbreads.net, (313) 832-0008.*

Bakersfield - With its Edison-bulb pendant lights, exposed ductwork, central industrial-style bar, large mural, and biergarten-style tables, the chic interior feels at once warm and approachable, and au courant. Bringing California-style tacos to Detroit by way of Cleveland, Bakersfield offers many traditional Mexican dishes, but also fare with some delicious, decidedly north-of-the-border ingredients like kale slaw, buttermilk dressing, and toasted almonds that are unique among the city's Mexican options. Though the menu is all strikes and no gutters, the tacos stand out. The carnitas tacos (pork beer-braised to perfection, guacamole, tomatillo crema, pickled red onion, and cilantro) and baja shrimp tacos (crispy shrimp, chipotle lime crema, guacamole, red cabbage, pickled fresno, and chive) are not to be missed, and the rotating, seasonal tostadas are gluttonous, filling masterpieces. Other winners include the Johnny salad, cochinita pibil, seasonal tostadas, and huitlacoche. Having a queso the mondays? You're in luck: Half of the menu is devoted to beer, wine, and liquor, including a thoughtfully curated selection of domestic, craft and Mexican beers as well as a diverse array of signature cocktails and margaritas. *3100 Woodward Ave., www.bakersfieldtacos.com, (313) 974-7040.*

Bikes & Coffee - At one point, milk and cookies probably seemed like an unusual pairing, too. Owner Ben Kehoe seamlessly marries bikes and coffee in this easygoing, Pacific Northwest-style coffee house. The clean, open, minimalist, loft-like aesthetic highlights the simple beauty in the exposed brick walls and antique wood floors, and makes a focal point of the abundance of bicycles along the back wall. The stylish central coffee bar greets enthusiastic customers with pour-overs and espresso drinks—all made using local Hyperion Coffee, alongside bagels from Detroit Institute of Bagels (see separate entry) and fresh pastries. Farther back, the rear of the space is kitted out for bicycle repair and custom builds, with the hum and clicks of professional mechanics creating a gentle, if accidental soundtrack. *1521 Putnam St., www.bikes-coffee.com, (313) 288-0201.*

Block - Simultaneously hidden within and anchoring the middle of the Garden Theater block in one of the city's most bustling neighborhoods, the aptly named Block specializes in well-executed, traditional American comfort food. The restaurant features a warm, industrial-urban interior, with exposed brick walls, and an elongated linear bar. The casual American menu spans small-plate shareables and all-inclusive entrees, with highlights including the many varieties of slathered gourmet wings (including Rock N' Rye and Bacon Bourbon), the Shotgun Shrimp (battered shrimp smothered in sweet chili sauce), and the decadent and gooey mac and cheese. In addition to offering a popular brunch, lunch, and dinner, the Block's happy hour is especially notable and affordable, with a 313 menu (so named for the city's area code) where all items are just $3 (most food and shots) or $1 (beer!). *3919 Woodward Ave., www.theblockdet.com, (313) 832-0892.*

Bolero - A new venture from the team behind Vicente's Cuban Cuisine (see separate entry), Bolero offers a menu with more of a regional focus than that of a particular country. Dishes and drinks can be found from throughout Central America, as well as the South American nations of Peru, Brazil, Argentina, and Chile, in an elegant translation of Latin cuisine. The kitchen offers exquisite and vibrant paellas (or favorite is the Paella del Mar), tangy and refreshing ceviches (try the Ceviche Classico), and a complement of Latin-themed tapas, which include highlights like duck empanadas and toothsome yuca fritas. The full bar offers thematic cocktails that pair well with the food, like the distinctive Pisco Sour. Guests will find that the interior offers a comfortable elegance, with its dramatic crimson coloring. Weekend diners can usually look forward to flamenco guitar performances, Samba nights, and other events. While it's not scenic per se, Bolero offers a patio in warmer months. *51 W. Forest Ave., www.bolerodetroit.com. (313) 800-5059.*

The Bottom Line Coffee House - With fine coffee and a handsome interior to match, this quaint subterranean coffee shop has won the hearts of many in the neighborhood. The bright and lively interior features exposed brick walls, vintage and topical prints, and contemporary woodwork. The soft music, aroma of fresh ground beans, and friendly student customers all contribute to the charming neighborhood hangout atmosphere. Owners Al and Pat Harris have good taste in food and coffee, using Intelligentsia beans from Chicago, locally roasted coffee from Righteous Bean, and baked treats from nearby Traffic Jam and Snug (see separate entry). All of the drinks on the menu—from espresso drinks including cafe con panna and macchiato, to a variety of hot teas—are nectarous and priced to sell. *4474 Third Ave., www.tblcoffeehouse.com, (313) 638-2759.*

★ **The Bronx Bar -** A beloved, straightforward shot-and-a-beer stronghold in the heart of the Cass Corridor, the Bronx Bar is known as a stalwart destination for those looking for a pint of beer without an ounce of pretension. This popular firewatering hole is known for its bright, vintage neon-basted exterior with its wrap-around deck, and its dark interior dominated by classic arcade machines, a pool table, a drink board, and a handful of gewgaw antiques atop the beautiful antique bar. Without TVs and with everything from

Etta James to LCD Soundsystem pouring from the two jukeboxes—perfectly curated by bartenders and regulars—the bar has a mellow atmosphere made for conversation. Customers can get both noshed and sloshed, thanks to a full line of liquor, a solid stable of drafts and bottles, and one of the city's tastiest assortments of bar fare—including the outstanding Bronx Burger, black bean burger, and the Veggie Machine, all served on incredible butter-grilled Iraqi bread. Conscientious owners Paul Howard and Scott Lowell have a personable staff, including affable cocktailian Chris and Charlene, a dry-witted charm school dropout. Although updated, the bar stays true to tradition, and remains a place where working class and brunching class rub elbows. *4476 Second Ave., (313) 832-8464.*

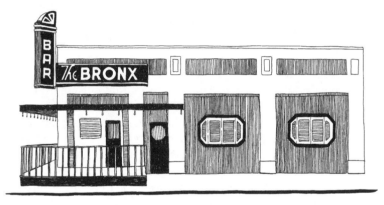

Byblos Cafe and Grill - Named for a city along the Mediterranean Sea, Byblos is an oasis for Middle Eastern, Lebanese, and African cuisine right in the heart of Midtown. Behind the unassuming brick exterior of one of the area's newer buildings, this sleek and modern restaurant offers tasty renditions of popular Middle Eastern favorites such as shawarma, falafel, and mujadara, as well as lesser-known dishes like sambousek (fried dough and cheese). Though it's an economical destination for both vegetarian and omnivore fans of Mediterranean food, less adventurous palates will be more at home with available diner fare. *4830 Cass Ave., www.bybloscafeandgrill.com, (313) 292-5678.*

Cafe 78 - A minimal, wood-rich, stand-alone bar and restaurant inside a central gathering space in the Museum of Contemporary Art Detroit (see separate entry), Cafe 78 offers a curated and refined program overseen by **The Detroit Optimist Society**, of

Sugar House fame. Due to its location, the establishment offers guests an ever-changing interior landscape that evolves with the museum's physical shows and live performances. No matter the time of year, patrons are treated to the beautiful, raw, quasi-industrial space, which is filled with natural light and floating ornamentation, and is always buzzing with activity. On the menu, the cafe offers treats from local bakeries, soup, and gourmet grilled-cheese (such as swiss and red onion marmalade on sourdough), as well as a full complement of coffee and espresso drinks. However, the true highlight of Cafe 78 is behind the bar, where the expertise of the Optimists comes into play in the form of elevated cocktails that fuse seasonal ingredients with inventive takes on accessible classics. Beer and wine also available. The cafe sticks to museum hours, so generally shutters early unless there is a late-running event. *4454 Woodward Ave., www.mocadetroit.org/about/cafe-78, (313) 832-6622.*

Cass Cafe - A hub for artists, students, and neighborhood folks of all stripes, the Cass Cafe is a casual bar and restaurant in an informal, contemporary gallery setting. Showcasing prominent and up-and-coming local artists through monthly art exhibitions, the rotating artwork that fills the expansive walls of the restaurant informs the atmosphere of the understated, unpretentious industrial theme. Offering a thoughtful, vegetarian-friendly menu with daily specials, favorites include the Monterey turkey burger, curried-lentil soup, and the killer lentil walnut burger. Of course, all options are best augmented with the Love Basket—a crowd-pleasing mix of fries and onion rings. The full bar offers a selection of local brews and some of the neighborhood's best nightly drink specials, including $3 margaritas and $1 beers. Look for regular DJ nights, music, and spoken-word performances. *4620 Cass Ave., www.casscafe.com, (313) 831-1400.*

Castalia - The intimate, one-of-a-kind scented craft cocktail bar in perfumery Sfumato, see details in that entry. *3980 Second Ave., www.castaliacocktails.com, (313) 305-1442.*

Cata Vino Mercato and Wine Bar - Building upon the success of their tapas venture next door, La Feria (see separate entry) owners Pilar Baron Hidalgo and Elias Khalil again charm guests with aperitif culture at Cata Vino, their lauded Andalusian-style Spanish wine outfit. Inside the intimate space, a leathered granite bar, exposed brick, custom wine-barrel fixtures, open ceilings, and ample earthtones lend a rustic air that helps this wine shrine shine. The long bar serves up an impressive selection of wines of mostly Spanish origin—including an outstanding selection of sherries—by the glass, bottle, or flight. The small kitchen in the back puts out a curated selection of high-end tinned seafood bites, including octopus, tuna, and anchovies. The far-wall retail area allows guests to take a bottle home, as well as shop gourmet speciality items including olive oil, paprika, and olives. *4130 Cass Ave., (313) 285-9081.*

★ **Chartreuse Kitchen and Cocktails** - Among just a handful of elite restaurants that define New American hospitality in Detroit, Chartreuse Kitchen and Cocktails never fails to offer inspired farm-to-table fare, lovely wines, and some of the city's best cocktails. With a charismatic, bright green, vegetal interior, your experience begins at the door, with a dreamy mural by local artist Ouizi, and continues with botanically inspired installations throughout. Seating vignettes accommodate a spectrum of occasions: a glass of wine among the emerald and kiwi lounges or cocktails at the commanding concrete bar; a romantic first date at the farm tables; or a fine dining experience at the chef's table, tucked away in its own secret garden. Featuring Detroit-grown produce, Chef Doug Hewitt's seasonal menu never disappoints. For lunch, try the twice-cooked egg, which anoints a bed of locally-grown frisee, brussels sprouts, salty cheese, and warm shallot vinaigrette; or sample the oft-praised fish sandwich, served on brioche, with a brussels slaw. Explore the dinner options with the expert staff and you'll find something exquisite, like the popular cap steak. Don't leave without excavating the selection of Chartreuse liqueurs, or sampling a classic Detroit cocktail, the Last Word. Reservations encouraged. *15 E. Kirby St., www.chartreusekc.com, (313) 818-3915.*

Chili Mustard and Onions - An answer to the proverbial vegan quandary, how will I survive without that *one* guilty pleasure, Chili Mustard and Onions (CMO) slings uncanny and ridiculously good all-plant-based and mostly organic versions of all your fast food favorites. Indeed, in all the best ways, this is not a rabbit food vegan joint. No sir, CMO is an unabashed, fabulous vegan fatty finger food festival of the highest and most delicious order. Offering highlights like the Big Mock, a "wait, is this really vegan?" imitation of the golden arches classic, gyros, chili-cheese fries, and their signature CMO Coney Dog—an all-plant-based take on the classic and sloppy Detroit-style chili dog—this epic neighborhood spot will delight herbivores and impress carnivores everywhere. Wash down your meal with a soda or a (vegan) working man's beer. After all, that's the best way to enjoy a coney. *3411 Brush St., (313) 462-4949.*

Cobb's Corner - The Cass Corridor of the 1970s was rough-and-tumble and brimming with life, populated by a cast of neighborhood characters, including artists, musicians, and creatives looking for a cheap place to lay their head and make their art. Cobb's Corner, which opened early in the decade, was a hotspot for live jazz, and a favorite haunt in that community, as well as what one article at the time affectionately called "neighborhood winos." However, the bar succumbed to the same fate as many other neighborhood businesses during that period, and shut its doors in the early 1980s. In 2018, the bar's original owner, Robert Cobb, revived the legendary neighborhood institution—in the same location—bringing live music and revelry back to this cozy corner bar with an artistic flair. Inside you'll find an enormous vintage wood bar, eclectic artwork filling the walls, and hopefully some Cass Corridor neighborhood characters. Belly up, grab a brew, and take in the excellent local acts at this new-old Detroit bar—you just might be seeing the next Marcus Belgrave or MC5. *4201 Cass Ave.*

Common Pub - Occupying the ground floor of the historic Belcrest building on the Wayne State University campus, the Common Pub is a recent entrant to the dining scene. With simple, modern decor, outdoor (poolside) dining, and a sophisticated but balanced drink and food menu, it is an ideal location for a midtown tête-à-tête, either with friends or colleagues. The restaurant is the product of Executive Chef Zachary Stotz, and uses a smart, meat-forward menu of pub grub and refined fare at reasonable prices. The menu emphasizes elevated variations on traditional food: Their French fries are prepared in duck fat, and are available as poutine (with specials daily), the chicken is brined in brown sugar before being fried, and burgers offer fried egg as a standard add-on. In addition to serving food until 2am, and offering a solid weekend brunch, Common boasts an everyman's happy hour special: Five bucks for a burger, fries, and draft PBR. Vegetarians won't starve, but they might want to plan ahead. *5440 Cass Ave., www.commonpub.com, (313) 285-8849.*

Detroit Shipping Co. - Finally bringing the coastal food hall craze to Detroit, the Shipping Co. docked in the city in 2018. A classic example of inside-looks-bigger-than-the-outside architecture, this well-designed two-story steel behemoth is assembled from 21 stacked shipping containers, and features an option-laden indoor-outdoor layout with two bars, five food truck-style eateries, copious biergarten seating, a stage, and other amenities. Look for a wealth of food options, with dishes both adventurous and pedestrian—and probably dishes for adventurous pedestrians, too. Current offerings include: **Brujo Tacos & Tapas** (tacos, montaditos, and Spanish latillas), **Bangkok 96** (creative and uncommonly good thai street food), **COOP Caribbean Fusion** (jerk chicken, and other Jamaican delights), **320 Coffee & Creamery** (coffee and nitrogen-frozen ice cream), and **Motor Burger** (creative burgers and poutine). Complementing the food, guests can find cocktails, wine, and beer at the dueling bars, as well as ongoing art shows (generally on the second floor), and DJs, comedy guests, and other entertainment. However, if a musical guest is on deck, expect the volume to be kicked up to 11 and be warned that this food hall—popular gathering spot walled with metal that it is—is often on the loud side of restaurant ambiance, so set your watch to party o'clock. Open late. *474 Peterboro St., www.detroitshippingcompany.com, (313) 462-4973.*

El Taco Veloz and Juice Joint - The best food counters inside a liquor store this side of anywhere, these two gems tucked inside **Marcus Market**—arguably Detroit's best party store, with a perfect mix of hipster indulgences, real Detroit necessities, and vice—are the salvation of Midtowners looking for a pick-me-up or a bring-me-down. Giving a new spin to health and convenience, **Juice Joint** boasts a tropical selection of freshly blended juices, immunity shots, and smoothies for customers suffering from vice or virtue. Cured of what ails you for $6? That's bananas! The Coffee Nut and The Boss smoothies add in a kick of critical caffeine (cold brew and matcha tea respectively) while The Cure practices what it preaches with a healthful dose of ginger and turmeric. As for **El Taco Veloz**, you've heard of Fresco Cali-Mex—this ain't that. Bringing the best in refried bean and cheese-filled Southwest Detroit-style Mexican to the neat streets of Midtown, Taco Veloz is as tasty and satisfying as it is guilt-inducing. With a simple à la carte menu, choose from a stable of staples—burrito, taco trio, salad, quesadilla, or tortas—and pack it with your salsa, toppings, and protein of choice, including spicy chorizo and vegan-friendly fake meats. Breakfast burritos are also available! Both spots are chiefly take-out joints, but you can perch at their respective counters, if you can nab a spot, or dine on the patio. If you do dine in, may we suggest you plan to use the commode elsewhere? This is a liquor store, after all. Taco Veloz is open late, but

Juice Joint keeps yoga hours. *4614 Second Ave, Inside Marcus Market. El Taco Veloz: (313) 315-3193, Juice Joint: (313) 315-3192.*

Empire Kitchen and Cocktails - From the vantage point of a seat on the all-season patio at Empire Kitchen and Cocktails, peering above a row of bright green fronds, you can watch the theater of city life play out before you: an old man greeting his friend, a pair of women on an evening stroll, teenagers whizzing by on scooters. This patio, with its view of Detroit, is just one of many wonderful things about Empire, which is a short block from Little Caesars Arena (see separate entry). Another is the restaurant's approachable-yet-haute cuisine, as perfect for a first date as for a pre-game meal. Share a pizza with friends, or roll solo with the delicious spicy chicken sandwich, whose golden crust belies an irresistibly juicy bite. If you're in the mood for libations, Empire's ace bartenders (alumni of the legendary Sugar House, see separate entry) serve up a menu of rotating beers and cocktails, and are more than willing to make you something special— pick your poison. For the teetotalers or hungover among us, Empire offers a unique selection of soft cocktails, too. *3148 Woodward Ave., www.empirekitchenandcocktails.com, (313) 315-3131.*

For the Love of Sugar - The only macaron shop in Detroit, this compact, fanciful spot will tempt even the tepid sweet tooth. For the uninitiated, macarons are two toothsome, colorful cookies sandwiching a dollop of buttercream. Inside, customers will find an accessible, laid-back cafe with princess-worthy touches, such as chandeliers, tufted paneling, and gold-painted accents. Though several classic options are available, such as pistachio and chocolate, the menu largely eschews traditional French macaron flavors for playful American varieties, such as Birthday Cake and Fruity Pebbles. In addition to these signature treats, Love of Sugar offers a varied menu of other decadent delights, ranging from cinnamon rolls to cookies—in addition to a full spectrum of house-made coffee and espresso drinks. *100 Erskine St., www.fortheloveofsugar.com, (313) 788-7111.*

Founders Brewing Co. - The repurposed brick storefront may not look like a temple, but you're about to have a near-religious experience. This massive Detroit outpost of the renowned Grand Rapids-based brewery—only their second location—uses a list longer than Santa's as a beer menu, but unlike Santa's, everything on this list is really nice. Founder's beers are routinely voted among the nation's best, and the entire quaffable cast makes an appearance behind this bar, from the crisp All Day IPA, to the indulgent Canadian Breakfast Stout and refreshing Honey Wheat, as well as exclusive Detroit-taproom-only options. Those who insist on having a solid supper will be greeted by a menu with an array of locally inspired, elevated pub fare options, such as bourbon-barrel smoked wings, a vegan sloppy joe, a barrel-smoked pulled pork sandwich, and caprese salad. All of these strong flavors are complemented by the relaxed atmosphere. The taproom—an enormous contemporary, industrial reimagination of a former grocery store—features factory-like pendant lights, exposed ductwork, and a wall of glass roll-up doors that overlook the year-round patio. Don't miss the gift shop on the way out. *456 Charlotte St., www.foundersbrewing.com/brewery/detroit, (313) 335-3440.*

Fourteen East - Just a few yards from the triumphant stone steps of the Detroit Institute of Arts stands Fourteen East, a coffee bar dedicated to perfecting the art of coffee in an aesthetically pleasing atmosphere. Order a cup of Michigan-roasted Chazzano Coffee (you can choose from drip, French press, or vacuum siphon methods of preparation) and be sure to try a few of the French macarons. The walls of local art, custom-made light fixtures, and beautiful molded-plywood seating invite you to leisurely sip your beverage and take in the thoughtful, contemporary decor. *15 E. Kirby St., www.14eastcafe.com, (313) 871-0500.*

Go! Sy Thai - With a sassy and snappy contemporary aesthetic (we see you, picture of rapper Ice Cube on the ice dispenser), this kid brother to the flagship suburban location is a student super-favorite, with lines sometimes literally out the door. The menu includes solid renditions of all of the Thai favorites, but we especially love their curries, which have a perfect spicy kick (not to mention that some options include decadent fried potatoes). For the herbivores amongst us, one of the best features of Go! Sy Thai is their vegetarian-friendliness. Because everything is made in-house, they can make any dish vegan, with tofu and fish-sauce alternatives. Though there are plenty of self-serve tables, the heart of this fun joint is takeout. On sunny days, guests should consider enjoying their meal at one of the many nearby parks. A second location is open in Downtown's Capitol Park (see separate entry). *4240 Cass Ave., www.gosythai.com, (313) 638-1467.*

Great Lakes Coffee - Self described as an Institute for Advanced Drinking, owner James Cadariu takes coffee—roasted nearby under the Great Lakes label—as seriously as he does imported wine, craft beer, and fine cocktails. Inviting patrons to hydrate, caffeinate, and inebriate, Great Lakes offers a wide selection of gourmet coffee—including cold brew on tap in the summer—and espresso drinks, as well as an exceptional, curated bar, with innovative offerings, many of which incorporate java and booze. Though Great Lakes doesn't offer a full menu, its sweets, baked goods, and cheese plates—including a vegan "better than cheese" plate, which is a highlight—are delicious ways to stave off hunger. Located in a beautifully renovated historic building, the design of the stunning 2,000-square-foot interior innovatively incorporates exposed brick, reclaimed wood from demolished homes in Detroit, and adapted industrial components. Those who prefer outdoor refreshment can enjoy the covered street side patio. *3965 Woodward Ave., www.greatlakescoffee.com, (313) 831-9627.*

Grey Ghost - Looking for a steak tartare, oysters, or a perfectly medium-rare filet mignon—without the high-end steakhouse pretension? Grey Ghost balances upscale cuisine and thoughtful contemporary decor with all-around Midwestern comfort. Pair your lamb chops with fried bologna. Order chicken wings and a dry-aged New York strip. Or skip the steak all together and head in late night to enjoy a burger and a mountain of fries, paired with a shot of whisky and an ice cold can of Hamm's—all for under $20. While Grey Ghost's menu is unmistakably meat-centric, a "Not Meat" section of the restaurant's menu includes seasonal vegetable offerings like heirloom tomato ravioli and miso-cured cabbage to offset your inevitable protein intake. Expect friendly, knowledgeable service and a stellar cocktail program with options (including draft cocktails!) to accommodate any palate. And don't miss out on Grey Ghost's brunch, available from 10am-2pm on weekends. We're glad the dress code is casual, because with highlights like bananas foster beignets, angel food pancakes, and pulled pork eggs benedict, you're going to want to wear your comfy pants. *47 Watson St., www.greyghostdetroit.com, (313) 262-6534.*

The Griot - Borrowing its name from a West African term for storytellers, poets, and musicians, the Griot is a cozy music-filled speakeasy with an outsized, welcoming aura. With more than 1,000 vinyl records, twin turntables in constant rotation, and walls dotted with paintings of iconic soul and jazz legends, music is integral to the experience at this homegrown lounge. On a nightly basis, well-versed DJs spin the best in classic jazz, blues, soul, and R&B to an often packed house—which spills out onto the adjacent patio—creating an uncommonly authentic living room experience where guests unwind while listening to the soundtrack of the city. The bar offers a full range of spirits, and a curated selection of wines, house cocktails, and craft beers. Though there are occasionally pop-up food features, The Griot is primarily a watering hole. *66 E. Forest St., www.griotdetroit.com, (313) 289-3813.*

Gus's World Famous Fried Chicken - Originally from Memphis, Tennessee, the Detroit outpost of this wildly popular chicken mini chain—which has locations in 12 states—opened in 2016. The decor is industrial-meets-countryside, with retro metal signs, checkered tablecloths, and charmingly mismatched chairs. Feel free to grab a beer at the bar and catch a game, but the main attraction is Gus's signature spicy fried chicken, a family recipe that dates back more than 60 years. Classic comfort food sides like macaroni and cheese, coleslaw, greens, potato salad, and okra round out any proper meal, but you also shouldn't miss the appetizers, like fried pickles and green tomatoes. And definitely save room for a slice of chocolate chess pie for dessert. Vegetarians may be happier dining elsewhere. Beer available for dining in. *4101 Third Ave., www.gusfriedchicken.com, (313) 818-0324.*

Harmonie Garden - Nestled in the digs of a former bar, Harmonie Garden is a Middle Eastern restaurant committed to serving affordably priced, healthy, diverse cuisine with plenty of vegetarian and vegan options. Classics like falafel, homemade lentil soup and shawarma are popular options, but the menu also offers a unique spin on classics, such as beet hummus, fruit and nut fattoush, and a category of "Special Falafel Ideas" which includes the amazing Falamankoush (veggies, falafel, and Syrian cheese between two pieces of grilled zatar bread) and Flobby Joe (something resembling a sloppy joe, but with falafel). Patrons dine casually along the carved wooden bar with matching wood overhang, or sit at cozy tables or booths under hanging lamps. With an impressively large weekend breakfast buffet, Middle Eastern coffee and fresh juice round out the reasons why so many people have become fans of this quirky neighborhood staple. *4704 Anthony Wayne Dr., www.harmoniegarden.com, (313) 638-2345.*

Harry's Detroit Bar and Restaurant - Harry's is a comfortable, modern bar on the edge of Foxtown offering quality food and a well-stocked drink selection. The interior is open, spacious, and clean, but sports fans—Harry's main clientele—will appreciate the eight televisions ringing the first floor, with four more on the upstairs patio (open on most warm home game days). Harry's has daily food and drink specials, and those working downtown can enjoy happy hour specials anytime. Darts available. *2482 Clifford St., www.harrysdetroit.com, (313) 964-1575.*

★**Honest John's** - No matter what day of the week, if it's 1am and you find yourself craving dinner, a cold glass or 40-ounce of beer, and some sweet old-school jams, get thee to Honest John's. Well known and dearly loved for its colorful, year-round retro Christmas tree lights, personality neon signs ("Men Lie," "Hoover Sucks"), and for serving food every night until 2am, Honest John's is an indispensable Cass Corridor neighborhood bar with a generous menu and booths (almost literally) the size of Buicks. The food—pleasing for both vegetarians and omnivores alike—ranges from the deliciously greasy (a grilled coleslaw Reuben called the Eastsider and a spinach artichoke melt) to the less detrimental but still delicious (hearty bean chili and a veggie and feta pita called the Pocket of Joy). Be sure not to miss breakfast, featuring the famous smothered hash and served 'til 5pm on weekends for the hungover set. *488 Selden St., www.honestjohnsdetroit.com, (313) 832-5646.*

HopCat - "I wish this place had more beer," said nobody ever. With a whopping 130 rotating, seasonal taps, this location of this modern Michigan institution, which has branches in several cities around the state, is a veritable heaven for beer lovers. Though the massive, two-story bar (the company's largest) does offer a bountiful, solid menu of pub-style American classics—with favorites that include a bacon, jalapeño, and barcheese-tinged burger; the Loaded Pretzel Nuggs; and the much ballyhooed, seasoned Crack Fries—dad pop is definitely the main event. The sprawling menu of drafts, which changes daily, is divided into 11 categories, spanning every major style of craft beer, from Belgians to wheats, including ciders and meads. While dozens of Michigan-made beers are highlighted on the menu at any given time, patrons can sample beers from every corner of the brewniverse, with an especially strong selection of Belgian and American beers. Downstairs, the bar is adorned with kitsch celebrating Detroit's cultural heritage (yes, that's a velvet painting of Bob Seger). Upstairs, patrons can enjoy the three-season patio, or check out the **Humaroom**, which hosts local and regional touring acts. Since this beer behemoth can be popular with the beer-pong set, visiting on quieter weeknights is sometimes your best bet. *4265 Woodward Ave., www.hopcat.com/detroit, (313) 769-8828.*

International Institute of Metropolitan Detroit - Since 1919, the International Institute has helped welcome immigrants to the Detroit area by offering English language courses and guidance on the path to American citizenship, and cultivating understanding among the city's many ethnicities and cultures. Highlights of the facility include an auditorium with a display of flags from more than 80 countries, an expansive collection of dolls modeling traditional clothing of world nations, and a large collection of models of historic ships that brought immigrants to the United States. However, the institute's most popular feature is the **International Cafe**, which offers an expansive, delicious, and affordable menu of traditional Indian, Italian, Mediterranean, Mexican, and American dishes. Welcoming diners every weekday from 11am to 2:30pm, the cafe allows visitors the rare opportunity to inauthentically pair tasty authentic dishes (would you like samosas and hummus with your quesadilla?). *111 E. Kirby St., www.iimd.org, (313) 871-8600.*

Jolly Old Timers - It's a perpetual party that could teach New Orleans a thing or two. An open secret hidden in plain sight, this crowded 1950s basement watering hole is one of the few remaining pre-Civil Rights Era private black social clubs. To get inside, find the two-story building with an "open" sign and few other indications of a bar inside, ring the bell, and flash a friendly smile—a member of the private club will almost certainly let you downstairs. Inside, the constant northern soul soundtrack, vintage wood paneling, linoleum tile floor, low-slung ceiling, and numerous pieces of Detroit and Jolly Old Timers memorabilia combine to create an irresistible mix of nostalgic comforts. The atmosphere is inviting and warm, with members frequently enlisting guests to join dance parties, lively conversations, or remarkable dinners. The bar has a solid, diverse collection of domestic and imported beers as well as a mass-market liquors. Outstanding comfort food—often fried chicken—is available occasionally. Non-members are welcome on Monday, Wednesday, and Friday evenings, or when the "open" sign is on. *641 W. Forest Ave., (313) 831-5342.*

Jolly Pumpkin - The Detroit outpost of this popular Michigan institution, which has a handful of other locations, Jolly Pumpkin features a warm, lodge-inspired industrial interior, a comprehensive menu of upscale pub grub, and an extensive list of thoughtfully crafted ales. The company is most well-known for its artisanal sour beers, which are tart, complex, and fruity—and have gained notoriety in the brewing world. However, the bar also offers a full slate of traditional beer from the affiliated North Peak Brewing Company, as well as wine and craft cocktails. Despite being located in a former Jeep factory, the space is wood-rich and cozy, with creative treatments and inventive accents, which make it a great place for a casual meal. The menu is an thoughtful take on American fare, with elevated burgers, fries, and salads—and excellent flat-crust pizzas. Highlights include the signature burger (served on a challah roll with smoked bacon and cheese), truffle fries, a solid black bean burger with chipotle mayo, and a shaved brussels sprout pizza. Barack Obama visited in 2016, which we're confident makes him the first sitting President to have had a cheeseburger in the Cass Corridor. *441 W. Canfield St., www.jollypumpkin.com, (313) 262-6115.*

Jumbo's Bar - A beloved, classic neighborhood dive, Jumbo's is an oasis in the southern Cass Corridor desert. On an otherwise barren stretch of Third Avenue, windowless Jumbo's always looks as though it might be closed, but it isn't. Step into the front door (or park in the lot and walk in the back door where you'll find smokers huddled), and you'll be greeted by a warm, brass-tacks interior, a pool table, several tables with chairs, ephemera from the bar's history, and a pair of killer touch-screen machines at the bar. Family-owned, you can find sisters Holly and Stephanie tending bar most nights. Sassy, friendly, and down-to-earth, they'll fix you a stiff drink (and the occasional shot on the house if you're a regular) or pour you a $2 beer while you strike up a conversation with an unexpected array of neighborhood folks. Spend the warmer months outside on the cozy patio or playing horseshoes. Be on the lookout for regular karaoke nights and occasional rock shows. Have a dog or a bike with you? Walk or wheel 'er right on in. *3736 Third Ave., (313) 831-8949.*

★ **La Feria** - Detroit's finest destination for Spanish tapas, refreshing and tart sangria, and a truly festive atmosphere, La Feria is a Midtown dining anchor and all-around delight. Named for the annual fair in Seville, the convivial ambiance of La Feria is evocative of its namesake. The welcoming restaurant is housed in a panel-clad, angular, contemporary building, which contrasts with the warm interior, featuring exposed brick, a reclaimed-wood bar and tables, and thematic decor that makes every visit a party. On an impressive Mediterranean-inspired menu of small plates, favorites include Manchego y Membrillo (cheese and quince paste), Berenjenas Fritas (succulent fried eggplant with a honey drizzle), Bombas (spicy beef-filled potato croquettes with tomato sauce), Gambas al Ajillo (seared shrimp with garlic and chilis), and the crowd-pleasing Patatas Bravas (fried potato with spicy tomato salsa and creamy aioli). The extensive wine list, locally renowned sangria, and unusual varieties of gin and tonic only enhance the festival atmosphere. Come for the bright, flavorful touches, and stay to soak up everything else. During the summer months, don't miss La Feria's enjoyable, breezy patio. *4130 Cass Ave., www.laferiadetroit.com, (313) 285-9081.*

La Palma - Appropriately nestled near the heart of the Detroit Medical Center, this Mediterranean restaurant offers a healthier choice for lunch on the go. With a warm, brick interior, the dining room is tidy and inviting, and provides booths and tables of all sizes for groups, or the lone (and hungry!) nurse or resident. Generous portions are just what the doctor ordered, and there are many favorites to choose from—and ideally share. The chicken shawarma and lamb dishes are neighborhood favorites, and the fresh, warm pita and toum (garlic sauce) is free flowing—a perfect complement to any entree. Featuring traditional sweets and pastries from the legendary Dearborn bakery, Shatila, make sure you save space for a tasty post-meal treat or two. *113 E. Canfield St., www.eatatlapalma.com, (313) 833-5000.*

La Pita Fresh - The perfect campus Mediterranean restaurant, La Pita Fresh is the fast-casual dining spot of choice for many Wayne State University students and faculty, as well as fans from across Midtown. From business lunches in the main dining room, to quick study breaks in the lofted second floor, the straightforward menu offers a wide range of Middle Eastern staples: crisp fattoush, zesty almond rice salad, ample falafel, an epic list of pita sandwiches, a tasty crushed-lentil soup, a liquid health bar (juices and smoothies!), and much more. An oasis for vegetarians and vegans, the Vegan Dream and spicy mujaddara sandwiches are especially popular among the meat-free set. A house speciality is the array of Man-Ushi sandwiches—your choice of fillings packed between grilled oregano and sesame bread that is as savory as it is satisfying. Whether you are dining in or carrying out, the friendly and fast service is sure to allow you time to relax and savor the moment—and every last bite. *5056 Cass Avenue, www.lapitafresh.com, (313) 831-4550.*

Magnet - The bottom of the food pyramid reigns supreme at this high-concept restaurant, famed for an elemental, handmade ethos. The celebrated second act from the team behind the renowned Takoi—owner Phil Kafka and chef Brad Greenhill—calls the once-derelict Magnet Radiator Works building home. Inside the minimalist industrial space, the 14-foot exposed ceilings, open kitchen, recessed bar, and low-slung booths allow the handsomely appointed dining room to feel open and airy even when busy. The menu continues this sophisticated tribute to simplicity. All dishes on this spectacular, globally inspired, plant-centric menu are cooked on a wood-fired grill or a wood-burning hearth, and emphasize house-made cheeses and sauces. Though the menu rotates, standouts include ash-cooked recaldo Japanese pumpkin with clotted cream, pao pepitas, and bitter greens; peperonata with green chili salsa verde, smoked labneh, and hazelnut dukkah; and a daily indulgence, such as a lamb shoulder, pizza, or steak. A thoughtful, curated beverage program is also available. Magnet is expected to open to the public in early 2019. *4848 W. Grand River Ave.*

Mario's Italian Restaurant - A Cass Corridor icon since 1948, Mario's is an upscale Italian restaurant and supper club. The traditional interior, dignified ambience, and fine woodwork contribute to an old-school charm that feels untouched by time. Despite the elegance, the mood is unpretentious and laid-back. The cuisine is no different—the decadent offerings, including the renowned Scaloppine Siciliana, Tournedos Maison, and Chicken Cacciatore, are served unassumingly. The diverse menu offers a host of hearty options and comprehensive beer, wine, and liquor menus. The six-or seven-course meals—bread, antipasto, soup, salad, pasta, and main course—and other amenities—such as tableside cooking—take time, so plan accordingly. As a supper club, Mario's offers live music and ballroom dancing on weekend nights. *4222 Second Ave., www.mariosdetroit.com, (313) 832-1616.*

★ **Motor City Brewing Works** - Since 1994, the small but mighty Motor City Brewing Works has made a name for itself as one of Michigan's finest microbreweries, and in this beer-rich state, that's saying something. Serving out of its constantly packed taproom dotted with locally designed tile mosaics and metalwork, owners John Linardos and Dan Scarsella offer a stable of handcrafted beers anchored by the signature Ghettoblaster, "the beer you can hear." Flanked by seasonal varieties such as Pumpkin Ale and the popular Summer Ale (best with an orange wedge), tasty house-made sodas, and locally made wines, the brewery has a beverage for every palate. If the beverages weren't enough, the neighborhood institution also boasts delectable thin-crust brick-oven pizza made with locally grown ingredients, from the Bronx Bomber (cheese and meat heaven) to Roasted Pear and Fig. During warmer months, Motor City offers a rooftop deck, and a lovely, brick-paved biergarten-style patio. Bottled brews are distributed regionally, and growlers of soda and beer are available to take home. *470 W. Canfield St., www.motorcitybeer.com, (313) 832-2700.*

New Order Coffee - New Order Coffee is a gorgeous, light-filled cafe for those with a lighthearted take on serious coffee. The modern, mostly white- and birch-filled space is punctuated throughout with bright pops of the cafe's signature colors, orange and aqua. As lovely as the views are, especially those from the heated patio, it's what's behind the counter that really sets New Order apart. This cafe is the only place in Detroit where you'll find a micro-brewed cup of coffee, meaning that when you order a black coffee, it's ground and brewed in less than a minute, one cup at a time! A range of bean options (all perfectly small-batch roasted on site) means that drinks are entirely customizable. The cafe also offers delicious, locally made baked goods, and a full-slate of espresso drinks, including a rotating selection of lattes with fanciful ingredients like cereal milk, marshmallows, and M&M ganache. *3100 Woodward Ave., www.newordercoffee.com, (313) 784-9164.*

★ **The Old Miami** - Officially a veterans bar ("Miami" is short for Missing in Action Michigan), this grade-A dive is welcoming to everyone and draws a diverse crowd of streetwise veterans, Cass Corridor old-timers, and discerning 20- and 30-somethings who know a quality juice joint when they see one. The back bar and walls are covered with a thousand relics that tell as many stories, from vintage firearms, to a cheery painting of (controversial) Mayor Coleman Young, and a stuffed beaver that's more often used as a beer stand than admired. Though in colder months, patrons congregate around the pool table and sit in the mismatched comfy chairs, a highlight of the place is the exterior greenery. When weather permits, guests spill out into the gargantuan backyard, which is decked out with Vietnam paraphernalia (Missile? Check! Sign directing you to Saigon? Check!), a cozy bonfire pit, dozens of lawn chairs, and a koi pond. On select nights, the stages (there's one inside and one outside) play host to indie, punk, and metal bands, as well as local DJs (check out Nothing Elegant to shake it down). *3930 Cass Ave., (313) 831-3830.*

Olympic Grill - Located on the southern edge of Wayne State's campus, this popular student hangout serves patrons fast, affordable meals from a menu of the usual suspects: coneys, wraps, grilled sandwiches, and burgers—with a few specials like saganaki and yogurt smoothies thrown in. Fare is filling and tasty, served in a clean, comfy, and welcoming setting—padded cloth and vinyl booths, hardwood tables, a few lamps, checkered-tile pillars, and an open kitchen. Hours are based around the university crowd: open early and closed before the last classes let out. *119 W. Warren Ave., (313) 832-5809.*

The Peterboro - With a menu best described as haute cui-Sino and a stunning industrial interior, owners Chuck Inchaustegui and Dave Kwiatkowski, of Sugar House fame (see separate entry), have set a new standard for contemporary Chinese fare in the city. The distinct interior of the restaurant features a sweeping horseshoe bar set against indigo subway tile, an oil painting of a tiger, hovering Chinese lanterns, jade leather booths, brick and Shou Sugi Ban cedar walls, and concrete countertops that together offer a rustic, stark aesthetic with a nod to traditional Chinese restaurant decor. Though Chef de Cuisine Brion Wong's elevated take on almond boneless chicken is worth all the tea in China, the crab rangoons, cheeseburger eggrolls, and salt-and-pepper shrimp (galangal- and coriander-spiced whole prawns with jalapeño confit) offer strong supporting roles on a menu that balances sophistication and whimsy. But The Peterboro puts more between the chopsticks than just food. Don't miss the heavyweight drink menu, with strong craft beer, wine, sake, and cocktail options including the stellar shiso sour, which masterfully combines Batavia Arrack, lemon, shiso, simple syrup, and yuzu. *420 Peterboro St., www.thepeterboro.com, (313) 833-1111.*

Pho Lucky - For a fan of simple yet sensuous noodles, Pho Lucky offers an attractive hideaway. The restaurant serves diners hearty portions of Vietnamese comfort food: Classic pho, with heaps of rice noodles in beef broth with sweet herbs, bean sprouts and your choice of protein, or Vietnamese rice plates topped with fried egg (piling on herbs, chili paste, and bean sprouts is highly recommended). Though there are a handful of Pho Lucky locations around metro Detroit, visitors to the Midtown location are treated to a relaxed contemporary dining room with some remnant Art Deco features, and floor-to-ceiling views of Woodward Avenue, the latter especially being an engaging sight to take in while slurping soup or sipping iced coffee. For the uninitiated, Pho is pronounced "fuh," and, as a culinary category, it is a must-try. You've got to ask yourself one question: do you Pho Lucky? Vegetarian options are available, and beer, wine, and Vietnamese digestifs are on hand for the dinner crowd. *3111 Woodward Ave., www.pholucky.net, (313) 338-3895.*

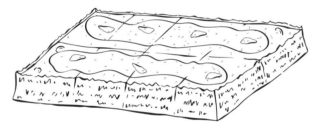

★ **Pie-Sci** - To the chagrin of waistlines everywhere, this science-themed pizza destination has made an art of the pie, and has become a byword for deliciousness—especially for daring pizza enthusiasts—thanks to its ambrosial, inspired combinations of *weirdough* toppings. Inside, the restaurant is charming and comfortable, with laboratory accoutrements, bright red pendant lights, butcher block two-tops, and a spirited psychedelic mural of a pizza-monster bicycle race. From the open kitchen, owner Jeremy Damaske is renowned for his seasonal, punny menu of round and Detroit-style square oven-blistered beauties topped with things like roasted pickled beets, savory white grits, and Tater Tots; and most pies are finished with a special drizzle, like herbed mayonnaise or lemon tahini. Favorites on the seasonal menu include the Lil' Kimchi (a white pie with kimchi, chicken, and Thai peanut drizzle) and the DevasTater (a red pie with Tots, ground beef, and a curry ketchup drizzle). For those in the mood for something more traditional, there's pepperoni and cheese here for you, too. Impressively, all pies are offered with meat, vegetarian, vegan, or gluten-free variants. In the warmer months, don't miss the breezy, relaxing patio. *5163 Trumbull Ave., www.piescipizza.com, (313) 818-0290.*

The Potato Place - Starch lovers, here's your haven. Offering crazy 3-pound potatoes the size of a small child, pile your spud with your choice of toppings (broccoli to taco), cheese, and butter, and watch the calories roll in. The loaded, perfectly textured, and creamy potatoes go down easy but are nearly impossible to finish in one sitting—though you'll likely try. While the focus of the place is obviously on everybody's favorite tuber, you can opt to swap your tater for a heaping plate of pasta smothered with your selection of vices. Don't have the appetite for a 3-pound potato? Split a spud with a friend or try the salads, house-made soups, baked goods, and award-winning ice cream. Keep in mind that "this is not a fast food restaurant" (as the sign by the register reminds patrons), so call ahead if you're in need of a quick fix. *107 W. Warren Ave., www.thepotatoplace.com, (313) 833-8948.*

★ **Rocco's Italian Deli** - Since opening in 2018, this deli-cocktail-bar hybrid has been gobbling up praise like Pac-Man. The restaurant is a bright, contemporary space punctuated by crisp white subway tiles, an open kitchen, marble countertops, and all white walls and ceilings. This elegant simplicity in design draws welcome attention to the food. On the menu, look for careful compositions of exquisite flavors that elevate the deli fare genre. The Hard Proof Prosciutto Means Love sandwich (prosciutto di parma, fresh mozzarella, oven-dried tomato, basil pesto, and lemon on an Italian roll softer than a baby's bum) is a particular standout, while Mozz and Mozz of Fun (their killer take on a caprese) is unspeakably divine. Somewhere, up above, the Earl of Sandwich is beaming with pride. The Whenever You're Feeling Blue salad, Chop Chop salad, and Want Nonna to Make You a Meatball? sandwiches are also also outstanding. Rocco's also offers a thoughtfully curated cocktail and beer menu, as well as wine and champagne. Once you've satiated your hunger, shop the curated deli and dry goods displays, which feature exceptional local and imported cheeses, meats, olives, anchovies, and other groceries. *3627 Cass Ave., www.roccosdetroit.com, (313) 315-3033.*

Rock City Eatery - Leaving their original home in Hamtramck, Rock City Eatery settled into these more spacious digs in 2016. The popular restaurant specializes in creative takes on global comfort food, from mac and cheese to tacos to Korean Hot Pot. Originally lauded for his pies, chef and owner Nikita Sanches has moved far beyond dessert to develop a robust menu that changes often "with respect to inspiration, ingredient, or season." The space, which was a Packard automotive showroom in a distant past life, is raw, industrial, unfussy, and modern with exposed brick walls, iconic Detroit rock 'n' roll photos, and mismatched chairs. Delicious standbys on the expansive and diverse menu include the spicy roasted brussels sprouts, duck fat fries, and the wildly flavorful lamb burger. Vegetarian and vegan diners will find a well-rounded selection, too. Wine, cocktails, and beer available. *4216 Woodward Ave., www.rockcityeatery.com (313) 265-3729.*

Royale with Cheese - While the name—a reference to an iconic scene in the film Pulp Fiction—might lead you to believe otherwise, the interior of this elevated burger spot bares only one (albeit large) reference to the popular film. Though the distracting allure of the burger in front of you make it easy to miss, Royale with Cheese is a contemporary place, with exposed ceiling joists and brick walls, Edison-bulb fixtures, an open kitchen, and yes, a floor-to-ceiling muraled homage to the film that inspired the name. The outstanding signature Royale burger—with its thick patty, smoked brisket, southwest corn relish, caramelized onions, avocado, creamy coleslaw, and smoked gouda fondue—generally keeps regulars from ordering other sandwiches, though the only poor option is not ordering. For those unmoved by the Royale, the nacho cheese ravioli, vegetarian falafel burger, and fairway salad are also sure bets. Whatever you choose, some herb and garlic parmesan fries would be a perfect sidekick. If you crave a little more, the strawberry milkshake makes for an outstanding finish. During warmer months, enjoy the shady patio. As Samuel L. Jackson's character Jules would say, "That *is* a tasty burger!" *4163 Cass Ave., wwwroyaledetroit.com, (313) 315-3014.*

Second Best Bar - Challenging the idea that "upscale dive bar" is an oxymoron, Second Best Bar pairs elevated bar food and a rigorous cocktail program with kitschy doodads and Up North comfort. The bar is popular with children of the Carter and Reagan Administrations, perhaps thanks to the 90s and aughts-heavy soundtrack, a general getting-drunk-in-your-parent's-basement vibe, period touches like an "Ice a friend" menu item, and dome hockey. Inside, the exposed brick walls, plaid banquettes, vintage stained glass pendants, glass garage door wall, mid-century stools, and ample taxidermy create an environment that is at once approachable, comfortable, stylish, and nostalgic. The food and drink menus follow suit. On the drink menu, look for a thoughtful assortment of bottled beers, a highly curated draft selection, and a relevant yet irreverent cocktail list, offering options like a House Zima, My First Old Fashioned, and an adult Boston Cooler. Soak it all up with a pizza puff du jour, some pulled pork hush puppies,seven layer deviled eggs, or something else off of the tasty, appetizer-centric food menu. *42 Watson St., www.secondbestdetroit.com, (313) 315-3077.*

★ **Selden Standard** - With exceptional lunch, dinner, and weekend brunch menus, Selden Standard is one of Detroit's finest restaurants, and continues to set the standard for New American cuisine in the city. The space is an intoxicating blend of modern textures, from the dark grey walls and concrete floor, to the copious subway tile, wood bar and tabletops, and warm filament lights that illuminate the space. On the menu, the wildly popular restaurant employs a small-plate concept. While the offerings are dictated by the seasons, look for standouts like a succulent grilled pork belly, well-balanced beef tartare, and flavorful, aromatic lamb chops. However, vegetarians also love Selden, with highlights like a bright, shaved vegetable carpaccio, flavor-packed roasted carrots, dramatic herbed flatbread, and a creamy, decadent polenta. The ever-changing dessert menu should also not be overlooked, as 2018 saw the nomination of pastry chef Lena Sareini for the prestigious James Beard Rising Star award. Behind the bar, Selden offers one of Detroit's best cocktail programs, as well as a full complement of beer and wine. Weekend brunch can be an approachable (and more affordable) way to explore the restaurant, with crowd-pleasers like a seasonal frittata, beef brisket hash, and a daily breakfast pastry. In warmer months, the spacious, shaded outdoor patio is the perfect hideaway and setting for your meal. *3921 Second Ave., www.seldenstandard.com, (313) 438-5055.*

★ **Seva Detroit** - To the delight of vegetarians (and everyone else), Seva—based out of Ann Arbor since 1973—opened a Detroit outpost in 2011. Attached to the N'Namdi Center for Contemporary Art, Seva offers patrons two dining rooms that feature a refined, industrially oriented contemporary gallery setting with concrete floors, exposed ceilings, floor-to-ceiling windows, and artwork that colorfully fills the walls. The expansive and versatile menu offers a wide range of vegetarian and vegan cuisine, with options that will satisfy even the heartiest appetite or the most particular palate. Highlights among the many appetizers, sandwiches, salads, and entrees include the indulgent deep-fried goodness of General Tso's cauliflower, a solid cilantro peanut stir-fry, a yummy club sandwich (amazing smoked-coconut pinch-hits for bacon), and a rotating menu of flavorful and filling salads. Also offering a full bar backlit by a glowing white wall, the beverage menu itself is four pages long, offering homemade sodas, fresh juice combos, signature cocktails, and a slew of local beers and wines. Don't miss the daily happy hour food and drink specials (yes, gouda tots are as good as they sound) and a weekly Sunday brunch. *66 E. Forest Ave., www.sevarestaurant.com, (313) 974-6661.*

Sgt. Pepperoni's Pizzeria & Deli - Although most popular at 2am when three sheets and looking for treats, the speedy service and tasty slices will leave customers of any blood-alcohol level saluting the Sergeant for a job well done. Complementing the golden crust and gooey cheese, the rich sauce offers a distinct, slightly spicy and slightly tangy, piquant flavor, making all of the signature thin-crust pies pretty tasty. While the individual slices are celebrated by the inebriated, Sgt. Pepperoni's offers whole pies, alongside a stable of salads and sandwiches—including the yummy grilled veggie reuben and baked Italian sub. Although the toppings mostly remain in familiar territory, visitors can opt for vegan cheese, bleu cheese, or chevre. Open late. Limited delivery available. *4120 Woodward Ave., www.majesticdetroit.com/sgt-pepperonis-detroit, (313) 833-7272.*

Shangri-La - Since opening in 2009, Shangri-La has quickly become a destination for authentic Cantonese cuisine in the city. An open, bi-level, contemporary space, Shangri-La is an inviting and lively setting featuring a wealth of Eastern decorations. While owner Cholada Chan is renowned for her innovative, flavorful, and delectable dim sum, the other dishes available, from sushi to massaman curry are also notable. Shangri-La offers a full bar, with an impressive selection of potables, including sake, Asian wines and beers, as well as all the usual suspects. *4710 Cass Ave., www.midtownshangri-la.com, (313) 974-7669.*

★**SheWolf Pastificio & Bar** - Named for the Roman origin legend (the empire's founders, Romulus and Remus, were nursed and raised by a wild she-wolf), this stunning restaurant is rooted in the classical Roman tradition, but is delightfully contemporary in its execution. Looking out onto the rapidly evolving Selden corridor, the minimalist, glass-filled space centers around a square bar, and features an open kitchen and a glass-encased pastificio (pasta factory to the rest of us). The inventive menu is solidly upscale, and small-plate oriented. In addition to a tour through ten traditional noodle presentations—all perfectly al dente and made on-site with house-milled flour—the menu includes focaccia, vegetable preparations, and fine meats, which run the gamut from seafood to veal, to balance your meal. Each dish is beautifully plated, and features stunning, herb-rich flavors. The meals are rounded out by the inventive cocktails—which range from contemporary American twists on Italian classics to Italian twists on American classics—and are only matched by the impressive wine list. Word is out, so reservations are highly recommended. We just wish it were socially acceptable—and our wallets could stomach—to eat SheWolf pasta at every meal. Yes, gluten-free pasta is available! *438 Selden St., www.shewolfdetroit.com, (313) 315-3992.*

Slows To Go - Offering a delectable, sapid homage to the deep south, Slows To Go follows in the footsteps of its revered Corktown parent, Slows Bar B Q (see separate entry). Housed in a 1926 building that has variously been a bank and storefront church, the interior of the beautiful restaurant features high ceilings, contemporary wood details, and engaging artwork on the brightly colored walls. Slows To Go offers Midtown Slows Bar B Q's renowned, toothsome entrees, such as the pulled pork, ribs, wings, as well as Slows signature sandwiches, such as the ambrosial Amish chicken and mushroom Yardbird, and the incredible vegetarian TVP and slaw Genius—alongside its own tacos and turkey offerings. If able to spare the stomach space, visitors should indulge in one of the revered sides, such as the rich, creamy mac and cheese, or the sweet, tangy pit-smoked baked beans. Although primarily a carryout location, visitors can dine in or picnic al fresco at the enormous table located to the south. The Old Miami (see separate entry)—just up the block—makes a great place to enjoy Slows To Go over a cold brewski. Internet ordering available. *4107 Cass Ave. www.slowstogo.com, (877) 569-7246.*

Socra Tea - A playful nod to the ancient Greek philosopher, Socra Tea is located on the garden level of historic 71 Garfield, and offers guests a cozy atmosphere, wholesome food, and an impressive selection of organic teas. Built with reclaimed components, the shop is a lesson in how such materials can be used to reinvent a space artfully, from the counter constructed with lath and discarded marble floors, to the leaded glass windows incorporated into one of the interior walls.

However, proprietor Meg Jones has put as much thought into her product as her decor. The shop carries more than 95 loose-leaf teas, including black, pu-erh, oolong, green, white, rooibos, and herbal varieties. The menu also features signature lemonade, iced teas, and tea lattes, as well as elevated sandwich classics with a bevy of vegan and vegetarian options. In this earthy, tranquil hidden gem, you'll often find students studying as they sip, and quiet meetings taking place over a light lunch or warm cup. As a perfect complement, handmade ceramics from neighboring **Sugar Hill Clay** are available for purchase. *71 Garfield, Ste. 50, www.socrateadetroit.com, 313.833.7100.*

Spread Deli & Coffee House - Spread is a Midtown deli and coffee shop with a mission: For every ten sandwiches they sell, they donate one to a person in need. Serving down-to-earth—and supremely high-quality—sandwiches with hyper-local ingredients like bread from next-door-neighbor Avalon, along with Eastern Market veggies, meats, and cheeses, Spread has a spread that will please any palette. The neighborhood deli complements their drool-worthy eats with a fun and artistic setting in which to enjoy them. Look for a clean and modern aesthetic with fanciful, cascading alphabetical decor. Along with tasty eats, the neighborhood deli also offers excellent fresh-roasted coffee options. *4215 Cass. Ave.*

Temple Bar - Visit the Temple Bar and meet the owner, George—Detroit's most opinionated, whimsical, mercurial, and charming bartender. The bar has been in George's family since the 1920s (and holds one of city's first 100 liquor licenses), but it's hard to imagine the joint without its modern day, larger-than-life proprietor. While the Temple Bar is pretty much the last business on this stretch of Cass Avenue, and the area is a little rough, you'd never know it once you get buzzed in the front door. This charmingly tarnished jewel of an Art Deco bar was a haven for African-Americans in the 1920s and interracial couples in the 1970s, before attracting its current mix of grizzled Corridor residents, drag queens, and hipsters. Today, its disco-ball-adorned dance floor is home to some of the city's best see-and-be-scene dance nights. To top it all off, the liquid courage doled out from behind the bar is stupid cheap. Dollar drafts? Eight-dollar microbrew pitchers? That's what we're talking about. But go quickly: word on the street is that with the new stadium around the corner, the bar's days might be numbered. Which is a damn shame, because they don't build local color like this anymore. *2906 Cass Ave., (313) 832-2822.*

Third Street Bar - Though it bills itself as a "rustic urban oasis," Third Street is a hip, tastefully decorated haven of hooch. With a gorgeous wood-laden, high-ceilinged interior illuminated by muted Edison-bulb lighting, the roomy bar features historic tin ceilings in the restroom, a wood-burning fireplace, and a hand-hewn bar and tables to match. The bar gives off a laid-back, mountain lodge atmosphere, complete with shuffleboard, darts, Internet jukebox, and old-school movies on the TV above the bar. Though Third Street is a full bar with 30 imported and domestic beers in bottles, the bar offers only three drafts, and liquors are limited to favored call mixers. In the summer, patrons can eat or drink al fresco on the patio. *701 W. Forest Ave., (313) 833-0603.*

Tony V's Tavern - The new Wayne State campus watering hole, Tony V's is heir to the throne (and location) of Cass Corridor bacchanal of yore Alvin's. The current iteration still has plenty of sauce and suds to keep students in the seats, but the resurrected bar features a more upscale touch, with hand-crafted pizzas, and a breezy, comfortable setting that includes patio seating. Owner Tony Vulaj brought some notable touches to the space, including a wrought iron chandelier, a carved wooden bar with accompanying rivulet molding, and a house interior coated in a deep terracotta. Tony's opens a garage door in fairer weather, so patrons can munch and mingle in the silhouette of locust trees. Be sure to visit during the bar's generous happy hour to take advantage of rotating food and drink specials. *5756 Cass Ave., www.tonyvstavern.com, (313) 833-5595.*

Tou & Mai - Midtown's only boba tea (or bubble tea) destination, this extension of neighborhood favorite Go! Sy Thai (see separate entry) ensures that you can enjoy a wide-variety of treats and appreciate the richness of Hmong culture. From milky taro tea with tapioca pearls, to Thai tea and flowering tea varieties, fresh fruit smoothies, and the cutest macarons in town, fun refreshment reigns supreme at Tou & Mai. Boba devotees can customize their selection with a wide range of exotic garnishes, including basil seeds, litchi jellies, and mango popping boba. The "sweet life" house specialities are also popular—especially the Black Tea Milk Cap, with a rich foam. The modern, open counters lead you to a well-curated market of popular snack treasures, mainly from Japan, including matcha Kit Kats, mochi, Pocky, and a slew of other delights you have and haven't heard of. Seating is limited, so it's best to snag a table outside, weather permitting and sip away in the sunshine. *4240 Cass Ave., www.touandmai.com.*

Traffic Jam & Snug - A Detroit institution since 1965, the Traffic Jam is famous for its eccentric decor and quality American fare. Bedecked with old school pieces of Americana, the beautiful interior boasts exposed brick, classic red tile, knotty pine woodwork, and a laid-back atmosphere. The diverse menu approaches American cuisine with an emphasis on fresh, local ingredients and an innovative eye. Although the menu is mostly strikes and no gutters, a few options shouldn't be missed, including the Portobello mushroom soup, the Tex-Mex lentil burger, the madras meatloaf, the vegetarian lasagna, the Traverse City dried cherry and pecan salad, and the house-brewed dopplebock-braised beef brisket panini. The fine restaurant is also home to an in-house brewery, dairy, and bakery, and visitors can pick up some of these fresh treats near the entrance. Those looking to drink their meal should visit the Snug, the attached, cozy bi-level bar, which offers house brews and mixed drinks and ice cream to go. *511 W. Canfield St., www.trafficjamdetroit.com, (313) 831-9470.*

Treat Dreams - Filling a conical void, in 2015 this satellite location of the popular Ferndale creamery finally gave Midtowners a way to properly beat the heat. Though Treat Dreams offers smoothies and coffees, as well as a small selection of homemade baked goods, the focus here is the incredible scooped ice cream (including vegan and lactose-free options) made daily in small batches at the Ferndale location. Of course, you can always find "safe" flavors like vanilla and chocolate, but it's the envelope-pushing one-off experimentations that keep us coming back. Expect to find an ever-changing cast of gourmet (and sometimes whimsical) flavors like bourbon ginger; mango cayenne; honey, goat cheese, and fig; beet, orange zest, and poppy seed; maple, bacon, and waffles; or froot loops and cream. These flavors always magically work—and work best in a homemade waffle cone—but with free tastes, you can be sure to make a wise selection. Seating is available inside, as well as streetside in warmer months. *4160 Cass Ave., www.treatdreams.com, (313) 818-0084.*

Union Street - Signaled by the iconic retro neon sign, Union Street has been a staple of the neighborhood dining experience since the 1970s. Offering patrons an elegant but casual Art Deco dining experience, the establishment features a stunning atmosphere highlighted by mirrored walls, lush red lighting, and historic dark wood fixtures, the touchstone of which is the simple yet incredible, curvy Deco bar. The moderately priced menu runs the gamut of sandwiches, pastas, and a bevy of classic entrees in the American tradition—a favorite of which is the jambalaya (thick, meaty Creole stew over rice). The bar, which is often lined with thirsty customers, offers an impressive 15 beers on tap and 100 in bottles, in addition to a full line of wines, liquors, and craft cocktails. Don't miss the popular Sunday brunch. *4145 Woodward Ave., www.unionstreetdetroit.com, (313) 831-3965.*

Urban Ramen - Bringing authentic, flavorful ramen to Detroit by way of L.A., Urban Ramen marries mastery of the Japanese culinary artform with a touch of American, big-city grit. This mashup is exemplified by the enormous graffiti mural that graces the back wall and somehow references Detroit street culture, the ear of buddha, and the signature noodle dish, and sets the tone for the approachable and friendly spot. The menu of slurp-worthy ramen is concise, but has something for everyone, from their signature Chicken Paitan Ramen (which features a rich chicken broth with pork chashu, vegetables, and marinated egg) to their Shoyu Vegan Ramen (which features a flavorful vegan broth, vegetables, and maitake mushrooms), as well as a bevy of optional additional toppings and traditional sides. All of the toothsome ramen noodles are made on site daily and aged to perfection to achieve a rare texture and flavor. If you're lucky, you can witness the magical process in the front window. *4206 Woodward Ave., www.urbanramen.com, (313) 285-9869.*

Wasabi Korean & Japanese Cuisine - Korean and Japanese restaurants are hard to come by in Detroit, but Wasabi's dual menu serves up a solid version of both cuisines. On the Korean side, the dolsot bibimbab is especially tasty (including the delectable vegetarian tofu variation), and the Japanese menu features a full range of sushi and traditional noodle dishes, along with a selection of sakes. Nestled in the ground floor of the Park Shelton, the interior is cozy, clean, and modern. If you find yourself visiting day after day, it might be worth your while to invest in one of the prepaid meal plans, from $150 for 17 lunches, to $1,300 for 100 lunches and dinners. *15 E. Kirby St., www.wasabidetroit.com, (313) 638-1272.*

The Whitney - A romantic restaurant set in a mansion of unparalleled extravagance and sophistication, the Whitney is a highlight on any culinary—or architectural—tour of Detroit. Once described as "one of the most elaborate houses in the West," the Romanesque Revival residence, which was built by lumber baron David Whitney Jr. in 1894 and converted to a restaurant in 1986, is indeed magnificent. From the stately exterior, to the 52 exquisitely appointed rooms, to the Tiffany glass windows, the restaurant offers surroundings that do its food justice. The menu, which changes seasonally, covers wide gastronomic terrain, but favors succulent and savory American flavors, with exceptional fowl, fish, and steak. Oenophiles will be equally pleased by the wine cellar, which offers a generous selection of local and international varieties. In addition, the Whitney offers a buffet-style Sunday brunch and a rotating lineup of entertainers in its garden and at the more casual **Ghost Bar** on the third floor. Though the restaurant has no formal dress code, business casual attire is recommended at a minimum. *4421 Woodward Ave., www.thewhitney.com, (313) 832-5700.*

Woodbridge Pub - Featuring vintage touches like antique tin ceilings, salvaged leaded glass, gorgeous historic paneling, and a reconstituted 1890s oak bar, this beautiful pub and neighborhood gem offers an eclectic, locally sourced menu reflective of the seasons. Although personable owner Jim Geary's menu features a stable of palate-pleasers, the Stevers McFever black bean burger (with zing from a balsamic reduction), buffal-pho, toasted pumpkin ravioli, and Trumbull ham pot pie are not to be missed. The pub boasts an impressive selection of beers including rotating Michigan-brewed selections and a full line of liquors. On Sunday mornings, make a beeline for Woodbridge for the special brunch menu and bottomless mimosas. The pub plays host to a fun roster of weekly events, including pub trivia on Wednesdays and a slow jam night each Monday. *5169 Trumbull Ave., www.woodbridgepub.com, (313) 833-2701.*

Zef's Midtown - The newer, but less character-filled, Midtown outpost of this popular Coney and diner. See Zef's Coney Island (separate entry) for more details. *4160 Woodward Ave., www.midtownzefsgrill.com, (313) 831-1210.*

SHOPPING & SERVICES

1701 Bespoke - Service in style. Welcome to 1701 Bespoke, a Midtown suit and tuxedo tailor aiming to restore panache to Detroit dresswear. Sourcing fabric from a half dozen top European fashion mills, the shop provides guests full concierge suiting, as well as unique silk ties, pocket squares, and other accessories. The suiting process begins with a preliminary ninety-minute meeting, where a tailor performs twenty measurements and counsels on design elements. When the garment is completed, the shop re-measures to fine-tune the fit and shape, and then puts the finishing touches on the suit that will last a lifetime. The shop emphasizes modern Italian fashion, with lighter-weight, breezier jackets, wine-bottle pockets, and soft lapels, which complement the aesthetic of the space, which is clean and contemporary. While you wait for your appointment, pour yourself a cocktail and enjoy the mezzanine view of Midtown. Look for biannual trunk shows and soirees to meld sophistication and socializing. *4160 Woodward Ave., www.1701bespoke.com, (313) 444-3680.*

Architectural Salvage Warehouse of Detroit - As the answer to the question "Where can I purchase gently used 2x4s, a working refrigerator, antique corbels, and ornamental balustrades?" the Architectural Salvage Warehouse is Detroit's reigning king of architectural salvage. Though active in advocacy and education, the backbone of the organization—and what it is best known for—is its successful (and legitimate) deconstruction and architectural salvage operation. All of the components that the facility collects and saves from landfills—from the historic to the mundane—are organized by type and laid to bare (and priced to sell) in the organization's massive two-story disposition center. Though its website is fairly comprehensive, it's not always completely up-to-date, so phone inquiries or in-person visits are recommended. *4885 15th St., www.aswdetroit.org, (313) 896-8333.*

Armageddon Beachparty - Founded by Detroit natives Elena and Aubrey Smith, known as Kozma and Motu—or even better known by fans as Armageddon Beachparty—this gallery, retail store, and lounge is dedicated to their artistic practice. This dynamic art duo has been collaborating creatively since 2013 to produce an impressive body of work including acrylic paintings, mixed-media pieces, and large-scale murals in their signature pop-surrealist style drawing from psychedelia, tiki culture, and sci-fi. The shop offers collectors' pieces at all price points, from inexpensive prints to original art pieces and mugs, pins, and textiles, as well as a selection of vintage clothing and kitsch. Regular events include live music, film screenings, burlesque, open mic, and dance parties. Check their website and social media for a calendar of events. *1517 Putnam St., www.armageddonbeachpartydetroit.com, (313) 704-4407.*

Art Loft - A popular retail mainstay in suburban Birmingham for more than 20 years, owner Rachael Woods brought Art Loft to one of Detroit's most vibrant retail districts in 2015. While the displays are contemporary and minimal, they highlight the vivid, colorful, whimsical and funky design objects that the store is known for—and the shop is packed with goods! The selection includes refined design goods by Alessi, Jonathan Adler, and others, as well as gorgeous, bright African textiles from Woods' native Ghana. In addition to a selection that is unique in the neighborhood, Art Loft offers free gift wrapping and jewelry repair. *4160 Cass Ave., www.artloftonline.com, (313) 818-0023.*

The Black Dress - A women's clothing boutique, The Black Dress is stocked with contemporary wardrobe essentials to outfit you from career to cocktails. Owned and operated by mother-daughter duo Sandra Allen and Missy Lewis, The Black Dress has become a local dress-tination for the classy, sassy 30-and-up crowd on the hunt for fun printed separates, sleek cocktail dresses, chic pullover ponchos, unique handbags, accessories, jewelry, and more. Although it carries a full range of sizes, The Black Dress specializes in larger sizes up to 5X. If you love a garment but would love it more if altered to your personal measurements, simply ask Sandra, a seamstress at heart. *113 E. Canfield St., www.theblackdressonline.com, (313) 833-7795.*

Bob's Classic Kicks - Don't let the "classic" in the name fool you, BCK is Detroit's best place to find old-school and new school sneaks. With its colorful murals, high ceilings, and open and airy feel, the hip, tightly curated boutique slings whatever stylin' Reebok, Adidas, and Nike kicks your feet desire—whether you're looking for classic, cutting edge, or locally designed foot fashions. In addition to quality footwear, the boutique also stocks a selection of flat-brim hats and locally designed tees. On the last Saturday of every month, Bob's hosts The Air UP There, an intimate hip-hop performance and party. *4717 Woodward Ave., www.bobsclassickicks.com, (313) 832-7513.*

Busted Bra Shop - Nestled in the back of the Park Shelton, Busted is the city's only full-service bra shop, and helps take the mystery out of the bare necessities. The expert staff offer friendly and efficient fitting services. Get ready to get personal and talk about all the most common bra issues, while learning more about fit, form, and the various styles. The team works from your measurements and rapidly combs through their enormous, well-organized collection, so that you can efficiently try the goods on your goods. With an inclusive range of skin tones, fun brights, smooth basics, and lacy and racy options, the shop has every woman in mind. You'll find AAA-N cups, 26-56 band measurements, and innumerable functions, sizes, uses— and most importantly—price points. Complementing the selection of bras are all things lingerie, including matching sets, stockings, shapewear, and fine washing accessories. Busted proves time and again that a great foundation is fundamental for all fashionable Detroiters. *15 E. Kirby St., www.bustedindetroit.com, 313.288.0449.*

Carhartt - Founded in Detroit in 1889, and still going strong, few companies represent the city's tenacity and hardscrabble attitude better than Carhartt. This store, the company's flagship location, and only retail presence in their home state of Michigan, channels that ethos, as well as the their deep heritage in the city—the fifth generation family-owned company was founded in Corktown, and is now headquartered in nearby Dearborn. The Midtown location is decorated in the brand's signature industrial style, and carries the full line of Carhartt workwear, daily wear, and accessories, as well as gifts for the working man or woman, including rugged retro lunch pails and leather goods. An impressive example of adaptive reuse, the store was built into the enormous, historic Dalgliesh Cadillac building—the practical upside being that there is convenient attached parking, but it can easy to miss—look for the driveway immediately north of the front entrance. Make sure to check out the enormous, beautiful murals decorating the north facade of the building, designed by local illustrators Michael Burdick and James Noellert. *5800 Cass Ave., www.carhartt.com/content/content-retail-detroit, (313) 831-1274.*

Cass Corridog - With nearly everything but the kitten sink for your four-legged toy destroyer, Cass Corridog offers a wide array of toys, treats, food, and care supplies for dogs and cats. The barker-friendly 800-square-foot shop is a bright, sunny space with boutique proportions and three aisles lined with dense, ever-changing displays. The shop carries a selection of standard critter-care essentials, but emphasizes local and natural options—look for staples such as Detroit-themed leashes, collars, and outfits, houndstooth pet blankets, as well as locally-made products like PetFection oils, handmade toys, and natural food and treats from Old Mother Hubbard and Taste of the Wild. The shop also addresses less pressing issues on the hierarchy of pets' needs, with an abundance of toys and novelties, including tennis ball guns, dog marshmallows, and pet costumes. Don't miss the bakery case of baked treats for furry friends on your way out to the Shinola Dog Park across the street. *4240 Cass Ave., www.casscorridog.com, (313) 775-1018.*

★ **City Bird** - The oldest store on bustling West Canfield Street, siblings Andy and Emily Linn opened this popular shop in 2009. City Bird offers its own singular line of Detroit-themed items, as well as housewares, jewelry, stationery, paper goods, apparel, accessories, and home decor by hundreds of other artists and designers. The Linns began making their own distinctive city-oriented products in 2005, which now run the gamut from this guidebook to exclusive glassware, T-shirts, notebooks, art prints, housewares, greeting cards, and other Detroit souvenirs for Detroiters. This expansive range of goods is displayed in the warm, friendly, sun-drenched shop with antique wooden fixtures, artful displays, and hints of Detroit's industrial history. City Bird is especially popular for its affordable jewelry by American designers, its delightful candles and soaps, its revolving selection of specialty Detroit T-shirts, and a bevy of one-of-a-kind gifts at a variety of price points. To top it off, with more than 500 different illustrated greeting cards by independent designers—many hand-printed—their card selection is something to write home about. *460 W. Canfield St., www.citybirddetroit.com, (313) 831-9146.*

★**Detroit Antique Mall / Senate Resale** - Though, depending on the sign, it's alternately known as the Detroit Antique Mall or Senate Resale, by either name, the 12,000-square-foot shop is one of Detroit's largest and finest antique stores. Boasting 12 vendors spread over two gigantic floors, the neatly compartmentalized antique mini-mall is organized by vendor—each of which specializes in a unique area of antique and vintage expertise. Once buzzed in, customers are greeted by a relatively neatly ordered and wide selection of Art Deco, Mid-Century Modern, Arts and Crafts, Victorian and Mission furniture and decor, architectural salvage, 1950s and 1960s collectibles, lighting, jewelry, periodicals, and numerous other facets of the antique experience, making it hard to walk out of the large emporium without finding a treasure. *828 W. Fisher Fwy., (313) 963-5252.*

Detroit Clothing Circle - Expect the unexpected in the first floor of this Victorian stunner on Second Avenue—a well-curated resale shop that is packed with personality, and focused on helping you craft your signature look through designer finds, vintage gems, and a diverse selection of clothing for men and women. With organized racks and digestible sections throughout the warm, brick interior, you truly feel that each piece has been chosen with a purpose, and a person, in mind. Speciality sneakers and shoes are hand selected—as are the large selection of jackets, denim, and accessories—which will make any outfit stand out. New apparel from Detroit designers is also featured, and the on-trend shop regularly hosts music, events, and other happenings. *3980 Second Ave., www.detroitclothingcircle.com, (313) 887-1370.*

Detroit Surf Co. - Beautifully arrayed in this sliver of a retail space in Midtown's Auburn building, this flagship store for the Detroit Surf Co. highlights the gorgeous signature line of this hot, idiosyncratic brand. As the story goes, the company was an idea that grew from a one-off, novelty T-shirt to localized production and a dedicated showroom in the space of twelve years. Today, the company produces its line of Detroit-themed surfboards, paddle boards, snowboards, longboards, and skateboards locally, using US-made materials. Most of the heirloom pieces feature all-wood construction, as well as detailed engravings that depict Detroit iconography, city maps, and the company logo. In addition to their signature boards, the store also stocks Detroit Surf Co. branded apparel and gear. And yes, there is photographic evidence that it is possible to catch a wave on the Great Lakes. Cowabunga! *4240 Cass Ave., www.detroitsurfco.com, (313) 744-3727.*

Downtown Detroit Bike Shop - Detroit is in the midst of a bicycle renaissance. No longer a maligned mode of transportation in the Motor City, bikes are popping up everywhere—from friendly joy rides like Slow Roll (see separate entry), to city bike tours, to two-wheeled work commuters. So, where can bicycle buffs get their fix? Downtown Detroit Bike Shop, a new Cass Corridor staple, and sister location to the Downtown Ferndale Bike Shop, offers something for all levels of enthusiasts, from hobbyists to hardcore cyclists. Get your beloved fixie fixed at their full-service repair shop, or find a new whip to tool around town—and buy some accessories to trick it out while you're at it. Downtown Detroit Bike Shop will have you Lance Armstronging Motown's bike lanes in no time. Just don't forget your helmet! *412 Peterboro St., www.downtown-bikeshop.com, (313) 818-0075.*

Filson - A Seattle-based heritage brand, Filson operates 19 stores globally, including New York, London, and Tokyo. Opened in 2016, this location calls the bustling Canfield Street home, and the shop adds a rugged outdoorsy grit—and a bevy of flannel—to the neighborhood's offerings. Founded in 1897 to outfit Alaskan gold seekers, the company specializes in handsome, timeless styling and durability. Their signature wool coats, rugged apparel, and accessories for men are prominently featured and beautifully displayed throughout the lodge-like store. The shop can quickly transform a city slicker into an outdoorsman, or at least have them looking the part. These heirloom-quality pieces are built to last a lifetime—and they're backed by a generous warranty—but priced accordingly. Though Filson's focus is menswear, the shop does offer a limited selection of items for women. *441 W. Canfield St., www.filson.com, (313) 285-1880.*

★ **Flo Boutique** - Inside Felicia Patrick's cozy, lively, eclectic clothing boutique, you'll find a collection of effortless style and soul. Think feminine dresses, comfy cotton separates, patchwork denim skirts, and all the right accessories to go with them, from wooden bracelets to fashionable fedoras, leather wallets, and fabulous shoes. Alongside the goods for women, Flo carries a smart collection of gear for men, all artfully displayed in her inviting shop with vintage and natural accents. Named for her mother, Patrick's store is the fulfillment of her lifelong dream of opening a shop and her love of fashion. Don't forget to take a whiff of one of the fragrant essential oils and grab a chic envelope clutch made from upcycled jute coffee bean sacks. *404 W. Willis St., www.flowingflava.com, (313) 831-4901.*

Frida - With clothing, accessories, and boho baubles, Frida embraces colors and textures, while emphasizing wearability and comfort. Facing Woodward, in the first floor of the Park Shelton building, the shop interior features a striking, vibrant chandelier and tassels galore set against clean, cool white walls. Though the boutique is dense with vibrant, colorful merchandise, there is space to shop and browse the curated vignettes and accessorized ensembles. The worldly, Bohemian offerings include a wide selection of independent and mid-size designers, like Amano Studio and Johnny Was, as well as eclectic displays influenced by Frida Kahlo (the muse and inspiration for the shop itself). Did we mention color? The spirited offerings (in a full range of sizes!) are sure to perk up your closet, while sassy notecards, salty socks, and other kitschy goods will make you chuckle. Thoughtful, friendly staff can point you in the right direction and are more than happy to assist as you treasure hunt. *15 E. Kirby St., 313-559-5500.*

The Hub of Detroit - Greetings from the land of used vintage bicycles! The Hub is Detroit's cyclery-with-a-conscience and home to perhaps the state's largest selection of used bicycles in various states of repair.

This lively, unpolished shop is known for its friendly staff, affordable repair services, and its unparalleled collection of used parts—from Italian threaded bottom brackets to indicator spindles. The Hub stays true to the values of its nonprofit roots, and works to train local youth in bike repair, help them earn bikes, and offers them jobs in the shop. If you know your way around a cone wrench and chain whip—or want to learn—you can take classes and volunteer at the affiliated nonprofit **Back Alley Bikes** on the second floor. The Hub accepts donated bicycles. *3611 Cass Ave., www.thehubofdetroit.org, (313) 879-5073.*

★**Hugh** - Born as a retail pop-up "happening" in 2010, after 65,000 votes were cast, owner Joe Posch emerged the popular victor in the first annual Hatch Detroit retail competition, granting him the startup capital needed to make his store a permanent fixture on the Detroit retail scene. Hugh is an enthusiastic celebration of classic 1950s and 1960s bachelor-pad style. Impeccably decorated in a manner that would make Don Draper proud, the store's stunning mid-century wood fixtures display a wide selection of classic barware, men's accessories, smoking accoutrements, new and vintage glassware, furniture, and home decor. Patrons will find flasks (including one tastefully concealed in a book), myriad cocktail shakers, stylish cufflinks, artful ashtrays, and even a selection of vintage Playboy magazines. Offering items at a wide range of price points, Posch, with his stunning taste and advice, can help every man—or the man in everyone's life—be outfitted in timeless style. Thank Hugh. *4020 Cass Ave., www.lovehughlongtime.com, (313) 887-0900.*

★**Little High Flyers** - This bright and playful destination children's clothing boutique features stylish, organic, gender-neutral products from small, women-owned brands from around the world. The merchandise is beautifully displayed on custom wooden fixtures, including shelving designed to look like little houses, and the bright green floor makes the whole shop pop. Primarily stocking stylish high-quality apparel and accessories, they also carry complementary toys, books, decor and gifts for babies and toddlers. From panda sweaters to rocket moon leggings, cute aviation-themed hats to buttery soft baby shoes, Little High Flyers will have the children in your life on cloud nine! Feel free to bring your little ones along while you shop, too. They can entertain themselves in the little playroom in the back, which is stocked with crayons and books. *4240 Cass Ave., www.littlehighflyers.com, (313) 818-3748.*

Mongers' Provisions - Since opening in 2018, this flagship outpost of the popular Ferndale charcuterie and cheese purveyor has found an enthusiastic audience. With its relaxed, airy, gallery-like atmosphere, the inspired artisanal food shop offers a reprieve from the bustling Cass/Canfield shopping district. Inside, owners Zach Berg and Will Werner stock their 12-foot cheese case with a rotating, globe-trotting, selection, from Idyll Gris, Alp Blossom, and Crottin to clothbound Cheddar, aged Gouda and Pecorino Toscano. The similarly diverse charcuterie selection varies from the rustic to the refined. A curated selection of meats from local outfit **Farm Field Table** includes a complementary salumi, terrines, rillettes and cured hams, alongside a diverse stable of fresh and frozen steaks and traditional sausage. The shop also offers a gloriously plentiful selection of some of the world's finest chocolates. A thoughtful collection of olives, dried fruit, nuts, olive oils, jams, cheese boards and knives, and books is available, as well as pre-assembled charcuterie platters, tastings, and classes. *4240 Cass Ave. #111, www.mongersprovisions.com, (313) 651-7119.*

★**Nest -** Brought to Detroit by the brother-sister duo behind City Bird next door, this sunny shop opened in 2011 and features accessible design, with a focus on gifts and home goods. With a long wall of 1920s oak library shelves rescued from the now-demolished, historic Cass Tech high school, 1920s rolling shelves from a shoe factory, a meticulously restored general-store counter, and nearly floor-to-ceiling windows, the warm, light-filled, wood and brick interior of this former industrial space is the perfect backdrop for the beautiful glass and barware, modern decor, old-timey toys, and local foods. However, Nest is most popular for its lush plants and addictive candles and soaps. The shop offers a curated but diverse selection of live plants, including succulents and airplants, and accompanying plant-related decor, including hanging glass globes, terrariums, and contemporary planters. They also offer one of the city's most extensive and tempting selections of fine candles, luxury soaps, and apothecary items, with numerous options for every taste and budget. *460 W. Canfield St., www.nestdetroit.com, (313) 831-9776.*

★**Nora -** A collaboration between local entrepreneurs Liz Boone and Toby Barlow, Nora is a stunning design shop. The bright, airy, white space with natural, open wooden shelves is punctuated by the artfully displayed products that are the store's focal point. Specializing in thoughtful, contemporary design from a wide range of influences, the light-filled shop has a gallery feel and features a well-curated selection of Scandinavian housewares, Japanese ceramics, and work by select local designers, as well as textiles, jewelry, periodicals, apothecary, children's and decor items. Be sure to check out their extensive selections of Hasami and Mud Australia ceramics and their exquisite cookbook, 4 Detroit, which features recipes from the founding chefs of four beloved local restaurants. *4240 Cass, Ave., www.noramodern.com, (313) 831-4845.*

The Peacock Room Park Shelton - The smaller, sister location of the popular Fisher Building flagship, this satellite boutique is located in the gorgeous former formal dining room of the historic Park Shelton, which was built as a hotel in the 1920s, and hosted the likes of Diego Rivera and Bob Hope. The beautiful architecture creates the perfect atmosphere for simultaneously upscale, affordable shopping. See the entry for The Peacock Room Fisher Building for more details about this lovely shop, which has become a Midtown institution. *15 E. Kirby St., (313) 559-5500.*

RUNdetroit - Located in part of a former Willys Overland Jeep factory, RUNdetroit now gets Detroiters moving with a different kind of tread. Since opening in 2013, owner Justin Craig's mag-run opus has become an institution with workshops and group runs alongside a traditional retail program. With its muted green walls, bright lighting, comfortable couches, handsome wood floors, and clean aesthetic, RUNdetroit's boutique approach and minimalist space spur an immersive focus on the product. On the racks, look for shoes from the likes of Saucony, On, Skechers Performance, New Balance, and Newton, alongside running glasses, water bottles, headbands, hats, Swiftwick socks, nutrition and hydration aids, and a variety of technical athletic wear for men and women in extended sizes. The service and customer attention, however, is where the shop really runs circles around the competition. Led by Craig, the passionate, knowledgeable, staff offer scientific sizing, gait analysis, and biomechanical assessments, and they hold workshops and runs throughout the week. *441 W. Canfield St., www.run-detroit.com, (313) 638-2831.*

Sfumato - Located in a Victorian mansion in the heart of Midtown, this dynamic destination is equal parts boutique perfumery and craft cocktail hideaway. By day, the artfully designed space serves as the flagship retail location for **Sfumato**, a Detroit-based fragrance house specializing in all-natural and gender-neutral fragrances that utilize natural and organic ingredients. All of the diverse aromas are intoxicating, deep, and complex, but our favorite is Siren Song, a delightful perfume with floral, clove, and pepper notes. By night, murphy tables and benches unfold from around the shop's dark wood shelves, transforming the garden-level space into **Castalia**, an intimate, art deco-inspired bar that serves cocktails created specifically to pair with the shop's signature scents. Offering a one-of-a-kind cocktail experience highlighting the sensory interplay of smell and taste, whether you choose your drink based on flavor or on fragrance, the harmony and balance of Castalia's cocktails (served with scented napkins) truly piques the senses. Unique cocktail ingredients like small-batch bitters are also available for purchase. *3980 Second Ave., www.sfumatofragrances.com and www.castaliacocktails.com, (313) 305-1442.*

★**Shinola Detroit** - Launched in 2011 by Tom Kartosis, the founder of Fossil, Shinola is a powerhouse luxury goods maker, manufacturing (and/or assembling) quality watches, bicycles, leathergoods, and other items in their storefront and 30,000-square-foot factory in New Center, an operation that employs upwards of 400 workers in Detroit. Opened in 2013, and housed in a former factory space, the gorgeous, light-filled Canfield Street storefront is massive and engaging. Enormous skylights punctuate the ceiling, and the refined space bustles and constantly takes on new forms. The retail floor features displays highlighting the full Shinola range, a large open bicycle assembly workshop, and glass bays that rotate in use—from bringing aspects of the manufacturing process onsite, to highlighting specific products, to hosting long-term pop-ups. For the uninitiated, the Shinola line is firmly within the luxury spectrum, but it is incredibly diverse, including not only watches (starting at

$550), bicycles (starting at $1,000), and everyday leather goods, but high-quality items as disparate as elaborate totes and backpacks, baseballs, record turntables, and headphones—an impressive offering. But don't worry, you can purchase a sleek, branded journal ($16) and walk out with an iconic black shopping bag, too. Near the entrance to the store, visitors will also find the **Shinola Cafe**, a premium full-service cafe, with pour-over coffee, espresso drinks, cold beverages, and an assortment of locally baked treats. For a tour of the New Center Factory, call 844-744-6652. *441 W. Canfield St., www.shinola.com, (313) 285-2390.*

Source Booksellers - This cozy neighborhood bookstore started as a passion project for owner Janet Webster Jones, who spent 40 years as an educator in the Detroit Public Schools before founding Source Booksellers in 2002. The focus here is firmly on non-fiction, where the well-curated shelves are stocked with tomes detailing everything from ancient African history and stories of the civil rights movement, to studies of the metaphysical and spiritual, to guides on urban gardening and bicycle maintenance. The large children's section is filled with many lesser-known gems, particularly if you're looking for books that focus on social justice or under-represented communities. Janet and her warm team offer unprecedented knowledge of the store's foci, ensuring that you'll walk away a little bit smarter—and with what you need. The shop also regularly hosts a variety of community events ranging from author readings to musical performances to tai chi and yoga workshops. *4240 Cass Ave., www.sourcebooksellers.com, (313) 832-1155.*

Spiral Collective - Detroit artist Dell Pryor opened this Cass Corridor space in 2002 as a supportive community for female entrepreneurs and a venue to promote African-American artists. When you enter the cozy space, expect to be greeted with soothing, earthy scents and friendly smiles that will invite you to stay the whole afternoon. While several businesses have been a part of the collective over the years, it currently houses two:

- **Dell Pryor Gallery -** Dell Pryor is an institution of the Detroit art scene. An interior designer herself, she has been promoting and showing work by African-American artists in Detroit since the 1970s. First located in Eastern Market, she moved her gallery to Greektown and then Harmonie Park before founding this collective. In addition to varied relevant exhibitions, the gallery hosts artist talks, lectures, readings, and other special events.

- **Tulani Rose -** A charming lifestyle gift boutique, owner Sharon Pryor opened her shop in Harmonie Park in 1997 before moving to this collective on Cass when it was founded by her mother. The perfect place to find thoughtful gifts such as fine soaps, candles, decorative notebooks, scarves, Detroit tote bags, and jewelry, Pryor's warm personality, taste, and knowledge of the neighborhood always makes it a pleasure to visit.

4201 Cass Ave., www.dellpryorgalleries.com, (313) 833-6990 (Dell Pryor Gallery), (313) 832-2477 (Tulani Rose).

★ **Third Man Records Cass Corridor -** A Detroit native, Jack White, of the White Stripes, launched Third Man in 2001. Once a small imprint, the label has a large, devoted following and is a leader in the vinyl revival movement. This location, the second for the company, opened in 2015, and is located not far from where White earned his stripes. Equal parts store, musical attraction, vinyl pressing plant, and venue, the destination is a must for music lovers. Visitors can buy records—which are pressed on-site—including the work of White and other contemporary artists, archival re-reissues from Motown and other labels, and documentary compilations—as well as a diverse and fanciful selection of branded merchandise, ranging from wiffle ball sets to high-end turntables. The store, housed in a former industrial space, is stunning and polished, decked to the gills with Third Man's trademark day-glo and the White Stripes' trademark starlight mint, with something curious to admire around every turn. Look for curiosities like an antique voice-to-record booth ($20 per session), a black-and-yellow photo booth, an animatronic jukebox, and a viewing area where guests can watch the fascinating record-pressing process in action. Located in the rear of the store, the full-scale pressing plant is one of just a handful in the United States and it is a captivating wonder. Third Man also hosts frequent shows, including local bands, national acts, and occasionally White himself, which are often recorded direct to acetate for the Live at Third Man series. *441 W. Canfield St., www.thirdmanrecords.com, (313) 209-5205.*

Third Wave Music - Operated by the endearing Jen David and Jeffrey Thomas, who earned their stripes as fixtures on Detroit's vibrant music scene, Third Wave is Detroit's only full-service musical instrument shop. Located on the garden level of the historic Forest Arms building, the store is a charming, welcoming, friendly space for musicians of all persuasions and abilities. The shop offers new, used, and vintage instruments and equipment (for when you decide that you want to try your hand at guitar), a suite of repair services (for when you rock a little too hard), a full slate of lessons (for when you realize you need a little help actualizing your potential), as well as trade-ins (for when you realize you're definitely more of a synthesizer person). *4625 Second Ave., www.thirdwavedetroit.com, (313) 312-0995.*

Wayne State University Farmers Market - Founded by an Urban Planning professor at the school, the Wayne State University Farmers Market is a small but mighty open-air market in front of Wayne's Business School Building, a modernist gem designed by Minoru Yamasaki. The market boasts one to two dozen vendors every week, including farmers, horticulturists, local bakeries, and restaurants. Though it's relatively new to the neighborhood, it's become a popular lunchtime destination during the sunnier months. The market is open from 11am to 4pm on Wednesdays from June to October. *Cass Ave. between W. Kirby St. and Putnam St. www.clas.wayne.edu/seedwayne.*

Will Leather Goods - This stunning leather palace is truly a paradise for fans of finely crafted leather goods—a fact that's evident from the aroma that wafts through the door upon opening it. Though originally a Detroiter, Will Adler founded the premium brand in his adopted home of Oregon, and now has eight stores in as many cities. This location, one of the company's largest, is housed in an enormous, airy, light-filled space with 20-foot ceilings, and a small mezzanine level. Centered around an elaborately constructed cow-hide teepee (demonstrating the historical use of hides in the American west), the character-filled space is dotted with eye-catching antique displays and a bounty of the signature line. The gorgeous selection spans heirloom-quality bags, totes, clutches, purses, notebooks, sports equipment, and accessories including belts, wallets, bracelets, sandals, gloves, keychains, and just about everything in between. As an added bonus, almost all products can be custom-embossed on-site. If you've got the cheddar, check out this leather—the store is gorgeous and worth a visit. The space also features an occasional pop-up coffee shop as well as a small community-oriented gallery. *4120 Second Ave., www.willleathergoods.com/pages/detroit-store, (313) 309-7892.*

CULTURAL ATTRACTIONS

Center Galleries - Since 1997, the College for Creative Studies has enriched Detroit's cultural scene with inspiring art exhibitions, literary readings, artist forums, and film screenings through Center Galleries, a cluster of four modern spaces housed in the Manoogian Visual Resource Center. The building itself stands as a work of art, featuring geometric orange metal ornamentation atop its contemporary cement-slab roof. Inside, the lobby features student art exhibitions, which leads to the Alumni and Faculty Hall, the College's Permanent Collection Gallery, and the Main Gallery. Each space hosts rotating exhibitions and special events—check the website for upcoming happenings. When in the building, check out the Manoogian Visual Resource Center Library, which holds more than 40,000 art and design books and 250 periodicals. Only CCS students can check out library materials, but the public is welcome to browse its fantastic collection of hard-to-find magazine titles. Main gallery closed in the summer months. *301 Frederick Douglass Ave., www.collegeforcreativestudies.edu/center_galleries, (313) 664-7800.*

★ **Charles H. Wright Museum of African American History -** Founded in 1965 by its namesake physician, the Charles H. Wright Museum has grown to become one of the largest institutions dedicated to African-American history in the world. The monumental, Sims-Varner-designed structure features a beautiful 100-foot-in-diameter stained glass dome, and a contemporary, minimalist facade adorned with aluminum and gold ornamentation by artist Richard Bennett crafted in the style of Malian Bambara masks. The 120,000-square-foot museum houses a permanent collection of more than 30,000 artifacts and archival materials, seven exhibition areas, a 317-seat theater, the Latimer Cafe refreshments area, as well as four research repositories and historical collections. In addition to rotating special exhibits, the museum offers a 22,000-square-foot core exhibition, "And Still We Rise: Our Journey Through African American History and Culture," which uses interactive installations to chronicle African-American history from prehistory to present. The stunning Ford Freedom Rotunda—and its *Ring of Genealogy*, a 37-foot-wide terrazzo tile mosaic by local artist Hubert Massey—shouldn't be missed. *315 E. Warren Ave., www.thewright.org, (313) 494-5800.*

College for Creative Studies - This Midtown anchor arts college offers undergraduate and graduate degrees in its varied, highly regarded programs from automotive design to crafts, industrial design, photography, and illustration. Members of the public can attend CCS' Toyota Lecture Series on art and design, featuring acclaimed artists and designers such as Stefen Sagmeister and Ken Walker. Additionally, CCS offers a comprehensive, affordable summer and semester-long continuing education courses in a wide array of art and design disciplines for adults and youth in ten-week, three-week, and workshop formats. *201 E. Kirby St., www.collegeforcreativestudies.edu, (313) 664-7400.*

Detroit Artists Market - A nonprofit contemporary gallery, the Detroit Artists Market was founded in the 1930s by a group of local art patrons as a venue for young Detroit artists to exhibit and sell their work. Within a few years, the gallery grew to exhibit emerging and established artists of all ages. These days, DAM continues to do wonderful work in the city, featuring contemporary work from Detroit and the region in creative and thought-provoking exhibitions installed in its gorgeous, modern gallery space. The gallery shop carries a wonderful assortment of smaller artwork, jewelry, and paper goods year-round and expands into the whole gallery during the holidays, making it a favorite destination to shop for affordable smaller artworks and crafts for gift giving. The annual design show is a highlight of the year. *4719 Woodward Ave., www.detroitartistsmarket.org, (313) 832-8540.*

★ **Detroit Historical Museum** - Since its founding in 1928, the Detroit Historical Museum has grown to become one of the nation's largest museums dedicated to metropolitan history, attracting 100,000 visitors a year. In 2012, the museum underwent a $20 million renovation and modernized its beautiful 78,000-square-foot space. The museum's impressive collection spans 250,000 items, including a Ty Cobb game-used bat, a Purple Gang Tommy gun, an Art Deco fountain from Detroit's Hudson's department store, and one of Bob Seger's guitars. Strolling through the exhibits, visitors can experience Detroit's 300-plus-year history, evolving from a French trading post to the Motor City to Motown to present-day Detroit. Among the museum's many offerings, our favorites include:

- **Streets of Old Detroit** - This life-size exhibit puts you in a re-created vision of 19th-century Detroit, complete with brick streets and period storefronts, including a blacksmith, barbershop, bicycle shop, pharmacy, Sanders confectionary, and more.

- **America's Motor City** - Learn how and why Detroit became the automotive capital of the world, view a rotating collection of classic and rare cars, and learn how automobiles go from the pages of a sketchbook to the city streets. Visitors can even watch a Cadillac body being lowered onto its frame—a piece of a real assembly line from a now-defunct factory.

- **Kid Rock Music Lab** - As an homage to the city's music legends and their contributions to rock, gospel, jazz, soul, techno, and funk, this interactive exhibit features original photos and posters, historical memorabilia, videos, countless artifacts, such as Kevin Saunderson's mixing board, and an interactive kiosk that allows visitors to mix songs.

- **Detroit: The Arsenal of Democracy** - This exhibit highlights the city's contribution to World War II war efforts and the conflict's effect on Detroit, through thoughtful installations of ephemera, historical documents, photos, and interactive displays. The exhibit is organized into three focus areas: the factory, the community, and the home.

- **Doorway to Freedom - Detroit and the Underground Railroad** - To better understand the city's role in the network of safe houses and abolitionists that comprised the antebellum Underground Railroad, visitors follow an interactive, experiential, information-packed trail illustrative of those taken by Canada-bound slaves.

- **Legends Plaza** - An outdoor plaza featuring the handprints and signatures in cement of dozens of notable Detroiters, including Thomas Hearns, Sam Raimi, Elmore Leonard, Juan Atkins, Dave Bing, Alice Cooper, and Al Kaline.

5401 Woodward Ave., www.detroithistorical.org, (313) 833-1805.

★ **Detroit Institute of Arts** - One of the finest art museums in the country, the DIA is an essential stop, not only for art lovers, but for any visitor to the city. Its encyclopedic collection, consisting of more than 65,000 works, includes art from around the world and from prehistory to today. The breadth and quality of the collection—on view in more than 100 galleries—is what sets it apart, and there is an abundance of extraordinary work in every collection, from ancient Egyptian to contemporary. Of particular note:

- The astonishing, 27-panel *Detroit Industry* fresco cycle by Diego Rivera, painted between 1932 and 1933. Commissioned by Edsel Ford and museum director William Valentiner, Rivera considered these frescoes to be his best work.

- Large-scale outdoor works by notable artists, including August Rodin's *The Thinker*, Alexander Calder's *Jeune Fille et sa Suite*, and a 30-ton, 27-foot tall geometric 1961 Tony Smith sculpture, *Gracehoper*.

- The DIA's African art collection (which is one of the finest in the country) including works from nearly 100 cultures. A highlight is a masterpiece 19th century *Kongo Nail Figure* sculpture.

- The American galleries in general, and specifically John Singleton Copley's *Watson and the Shark*, Frederic Edwin Church's *Cotopaxi*, James Abbott McNeill Whistler's *Nocturne in Black* and *Gold: The Falling Rocket*, John Singer Sargent's *Mosquito Nets*, and John Sloan's *McSorley's Bar*.

- The colorful brick Dragon from the *Ishtar Gate* at Babylon (604–562 B.C.E.).

- The Asian galleries including the popular *Reeds and Cranes* screens by Suzuki Kiitsu.

- An incredible 15th-century Qur'an written on colored Chinese paper.

- Exquisite Native American textiles and beadwork.
- Small but popular galleries exhibiting Egyptian mummies and artifacts.
- The awe-inspiring Great Hall off the Woodward entrance, lined with suits of armor.
- The European art collection, which is one of the largest and most distinguished in the country, was founded with a gift of 100 Old Master paintings from newspaper magnate James Scripps in 1889, and features a broad range of media from across the continent spanning periods from ancient Greece to modern works from first half of the 20th century. Notable artists include Pieter Bruegel the Elder, Giovanni Bellini, Titian, Rembrandt van Rijn, Andrea and Luca Della Robbia, Edgar Degas, Paul Cézanne, Georges Seurat, Caravaggio, Peter Paul Rubens, Auguste Rodin, Vincent Van Gogh, Pablo Picasso, Henri Matisse, and many, many others. The German Expressionist collection is one of the museum's strengths, and the DIA was the first American museum to collect a painting by Van Gogh—*Self-Portrait with Straw Hat*, from 1887.
- The Department of Prints, Drawings, and Photographs is one of the museum's most diverse collections, with about 35,000 prints, drawings, photographs, watercolors, posters and artists' books from the 16th century to the present including studies by Michelangelo for the Sistine Chapel and prints by Albrecht Durer.
- The museum's GM Center for African American Art was one of the first curatorial departments dedicated to African-American art at any museum. Established in 2000, highlights of the collection include works by Benny Andrews, Romare Bearden, Jacob Lawrence, Martin Puryear, Lorna Simpson, and Carrie Mae Weems.
- The James Pearson Duffy Department of Contemporary Art collection, which spans the period from the mid-20th century to the present day, including notable works by Willem de Kooning, Donald Judd, Andy Warhol, Eva Hesse, Alberto Giacometti, Claes Oldenburg, Judy Pfaff, Francis Bacon, and many others, including numerous younger contemporary artists.

Founded in 1885, the DIA moved to its current location 1927, an incredible, stately Beaux-Arts building designed by Paul Cret. Two wings were added in the 1960s and 1970s, and a major renovation and expansion was completed in 2007 making the museum its current 658,000 square feet. The DIA hosts crowd-pleasing special exhibitions, regular Friday night music performances that are free with admission, and a variety of special events, including free art-making workshops every Friday, Saturday, and Sunday and lectures by important contemporary artists, designers, and critics. It also houses the **Detroit Film Theatre** (see separate entry), an elegant cafeteria, a great gift shop, a 380-seat lecture hall, a coffee shop housed in an astounding formerly open-air courtyard, a state-of-the-art conservation laboratory, and a research library holding a quarter million volumes. In 2012, three Southeastern Michigan counties (Wayne, Oakland, and Macomb) came together to pass a millage to support the museum, in a reassuring show of regional support for this incredible cultural jewel. As a result, residents of these counties have free, unlimited general museum admission and access to expanded programs. If you happen to not be an art lover already, the DIA is the place to become one—the information-rich interpretive displays don't assume that every viewer is an expert, and curators and educators take time to contextualize the work for a broad audience. *5300 Woodward Ave., www.dia.org, (313) 833-7900.*

★ **Detroit Main Library** - This treasure trove is the anchor of the massive 4.2 million-volume Detroit Public Library system, which, after the University of Michigan's collection, is the second largest in the state. Within the walls of the building—completed in 1921 and designed by U.S. Supreme Court architect Cass Gilbert—the library's vast collection includes books, vinyl records, and contemporary media. Of special interest are:

- The massive **Burton Historical Collection** of Detroit historical documents, which is a boundless and essential resource for genealogists and historians and is where visitors can peruse and touch authentic maps, photographs, records, and histories from the past 300 years.

- **The Ernie Harwell Sports Collection**, seeded by a donation from the legendary Tigers sportscaster in 1966, consists of books, team annuals, media guides, programs, scorecards, baseball cards, clippings, photographs, recordings, and artifacts from the city's rich sports history.

- **The E. Azalia Hackley Collection of African Americans in the Performing Arts**, which opened in 1943, includes books, manuscripts, and historical documents, with dance, blues, jazz, soul, and electronic music well represented. Documents from Motown Records are a special highlight.

- The Rare Book Collection, which opened in 1948, includes a Babylonian tablet, a Gutenberg Bible, original manuscripts to the *Little House on the Prairie*, *Tom Sawyer*, and *Huckleberry Finn*, an irreplaceable facsimile copy of Handel's original Messiah score (complete with cross-outs and droplets of perspiration), as well as thousands of other priceless first editions and other printed artifacts.

- The media libraries which, in addition to sizeable CD and DVD offerings, still lend from their incredible library of vinyl records.

- A Microfilm library of historic American newspapers, including the *Detroit Free Press*, *Detroit News*, and *New York Times* dating back to 1873—as well as digital access to even older materials.

201 Woodward Ave., www.detroit.lib.mi.us/branch/main, (313) 481-1300.

Elaine L. Jacob Gallery - This beautiful, bi-level gallery on the campus of Wayne State University presents work by contemporary regional, national, and international artists across media. It opened in 1997 as part of a mid-1990s addition to Old Main (see separate entry), the 1897 architectural symbol of the university. Its clean design, elegant spiral staircase, and abundant light provided by a dramatic 20-foot-by-40-foot wall of windows make it an exquisite space in which to encounter a variety of exceptional work. *480 W. Hancock St., www.art.wayne.edu/jacob_gallery.php, (313) 993-7813.*

Galerie Camille - Originally founded in Boston in 1987, Galerie Camille opened this larger, permanent space in Midtown, Detroit in 2013. Occupying the back suite of a building that was once a truck car wash (look for the large metal door inside), visitors can step into this serene environment to enjoy high-caliber contemporary art secluded from the bustle of the Cass Corridor. Featuring established and emerging artists from Detroit and abroad, the artwork shown is a mix of painting, photography, sculpture, and installations. Exhibitions are up for approximately five to six weeks. Regular programming includes opening receptions, artist talks, and events, including yoga, pop-up exhibitions, and performances. The gallery spans three rooms, with an impressive central space with soaring ceilings, and is available for event rental. *4130 Cass Ave. Suite C, www.galeriecamille.com, (313) 974-6737.*

Gordon L. Grosscup Museum of Anthropology - Named for famed Wayne State University archaeologist Gordon Grosscup, the Grosscup Museum is a small, well-curated, 1,500-square-foot museum featuring an array of permanent and travelling exhibits. Although it offers exhibits on a range of topics—from Congolese fetish figures to Anishnabeg artifacts—some of its most compelling installations draw from Wayne State's long work performing archaeological digs at major downtown development sites. The artifacts extracted from sites such as Kennedy Square, 150 West Jefferson, the Hotel Pontchartrain, and the Renaissance Center tell fascinating stories about Detroit's earliest residents and contemporary development projects. The incredibly friendly and knowledgeable staff can help you use the impressive research equipment, including binocular and polarizing microscopes, thin-sectioning equipment, and a kiln. *4841 Cass Ave., 1st floor Old Main, www.clas.wayne.edu/anthromuseum, (313) 577-2598.*

★**G.R. N'Namdi Gallery -** The G.R. N'Namdi Gallery is the focus of the spectacular **N'Namdi Center for Contemporary Art**, housed in a vast, 16,000-square-foot facility punctuated by a cobalt blue facade. Prominent local collector George N'Namdi founded the gallery in Harmonie Park in 1981, and after several moves, found a home in this renovated former auto garage in 2010, as a cultural anchor of the recently resurrected historic Sugar Hill Arts District. The interior, with its soaring, open ceilings and warm, reclaimed wooden floors, houses four exhibition spaces, as well as a performance space called the Black Box. Originally intended to showcase N'Namdi's extensive collection of African-American art (including works by the likes of Benny Andrews, Romare Bearden, Chakaia Booker, Jacob Lawrence, and Hughie Lee-Smith), the gallery's focus has broadened to include an exciting exhibition schedule of work in a range of styles and media by local, national, and international artists. *52 E. Forest Ave., www.nnamdicenter.org, (313) 831-8700.*

Hellenic Museum of Michigan - A young cultural institution celebrating Greeks and their rich contributions to Detroit—and the world—the Hellenic Museum opened its doors in 2009. While the organization—which is housed in the exquisite historic Sherer Mansion (notably the birthplace of the gel capsule)—is still expanding its scope, it aspires to be a "mouseion"—a "house of muses"—where visitors can learn about Hellenic culture through exhibitions, workshops, and programming. Currently, the museum exhibits a selection of ephemera from Greece and the golden age of Greek Detroit—including the ornate original door from the legendary Greektown restaurant New Hellas—and holds regular events, including film screenings, social hours, cultural celebrations, demonstrations, and tastings. Look for upcoming events on the museum's Facebook page. *67 E. Kirby St., www.hellenicmi.org, (313) 871-4100.*

Josephine F. Ford Sculpture Garden - Built in 2005 in a collaboration between Cultural Center behemoths the Detroit Institute of Arts (see separate entry) and College for Creative Studies (see separate entry) with funds from Josephine Ford (granddaughter of Henry), this majestic sculpture garden is the only one of its kind in the city. Stop here to take a break or have a picnic lunch while basking in the presence of nine large-scale, jaw-dropping works from the DIA's collection, including pieces from 20th-century art-world heavy-hitters Richard Serra, Beverly Pepper, and Alexander Calder. In addition to the art, the 2-acre garden features an elliptical walkway that connects CCS buildings, benches along the walk, and a variety of trees and plantings. Open to the public 24 hours a day. *John R. St. and E. Kirby St.*

★ **Michigan Science Center** - The Michigan (née Detroit) Science Center has existed to provide youthful and inquisitive minds a venue to engage and explore scientific concepts since opening in 1970. Now the tenth-largest science museum in the country, the original storefront science center has been expanded repeatedly over the years, becoming a polished and modern facility that provides hundreds of hands-on exhibits ideal for families, groups, or simply the curious. Explore everything from space, health, physical science, engineering, and more through live stage shows and science demonstrations: the Smithsonian Spark!Lab that engages children in the process of invention and entrepreneurship; Kids Town gallery, a child-size town that encourages social and motor skill development; and the STEM Playground, where kids learn how science applies to the real world. The science center also boasts the largest movie screen in Michigan, a domed IMAX which doubles as a planetarium, and a 4D theater, in addition to a an auditorium for examining electromagnetism and other principles at play, and rotating exhibits. Science education can be stereotyped for being too dry or abstract— but the Science Center's method of using colorful, stimulating, and educational activities guarantees this won't be a problem. Open Tuesday through Sunday. *5020 John R. St., www.mi-sci.org, (313) 577-8400.*

★ **Museum of Contemporary Art Detroit** - Located in the Sugar Hill Arts District, the Museum of Contemporary Art Detroit presents art at the forefront of contemporary culture. The museum opened its doors in late 2006 and has featured work by internationally renowned contemporary artists like Barry McGee, Kara Walker, Alex Melamid, Martin Creed, Yona Friedman, Mike Kelley, Dave Eggers, and Rob Pruitt, along with local favorites like Gordon Newton, Tyree Guyton, and Carey Lorenn. The raw and industrial, 22,000-square-foot former auto dealership transforms every three months to showcase a new temporary exhibition. Each exhibition is accompanied by a series of public programs that include musical performances, films, readings, lectures, creative and family workshops, gallery tours, and sometimes raucous dance parties. The museum also houses the MOCAD Store, which features art and design books, art objects and other hard-to-find goods, as well as the exceptional Cafe 78 bar and cafe (see separate entry). Except for openings and special events, admission is free. Guided tours are available on a regular basis. *4454 Woodward Ave., www.mocadetroit.org, (313) 832-6622.*

Scarab Club - Founded in 1907 by a group of artists, the venerable Scarab Club built this Renaissance Revival building in 1928 to serve as its clubhouse. The interior features exquisite tilework from Pewabic Pottery, warm woodwork, a bright gallery space, and a charming outdoor brick-walled garden. Walk upstairs to visit the six gorgeous artist studios and the cozy upstairs lounge with ceiling beams signed by acclaimed artists who have visited, including Diego Rivera, Marcel Duchamp, Norman Rockwell, Marshall Fredericks, and John Sinclair. In the club's early years, its annual costume balls were the most important social occasion in the city—*Life* magazine even published a two-page spread of photos of the 1937 "Scarabean

Cruise" ball. Today, the institution maintains its identity as a lively club for working artists with a full exhibition schedule and classes, workshops, and events for members and the public. The space is available for private events. *217 Farnsworth St., www.scarabclub.org, (313) 831-1250.*

★ **Simone DeSousa Gallery** - One of the few galleries in the city to actively represent local artists (in addition to showing their work), owner and director Simone DeSousa's namesake space exhibits stunning contemporary works and actively engages with the community to foster a new culture of art appreciation. The gallery's mission is to make art accessible and personally meaningful to metro Detroiters, and the space usually presents solo and group artist shows—including the occasional performance piece or inventive installation on the patio. The gallery has highlighted significant work from legendary Cass Corridor artists, including Jim Chatelain, Michael Luchs, Ellen Phelan, and Robert Sestok. Adjacent to the space is the gallery's store **Edition**, where you can see and purchase unique limited-edition art and design pieces—including ceramics, art prints, crafted jewelry, and design objects—by artists from Detroit and beyond, including some of city's most prominent contemporary talents. *444 W. Willis St., www.simonedesousagallery.com, (313) 833-9000.*

Walter P. Reuther Library - Located on the Wayne State University campus, the Walter P. Reuther Library is a contemporary four-story concrete and glass building that has the distinction of being North America's largest archive dedicated to labor and urban affairs. With a mission "to collect, preserve and provide access to the documentary and visual heritage of the American labor movement," the library boasts more than 2,000 distinct collections related to labor, with topics ranging from the history of mainstream organizing, to minorities in the labor movement, to radical splinter initiatives. In addition, the library also contains healthy archives of historical information related to the city of Detroit, social welfare, health care, politics, civil rights, women's rights, Detroit's regional social communities, and Wayne State University's history and development. In recent years, the institution has made efforts to increase accessibility through digitization of documents and artifacts, some of which date to the 1800s. Generally, an appointment is needed for access to the archives. *5401 Cass Ave., www.reuther.wayne.edu, (313) 577-4024.*

Wayne State University Art Department Gallery - Since 1956, Wayne State University has featured artwork by prominent Michigan artists and WSU students and faculty in this gallery, where tall windows stretch floor to ceiling along one long side of the space, creating a light-filled, clean, white setting that is perfect for showcasing the work. Highlights of the annual exhibition schedule are the WSU Undergraduate, MFA thesis, and faculty exhibitions. Because this gallery caters to students, it is closed on weekends and has more limited summer hours, so check the website before going. *5400 Gullen Mall, www.art.wayne.edu/communityarts_gallery.php, (313) 993-7813.*

Wayne State University Planetarium - A longtime favorite among children, stargazers, and guidebook writers alike, the Wayne State University Planetarium is a large, state-of-the-art digital projection facility. This 59-seat planetarium hosts weekly 90-minute events on Friday nights. While every event includes interactive demonstrations and current night sky presentations, all conclude with one of its many full dome films, from the scientific documentary *Black Hole: The Other Side of Infinity*, to the children's animated adventure video *Zula Patrol: Down to Earth*. To ensure a seat, planetarium-hounds typically come 15 to 20 minutes early. Visit its website for schedules. *4841 Cass Ave., www.planetarium.wayne.edu, Room 0209, (313) 577-2107.*

ENTERTAINMENT & RECREATION

Bill's Recreation - The last of an old breed, Bill's is strictly a pool hall—there's no alcohol or gambling, just pool played by a contingent of a few dozen regulars, mostly older men who come to play specialty skill games like bank or one-pocket for a modest hourly rate. Built in 1921, the hall itself is a den of staid utility. The lamps are low-slung fluorescent tubes, small black chalkboards used to keep score are tacked to the building's columns, old strands of beads used to score straight pool are slung over tables, and the solid wood tables— estimated to be more than 60 years old—are set with wood racks. The hall was used as a filming location for the movie *Sparkle*, which paid for all the tables to be resurfaced. Newcomers are welcome but should arrive with the necessary chops to keep up. Bottled G-rated drinks and snacks available. *3525 Third Ave., (313) 833-4238.*

Bonstelle Theatre - One of two landmark theatres owned by Wayne State University featuring student actors, the Bonstelle is housed in a century-old Beaux-Arts neoclassical building that emulates the

Pantheon. Originally the Temple Beth-El Synagogue, the building was designed by Albert Kahn and completed in 1902. In 1924, C. Howard Crane was retained to oversee a conversion of the building into a theatre. Unfortunately, the Bonstelle had to shed its front columns when Woodward was widened in the 1930s, but the sizable auditorium, with its ample apron, is still striking and comfortably seats 1,200 patrons for its regular live performances and Broadway-style plays. The players at Bonstelle—WSU undergraduates—perform dramas, comedies, musicals, and show pieces, with full-run shows running four times per year. *3424 Woodward Ave., www.bonstelle.com, (313) 577-2960.*

Cinema Detroit - Located in a space that took turns as a school and furniture store before becoming Midtown's homey, local microtheater, Cinema Detroit is where you can get cozy next to strangers on vintage couches and loveseats while enjoying the latest films. The theater is run by lifelong Detroiters (and lifelong movie lovers) Paula and Tim Guthat. It seems only fitting that when the two met, Tim was the entertainment editor of the college newspaper and Paula was the movie reviewer. That sounds like a rom-com in the making! Cinemagoers today will find a curated selection of the best in independent, foreign, arthouse, genre, and cult classic films, along with the occasional big-budget blockbuster, special event, and focused, eclectic series. Don't miss the classic snacks, including Sour Patch Kids, Faygo sodas, and other treats starting at just $1—and absolutely don't miss the freshly made popcorn! Siskel and Ebert would have given Cinema Detroit "two thumbs up." *4126 Third Ave., www.cinemadetroit.org, 313.482.9028.*

★**Detroit Film Theatre** - Attached to the Detroit Institute of Arts (see separate entry), the Detroit Film Theatre is where local cinephiles go to see movies they aren't likely to find anywhere else in Metro Detroit. Specializing in art films, documentaries, international, and classic cinema, the DFT is also known for its outstanding special programs, including live film accompaniment, lectures by noted filmmakers, and themed series. (Recurring programs of note include Academy Award-nominated short films, an animation showcase, high-definition opera broadcasts, and annual performances by silent film accompanists The Alloy Orchestra.) Every DFT season is a carefully curated treasure trove of new and classic cinema that brings the wide world of film art to Detroit. And the grand 1927 theatre itself, with its resplendent architectural detail, is nothing to sneeze at; in the age of the multiplex, it remains a true movie palace. Before screenings, enjoy a snack and a glass of wine in the second-floor Crystal Gallery Cafe. *5200 Woodward Ave., www.dia.org/dft, (313) 833-7900.*

Detroit Masonic Temple - As the largest Masonic Temple in the world, this Neo-Gothic limestone giant is a sight to behold. Designed by renowned architect George D. Mason, the cornerstone of the building was laid in 1922—with the same trowel used by George Washington to ceremonially start construction of the United States Capitol—but the gargantuan structure was not completed until 1926. The landmark, which towers over the lower Cass Corridor, is ornately decorated inside and out, with beautifully carved marble, sweeping staircases, and floor upon floor of tile mosaics, making the building one of the most opulent in Detroit. The temple is a labyrinth of hallways, corridors, and passageways, and boasts 1,000 rooms, including numerous ballrooms, sanctuaries, theaters, a cathedral, a drill hall, and a signature seven-story auditorium. Since the day it opened, the Masonic Temple has hosted a variety of events, shows, and organizations, a tradition that continues today, as visitors come weekly for fairs, elaborate parties, a wide range of concerts, theatrical performances, off-Broadway shows, and the Detroit Derby Girls (see separate entry), who are based out of the venue. Come for an event or a tour and try not to get lost. It's purported that the temple is haunted! *500 Temple St., www.themasonic.com, (313) 832-7100.*

Detroit Roller Derby - Roller derby is a competitive, full-contact extravaganza played on a flat track in which each team of five roller skaters attempts to help their offensive player, or "jammer," lap members of the opposing team by any means necessary. The Detroit Roller Derby league first introduced the Motor City to the sport in 2005. Comprised of four all-female home teams—with names like the Detroit Pistoffs and the Grand Prix Madonnas—that regularly battle one another, the league also fields three All-Star teams that take on challengers nationwide. Detroit Roller Derby bouts are bound to please, with halftime rock bands, glammed-out referees, and punk cheerleaders ensuring that every outing is a spectacle. Don't be intimidated by the brawling lasses. Though they have pseudonyms like Ruthless Bader Ginsburg, Wham!tramck, and Biscuits N Crazy, they come out and sign autographs after games. The regular season runs from November to June, with most matches at the Detroit Masonic Temple (see separate entry). *500 Temple St., www.detroitrollerderby.com.*

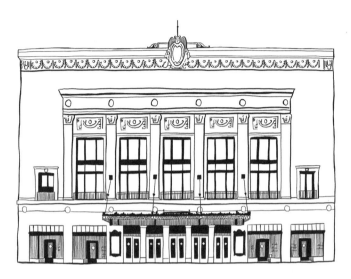

★ **Detroit Symphony Orchestra / Orchestra Hall / Max M. & Marjorie S. Fisher Music Center** - A major anchor of Midtown, the 2,014-seat historic **Orchestra Hall**, designed by C. Howard Crane in 1919, and famous for its perfect acoustics, is home to the world-renowned Detroit Symphony Orchestra (DSO). Though the symphony was founded in 1914, it was during the 1920s, on the back of the booming automobile industry, that the DSO became one of the most prominent orchestras in the country, performing with spectacular guest artists such as Enrico Caruso, Igor Stravinsky, Richard Strauss, Marian Anderson, Sergei Rachmaninoff, Isadora Duncan, Anna Pavlova, Jascha Heifetz, Pablo Casals, and others. Because of the strain of the Great Depression, the symphony was forced to leave its home in 1939, and though the hall enjoyed a stint as a jazz venue called the **Paradise Theater**—hosting greats such as Count Basie, Billie Holliday, Ella Fitzgerald, and Duke Ellington—and then became a church, it was scheduled for demolition in 1970. However, after a dedicated preservation effort, the hall was saved and was beautifully restored, and it became home to the symphony again in 1989. In 2003, a massive expansion was undertaken and the facility became known as the **Max M. & Marjorie S. Fisher Music Center**. Today, under Music Director Leonard Slatkin, the DSO enjoys a reputation as one of the top 10 orchestras in the United States. Regular offerings include a variety of concert programs for every age and taste, including classical, jazz, movie music, big band, seasonal performances, and more.
3711 Woodward Ave., www.detroitsymphony.com, (313) 576-5111.

★ **Garden Bowl -** A part of the Majestic Theater Complex and in business since 1913, the Garden Bowl is America's oldest continually operating bowling alley. Though it offers a full bar, it boasts a family-friendly environment during the day and is perfect for birthday parties or field trips. At night, the black lights come on, and the illuminated lanes lend a spacey, campy feel and the party starts. A variety of DJs keep the atmosphere upbeat, spinning anything from classic R&B to lo-fi punk rock. In addition to the regular revelry, the alley occasionally hosts concerts, with a stage suspended above the lanes, so one can quite literally "rock 'n' bowl." *4120 Woodward Ave., www.majesticdetroit.com, (313) 833-9700.*

The Garden Theater - After decades in ruin, and a modern stint as a blind pig, the richly historic Garden Theater was officially reopened in 2013. Constructed in 1912, and designed by acclaimed theater architect C. Howard Crane (of Fox Theatre fame, see separate entry), The Garden Theater originally featured an opulent garden theme, with a forest of live plants. While much of the interior was lost to time, the structure has been lovingly restored, with exposed brick walls and industrial touches that give the space a contemporary feel, complementing the ornamental and opulent original ceiling. The space features a split-level first floor, as well as a balcony, so depending on the event, the venue can host standing, seated, or tabled events. See the venue's website for a current schedule. *3929 Woodward Ave., www.thegardentheaterdetroit.com, (313) 832-0888.*

Hilberry Theatre - The repertory theatre for Wayne State University's competitive graduate theatre program, Hilberry productions leave crowds mesmerized and coming back. The theatre is based out of the former First Church of Christ Scientist building which was completed in 1917 in a neoclassical style with eight ionic columns set off by compound ramps greeting visitors from its Cass Avenue entrance. The Hilberry became Wayne State's graduate repertory theatre in 1964, after the building was remodeled to feature an intimate, 500-seat theatre with an oval, open stage. The season offers six to nine shows per year featuring canonical and contemporary comedies and dramas by MA and MFA students. Recently added to the basement is the Studio Theatre, an intimate 100-seat space for experimental works. *4743 Cass Ave., www.hilberry.com, (313) 577-2972.*

Lexus Velodrome - One of the nation's only indoor track-bicycle courses doubles as one of the city's most engaging cocktail spots. On the outside, this 64,000-square-foot behemoth resembles the Michelin Man's igloo. Inside, the space reads utilitarian, thanks to the imposing patchwork of metal supports and blond wood track anchoring the room, and the infield's central contemporary couches and concrete floor. The Velodrome offers three fields of play: the elevated, pitched tenth-of-a-mile bicycle track for Olympic-style sprints, scratches, and pursuits; a level perimeter track for jogging, walking, and inline skating; and a relaxing, lounge-like, track-side cocktail bar called **SpokeEasy** in the center. Guests can make use of the tracks through scheduled classes, open sessions, or weekly races, all booked online. With its primetime views of the elevated track, the spacious SpokeEasy offers craft and domestic bottles, a thoughtful selection of inventive cocktails, and an uncommonly diverse selection of wines, alongside a limited selection of bagged bar snacks. *601 Mack Ave., www.lexusvelodrome.com, (313) 265-6725.*

Little Caesars Arena / The Detroit Red Wings / The Detroit Pistons - Affectionately (and unaffectionately) called Pizzarena by locals, Little Caesars Arena (LCA) is home to not only one of the greatest hockey franchises in NHL history, but also a beloved and gritty NBA team. Completed in 2017, the arena has a capacity of 22,000, and features a unique glass-covered concourse called the Via, which connects the below-grade playing surface to shops, offices, and a slew of amenities. The arena cost a whopping $862.9 million to build, which was highly controversial, as taxpayer funds were tapped to make the project possible, and historic buildings were aggressively demolished to make way for construction. The interior features some compelling diversions, including signage from long lost **Olympia Stadium**, the player bench from **Joe Louis Arena** (which includes player standees, making it a popular photo opportunity), as well as unique action statues of famous Wings, historical exhibits, and memorabilia, but the anchoring restaurants—namely **Kid Rock's Made in Detroit** and **Mike's Pizza Bar**—should be considered more passing novelties than destinations. Despite a bevy of bells and whistles, Pizzarena's main attractions are Red Wings and Pistons games, as well as popular A-list musical acts, from Radiohead to Elton John. *2645 Woodward Ave., www.olympiaentertainment.com, (313) 471-7000.*

- **The Detroit Red Wings:** The most successful American National Hockey League (NHL) team of all time, and a member of the original six, Detroit's beloved Red Wings have 11 Stanley Cup Championships, and an endless roster of legendary Hall-of-Famers, including Gordie Howe (the NHL all-time points leader), Alex Delvecchio, Ted Lindsay, Nicklas Lidström, "The Captain" Steve Yzerman, and countless others. Their record-breaking success makes their popularity well justified, and is the reason that many still call Detroit Hockeytown. Even though the wings are in the beginning stages of a "rebuilding phase," the games are still thrilling and pack an exciting punch. The NHL season runs from fall to late spring. *www.redwings.nhl.com*

- **The Detroit Pistons:** One of eight remaining charter members of the National Basketball Association (NBA), the Detroit Pistons have led a storied existence since their founding in 1941. Playing in the Association's Eastern Conference Central Division, the Pistons have had many successful seasons, including championships in 1989, 1990, and 2004. However, the proudest time in the franchise's history was arguably the late 80's and early 90's when the Pistons gave Detroit the Bad Boys era of highly entertaining rough play—and consecutive championships in 1989 and 1990. Legendary Detroit Pistons include Isiah Thomas, Joe Dumars, Grant Hill, Ben Wallace, Jerry Stackhouse, Dave Bing (later elected Detroit's Mayor), Bill Laimbeer, and Dennis Rodman. Recent reshuffling and some smart trades have made the Pistons somewhat competitive again and a team to watch. The NBA season runs from fall to late spring. *www.nba.com/pistons.*

Magic Stick / Alley Deck - Located above the Garden Bowl (see separate entry), the **Magic Stick**, a vital part of the Majestic Theatre complex, served as a backbone to Detroit's explosive garage rock revival in the late 1990s and early 2000s. Bands such as The White

Stripes, The Von Bondies, The Detroit Cobras, The Dirtbombs, and more played here before touring the rest of the world, fuzz pedals and cigarettes in tow. Nowadays, the venue is consistently booked with local bands and national-touring acts, primarily of the indie rock variety, but with sizeable proportions of hip-hop, reggae, metal, and electronic, as well. With a standing capacity of about 250, the venue is spacious enough to relax by the bar and get a beer, yet intimate enough to catch the sweat dripping off of whatever sultry lead singer you're eying from the front row. Open seasonally, the **Alley Deck** is a second-story outdoor bar and patio located just outside of the Magic Stick, which subs in for an almost tropical getaway, complete with torch lighting and tiki decorations. Every Sunday morning, weather permitting, the Alley Deck is home to Bloody Marys, mimosas, cinnamon rolls, and other goodies guaranteed to stop a hangover—or at least delay its onset. *4120 Woodward Ave., www.majesticdetroit.com, (313) 833-9700.*

Majestic Theatre - At the time it was built in 1915, it was the largest movie-only theatre in the world. Undergoing numerous transformations through the years, including the addition of a glorious Art Deco façade prompted by the expansion of Woodward Avenue and requisite demolition of the original, historic frontage in the 1930s, the space became a live music venue in 1987. With the largest capacity of any venue in the Majestic Theatre complex, the venue plays host to everything from successful independent acts like Yo La Tengo, to world beat and hip-hop groups, and Juggalo gatherings. Note that the venue offers no seating aside from the bar, so plan to stand. *4120 Woodward Ave., www.majesticdetroit.com, (313) 833-9700.*

Trumbullplex - Established in 1993, the Trumbullplex is an anarchist collective that sprawls over two slightly disheveled turn-of-the-century Victorian mansions, an enviable vegetable garden, a chicken coop, a campfire pit, a large indoor performance venue, and a huge swath of green space. While the complex is not public per se, as it is home to at least a dozen residents at any given time, members of the collective are welcoming to passersby, especially like-minded allies of activism. The performance venue between the Victorian homes is a popular punk, metal, and folk venue for both local and indie touring acts. Additionally, among other offerings, the Tplex hosts parties, potlucks, and public open hours in its expansive zine library. An up-to-date schedule of events and hours can be found on the Trumbullplex website. *4210 Trumbull St., www.trumbullplex.org.*

Wayne State Warriors Football - Rah-Rah-Rah-Cis-Boom-Bah! Since 1918, the Warriors, who until 1999 were known as the fighting Tartars, have graced the gridiron at Wayne State University. Though the NCAA Division II team has historically been an underdog, they've been competitive in recent years, and play with heart and determination that is frequently missing from pro ball. While the team's home, Tom Adams Field, seats only 6,000, tickets are a bargain at just $8. Be sure to dress warmly in colder months. *5101 John C. Lodge Fwy., www.wsuathletics.com, (313) 577-0241.*

Willis Showbar - An Art Moderne gem inside and out, The Willis Showbar is a quadruple threat, offering not just good looks, but tasty cocktails, timeless entertainment, and an infamous, lurid past. If these walls could talk, they'd need to go to confession. An "entertainment" mainstay in the glory days of the rough and tumble Cass Corridor, legend has it that it wasn't what happened *in* the bar, but rather what happened *on* it that was so debaucherous. However, those days are past, and after forty years of quiet vacancy, the lovingly restored bar is now a showpiece. Stroll into the foyer, and peel back the curtain to reveal the dazzling delights inside. Reminiscent of the golden age of jazz, the centerpiece of the cozy showbar is the unusual cabaret stage, which is set behind the bar, granting patrons an unparalleled, intimate experience. With live jazz, blues, burlesque, and DJs nightly, perch at the bar or slide into the leather booths to soak in the atmosphere. The experience is only elevated by the elegant and perfectly prepared classic cocktails that feature contemporary twists to keep them interesting. *4156 Third Ave., www.willisshowbar.com, (313) 788-7469.*

SITES

Brush Park - In 1825, the completion of the Erie Canal enabled immigrants and industry to travel to Detroit by ship, spurring the growth of new development and opportunity in the city. In the early 1850s, enterprising developer Edmund Brush (son of the city's second Mayor, Elijah Brush) began developing his grandparents' ribbon farm into a stately neighborhood for the city's burgeoning contingent of wealthy residents. His development grew to encompass 300 two- and three-story homes across 24 blocks, and, to this day, it boasts magnificent brick homes built in the Second Empire, Gilded Age, Queen Anne, French Renaissance Revival, Romanesque,

and other Victorian styles. The structures showcase the skill and craftsmanship of the period, with mansard roofs, Romanesque columns, and cornices with intricate dentition. The streets in the area still carry the names he chose, including Adelaide for his mother, Alfred for his brother, Edmund for himself, Brush for his family, and Winder for his friend Colonel John Winder. However, a century after the neighborhood's meteoric rise, it began a long descent, with population loss and demolition taking heavy tolls. Although some blocks remain relatively historically intact, many have just two or three remaining original structures. Long a ghostly and poetic setting, with gorgeous 19th century homes—many of which were the worse for wear—juxtaposed alongside fields of tall weeds, a recent wave of development has hit Brush Park. Today, nearly all of the remaining original homes have been restored, and massive new-construction projects, including The Scott and City Modern developments, have brought increased density, and altered the character of the neighborhood. *Bounded by Mack Ave., Woodward Ave., Beaubien St., and the Fisher Fwy.*

Cathedral Church of St. Paul - This reserved architectural gem is one of the first examples of the late Gothic Revival style perfected by architect Ralph Adams Cram, who designed the century-old building. Though the church itself was completed in 1908, the parish dates to 1824, making it the oldest Episcopalian parish in the state. For the design of the building, Cram forewent a contemporary steel framework, favoring medieval construction techniques, so that the limestone structure is supported by only its own weight, and is an authentic representation of the period it emulates. The highlights of the relatively understated exterior of the cathedral are the towering pillars, pointed arches, and vermillion doors, while the interior is more ostentatious, with wide expanses of richly colored stained glass done in 13th- and 14th-century English styles—some of which was imported from a medieval Spanish cathedral, distinct Pewabic tile floor inlays, and an intricate wood reredo, which is representative of the elaborate woodwork throughout the cathedral. The building's impregnable stone construction creates the impression of a cloistered fortress for worshippers, but the parish of St. Paul—the home to the Episcopalian diocese of Michigan—is extremely active in community outreach. *4800 Woodward Ave., www.detroitcathedral.org, (313) 831-5000.*

City Sculpture - This art park features the large-scale metal sculptures of artist Robert Sestok, a leading figure in Detroit's Cass Corridor art movement throughout the 1960s and 1970s. Titled City Sculpture, the 29 welded sculptures that comprise the park are neatly laid out in a grid format, in what was once an abandoned lot alongside the John C. Lodge Service Drive. With the largest sculpture stretching 12 feet tall, and weighing in at about two tons, the pieces are massive, but also unique in form, and a study in deconstructivism. To fabricate the impressive pieces, Sestok made use of recycled material, such as propane tanks. Tip: Visit early or late in the day to see the interesting shadows cast by the sculptures. Check the park's website for a rotating exhibition schedule and events program. *955 W. Alexandrine St., www.citysculpture.org.*

East Ferry Street Historic District - Historically an upper-class Jewish and then black enclave, the neighborhood, comprised of East Ferry Street between Woodward Avenue and Brush Street, is a National Historic District, primarily featuring homes in the Late Victorian, Romanesque, and Queen Anne styles. The neighborhood was established when local farmer Dexter Ferry—founder of what is now the Ferry-Morse Seed Company—began to subdivide his farm in the 1880s. Though the neighborhood was built out with elaborate residences by the 1890s, it became a destination for ascendant Jewish professionals before the First World War. In the 1920s, a second demographic shift took hold, and the neighborhood became an upper-class extension of the vibrant, primarily African-American, Paradise Valley neighborhood, as white-collar black families began to move into the mansions in the area. Today, anchored by The Inn on Ferry Street and Wayne State University, the neighborhood is a stable—largely institutional—scenic destination for architecture aficionados. Though the East Ferry Historic District features an inspired array of stately homes from the end of the 19th century along the vernal stretch of closely-plotted residences, notable highlights include:

- **The Charles Lang Freer House:** A Queen Anne residence by architect Louis Kamper built of blue limestone. *71 E. Ferry St.*

- **The Colonel Frank J. Hecker House:** A distinct, awe-inspiring, Chateauesque design with stone turrets. *5510 Woodward Ave.*

- **The Inn on Ferry Street:** A four-home complex comprised of a mix of stately, well-preserved Victorian mansions. *84 E. Ferry St.*

- **The Lewis College of Business:** A Colonial Revival residence that is now the home of the Detroit Association of Women's Clubs. *5450 John R. St.*

- **Omega Psi Phi Fraternity:** A converted Romanesque Revival mansion. *235 East Ferry St.*

First Congregational Church - Originally located on the Detroit River when the parish was founded in 1844, First Congregational moved to its present location, a temple of impressive red limestone, in 1890. The building was designed in a mix of Romanesque and Byzantine styles by architect J. L. Faxon, featuring a campanile tower topped with an 8-foot green copper statue of the archangel Uriel. The church has a sanctuary and chapel resplendently decorated with ornate woodwork gilded with quotes from scripture. Visitors are treated to rose windows, cruciform brass chandeliers, an imposing organ installed over its wood foyer, and a domed ceiling ornamented with hagiographic paintings of the four Gospelers. The church considers itself a living museum, and so is open to the public to view its architecture, examine exhibits about the history and culture of the church, and visit the **Underground Railroad Living Museum**, a theatrical program of a tour and narrative storytelling about the Underground Railroad, including First Congregational's role in sheltering escaped slaves in the original church's basement while they awaited final transit to Windsor (charges apply, must be arranged in advance). *33 E. Forest Ave., www.friendsoffirst.com, (313) 831-4080.*

Grand River Creative Corridor - Cruise down this stretch of Grand River Avenue to see an outdoor art gallery that features more than 100 vibrant murals and free-standing art installations. Conceived of as a neighborhood revitalization initiative, the project is overseen by a non-profit called P.A.S.S.E.S. and continues to evolve with new work, both sanctioned and not. The artwork is most heavily concentrated between Rosa Parks Boulevard and Warren Avenue but works can be found as far north as Grand Boulevard, where the African Bead Museum stands (see separate entry). Many murals are on the sides or backs of buildings or off side streets from the main road; for example, make sure to go around the entirety of the American Integrated Supply and North End Studios (4250-4264 Grand River Avenue). A tip if you're driving: Start from one end and then turn around and drive back the opposite direction to get a second look and discover some hidden gems. *Grand River Ave. between Rosa Parks Blvd. and Grand Blvd.* Some notable murals to catch:

- **Abe in Shades** by Desiree Kelly, a humorous depiction of the 16th U.S. president in kaleidoscopic glasses. *4239 Grand River Ave.*

- **The Detroit Portrait Series** by Nicole Macdonald, a warehouse that features 16 "window" portraits of leaders and pioneers of justice, artists, and inventors from Detroit. *5729 Grand River Ave.*

- **World Peace** by Renda Writer, a striking meditation on the title. *Southeast corner of Grand River and Rosa Parks.*

- The cute, untitled cartoonish creatures by Patch Whisky. *4120 Grand River Ave.*

Old Main - A gargantuan icon of Midtown, Old Main—with its unmistakable clock tower, pitched roofs, and yellow bricks—is the most recognizable structure on Wayne State's campus. Originally Detroit's Central High School, the sprawling building hosted 2,000 students when classes began in 1896, the building's inaugural year. In 1917, after four years of offering college-level courses, the College of the City of Detroit began operating as a two-year college in the building. By 1925, the college, which eventually grew into Wayne State University, was the third largest in the state. Today, Old Main houses the College of Liberal Arts and Sciences as well as classes for students in the dance, visual arts, music, and geology programs. The building houses the William Grosscup Geology Museum, The Wayne State University Planetarium, and the Elaine L. Jacob Gallery, which are public, but have their own separate entries. *4841 Cass Ave.*

St. Josaphat Catholic Church - Constructed in the Victorian Romanesque style with Gothic and Baroque flourishes, St. Josaphat—established to accommodate Detroit's growing community of Polish immigrants—became the city's third Polish-speaking church in 1889. The exterior is comprised of red brick, carved sandstone, and a triad of steeples, sheltering an interior featuring Polish-style stained-glass windows—produced in 1903 by Detroit Stained Glass—ornate religious statuary, and elaborate murals beneath a vaulted ceiling. The nave is spectacular, and illuminated by a galaxy of small lights, evidence of the historical fascination with the electric light bulb—a technology that was en vogue when the building was completed more than 100 years ago. Additionally, there are five decorative altars, as well as murals with liturgical paintings above the confessionals. For travelers on southbound I-75, the church is one of the city's most popular architectural curiosities, as the three spires of the landmark line up perfectly with the towers of Downtown's Renaissance Center.

Traditional Tridentine Latin Mass is offered every Sunday morning. *691 E. Canfield St., www.historicstjosaphat.org, (313) 831-6659.*

West Canfield Historic District - A beautiful, stunningly preserved block of houses occupies Canfield Street, between Second and Third Avenues. In 1869, sisters Matilda Cass Ledyard and Mary Cass Canfield, daughters of Territorial Governor Lewis Cass, subdivided the block from their property and named Canfield Avenue after Mary Cass's late husband, Captain Augustus Canfield. Attracting prominent attorneys, architects, doctors, and dentists, to the area, the resulting, spectacular two- and three-story residences followed between 1870 and 1890 and feature a variety of styles, including Gothic Revival, Italianate, Second Empire, and Queen Anne. To this day, the intricately preserved mansions offer slate shingles, metal cresting, and ornate wooden trims, painted in era-appropriate colors. The West Canfield Historic District became Detroit's first local historic district in 1970, and it was listed on the Natural Register of Historic Places in 1971. Any visitor to Midtown should consider a stroll along the one-block historic street, which affords sightseers a picture-perfect cobblestone road, Victorian-style streetlamps, and tall, shady trees to complement the beautiful homes. *Canfield St. between Third Ave. and Second Ave.*

Woodbridge - Thanks to a strong, active community, Woodbridge, which is known for block after block of historic homes, was relatively unscathed by Detroit's historical penchant for demolition and redevelopment in the area. The neighborhood, which features houses and duplexes in the Victorian, Queen Anne, Colonial Revival, and Georgian Revival styles, was named for Michigan's second governor, William Woodbridge, who owned much of the property on which the neighborhood sits today. Housing demand created by the advent of the automobile industry and active streetcar lines on Trumbull Street and Grand River Avenue positioned the neighborhood as an early white-collar bedroom community for downtown office workers, and the area exploded between 1900 and 1920. However, after World War II, the population and stability of Woodbridge began to decline, as a countrywide trend of suburban migration took hold. In a misguided response to the neighborhood's perceived instability, in the 1960s, the City of Detroit and Wayne State University began an aggressive "urban renewal" campaign and razed as much as one-fifth of the neighborhood—mostly east of Trumbull—to make way for public housing and the expansion of the university. Fortunately, the dynamic neighborhood community responded with a formidable preservation effort, and the destructive attack was halted. Today, the Woodbridge area is a stable mix of families and students and boasts a strong sense of community and renewal. Neighborhood gardens have taken root in formerly vacant lots, and brightly hued art installations have popped up throughout the neighborhood. While nearly every home in the shady tree-lined neighborhood is stately, yet reserved, highlights include:

- **Northwood-Hunter House:** An inordinately elaborate French Renaissance mansion. *3985 Trumbull Ave.*

- **Castle Lofts:** A sprawling, stunning mansion in the French Châteauesque and French Renaissance styles that served for a time as the Eighth Precinct Police Station. *4150 Grand River Ave.*

- **The Ty Cobb Duplex:** The modest historic home of legendary Detroit Tiger Tyrus Cobb from 1913 to 1915. *4115 Commonwealth St.*

The remaining historic portion of the neighborhood is bounded by I-94 to the north, Lincoln St. to the east, Grand River Ave. to the south, and Avery St. to the west.

Yamasaki Architecture on the WSU Campus - In 1957, one of the 20th century's most prominent architects, Minoru Yamasaki, was hired by Wayne State University to develop a master plan that grew to include many of the features that define the campus today, including the streets closed to automotive traffic and the large internal courts and pathways. However, his greatest contributions to the campus were the four buildings that he designed for the university after he completed the plan. These gifts to the city's architectural landscape are small masterpieces that demonstrate Yamasaki's reserved brilliance while retaining an approachability not demonstrated in the skyscrapers he designed later in his career. Among them, our favorite is the **McGregor Memorial Conference Center**, which is arguably both the crown jewel of the campus and Yamasaki's most beautiful and intricate structure. Completed in 1958, the two-story building is constructed with travertine marble and Mankato stone, and features a triangular glass motif that brilliantly weds Western modernism with Eastern traditionalism. Though the exterior is wrapped by a reflecting pool and sunken sculpture garden, the interior atrium, with its soaring tessellated glass skylight, marble floors, and Mies van der Rohe furniture is the highlight of the structure. Steps away lies the four-story **College of Education Building** which, built in 1960, features narrow windows and a light pre-cast concrete exoskeleton that stylistically foreshadows Yamasaki's later work. Southeast of these buildings lies **Prentis Hall**, which was completed in 1964 and defies nature with a vertical, angular pre-cast concrete motif that appears to float above an airy glass first story. Adjacent to Prentis Hall and designed to harmonize with it, is the **Helen L. DeRoy Auditorium**. Built concurrently with Prentis Hall, and connected by an underground tunnel, the auditorium is curvy, yet monolithic and windowless, with an empty reflecting pool that now serves as a moat and makes the building a fascinating oppositional complement to the architect's other nearby works. All of the buildings are generally open to curious—and courteous—visitors and are within a short walk from one another. *The McGregor Memorial Conference Center is located at 495 Ferry Mall, the College of Education Building at 5425 Gullen Mall, Prentis Hall at 5201 Cass Ave., and the Helen L. Deroy Auditorium behind it to the west at 5203 Cass Ave.*

POINTS OF INTEREST

Art Center Community Garden - Founded in 2010, this raised-bed community garden is managed by the University Cultural Center Association. Neighbors pay an annual fee to grow vegetables and plants in their own dedicated bed. *John R. St. and Palmer St.*

Automotive Mural - This 6-foot-by-40-foot mural, originally finished in 1941 by artist William Gropper for placement in a Detroit post office that has since been demolished, is striking in its explicit references to Diego Rivera's *Detroit Industry* mural at the DIA. Whereas Rivera was concerned with the intersection of technology and life, Gropper's work seems to place emphasis on the power of labor. *Anthony Wayne Dr. and W. Palmer Ave.*

Brewster Wheeler Recreation Center - Scenes for Ryan Gosling's film *Lost River* were filmed on the grounds of this historic, vacant recreation center, which was built in 1929 to serve residents of the then burgeoning, and largely African American, Paradise Valley and Black Bottom neighborhoods. *2900 Saint Antoine St.*

Casey Kasem Home - The famous Top 40 host spent his early years in Detroit in this brick Midtown apartment building. *454 W. Alexandrine St.*

Charles Lindbergh Home Site - Though the original structure, a historic single-family home, is long gone, it was the birthplace of this legendary pilot and American folk hero. *1120 W. Forest Ave.*

Charles McGee Mural - This 20-foot-tall black and white abstract sculpture by local artist Charles McGee was created in remembrance of the Detroit uprising in 1967, and is displayed prominently in front of the Charles H. Wright Museum of African American History. *315 E. Warren Ave.*

Chase Scene from Beverly Hills Cop - The action-packed post–drug bust chase scene in the 1984 film *Beverly Hills Cop*—that starred Eddie Murphy as hardscrabble Detroit detective Axel Foley—incongruously skips around the city, including a romp through this intersection. *Henry St. and Park Ave.*

The Detroiters Houses - These two stately Victorian homes in Woodbridge are the fictional residences of characters Sam Duvet and Tim Cramblin in the hit Comedy Central show *Detroiters*. *4214 & 4208 Avery St.*

The El Moore Lodge - This gorgeous 1898 red sandstone apartment building stood vacant for years, but was stunningly redeveloped, with numerous green features and reclaimed components, and re-opened in 2015. The development includes new satellite structures built from other deconstructed buildings, and a public gathering space with a grand entryway constructed from a salvaged water tower. The Lodge includes rooftop "cabins" that are available for short-term stays. *624 W. Alexandrine St.*

Former Translove Energies Site - Now the site of a strip mall, this location was the late 1960s headquarters for counterculture luminaries John Sinclair, the MC5, and other self-proclaimed "hippies." *4857 John C. Lodge Fwy.*

Fortune Records - This vacant lot was once home to Jack and Devora Brown's label that, in its run from 1946 to 1995, recorded artists ranging from John Lee Hooker and Nathaniel Mayer to doo-wop artists Nolan Strong and The Diablos. *3942 Third Ave.*

Fresh Cut Flower Farm - Sarah Pappas founded this quarter-acre flower farm next to her home in 2013. This hoophouse and outdoor garden produce beautiful blooms throughout the growing season, which are featured in businesses and homes throughout the city. *1760 W. Forest Ave.*

Gold Dollar - Right in the heart of the Cass Corridor, this shuttered club was once the beating heart of late 1990s Detroit garage rock, helping to launch the White Stripes, among others, to stardom. *3129 Cass Ave.*

The Green Garage and Cass Farms Green Alley - An incubator for environmentally conscious businesses, the **Green Garage** is housed in a sustainably renovated, 12,000-square-foot former Model T showroom built in 1920. The Garage is a beautiful example of preservation, with thoughtful design elements at every turn. The adjacent **Cass Farms Green Alley** is paved with permeable reclaimed materials and populated with native plants, making it an inspiring and inviting public space. *4444 Second Ave.*

Hygienic Dress League Wheat Pastes - This series of wheat pastes continues the artists' exploration of the pervasiveness of marketing in American culture though their prolific promotion of the anonymous, mysterious, and ominous Hygienic Dress League brand. Look for their elaborate and intriguing wheat pastes, murals, and installations throughout the city. *70 W. Alexandrine St.*

Marquette, LaSalle, Cadillac, and Richard Sculptures - Originally made for display in Detroit's 1871 Old City Hall, these sandstone sculptures depicting four of the city's most important French pioneers were saved from the wrecking ball that brought down the building in 1961. The figures, sculpted by artist Julius Melchers and architect John Donaldson in 1874, were moved to their current location in 1974. *Anthony Wayne Dr. and W. Warren Ave.*

Mike Wallace Home - While he was working for WXYZ radio in the early 1940s, the *60 Minutes* mainstay lived in this apartment building just south of Wayne State University. *4863 Second Ave.*

North Cass Community Garden - Created in 2009, this community garden turned a blighted piece of land into a place where the residents of the Cass Corridor could try their hands at gardening in individual raised beds. *611 W. Willis St.*

Only Lovers Left Alive House - This magnificent Queen Anne mansion, now fully restored, was the grand, dilapidated setting for Jim Jarmusch's 2013 vampire film Only Lovers Left Alive. *82 Alfred St.*

Peck Park - This lovely little park tucked behind the College for Creative Studies features playsets for kids and often, outdoor movie

screenings in the summer. Across the street, visitors will see *Patterns of Detroit*, a multicolored glazed-tile installation celebrating the area's diversity, created by artist Hubert Massey.
E. Kirby St. and Brush St.

People Have Power Mural - This vibrant, reverent ode to Patti Smith, the people of Woodbridge, and beloved neighborhood wildlife (those bees and pheasants!), was completed by local artist Jake Dwyer.
3714 Trumbull Ave.

Ransom Gillis Mansion - Built in 1878, this Venetian Gothic masterpiece has a few claims to fame. One of the home's early occupants, Mary Chase Stratton, founded Pewabic Pottery here in 1903. Later, while abandoned, it was used as a shooting location in *Batman v Superman: Dawn of Justice*. The home's rehab was later subject of an HGTV special with Rehab Addict "star" Nicole Curtis.
205 Alfred St.

Robert Burns Sculpture - This George Lawson sculpture, dedicated in 1921 with help from Detroit's Burns Club, catches the young Scottish poet in a moment of seeming contemplation. *Second Ave. and Temple St.*

Society of Arts & Crafts Building - The original home of the School for the Society of Arts & Crafts, this mid-century gem, which is recessed from campus, was designed by Minoru Yamasaki. The elegant building features a tapestry of brick which forms a screen, and the Architect's signature use of glass. The building currently houses the business administration offices for CCS. The building located northeast of the Josephine F. Ford Sculpture Garden.
201 E. Kirby St.

TARDIS Library - Dr. Who fans will immediately recognize the iconic phone booth sitting on this vacant lot on the edge of Woodbridge. Visitors, however, will discover not a time machine inside, but a cozy little library of free books. *1944 W. Warren Ave.*

Warrior Demonstration Garden and St. Andrew's Allotment Garden - Located on the campus of Wayne State University, these gardens are designed to let students get involved in the growing urban gardening movement in the city. The gardens' produce ends up in student meals, sold at the campus farmer's market, or is donated to charitable organizations. *656 W. Kirby St. and 5105 Third Ave.*

Welcome to Woodbridge Mural - This huge colorful giraffe mural—created by the organization Summer in the City—presides over the southern end of Woodbridge, a piece that gets a lot of views thanks to the city's slowest traffic light at the nearby intersection. *3530 Grand River Ave.*

Woodbridge Bikes Art Installation - Sponsored by local developer Larry John, this vibrant public art installation features sculptures of colorful, abstracted bicycles, and murals. *5086 Commonwealth St.*

CHAPTER 3
EASTERN MARKET

Come soak in the sights, sounds, smells, and tastes of the largest and oldest historic public market district in the United States, and enjoy the delicious bounty of farms from across Michigan, Ohio, and Ontario. A venerable Detroit landmark since 1891, Eastern Market attracts more than two million visitors each year to its lively, charming open-air markets.

Although geographically the smallest neighborhood in this guide, Eastern Market is a dense historic commercial district anchored by the market itself, which has been in continuous operation as an outdoor market space since 1850. Located about a mile northeast of the city's central business district, as defined for this book, the neighborhood is bounded by Mack Avenue to the north, Gratiot Avenue to the south, and I-75 (the Chrysler Freeway) to the west.

In the 1850s, Eastern Market was just one of three large-scale outdoor markets in the city, the others being Western Market on the former site of Tiger Stadium in Corktown, and Central Market in Cadillac Square downtown. However, in 1891, the three markets were consolidated, and Eastern Market was designated as the region's primary public market area. In the following decades, Eastern Market grew substantially. During the 1920s, the public market area grew as new sheds were added. In the late 1940s, the market cemented its position as the hub of the regional wholesale food distribution industry, as a substantial number of wholesalers and food processors moved into the area. The public market area was overseen by the city until 2006, when a public-private partnership was forged, and administration and development of the area was ceded to the Eastern Market Corporation, which has overseen substantial improvements of the market, including the restoration of the historic sheds, the addition of the Tuesday market day, the transition of the neighborhood into an active, mixed-use district, and the planned construction of new facilities.

While the outdoor farmers market itself, which is detailed below, is open on Tuesdays seasonally and Saturdays all-year, playing host to more than 225 vendors and as many as 40,000 visitors every weekend, the area is also home to more than 100 permanent speciality wholesalers, retailers, and restaurants which make it a vibrant destination all week. Dotted with quaint historic brick commercial buildings, Eastern Market is not only a destination for produce, poultry, livestock, spices, flowers, and other fresh products,

but it is an epicenter of city life and, increasingly, a center for high-concept restaurants and high-energy art galleries.

In recent years, a flood of public art and peripheral businesses have only intensified this incredible energy. Each fall, the market cedes blank warehouse walls to a new, wordly group of artists for a week-long Murals in the Market program. The cumulative impact has left the market with a jaw-dropping collection of outdoor art that is thoughtful, beautiful, and ever-changing. At the same time, a growing slate of shops, galleries, and restaurants have opened along the market's periphery, on Gratiot Avenue, particularly between Russell Street and Joseph Campau Avenue. This burgeoning adjacent commercial district has furthered the area's reputation as center for art and food all week long.

Please note that most businesses in Eastern Market are closed on Sundays and Mondays and some have more limited hours, so be sure to call before visiting. On football Sundays, Lions fans take over the market to tailgate for $45 per car.

★ THE MARKET

The primary commercial and cultural anchor of its namesake neighborhood, the market spans five sheds across five city blocks and is home to more than 225 independent vendors and merchants who sell fresh fruit, vegetables, dairy, baked goods, fresh-cut flowers, cider, honey, jam, syrup, grass-fed meat, plants, prepared foods, and an eclectic mix of home goods. Open year round, the market's specialties follow the seasons from affordable flats of perennials in the spring, to fresh seasonal produce all summer long, and from Michigan apples and squash in the fall, to Christmas trees and wreaths in the winter. The Saturday markets are a vibrant urban experience, an authentic Detroit tradition, and a destination for shoppers looking for incredibly fresh produce at bargain prices. The months from June to September bring additional, smaller market days on Tuesdays.

First-time visitors should come on Saturday to experience the widest array of vendors. The market is open from 7am to 4pm and the best selection is available in the morning, however, vendors gradually lower their prices in the afternoon, to sell through their stock. Depending on the length of their shopping list, veteran shoppers bring tote bags, wagons, or carts with them, as many vendors don't offer bags. Eastern Market is not credit card territory, so be sure to bring cash.

Most visitors begin their trip at the southernmost shed, Shed 2, which is located at the corner of Russell Street and Winder Street, and gradually work their way north, toward Shed 6, where goods become increasingly specialized. Enjoy the interstitial space between the sheds, where historic architecture, buskers, and the smell of barbecue offer a delightful complement to the commercial commotion of the sheds. Visit the **Welcome Center** at 1445 Adelaide to get a map to plan your visit or to find an ATM or restrooms.

In addition to the regular markets, Eastern Market is home to a number of annual and seasonal events. Our favorite events are Flower Day in May, Eastern Market After Dark in September, Murals in the Market in September, the Detroit Fall Beer Festival in October, and occasional food truck rallies throughout the year. *www.detroiteasternmarket.com.*

BARS & RESTAURANTS

Al's Fish, Seafood & Chicken - One of Detroit's many "you buy, we fry" locations, Al's Fish Market stands apart from the rest because of its large selection of fresh fish, seafood and chicken and giant selection of spices and batters. To the left, shelves of bulk spices, rice, and condiments line up next to a mountain of cardboard boxes that are ready to be filled with large to-go fish orders. To the right, a long glass counter full of catfish, perch fillets, shrimp, prawns, and crab legs lines the wall. In the back, to-go cooks fry up battered shrimp, chicken, and fish in affordable lunch specials or by-the-pound prices. Just grab a number, take a seat on a red vinyl chair, and watch your fish fry. *2935 Russell St., (313) 393-1722.*

Amore da Roma - Established as Roma Cafe in 1890, Amore de Roma is the most recent incarnation of Detroit's oldest restaurant, identified by the cheerful red-and-white awning outside. This historic business began life as a boarding house for local farmers before transforming into the old-school Italian eatery it is today. In 2017, the restaurant changed hands when owner Janet Sossi Belcoure, whose family had run the restaurant since 1918, retired. Happily, new owner (and former executive chef of Roma Cafe) Guy Pelino has retained the spirit of the original, with its excellent service and upscale Italian favorites—now with updated furniture and decor. House specialties include succulent veal in the classic variations from cacciatore to piccante, fried calamari, homemade fettuccini, a thick minestrone soup, and stupendous desserts like cannoli and Chef Guy's tiramisu. As one would expect, Roma offers a healthy selection of wines and a full bar. Don't miss the all-you-can-eat, diet-destroying buffet on Monday's, or the new Sunday brunch. Sports fans should note that Roma is a popular post-practice pit stop for the Detroit Red Wings, who are often spotted dining at the restaurant. *3401 Riopelle St., www.amoredaroma.com, (313) 831-5940.*

Beau Bien Fine Foods - French for beautiful and well, and a clever play on the Detroit street name Beaubien, Noelle Lothamer's Beau Bien Fine Foods has built a well-deserved reputation as Detroit's finest producer of gourmet jams, marmalades, and preserves. Beyond the humble, white-brick facade and familiar illustrative logo, visitors will find the small company's headquarters, production facility, cafe, and retail store. The space features a refined, minimal, contemporary aesthetic with hexagonal floor tiles, a crystal chandelier, and dramatic dark accents. In addition to getting a peek behind the figurative curtain, patrons can sample exclusive, experimental seasonal jams, shop the entire line of sought-after jarred goods, and enjoy the divine cafe menu. Serving breakfast and lunch most days of the week, Lothamer pairs her jams with gourmet vegetables and deli items to create a mouth-watering menu of ever-changing, seasonal soups, sandwiches, and baked goods.

Think corned beef, Swiss, juniper caraway sauerkraut, and Beau Bien apple mustard on rye; or baked eggs with monterey jack, cilantro, scallions, and tomato preserves on a house-made biscuit. *2478 Riopelle St., www.beaubienfinefoods.com, (313) 800-1363.*

★**Bert's Marketplace** - Anyone who has visited Eastern Market on a Saturday has probably been enticed by the smoky flavors wafting from Bert's outdoor metal barrel grill and the grooves emanating from the raucous karaoke patio party. But Bert's is an all-week affair, and like all good parties, cocktails, barbeque, and live music drive this celebration of Detroit's history and culture. The interconnected, multifaceted complex hosts several different businesses, including the **Motown Bistro & Oyster Bar**, the Jazz Room, Eat at Bert's, and **Bert's Warehouse Theater**. The oyster bar is a sleek, upscale seafood and steak spot with contemporary woodwork, outstanding lobster mac and cheese, and miracles in a halfshell. Next door, Bert's Warehouse is a raw, industrial space hosting ticketed, live jazz, blues, soul, and R&B shows. Further down, the **Jazz Room** delights crowds with glitzy chandeliers, speciality cocktails, a lively dance floor, and live jazz and R&B most nights. Next door, **Eat at Bert's** is an old-timey, well-worn barbeque joint famous for Rust Belt portions and dreamy ribs slow-cooked to perfection with a heavenly balance of chew and char. Keep a lookout for gold records, grammy awards, and colorful Motown murals tucked away throughout. *2727 Russell St., www.bertsentertainmentcomplex.com, (313) 567-2030.*

Beyond Juicery + Eatery - Though it's relatively new to Eastern Market, this popular juice and smoothie shop has been a metro Detroit staple since 2005, with five locations throughout the region.

It seems only fitting that one of those should neighbor the country's largest and oldest open-air market! Really, who doesn't want to follow up a fruitful morning at the farmer's market with some Razzle Dazzle liquid fuel? (to be clear, that's a raspberry, strawberry, banana, coconut water, honey, vanilla, and lime smoothie). This shop, with its refined industrial interior, prides itself on fast, healthy fare, and the choices extend far beyond just exceptional smoothies. As the name would suggest, look for fresh juices, as well as crisp salads, hearty sandwiches, and especially delicious quinoa bowls. For those times when you need more than just a single juice to reset, you can also order your choice of a 24, 48, or 72 hour juice cleanse through the shop! 2501 Russell St., *www.beyondjuicedetroit.com*, *(313) 818-3502*.

★ **Cøllect** - Owners Kyle and Lea Hunt have brought simple design and complex beers to this sophisticated second story craft beer destination. If you take design cues from the artist Robert Ryman, you're likely to love the bright white space, with its milk glass lights, subway tile, and general Scandinavian elegance. Punctuating the space is a colorful, abstract botanical mural by renowned Australian muralist David "MEGGS" Hooke, and a single projector silently playing local sports. The floorplan eschews traditional tables in favor of ample bar seating and benches along the perimeter in a way that furthers the open, airy feel. On the thoughtfully curated beer list, look for a rotating selection of outstanding, often obscure, craft options from the likes of Mikkeller, Grimm, Bloom Ferments, and Batch. The 14 taps vary, but emphasize IPAs, sours, and saisons. Gratis popcorn with a delicious faux-rito seasoning available, though for more serious eats, head downstairs to Gather (see separate entry). In warmer months, head upstairs to the beautiful rooftop deck. *1454 Gratiot Ave., (586) 850-0205.*

Cutter's Bar & Grill - Located on the periphery of the market, this neighborhood dive serves pub grub, including one of the freshest and most admired hamburgers in the city. If its eight-ounce "slider" isn't enough for you, consider upgrading to the 16-ounce version— as long as, hunger permitting, you don't rule out buying the two-pounder. For looks, Cutter's is a hole-in-the-wall, but it's always hopping, domestics are cheap, and cocktails are generous. Known as a destination after-work eatery and sippery, Cutter's may wind up getting some patrons to stay longer than they anticipated. Closed Sundays except for during Lions games. *2638 Orleans St., www.cuttersdetroit.com, (313) 393-0960.*

Detroit City Distillery - Step inside this inviting, darkly romantic space in Eastern Market and feel like you've been transported to a Prohibition-era speakeasy. Once a slaughterhouse, the space has been transformed into a raw, moody hideaway, with a stunning antique bar, exposed brick, and bourbon-barrel accents. The eight childhood friends that opened the distillery and tasting room wanted to harken back to the legacy and lore of Prohibition-era Detroit, and they succeeded. Today, the team makes award-winning, small-batch, artisanal rye, whiskey, gin, and vodka using locally sourced and Michigan-grown ingredients. The menu offers a rotating mix of classic and inventive drinks shaken or stirred to perfection. We're especially fond of the Rye of Fire, an intoxicating blend of rye whiskey, mango habanero, honey, ginger, and lemon, with just the right amount of kick. If you're feeling extra adventurous you could always opt for the Omakase, Japanese for "I'll leave it to you" (dealer's choice). Tours of the on-site distillery, as well as the larger-scale operation at the old Stroh's plant, are readily available. Make arrangements through the tasting room. *2462 Riopelle St., www.detroitcitydistillery.com, (313) 338-3760.*

Eastern Market Brewing Company - With its houseplant wall, decorative historic ironwork salvaged from Old City Hall, black pipe and plank tables, large distressed mural, industrial lighting, and reclaimed church pews, this taproom seamlessly evokes the city's history while offering an of-the-moment brewery aesthetic. Since joining the city's burgeoning brewery scene in 2017, Eastern Market Brewing Coming has developed a reputation for using local ingredients to brew traditional, true-to-style beer with a speciality in India pale ales. On the rotating, seasonal, double-digit beer list, look for standouts like the Nitro Irish Stout, Market Day IPA, Elephant Juice Double IPA, Nitro Vanilla Lavender, and the Summer Saison, all of which will leave you planning for a roadie growler before you finish your first pint. If you were unable to conquer your thirst on site, the taproom's can seamer makes carryout cans of any draft. The bar sells snacks like popcorn, gourmet nuts, and chips, though those looking for something more substantial can bring in carry out, or try the pop-up food truck on weekends. Dog friendly. *2515 Riopelle St., www.easternmarket.beer, (313) 502-5165.*

Eastern Market Food Trucks - Especially during market days, Eastern Market boasts an impressive fleet of food trucks—which often overlap with the workweek trucks that serve Downtown. See separate Downtown Food Trucks entry for more information.

Eastern Market Seafood Co. - Yes, the Eastern Market Seafood Co. specializes in seafood and slings a wide array of relatively inexpensive fresh and frozen seafood, from standard fare to delicacies like king crab legs, alligator, and the largest, mutant-size jumbo shrimp you've ever seen. However, the real attraction—especially on Saturdays, when it often draws a line out the door—is its three-sausage pita sandwich. Your choice of three sausage varieties (the options include everything from bratwurst to Cajun andouille) are diced and laid out over lettuce, tomato, and onion and then smothered in mustard, which makes the $4 sandwich a steal. *2456 Market St., (313) 567-8359.*

Farmer's Restaurant - Open at 5am on Saturdays for hungry farmers traveling from afar, Farmer's Restaurant is one of Eastern Market's premier diners, serving up a hearty portion of hotcakes and sausages. Most of its ingredients must come from the market, because its omelets are always fresh and its hash browns always delectable. Located just east of Shed 3, next to the Cultivation Station, Farmer's Restaurant is one of the only places in Detroit to get a good omelet and great service for the early breakfast set. Be forewarned that you'll most likely need a box for your leftovers—it's like two meals for the cheap, cheap price of one. *2542 Market St., (313) 259-8230.*

Gather - The category of New-American small plates restaurants is a crowded field, but Gather is exceptional. Reshaping what Eastern Market dining has to offer, this compact restaurant dishes out masterpieces from its diminutive open kitchen. While the delectable, locally sourced menu changes seasonally, look for fluffy, perfectly soft gnocchi, beautifully prepared white fish and mussels, and particularly innovative, flavorful, and delicious seasonal vegetable dishes. While the aesthetic is minimalist and contemporary, with simple metal community tables, diffused fluorescent light, and reclaimed school chairs, the jovial mural on the western wall is a reminder that that this welcoming restaurant doesn't take itself all-seriously, and it is an easygoing, familial space that seems to inspire friendly conversations between perfect strangers. A full bar and limited cocktail menu is also offered. *1454 Gratiot Ave., www.gatherdetroit.com, (586) 850-0205.*

Germack Coffee and Tea Shop - Under the same roof as the storied Germack Pistachio Company (see separate entry), the Germack Coffee and Tea Shop is a great pitstop for a jolt of caffeine and a snack during market day—or any other day of the week. Amid a thoughtful atmosphere of wood floors, exposed brick, sliding industrial doors, and antique accent pieces, Germack offers a full selection of espresso drinks, pour-over, drip coffee, cold brew, and teas. It uses a wide variety of beans roasted on site and you can even sneak a peek of the roasting process in the back! In addition, it sells its own coffee roasts by the bag, fresh spices by the ounce, and a curated selection of pantry items and caffeinated-beverage-related housewares to facilitate your addiction. *2509 Russell St., www.germack.com, (313) 556-0062.*

Louie's Ham and Corned Beef - A little thing most people don't know about Detroit: It's corned beef country, and Eastern Market is the hub. At Louie's Ham and Corned Beef, breakfast is served any time, and that includes its selection of 18 massive three-egg omelets (in fact, all portion sizes at Louie's are massive, so be sure to come extra hungry). The menu is vast, and it has a wide variety of Detroit-area diner specialties. But the name says it all: When you go to Louie's, you get the ham or the corned beef. The corned beef comes from the infamous Wigley's, also located in Eastern Market. For the holidays, order a whole ham from Louie's (from Dearborn Ham Co.) or satisfy your craving with a mound of meat stuffed between two slices of rye. There's even an improbable (but somehow completely reliable) drive-through. *3570 Riopelle St., www.louieseasternmarket.com, (313) 831-1800.*

Louisiana Creole Gumbo - Althought there is a satellite location in Northwest Detroit, this original carryout location of Louisiana Creole Gumbo is the main event, and welcomes visitors with a large, toothy brass gator that stretches across the storefront's bay window. The gator remains the signature mascot for this delicious establishment, which has a variety of gumbos and classic jambalaya that include seafood, sausage, and crab. Visitors can dress up any order with bacon, cheese, and other tasty toppings for less than a dollar more. Vegetarian options include red beans and rice, award-winning cornbread, and famous candied yams. Gumbo-lovers, note that Creole gumbo is less spicy than the Cajun style, but packs a ton of flavor! A friend once claimed that if the gumbo was this good in Louisiana, she never would've moved here. *2051 Gratiot Ave., www.detroitgumbo.com, (313) 446-9639.*

Mike's Pita & Grill - Coated inside and out with sunny yellow paint, this cozy coney island offers hot pita sandwiches, hot dogs, hot soups, and warm welcomes to visitors. Because of the affordable lunch specials, Mike's gets hopping around noon. Sit-down diners might have to wait for a space during the lunch or dinner rush, since there's just enough room for a grill top, black-cushioned stools at the counter, and a few tables and chairs—but that all adds to the cozy coney experience. If hurrying through a lunch break, call ahead for extra-snappy carryout that's easy on the wallet. *2719 Russell St., (313) 259-8151.*

Milano Bakery & Cafe - Conveniently located on the northern edge of the market near Midtown, Milano is a solid bakery with a large selection of affordable classic cakes, cookies, pastries, coffee cakes, Kosher breads, rolls, and breadsticks. The space is airy, spare, and clean, and service is usually quick and friendly. While many of the cakes are quite basic, the carrot, pineapple-upside-down, German chocolate, and red velvet are especially tasty and a good value. Order ahead or take your chances and choose from the case—though not extensive, there is usually a selection of small and large pre-made layer cakes to choose from, and employees will happily add a custom message on the top. Milano also offers a nice menu of salads, soups, sandwiches, and pizza—with large portions for a reasonable price—available for carryout or dining-in in the pleasant, bright cafeteria-type setting. *3500 Russell St., www.milanobakerydetroit.com, (313) 833-3500.*

Mootown Creamery and More - Open since 2011, Mootown's delicious frosty treats are popular with hoards of summertime market shoppers. It specializes in classic Michigan products, including Faygo soda, Vernors ginger ale, Sanders fudge, Better Made chips, and delicious Hudsonville ice cream. Ice cream flavors range from classic favorites (like chocolate or butter pecan) to state-themed varieties (such as Grand Traverse Bay Cherry Fudge, Sleeping Bear Dunes Bear Hug, or Michigan Deer Traxx). Prices are reasonable, and the yummy scoops are generous. *2641 Russell St., www.mymootown.com, (313) 393-6016.*

★**Russell Street Deli -** This popular deli serves up some of Detroit's tastiest eats for carnivores and vegans alike in a clean, contemporary setting. From classic deli sandwiches like the BLT (made with double-smoked hickory bacon) and reubens stuffed with corned beef, to hearty vegetarian options such as the Avocado Melt and the TLT (tofu, lettuce, and tomato), all of Russell's sandwiches hit it out of the park. If sandwiches aren't your bag, RSD is known for tasty salads and the best soups in town, offering five or six options each day, made from scratch in-house with all-natural, local ingredients. Try our favorites—black-eyed pea with collard greens, Tuscan potato, or Moroccan chickpea—or just flip a coin. They don't disappoint! In the summer, RSD's mint iced tea or fresh lemonade are a must. Expect a long wait for Saturday breakfast and note that all the deli's tables seat six, so be prepared to share a table if you come with a smaller group or split up if you have a larger party. Only open for breakfast and lunch. *2465 Russell St., www.russellstreetdeli.com, (313) 567-2900.*

Sala Thai - An antidote for coney fever, Sala Thai serves up some of the city's finest Thai food from its home in a retired 1888 firehouse. The menu offers all of the de rigueur Thai options—like pad Thai, pad prik, pad khing, and gaeng phanaeng—alongside more adventurous options, such as shrimp-and-mussels-stuffed squid— all of which are equally delectable. Although the menu is almost exclusively Thai, it includes a diverse selection of fresh, visually stunning sushi, including octopus, white tuna, red snapper, and eel. Setting the right mood for diners, Sala Thai eschews the Thaikea ambiance of other Thai restaurants in favor of a more authentic feel, including bamboo-thatched booths, door gods, and beautiful murals and sculptures. In addition to the food offerings, Sala Thai offers a full bar, with a superior selection of sakes, plum wines, and Asian beers like Sapporo and Tsingtao. Vegetarians beware: There are few non-fish-sauce options available, although the veggie sushi is popular. *3400 Russell St., www.salathaidetroit.com, (313) 831-1302.*

Stache International - These days, this former slaughterhouse just slays the sandwich game. With a TV playing something between Bob Ross and international soccer, a heap of board games, local art on the walls, a bearded refrigerator, and carousel horses punctuating the bar, the spot has a vibe that is at once inviting, fun, lively, and eclectic. The menu, in contrast, is all business. Showcasing house-smoked and -cured meats, the menu emphasizes creative applications of familiar flavors. Look for toothsome offerings like the Wings ala Zorba (Mediterranean-style wings), Brooklyn Bites (an egg roll and cheese stick hybrid), and the Russian-style Moscow Cheesesteak. There's a reason, however, that the Turkey Mondulo is at the top of the menu. Its house-smoked chipotle and modelo-marinated pulled turkey, honey cilantro cabbage slaw, rosemary garlic aioli, and sourdough create a chorus of flavors and textures that will make you a regular in just one bite. On the liquid side, look for creative cocktails with whimsical garnishes—like Rock & Rye ice cubes, circus peanuts, and cotton candy—and a thoughtful roster of domestic and craft beers. *1416 E. Fisher Service Dr., www.stacheinternational.com, (313) 974-6895.*

★ **Supino Pizzeria** - Believe every word of praise: Supino serves up metro Detroit's best traditional thin-crust brick oven pies. Inspired by relatives in the village of Supino, Italy, owner and maestro Dave Mancini painstakingly honed his craft before he opened up shop in 2008. Melding balanced, rich, traditional flavors with perfectly textured New York-style crusts, Supino's enormous pies are delights that never disappoint. Though there are dozens of options, adventurous meat-eaters should try the Bismarck: homemade red sauce, fresh mozzarella, and salty prosciutto, with an egg cracked in the middle, blending brilliantly with the tomato and cheese. Vegetarians (and anyone who likes delicious food) shouldn't miss the Supino: homemade red sauce, fresh mozzarella, sublimely roasted whole garlic cloves, olives, and fresh ricotta. Though Supino does a steady carryout business, it also offers a delightful dine-in experience, with a sit-down menu rounded out with house-made italian classics; a well-appointed sit-down space that features reclaimed hardwood floors, contemporary decor, and tin ceilings; and a full bar with wine, beer, and choice craft cocktails. *2457 Russell St., www.supinopizzeria.com, (313) 567-7879.*

Thomas Magee's Sporting House Whiskey Bar - The signature house cocktail is Irish coffee. It's a fitting choice for a bar that can easily claim the mantle of classiest sports bar—partly because it has a mantle—and is dedicated to showing every game, even European soccer games that air live at dawn. With a beaver's dream worth of floor-to-ceiling dark wood paneling, a matching long bar, and a historic tin ceiling, the bar exudes an uncommon sense of class. The long and narrow structure of the bar gives every seat in the house a good view of the seven big screens on the wall, which play just about every game, fight, match, and race. Behind that long bar, look for an extensive selection of beers, ciders, and liquors ranging from local beers and imported Irish ciders to deep-cut spirit options, not to mention an epic selection of whiskeys of all stripes. All that booze leaves little space for a kitchen, but owner Erik Olson encourages guests to bring carryout. Don't miss the rear game room with Golden Tee, bubble hockey, darts, and foosball. *1408 E. Fisher Service Dr., www.thomasmagees.com, (313) 263-4342.*

Vivio's - Vivio's has been an Eastern Market tradition for more than 40 years. Whether tailgating before a Lions game on Sundays, enjoying a boozy Saturday brunch, or savoring the succulent burgers or mussels on just any old day, Vivio's is a Detroit favorite. Known best for its signature Bloody Mary—made with a house mix and served in a pint glass with a beer chaser—Vivio's is a popular spot centrally located in the Eastern Market district. The first floor is a quaintly decorated bar space with historic decor and cozy booths, while the upstairs has a more relaxed atmosphere with comfortable couches. Though the menu is specialized, the friendly staff is extremely knowledgeable and accommodating. Vivio's offers a complimentary shuttle bus for most sporting events making it a popular pre-game destination. If you haven't finished scratching your Bloody Mary itch by last call, pick up some of the bottled house-made mix on your way out. *2460 Market St., www.viviosbloodymary.com, (313) 393-1711.*

Zeff's Coney Island - A mainstay of the market's Russell Street restaurant strip, Zeff's has been around longer than neighbors Russell Street Deli, Supino Pizzeria, and Mootown Creamery combined. The food is great, the staff is friendly, the huge portions are relatively inexpensive, and its charming classic diner counter and airy front windows make dining-in a pleasure. At first glance the menu seems pretty standard as far as coney islands (they have basic coney dogs, hot dogs, loose burger, and the coney taco down to a science), but Zeff's uses quality, market-fresh ingredients, including Wigley's corned beef (which is as delicious as it is famous). Its coffee is tasty and employees will happily keep it full, especially if you've brought your laptop and are grinding away the hours working on their free Wi-Fi—just don't expect to be able to sit with your computer all day on a Saturday, because you'll barely be able to get a table. *2469 Russell St., (313) 259-4705.*

SHOPPING & SERVICES

3 Dogs 1 Cat - Finding a purr-fect gift for a pet isn't ruff at this fun and hip, self-described "urban petshop," with as much of an eye towards pet essentials as essential pet gifts. The unique space, in an adapted Eastern Market agri-industrial storefront, features exposed wood joists, a sliding barn door, and a collection of industrial and antique fixtures that give the store an unexpected and delightful design-oriented appearance with more than a nod towards history. The shop offers a well-curated array of everyday items for dogs and cats, like bedding, toys, leashes, accessories, and food, as well as special edible treats like meat sticks and "bagels," and the city's best selection of Detroit-themed pet apparel and accoutrements. Look for canine CEO Mr. Elroy, who holds court over the front counter. *2714 Riopelle St., www.shop.3dogs1cat.com, (313) 888-9803.*

Boro Resale - The most dynamic resale shop in the city, Boro is at home near Detroit's vibrant Eastern Market, and it stocks designer, vintage and independent clothing and accessories for women and men. From Madewell to Missoni, Levi to YSL, owner Miriam Pranschke is a master curator and purveyor, and she finds unique and irresistible consignment items at an almost exhaustive pace. The sunny space is elegant, with high ceilings, restored, intricate details (check out that crown molding!), and a spiral staircase that winds itself like a corkscrew up to the lofted second story. The shop offers a wide range of price points (most very accessible), as well as a range of inclusive sizes—and on-point style advice—ensuring that everyone can walk away with a killer find. Adding a socially conscious component, a portion of all proceeds is donated to community organizations. *1440 Gratiot Ave., www.bororesale.com, (313) 888-9648.*

Cheap Charlies - Need a rug, work boots, gently used work shirt, socks, shopping cart, underwear, utensil, pocketknife, stockpot, lucky rabbit foot, or oversize piggy bank? If you need any of these items— or pretty much anything else for that matter—Cheap Charlies probably has it for you, packed into its pleasantly cluttered heaping displays. The sign above the door reads "THE WORKING MAN'S STORE," and it doesn't lie: in addition to a healthy stock of every type of work-related apparel, its goods are priced to sell, and it's hard to step foot inside without picking up a steal. *1461 Gratiot Ave., (313) 567-7788.*

Cost Plus Wine Shoppe - This family-owned and-operated wine shop boasts a fabulous variety of more than a thousand wines at reasonable prices. A market institution since it opened on St. Patrick's Day in 1986, the selection is also well curated. Enjoy reading the descriptive signs and perusing the bottles sold from boxes stacked high on the worn wooden floors, or ask for advice— the staff members really know their stuff and have a knack for helping to select the perfect variety for your menu and budget, whether you are an oenophile or just turned 21. The store sells a nice selection of Michigan wines—from labels like Chateau Grand Traverse, Black Star Farms, and Peninsula Cellars—and also carries a great selection of specialty, Michigan, and imported beers. *2448 Market St., (313) 259-3845.*

The Detroit Mercantile Co. - Located in a historic fire station just a little north of the main drag of Eastern Market, The Mercantile opened in 2012. Although the shop hasn't yet hit the decade milestone, it oozes authentic history and feels as if it's been in the market for a century. Watched over by its stuffed mascot, Coleman the Buffalo, this beautifully merchandised shop features American-made brands and a broad range of old-timey takes on classic household items, from hand-built bicycles to cloth-covered extension cords, as well as a curated, but healthy, selection of high-end antiques and a wide assortment of topical T-shirts from Detroit Manufacturing. They get new antiques in frequently and many of the objects offered are truly special and Detroit-centric—such as an awe-inspiring vintage pull-down map of Detroit. *3434 Russell St., www.detroitmercantile.com, (313) 831-9000.*

Detroit Vs. Everybody - Few brands have captured the swagger, attitude, tenacity, and grit of 21st century Detroit as well as Detroit Vs. Everybody. Established in 2011, the label has grown into a small empire, with its goods available throughout the region. Here, in this polished garden-level space, guests can find the slogan emblazoned on glassware, accessories, hoodies and the company's iconic black T-shirts. They say imitation is the sincerest form of flattery (looking at you Ohio and London!), but Walker's line is the original and (in our unbiased opinion) best. So, pick something up, and you'll be in good company—Eminem, Big Sean, and a laundry list of other celebrities are noted fans. The brand's original homebase is still open at 400 Monroe Street in Greektown, but this larger location is the place to go. Don't miss the spirited, eponymous music

video, which is a who's who of Detroit hip-hop. *2501 Russell St., www.vseverybody.com, (800) 478-3218.*

★ **DeVries & Co. 1887** - Founded by Rudolf Hirt Jr. in 1887, and still family-owned, an incarnation of this shop has been an Eastern Market staple for generations. DeVries is Detroit's OG cheesemonger, and with its high ceilings, wooden floors, history-drenched decor and fixtures, and friendly counter service, shopping here is a charming experience from another time. The knowledgeable staff will happily recommend a cheese to suit your fancy, and sampling is encouraged. In addition to its vast array of cheeses, this fine specialty foods shop carries an impressive array of imported dry goods including European mustards, shortbreads, jams, chocolates, crackers, local dairy products, and teas. Be sure to also check out the selection of gifts and homegoods upstairs—if you can hitch one, a ride on the old-timey elevator is worth the price of admission alone. *2468 Market St., www.devries1887.com, (313) 568-7777.*

Division Street Boutique - Known for its ever-popular apparel emblazoned with the phrases "Detroit Hustles Harder" and "RUN DET," the Division Street Boutique is the home base of Aptemal

Clothing, the company that hand-prints everything in-house, up the stairs on the second floor. When the store's open, the large garage door opens up to the street, just off of the market's main drag, to show off all the goods and welcome visitors. Though it's a small store, it's brimming with awesome, hip apparel and accessories for gents and ladies, too. While Aptemal Clothing is also available elsewhere, this is the company's flagship location and is the best place to find the entire line. Insider tip: Keep your ear out for parties that happen after close. They're not to be missed. In the attached spaces, you'll find **Blue Velvet Vintage**, which is filled with fashionable treasures for men and women who appreciate classic looks, as well as **37th Shield Library**, which features a wide selection of records, tapes, collectables, and bric-a-brac that will make you smile, and **Detroit Design Reworked**, which artfully repurposes building materials into beautiful benches, tables, and fixtures for your home. *1353 Division St., www.divisionstreetboutique.com, (313) 412-3337.*

Eastern Market Antiques - This favorite of antique lovers glows with the light of glass saloon bar lamps, vintage chandeliers, and modern light fixtures that drape above the entire first floor showroom. The extra lighting illuminates collectibles from more than 15 vendors selling vintage aprons, secondhand furniture, 1990s computer games, comics, posters, wall hangings, typewriters, tools, even Detroit salvage pieces, such as theater seats. Upstairs, it's all about the rarer things: 1950s postcards from each of the 50 states, designer turn-of-the-century hats and dresses, and even taxidermy animals. *2530 Market St., www.easternmarketantiques.com, (313) 259-0600.*

Eastern Market Meat Cutters - The patchwork string of butchers and meat counters on the eastern edge of the market area is a treasured, integral part of the Eastern Market experience. Even when not shopping for fresh meat and seafood, the mix of historic buildings, knowledgeable staff, and butchering-process backdrop—from truck to yuck to pluck—makes for a worthwhile visit. While shopping amongst the scores of chefs and grocers, customers get impromptu, across-the-counter consultations about cuts, preparation, and selection. These shops—located along Russell, Market, Riopelle, and Orleans Streets—are open during the week and are welcoming of retail customers, though some only sell in bulk quantities. At the southern end of the market, **Capital Poultry** offers freshly butchered chicken cut to order, pekin ducks, farm fresh eggs. A block over, **Berry**

& Sons Islamic Slaughter offers Halal cuts of grass-fed lamb, beef, and goat from family ranches. Up the block, **E.W. Grobbel Sons, Inc.**, the country's oldest corned beef company and the Free Press-anointed champion of the category, is renowned for its subtle spice and signature cure. Through a Sinclair-esque cooler of hanging whole pigs, **Kap's Wholesale Meats'** professorial butchers offer individual cuts of steak, pork chops, amish turkey and chicken, condiments, barbecue spice rubs, and cheeses. Up the street, **Dugagjini Meats'** beet-red facade and plump grazing-animal mural invite customers to its dense warren of wholesale groceries and a renowned meat counter with beef, pork, fish, poultry, lamb, rabbit, and goat. A block over, owner Aref Saad's **Saad Wholesale Meats** offers high quality halal cuts of goat, lamb, poultry, veal, and fresh and frozen fish. At the northern end of the market, **Frank's Meat & Produce** offers an extensive, full service meat and deli counter with fresh Amish poultry, cut-daily steaks and chops, and Wigley's exceptional corned beef. *2400-3400 Russell St., Market St., Riopelle St., and Orleans St.*

★ **Floyd** - If the proliferation of ugly, heavy, disposable, cheaply-made, assemble-yourself furniture makes you cry a little on the inside, you'll love Floyd. A Detroit-based startup, the company was founded on the principle that furniture should embody the best of contemporary design, while being of lasting quality, and conducive to the modern nomadic lifestyle. This flagship store and headquarters for the brand highlights everything to love about Floyd. The minimalist space includes a showroom for the line, including their beautiful and simple beds, tables, chairs, and sofas. The airy space features dynamic displays that highlight each piece's contemporary stylings and vibrant colors, including an interactive game where customers can time themselves constructing the intuitive-to-assemble furniture—which often takes less than a minute. Each made-in-the-USA heirloom collectable is modular and customizable, and comes with free shipping to its final destination. *1948 Division St., www.floydhome.com.*

Gardella Furniture - Decorating Detroit area homes from the same gorgeous brick building since 1939, Gardella Furniture fills three floors—20,000 square feet—with the latest in classic, modern, and contemporary furniture. The exposed brick walls are decorated with unique decor for the home and office, and reproduction antiques, including a linen travel map of Detroit from the 1700s. A rounded glass-block corner window sheds light on the large selection of bedroom furniture and couches, fabric swatches, dining tables, chairs, kids furniture—even drapery, light fixtures, and rugs. The large selection may seem overwhelming, but interior designers are on-hand to offer consultations. Closed Thursdays and Sundays. *2306 Gratiot Ave., www.gardellafurniture.com, (313) 567-7470.*

Germack Pistachio Company - Long a staple in Detroit and a household name throughout Michigan, the Germack Pistachio Company has been roasting pistachios since 1924, which makes it the oldest such roaster in America. Since the early days, their product line has grown substantially. Today, in small batches, Germack roasts and manufactures a wide variety of nuts, seeds, dried fruits, spices, coffees, chocolates, nostalgic candies, and other items, selling them wholesale and retail out of their Eastern Market shop. Located on Russell Street, in the heart of Eastern Market, Germack's storefront features beautiful wood floors, exposed brick, and heavy industrial doors, making it the perfect fit for such a storied business—and a perfect place to buy old-timey treats, sweets, and pantry items, both in bulk and in consumer quantities. *2509 Russell St., www.germack.com, (313) 393-2000.*

★ **Henry the Hatter -** A Detroit tradition since 1893, Henry the Hatter is a beloved haberdashery and Detroit icon. After 124 years in various locations downtown, this shop, purportedly America's oldest hat retailer, moved to its current Eastern Market location in 2017. Once past the iconic old-timey neon sign above the door, visitors will find a beautiful, long, narrow store with mint-colored shelves and antique racks bursting with men's hats and caps. Whether you are in the market for a bowler, derby, fedora, homburg, driving cap, or any other variety of formal headwear, you are bound to find a number of options among the large selection of hats from respected brands, including Bailey, Biltmore, Borsalino, Dobbs, Giorgio Cellini, Henschel, Kangol, Selentino, Stetson, and Tilden. President Dwight D. Eisenhower's inauguration hat was from this shop, and contemporary customers include LL Cool J, Run DMC, and Kid Rock. *2472 Riopelle St., www.henrythehatterdetroit.com, (313) 962-0970.*

Marketplace Antiques - On busy Gratiot Avenue, you'll find one of the city's best-kept secrets for lovers of quality antiques, including beautiful historic furniture, art, collectibles, and much more. Marketplace Antiques is known for offering high-quality pieces in excellent condition, and given their curated selection, more than reasonable prices. Stop in after you do your Eastern Market shopping and you just might find that Art Deco sofa you've always dreamed of. *2047 Gratiot Ave., (313) 567-8250.*

Modele Dress and High Street Tie Shop - Perched on the second floor of this Eastern Market warehouse, this pair of conjoined sister stores offers high fashion, a runway-worthy gallery, and an absolutely unique view. With vintage dresses, contemporary business and formal wear, and a range of blouses in every color of the spectrum, **Modele Dress** is an imaginative and size-inclusive shop that has something for every Detroit lady, with the perfect amount of natural light and space to try it all on. From stunning geometric shapes to bold details and sophisticated patterns, an array of accessories, scarves, and other finishing touches, the dress shop is sure to make an impact on your style. In a true his-and-hers format, the adjoining **High Street Tie Shop** provides the dapper fellow a touch of flair, class, and distinction. With walls of stylish ties, statement blazers, genteel objects like pocket scarves, and more than an occasional bow tie, the shop supplies everything you need to be a true gentleman, or at least look like one. *2362 Russell St., www.modeledress.com, (313) 918-6655.*

Orleans + Winder - This dreamy, high-end boutique offers up a thoughtfully curated selection of clothes, art, and objects that almost feel too beautiful to touch. Almost. Owner Erin Wetzel, whose inspirations include film, fashion, and theater, has made a space that feels more gallery than clothing store. In her lucent space on Gratiot Avenue, just outside of Eastern Market, she supports and showcases the talent of designers who opt away from mass production, including the emerging Chinese designer Uma Wang, the young Los Angeles-based Shaina Mote, and the Italian shoe-making house, Guidi, which has been honoring leather traditions for more than 120 years! You'll also find a curated selection of gorgeous apothecary products such as palo santo bath soaks and volcanic hot spring bath salts. *1410 Gratiot Ave. Ste. 102, www.orleansandwinder.com, (313) 409-6343.*

★**People's Records** - Arguably Detroit's most lauded record store, especially among soul and funk heads, People's is a storied destination for rare and sought-after vinyl. The shop was hailed as one of America's top 50 record shops by *Rolling Stone Magazine* in 2011, and is often singled out by the *New York Times* as a must-visit. Consequently, fans travel from around the globe (yes, literally) to tap into down-to-earth owner Brad Hale's encyclopedic music knowledge and dig through his crates. Spread over two rooms, the shop offers a well-organized, comprehensive selection of pre-loved LPs and 45s, with especially strong selections of blues, jazz, and rock, but the store's legendary status stems from the ungodly number of soul and funk 45s sorted by label, style, and artist, and stored in charmingly hand-painted boxes. With records coming in daily from forgotten attics and garages, People's is *the* place to score extremely rare limited pressings from obscure Detroit artists of the 60s and 70s. Hales also curates the **MAHS Museum** of historical Detroit music memorabilia and photos, and exhibits the collection in his shop. A second, smaller location, People's North is open on the Avenue of Fashion (see separate entry). *1464 Gratiot Ave., www.peoplesdetroit.com, (313) 831-0864.*

People's Restaurant Equipment Company - Occupying a four-room warehouse with a freshly painted brick facade and sign inviting shoppers to "the party place," People's is packed with every supply imaginable for kitchens and restaurants. Think everything from five-gallon barrel barbecues to drink muddlers and strainers, giant margarita glasses, party picks, chef uniforms, basic glassware, beer pitchers, knives, a rainbow of tablecloths and matching napkins, and even commercial stainless steel tables, deep fryers, and barstools. Even though the store caters to restaurants and commercial clients, it stocks a wide variety of goods useful for home kitchens, and individuals are welcome to stop in to shop. *2209 Gratiot Ave., www.peoplesrestaurantequipco.com, (313) 567-1944.*

Rocky Peanut Company - In the produce-delivery and peanut-roasting business since 1931, the Russo family's enterprise became a Detroit institution when brothers Dominic and Rocco—aka Rocky—opened their brick-and-mortar location in Eastern Market in 1971. Though the east side classic offers a mind-blowing selection of sweet and savory seeds, nuts, and peanuts, they also offer a completist's selection of pantry items, including bulk options, such as fine coffee, dried beans, spices, flour, sugar, dried fruit, and old timey candies. Though we're always suckers for the chocolate-covered nuts, Rocky's fresh honey-roasted almonds are conveniently located by the register, so they're hard to pass up. *2489 Russell St., www.rockypeanut.com, (313) 567-6871.*

Savvy Chic - An Eastern Market staple, Savvy Chic's cream and crème de menthe interior feels like a stylish boutique in the French countryside thanks to the creative expertise of owner, and College for Creative Studies alumna, Karen Brown, who has lovingly filled her hand-painted space with a large selection of modern, Earth-friendly made-in-America housewares, one-of-a kind antique decor, and unique women's fashions with a decidedly French flair. Stop in Tuesday through Saturday to find vintage Victorian chairs, floral cloth napkins and aprons, an antique crafted in-Detroit oven, gardening tools and golf gifts for dad, luscious bath and candle products, and a bit of imagination! While you're there, don't forget to pick up one of the city's best cups of java (and a delicious bite to eat) at **Cairo Coffee**, located inside the boutique. The welcoming baristas, including owner Monica Isaac, will make you feel right at home as they prepare your pour-over or espresso from an ever-changing selection of excellent roasters. *2712 Riopelle St., (313) 833-8769.*

★ **Signal-Return** - Signal-Return is a modern, open space full of presses, antique letter blocks, working artists, and wordsmiths alike. The space reverberates with creative energy as artists work at long blonde wooden-block tabletops, surrounded by exposed brick walls and orange and white ceiling beams. Separating the retail and workshop areas are shelves stacked with chapbooks and art and design publications, as well as blank postcards, envelopes, and notebooks ready to be printed! A long string stretches along the length of the store, clothes-pinned with the latest screen prints and letter-pressed memorabilia for sale. The studio offers a variety of great classes (including letterpress printing, book binding, and linocut printing) and after taking two, students are eligible to use the shop's presses during open studio hours. *1345 Division St., www.signalreturnpress.org, (313) 567-8970.*

★ **SMPLFD** - An anchor retail store in an historic art deco commercial building on that block of Gratiot Avenue, SMPLFD (pronounced Simplified) is a stunning graphic apparel and accessories shop that continues to raise the bar for casual wear in Detroit. From the street, the expansive windows reveal the beautiful store, which blends the original tin ceiling and mercantile pendant lighting with an otherwise all-white, minimal interior punctuated by pops of color from the innovative displays, contemporary styles, and abstract neon accents. The bad boys of the Detroit apparel scene, the gentlemen behind SMPLFD are seemingly always unveiling another clever or well-designed concept, whether it's their mashup of Detroit Vs. Everybody and Detroit Hustles Harder (Detroit Hustles Everybody), their mashup of the Supreme brand and the Supremes band, their everyday line of minimal urban wear, or their expansive range of timeless original throwback Detroit sports gear. Whatever your fancy, the shop's snappy selection is the perfect way to punch up your wardrobe—or someone else's. It's shopping, simplified. *1480 Gratiot Ave., www.buy.smplfd.com, (313) 285-9564.*

CULTURAL ATTRACTIONS

K.OSS Contemporary Art - A new player in the Detroit art scene, K.OSS Contemporary Art opened in early 2018 on Gratiot. Gallery director Kristina Oss and her husband originally hail from Russia and lived in New York City and San Francisco before moving to Detroit and purchasing the building which now houses the gallery. With a background in art, and drawing on her travels and time spent in different locales, Oss casts a wide net, bringing established world-class artists from around the globe to her space. You'll find thought-provoking abstract contemporary art including paintings, sculptures, and installations, with new exhibits presented every two months. The tall ceilings with exposed ductwork and brick walls are an elegant backdrop, and contrast perfectly with the serious art pieces on display. Check their website for event programming, including opening receptions and film screenings. *1410 Gratiot Ave., www.kossgallery.com, (248) 599-2232.*

Playground Detroit - Paulina Petkoski and Samantha Banks Schefman founded Playground Detroit in 2012 while they were living in New York City, showcasing Detroit artists on the East Coast. Both returned to their native Michigan and renovated this space in a building built in 1877, which was once a hardware store. The pair opened their doors in 2017 and—staying true to their mission of attracting, developing and retaining talent in Detroit—they focus on locally based emerging and mid-career artists. The impressive gallery space and meticulously curated exhibitions attract an in-the-know crowd of young art collectors and their hip contemporaries. The gallery runs a robust program of exhibitions and events, including artist talks, dinners, yoga classes, and performances. Additionally, Playground Detroit publishes an online magazine of Detroit art, music, and cultural happenings. *2845 Gratiot Ave., www.playgrounddetroit.com, (313) 649-7741*

Red Bull Arts Detroit - When approaching the building, an unassuming, industrial entrance leads into the open floor plan of first-floor studios. Visitors will find that there's a hyped-up, collaborative feeling throughout the workspaces, which are occupied by a range of visual artists. However, it's in the gallery space, on the lower level, where visitors can expect to be blown away. A dark corridor of stairs leads to a series of brick-walled tunnels, almost subway-like in appearance, glowing under ambient neon lights. The tunnels lead past a bar and some sitting areas, to what feels like another world: a vast, wide-open gallery. You'll feel as if you've been transported to New York's Meatpacking District, especially on their busy opening nights, in this magnificent industrial space exhibiting works by emerging and established artists. Refreshingly, corporate logos are tastefully absent from the complex, aside from a couple of displays stocked with (free!) cans of the energy drink. *1551 Winder St., www.redbullarts.com/detroit.*

★**Wasserman Projects** - Gary Wasserman returned to his native Detroit to open this dynamic interdisciplinary space in 2015, breathing new life into the engine house of a former fire station. The brick-walled venue is impressive, and spans more than 5,000 square feet, which provides more than ample room for larger scale installations. Wasserman Projects operates in the vein of a *kunsthalle*, as well as a performance space presenting local and international artists working across all disciplines. At the helm, Director Alison Wong curates immersive exhibitions, collaborations, and projects that push the boundaries of what one might expect from a gallery—from an artist's project of breeding live chickens to Old Master paintings. The space hosts a robust program of events, including concerts, performances, and panel discussions. Enter through the red door on the north side of the building next to the parking lot. *3434 Russell St. #502, www.wassermanprojects.com, (313) 818-3550.*

ENTERTAINMENT & RECREATION

★**Trinosophes** - Much more than a cafe, Trinosophes is like your cooler, more worldly older sister who reads 1970s radical leftist literature with her pour-over in the morning, shops for Sun Ra LP's at lunch, and attends experimental gong shows at night. And at this cafe/gallery/music venue, she can do all three in the same place. The sprawling interior, which was formerly a spice market, is separated into a cozy daytime cafe and a nighttime gallery/ performance space. The coffee is on point—lovingly prepared using beans from local roasters Anthology (see separate entry)—and is a perfect complement to the beautiful Algerian pastries from Warda Pâtisserie sold alongside it. For those who want to make a day of it, you can also wander into the attached People's Records (see separate entry) for some vintage vinyl, as well as peruse the personal book collections of local activists Jim Kennedy, Brad Duncan, and Ronald Arson. In the evenings, Trinosophes co-owner Joel Peterson curates an eclectic lineup of boundary-pushing acts, from contemporary classical, to world, to jazz, to garage rock, making this the premiere venue in Detroit for avant garde music of all genres. *1464 Gratiot Ave, trinosophes.com, (313) 737-6606.*

SITES

C.A.N. Art Handworks - If the spinning windmills and giant origami cranes don't catch your eye, the enormous metal letters spelling out "DETROIT" definitely will. Originally from Germany, Carl A. Nielbock learned the metal crafting trade through formal training as a blacksmith, and moved to Detroit in 1984. Though he worked originally as a conservationist on Detroit landmarks, more recently he has taken on large-scale artistic and conceptual projects, like the Skybox, a towering open structure of plants and seating, which can be seen through the ornamental gates that lead to his outdoor workspace. Today, dozens of his immense, beautiful works erupt out of his fenced yard, or are on display outside. While many of the large-scale works can be admired from the street, the area beyond the gate is Neilbock's live-work area, and should not be entered without making prior arrangements. In addition to admiring work from in front of his studio, there is an open park area just to the west, that features several Nielbock pieces commemorating the Battle of Bloody Run of 1763. *2264 Wilkins St., www.canarts.portfoliobox.io, (313) 392-0116.*

Murals in the Market - Eastern Market's walls, home to the neighborhood's many produce warehouses and slaughterhouses, serve as the canvas for international artists who have transformed the district with more than 125 massive, stunning works of public art since 2015. The work of more than 100 artists, these murals have been produced by **1xRUN**, a gallery and art publisher, and the Eastern Market Corporation. More murals are created every September, as part of the lively Murals in the Market festival (see separate entry), which features live painting, art shows, artist talks, and special events. Pick up a free official map of all current works from the Eastern Market Welcome Center (see separate entry), or find a map of the past year's additions on the Murals in the Market website. Walk, drive, or bike the area, but don't forget to bring your camera. Most of the murals are concentrated in Eastern Market: Between Rivard St. to the west, Mack Ave. to the north, and Gratiot Ave. to the east and south. *www.muralsinthemarket.com.*

Some notable murals to look for:

- Gigantic sharks by the artist Shark Toof. *2630 Riopelle St. and another at Division St. overlooking the Dequindre Cut.*

- Whimsical cartoon-like faces by Kevin Lyons. *Gratiot Ave. near St. Aubin St.*

- The many gorgeous floral motifs of Ouizi. Among many, a highlight is located at *2628 Orleans St.*

- A marching band playing disintegrating auto parts and industrial refuse by Pat Perry. *1898 Wilkins St.*

- A powerful commentary on race in America by Sydney G. James. *Division St. near Orleans St.*

POINTS OF INTEREST

Aretha Franklin Pothole Mosaic - Located in Eastern Market, this unusual tribute to the Queen of Soul is literally set in stone (well, in a pothole, at least). With a blue and gold mosaic by artist Jim Bachor, this delightful piece commemorates Franklin's Detroit roots and her timeless appeal. *Intersection of Rivard St. and Adelaide St.*

Brixel Murals - Conceived by artist Cedric Tai, these "brixel" murals (a mash up of brick and pixel) transform the uniform bricks on the sides of buildings into stunningly colorful geometric patterns. Although these murals have spread across the city, this is one of our favorites. *1492 Gratiot Ave.*

Coriander Farm - This half-acre farm, just east of Eastern Market, provides much of the produce for local pop-up restaurant and catering company Coriander Kitchen. *2840 Scott St.*

Eastern Market Cold Storage Mural - This colorful mural adorning the side of a warehouse features a bounty of fruit whimsically arranged to depict a heifer. The mural is the handiwork of architect Alexander Pollack, who painted the piece in 1972 in an effort to enliven the market. At four stories tall, you can't miss this piece. *2531 Riopelle St.*

Eastern Market Welcome Mural - One of the popular large-scale commercial works painted in the market by artist Alexander Pollack in 1972, this mural depicts a forklift hauling what might be the world's largest watermelon and pulling cartloads of less absurdly scaled fresh produce. *2451 Napoleon St.*

Transmat Records - The headquarters for techno pioneer Derrick May since 1986. *1492 Gratiot Ave.*

Vertical El Camino - This 1973 El Camino was installed by London Artist Anthony Gross as part of Murals in the Market in 2016. It looks as if it was dropped from the sky, nose-first. *1942 Alfred St.*

CHAPTER 4
CORKTOWN

A historically working-class neighborhood, Corktown, which is characterized by its quaint, pastel-colored workers cottages and destination commercial outlets, is not only Detroit's oldest standing neighborhood, but one of its most charming. For the purposes of this guide, the area defined as Corktown is about two-and-a-half square miles, roughly bounded by Grand River Avenue to the north, M-10, the Lodge Freeway to the east, the Detroit River to the south, and a private railroad line and 16th Street on the west.

Comprised of French ribbon farms through the 1700s, Corktown began to develop as a neighborhood community when Irish immigrants flocked to Detroit to escape the Irish potato famine of 1845 and settled in the eighth ward of the city, which included this neighborhood. Because immigrants to this area specifically were primarily from the County Cork in Ireland, the neighborhood became known colloquially as Corktown. Developed as a working-class immigrant community, the tree-lined neighborhood rose quickly, as the small pastel, wood-frame workers' cottages and multi-family row houses were constructed expeditiously—and mostly built by the 1860s. Though the tight-knit Irish immigrant population diffused over the years, as newcomers arrived from Germany, Malta, Mexico, and the American South, the historic association with Ireland has remained, including many subtle nods to the heritage in businesses around Corktown, and the neighborhood playing host to the raucous, annual St. Patrick's Day Parade.

Through the late 20th century, the neighborhood has been challenged by freeway construction, industrial development, the closure of Michigan Central Station, and, most recently, the move of the Tigers—and eventual demolition of the historic stadium—which had been a vital part of the neighborhood since 1912. However, despite these setbacks, Corktown has persevered and even flourished. Today, though home to just 6,000 people, the neighborhood is frequently in the national spotlight for the unprecedented growth in small business and entrepreneurship, urban agriculture, grassroots development, and the arts.

Because of the path of I-75 (the Chrysler Freeway), the area is commonly separated into two neighborhoods, Corktown and North Corktown. While they have a shared history, they have somewhat distinct personalities. The traditional Corktown neighborhood, which is south of I-75, is more historically intact, and is where the Irish enclave began to establish itself. Today, it's a dense, active neighborhood that has seen substantial growth and development, especially around Michigan Avenue, including—most notably—the anticipated reopening of Michigan Central Station. Characterized by its distinctive, charming streets, the neighborhood offers many walkable and bikeable amenities and is an enticing place to visit. North Corktown is composed of parts of the historic Core City and Briggs neighborhoods. Though the area went through a period of decline, recently, it has been reborn as a center for activism and urban farming, offering residents historic homes in close proximity to downtown, as well as open green space for gardens, greenhouses, and creative projects.

Every visit to Detroit should include a visit to Corktown. The neighborhood's convenient location, well-earned reputation as a destination for exceptional dining and drinking options, and walkable density make it worthy of inclusion on even the briefest of itineraries. Those with limited time might consider live music at PJ's Lager House and the UFO Factory; dinner at the legendary Slows Bar B Q, noodle hotspot ima, slider haven Green Dot Stables, or avant garde Thai option Takoi; or drinks at nanobrewery Batch Brewing or cocktail mainstay the Sugar House; or perhaps the greatest priority of all, a walk down quaint streets of colorful gingerbread cottages.

BARS & RESTAURANTS

★**Astro Coffee** - Serious coffee nerds, lovers of incredible homemade fresh sweets and sandwiches, and pretty much everyone else rejoiced when husband and wife team Daisuke Hughes and Jess Hicks opened this gem in 2011. A daily ritual for neighborhood folks and a destination for those from afar, Astro offers a near-endless rotation of high-quality and fair-trade beans from across the world (looking for a Guatemalan roast with a thick mouth feel and notes of caramel apple? The chalkboard wall behind the baristas will give you tasting notes on your daily options). These are perfectly complimented by Jess' locally sourced, made-from-scratch, mouthwatering treats, though we caution that their polenta cakes, coconut Anzac cookies, and crème fraiche and egg sandwiches are proven to be dangerously addictive. Take a seat at the back counter, at a charming café table in the sunny front windows, or at the large communal table in the back and soak in some Corktown culture with your coffee. *2124 Michigan Ave., www.astrodetroit.com, (313) 638-2989.*

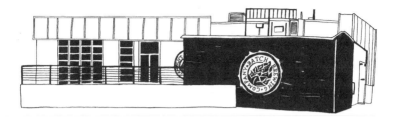

★ **Batch Brewing Company** - In a building that once housed a railroad-themed bar (look for a few remaining clues), dedicated homebrewers Stephen Roginson and Jason Williams opened this celebrated nano-brewery, where each batch is limited to three barrels or less, empowering delicious creativity and experimentation. During a painstaking, year-long DIY rehab, the formerly drab interior was transformed into an intimate, open-concept beer hall where every phase of the brewing process is visible. In the beautiful white-walled space, patrons line long, hand-built communal tables under the warmth of patio string lights, evoking the charm of a German biergarten, with a twist of refined contemporary simplicity. Because this heaven-sent tap temple is a nano-brewery, the beer selection changes daily, but boasts as many as 18 exclusive brews, including ales, Belgians, IPAs, porters, saisons, stouts, sours, experimental amalgamations, and inspired collaborations. However, this is not just a watering hole. Behind the grill, Chef Matt creates a curated, but consistently mouthwatering weekly menu rooted in traditional pub fare, with nods to Northern Michigan comfort food. Expect to find a weekly pretzel (the best in Detroit), loaded risotto ball, and savory pasty, as well as a diverse, evolving menu of sandwiches and other surprises, with options for omnivores and vegetarians alike. *1400 Porter St., www.batchbrewingcompany.com, (313) 338-8008.*

Bobcat Bonnie's - Opened in 2015, the interior of this soon-to-be classic is a sun-filled, airy space, with a contemporary loft-like atmosphere anchored by a beautiful wooden bar, Edison bulbs hanging from the open ceiling, bright geometric wallpaper, and exposed-brick walls bespeckled with cacti and chic bibelots. On the seasonal menu, expect piquant contemporary American options, including highlights like the rodeo-style Bobcat Burger (beer-battered onion rings, cheddar, bacon, and barbeque sauce on a fresh-ground patty) and arugula salad (figs, prosciutto, pecan-encrusted goat cheese and balsamic fig vinaigrette on a bed of the namesake greens)—though the fish tacos, chicken tikka masala, Captain Crunch chicken fingers, and plentiful vegetarian options are also standouts. Behind the enormous wooden bar, expect friendly, lead-handed bartenders who oversee a thoughtful cocktail menu and extensive beer and wine list. Drink a few, so you can sneak off to the arcade and pinball area while en route to the latrine. *1800 Michigan Ave., www.bobcatbonnies.com, (313) 962-1383.*

Brew Detroit - One of Detroit's best kept secrets for beer lovers, this gargantuan 68,000-square-foot warehouse complex is hiding in plain site on a quiet stretch in Corktown. While the facility is Michigan's largest contract brewery—conducting private label brewing for Atwater, Motor City Brewing Works, Stroh's, and others— the public face of the operation is their 7,000-square-foot tasting room. Look for the lone neon sign on Abbot and enter through the parking lot. Set in a refined industrial atmosphere, the bar offers two floors of the best in tasteful man-cave comfort, with pool, shuffleboard, darts, air hockey, foosball, a curated arcade, bountiful comfortable seating, and six 50-inch screens to catch the big game. However, the highlight here is what flows from the taps. They say a pitcher is worth a thousand words, and the tasting room offers plenty, with four handles dedicated to highlights from the current roster of premium craft brewing on site, and six handles dedicated to on-site exclusive, one-off nano-brews—exceptional seasonal brews that are only made in four-barrel batches, and never made twice! *1401 Abbott St., www.brewdetroit.com, (313) 974-7366 ext. 6.*

Brooklyn Street Local - This diner emphasizes locally sourced from-scratch meals for breakfast and lunch and is operated by two former Torontonians who decided to follow their dream of owning their own restaurant and moved to Detroit to make it happen.
Located on Corktown's main drag, visitors traveling west on Michigan won't be able to miss the flowing, abstract mural by street artist Reyes that covers an entire side of the building. Inside, the establishment offers a warmer feel, a contemporary take on the classic diner aesthetic. Though Brooklyn Street serves all of the hearty home-cooked diner staples, with a fresh, local spin, it also offers a strong menu of vegetarian and vegan options—and even brings a touch of Canadian flavor to the menu with pea meal bacon and the best poutine this side of the Detroit River. *1266 Michigan Ave., www.brooklynstreetlocal.com, (313) 262-6547.*

Bucharest Grill Corktown - The Michigan Avenue outpost of this insanely popular (and rightfully so) Romanian/Middle Eastern/American mashup restaurant, offering carryout and counter seating. See separate Bucharest Grill Rivertown entry for more details. *1623 Michigan Ave., www.bucharestgrill.com, (313) 965-3111.*

Corktown Tavern - It was at ground zero when the Detroit Tigers decided to pack up and head downtown in 1999 (spitting distance from the ballpark is hardly an exaggeration). Today, it's a little rough around the edges, but the Corktown Tavern soldiers on with a mix of neighborhood regulars, hard-core Tigers devotees, rockers, bikers, and their kin. While at times you get a sense of a devil-may-care attitude from the bartenders and patrons alike (those plastic cups aren't for drinking water), there's plenty of vibrancy left in this Corktown dive. Take a walk up the creaky, narrow staircase in the back: Depending on the night, you might catch a DJ spinning classic punk records, your favorite new up-and-coming band, or the occasional full-fledged, packed-to-the-gills dance party. *1716 Michigan Ave., www.corktowntavern.com, (313) 964-5103.*

★ **Detroit Institute of Bagels -** With its contemporary atmos-shmear and exceptional, traditionally styled bagels, owner Ben Newman's popular bagel shop has built a sterling reputation. After an intensive renovation in 2013, this nineteenth-century onetime-furniture store shines with exposed brick walls, bright white fixtures, and its trademark, whimsical, illustrated murals on the walls. The signature matchless rounds are made from scratch the traditional way, boiled and baked, with a dense and chewy body and a distinctive, crackly crust. The menu emphasizes standards like sesame, cinnamon raisin, and everything, alongside a limited selection of more inventive, but equally delicious, house recipes like fragrant rosemary olive oil or cheesy jalapeño cheddar. Breakfast and lunch sandwiches are nothing short of stacked, tasty masterpieces, especially the DIB Griddle (sausage, egg, cheese, hot sauce, and maple syrup), and the eponymous Ginsberg (Sy Ginsberg corned beef, Swiss cheese, coleslaw, and Russian dressing). The house shmears are prepared with the freshest ingredients, including the luxe lox cream cheese or a dozen other strong options. In warmer months, take your sandwich and Zingerman's coffee outside to the brick patio and sun-drenched Adirondack chairs. Don't miss their weekly soup specials! *1236 Michigan Ave., www.detroitinstituteofbagels.com, (313) 788-7342.*

★ **Folk** - This bright and airy cafe features some of the freshest and most beautifully plated dishes in the city. Owned and operated by the folks behind The Farmer's Hand (and located in the same building, see separate entry), Folk uses the same fresh and local ethos behind the nearby market to create a uniquely satisfying breakfast and lunch destination. The restaurant is impeccably designed, with copious white tile, beautiful contemporary fixtures, and visual surprises everywhere. The menu, which changes regularly as ingredients come into and go out of season, features housemade granola, a variety of decadently topped toasts, and bowls featuring noodles and greens. The flavored milks, pastel-tinted with matcha and rose, taste just as beautiful as they look. And if you're still hungry after lunch, you can grab a cone of Detroit's own Reilly Craft Creamery ice cream, take a seat outside, and watch the Corktown traffic drift by. *1701 Trumbull Ave., www.folkdetroit.com, (313) 290-5849.*

Gaelic League and Irish-American Club of Detroit - Founded in December 1920 with the aim of preserving and promoting the "Irish race" in Detroit and beyond, the League remains a staple of the Corktown neighborhood with its historic dance hall and cozy tavern that look much the same as they did nearly a century ago. Known for its St. Patrick's Day festivities, the club documents parades gone by with a commemorative Master of Ceremonies plaque wall and scattered black and white photos. Though many of the social activities hosted at the League are reserved for members or the Irish-American Club (just $20 annually), don't be intimidated by the "members only" sign on the door—anyone can enjoy a pint at the quaint bar inside. As an added incentive, lucky visitors can often catch live Irish folk tunes in the tavern. *2068 Michigan Ave., www.gaelicleagueofdetroit.org, (313) 964-8700.*

★ **Gold Cash Gold** - After dining, hope for memory loss or you'll never go anywhere else. With a name that harkens back to the space's past life as a pawnshop, Chef Brendon Edwards has combined a reverence for Southern culinary traditions, a dedication to Midwestern ingredients, and a distinctly Detroit design aesthetic to create a dining experience that is a perennial favorite among local food critics. The interior of the modern, airy space, is an irresistible mix of reclaimed materials and photogenic flourishes, punctuated by geometric stained glass, a large painted golden eagle emblazoned across the salvaged gym flooring, and a colorful wall of jarred pickled vegetables. Though renowned for their pickle-brined fried chicken and pepper gravy, the curated seasonal menu boasts many dishes worthy of the same fame. The carrot and cashew soup, duck dumplings, and cassoulet-stuffed quail should not be missed. As for the liquid portion of food pyramid, the restaurants boasts a splashy cocktail program and thoughtful selection of craft beers and ciders. *2100 Michigan Ave., www.goldcashgolddetroit.com, (313) 242-0770.*

★ **Green Dot Stables -** This equestrian-themed bar and slider joint is massively popular, and with good reason! Though it's often difficult to nab a seat, the fun, tasty, and affordable menu of eclectic sliders, deliciously seasoned specialty fries, craft beers, and house cocktails is well worth the wait. Mosey in through the swinging saloon doors and enjoy a drink at the bar by the cozy faux gas lamps while watching the ponies on TV, cuddle up in a booth under the cedar shake shingles, or bring a group and sit at one of the larger tables. The à la carte menu boasts nothing outside of the $2-4 range (literally nothing—cocktails and draft beer included), so pick out a slider or three and be sure to get some fries. While you can get a classic meat-and-cheese, the menu boasts 24 sliders, many with creative flair, like a venison coney, Korean (beef, kimchi, and peanut butter), tofu banh mi, or pork shoulder. Look for plenty to please omnivores and herbivores alike (Green Dot usually offers five vegetarian or vegan slider options). The spot features a fantastic yard and a three-season patio, to boot! *2200 W. Lafayette Blvd., www.greendotstables.com, (313) 962-5588.*

★ **ima -** The atmosphere at ima is fitting for a noodle spot that makes an art of udon. The restaurant's stark white walls, exposed ductwork, industrial pendant lights, and birchwood tables combine to create a contemporary yet comfortable gallery-like space. As for the art, all of Chef Mike Ransom's broths are cooked spot-on on-site for 12-14 hours, and are remarkable for their rich, deep, savory flavors that are at once balanced and complex. On a menu of strong options, the spicy pork udon—toasted chili broth, smoked pork loin, soft egg, gai lan, nori, and scallion—stands out, though the curry udon and golden curry riche would easily top the medal podium at most restaurants. Vegetarians will enjoy the boombap rice, yaki udon, or forest udon. Add-on options abound, and customers are encouraged to customize their dishes by adding ginger beef, roasted tofu, or one of the 22 other toppings. On the other side of the menu, look for a curated selection of beer, sake and shochu. Al fresco dining available on the covered, heated patio. *2015 Michigan Ave., www.imanoodles.com, (313) 502-5959.*

Iridescence - Sitting atop the MotorCity Casino Hotel, 17 stories in the sky, Iridescence offers soaring views of the Detroit skyline from 40-foot-high windows that stretch 180 feet across in what is easily one of the most dramatic, if slightly ostentatious, dining rooms in the city. Hundreds of pendant lights in glass bubbles float overhead while LED-lit panels subtly illuminate the walls and ceiling in a pearly glow of jewel-colored neon. And all of that is merely parlor dressing for the food. A multi-time recipient of the AAA four-diamond award and the Wine Spectator Award of Excellence, Iridescence truly does take fine dining to new heights. Drawing on French and Asian influences, Iridescence presents "deconstructed" American classics in a way that is nothing short of art. The 40-foot wine wall with an electronic pulley system that rotates its 300 or so on-hand labels will delight even the most casual oenophile. *2901 Grand River Ave., (313) 237-6732.*

★**Lady of the House -** Like the food, the space delightfully defies ready definition. The whitewashed hardwood paneling, green velvet banquettes, soft lighting, mismatched vintage china, and riverstone fireplace create an atmosphere that is at once cozy and handsome, upscale and rustic. The food is similarly complex. By elevating simple vegetables—think carrot steak—and cooking nose-to-tail, chef Kate Williams combines international inspiration and local ingredients to create an unforgettable menu. There's the savory roasted cauliflower with parmesan and fennel; the locally raised young farm greens salad with Basque cheese and tarragon vinaigrette; the succulent steak tartare, perfectly paired with charred leeks and an oyster aioli; and the crispy, creamy potato doughnuts served with sprigs of candied thyme, that are each easily worthy of another paragraph. The bar program is no slouch, either. The seasonal cocktail menu and extensive beer, wine, and cider options leave few reasons to go home thirsty. *1426 Bagley St, www.ladyofthehousedetroit.com, (313) 818-0218.*

LJ's Sweetheart Bar - Between the original mirrorball pillars, Budweiser "Great Kings of Africa" portraits, and the massive fish tank perched behind the bar, LJ's Sweetheart Bar—sometimes known as LJ's Lounge—is Detroit character with a capital "C." This Michigan Avenue dive attracts a cross-section of Corktown regulars, rock scene fashionistas, and awestruck tourists with its cheap beers and only-in-Detroit time-capsule comforts. It's been home to some of the city's most legendary (and mostly defunct) DJ nights, piloted from the bar's one-of-a-kind record library and DJ booth in the back. These days, don't miss Prankis with Bart Dangus on Monday nights, a proving grounds for Detroit's up-and-coming improv comics. For extra localist-points, keep an eye out for Charlie, the blue-shirted spirit who's rumored to haunt the bathroom hallway at the back of the bar. *2114 Michigan Ave., (313) 962-0013.*

Lucky Detroit Coffee - Detroit is fortunate indeed to have this gorgeous second-floor coffee shop, which sits above a men's barber shop. With exposed brick, vintage fixtures, and a chic, industrial vibe, this recent addition to Corktown's flourishing coffee scene features one of the city's best pour-overs. Or opt for a quick jolt of java with an espresso, ordered at the exquisite antique wooden bar (complete with stools that look right out of a Victorian soda shop). Once you've made your selection, grab a seat by the oversized windows and watch busy Michigan Avenue below. Best of all, the shop is open until 8pm during the week, which means that night owls can get their caffeine fix too. *2000 Michigan Avenue (2nd Floor), www.luckydetroit.com.*

Maltese American Benevolent Society - In the heart of the Michigan Avenue Corridor lies the Maltese American Benevolent Society, where Maltese Americans—real, honorary, and self-declared—sip domestic beers or basic cocktails and swap news from Malta or downtown Detroit. The interior of the space will make even the unacquainted nostalgic for the home country: Pictures of Malta's sandy coastlines, architecture, star soccer players, and influential citizens decorate the club. For a couple of quarters, visitors can crank up the volume on a classic jukebox full of '90s hits and Motown classics. But the real fun here is to be had with the gracious and hospitable regulars, who are known to buy a drink for a fresh, friendly face. While food isn't normally served, on Sundays visitors can buy delicious a Maltese pastizzi pastry, full of ground beef, peas, and cheese. Although the club is membership-based, the public can join the fun on Thursday through Sunday each week. *1832 Michigan Ave., (313) 961-8393.*

McShane's Irish Pub and Whiskey Bar - The handiwork of Sean, Ryan, and Bobby McShane, this spot is a contemporary, upscale take on the classic sports-orientated shuttle bar format and a lively pre-game watering hole. Opened in 2012, this popular sports bar offers a host of distractions from the game, including billiards tables, 17 TVs, a shotski (four shots affixed to a ski), jukebox, and an impressive draft list packed with Michigan craft beers. If you'd like to fill up before being tempted by a rink-side wiener, you're in luck—the food is tasty. The menu is best described as upscale bar fare with an Irish slant, including a veggie Philly supreme, Irish egg rolls, killer fish and chips (with thyme-seasoned fries), baked macaroni and cheese, and the Hammer of the Gods—a thick pile of ham, gouda, lettuce, and tomato on challah. *1460 Michigan Ave., www.mcshanespub.com, (313) 961-1960.*

Mercury Burger & Bar - Mercury Burger & Bar delivers upgraded, home-style versions of American favorites: delicious burgers ground fresh daily, classic sandwiches, dogs, fries, homemade onion rings, tasty salads, and dreamy tater tots, served in paper-lined baskets. They've got a full bar featuring Michigan craft beers and decadent hand-dipped milkshakes with addictive boozy "grown-up" versions available. The vibe at Mercury is casual and fun with a clean, subway-tile-and-chrome retro diner feel, a long bar, comfortable booths, and a handful of references to "Mercury," including a cool mercury-dime bar, and a larger-than-life Lincoln-Mercury photo. In the summer months, munch al fresco on the patio with a view of the iconic train station. *2163 Michigan Ave., www.mercuryburgerbar.com, (313) 964-5000.*

Motor City Wine - One part bar, one part wine shop, and one part live music venue, Motor City Wine takes on many faces, depending on when you stop in. Housed in an unassuming little building right in the middle of Corktown's busy Michigan Avenue, locals in the know flock to this shop for its thoughtfully curated collection of wines from around the world. The bar inside is dark and cozy, while a back door leads to a surprisingly bright and airy outdoor patio. Rotating selections of charcuterie and cheese are always available to go alongside big pours of the shop's diverse selection of wines, and pop-up food events happen regularly. Live music, ranging from jazz trios to techno, often transforms the normally quiet atmosphere inside into something completely different. And there's never any need to be intimidated by the wine list here—the bartenders are some of the friendliest and most knowledgeable in town. *1949 Michigan Ave., www.motorcitywine.com, (313) 483-7283.*

★**Mudgie's Deli** - In Detroit, meat is king—and Mudgie's is a top contender for the deli sandwich crown. This massively popular, once diminutive corner eatery has grown from a small neighborhood joint into a charming, homey labyrinth that encompasses several historic commercial spaces and homes. The eatery builds on the traditional deli model with an epically large menu and innovations such as its locally made Sy Ginsburg corned beef, adventurous daily soup specials, and a delectable apple potato salad. At both lunch and dinner, it's packed but never overrun, and its Sunday brunch is a gem. The only frustrating thing about this spot is selecting from its 40+ sandwich menu, forcing carnivores and vegetarians alike into fits of indecision over which house specialty to devour—though standouts include the Madill (turkey and smoked bacon), a perfected Reuben, and a vegetarian delight called the Tempeh of Doom. To top things off, the place offers an impressive selection of wine, beer, and craft sodas, as well as an intimate and cozy patio hidden away in the back. *1300 Porter St., www.mudgiesdeli.com, (313) 961-2000.*

★**Nancy Whiskey** - If the bartenders like you—REALLY like you—they might pull out the tattered book with photos of Nancy riding a horse through the bar on St. Patrick's Days of yore. This beer-and-a-shot joint carries a liquor license dating to 1902, making it one of the oldest watering holes in the city. The veteran Corktown establishment has benefited from a massive, historically respectful facelift following a near-devastating 2009 fire but still makes good on the traditions that made it a Corktown legend: neighborhood vibe, live blues on the weekends, and enough Irish whiskey to kill... well, a horse. Be sure to let your bartender know if it's your first time in—he or she might have a special treat for you. *2644 Harrison St., www.nancywhiskeydetroit.com, (313) 962-4247.*

Nemo's - It's like Field of Dreams, but in reverse: One of Detroit's longest-standing and most-revered sports bars did booming business for decades, thanks to the crowds that flocked to Tiger Stadium a few blocks away. But once the Tigers moved downtown to Comerica Park, the crowds kept coming. This devotion makes Nemo's the city's ultimate sports bar to this day. During home games, the rear parking lots are packed with tailgaters, and the bar's fleet of buses (painted in Corktown green and white) shuttle hundreds of fans to the sporting events of the season. Inside, of course you'll find plenty of big-screen TVs, but the main decor of the tin-ceilinged bar consists of dozens of framed newspapers chronicling the city's sports glory. With bartenders who could fill in for TV color commentators without breaking a sweat, and a hilariously no-frills food menu (burgers and chips, please), Nemo's is where the sporting crowd's true believers congregate. If you want to get a seat at the bar on Opening Day, get there early. *1384 Michigan Ave., www.nemosdetroit.com, (313) 965-3180.*

Ottava Via - Head West, young pizza-seekers! Housed in a historic bank building, with exposed ductwork and walls decorated with antiques, the interior of Ottava Via is at once loft-like and vaguely historic Tuscan. A contemporary pizza-oriented Italian restaurant with a clear appreciation for the past, this popular Corktown spot has the menu to match. Though guests will find outstanding paninis, porchetta, and pasta, veterans cut straight for the pizza, which is hard to top. Ottava Via makes a traditional Tuscan style pizza, noted for its thin, flaky crust and high sauce-to-topping ratio, which makes for an exquisite pie. The Rustica pizza (with potato, pancetta, egg, rosemary, and smoked provolone) and Artichoke (with roasted garlic, spinach pesto, arugula, cipollini onions, and tarofu cheese) are standouts. Don't miss the massive antique bar (though it would be hard to), with a well-appointed liquor selection and knowledgeable bartenders. During the summer months, enjoy the charming backyard patio, which features two traditional bocce lanes. *1400 Michigan Ave., www.ottavavia.com, (313) 962-5500.*

PJ's Lager House - Continuously operated as a restaurant, bar, or speakeasy since 1914, the Lager House has forged a reputation as one of the best joints in the city to catch local and national indie, punk, and garage rock 'n' roll. Since purchasing it in 2007, owner and music guru PJ Ryder has breathed new life into the venue, which now hosts shows—and draws crowds—almost every night. In addition to bringing the jams, the bar boasts food a cut above normal bar fare, with solid options for vegetarians and meat eaters alike, aptly billing it as a "kitchen with Detroit attitude and a dash of New Orleans flavor." Think homemade burgers—both meat and veg—burritos the size of your head, real deal po' boys, and gumbo. On off-nights, and before shows, there is often ping pong in the Jerome P. Cavanagh Social Room or, of course, you can just hunker down with a Stroh's at the long, history-laden bar. *1254 Michigan Ave., www.pjslagerhouse.com, (313) 961-4668.*

Red Dunn Kitchen - Business in the front, party in the back, this trendy New American destination is hidden away inside the Trumbull and Porter Hotel. Just look for a mural depicting a dapper gent's feet caught up in Detroit's infamous steamy streets. A restaurant and bar set by the firm that set the bar, Patrick Thompson Design—the name attached to some of Detroit's most celebrated recent interior design—the restaurant (and hotel for that matter) is contemporary and beautifully designed. With exposed concrete ceilings and floors and a distinguished atmosphere with lively accents, diners can choose between the cozy bar where they can ease into stylish booths, or the bright, courtyard-facing dining room. Allegedly, Red Dunn is slang for chicken, so it's no surprise that poultry is prominent, with creative stunners like fried chicken roulade and Korean barbecued chicken poutine. However, the deep breakfast-to-dinner menu will delight most, with simple crowd pleasers (e.g. a burger), vegetarian options (don't miss the cauliflower or popover), and even green eggs and ham. The spot offers a full bar, including house speciality gin and tea cocktails, as well as an outdoor courtyard bar, called the **Pump Room**, open during warmer months. *1331 Trumbull St., www.reddunnkitchen.com, 313-887-9477.*

★ **Slows Bar B Q -** Often cited as a shining example of local business in Detroit, Slows' soul-satiating cuisine has won over the hearts of longtime Detroiters, new transplants, suburban old-timers, and New York Times critics alike. Established in 2005, Slows boasts a well-designed, contemporary interior built mainly of reclaimed wood in an urban-yet-homey atmosphere perfect for the comfort food it serves. In general, the brisket, ribs, and pulled pork are revered, and the must-try sandwiches include The Yardbird (pulled smoked Amish chicken, mustard sauce, bacon, mushrooms, and cheddar)—which was named one of the top three sandwiches in America by the Travel Channel—The Longhorn (beef brisket, onion marmalade, smoked gouda, with a spicy sauce), and The Reason (smoked pulled pork butt, coleslaw, and pickle strips). Vegetarians love the place, too, for The Genius—a faux chicken wonder. Round out your meal with one or two of the life-affirming sides: succulent waffle fries, the homemade mac and cheese, sweet-potato mash, green beans, cornbread, old-time applesauce, and split pea and okra fritters—all of which are excellent receptacles for the many house-made sauces. Blame it on the huge selection of beers and bourbons, the mouth-watering entrees, or the overall affordable prices, but Slows gets packed at peak hours. Reservations are accepted for parties of six or more; otherwise it's recommended to come early—or wait it out at one of the many nearby bars in Corktown. *2138 Michigan Ave., www.slowsbarbq.com, (313) 962-9828.*

★ **The Sugar House -** With an emphasis on pre-Prohibition refinement, the Sugar House is home to some of Detroit's most exceptional craft cocktails. In an elegant atmosphere replete with taxidermy, vintage photos, and dramatic brass chandeliers, vest-clad bartenders and servers tend to candlelit tables. Following the grand tradition of fine cocktails, all syrups and juices are freshly house-made, so you won't find any artificial flavors at this dram shop, only high-quality ingredients and a carefully vetted drink menu of the highest caliber. If the selections on the seasonal menu don't strike your fancy, and you aren't drawn to one of the listed "101 classics," there's always "dealer's choice"—select a favorite liquor or theme and let the bartenders expand your palette. Though there isn't a full menu, the bar offers a selective assortment of gourmet small plates and bar snacks. Visit on Saturday or Sunday afternoons for their "eye-opener menu," featuring Bloody Marys and bagels. If you're lucky (or check the schedule) you can catch Spanish guitar, DJs, or jazz music throughout the week. *2130 Michigan Ave., www.sugarhousedetroit.com, (313) 962-0123.*

★ **Takoi -** On Corktown's western border, this restaurant—one of Detroit's finest and most creative food destinations—sits unassumingly inside of a windowless, single-story cinder block building, surrounded by an imposing sixteen-foot-tall chain link fence. Step inside, however, and you'll be transported to an entirely different place, an otherworldly space-scape accented by soft brightly colored lights and glowing decor in a rainbow of colors, a warren of low geometrically-patterned booths, and the aromas of Southeast Asia. Since opening in 2016 (then known as **Katoi**), Takoi's riffs on Thai food have earned heaps of praise, garnering awards and nominations from the *Detroit Free Press*, *Eater*, and the James Beard Foundation. Alongside more traditional fare like spicy papaya salad and bowls of curry noodles, you can indulge in crispy spare ribs coated in fish sauce caramel, whole fried snapper with mounds of fresh herbs and sticky rice, and egg rolls stuffed with short rib and chilies. Don't miss out on the fantastic cocktails, which often incorporate Thai teas, fresh herbs, and syrups infused with Southeast Asian flavors. Especially on weekend nights, expect a wait, but believe us, it's worth it! *2520 Michigan Ave., www.takoidetroit.com, (313) 855-2864.*

★ **Two James Spirits -** When the founder of a distillery is a self-described 'spirit snob' with a background as both a sommelier and a mixologist, you know the drinks are going to be good. Located in a historic industrial building, this popular Corktown tasting room and small-batch distillery sits in the shadow of the majestic Michigan Central Station (see separate entry). The stunning interior impresses with its mix of rough and refined textures, from the concrete bar in-the-round, to the patterned tin globes that hover above it, to the wall lined with whiskey barrels. Peer through one of those barrels—or get a tour—to view the masterful distilling process. At the bar you'll find inventive cocktails that use the house-made gin, bourbon, rye, vodka, rum, absinthe, and mezcal. The craft cocktail menu is among the best in Detroit. Though it changes with the seasons, a couple favorites include Fresh to Death (a crisp mezcal selection with a bit of kick) and A Rare Bird (a rye sour variation with pineapple and molasses). However, if you prefer to go with a classic, the cocktailian bartenders are masters, and will shake or stir their way to your heart. *2445 Michigan Ave., www.twojames.com, (313) 964-4800.*

★ **The UFO Factory** - A secret Eastern Market art space turned MOCAD art installation turned leading independent music venue and bar, the resilient UFO Factory was almost lost to a neighboring construction accident gone horribly awry, but thankfully it re-opened in 2018. Unlike any other bar in Detroit (and maybe the world), the interior of the other-worldly UFO Factory features an all-metallic silver paint job, gently pulsing alien lights, and cloud-inspired mirrors—and is marked by an unusually large satellite dish atop the roof. The venue features some of the city's best independent booking, and it's a great place to check out local acts like Protomartyr, as well as touring bands like The Blow, Shannon and the Clams, and Frankie Rose. Bonus if you enjoy your live music (or your karaoke, or your jukebox picks) with some of Detroit's tastiest and most creative hot dogs! Home to **Laika Dog** (named for the first animal to orbit earth, RIP), these wildly delicious meat or vegan franks come in inventive combinations that include banh mi, loaded nachos, kimchi, and others—or build your own. Add a side of custom, loaded tots, and now we're talking. If you need a little more, don't miss the free popcorn! *2110 Trumbull Ave., www.ufofactory.com.*

SHOPPING & SERVICES

Detroit Athletic Company - Located in a charming old building steps away from the site of where Tiger Stadium once stood, this athletic-wear emporium has something for every Tigers, Pistons, Red Wings, or Lions fan. Though not a huge store, it packs in the merch and, in addition to a stellar selection of T-shirts, caps, and sweatshirts (including some classic vintage throwback styles), it has an impressive array of other goods emblazoned with your favorite team's logo. From simple T-shirts to lapel pins to Tigers-themed BBQ sets to photo-realistic woven Red Wings blankets, the Detroit Athletic

Company is a one-stop shop to stock up on goods to show your team pride. *1744 Michigan Ave., www.detroitathletic.com, (313) 961-3550.*

★ **El Dorado General Store** - After a stint in advertising in New York, Erin Gavle returned to her hometown of Detroit to open El Dorado General Store. Fittingly named for the lost city of gold, Gavle's store is a treasure, perfectly blending elements of mysticism, the American West, and Bohemian culture to create this inviting, sun-filled boutique packed with with curious and beautiful objects at every turn. An adventure seeker, Gavle makes frequent journeys out West—living out of her "vansion"—to explore and find new treasures. These treasures come in the form of the well-curated items that make up her shop: vintage clothing for both men and women, mystical talismans and crystals, select antiques, and handcrafted jewelry, accessories, and homegoods, including candles and decor. As Gavle says, she tries to stock her general store with objects that will delight almost every visitor. You'll walk away inspired by the magical atmosphere of this destination speciality store. *1700 Michigan Ave., www.eldoradogeneralstore.com, (313) 784-9220.*

The Farmer's Hand - Tucked into a pint-sized space inside of a beautifully renovated turn-of-the-20th-century building, The Farmer's Hand may be the ideal neighborhood corner store. The emphasis here is firmly on the local. Fresh bundles of Corktown-grown sunflower shoots sit next to barrels of purple potatoes and onions grown right outside the city limits. In addition to the beautiful local produce, at its best in the summer and early fall, the shelves are always stocked with bread, jam, coffee, meat, ice cream, cheese, beer, wine, and more—nearly all of it locally sourced. If it's a quick bite you're after, European-style baguette sandwiches, salads studded with quinoa and local greens, and big slices of pie (carted in from West Village's celebrated Sister Pie, see separate entry) are all on offer. Lunch here is a special treat in the summer, when the store's limited seating doubles with the addition of shaded patio tables. *1701 Trumbull Ave., www.thefarmershand.com, (313) 377-8262.*

Franklin Furniture - Equal parts office furniture store and alternate view of Detroit businesses past, Franklin Furniture is crammed with inventory. Owner Jim Snyder procures furniture from defunct Detroit-area businesses—often with old documents still in the filing cabinets! You can wander through the dimly lit furniture-lined hallways to find vintage pieces or hang out in the front of the shop to browse through smaller office supplies. The warehouse doesn't have a distinct sign, but visitors can enter through what looks like a back door facing the street in the winter months and an open garage door in the summertime. Once inside, you'll be overwhelmed by the seemingly endless supply of often vintage office chairs, desks, conference tables, filing cabinets, and just about every other office accoutrement you can imagine. *5062 Loraine St., (313) 393-2500.*

★ **George Gregory** - After making a detour in Chicago, owner Caitlin Riney brought her penchant for men's fashion to Corktown in 2017. Now a popular destination for style-forward fellows, George Gregory is an exquisite store, from the historic storefront, to the hardwood floors, to the contemporary, industrially inspired displays, and the well-curated, quality apparel and accessories that she highlights. Not only is this Detroit's best selection of chambray button-ups, colorful patterned shirts, quality denim, style-forward accessories, shoes, and plaids for lads, but the offerings are available in sizes small to triple XL, with prices from $15-$115, so that a diverse array of gents can indulge in the sensible, stylish offerings. Look for perfect options for a sunny Sunday, a fashionable Friday, a notable night out, and everything in-between. *1422 Michigan Ave., www.shopgeorgegregory.com, (313) 285-8345.*

★ **Hello Records** - Small in size but stacked with wax, Hello Records is a great place to load up on music at fantastic prices. With beautiful hardwood floors and wall-to-wall record shelves, this unassuming store has a laid-back atmosphere made for browsing. Although they stock rock, soul, gospel, funk, jazz, disco, techno, hip hop, and folk LPs and 45s from all eras, this shop is especially popular among collectors looking for jazz, soul, and dance platters—particularly forgotten soul gems from Detroit's hundreds of local music labels. With Hello's low prices, customers can buy an album for a song, even on the deepest cuts. Knowledgeable owner Wade Kergan is without pretense, and his friendly staff is approachable and excited to introduce customers to new artists, albums, and genres. The store's popularity among both buyers and sellers leads to a constantly changing inventory. If you don't find what you're looking for, come back after lunch. *1459 Bagley St., www.hellorecordsdetroit.com, (313) 300-5654.*

★ **John K. King Used & Rare Books** - If you're looking for an in-town escape, lose yourself in books at Michigan's largest used and rare bookstore, and one of Detroit's best and most beloved shopping experiences. This four-story former glove factory, once moved from its original moorings to make room for a highway six decades ago, is a bibliophile's sanctuary. With a collection of more than one million books, you can treasure hunt for hours through aisles upon aisles of floor-to-ceiling stacks. If you're not browsing for bargains, peculiarities, or happy accidents but have something particular in mind, just ask one of the incredibly helpful and knowledgeable staff members to point you in the right direction. Thankfully, the titles are well-organized. *901 W. Lafayette Blvd., www.rarebooklink.com, (313) 961-0622.*

Mama Coo's Boutique - Located in what was once a dusty-shelved liquor store, Mama Coo's is a treasure trove of vintage goodies of another kind: gorgeous clothing, accessories, and curios to please all tastes—from minimalist to psychedelic. Full of unique pieces (1980s turquoise leather skirt? Yes, please!) and homemade items, every visit to Mama Coo's is different—a kaleidoscope of colorful shirts, dresses, jewelry, and much more. Snag your favorite piece before it's gone, and don't worry—great deals abound, so you won't do too much damage on your wallet. Step inside this friendly neighborhood shop and you're sure to find something for a new flirtation, an old friend, or yourself. *1701 Trumbull Ave., www.mamacoosboutique.com, (313) 404-2543.*

Meta Physica Wellness Center - Featuring raw organic juices, smoothies, and elixirs, the juice bar at Meta Physica is the ultimate recovery companion to a deep tissue massage or an hour of detoxing in one of this wellness center's infrared saunas—not to mention the perfect antidote to a night (or even a long weekend) of overindulgence. Meta Physica's beverage offerings are bold in color and flavor (think pungent wheatgrass shots and vibrant turmeric tonics) and its holistic menu emphasizes ingredients that are as nourishing as they are delicious. Still debating whether to stop in for an alkaline, anti-inflammatory green juice packed with chlorophyll, vitamins, minerals, and the full spectrum of amino acids, or just hitting the Whole Foods smoothie bar? Let aesthetics guide your decision and consider that at Meta Physica, instead of dodging shopping carts you'll be perched comfortably at a marble bar top beneath the mood lighting, enjoying a space designed expressly for relaxation. *1701 Trumbull Ave., www.metaphysicamassage.com, (313) 303-7611.*

Metropolis Cycles - This popular Corktown bike shop looks as sleek on the outside, with its slate grey-and-white color scheme, as it does on the inside, with its raw, contemporary interior, pleasantly spacious layout, and meticulously organized bikes and accessories. (It's also not often you find a bike shop with such a lovely collection of thriving, potted plants!) The knowledgeable and enthusiastic staff is always ready to help you with whatever ails your bike, and the full service shop can give you a tune-up, find new parts for your bike, or just fill your tires with air. Their new and used bike selection is well-curated, with choices in top condition and prices accomodating a range of budgets. Whether you wear spandex or denim while riding (we won't judge), Metropolis has a plethora of styles to choose from, including commuter bikes, touring bikes, stunning road bikes—and the occasional hooptie. *2117 Michigan Ave., www.metropoliscycles.bike, (313) 818-3248.*

National Dry Goods Co. - Since 1921, National Dry Goods has supplied Detroit with affordable, "durable, rugged, and comfortable" clothing and shoes for school, work, and play. Women, men, and children can find everything from school uniforms to Dickie's work pants to Carhartt coats, gloves, and jumpsuits. The store also offers custom screen-printing services. Other accessories— including umbrellas, colorful roll socks, wool berets, and ball caps—keep customers coming back to this one-stop apparel shop. *1200 Trumbull Ave., www.nationaldrygoods.com, (313) 961-3656.*

Rachel's Place - Tucked away in a brownstone row house on a residential street just north of Michigan Avenue, Rachel's Place always seems like a wonderful secret, even though it's popular with in-the-know vintage lovers and is just steps away from all the

Corktown action. Owner Rachel Leggs' fabulous style and eye are apparent in the selection and organization of this bountiful and well-curated store. Her friendly welcome will make you feel at home from the second you first set foot in the door. After only a couple of visits, when you walk in, she's likely to pull out spot-on finds that she's been holding behind the desk for you. If you like vintage clothes, it's nearly impossible to set foot inside without finding something to buy. *2124 Pine St., (313) 964-9008.*

Salvation Army - The Fort Street Salvation Army is a colossal thrift store with a choice selection of small housewares, linens, and tchotchkes for the discerning thrifter. The clothing selection is above average and extremely plentiful. In addition to these items, the store sells furniture, though this is not its strong suit. As a perk, this Salvo is cleaner than other area thrift stores and boasts restrooms and fitting rooms, which are fairly uncommon in similar outfits. *1200 W. Fort St., www.salvationarmyusa.org, (313) 309-3372.*

Xavier's 20th Century Furniture - Since 1985, Xavier's has brought the finest collection of modern, functional, and famous names in furniture design to Michigan Avenue. Here, owner James Slade keeps things fresh and lively from his burgundy brick building, which is accented with popping robin's egg blue trim and stunning window displays of his latest vintage furniture finds. Shoppers will not only admire modern pottery and glass, coffee tables, sofas, elegantly framed paintings, and rare Hudson's fur hats, but they will hear the history behind each piece and the story of each designer from Slade himself. Collectors will appreciate Slade's eye for Gilbert Rohde and Charles and Ray Eames pieces, as well as modern and contemporary furniture from the 1920s through the 1980s. Rare pieces, such as Art Deco Chase chrome candlesticks, appear as Slade discovers gems at antique malls and estate sales across the country. Xavier's cult following of customers snatches up these exciting items quickly, so be sure to visit often. Filmmakers and photographers are also welcome to inquire for prop rentals. *2546 Michigan Ave., www.x20th.com, (313) 964-1222.*

CULTURAL ATTRACTIONS

Ponyride - One of many projects launched by model-turned-restaurateur-turned-philanthropist Phil Cooley, Ponyride transformed a declining 30,000-square-foot industrial office complex into a community-driven art space where tenants, composed of fledgling creative enterprises, pay just 10 to 20 cents per square foot in exchange for sharing their craft and expertise with the surrounding community. The result is an inspiring, aesthetically beautiful space that is filled with surprises around every corner. As of the writing of this guide, some of our favorite enterprises housed in the facility include celebrated java slingers and roasters **Anthology Coffee**; the **Beehive Recording Company** record label; **Rebel Nell**, which employs women across Detroit to design and create jewelry made from pieces of graffiti; and **Detroit Tango Dojo**, an Argentine dance workshop. Because the building itself does not hold regular public hours, be sure to contact the party you intend to visit prior to your trip, or join one of the weekly public tours held every Wednesday at 2pm. *1501 Vermont St., www.ponyride.org.*

ENTERTAINMENT & RECREATION

The Corner Ballpark and Willie Horton Field of Dreams - For more 100 years, the Tigers called this corner—"The Corner"—home, from Bennett Park, to Navin Field, to Briggs Stadium, and finally **Tiger Stadium**. Evolving with each successive owner and expansion until its final game on the eve of the millennium, the site has seen many sacred baseball moments: Ty Cobb stealing three bases on three consecutive pitches in 1911, the team's first World Series victory in 1935, the end of Lou Gehrig's streak of 2,130 consecutive games in 1939, Denny McClain's 31st win in the team's '68 championship season, Dave Bergman's dogged 13-pitch walk-off home run in '84, and Robert Fick's grand slam in 1999 as the last home run, RBI, and hit at Tiger Stadium. While the original stadium was lost in a dogged preservation fight between the Old Tiger Stadium Conservancy and a city agency in 2009, the heroic non-profit, led by President (and guidebook editor Dad) Thom Linn ultimately triumphed. Teaming up with **The Detroit Police Athletic League (PAL)**, the organizations raised more than $20-million to fund the construction of a new stadium on the site—meticulously preserving the historic field's dimensions and rich legacy. Now the headquarters of Detroit PAL, the site hosts youth athletic programming for more than 15,000 local kids each year, with seasonal daily amateur ball games that the public can attend. The facility also offers rentable banquet space and exhibits that highlight Tiger Stadium artifacts and detail the history of the "The Corner," one of the most hallowed grounds in baseball. *1680 Michigan Ave., www.detroitpal.org, (313) 833-1600.*

MotorCity Casino - Since opening in 1999, the MotorCity Casino has become renowned among area gamblers for its unique ambiance, attentive staff, dining options, and array of gaming machines. In a Las Vegas style reminiscent of a concept car, the exterior's wavy chrome and ostentatious neon light display complement the building's interior, which draws design and aesthetic inspiration from local automotive tradition, including fixtures modeled after automobile parts interspersed with architectural elements custom-made by West Coast automotive designer Chip Foose. The on-site casual dining options, including the **Assembly Line Buffet** and **The Lodge Diner**, offer unparalleled selection, and pay further homage to the area's automotive heritage. For an upscale option, try Iridescence (see separate entry), which offers inventive New American cuisine and breathtaking views of the city. While even the most seasoned card shark will enjoy the wide assortment of table games, MotorCity Casino is better known for its gaming machines—especially its loose slots and video poker. The casino's 2,800 games include classic reel games, fivereel options, video poker, and video slots—and come in denominations from $.01 to $50. *2901 Grand River Ave., www.motorcitycasino.com, (313) 237-7711.*

SITES

★**Michigan Central Station -** Once a hauntingly beautiful, captivating image of urban blight, Michigan Central Station was closed for three decades before being purchased by Ford Motor Company in 2018—an event that stunned and delighted fans of the iconic Beaux-Arts building. In its long-ruined state, the station, which is set on the apron of Roosevelt Park, is one of the city's most popular (and beautiful) buildings—long a favorite destination for clandestine urban spelunkers, as well as an occasional backdrop in major film and television productions, including *Transformers and Batman v Superman: Dawn of Justice.* Opened in 1913, the station clocks in at an impressive 500,000 square feet and stands eight stories. However, despite ambitious neoclassical flourishes—such as ionic columns and vaulted ceilings in marble rooms made to mimic Roman bath houses—the building faced challenges from the start. The construction of MCS was rushed because of a fire at the city's

prior train depot, and consequently, the upper floors of the building were never completed or occupied. Once Detroit's streetcar system was dismantled, in the postwar years, the station became hard to access, an issue only magnified when the city's freeways began to make driving more attractive than train travel. Consequently, the station struggled during the second half of the 20th century, and was gradually wound down before being closed in 1988. Left vacant, as it fell into ruin. Despite being considered "unsaveable" by some because of its massive size and lengthy period of abandonment, in 2018, Ford announced its intention to complete more than $740 million in renovations to make Michigan Central Station its hub for a new Corktown campus focused on the future of transportation, ushering in a new era for the building—and the city. *2405 W. Vernor St.*

Worker's Row House - Built in 1849, and one of the oldest surviving homes in Detroit, though now empty, this unassuming three-unit row house was occupied continuously for 150 years, originally by Irish immigrants, and then a steady succession of other hardworking Detroiters. In the early life of the building, density and rental rates were so high that as many as 12 people lived in each of the three 560-square-foot units at a given time. Though threatened by the development of a church parking lot, the Greater Corktown Development Corporation, which plans to develop the structure into a workers museum, rescued the historic building from the wrecking ball. In the meantime, Wayne State University is in the midst of a long-term archeological dig on the site, recovering everyday artifacts of 19th century Detroit life. *Located on Sixth St. between Bagley St. and Labrosse St.*

POINTS OF INTEREST

Batman v Superman Church Location - This church, the angular and historic Most Holy Trinity, was a prominent filming location for the movie *Batman v Superman: Dawn of Justice. 1050 Porter St.*

Brian 'Sintex' Mural - In this politically relevant mural cycle, artist Sintex (aka Brian Glass) has rendered civil rights heroes, symbols of resistance, and remembered victims, including Chief Crazy Horse, Elijah Muhammad, and Malice Green into present day Core City. *4731 Grand River Ave.*

Brother Nature Farm - This urban farm supplies a number of local restaurants with fresh produce, runs a community-supported agriculture (CSA) operation, and can be found at its stand every Saturday at Eastern Market. About once a week, the farm also sells prepared foods from an old Airstream trailer located next to its farmland. *2913 Rosa Parks Blvd.*

Fisheye Farms - Andy Chae's urban farm, located just south of the True North Quonset Hut development, features long rows of greens, radishes, and other produce. Most of the harvest makes its way onto menus at high end restaurants throughout town, however you can grab some more yourself at the Wayne State Farmers Market on Wednesdays in the summer. *2334 Buchanan St.*

Hope Takes Root Garden - One of the older community gardens in the city, the plants here get a boost from the bees that the members keep on site. *2829 Wabash St.*

Joe's Auto Truck Welding Perforated Metal Installation - This abandoned auto repair shop received a striking makeover in 2012, when University of Michigan graduate students filled in its missing windows with undulating, geometric metal sheets. *2223 Perry St.*

Mary Ellen Riordan Mural - This otherwise unassuming North Corktown duplex features an impressive mural along its northern face commemorating former Detroit Federation of Teachers president Mary Ellen Riordan, best known as the first woman in America to head a major labor union. *3437 Cochrane St.*

Monumental Kitty - Artist Jerome Ferretti's brick sculpture of a huge cat head, paw, and tail was inspired both by the nearby former Tiger Stadium site, as well as the abundance of cats hanging around in North Corktown. *1717 Fisher Fwy.*

Spirit of Hope Farm - Operated by the adjacent Spirit of Hope Church, this farm aims to beautify the neighborhood, stock the church's food programs, and provide an educational opportunity for local children and adults alike. *1561 Myrtle St.*

True North - These contemporary arching metal quonset huts, inspired by military and industrial designs, won multiple architectural awards when they were completed in 2017. They host a unique live/work community of artists, writers, and entrepreneurs. *4711 16th St.*

CHAPTER 5
SOUTHWEST

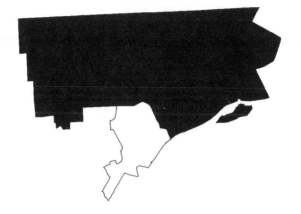

No visit to the city is complete without a trip to Southwest Detroit. This collection of historic neighborhoods is a regional destination for its Central and South American cuisine, vibrant commercial districts, and local cultural amenities. Foodies, history buffs, art and music lovers, bargain hunters, and architecture fans can spend a lifetime— or an afternoon—exploring Southwest Detroit and never soak everything in. As we define it, Southwest Detroit spans 16.2 square miles, and is bounded by Tireman Avenue, I-75, the Detroit River, and the city limits.

Since becoming part of Detroit between 1857 and 1922, Southwest Detroit has remained one of the most ethnically, religiously, and racially diverse areas in the city. Drawn by the promise of Ford's $5 day at the neighboring Rouge Plant, waves of German, Hungarian, Irish, Italian, Russian, Romanian, Czech, Armenian, Appalachian, and African-American workers flocked to Southwest Detroit through the postwar era. Today, this legacy of popularity among immigrants continues through the many South and Central Americans living in, and moving to, the area. Southwest is home to more than 75,000 residents and is growing, by most accounts. Many know parts of Southwest Detroit as Mexicantown, but alongside the many residents of Mexican heritage are smaller contingents of people of Argentinian, Bolivian, Chilean, Colombian, Cuban, Ecuadorian, Dominican, El Salvadorian, Guatemalan, Honduran, Nicaraguan, Panamanian, and Puerto Rican ancestry. New immigrants are increasingly of South and Central American heritage, a fact reflected in the ever-more diverse restaurant options in the area.

Southwest Detroit is home to a diverse group of neighborhoods, each with unique identities, development patterns, and evolutionary directions. Among other neighborhoods, Southwest Detroit is home to Boynton, Carbon Works, Claytown, Delray, Hubbard Farms, Hubbard Richard, Mexicantown, Michigan Martin, Oakwood Heights, and Springwells. Although each of these neighborhoods offers a distinct character, their shared historical popularity among immigrants has created many physical and aesthetic similarities. Because of the past—and in some neighborhoods, current—influx of immigrants and working-class residents, the area features blocks upon blocks of brick and wood frame homes in Foursquare, Craftsman, and Colonial Revival styles, most typically of between 1,000 and 2,000 square feet, and built between 1890 and 1930. The streets of Southwest Detroit are typically narrow, highly walkable, and flanked by beautifully aged trees. Along many residential blocks, visitors will find charming neighborhood bars or corner markets tucked away, far from major roads. Many Southwest neighborhoods straddle or abut the area's primary commercial artery, West Vernor Highway, which despite its name, is a stroll-worthy, narrow commercial corridor, with tree-lined shopping districts corralling unusually congenial traffic congestion, parking-lot taco trucks, summer popsicle vendors on bikes pedaling in and out of side streets, and scores of independent businesses packed with locals. The T-shaped corridor formed by West Vernor Highway from Lawndale Street to Beard Street, and Springwells Street from West Vernor to I-75, is especially dense with activity. This area is also awash with stunning, high-caliber murals and public art.

Although nearly every neighborhood in Southwest has reasons to visit, a few areas rank among our favorites. Those looking to enjoy a bustling, diverse urban neighborhood awash with delightful Mexican history, culture, and flavors should explore Mexicantown and the West Vernor corridor. Visitors looking to soak up some vintage character at a corner dive should follow their boozy divining rods to Springwells, where character-rich watering holes are seemingly tucked around every corner. Visitors looking for Central and South American restaurants—such as Pupuseria Y Restaurante Salvadoreno, and El Rey de las Arepas—should explore the northern reaches of the neighborhood, particularly north of John Kronk Street. Those exploring Detroit for extended periods may want to explore Delray, the largely industrial area south of Fort. The area is home to charming old-timey establishments such as Motz Restaurant and the Carbon Athletic Club that many fear may relocate in the face of the construction of the Gordie Howe International Bridge nearby. Visitors looking to stroll through a beautiful, tree-lined, historic neighborhood amid the sweet smell of fresh tortillas and admire fine Romanesque, Colonial Revival, Cape Cod, Foursquare, and Craftsman architecture should look no further than Hubbard Farms.

BARS & RESTAURANTS

★**Abick's Bar** - Don't tell anyone, but Abick's might be the classiest secret in the neighborhood. Behind the unassuming facade of this bar at the intersection of two residential streets in Southwest Detroit lies a century-old family tradition. Until she passed, Maya Abick

Soviak, the octogenarian owner and barkeep, lived her entire life in the apartment upstairs and had a reputation for fine cocktails and legendary stories. The barkeeps who tend bar at Abick's today carry on Soviak's tradition. Patrons are welcomed into a cozy, well-worn front room complete with a tin ceiling, beautiful brass cash register, and a bar-long wooden liquor cabinet featuring stained-glass windows. The bar offers a secluded, plush cigar lounge in the rear, which features two TVs, rental lockers, and a curated selection of cigars for sale. Bring a treat for Samson, the friendly and endearing bull mastiff and unofficial mascot. The bar also features a pool table, darts, and limited menu. *3500 Gilbert St., (313) 894-9329.*

Angel's Place - Angel's is an excellent option for the peckish looking for lunchtime variety. This cheap, delectable Puerto Rican carryout joint on Michigan Avenue is easy to spot, with its bright red patriotico paint scheme, and is tough to mistake for any other restaurant once inside. Dine-in service is possible at a few red-and-white clothed tables, but ambience skews toward the Spartan. Quick, cheap takeaways—like alcapurria (fried banana mash stuffed with chicken), pasteles (meat and potato stuffed fritters), and tostones (fried flat bananas)—are kept warm instead of made to order, so arriving earlier is better. Dinners of beef, chicken, and pork are served with traditional rice and beans. For beverages, customers may choose between Malta and Pepsi. *7824 Michigan Ave., (313) 846-7381.*

Antojitos El Catracho - Translated, the name Honduran Snacks only describes the first page of the menu. This pleasant surprise in an otherwise archetypal strip mall offers delicious, loosen-your-belt portions of *really*-south-of-the-border specialities from Guatemala, El Salvador, Nicaragua, and Honduras. Aside from a small mural of a campesino and several Central American flags, the otherwise unadorned, Spartan white walls and simple beige tile floors showcase an attention to cleanliness. On the extensive pan-Central American menu, the pupusas (with their pleasing crisp, cheesy finish, loroco crunch, and cabbage bedding), and painstakingly crafted tamales, with their distinctive moist texture, and subtly sweet flavor, are reason enough for a visit. The outstanding tostones, yuca fries, tajadas, bistec encebollado, and carne asada are reason enough never to leave. Though many Eliot Ness-approved beverage options are offered, many guests bring their own beer and wine. *4627 Vernor Hwy., (313) 784-9361.*

Armando's Mexican Restaurant - A favorite stop for many a hungry Detroiter, this charming Mexican restaurant offers large portions at small prices. Setting the scene with a tiled decor, a welcoming atmosphere, and traditional Mexican music, the kitchen whips up classic favorites, as well as Tex-Mex options, with standards like botanas, tacos, and enchiladas (with a special zesty sauce) serving as consistently stellar options. Every weekday, the spot hosts a flavorful all-you-can-eat lunch buffet, complete with homemade salsas and pitchers of margaritas. Open until 2am on weekdays and 4am on weekends, the place is an ideal postbar destination. For those lucky enough to skeeter in before last call, Armando's has a full bar, with extra-solid margaritas and mojitos. *4242 W. Vernor Hwy., (313) 554-0666.*

Asty Time Dominican Cuisine - The outside of this hidden gem is modest and easy to miss, but you'll know you're getting warmer when you catch the aroma of masterful grilling that wafts from the many outdoor stands that surround what locals call "Dominican Corner." Enter through the knotty pine vestibule to find this warm, inviting, and tidy family restaurant, painted with folksy murals of farming and, curiously, the Mayan ruin Chichen Itza. Originally a secret, in-home carryout operation, Asty Time has always been about working together as a family: Parents Asty and Edra Acosta run the kitchen, while their endearing kids serve and host. Small but mighty, the menu features two dozen traditional dishes from the Dominican Republic, a cuisine that draws on Spanish, Caribbean, and African influences. Highlights include Tostones (fried plantain), Arroz con Hibichuela (rice and stewed beans), Mangu de Platano (mashed plantains), Mofongo (fried, garlicky mashed plantains with pork), Chuleta Frita (fried pork chops marinated in sofrito, an aromatic sauce), and Carne de res Guisada (stewed, sofrito-soaked beef). Don't miss Asty's special condiment, a mayo and ketchup concoction—you should dab some on your plantains, some on your rice, and probably on everything else, too. *7340 McGraw Ave., www.astytime.com, (313) 285-9390.*

Black Horse Cantina - Rarely is a bar name phone-book perfect, so that a person who doesn't know it can get a sense of the place just by landing on it with their index finger. Black Horse is exactly such a place. Less a dive bar than a rebuke of more polished establishments, the place is what it says it is, notwithstanding the obscure and manifold meaning the animal portends. The cantina is kelly green, cavernously large, and adorned with pulsing strobes, video poker monitors, occasional lounge furniture, and a long wooden bar. "Cerveza" is on the menu, but so are dozens of top-shelf tequilas, making this dark den one of the finest spots in Detroit for sipping distilled agave. Black Horse benefits from its surroundings, such as it can and such as they are: The watering hole is situated across from the sleepless steel plant on Zug Island (see separate entry), and offers visitors a post-apocalyptic nightly "fireworks" show, as the island shoots flames into the night sky. There are other nearby Black Horse locations, but this is our favorite. Cash recommended. *7844 W. Jefferson Ave. (313) 846-3036.*

Brooksey's - While it hasn't always been Brooksey's, there has been a bar at 7625 W. Warren since 1925. Ownership has changed, but the antique dark wood bar and back bar remain, adding a touch of old-timey class to a modern social spot. Inside is a deep, cavernous place with a well-loved dance floor flanked by two poles available for use as long as patrons keep clothed, with amber-tinted lights around a brass-colored ceiling rail turned on when action mellows. Brooksey's brings a variety of visitors and is known among locals as a familiar spot. The outside wall bears a mural of the bar's namesake—the owner's departed father. Brooksey's maintains a community interest—open mic nights, open pool nights, and event rental are offered. *7625 W. Warren Ave., (313) 898-8099.*

Camino Real Mexican Grill - With its airy, expansive patio, and conifer-hued Mexican lumberjack-fantasyland dining room, Camino Real has been luring customers past all of the more on-the-beaten-path options for years. Inside, the restaurant boasts scads of knotty pine paneling and furniture as well as vivid Mexican art, wagon parts, and climbing ivy in an L-shaped space that flanks the large patio. The extensive menu checks all of the typical boxes—tacos, tortas, tostadas—but keeps going to include numerous unusual options for soups, breakfast, and seafood. Visitors should not miss the birria (a spicy goat stew), ostiones preparados (delicately seasoned oysters), and, for the more adventurous, cabeza (head meat). Leave room for a double watermelon cone at the patio-side ice cream parlor on the way out. *1100 Central Ave., www.restaurantcaminoreal.com, (313) 297-8804.*

Carbon Athletic Club - If your idea of a balanced diet is a Labatt in each hand, you'll fit right in. Situated at the intersection of two busy train tracks on a rough-and-tumble corner of Delray, this dive bar is a private social club frequented by colorful retired steelworkers, though friendly strangers can typically silver tongue their way inside for a visit. As you pass the old anti-tank gun in the parking lot and make your way inside, you'll be struck by the 1950s wood-paneled walls clad with 1930s amateur football memorabilia, antique tin ceiling, and vintage wood bar—all of which dances a bit every 15-20 minutes as trains pass. As an old-time shot-and-a-beer spot, the menu has a solid selection of domestic and imported beers in cans and bottles, as well as a respectable stable of mass market liquor, all at prices that would have been considered cheap during the Nixon Administration. Though there's no food—aside from the complimentary cheeseballs and Chex mix—guests can bring takeout. *111 Gates St., (313) 554-3518.*

Cas Bar - A play on the name of the adjacent Casper Street, the understated curiosity-inviting vintage neon sign shining through the bar's hexagonal window is indicative of the tarnished treasure inside. While the galley-style bar, which caters almost entirely to grizzled neighborhood regulars, isn't polished by any means, it's an inviting and friendly verbal repository of Southwest Detroit lore. So, if you're feeling social, order a Stroh's, and prepare to talk shop. There's a pool table in the back. *7800 Michigan Ave., (313) 581-9777.*

Charlie's Bar - Detroit's response to the international shortage of Art Deco dive bars, Charlie's Bar draws from the best of 1930s style, 1970s entertainment, and 1980s drink prices. A small, friendly neighborhood bar on a lively strip of Springwells, Charlie's is a quiet space offering Centipede, a large projection screen, a pool table, darts, and a jukebox alongside the intricate Art Deco woodwork behind the bar. The impressive projector makes this a solid choice to watch the game, but the woodwork, darts, and pool table make this a great place to work on your elbow bends with friends. In contrast to most dives, cocktail drinkers will be impressed by the selection of liquors. *1503 Springwells St., (313) 849-3951.*

Chicago's Pizza - Whether you're craving a classic round or a deep, saucy, cheesy Chicago-style pizza pie, this family-owned carryout pizza joint has the pie for you. Not only does Chicago's Pizza serve up the classic sauce-on-top deep dish at a few dollars cheaper than Pizza Papalis (see separate entry), but delivery is also available. Wings and subs make great supplements to the spot's iconic specialty, the Mexican Pizza, which piles Chorizo, ham, pepperoni, beans, onions, and peppers atop a classic round crust. Open late. *4650 W. Vernor Hwy., www.chicago-pizza-detroit.com, (313) 843-3777.*

Colombo's Coney - An adorable little old-school diner that's clean but not overly bright for those still recovering from late-night indulgences, Colombo's features a shiny new exterior, overstuffed red booth seating, and plenty of counter stools for a good view of the grill top. Scrape together the last of your change to grab a deal your out-of-town friends will envy: a $2 breakfast special of eggs, toast, and hashbrowns (served 6am–11am) or splurge and pay an extra dollar to get some meat with that breakfast. *5414 W. Vernor Hwy., (313) 849-0995.*

Detroit 75 Kitchen - Chef Mike Nassar's stationary food truck, Detroit 75 Kitchen operates near Junction and Fort in southwest Detroit. A Detroit native, Chef Mike started serving from his Fort Street truck in 2016 to anchor the neighborhood with unique Mediterranean fusion food. The truck offers elevated street food with an emphasis on fresh, local ingredients, distinct flavor combinations, and remixes of familiar dishes. In addition to several shawarma and falafel options, the menu includes gooey barbecue chicken egg rolls, loaded Philly sandwiches, piquant garlic-cilantro fries, fresh lemonade, and recurring specials like Applewood smoked chicken. Dine-in guests can enjoy Detroit 75's patio dining area, with Fort Street traffic acting as a fourth wall and I-75 concealed in the back. Strange as it sounds, the juxtaposition works, as the patio feels legitimately secluded, thanks to dozens of herb and flower boxes, picnic table furniture, street art, a fountain, and a canopy of shade umbrellas. Delivery available. Closed on weekends. *4800 W. Fort St., www.detroit75kitchen.com, (313) 843-3215.*

Dino's Cafe - Tucked between some railroad tracks and an abandoned thermostat plant, this shot-and-a-beer joint is easy to miss, but worth the U-turn. The inside of this dark, strikingly unpretentious spot is adorned with NASCAR hoods, beer memorabilia, Christmas lights, and general dive detritus, all tied together by an oversized mural of a green and brown ribbon encircling the room. Behind the bar, owner Dino Carrer showcases his Tetris skills, keeping an expansive selection of liquor and mixers; a comprehensive stable of domestic and imported beers; several racks of snacks and smokeables; a lighted glass-block display; and a fully stocked grill and fry station all within the confines of this antique wooden 12-seater. The 13-item Guy Fieri-style menu offers a healthy mix of pleasantly unhealthy options including fried

cheese sticks, fried mushrooms, french fries, fried pizza sticks, fried wing dings, onion rings, and an outstanding hamburger. Ashtrays provided. Baby shower catering available. *1601 Waterman St. (313) 842-6006.*

Donovan's Pub - This pub wears the title "dive bar" with pride. Cheap, cold beers, the occasional musical act, and an off-the-beaten path vibe are sure to welcome you on any given night. The bar embraces a nonchalant joie de vivre—the Christmas lights, antique breweriana, and Detroit ephemera hanging on the walls are emblematic of the laid-back vibe and easygoing staff. From behind the old-timey bar, the affable staff digs into its deep inventory of greasy bar food, call liquors, and bottled beers to the sounds of classic rock, pop, and country. On the right nights, local bands grace the stage, but one thing remains the same: no frills. If you're looking for a friendly barkeep and a place to drown your sorrows without having to worry about a whopping bar tab, you've found your match. No drafts. *3003 W. Vernor Hwy., (313) 964-2267.*

Donut Villa - With the vintage modernist signs and pungent doughnut aroma drawing customers in from throughout the neighborhood, it's no wonder that it's usually hard to find a seat at the counter. Open since the Eisenhower administration, Donut Villa is a thrifty sweet tooth's paradise: The cheerful staff makes all of the more than 30 varieties of 65-cent doughnuts—including the ever-popular pumpkin doughnuts—and coffee all day, ensuring you're always getting fresh treats. Don't leave without ordering a handful of nickelnuts—the renowned 5-cent doughnut holes. Gambling fans will be relieved to know you can purchase lottery tickets at the counter. *5875 W. Vernor Hwy., (313) 849-4752.*

★ **Duly's Place Coney Island -** Not a place for claustrophobics, Duly's is at most a 12-foot-wide shotgun style diner with a handful of tightly packed tables reminiscent of a Depression-era lunch counter—with Depression-era prices. Open 24 hours, the coney is dotted with memorabilia, newspaper clippings, photographs, and regulars who look like they've been there since the place opened in 1921, giving it a certain indescribable charm. While the faithful who ascribe to the Duly's dogma will attest to the fact that the counter serves up the best coney in the city, this is an argument for the ages—one that can be settled only with a first-person sample. Those who aren't coney fans can sample the breakfast, which is served all day and night, or the tasty homemade soups. Just look for the logo that's the well-dressed hot dog equivalent of Mr. Peanut. *5458 W. Vernor Hwy., (313) 554-3076.*

★ **El Asador Steakhouse -** The term steakhouse sells the place short. Though the ribeyes, sirloins, and New York strips are divine, chef and owner Luis Garza has mastered the surf side of the menu, too. El Asador offers Cadillac food at Chevy prices—an elevated take on Mexican food, with dueling steak and seafood specialities and a menu boasting sophisticated ingredients such as aged sirloin, lobster, shrimp, squid, and mussels. From appetizers to desserts, the whole menu is a model of epicurean taste, though the camarones en salsa de langosta (cheese-stuffed, lightly-battered king prawns with a lobster poblano sauce), flakey mahi mahi fish tacos with citrus-cucumber relish, and guacamole, prepared theatrically tableside, are not to be missed. The restaurant is dry, but encourages guests to bring their own beer or wine. *1312 Springwells St., www.elasadordetroit.com, (313) 297-2360.*

★ **El Barzon -** Although you might think serving both Italian and Mexican food is a novelty act, it's anything but. Tucked into a quiet Southwest Detroit neighborhood, El Barzon owner and head chef Norberto Garita offers cheap tickets to Puebla and Rome with his exquisite, split menu. The restaurant's exposed brick walls, white tablecloths, wooden chairs, and marble-top bar imbue an atmosphere of casual elegance, and the menu reflects this decor. Through both his Mexican heritage and Italian culinary training, Garita demonstrates a faith in the power of fine, fresh ingredients, which lends dishes on both the Italian and Mexican sides of the menu an unparalleled zest and intensity. Although revered for the delightfully rich, citrusy homemade mole sauce and the incredible and celebrated homemade pastas, guests can explore the diverse menu with confidence—nary an option misses the mark. The Involtino di Vetello (veal stuffed with prosciutto), Vongole Ecozze all Arrabiata (mussels and clams in a tomato broth), and Barbacoa de Chivo al Horno (poblano goat barbecue) are all peerless and make excellent options on a third visit, after a thorough sampling of the mole and pasta. Each of these choices will leave guests snitching from the doggy bag on the way home. If you leave room after your delicious, affordable meal, try the lemon ripieno sorbet. The beautiful covered patio in the rear makes a perfect summer hideaway. *3710 Junction St., www.elbarzonrestaurant.com, (313) 894-2070.*

El Rancho Restaurant - Serving up authentic Mexican fare inspired by flavors of their hometown of San Louis Potosi, owners Lucia and Alfonso Avila have built upon their stellar reputation since opening in 1983. Charming murals of Mexican towns adorn the sunny-yellow walls and traditional weavings and cowboy hats rest above the comfortable, cushioned brown booths. In addition to the extremely affordable lunch specials—entree, soup, chips and two varieties of delicious salsa for $5—El Rancho offers a comprehensive, tasty, dinner menu, including delicious flautas (deep fried tortillas stuffed with beef or chicken), camarones al a veracruzana (shrimp in tomatillo sauce), and menudo (tripe soup). The breakfast options shouldn't be overlooked either, particularly the chilaquiles (scrambled eggs with corn tortillas, cheese, and vegetables). A full-service bar also offers a wide selection of tequila and Mexican beer. Complete your meal with El Rancho's famous flaming ice cream dessert (think Baked Acapulco). *5900 W. Vernor Hwy., www.elranchomexrest.net, (313) 843-2151.*

El Rey de las Arepas - Follow the yellow tile walkway to meet the wizards of Oz-repas. Owners Zoraida and Rayner Gutierrez harness their mastery of Venezuelan cooking to host this physical and culinary celebration of their home county. From the Venezuelan flag paint job on the exterior, and the quiet South American music playing, to the walls clad with photos of local celebrities and souvenirs of the old country, the restaurant's atmosphere is at once simple, convivial, and bright. On the menu, expect outstanding renditions of cachapa (corn pancakes with cheese, tostones), deep-fried plantains with salami, grilled cheese and eggs, and pabellon (white rice, shredded beef, beans, and plantains). It is the arepas, however, that will have you checking Venezuelan visa requirements between bites four and five.

The lightly grilled corn cakes offer a delicate crunch and a pillowy texture with a range of stuffing options, including reina pepiada (chicken and avocado), shredded beef, ham, steak, black beans, and chicharrones. Wash it down with a passion fruit juice, papelón con limón, chicha, or malta. Avocados, cheese, or eggs are happily substituted for meat. *7701 McGraw Ave., (313) 307-2210.*

El Salpicon - If the only impression a customer ever gets of Nayarit cuisine is that it is a sumptuous, gonzo, and satisfying mix of seafood, El Salpicon has done its job. This Mexican mariscos restaurant grew into a brick-and-mortar location after owner Aldo Dominguez Perez outgrew his popular food truck. The beach-decorated, summery restaurant has quickly grown into a well-loved neighborhood destination in its own right, and has also developed a reputation as a regional draw for live Mexican music. The aesthetic touches at El Salpicon (literally "medley" or "mélange") are not subtle, but the desired effect (seafood coma) is not subtle either. There is a cantina bar, rooms divided in monochrome by function—dining room, dance floor, and stage—and there are also Leviathan platters of seafood. Look for standouts like stuffed lobster, prawns in hot sauce, and seafood-stuffed pineapple, as well as big-gulp-size Micheladas (basically, beer bloody marys). Diners are encouraged to share, plan ahead, and wear loose-fitting clothing. Vegetarians can ask for their Micheladas shrimp-free. *8600 W. Vernor Hwy., www.elsalpicondetroit.com, (313) 914-2214.*

Evie's Tamales & Family Restaurant - Evie's is a Mexican restaurant famous for its satisfying tamales, but also drawing crowds for cheap and generous breakfasts and lunches. Breakfast here hits the main points—an emphasis on eggs and meat with large quantities at good prices, but flavors are tart and spicier; grits or potatoes are swapped for rice and beans; tortillas pinch-hit for toast. The trappings are basically low-key: Earth tones, nods to Detroit icons like the Boblo boat, and Mexican trinkets, but the menu—full of Mexicantown standards—makes Evie's a real draw. Dine-in tamales are served with homemade salsa and run only 70 cents a pop, while terrines of rich and hearty pozole (pork and hominy soup) or menudo (hominy and tripe) will slake any appetite. Word of caution: Restrooms at Evie's barely outsize airplane johns. *3454 Bagley Ave., (313) 843-5056.*

Family Treat - Family Treat's motto, "Serving Southwest Detroit's best foot-long coney for more than 54 years," is a perfect description of this retro neighborhood diner. With the original vintage decor and seemingly original prices—including 99-cent ice cream cones—this neighborhood spot serves as much charm as it does delicious foot-long coney dogs. While the entire menu is popular, the foot-long dogs, fried mushrooms, fishwiches, and all 12 flavors of milkshakes are renowned. Stop by on Tuesday for taco night or Thursday for foot-long night. Closed November through January. *2010 Springwells St., (313) 841-3522.*

★ **Flowers of Vietnam** - What began as a weekend evening pop-up inside of Chef George Azar's father's diner has transformed into one of Detroit's most acclaimed restaurants, earning accolades from national press, and a rabid local following. Nestled into a nondescript building along bustling Vernor Highway, Flowers of Vietnam's past as a Coney Island diner is on full display in the barstools facing the open kitchen, the dining booths, and the "Vernor Coney Island" neon sign that still hangs in the window. The food, however, draws inspiration not from greasy spoons but rather from the bright, sour, and spicy flavors of Vietnam. Here you can find Korean fried caramel chicken wings, crunchy head-on salt and pepper prawns, and big steaming bowls of pho. Large plates full of crispy rice, topped with Chinese sausage, grilled pork chops, and shrimp are best shared at a big table with friends, alongside one of the restaurant's fantastic cocktails, which are often accented with coconut, lemongrass, and basil. The egg cream coffee, and its accompanying cookie, make for a perfectly sweet finish. *4430 Vernor Hwy., (313) 554-2085.*

Giovanna's Lounge - With bartenders as gifted with gab as they are with muddlers, a vibe as friendly as it relentlessly unpretentious, and drinks as cheap as they are delicious, plan on a few rounds. This paradigmatic hidey hole has a distinct south-of-the-border twist, thanks to novelty slot machines, chalk figurines of men in sombreros, paper Mexican lanterns, Dos Equis pennant strings, and an ambiance so dark, Goths might need crossing guard vests. Though a full range of liver ticklers are available—look for major label liquors alongside domestic and imported beers—Giovanna's is famous for bartenders with a flair for cocktails and a strong selection of Mexican beers. If your interests extend beyond draining a glass, try the aforementioned slot machines, the solitary pool table, or watch the sunset on one of Detroit's finest bar patios out back. When hunger strikes, and the chicharones behind the bar aren't singing to you, take advantage of the bar's embrace of outside food at the taco truck in the parking lot, or the pizza place across the street. *3537 Vernor Hwy., (313) 554-9391.*

Giovanni's Ristorante - Arguably the best Old World Italian food in the city, Giovanni's is a hidden jewel. Part of a stalwart Italian enclave that has survived the encroachment of surrounding industry, the restaurant opened in 1967 and still oozes pride and tradition. Though the decor in the three dining rooms is reserved, the gentle accent lighting, black tablecloths, and light-hued walls are complemented by classy touches, such as photographs of Tony Bennett and Frank Sinatra dining at the establishment—which are as good an endorsement as any. The cuisine is exceptional, evidenced in the preparation and subtlety of what is served. Of the many varied options, standouts are the homemade pastas (all made from scratch on-site), the alfredo gnocchi, ricotta cannelloni, braciole (beef tenderloin rolled with prosciutto, braised in a tomato sauce), and richly flavorful tiramisu. Foodies looking to brush up on their Italiano will be pleased to know that Berlitz-style "learn Italian" dialogues are broadcast in the restrooms. As a suggestion, those traveling from the east should make it a point to travel across the Oakwood Avenue Bridge, a small engineering splendor from another time. *330 Oakwood Blvd., www.giovannisristorante.com, (313) 841-0122.*

Gonella's Italian Foods - On a quiet block in Oakwood Heights lies this charming corner Italian grocery and deli that has kept Detroiters well fed for more than 70 years. This neighborhood corner market puts its Italian pride on display inside and out, from murals of the Tuscan countryside painted above the refrigerators to the green, white, and yellow storefront awning. The highlight of the place is at the large deli counter, where Gonella's serves renowned, layered Italian subs built with fine, fresh-cut deli meats and fresh-baked hard and soft rolls. Although customers can order from the menu, veterans go custom, selecting from the wide variety of meats— including ham, turkey, bologna, salami, capicola, prosciutto, and pancetta—and delicious assortments of cheeses, vegetables, and dressings. One word describes what you're about to enjoy: delizioso. Aside from the beloved deli counter and a selection of prepared pasta and salads, Gonella's sells cannolis that are hand filled by a local Italian grandmother, alongside a fine selection of olives, olive oils, homemade sausages, pillowy Italian breads, balsamic vinegars, wines, and a variety of other Italian kitchen staples. *295 Oakwood Blvd., (313) 841-3500.*

Ham Palace / A&L Restaurant - Though "palace" might be overselling it a bit, A&L is a haven for grabbing a cheap, tasty, quick, and filling breakfast or early lunch. This diner on the edge of Delray, decked in patriotic tri-color paint, fits the bill for a convenient stop-in—customers can choose from thick-cut off-the-bone ham, breakfast specials with amply portioned sides, and grilled sandwiches. The setup at A&L consists of worn vinyl stools for counter patrons, cozy booths, and a smattering of porcine set pieces from piggy banks, to cookie jars, to just plain decorative pigs. Patriotism and piety accompany succulent ham here—icons of the Madonna, the Messiah, and Mother Teresa preside over all service, which is friendly and conversational. *9405 W. Fort St., (313) 841-1309.*

★ **Hygrade Deli -** The sparkly blue, red, and gold vinyl seats, vintage fixtures, old-school wood paneling, and Art Deco-esque facade make a marvelous stage for the real stars of this show: the corned beef and pastrami. Since opening in 1955, owner Stuart Litt's deli has built a legion of adoring fans that love tender texture, glistening presentation, exceptional flavor, and outstanding, perfectly brackish corned beef. Although beautifully shaved in house, the corned beef and pastrami are made up the street at United Meat and Deli, keeping the meat juicy, and aromatic. Lunch customers can't miss with the renowned mile-high reuben, egg salad sandwich, hot pastrami, corned beef on rye, and split pea soup. If you're an early bird, try the corned beef hash—it's so divine, you'll find yourself contemplating abandoning silverware and eating like a caveman. After you fall in love with Hygrade, you won't be alone—the affable staff serves 400 pounds of corned beef a week. Look for the deli's appearance in the film *Batman v Superman: Dawn of Justice. 3640 Michigan Ave., (313) 894-6620.*

Johnny Noodle King - In the silhouette of the Ambassador Bridge, this snappy and hip, humorously named ramen spot rose from the ashes of a former truckers' diner called Johnny's Ham King. Brought to life by the team behind Green Dot Stables (see separate entry), the restaurant now lights up Fort Street with a can't-miss neon noodle bowl sign that invites patrons in for bowls of sumptuous Japanese ramen, house sakes, Japanese draft beer, and cocktails. The space is compact, but modern and inviting, with reclaimed wood elements and copious subway tile. For slurping purposes, Johnny Noodle King serves traditional ramen styles such as shoyu, a pork-based broth with soy sauce, as well as globally inspired modern incarnations like a Southwest bowl with green chiles and cilantro, and even a classic no-frills dorm-room ramen. Put more between your chopsticks by loading up your bowl with extras, including a slew of vegetables, eggs, meats, and spices, such as togarashi, Japanese seven spice. The restaurant offers dine in or carryout, and features a bevy of vegan and vegetarian options. Kanpai! *2601 W. Fort St., www.johnnynoodleking.com, (313) 309-7946.*

La Noria Bistro - In 2018, chef and owner Noberto Garita opened this sister location to the exceptional El Barzon (see separate entry). Like his original venture, La Noria offers an inventive marriage of Italian and Mexican cuisines. The front dining room was once home to a coney island and features a soaring ceiling and a eye-catching original tile floor, but the newly built main dining room is a series of bricked chambers, with natural light streaming in from skylights and garage doors that slide open during warmer months. Choose from Italian classics including veal parmesan and fresh, housemade pastas. On the Mexican side, Garita's hometown of Puebla is highlighted with specialties such as tacos arabes (a Puebla taco with a Middle Eastern influence) and cemitas (torta-like sandwiches). The open, wood-burning pizza oven churns out exceptional, thin-crust Neapolitan-style pizzas. Try the mole pizzas, a blend of Italian and Mexican flavors, or if you're feeling more adventurous, the chapulines pie (roasted grasshoppers). La Noria features a bevy of vegetarian options, as well as a full bar. *5517 Michigan Ave., (313) 338-3545.*

La Pasada - La Pasada is a fantastic neighborhood watering hole. You might want to move to the neighborhood once you've been. While La Pasada makes a good drinker's destination for a night in Southwest, it's a bar particularly propped up by its customers, who make the place come alive. A Saturday night is apt to feature dapper weekend cowboys, swirling Mariachi music, snapping pool balls, and some complimentary Mexican specialities, provided by the bar. The service and company are hospitable, with the bartender as prone to tell an earnest story as to listen to one. The bar itself is comfortable and warm. The floor is de-lacquered and char-spotted from decades of impromptu dancing, and there are flourishes like a matte-charcoal tin ceiling, a candlelit Christian shrine, and a cool, airy patio with walls constructed from shipping pallets. Cash recommended; Spanish language knowledge helpful, but not essential. *1601 Springwells St., (313) 406-5809.*

La Posada - A corner store-turned-family diner, La Posada ("The Inn") originally sold staples, but customer demand inspired owner Juan Romo to offer prepared food in the style of his home, Jalisco, Mexico. Eventually, La Posada evolved into more of a restaurant than a store, which is a good thing, as the food here can compete with the best of Southwest. The store has a carniceria (butcher), where fresh meat is prepared for retail and restaurant use—so every lengua, every sweet-spicy chorizo, every sticky-savory-oniony al pastor is maximally fresh, with the meat cut to exacting standards. While, undoubtedly, it's this feature that packs 'em in, the place offers several other distinct touches that show creativity and care. The homemade agua frescas are delicious, and include a creamy *horchata* and a tangy *Jamaica*; guests can daub freshly made jalapeño crema on their food; and patrons can snack on flaky chips with a spicy roasted pepper salsa. While the interior is unmistakably corner store-turned-diner, it features some decorative touches: The Jaliscan furniture has panels commemorating the 1910 Mexican Revolution, a large relief features Christian shrines, and the parking lot has a sweeping mural depicting the ascendant neighborhood. *1930 Springwells St., en.laposadadetroit.com, (313) 841-1690.*

La Rosa Bakery - Tucked away in a quiet stretch of north Mexicantown lies La Rosa, a corner bakery that's worth pulling over for. The shop sells a comprehensive slate of scrumptious bakery treats at bargain prices, and features stop-in items that make the neighborhood spot perfect for a workday carb load. Let's not mince words—the most forward ingredient will likely be sugar—but La Rosa offers tasty, super-affordable renditions of freshly made counter donuts and flake Danishes; Mexican sweets like churros, conchas, sweet empanadas; as well as traditional cakes like Seven Sisters and Tres Leches. The friendly spot also offers savory refueling snacks like pizza bread, and loaves of their distinctive freshly baked bread. The service counter may be a little old-fangled at La Rosa, but the friendly service and neighborhood charm is more than enough to make up for it—as are the delectable treats. *5401 Proctor St., (313) 894-0222.*

La Rosita - Welcome to Southwest Detroit's premier postprandial lethargy clinic. With its need-a-nap-after portions—think micheladas in glasses that could double as puppy baths—leaving on two feet can feel daunting. The food's origins, however, are more notable than their portions. While most area Mexican restaurants specialize in a variant of Jalisco cuisine, La Rosita offers tastes of Mexico City and Central Mexico. The almost-encyclopedic menu deliciously covers all the Mexican bases, though outstanding regional dishes like sincronizada, torta cubana, and arrachera steak help the place stand out. The hard-to-forget atmosphere—think pink and yellow ceilings, black walls, and a preponderance of paper party flags —doesn't hurt in this regard. The attached grocery store offers a curated selection of Mexican staples and speciality items. Full bar available. *7849 Mcgraw St., (313) 297-3145.*

Las Cazuelas Grill - If we told you that you could get some of the best American-style Mexican food in Detroit at a gas station, would you believe us? The original location that launched a small local chain, Las Cazuelas's humble digs inside a Citgo station in Southwest Detroit belie the tasty, fresh and inexpensive fare offered inside. All of your favorites are here—tacos, burritos, quesadillas and more—and they come loaded with fixings like onions, jalapeño and sour cream. Or try the unique Cazuelas pizza—a cross between a botana (a must-try Detroit "culinary" invention) and a chimichanga. Wash it all down with a fruit milk smoothie made in house. Visit on a Tuesday for an unbeatable deal: 10 tacos for 10 bucks—leaving just enough cash for a few lotto tickets on the way out the door. *4000 Livernois Ave., www.lascazuelasgrill.net, 313-361-1100.*

Las Palmas - Passing on the trivialities and decorative frills, Las Palmas is a neighborhood neveria (roughly translated, an ice cream shop) that serves tasty Mexican street food. The menu hits all of the right notes, with classic offerings like Dorilocos (still-bagged Doritos mixed with Japanese peanuts, chickpeas, cucumber, jicama, Tajin spice, and mayonnaise, creating a trail mix/nacho hybrid), Takilocos (Dorilocos but with Takis, a rolled corn snack), elote (kernel corn mixed with Tajin, mayonnaise, and cotilla cheese), and torta sandwiches. The place also offers a suite of sweets, including fresh, gooey crepes, strawberries and cream, licuados (milkshakes, but in flavors like plantain and guava), fresh juice, and coctels tropicales (akin to tangy-spicy fruit salads served in blossomed arrangements). Oh, there's also ice cream. Come early for best choice of ingredients. Closed Sunday. *7009 W. Vernor Hwy., (313) 914-5282.*

La Terraza - Though it's off the beaten path and has minimal signage, La Terraza has built a well-deserved reputation as a destination for tasty Mexican seafood. Patrons who make their way to the one-story brick building will find a pleasant but understated interior with dark hardwood tables and booths that afford guests a direct view of the action in the kitchen. Though traditional Mexican food is available, the house specialty is seafood. Offerings include a variety of fish and seafood soups, with highlights being a pre-Columbian pozole, unique fish and shrimp tostadas such as a Marlin tostada served in smoky Mazatlan sauce and garnished with avocado slices, and an incredible fish cocktail. La Terraza doesn't serve alcohol, but Jarritos, Mexican Coke, and delectable homemade agua fresca are solid substitutes. *8445 Vernor Hwy., (313) 843-1433.*

Los Altos Restaurant - Just a bit off-the-beaten-path, Los Altos is the favorite Mexicantown spot for many Detroiters and is definitely worth the minimal extra effort. Start your meal with complimentary chips served with four or more delectable house-made salsas and other dips, and then order one of Los Altos' plentiful, affordable entrees. If you only go once, a must-have is the taco al pastor—pork marinated to perfection and topped with cilantro and onions—though everything from burritos to botanas (and even the beans and rice) are outstanding. Wash it all down with a bottled Coca-Cola or horchata. Though its food is tops, the cozy dining room is part of the draw, with comfy booths aplenty and warm, charming lighting. *7056 W. Vernor Hwy., (313) 841-3109.*

Los Corrales - While most of Mexicantown's eateries are clustered together, Los Corrales is somewhat of an island north of Junction, but it's well worth the detour. Cheap, abundant food with a range of choice is the specialty here, including a selection of seafood dishes, such as fried whole tilapia, shrimp and cactus, or ceviche tostadas. Traditional Mexican tacos with an array of meats—chicken, tongue, brisket, pig stomach (crispy, salty, succulent), or tripe (perfectly cooked)—are especially delicious. All food ordered-in is served with fresh chips and a delectable variety of homemade salsas. The dining room has a terra cotta color scheme, red brick archways, and an ad hoc tiki cantina with a light assortment of call liquors to satiate thirsty guests. Though dubbed a "billar," the games are on hiatus, making food the main event. *2244 Junction St., (313) 849-3196.*

Los Galanes - One of the real highlights of the heart of the Mexicantown strip, this Southwest Detroit-family-owned restaurant has been a favorite since the early 1990s. The sprawling restaurant is great for large groups (check out the upstairs) or for an intimate meal for two in the colorfully painted and tiled dining room. The menu is vast and extensive—enjoy everything from traditional goat stew to a full menu of fresh seafood or some solid vegetarian options. The covered light-strung patio is a highlight of the summer and can't be beat for ambience and people-watching. Enjoy a margarita or several or a bevy of Mexican beers while a mariachi band serenades you. Visit the second floor on a weekend night to find Los Galanes transformed into one of the neighborhood's favorite dance spots. *3362 Bagley Ave., www.losgalanesdetroit.com, (313) 554-4444.*

Mangonadas Del Barrio - Easily spotted by a bold blue exterior, you'll find that these neighborhood snack and dessert shops are even more colorful once you walk inside. Choose either of the two southwest Detroit locations to avail yourself of the many classic Mexican street foods and beverages on offer, including cocktails de fruta con chile, agua frescas, and horchata. And don't miss their signature mangonadas, consisting of a cup full of frozen mangos covered in tart chamoy sauce, chili, and lime. Snacks like nachos, elote (Mexican-style grilled corn with chile, lime, mayo, and cotija cheese), and dollar tamales are the perfect savory complement to your sweets. If you're feeling extra adventurous, go wild on some Dorilocos, a popular snack in which bags of nacho cheese Doritos are topped with just about anything edible that you can imagine—cucumber, jicama, and nuggets of mango, plus hot sauce, nuts, and even gummi bears. *www.mangonadasdelbarrio.com; 1210 Lawndale St., (313) 724-6074 and 4029 Vernor Hwy., (313) 551-0883.*

Mariscos Mi Lindo San Blas - This Mexican seafood restaurant in the West Vernor Corridor makes curb appeal seem like a magic trick. Deceptively small and restrictive from the outside, Mi Lindo San Blas is enormous indoors, and has decorative touches that make diners feel truly immersed in the experience. The crescent-shaped dining room features murals of sea themes and coastal vistas, and the blue dining chairs seem to bob along the floor, which itself features custom sea-life designs. All this decor appropriately sets the mood for the Mexican family seafood restaurant; the menu is designed *en estilo* Nayarit (a Pacific coastal region south of the Baja Peninsula), which includes shrimp served head-on, seafood caldo (robust tomato soup), raw oysters, ceviche, and practically any aquatic life local to Nayarit. One distinguishing feature of Mi Lindo is its draft beer, which features a choice of six Mexican beers, all tapped and served impressively cold. The effect makes Mi Lindo seem like a mix of a marisco restaurant and a beer hall—and, indeed, Mi Lindo boasts that it makes the best Micheladas (beer bloody marys) in town. Reservations recommended for weekends and special events. *1807 Livernois Ave., www.milindosanblas.com, (313) 789-5100.*

Mexican Village Restaurant - For a cheesy, delicious, take on south-of-the-border comfort food in a fiesta atmosphere, pull into the secured lot. The ambiance is wonderfully kitsch, with vivid paintings of dramatic desert scenes, ponchos and sombreros on the wall, and colorful flowers and candles at every table. Open since 1958, owner Connie Azofeifa and her crack staff offer a dizzying array of delicious, rich, options on the comprehensive menu, most notably including the El Tejano Burritos (deep-fried burrito with the works), and Enchiladas Rancheras (enchiladas with ranchera sauce). Veterans start off with a Botanita Appetizer (kitchen sink nachos and what the menu calls "A Special Treat!!!"), which might be a white tablecloth's nightmare but a dream for the rest of us. Try an incredible homemade Sopapilla (fried pastry) if you've managed to save room. The ambrosial margaritas are available by the glass and the liter. *2600 Bagley St., www.mexicanvillagefood.com, (313) 237-0333.*

Mike's Famous Ham Place - To the chagrin of kosher diners everywhere, Mike's Famous Ham Place is so confident in the taste of their inexpensive, savory, and delectable sliced ham that it sees little reason to offer much else. Actually, since 1974, this legendary, charming, old-school diner has been dishing out one thing and one thing only: killer ham. Outside of the occasional pie or daily special, the menu includes only five items: a heaping plate of sliced ham; ham and eggs; bean soup (with ham); pea soup (loaded with ham); and the tastiest, largest ham sandwich known to man (garnished with ham). Portions are outrageously large, so be ready for a doggy bag. *3700 Michigan Ave., (313) 894-6922.*

★**Motz's Hamburgers -** Don't let the lack of a crowd fool you. Motz's distinctive large, juicy sliders have been among the best in the city since it opened in 1929. While the early White Tower architecture—replete with vintage dining counter and retro diner-facing grill—would be reason enough to visit, its renown is burger-based. Motz uses Eastern Market–fresh, never-frozen beef grilled on a bed of onions to create its big, rich, and tender sliders. Motz is not quite the carnivore stronghold it once was: Vegetarian visitors will enjoy the veggie burger sliders. *7216 W. Fort St., www.motzhamburgers.com, (313) 843-9186.*

Mutiny Bar - Bringing a splash of retro fantasy-Polynesian perfection to Southwest Detroit's main drag, Mutiny Bar expertly blends elements of Tiki kitsch and cocktail craft with an appropriate dash of timeless Detroit dive. Look for the subtle blue banner above the door (festooned only with a letter "M" and a hand clutching a dagger) and enter. Inside, you can belly up to the thatched-roof bar, and admire this charming, divey take on the classic Tiki aesthetic, with fishing nets, string lights, paper parasols suspended from the ceiling, and vaguely polynesian—and nautical—decor throughout (not to mention the mandatory anthropomorphic Tiki drinking vessels). Don't miss the framed photos and memorabilia from great

Tiki restaurants of Detroit's past, including the legendary Chin Tiki. Priced from $7-11, the cocktails (developed by owners the Detroit Optimist Society, of Sugar House fame, see separate entry) are delicious, fun, and inventive, without devouring your wallet. Our favorites are the Rye Tai (a Mai Tai with rye), the classic Painkiller (a rum and coconut delight), and their on-tap frozen cocktails: Junk Ship (a spicy bourbon, raspberry, and grapefruit number) and Walk the Plank (a whiskey, lemongrass, and ginger concoction). *4654 Vernor Hwy., www.mutinybar.com, (313) 406-4043.*

Neveria La Michoacana - La Michoacana's hand-painted signs and welcoming purple and teal chairs will carry visitors back to their own favorite childhood ice cream parlor—and make them wish that the Superman sundaes of their younger years had tasted as good as La Michoacana's frozen pineapple popsicle. Known for its homemade fruit popsicles and the giant $4 La Michoacana Sundae—featuring four scoops of classic ice cream flavors layered with desirable toppings—this shop has a huge selection of cold treats. Try an agua fresca (a fruit-juice-like drink that is sometimes made with cream), horchata, frozen chocolate-covered bananas, or delicious fresh strawberries drizzled in homemade sweet cream. Most menu items are listed in Spanish and English, accompanied by hand-painted illustrations, but the welcoming staff is happy to answer questions or offer you a sample to try before you buy. *4336 W. Vernor Hwy., (313) 658-3217.*

Paris Cafe Deli - Whichever arrondissement has the cafes with the thick piles of corned beef, heavenly peach cobblers, and bulletproof glass must be where this place comes from. On the right bank of South Fort, this charming hashery's chalkboard menus, checkerboard floor, newsprint formica tables, and Parisian knickknacks combine to create a modest space that feels bright, warm, and eminently likeable. The food options—all freshly prepared—center on outstanding salads and pita sandwiches, though wings, burgers, and hoagies are plentiful. The Eiffel Tower—with its three heaping layers of corned beef, coleslaw, Russian dressing, and melted Swiss cheese on a toasted pita—is perhaps as tall as its namesake, and a standout item not to be missed. Prepared the old-fashioned way, with hand-scooped ice cream, the delicious chocolate, strawberry, and vanilla milkshakes are a perfect occasional, no-occasion indulgence. *2709 S. Fort St., (313) 633-1040.*

Paul's Pizza - If James Bread Awards were a thing, Paul's Pizza would need a trophy case. Inside this laid-back neighborhood pizzeria, visitors are greeted by a bright, vibrant space dominated by walls clad with street signs and views of the open kitchen. From the vintage lunch counter dinette stools, guests can watch the bustling neighborhood go by or see the original 1962 brick oven in action. The oven is a near-legend in Southwest Detroit, known for making neo-Neapolitan pies with flakey, buttery crusts paired with sweet, smooth tomato sauce and a diverse array of toppings. Though the Super Special Pizza does a good job of showcasing the dough and sauce quality, the Thai Chicken Pizza—with spicy ginger sauce, Thai chicken, mushroom, and tomato—is outstanding. If you must select one item, however, the three cheese bread is the sure bet— wars have been fought over lessor dishes. The signature blend of cheeses and flaky bread create a juxtaposition of textures that leaves guests longing long after leaving. Those looking for lighter fare might try the turkey sub or Thai chicken salad. *7635 W. Vernor Hwy., www.paulspizza.net, (313) 843-1444.*

Perfect Beat Lounge - Imagine that the Old Vegas Strip and the set of Saved By The Bell have a Pina Colada-fueled, neon-backlit love affair. Now imagine that the resultant lovechild—bright, glittery, and full of '90s neon, lush faux plants, and mirrored surfaces of all kinds—is plopped down in the middle of a heavily industrial area of Southwest Detroit. This is the glory of Perfect Beat Lounge. With plenty of plush round booths for groups, and a friendly crowd to greet those riding solo, this old-school lounge is a perfect spot for a casual drink or to check out the free Sunday-night entertainment. The beers and cocktails aren't fancy, but they are generously poured, and strong. So, if you're "Looking for the Perfect Beat," as Africa Bambaata sang, look no further than this perfectly off-the-beaten path destination. Bonus points: This spot is highly #Grammable, as the kids would say. *1941 S. Fort St., (313) 388-6262.*

PizzaPlex - Step into PizzaPlex and you'll be greeted with a dimly lit space punctuated by cozy booths and illuminated by the soft glow of purple grow lights hovering above a DIY pallet-wall of herbs. In the adjoining room, you'll find the brightly lit "plex" side, which houses a foosball table and hosts movie screenings and neighborhood events. Owners Alessandra Carreon and Drew McUsic want their space to be as much about building community as it is about delicious pizza. But they *are* very serious about pizza. Carreon spent some of her early years in Naples, Italy, and the restaurant is the only pizzeria in the city (and only the second in the state) to be recognized and approved by the *Associazione Verace Pizza Napoletana*, the official governing body of Neapolitan pizza. (Yes, it's a real thing!) Look for exceptional, thin-crust, wood-fired pies with an especially toothsome crust. Favorites include the Pera (pear, arugula, and truffle oil) and the Porcini (fresh mozzarella, porcini mushrooms, pancetta, truffle oil, and fresh basil), but you can't go wrong on this menu. This friendly destination also offers a full bar. What isn't better with a little wine? *4458 W. Vernor Hwy., www.pizzaplex.wordpress.com, (313) 757-4992.*

Pollo Chapin - Pollo Chapin and its Guatemalan pride add a different dimension to the Mexican-restaurant-heavy Southwest neighborhood palate. The scent of perfectly seasoned fried chicken wafts from the restaurant, located in a renovated bright yellow house full of orange chairs, smiling patrons, and incredibly friendly servers. Though the house fried chicken is divine (available barbecue or spicy), the delectable sides with authentic Guatemalan flair are a highlight, including the Curtido beet and cabbage salad, the macaroni and cheese with jalapeño, and chocolate flan. While you wait for your order, take a peek at the colorful wooden display cases full of Guatemalan imported jewelry, woven bags, and trinkets for sale. *2054 Junction St., (313) 843-1885.*

★**Pupusaría y Restaurante Salvedoreño** - This small, cinderblock, hidden gem is set far back from the street in an unlikely neighborhood, and it's easy to miss. With eight booths and four tables for four, it's tiny, but festive with South and Central American, African, and Asian flags for decor. Pupusas are a traditional El Salvadoran empanada-like dish made of corn flour and filled with such delightful combinations as cheese, beans, and loroco flowers; pork, beans, and cheese; jalapeños and cheese; and chicken, squash, and cheese. In addition to the pupusas, the tamales, pasteles, and the fried plantains with crema and frijoles are to die for. Be sure to make heavy use of the delicious salsa and curtido accompanying your order. There's no booze, but there is a bountiful selection of non-alcoholic drinks, including a tasty horchata. To top it off, this joint is astonishingly cheap—you'll be belt-looseningly full for well under $10, including drinks and sides. *3149 Livernois Ave., (313) 899-4020.*

Red's Park-In Bar - Long a haven for Southwest Detroit's Appalachian community, this husband-and-wife-owned country-western dive endures in a changing neighborhood thanks to hospitable service, cheap drinks, and one of the best jukeboxes in Detroit. Red's, occupying the first floor of a red brick two-story, is darkly lit with a black ceiling, wood-paneled walls, and racing car hoods for decoration. A low-slung lampshade hangs above the pool table and illuminates nearby signs prohibiting gambling on pool. The jukebox has popular choices like Hank Williams, Ernest Tubb, bluegrass classics, and even pop crooners like Nat King Cole. Original owners Chuck and Sue still live upstairs, and their dachshund is usually around as a lookout. Red's opens around 10am and closes by 8pm or so. *4442 Central St., (313) 841-1858.*

Señor López Mexican Restaurant - The chiles rellenos alone are worth the trip. These culinary masterpieces are lightly battered and fried poblano peppers hand-stuffed with cheese and topped with unmatched ranchero sauce. The chiles rellenos, however, are not your only path to Mexican nirvana: the Cochinita Pibil (marinated pork), Chiles En Nogada (stewed poblano peppers over rice), and delicate yet straightforward tacos loaded with fresh-cut cilantro and onions and your choice of meat are all outstanding. Open since 2002, Señor López is extremely popular with the in-the-know locals, so getting one of the handful of tables can be difficult on some days. Carryout isn't a bad option, however, as the quiet, if not divey, atmosphere is rather unremarkable. *7146 Michigan Ave., www.senorlopezmexicanrestaurant.com, (313) 551-0685.*

Sidekicks Saloon - As a bar in a house turned storefront in the middle of an otherwise quiet block, this watering hole is a living reminder of an era when neighborhood bars were plentiful. When visiting for the first time, it's hard not be reminded of bars in Northern Michigan. The long Art Deco wood bar, vintage wood paneling, signs with faux-lksy wisdom like "drink triple, see double, act single" on the walls, old beer signs, and other nicotine-tinged trinkets, all further this feel. Behind the bar, consummate bartender Rene offers a healthy selection of domestic and imported beers in bottles and cans, along with all of the usual distilled suspects. Though the colorful bar banter—usually the type that could make a sailor blush—is likely entertainment enough, a jukebox, several TVs, and a pool table are available. Highly amusing, Eagles-heavy karaoke available on Fridays. *7023 Chatfield St., (313) 842-1094.*

★ **Southwest Detroit Taco Trucks and Grills** - Southwest Detroit is home to a wide array of tasty taco trucks and outdoor grills slinging Mexican street food. In general, at either trucks or grills (which sometimes include indoor seating) food is cheap, quick, and made from a variety of meats with other ingredients that are fresh, and a beverage selection that is limited to Coke products and water, with the occasional Jarritos. Food and service are the focus, while the typical parking lot ambiance takes a backseat. April to October is the surest time to catch the widest selection, but several joints are open year-round. Hours vary by eatery, but none open later than 11am or close before 7pm, and most are open much later. You'll find most of the taco trucks and grills between Junction Street and Lawndale Street, on or around Vernor Highway, Dix Street, or Springwells Street. All locations are cash only, and vegetarian options exist but aren't the strength of most vendors. These are a few of our favorite spots:

- **Detroit 75 Kitchen:** See separate entry.

- **El Primo:** A smaller selection of meat than others, but lightning-fast, generously portioned tacos for $1.25. Very popular. *Dix St. at Central Ave.*

- **El Taco Veloz:** The early bird's taco truck. Open at 8am, seven days a week, until as late as 11pm weekends. Excellent grilled onion or jalapeño, anyone? See separate entry for Midtown brick-and-mortar location. *6170 Toledo St.*

- **El Taquito:** Featuring shrimp quesadillas, and affordable as they come. The al pastor tacos are outstanding. Seven days a week. *6060 W. Vernor Hwy.*

- **La Mexicana Supermercado:** An outdoor grill connected to a grocery store. Serves delectable tacos, including pollo, carne asada, and lengua. Open until the cows come home, year-round. *7934 W. Vernor Hwy.*

- **Loncheria el Parian:** $1 tacos and a huge variety. The Springwells location has an authentic al pastor rotating spit. The charming Dix cart is reminiscent of a carnival wagon. Both offer delicious tortas. Open until 11pm on Friday and Saturday. Burgers and hot dogs available. Two trucks: *Dix St. at W. Vernor Hwy. and Springwells St. at I-75.*

- **Tacos El Caballo:** A fan favorite, featuring $1.50 corn tacos with your choice of meat, freshly and lovingly prepared. Simple, delicious, and incredibly satisfying. Look for the truck with the festive horse on the side and you'll know you're at the right place. *1436 Springwells.*

- **Tacos El Rodeo:** Grab a taco, tostada, torta, or burrito filled with a wide array of meats, or a great vegetarian option. With generous portions and some unique choices, including a "California burrito" complete with fries, you can't go wrong with this truck, which is typically parked in front of the What Pipeline gallery (see separate entry). *3501-3525 Vernor Hwy.*

- **Taqueria El Rey:** See separate entry.

Tamaleria Nuevo Leon - For more than 30 years, Tamaleria Nuevo Leon has served authentic, savory and sweet tamales by the half-dozen from its picturesque locale. Two friendly women work behind the counter of this family-owned spot, preparing masa to the perfect consistency and cutting meat for fresh tamales. For about $5 customers can feast on six tamales and a tasty side of salsa. Parking is available on the side street, Ste. Anne Street, making this little restaurant perfect for carryout. Just down the street from the infamous Michigan Central Station, you'll see the restaurant's charming terra cotta roof tiles and whitewashed facade nestled next to the curious blue "dome home." Veggie-friendly tamales available. *2669 W. Vernor Hwy., (313) 962-8066.*

Taqueria El Naciemento - In the thick of the vibrant West Vernor strip lies El Nacimiento, named for its owner's hometown in Jalisco, Mexico. Decidedly more authentic than some of its brethren down the street, this taqueria and full bar, which is popular with locals, might lay claim to the most extensive selection of taco, burrito, and torta fillings this side of Texas. Though all the bases are covered handily, if you're looking to move beyond the tenets of American-Mexican fare, this is your place. Expand your palate with expertly executed classics like fried pork carnitas, seafood, goat, steak, tongue, and chorizo, or push your boundaries with stomach, brain, or head. To complement the tasty edibles, the interior of El Nacimiento has a thoughtful, cozy Mexican villa feel that transforms into a neighborhood hangout when locals arrive, which is usually later in the evening. Don't miss out on the yummy homemade juice. Open until midnight during the week and 4am on Friday and Saturday. *7400 W. Vernor Hwy., www.elnacimientorestaurant.com, (313) 554-1790.*

Taqueria El Rey - Beyond the unpolished facade and aromatic siren song of grilled chicken, the unassuming Taqueria El Rey offers some of the city's finest Mexican food. While the prosaic atmosphere might remind you of an orthodontist's office or dive bar, the food might remind you of the Mexican food served behind St. Peter. Although the supporting cast is outstanding, the belle of ball on this menu is the grilled chicken. Cooked right outside at the adjoining walk-up taco stand, the excellent dry rub, smoky flavor, and perfectly cooked, tender texture of these slabs of heaven will leave you ordering seconds. Not a bird nerd? Look no further than the outstanding tostadas de camaron, hamburguesa de camaron, burrito estilo california, or torta de lomo adobado. If you need to take the edge off, try one of the renowned margaritas originales from the full bar. *4730 W. Vernor Hwy., www.taqueria-elrey.com, (313) 357-3094.*

Taqueria Lupita's - In a neighborhood flush with tasty Mexican options, and on a street that's one of the epicenters of the action, it can be hard for a taqueria to distinguish itself, but if you're willing to pass on the margarita, Lupita's does it with a bevy of inordinately inexpensive real-deal authentic Mexican street food. Highlights at this divey self-proclaimed "house of the original Mexican taco" include hearty pozole soup and chorizo, carnitas, and especially al pastor tacos, which are legendary in these parts. Don't be afraid to get adventurous here, that lengua taco won't eat itself. *3443 Bagley St., (313) 843-1105.*

Taqueria Mi Pueblo - Affectionately dubbed "Mexican Applebees"— more for its decor than the quality of the food—Mi Pueblo stands out among the many Southwest Detroit Mexican eateries as a spacious, cheery, and inviting restaurant, with broad appeal for various palates on a budget. It has all the Mexican staples in its many-page colorful, laminated menu—try the chorizo tacos, carnitas, and tamales—and that includes the really Mexican staples like menudo, beef head, and tongue tacos. The complimentary chips and salsa are plentiful and delicious, and there are plenty of vegetarian options. Flavors are bright and products are fresh. *7278 Dix St., (313) 841-3315.*

Taqueria Nuestra Familia - Aside from the brightly lit cashier's counter glowing from the back-lit images of delicious pork street tacos, fresh-pressed corn tortillas, and green-sauced enchiladas, patrons will admire Taqueria Nuestra Familia's rainbow of hand-painted tables and chairs depicting the tropical landscape scenes of Mexico. The colorful atmosphere matches the demeanor of the friendly wait staff, as well as the delicious taste of the house-made salsa. Enjoy the $2.95 taco lunch special or go for an evening out and sip on $4 margaritas or a glass of Pacifico at the full bar. *7620 W. Vernor Hwy., www.nuestrafamiliarestaurant.com, (313) 842-5668.*

★**Telway Hamburgers -** Open since 1944, the Telway is a "hamburger system" that offers sliders by the bag and the self-proclaimed "best coffee in Detroit" (a statement that's hard to dispute). The burgers are steamed on a bed of onions, giving the meat an incredibly tender, juicy, consistency that melts on your tongue and melds with the flavor of the wonder buns and gooey cheese. The onion rings and fries are made fresh and have an outstanding texture. Telway serves 3,000 hamburgers a day out of its beautifully vintage, all metal White Tower building from the 1940s. Eat your burgers at the counter or sit on your car in the parking lot. You'll never go back to White Castle. *6820 Michigan Ave., (313) 843-2146.*

Tommy T's Pub - Tommy T's Pub, a unique neighborhood dive bar in a residential area, emphasizes comfort and selection. The simple yellow awning outside belies a modern, sand-colored interior, which is clean, cool, and massive. In addition to a counter that stretches more than 50 feet, Tommy T's offers six pool tables for customers, who are usually locals, meaning that soccer is extremely popular television viewing, Mariachi is often heard on the jukebox, and Spanish is the lingua franca, though the staff is bilingual. The drink menu includes bottles of Pacifico and Modelo with Mexican Coke for teetotalers. *3511 Clippert Ave., (313) 897-5967.*

Tortitas El Rojito - If such a publication existed, *Gas Station Taqueria Connoisseur Magazine* would give this place five stars. Overlooking a taxicab maintenance yard, the bare-bones restaurant is located inside a nondescript Marathon station, and still features some vestigial signs from its days as a Taco Bell Express. Though the menu includes outstanding takes on steak, chorizo, and chicken tacos and quesadillas, the two delicious and unique menu items that make Tortitas El Rojito worth the trip are the tortas and hot dogs. The tortas, Mexico's answer to bahn mi, are served on perfectly toasted bolillo, most typically filled with a breaded chicken breast garnished with jalapeño, pico de gallo, lettuce, sour cream, and avocado. The real knockout here, however, are the hot dogs. These oversized tube steaks are wrapped in bacon and smothered with fresh grilled onions, diced tomato, cilantro, ketchup, yellow mustard, mayo, and hot sauce. Prepare to eat an embarrassing number. *2257 Waterman St., (313) 471-0012.*

Vicki's Barbecue & Shrimp - You can't miss Vicki's if you're in the neighborhood—where there's smoke, there's barbecue. Established in 1960, this carryout joint serves a focused menu of tender smoked ribs in either regular or hot sauce, oven-pit chicken, and fried shrimp. The restaurant is unmistakable for its distinctive sharp V out front and the tufts of deep, rich oven smoke continuously piping out of the building's roof. Step inside and you'll see the brick smoke oven with a steep black metal hood behind the kitchen glass from the vantage point of a small red brick colored lobby. Pro tip: The "sandwich" (which is actually just ribs with bread on the side) and fries with sauce on top are especially delicious. *3845 W. Warren Ave., (313) 894-9906.*

Vince's Italian Restaurant & Pizzeria - There's a reason they've been using the same recipes since 1960: Vince's is classic Italian food at its best. In a homey dining room that feels like a visit to your Italian grandparents' basement, bedecked with murals of Italian cities, this Springwells favorite is family-owned by four generations of the same family, and it shows. Founded by Italian immigrants Vincenzo and Maria Perfili, what began as a small pizza parlor serving up pies for workers at Southwest Detroit's Cadillac Fleetwood Plant grew into a beloved family restaurant. In addition to its popular old-school pizzas, Vince's serves house-made pastas and sauces as well as wonderful ravioli and manicotti. All the dishes are made to order, so it's not a good option if you're in a rush. Be sure to stay for dessert—the tiramisu is the best in town and the cannoli is sublime. *1341 Springwells St., www.vincesdetroit.com, (313) 842-4857.*

Xochimilco - One of the more popular eateries in Mexicantown, Xochimilco (that's pronounced "zo-she-mill-co," in case you were wondering)—which is "small" for the area with seating for only 240—is best known for its intimate, homey decor with dark rooms, antique chandeliers, and large velvet oil paintings hanging on the walls. With a menu leaning toward the Tex-Mex side of the spectrum, house specialties include botanas (Mexican small plates), cheesy nachos, boozy margaritas, and homemade chips and salsa. For night owls, both the kitchen and bar are open until 2am daily. *3409 Bagley St., (313) 843-0179.*

SHOPPING & SERVICES

California Wine Grape Co. - A little corner of Italy lies tucked away on West Fort Street, where the facade of California Wine Grape Company displays a sunny mural of rolling hills and tangled grapevines. This bright shop is a mecca for wine drinkers and winemakers alike. Inside the massive 10,000-square-foot showroom and warehouse, visitors will find rows upon rows of grapes (including 16 reds and 13 whites), juices, de-stemers, oak casks, demi-johns, custom glassware, presses, pumps, and starter kits. Shop owner and Abruzzo, Italy native Giuseppe Pracilio brings a great deal of sophistication to the craft, and often serves as an oracle of oenophilia to the scores of rookie and veteran home winemakers who come for advice. Pracilio makes his own legendary wines, which are highly sought after and available by the half gallon. The shop becomes a hive of activity each year when California Wine Grapes sells more than

20 truckloads of grapes over the six week harvest season in early autumn. *7250 W. Fort St., www.californiawinegrapeco.com, (313) 841-0590.*

Chilango's Bakery - This little panadería y pastelería—or bakery and pastry shop—carries a huge selection of authentic Mexican baked goods, including breads, pastries, and sweets. Self-serve style, use parchment paper and plastic tongs to make your selections from the long glass display case. Feel free to ask the friendly staff for explanations about each item, since the labels are listed in only Spanish. With huge portions and reasonable prices, the shop can be an economical alternative to some of the larger, better known bakeries in the neighborhood. *5427 W. Vernor Hwy., (313) 554-0133.*

Hacienda Mexican Foods - Supplying the public with wholesale Mexican goods and locally produced taco shells, tortillas, corn chips and tostadas since 1994, Hacienda Mexican Foods offers wholesale prices and wholesome service. From bulk spices, fresh avocados, and frozen chorizo to Mexican sodas and candy, owner Lydia Gutierrez takes pride in the outstanding quality of her goods, which are sold across the country, and available to the public in bulk quantities. The beautiful storefront includes an epic-scale mural by local artist Elton Monroy Duran, featuring a colorful Cinco de Mayo parade, Mexican ranchero singer Pedro Infante, and portraits of community members. Although offering limited options, hungry Detroiters can also get straight-from-the-factory tortillas at nearby **La Michocana Tortilla Factory**. *Hacienda: 6100 Buchanan St. (313) 895-8823; La Michocana: 3428 Bagley Ave., (313) 554-4450.*

Honey Bee La Colmena - A destination grocery store that offers a festive experience, Honey Bee has been constantly expanding since 1956 and is a beautifully managed, Mexican-oriented, full-service grocer. With a killer selection of fresh, inexpensive produce, every kind of hot sauce imaginable, lots of locally made tortillas, organic and vegetarian options, and completely incredible house-made guacamole and salsas (available for sampling at the entrance), this shop is a destination and a real treat. In addition to groceries, it carries a solid selection of Michigan and Mexican beers and Mexican sundries (like loteria cards, soaps, and candies), and it has a wonderful hot food counter at the back of the store featuring delectable burritos and tacos. If you're looking to round out your fiesta, check out the large and festive selection of piñatas for sale that are displayed around the store. *2443 Bagley St., www.honeybeemkt.com, (313) 237-0295.*

La Gloria Bakery - After being greeted by the aroma of baked treats and the cheerful staff, visitors should equip themselves with tongs and plastic trays and begin their self-guided cafeteria-style confection safari. This small, bright, and unassuming space is packed with cases upon cases of freshly baked pastries, cakes, tamales, breads, and tortillas set out on wooden racks. Take your time. In a room seemingly bursting with flans, turnovers, cannolis, conchas, galletas, pan de polvo, and tres leches, La Gloria rookies often miss some of the best delicacies. Although the racks are typically lacking in details or descriptions of the goods for sale, all of the options are delicious. The pan dulce, empanadas, and churros are held in especially high regard by regulars. Visitors can easily buy enough desserts to rot a tooth with pocket change, so stock up. *3345 Bagley St., (313) 842-5722.*

Mexicantown Bakery - This inviting, convivial bakery in the heart of Mexicantown is popular among locals for good reason: It provides customers a range of fluffy pastries and sweet treats for any sweet tooth, from Mexican cookies and pastries like conchas, to traditional favorites like cannoli and cake, indulgent renditions of classics like tres leches cake, pan de muerto, or budin de pan, and its own distinctly popular chocolate "mice" (vegetarian friendly). The beautiful, loft-like interior features exposed brick, hardwood floors, and bright displays of piñatas above the wall of pastry displays. Conveniently, they also stock a limited selection of Latin American groceries and beverages in the back of the store. *4300 W. Vernor Hwy., www.mexicantown.com/bakery, (313) 554-0001.*

Peoples Brothers Bakery - This charming bakery has been a neighborhood staple since 1976. From behind the mismatched stools and counter, the delightful house pastry chefs in flour-dusted white aprons pour fresh-brewed coffee and help customers select from the incredible selection of Southern-style baked goods. The mammoth pastry display cases are stuffed with delicious sweet and savory treats, including outstanding custard donuts, sweet potato pie, Danishes, cream puffs, lemon tarts, hand-iced cakes, and dinner rolls. Owner James Peoples' double-crust sweet potato pie, especially, is to die for—the rich flavor and creamy consistency are almost unparalleled. Sit down or carryout. Irregular hours. *2765 S. Fort St., (313) 383-9090.*

Rodriguez Vaquerita - With a name derived from the Spanish word vaquero, which means cowboy, Rodriguez Vaquerita specializes in western apparel. The understated storefront on West Vernor Highway is packed floor-to-ceiling with a wide variety of items, including racks of embossed leather cowboy and biker boots, timeless cowboy hats, fringed leather vests, silver belt buckles, denim clothes, and— perhaps best of all—pearl-snap cowboy shirts. Though the store focuses heavily on clothing and apparel of the cowboy variety, they also (curiously) sell children's communion clothes and shoes, as well as soccer gear. Yee haw! *5698 W. Vernor Hwy., (313) 849-0746.*

Sheila's Bakery - As a temple to the grain corner of the food pyramid, this pantheon of pastry is worth the pilgrimage. Located on a lively strip of Springwells Street, this large, modern Mexican bakery offers a diverse selection of sweet and savory treats in its nineteen bakery cases, as well as fresh-brewed coffee. Sheila's offers a wide variety of traditional and delicious Mexican treats including arroz con leche, conchas, and buneulos, as well as equally delicious, albeit unorthodox, offerings such as the "Ding Dongs Mexicana." However, the house specialty of this Southwest gem is its cake—specifically the to-die-for tres leches cakes, which are baked fresh frequently and always on hand. Cake customization is complimentary. Carry-out only. *2142 Springwells St., (313) 841-8480.*

Southwest Detroit Outdoor Mercado - A Southwest Detroit destination for down-and-dirty flea market action, vendors gather at this unmarked gravel lot on West Vernor Highway to sell everything from antique tools to knock-off purses. Everybody and their uncle shows up to shop between 7am and 7pm Friday through Sunday, but Saturday usually draws in the most customers—and the tastiest food trucks! Keep an eye out for savory delights from taco trucks and Middle Eastern food carts parked among the secondhand furniture vendors during the lunchtime rush. *6408 W. Vernor Hwy.*

Southwest Rides - This bike shop and youth job program in the Springwells neighborhood has helped develop a nascent bike culture in southwest Detroit. Aesthetically, things are a little crunchy at Southwest Rides, but its inventory and services more than compensate. The shop sells resale bikes and new skateboards at competitive prices, and also offers full-service bike and board repair. As part of the Urban Neighborhood Initiative, a regional nonprofit working to improve community development, the shop offers job training for local youths and also offers an Earn-A-Bike program, where members of the community can build a bike for personal use. The store leads a monthly Thursday night neighborhood youth ride and puts on an annual bike scavenger hunt. Bike donations accepted. *1824 Springwells St., www.swridesdetroit.com, (313) 315-2127.*

Xochi's Gift Shop - The word "xochi" means "flower" in Nahuatl, and there couldn't be a more perfect name for this blossoming depot of Mexican imports located in the heart of Mexicantown. Owned by the Rosas family since 1985, Xochi's stocks its space with a wide assortment of gifts and souvenirs from the floor to the ceiling. Get outfitted with multicolored sombreros, traditional ponchos, authentic Wrangler embroidered shirts, silver jewelry, and leather boots. Then deck out your home with classic margarita glasses, pottery, tapestries, and canvas paintings of Frida Kahlo, Our Lady of Guadalupe, Pancho Villa, and more. Heading to a fiesta? Bring a bouquet of the large, vibrant paper flowers (made by Xochi's) and a piñata (Xochi's makes those, too!). *3437 Bagley St., www.xochis.net, (313) 841-6410.*

CULTURAL ATTRACTIONS

Grey Area - After spending many years in Southern California, Eileen Lee and Christopher Taylor returned to their native Michigan to open this experiential gallery, shop, and studio. In the front of the space, guests will find a gallery that hosts an array of art exhibitions that feature a spectrum of outsider art, installations, and live performances. In the back and side of the space, visitors will find the store portion of the venture, and can shop a tastefully and carefully curated selection of vintage clothing, home goods, art objects, jewelry, and records. **Aura Aura**, the third component of Grey Area, is Lee's aura portrait photography practice. Contained inside a permanent dome installation inside the gallery, the studio employs a double exposure process to take colorful, psychedelic, and stunning otherworldly portraits that "make the metaphysical visible." Aura Aura accepts walk-ins on weekends, but it's highly recommended that you make an appointment to guarantee a time slot. Check Grey Area's social media for updated exhibition information. The entrance to the space is located on Scotten Avenue. *4200 W. Vernor Hwy., Rear Unit, www.auraaura.co.*

Ladybug Studios - This creative space nestled in the garden level of the Whitdel Building is a cooperatively run clay studio and gallery space. Home to an emerging co-operative of ceramic artists, teachers, and activists, Ladybug Studios provides the tools and space to create in a welcoming and encouraging environment. They offer workshops and tutorials to local artists, as well as a donation-based monthly community drop-in where anyone can come and work on a creative project. Pick up unique handmade gifts during the December drop-in when they host a special holiday sale of works by members. Check their Facebook page for a calendar of events. *1250 Hubbard St.*

Tuskegee Airmen National Museum - Inside Historic Fort Wayne, the Tuskegee Airmen National Museum is dedicated to commemorating the history of the African-American men who trained and flew as combat pilots during World War II. The legacy of the airmen, among whom former-Mayor Coleman Young is counted, is recounted through exhibits including authentic combat artifacts, films, and documents. The museum scored a coup in 2010, when it purchased an authentic 1943 T-6 aircraft used in training the Tuskegee airmen, though this is housed at City Airport and not on-site at the Fort Wayne location. Prospective visitors should plan on inquiring ahead; hours to view exhibitions are by appointment, and admission is not included with entrance to Fort Wayne. *6325 W. Jefferson Ave., www.tuskegeeairmennationalmuseum.org, (313) 843-8849.*

What Pipeline - Located in Mexicantown, if you didn't know what you were looking for, you might miss this unassuming, nondescript building with no signage. It sits in one corner of the parking lot for Giovanna's Lounge (see separate entry), and Tacos El rodeo, a popular taco truck, is usually parked out front. However, once you discover What Pipeline, you'll walk into a white-walled gallery space where you'll encounter some of the most cutting-edge and experimental contemporary art from emerging and established artists from Detroit and beyond. Founded in 2013 by Daniel Sperry and Alivia Zivich, the pair work tirelessly to stage new exhibitions and accompanying events throughout the year, and they have won awards and critical acclaim for their efforts. What Pipeline also works to introduce Detroit artists to an outside audience, showing work at galleries and venues in other major cities and at international art fairs like Art Basel Miami. *3525 W. Vernor Hwy., www.whatpipeline.com.*

ENTERTAINMENT & RECREATION

Clark Park - A lush, lively, 29.8-acre recreational, athletic, and cultural jewel set amidst old homes, a vibrant commercial corridor, and dense neighborhoods, Clark Park has been a vital center for Southwest Detroit for generations. Since its donation to the city by real estate and fisheries magnate John P. Clark in 1888 and more recent adoption by the nonprofit Clark Park Coalition in 1991, the park has built a reputation for both its fine physical amenities and its exciting programming. While most of the park's physical assets are located in the southern end of the park—south of Christiancy Street—the northern end of the park is a scenic wooded area built for strolling and picnics, with dense stands of trees that become beautiful with changing seasons. Among other amenities, the southern end of the park is home to a regulation-size outdoor ice rink, baseball and softball diamonds, playscapes, football and soccer fields, tennis courts, a clubhouse, basketball courts, a scenic wooded area, a number of public art installations, and an amphitheatre. The amphitheatre and ice rink, especially, play host to numerous festivals, performances, matches, one-time events, and tournaments, such as the annual Cinco de Mayo festival, Police Department/Fire Department hockey charity match, and Winter Carnival. Among the many attractions at the park, these stand out:

- **Ice Rink:** The regulation-size outdoor sheet, complete with stands, scoreboard, and dashing boards, offers free skating and skate rental and has been known to host outdoor Red Wings practices.

- **Public Art:** Between the storied Clark Park Sculpture Project and more recent art additions, such as ornamental brickwork by Lisa and Mary Luevanos and the mosaic installation *Bridge the Divide* (2012) by Gary Kulak and Vito Valdez, the park's northern portion makes for a scenic walk.

Bordered by W. Vernor Hwy., Clark St., Scotten St. and Lafayette Blvd., www.clarkparkdetroit.com, (313) 841-8534.

Detroit City Futbol League - A spirited co-ed recreational futbol (known stateside as soccer) league, the Detroit City Futbol League has united Detroit's neighborhoods through the "beautiful game" since 2010. Composed of teams assembled from Detroit's historic neighborhoods, the adult league debuted with 11 clubs, but now boasts 30. The teams compete each season for pride, bragging rights, and the illustrious Copa Detroit title, which is granted to the winner of the end-of-season tournament of the same name. The competitive but sporting games are lively and thrilling to watch, especially when some of the more colorful teams are playing, such as Cass Corridor and their "Suck it" flag, boombox, and PBR-swigging, or "upper crust" Indian Village and their postgame martinis. Games are free and open to the public and are played Tuesday and Thursday evenings throughout the summer. Games are played at Historic Fort Wayne (see separate entry). Check out the website for schedules and standings: *www.detroitcityfutbol.com.*

El Club - A triple threat in Mexicantown that's become one of the city's best destinations for live music, El Club also offers one of Detroit's most luxurious dive bar patios, and serves up phenomenal wood-fired pizza. Come for cheap tickets to see top indie rock, garage rock, hip-hop, and reggae from around the globe (think Ty Segall, GZA, and Lee "Scratch "Perry) as well as notable local bands (think Bonny Doon, The Gories, and the epic Trip Metal Fest). Stay for the incredible light shows, massive and serene outdoor patio, and pizza. El Club's pies are traditionally prepared, thin, and toothsome. Standouts include a margarita with house-made mozzarella, and a green arugula pie, but there are a slew of other exceptional meat-centric, vegan, and vegetarian options. The intimate space lived past lives as a Lithuanian social club and later a Mexican hall, and there are charming reminders of these histories, including a massive skylight with original plaster molding, and the venue's name: El Club. *4114 Vernor Hwy., www.elclubdetroit.com, (313) 279-7382.*

Latino Mission Society - Forty-five years ago, bowling was a major part of Detroit life and culture. So much so, in fact, that in addition to the 47 bowling alleys that once graced the city's neighborhoods, dozens upon dozens of Detroit civic, institutional, and religious buildings added private bowling alleys—from churches to the mayoral residence. Though most of these lanes and alleys have been lost to time, one of those that remains can be found in the basement of what was formerly the Bethlehem Lutheran School and is now the Latino Mission Society. Predating the Depression, the fully operational and nonmechanized four-lane alley is a curious marvel. Constructed almost entirely of wood, cloth, and leather, the alley requires "pin boys" to hustle and return balls on the rickety track while they reset the pins with the surprisingly efficient hand-operated contraption. In addition to the alley, which is private but available and economically priced for party rental, the secular organization offers performances, music classes, and nutrition courses for the community. Call for bowling rental. *1450 McKinstry St., www.latinomission.org, (313) 841-2377.*

Matrix Theatre Company - A beloved Southwest Detroit institution, Matrix Theatre was founded in 1991 and is a community-based, socially engaged theater company and venue. The organization offers and fosters creative original and heritage theater, as well as opportunities for youth and adult community participation. In addition to live theatre, Matrix creates and performs with impressive larger-than-life puppets on-site, throughout the city, and through schools and after-school outreach programs. Watching a play in the intimate theater is an experience not to be missed—check the website for upcoming performances. *2730 Bagley Ave., www.matrixtheatre.org, (313) 967-0999.*

RollerCade - Though this pint-sized skating rink in the city's Boynton neighborhood might seem unassuming at first glance, it is rich with history. As the first black-owned roller rink in the U.S., Rollercade has remained in operation and in the same family through three generations, hosting everything from kids' birthday parties to roller disco dance nights for more than six decades. Skate rentals are available for children and adults, so lace up and grab a snack at Rollercade's Roller Cafe. Rent the rink for a party of your own or glide in on a Tuesday night (when R&B tunes spin from 9pm-1am) to watch some of the fanciest footwork you'll ever see on eight wheels. *2130 Schaefer Hwy., www.rollercadedetroit.com, (313) 736-0832.*

SITES

Ambassador Bridge - One of the most notable landmarks in Detroit, the Ambassador Bridge is a graceful suspension bridge and a gleaming, towering testament to the beauty of Art Deco and Art Moderne design and the innovation of the Modern Age. It was the longest suspension bridge in the world when it was built in 1929, and the lights on the bridge's cables can be seen at night from miles around, glimmering and reflecting on the Detroit River. The busiest border crossing in North America, the bridge carries 25% of all trade volume between the United States and Canada and is privately owned by controversial billionaire Manuel "Matty" Moroun through

the Detroit International Bridge Company. As is standard with most international crossings, it's equipped with duty-free shops and a duty-free gas station (also owned by Moroun). *2744 W. Fort St., www.ambassadorbridge.com, (313) 963-1410.*

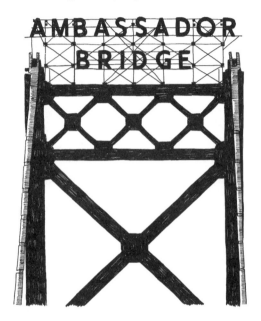

Bagley Pedestrian Bridge - In 2010, 40 years after being severed by the chasm of the I-75 and I-96 freeways, Mexicantown was re-connected by the Bagley Pedestrian Bridge. With a lofty mission of re-establishing communal unity, the bridge succeeds with a design that invites interaction. An impressive 417 feet across, the most distinct feature of the contemporary asymmetrical crossing—which is the only cable-stayed footbridge in Michigan—is the 155-foot tall angular pylon that towers over the bridge it supports. With a price tag of $5 million, the bridge is dotted throughout with decorative lighting, seating, and landscaping, which, combined with the fact that it allows visitors to sit atop 10 lanes of traffic—and affords an incredible view of the Ambassador Bridge—makes it an unforgettable destination for carryout from the many nearby restaurants. Of course, for those who aren't hungry, it can simply be a place to meditate on neighborhoods, development, and what being the "Motor City" has meant for Detroit. *The bridge starts at Bagley and the I-75 service drive on the west side, and Bagley and 21st on the east side.*

Dome Home - Built in 1998 by Leo Gillis, cousin of Jack White (née Gillis), the bright blue 4,000-square-foot residential mini-complex is based on the geodesic domes developed by Buckminster Fuller in 1948. The only geodesic domes in Detroit, the complex's reinforced concrete structure was constructed from a kit and cost $110,000 to build, including materials and labor. The structure is privately owned, so please restrict visits to the sidewalk. *Located at the intersection of W. Vernor Hwy. and Johnson St.*

Historic Fort Wayne - Situated on 96 acres along the Detroit River, Fort Wayne was originally built to repel a British invasion from Canada that never materialized. These days, the only battles you're likely to find are between competing bargain-hunters both eyeing the same tschotske at the fort's biannual flea market or simulated ones put on by Civil War re-enactors. The main, star-shaped fort building and stunning limestone barracks were constructed between 1843 and 1851, but additional construction continued until 1931, resulting in a number of smaller structures, including additional barracks, officers' quarters, stables and shops. Not all have been well-preserved, and many are off-limits to visitors, but history enthusiasts will have a ball wandering around the vast premises and exploring the buildings that are accessible. It's also a great spot for a picnic, a bike ride, or any number of events that regularly take place there, including the flea market and battle re-enactments, as well as races, veterans' events, historic commemorations, and holiday celebrations. *6325 W. Jefferson Ave., www.historicfortwaynecoalition.com, (313) 628-0796.*

Hubbard Farms - Bounded by West Vernor Highway to the north, Clark Street to the west, West Lafayette to the south and West Grand Boulevard to the east, the Hubbard Farms historic district is a two-century old enclave named for developer Bela Hubbard, one of the founders of what would grow to become the Detroit Institute of Arts. Historically, the land that now comprises the scenic neighborhood was a Pottawatamie village and was dotted by elaborate burial mounds, which were later joined by French ribbon farms (narrow plots designed to maximize fresh water access). However, both the remnants of the gravesites and the farms were cleared to make way for the city's increasingly explosive growth at the end of the 19th century. Largely developed between 1880 and 1920, the neighborhood attracted upper-class residents employed as managers in industry and manufacturing. Housing styles in the neighborhood—which has been well-maintained, especially in recent decades—include a range of attractive Victorian, Romanesque Revival, Beaux Arts, Italianate, and Colonial Revival residences. Though the neighborhood is more reserved in its grandeur than Boston-Edison or Palmer Woods (see separate entries) it makes for a scenic two- or four-wheeled historic home tour.

J.W. Westcott Co. - At the foot of 24th Street on the Detroit River sits the most unique post office in Detroit—and maybe the United States: a mobile marine mail delivery service that claims to be the only mail service in the world that delivers while vessels are under way. "Mail in the pail," as it's called, was first provided by John W. Westcott in 1874 from his rowboats to passing steamships, and the service expanded over the decades to come. In 1948, Westcott's company was assigned its own ZIP code—48222 (the only floating ZIP code in the United States)—and today the 24/7 operation averages about 30 deliveries in a solar day. A contract post office, walk-up customers can visit the land-based office to send mail to all destinations, floating or not, and purchase nautical charts, books of nautical history, and trade publications. Business is seasonal—J.W. Westcott operates from April to mid-December. Visitors should try to watch a delivery from the most optimal location, the adjacent Riverside Park, which provides fence-free seating on the waterfront. *12 24th St., www.jwwestcott.com, (313) 496-0555.*

Lawndale Market - With its walls, racks, and ceilings plastered with more than 10,000 Polaroid pictures of customers, Lawndale Market is more folk museum than liquor store. Between 1995 and 2008 (when Polaroid ended film production), owner Amad Samaan decorated his store with his celluloid garlands and wallpaper by photographing local children who did well in school and other customers who piqued his interest. This otherwise modest party store has an impressive selection of South and Central American beers. Hours vary wildly, so visitors should call ahead. *1136 Lawndale St., (313) 841-2531.*

Ste. Anne de Detroit - Considering its heritage as the second-oldest continuously operating Roman Catholic parish in the United States, it's appropriate that a church named for the grandmother of Jesus has provided sanctuary to Detroiters as long as the city has existed. Construction of the first church began just two days after the city's founder, Antoine de la Mothe Cadillac, arrived in 1701, though the parish was forced to rebuild eight times over three centuries because of urban renewal and fires, including a scuttling by the Fort Pontchartrain settlers themselves during the first Fox War. The current edifice was completed in 1887, and boasts elegant Victorian Gothic features, including some uncommon for American churches—soaring flying buttresses, spired wood pews, and an ornate carved-wood elevated pulpit. The church also has a shrine of the patroness saint (worshipped at special Novena services) and still retains the wood altar from the church constructed in 1818 in its chapel, where the renowned local 19th century priest Gabriel Richard is interred. There are also two majestic organs—one 26-rank organ above the entrance to the sanctuary, and another in the chapel. Detroit's history can be traced from the church's comprehensive historical records, which trace the city's evolution from a French colony to U.S. metropolis. Spanish mass offered. *1000 St. Anne St., (313) 496-1701 www.ste-anne.org*

Woodmere Cemetery - Founded in 1867, Woodmere is one of Detroit's oldest cemeteries and the resting place of many of its most influential businessmen, especially those who made their fortunes before the auto industry—in tobacco, lumber, steel, newspapers, shipping, and even soda. Established as a rural oasis

in the sleepy township of Springwells, today, Woodmere is part of this bustling neighborhood in Southwest Detroit. It's huge—more than 200 acres—so it helps to bring wheels, two or four, when you visit. *9400 W. Fort St., www.woodmerecemeteryresearch.com, (313) 841-0188.*

Notable burials include:

- **David Dunbar Buick (1854 - 1929):** Founder of Buick Motor Company, inventor of a method for enameling bathtubs still in use today. *Section Allendale, Lot 631.*

- **David Whitney (1830-1900):** Lumber baron whose former home is now The Whitney restaurant (see separate entry). *Section F.*

- **Ford Hunger March victims Joseph York, Joseph Bussell, Kalman Leny and Joseph DeBascio:** Killed March 7, 1932, during a labor demonstration. *Section Ferndale, Lot 18.*

- **Hamilton Carhartt (1857-1937):** Founder of the Carhartt line of work clothes. *Section North Lake.*

- **James E. Scripps (1835-1906):** Founder of the *Detroit Evening News* (today's *Detroit News*). *Section A5.*

- **James Vernor, Sr. (1843-1927):** Inventor of Vernor's Ginger Ale and longtime member of Detroit's Common Council. *Section D, Lot 146.*

- **John Judson Bagley (1832-1881):** Tobacco magnate, governor of Michigan, and one of Woodmere's founders. *Section D, Lot 149.*

Zug Island - Across a shipping canal from the hardscrabble Del Ray neighborhood lies Zug Island, a heavily industrialized dystopian iron island that belches smoke and fire like a post-apocalyptic volcanic monster. Originally a small peninsula in the Detroit River, the island was owned by furniture magnate Samuel Zug who fancied it for the site of his dream home, until it was found to be too swampy, vermin-infested, and inhospitable. In 1888, Zug permitted a canal to be cut through his property to allow ships easier access to the Rouge River, transforming the peninsula into an island. Zug sold the island in 1891, and it quickly became a compact industrial center, with the first of its three blast furnaces constructed in 1902. Today, the island is owned and operated by United States Steel and is formally called the Great Lakes Works, but we'll stick with Zug Island. It's connected to the mainland by only two bridges, but don't even think about turning onto one of them to try to enter the island. Few have seen the interior of this industrial works because of its intense high security level, and you'll be turned away. That's OK, though: You can marvel from the mainland at the strangely beautiful, jaw-dropping site with blast furnaces lighting up the sky and producing an entrancing glow that can be seen for miles. Though technically, the private island is located in River Rouge, it is best observed from Southwest Detroit. Trivia bonus: Zug Island was supposed to be the final destination of the ill-fated Great Lakes freighter the Edmund Fitzgerald that sank off of Whitefish Point in Lake Superior in 1975. *W. Jefferson Ave. and Zug Island Dr.*

POINTS OF INTEREST

Batman v Superman Chase Scene - This gritty industrial complex was the filming location of a priminant chase scene in the 2016 movie *Batman v Superman: Dawn of Justice. 4105 W Jefferson Ave.*

Big Mack Records - This vacant lot was once home to Ed McCoy's label, churning out R&B, soul, and gospel music from the likes of Edd Henry, the Grand Prix's, and Bob and Fred. *7018 W. Warren Ave.*

Cadillac Urban Gardens - In a former parking lot for GM executives, this urban garden features raised beds built from repurposed shipping crates. *McKinstry St. and Merritt St.*

Cloud Bridge - This cheerful transformation of a grimy overpass into a blue sky dotted with clouds was the work of local artists Davin Brainard and Dion Fischer. *665 W. Grand Blvd.*

Diversity Is Our Strength - In 1995, 18-year-old Arturo Cruz designed this huge mural on the side of the popular Mexican restaurant Los Galanes. The celebration of the diversity of people that make up the region was executed by a multicultural, multigenerational group of more than seventy people. *3362 Bagley Ave.*

Electric Kit House - With its oversized eaves and hipped gables, this modest home was purchased as a kit house from Sears, Roebuck, and Co., for $907. This simple bungalow, a Rodessa model, was advertised as "a pretty little home" when it was assembled here in 1921. *2516 Electric St.*

Ford Hunger March Site - On March 7, 1932, thousands gathered to march toward the Dearborn office of Henry Ford to demand better employment opportunities and the right to organize. The loud, but peaceful, protesters were met with violent resistance from the Dearborn Police and Ford Security, who sprayed machine gun fire into the crowd, killing five and injuring more than 60. *W. Fort St. and Miller St.*

Gabriel Richard Grave at Saint Anne's Church - The French-born Catholic priest served as a nonvoting delegate of the Michigan Territory from 1823 to 1825. Father Richard opened the first printing press in the city, was a cofounder of the Catholepistemiad of Michigania, which would later become the University of Michigan, and gave the city its motto (Speramus meliora; resurget cineribus; in English: "We hope for better things; it will arise from the ashes") shortly after a fire leveled the city in 1805. *1000 Ste. Anne St.*

Giant Bowling Pin - This enormous 10-ft tall bowling pin stands near the entrance to local favorite Taqueria Mi Pueblo. Why? Your guess is just as good as ours... *7278 Dix St.*

Hotel Yorba - Made famous by the White Stripes song and video of the same name, this once economical hotel is now long-term housing. *4020 Lafayette Blvd.*

Jack White Home - The White Stripes frontman spent his early years in this Southwest home, later turning it into a recording studio. *1203 Ferdinand St.*

Jimmy Hoffa Home - This is the childhood home of the infamous Teamsters president whose death remains a mystery to this day. *4742 Toledo St.*

Kitten Mural - This large-scale mural by artist MUCKROCK features adorable kittens batting at a missle. *5719 W. Warren Ave.*

Mail Pouch Tobacco Ghost Sign - Tabacco chew and vibrant colors comprise this almost-complete ghost sign, which encourages viewers to "treat yourself to the best!" *8914 Michigan Ave.*

Marka27 Mural - Painted by East Coast artist Victor "'Marka27" Quinonez, this vibrant, color-rich mural on the side of El Asador Steakhouse was designed as a traditionally rooted emblem of good fortune for Southwest Detroit. *1312 Springwells St.*

Old Boblo Docks - This oversize blue mural is all that remains of what was once the docking place for the steamers Columbia and Ste. Claire, which took happy families to Boblo Island, an amusement park located on an island in the middle of the Detroit River. *4436 W. Jefferson Ave.*

Our/Detroit Vodka - Home to a vodka distillery, event space, and glorious mural, Our/Vodka's Detroit home is the second international outpost for Pernod Ricard concept spirit and the first micro-distillery in the U.S. *2545 Bagley St.*

Romanowski Park - An example of grassroots volunteerism and dedication, this park, once little more than a weedy lot, now contains athletic fields, a 100-plus fruit tree orchard, and a handful of community gardens. *4401 Lonyo St.*

Rosa Parks Deconstructed Home Site - This vacant lot on the far southwest side was once home to Sylvester McCauley, Rosa Parks' sole sibling. It's rumored that Parks lived in this home in the late 1950s, after she moved to Detroit. The house was purchased by artist Ryan Mendoza in 2014 for $500, deconstructed, and controversially shipped to Berlin for an art exhibition. *2672 S. Deacon St.*

Salt Mines - About 1,200 feet below the city, this enormous mine, host to 100 miles of underground roads, has been intermittently in operation since 1910. It's currently producing rock salt used to de-ice roads. *12841 Sanders St.*

Saner Mural - This vibrant mural by Mexico City based artist Saner (Edgar Flores) features brilliant masked characters in serious conversation, or an ancestral ritual, alongside a ruddy, tropical forest. *1421 Springwells St.*

St. Francis D'Assisi Parish - Completed in 1903, the two five-story towers of the historically Polish Catholic Church flank the ornate three-story Corinthian-columned entryway. *4500 Wesson Ave.*

Target Mural - This 1975 mural by renowned Cass Corridor artist Robert Sestok was commissioned by James F. Duffy Jr., an avid patron of the Detroit art scene and the owner of the warehouse on which it's painted. The work connects itself to the city's industrial roots with a kinetic circle resembling a whirring sawblade or a cross-section of a working pipe. *5840 W. Jefferson Ave.*

CHAPTER 6
NEW CENTER AREA

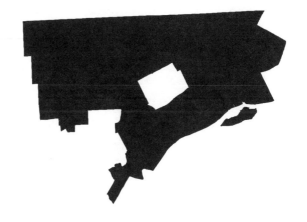

From renowned neighborhood shops and local eateries to authentic dive bars and live entertainment, the New Center Area of Detroit is the perfect destination to view stunning architecture, soak in the region's history, and admire diverse, character-rich local art. Collectively, the commercial and residential neighborhoods in this area are filled with big-city history, culture, and flavors that draw people from throughout the region.

The New Center Area, as we define it, covers more than seven square miles and is bounded by I-94, Hamtramck, Highland Park, Dexter Avenue, and Tuxedo Street. This area is home to a constellation of neighborhoods, including Arden Park, Boston-Edison, LaSalle Gardens, Milwaukee Junction, New Center, North End, Northwest Goldberg, and Virginia Park. Most neighborhoods within this area date to the earliest days of the city's automotive renaissance, having been annexed between 1827 and 1915, and originally built primarily between 1900 and 1929. The area is steeped in automotive history, and is home to Henry Ford's first plant, a neighborhood for automotive magnates, the former Fisher Body factory, the General Motors headquarters from its golden years, and large swaths of automotive workers' housing.

Today, the New Center Area is home to 27,000 people, and includes the city's most diverse collection of historic architecture, as well as an array of neighborhoods that have evolved in different ways due to the ongoing diminution of the local automotive industry. Although defined here together as New Center Area, the neighborhoods that collectively comprise the district have distinct histories, and disparate trajectories. Despite these differences, the area can be divided into three sections—southern, central, and northern/western—that are unified by similar histories and physical characteristics.

For shoppers and hungry or thirsty visitors alike, the New Center district proper—in the southern portion of this chapter—is among Detroit's most significant commercial corridors, and increasingly offers one of city's most diverse retail districts. The T-shaped area runs along Woodward Avenue from Harper Street to Grand Boulevard, and along Grand Boulevard from Oakland Avenue to Third Avenue, with the intersection of the two stretches as a focal point. This area's collections of restaurants, bars, and independent shops are set in some of the most breathtaking commercial architecture in the city, making it a destination for enjoying local art and culture, shopping, and flavors. In recent years, this pattern has intensified as scores of new shops, restaurants, and amenities have flocked to New Center.

This area serves as the northern terminus of the QLINE streetcar system, and perhaps as a consequence, it has been an epicenter of new development in recent years.

The central area of this chapter is a network of historic neighborhoods straddling Woodward Avenue, the collective neighborhoods' primary cultural dividing line and central commercial corridor. The area west of Woodward offers a string of largely-intact historic WWI-era neighborhoods with lush gardens, intricate masonry, and one-of-a-kind palatial mansions. These neighborhoods—Boston-Edison, Virginia Park, Historic Atkinson, Piety Hill, and New Center Commons—are popular with those looking to experience scenic, stately, historic urban neighborhoods. Many of the city's early auto barons and Motown celebrities once lived here, leaving noteworthy history around every corner. While the area west of Woodward was once a center of wealth, the area east of Woodward has a more working class history. This area, the North End, takes its name from its former role as the north end of Paradise Valley, a one-time center of African-American life that was dolefully cleared during the postwar years. Though less of the North End has been erased by urban renewal, the area is home to large swaths of vacancy. In this resurgent neighborhood, ambitious local residents have capitalized on abundant land and developed urban farms at a rapid clip. Led by the Oakland Avenue Urban Farm and Michigan Urban Farming Initiative, the area has developed a reputation as a regional leader in urban farming and gardening.

The northern and western areas of this chapter—those areas north of Boston Boulevard or west of the Lodge Freeway—offer a more archetypal cross section of the city. In general, these areas are home to a patchwork of typical west side Detroit neighborhoods—swaths of tudor, colonial, bungalow, and Romanesque homes on shady, tree-lined streets. Some blocks of these neighborhoods—including Herman Kiefer, LaSalle Gardens, Elijah McCoy, Dexter-Linwood, and Gateway Community—sit unchanged after a century, while other blocks more plainly bare the scars of vacancy. In recent years, several neighborhoods in this area have begun to see new patterns of investment. The Elijah McCoy neighborhood has seen an influx of street art and underground nightlife, thanks to increasingly popular sites like the Lincoln Street Art Park and the Marble Bar. Meanwhile, the Herman Kiefer neighborhood is the focal point of a nascent, massive redevelopment project affecting hundreds of homes.

BARS & RESTAURANTS

Avalon Cafe and Biscuit Bar - With a handful of other locations sprinkled throughout the city, this offshoot of the wildly popular Detroit institution specializes in biscuits. This sunny cafe is modern and polished—and made even sunnier thanks to bright splashes of yellow and orange. Situated alongside New Center Park (see separate entry), this bustling neighborhood hotspot offers up a slew of build-your-own-biscuit options. These range from sweet and simple, like the ricotta and jam, to more savory and intense, like the ham and gravy. Luckily for the vegans and vegetarians amongst us, the place offers a truckload of friendly options, including vegan gravy! Luckily for all of us, you can also grab a loaf of Motown Multigrain bread or a sea salt chocolate chip cookie, as this location comes stocked with all the non-biscuit Avalon baked goods that Detroiters fell in love with years ago. Best of all, breakfast is served all day! Why should egg and cheddar sandwiches be relegated to the morning, anyway? Closed Sundays. See separate entries for other Avalon locations. *2998 W. Grand Blvd., www.avalonbreads.net, (313) 800-5760.*

Baobab Fare - Thanks to its deliciously distinctive East African fare, social mission, and striking setting, this popular restaurant from Burundian refugees Nadia Nijimbere and Jamissi Mamba has developed a loyal following. With its distinctive East African cafe styling, the long, open dining room glows with natural light and colorful African accents, lending the space a lively, big-city atmosphere. The delightful, deeply savory menu is unmistakably Burundian, showcasing the East African cuisine's emphasis on aromatic spices, plant-based proteins, and tangible—if subtle—Middle Eastern and Belgian influences. Nijimbere and Mamba elevate staple vegetables while introducing ingredients like the tamarillo through a stable of sapid options including wali wa nazi (rice cooked in coconut water, with brochette beef and chicken), kuku (beautifully marinated chicken and onion), nyana and maharage (eggplant stew and seasoned yellow beans), and cassava (yuca). Morning fare tends towards flat bread, beef stew, omelets, eggs, and African teas and coffees, along with offerings from the full-line juice bar. *6568 Woodward Ave., www.baobabfare.com.*

Bucharest Grill Milwaukee Junction - The New Center outpost of this insanely popular (and rightfully so) Romanian/Middle Eastern/American mashup restaurant, offering carryout and counter seating.

See Bucharest Grill Rivertown (separate entry) for more details. *110 Piquette St. (313) 965-3111*

City Bakery - With six locations in New York and Tokyo, City Bakery opened its seventh in Detroit's historic Fisher Building in 2018. A staple of New York's Union Square since 1990, the Detroit location maintains the aesthetic cues of the others: A blue square-tile backsplash and white vaulted ceilings, alongside the trademark blue-and-white cups. However, the true signature of the popular cafe and restaurant remains its epic hot chocolate, a thick and indulgent beverage that has more in common with pure melted chocolate than we'd like to admit—and comes topped with a massive, artisanal square marshmallow. Be sure to try their full suite of delicious breakfast and lunch options, including breads, decadent pastries, seasonally oriented salads, and sandwiches. Keep an eye out for the epic pretzel croissant. We're sure it has nothing to do with French culinary traditions, but it has everything to do with being delicious. Located inside the Fisher Building. *3011 West Grand Blvd., www.thecitybakery.com, (313) 315-3036.*

City Wings - Owner Grant Lancaster's sleek, inviting, and modern space is a wing lover's paradise. The clean lines, bright colors, and industrial loft aesthetic of the large dining room offer a cheerful atmosphere, while the re-arrangeable nature of the small tables accentuates the social nature of wings. Visitors can see the open kitchen and watch as the cooks turn massive pieces of fresh Amish chicken into one of 16 flavors of chicken wings. Although every type of wing is outstanding, the hickory smoked BBQ, and Parmesan and garlic flavors are exceptional. City Wings' non-wing menu is also delicious. Standouts include the fried okra, baked beans, and turkey chili. Vegetarian options are limited, but the veggie plate—any combination of three sides—is available and tasty. *2896 W. Grand Blvd., www.citywingsinc.com, (313) 871-2489.*

Cuisine - Enjoy elegant, contemporary French-American cuisine by candlelight in this little gem tucked away in a charming historic home on a tree-lined street behind the Fisher Theatre. The cozy house was a speakeasy in the 1920s and has been a series of restaurants since the 1950s. It's not for the budget conscious, but it's worth every penny of the splurge. Cuisine offers a seasonal menu of innovative, fresh food with a French influence from chef and owner Paul Grosz, who studied under chefs in France, had a stint at Le Cordon Bleu, and was a chef at the Whitney in Midtown before opening Cuisine. The beef tenderloin and scallops are especially sublime, and the truffle mac and cheese is outstanding. The menu doesn't cater to vegetarians, but there's usually at least one veggie-friendly entree, such as an asparagus risotto. Ask the friendly servers for advice on wine pairings for your meal. *670 Lothrop Rd., (313) 872-5110.*

Firewater II Bar and Grill - Part bistro and part dance club, by day, this popular neighborhood joint is a New Center destination for mid-priced business lunch and low-key dinner and drinks. The raised round tables—and large open bar—offer a welcoming atmosphere for tuna melts, grilled salmon salads, ribs, and other mealtime staples. By night, the bar and grill transforms into a place "where class is a requirement, not a request," often requiring a $5 cover charge and a dress code: no boots or sneakers. On the central wooden dance floor, a cult following of eager Chicago steppers and other dancers ignites the bar with clapping heels in front of the DJ stage, which also plays host to live music on weekends. For those dancers who are a little green, lessons are offered on Tuesday afternoons. *6521 John R St., (313) 872-0812.*

★ **Kiesling -** Look for the glowing yellow letter "K" on this quiet strip of Milwaukee Junction and venture inside to be greeted by the mystery and splendor of this stunning bar. Borrowing its name from its long-ago turn as the German-American Kiesling Saloon, this gorgeously restored labor of love perfectly blends historical elements with reclaimed accents and sophisticated Art Deco flourishes. From the 30-foot wood-and-marble bar and the Deco-inspired eight-sided linear star-shaped chandeliers to the exposed brick walls and the enchanting fragments of original wildlife murals uncovered during the restoration, Kiesling is an inviting, romantic, and moody wonder. To quench your thirst, the bar offers a diverse menu of wines, craft beers (including rotating drafts), and a curated menu of well-crafted pre-prohibition-era cocktails. Among the latter, our favorite is the Honey Bearing, a deceivingly complex gin, Chartreuse, and honey delight topped with bee pollen. However, the bar is the perfect example of a two-way hitter, playing to both the gourmet and the working man: alongside the curated menu, the bar offers a daily $5 shot-and-beer special. A cozy, walled patio is available during warmer months. Only open after 4pm. *449 East Milwaukee Ave., www.kieslingdetroit.com, (313) 638-2169.*

Miss Virginia's Ice Cream Parlor - There's something old-school about this friendly neighborhood ice cream parlor in Detroit's North End neighborhood. It's the kind of place that a kid can walk to in the dead of summer, a couple dollars in his hand, and leave with two scoops of colorful, sticky, and rapidly melting bliss. Housed in a small corner building covered in cheery ice cream-themed murals, Miss Virginia's offers up everything from slushies to cones in nearly a dozen flavors, from classics like blue moon and mint chocolate chip, to less typical but tasty choices like black walnut and banana pudding. Stop by for a scoop (or two)—the selections may change, but Miss Virginia's always has nostalgia on the menu. *8801 Oakland Ave., (313) 649-7850.*

New Center Eatery - Despite a diverse menu loaded with delicious Southern staples—such as turkey sausage, grits, chicken fajitas, fried green tomatoes, gumbo, and baby back ribs—the belle of the ball on this Dixie menu is the chicken and waffles. Whether you're visiting this charming yet unassuming breakfast-and-lunch spot for hangover treatment, a social breakfast, or a business lunch, get the chicken and waffles and be prepared for a yin and yang combination of sweet and savory featuring lightly breaded chicken, fluffy waffles, juicy strawberries, buttery butter, and warm syrup. This New Center classic can be busy during weekday lunches, so many regulars get carryout and head over to the nearby New Center Park (see separate entry). *3100 W. Grand Blvd., www.newcentereatery.com, (313) 875-0088.*

Northern Lights Lounge - Decked out with mid-century swank, the Northern Lights Lounge is one of the classiest establishments in New Center. The bar is elegantly decorated with a retro lounge decor: dark wood trim, velvet upholstery, elevated vinyl booths, and candlelit tables. Step outside and you'll find one of the best patios in Detroit, complete with a bonfire for chilly fall days. Though shuffleboard is on the bill every night, there is frequently live entertainment, which varies from rock concerts—including a residency by Detroit legend and Funk Brother Dennis Coffey every Tuesday night—to burlesque shows or DJ nights. There are drink specials most nights, and food is served until midnight. The menu offerings are more dive bar than four-star, but with half off on Thursday nights, you can't complain. *660 W. Baltimore St., www.northernlightslounge.com, (313) 873-1379.*

Parks Old Style Bar-B-Q - Get ready for meltingly tender and mouthwateringly flavorful ribs served in Fred Flintstone–size portions. From within the sleepy building and its modest interior, owner and barbe-guru Constance Parks has been barbecuing some of the city's finest ribs and chicken since 1964. Although the slightly unkempt building and interior waiting area appear unchanged since opening, it is a very clean space, with a cheerful atmosphere and friendly staff. While the simple menu lists only two meats—ribs and chicken—customers can order them in a variety of preparations, including slabs, rib sandwiches, wing dings, half chickens, and rib tips. The barbecue chicken is, naturally, tender and perfectly cooked and seasoned, but the rib portions of the menu are the highlight. The ribs are outstanding, drawing a perfect balance between being well-done and juicy, sweet, and spicy. Perhaps most importantly, the ribs are smothered in the house vinegar-based barbecue sauce. Don't forget to ask for extra napkins. *7444 Beaubien St., www.parksoldstylebar-b-q.com, (313) 873-7444.*

Stella Good Coffee - Set just off the breathtaking lobby of the Fisher Building, with cafe seating under the ornate concourse, Stella is a small, European-style coffee shop in the most elegant of settings. The shop itself is beautiful and contemporary, with an interior that features elegant reclaimed wood fixtures, sleek subway tile, and a striking black-and-white mural in the rear that makes the space pop. Stella offers a full slate of coffees with their locally roasted house blends, including pour-over and well-executed espresso drinks. To augment its caffeinated offerings, the shop slings bagels, as well as a wide variety of fresh pastries, and breakfast delights. *3011 W. Grand Blvd., www.stellacafe.com, (313) 664-0400.*

Sweet Tooth Grill Ice Cream Parlor & Jet Detail Spa - Detroit's (and the world's?) only combination car wash and ice cream shop, this North End spot features some of the city's most charming commercial folk art. The building, which was a drive-in restaurant in a distant past life, is covered with an adorable old-timey mural that depicts anthropomorphic burgers, hot dogs, assorted frozen treats, and teeth (?!) frolicking down a yellow brick road and manning a grill. Patrons will find eight yummy flavors of hand-packed ice cream and a solid menu of American classics, including loaded burgers, loaded chili dogs, loaded footlongs, and fries. Take note that when we say loaded, we mean loaded. Look for wild specials throughout the week, including $1 scoop Sundays, or $2 for anything on Tuesdays. Of course, for the full experience, you can always get your car washed and detailed while you indulge. *9041 Second Ave., (313) 707-3557.*

Turkey Grill - Home to Detroit's turkey burger for more than 15 years, the Turkey Grill offers healthy and tasty alternatives to typical carryout at comparable prices. Order at the counter, and in about 10 minutes the turkey-tom goodness will arrive hot off the grill for you to enjoy to-go or at one of the spacious booths. From the classic turkey burger to breakfast specials with turkey sausage to Cajun-fried turkey wings, the Turkey Grill offers a tasty variety of Southern-style dishes for less than $10. Be sure to drop in Fridays for the Louisiana-style gumbo special. Fried sides and a few salads are vegetarian-friendly, but the main dishes offer turkey, turkey, or turkey! *8290 Woodward Ave., www.turkeygrilldetroit.com, (313) 872-4624.*

Woodward Cocktail Bar - Said to be the oldest operating gay bar in America still in its original location, the Woodward has been a nexus for the LGBTQ community to socialize, relax, drink, and dance since 1951. The address of the bar belies its rear entrance—patrons buzz to get in and are served in a den of exposed brick with a low ceiling and rose-tinted lighting. The dance floor is a raised wooden stage and features a colored light rig, with DJs spinning seven nights a week starting at 10pm. The Woodward is largely a destination bar for members of Detroit's African-American gay community, but there's no litmus test for prospective regulars. Standard pub grub and smoking patio available. Monday is drag night. *6426 Woodward Ave., (313) 872-0166.*

Z's Villa - Roll up your sleeves and get ready for bonfires, horseshoes, and volleyball over beers and pizza. Set in a deceivingly quaint home, this lively bar and restaurant specializes in what can only be described as "party food"—pizza, ribs, wing dings, potato skin boats, clam strips, and nachos. In addition to its yummy food, Z's has a well-stocked bar and a commendable beer list. While a favorite for lunch and dinner year-round, this spot is especially popular in the summer, when the horseshoe pits and volleyball court come alive. The free shuttle makes this a great option for catching some vittles before downtown sporting events. *42 Piquette St., www.zsvilladet.com, (313) 874-2680.*

SHOPPING & SERVICES

★**African Bead Museum** - Equal parts gallery, bead shop, and museum, it's hard to miss the mirage-like light shimmering from the thousands of fragments of mirrors adorning the exterior of the building and the colorful painting and sculptures in the adjacent lots. Its external ornamentation is only a preamble to an even richer interior: Visitors may stop in to shop from a selection of thousands of fascinating and beautiful authentic folk beads from throughout Africa, take part in African dance classes, or check out the museum's collection of African artifacts, which includes sculptures, textiles, and pottery from the last several hundred years. Founded in 1985 by celebrated local artist Olayami Dabls, the museum moved to this 17,500-square-foot location in 1998. Stop in any weekday or on Saturdays, and if you're lucky, you'll be able to enjoy a thoughtful conversation with Dabls himself about beads, art, African artifacts, and Detroit. *6559 Grand River Ave., www.mbad.org, (313) 898-3007.*

Clutch & Throttle - Clutch & Throttle was the dream of Brad Touchette, a Harley-Davidson engineer who wanted to open a shop dedicated exclusively to selling quality, affordable motorcycle gear. If this sounds like a niche market, think again. Touchette's store features unique apparel like Kevlar-padded blue jeans (to arrive in style safely), as well as classic Brando-approved black leather jackets, heavy flannel shirts, headgear, gloves, Pelican saddlebags, and all the appropriate gear to keep you comfortable and fashionable at seventy miles an hour. So, while the store's core demographic is bikers, the nature of high-end durable gear has broader appeal. Make no mistake, this place is a motorcyclist's motorcycle shop: In addition to retailing necessities and accessories, Touchette repairs bikes in the space, but visitors uninitiated with motorcycle culture will enjoy the well-designed store, with distinct touches like custom steel-and-hardwood tables, Turkish rugs, and a vintage barber's chair that's utilized for rotating barber pop-ups. Bikers looking for a fix-up should call ahead; patrons looking for outer wear can stop right in. *6544 Beaubien St., www.clutchandthrottle.co, (313) 656-4325.*

Detroit Gallery of Contemporary Crafts - Appropriately located on the first floor of the magnificent Art Deco Fisher Building, Detroit Gallery of Contemporary Crafts showcases traditional craftspeople and artists from across the nation. This store features handmade ceramics, jewelry, handbags, knits, tapestries, furniture, home decor, and even hand-dyed and handcrafted women's clothing and hats. The gallery has been the perfect place to find a meaningful gift or a unique personal piece for your home or wardrobe for more than 35 years. *3011 W. Grand Blvd., Ste. 104, (313) 873-7888.*

Dittrich Furs - Harkening back to Detroit's days as a fur-trading post for Ojibwe trappers and French merchants, Dittrich keeps the tradition of fine furs alive. As one of the oldest family-owned retail business in Detroit, Dittrich was founded in 1893 and is one of the leading fur retailers in the United States. The store offers a selection of more than 1,000 furs, as well as garment design and manufacturing services, garment repair and restyling, and state-of-the-art cleaning and storage. Known for wonderful service, Dittrich employees greet every visitor as if they had walked into the family's own living room. If for any reason you can't find what you are looking for at Dittrich, try **Silver Fox Furs** (3031 W. Grand Blvd., (313) 872-4260), which specializes in custom and one-of-a-kind fur apparel and accessories. *7373 Third Ave., www.dittrichfurs.com, (313) 873-8300.*

Ferne Boutique - A welcome addition to Detroit's women's boutique clothing scene, this charming and spacious shop in New Center is the well-curated outpost of the popular Bay City store. The trendy, minimal, and raw industrial space features flourishes and pops of color, like a paisley sitting area, a linear mural, and a central showroom mirror that all draw the eye. The polished and well-organized racks make it easy to shop and enjoy the selection of contemporary dresses, tops, rompers, and jumpsuits, with seasonally appropriate accessories, and a capsule collection of jewelry. Segmented vignettes help to break up the assembled ensembles and define different styles for shoppers, from stylish workwear to night-on-the-town. With affordable brands like Lush, Storia, Elan, Alternative Apparel, and others—as well as the of-the-moment suede hats, the store defines an elevated Midwest style that is fashionable, modern, and irresistible. *6529 Woodward Ave., www.ferneboutique.shoplightspeed.com, (248) 703-2858.*

London Luggage - Since opening in 1948, London Luggage has been outfitting area travelers and businesspeople with its extensive inventory of suitcases, briefcases, purses, satchels, writing instruments, and handbags. Enthusiastic owner Ward Dietrich and his staff have a passion for baggage, and love explaining products to customers, while helping them navigate the huge 6,500-square-foot showroom and warehouse. Though the window display showcases iconic luggage brands, such as the reliable Briggs and Riley, classic Samsonite, and sturdy Swiss Army, a wealth of options populate the contemporary sales floor. Dooney and Burke handbags, sturdy laptop cases, and fine briefcases are just a few items available in addition to first-rate luggage brands. In the sparkling glass showcases, admire the Mont Blanc fountain pens, Cross pens, and fine watches. *5955 Woodward Ave., www.londonluggage.com, (313) 831-7200.*

Offin River's Accessories Etcetera - Specializing in women's clothing that is chic, eclectic and, most of all, memorable, this boutique in New Center offers a range of sizes, from 8-3X. With apparel and bedazzled accessories that highlight ladies' individuality and style, the shop features independent local and national brands, with a focus on African-American millinery designers, including Suzette Couture and Gloria Bradley, as well as Rosebud for wearable art fashions. Kwame and Sharon Yamoah started the business in 1994, initially offering just scarves, but began adding handbags and jewelry to their collection. Fast forward to today, and this destination shop now carries vibrant, one-of-a-kind clothing and accessories for all seasons, from refined stone necklaces in turquoise and deep amber hues, to richly colorful sweaters, wraps, stoles, and hats that add true personality to any ensemble. *6080 Woodward Ave., www.offinriversboutique.com, 313-870-1630.*

★ **The Peacock Room Fisher Building -** Shopping at the Peacock Room is an elegant experience for distinguished ladies (and gentlemen!) who embrace pomp and circumstance, along with Swarovski crystals, and racks of dresses as far as the eye can see. An anchor of retail and splendor in the Fisher Building, this flagship location brings together new, consignment, and select vintage clothing in sizes 00 to 24, as well as an eclectic array of accessories—

from feather fascinators and the occasional tiara, to men's ties and scarves, and whimsical socks for everyone. The selection of glamorous night-out (and fanciful everyday) fashions are not the only reason to take a peek: The showroom also incorporates a small bridal boutique for non-traditional brides, and the gilded-age interior is a historic preservationist's dream, featuring stunning flourishes and architectural details. With an uncommonly helpful team, lead by proprietress and maven Rachel Lutz, be careful what you wish for, as you could waltz out of the Fisher with a whole new wardrobe, white opera gloves included! Look for the smaller, but also lovely original location in the nearby Park Shelton (see separate entry). *3011 W. Grand Blvd., (313) 315-3061.*

★**Pot + Box** - The verdant, visionary brick-and-mortar home base of the nomadic Pot + Box flower truck, this lush flower and plant store is located in the arcade of New Center's gorgeous, Art Deco Fisher Building. The brainchild of Lisa Waud, the imaginative shop, which is both environmentally friendly and socially conscious, features dreamy, fresh seasonal blooms, with many Michigan growers strongly represented in the summer months. Lisa and her team are on Detroit's floral design forefront, and they assemble stunning bouquets and arrangements that are guaranteed to make you or someone special smile. In this magical, ethereal space, you'll also find a curated selection of houseplants, often categorized by how much light they require, as well as accompanying vessels, along with soil and fertilizer, so that you can hone your green thumb at home. With a talented team at the helm, the space also offers an inspiring schedule of classes. *3011 W. Grand Blvd., Ste 130, www.potandbox.com, (313) 212-1869.*

★**Pure Detroit** - What began as a small T-shirt company and shop in the David Whitney Building in 1998 has grown into a thriving Detroit business and a beloved local brand. Though the company also maintains storefronts in two prominent Downtown architectural icons—the Guardian Building and the Renaissance Center (see separate entry)—its flagship store is located in the palatial Fisher Building. Accessible just off of the architectural gem's Lothrop Road entrance, the bi-level store offers the largest selection of Pure Detroit's signature Detroit tees, totes, sweatshirts, magnets, undies, pet leashes, and belts and purses made from old seat belts—as well as Detroit gifts such as mouth-watering Sanders treats, delicious McClure's pickles, and Faygo pop. Pure Detroit has become a destination for visitors and locals alike looking to stock up on some Detroit swag. *3011 W. Grand Blvd., Ste. 101, www.puredetroit.com, (313) 873-7873.*

Recycle Here! - If you've got a dash of trash to stash, steer your rear to Recycle Here! Home to numerous murals, cheerful staff, interactive art installations, and a free rummage trailer—the "junk hole"—Recycle Here! is Detroit's response to the recycling blues. The center offers residents a chance to recycle their paper, cardboard, plastic, glass, plastic bags, Styrofoam, and broken electronics while visiting with their neighbors and having a good time. Recycle Here! is a multi-stream facility, so recyclers must sort their recyclables into appropriate bins. Visitors should also plan on checking out the two sister operations: the **Greensafe Store**—which offers environmentally friendly disposable foodservice supplies, including sugarcane compostable bowls and cornstarch utensils—and the **Lincoln Street Art Park**, a self-described outdoor "Ghetto Louvre" which features art made from found and recycled materials, and an array of exciting, unorthodox, and curious outdoor events, as well as live shows. *1331 Holden St., www.recyclehere.net, (313) 871-4000.*

Urbanum - Located on one of the most bustling—and rapidly evolving—blocks in New Center, Urbanum is beautifully curated and thoughtfully arranged. The brainchild of Brigid Beaubien, a descendant of one of Detroit's founding families, the shop is an exquisite and spacious furniture and home decor store for the city dweller. Urbanum offers perfect versions of practical goods like home lighting and bed linens, with a side of delightful gift and personal items, including coffee accessories to enhance your morning ritual, eco-friendly lunch bags, gilded framed mirrors, chic decor items, coffee table books, cozy candles, and other gems—many with a retro look and feel. In keeping with this vintage aesthetic, Urbanum has taken care to retain, and even showcase, its history—a slice of wall unearthed during renovations that revealed gorgeous gilded wallpaper with images of chandeliers that perfectly parallel the shop's own opulent lighting. *6545 Woodward Ave., www.urbanumdetroit.com, (313) 771-4777.*

Vera Jane - Founded by the team behind Pure Detroit (see separate entry), Vera Jane has been offering New Center shoppers eclectic and stylish women's clothing, loungewear, accessories, and jewelry since 2003. Located in the Fisher Building, the store's clean, contemporary look, poured concrete floor, and exposed ceiling contrast pleasantly with the opulent brass and marble lobby outside. The store offers a curated collection—think boutiquette or cozier—but its selection is well-defined, with a unique mix of vintage finds and new pieces, including contemporary fashion, yoga accoutrements, faux-leather handbags, tasteful lingerie, an eye-catching selection of retro sunglasses, and specially commissioned jewelry pieces crafted from estate-sale finds. The store offers extended hours during Fisher Theater shows (see separate entry). *3011 W. Grand Blvd., www.verajane.com, (313) 875-4588.*

Workshop - A beautiful, warm, contemporary showroom for the company's one-of-a-kind modern furniture made from reclaimed wood, Workshop typifies the potential for material reclamation in Detroit. Rescuing old-growth lumber from abandoned demo-list homes in the city, this design-oriented, environmentally minded company turns the rich material bounty into stunning, finished pieces for discerning homes, and gives the historic lumber a third life. Open since 2013, Workshop designs and creates each piece for the showroom in their mezzanine-level studio above the shop. In addition to employing the company's signature, labor-intensive wood joinery, each piece is stamped with the street address of the origin of the materials, creating a unique narrative legacy. In addition to tables, benches, and other home goods, Workshop offers custom made-to-order work to fit almost any need. *3011 W Grand Blvd. #105, www.workshopdetroit.com, (313) 318-9029.*

YAMA - Tasteful pastels, pops of fluorescent colors, and flashes of geometric metallics give this women's shop a modern edge against the backdrop of the Fisher Building's Art Deco splendor. With architecturally inspired jewelry, accessories, and clothing, YAMA lifts inspiration from Minoru Yamasaki, whose legendary structures defined mid-century modern Detroit. From the inside of the Fisher, the narrow galley entrance leads you to a large, light-filled showroom with maze-like racks highlighting the many options and styles. Linear sheaths, shimmery shawls, and statement separates accompany full-on ensembles—and staff will eagerly show you where the newest arrivals perch. Bold brands like Joseph Ribkoff, Samuel Dong, and made-in-the-USA standout Beau Hous, are prominently featured throughout. YAMA offers an alluring selection for women of all shapes and sizes. *3011 W. Grand Blvd. #110, (313) 315-3060.*

CULTURAL ATTRACTIONS

The Baltimore Gallery - You'll know you're in the right place when you spy the diverse, colorful murals that envelope the exterior walls of this gallery and creative space in Milwaukee Junction. Founded in 2013 by artist and Detroit native Phil "Fresh" Simpson, the Baltimore Gallery presents mainly local artists working in photography, painting, sculpture, and other media, in a range of styles. Occupying more than 2,000 square feet, the gallery features exposed ceiling ductwork that gives the space a raw edge, juxtaposed with hanging chandelier lighting. New exhibitions open on a monthly schedule, and the gallery offers an active calendar of other events, including open mic nights, workshops, live music, and film screenings. Check the gallery's social media for event announcements. Stop in the gallery's retail shop to browse locally made apparel and goods from Simpson's own Smile Brand. *314 E. Baltimore Ave., www.thebaltimoregallerydetroit.com, (313) 768-6017.*

★ **Model T Automotive Heritage Complex -** Perhaps the nation's most significant automotive heritage site, the Model T Automotive Heritage Complex at the **Ford Piquette Avenue Plant** is an impressive museum in a storied 1904 structure. The building, a New England mill-style plant, was the first structure built by the Ford Motor Company and the birthplace of the Model T, the "Tin Lizzy." The beautiful three-story red brick building, with its original wooden columns, maple floors, and patches of original paint, untouched since 1910, affords visitors the opportunity to walk in history. The museum, spread across the second and third floors of the building, showcases a number of authentic vintage Piquette-era Fords, including several models of the Model T and earlier Model S.

In addition to the many antique Fords and period artifacts on display, the museum offers a constellation of innovative interpretive displays that explain the assembly process with original Model Ts and display panels that underscore the historic importance of these iconic cars and the people and building that created them. A museum gift shop sells a range of Model T memorabilia, clothing, and Ford-related items. In addition to regular programming and exhibits, the museum acts as a de facto Model T enthusiast's meeting place, and frequently, collectors are on hand to offer rides in one of the legendary cars. The complex is open from April to October, Wednesday to Sunday. Check out the original wooden elevator. *461 Piquette St., www.tplex.org, (313) 872-8759.*

★**Motown Historical Museum -** A mecca for music lovers from all over the world, the Motown Historical Museum is housed in **Hitsville U.S.A.**, the birthplace of Motown Records, one of the most influential and significant music labels in U.S. history. Between 1961 and 1971, Motown had 110 top-10 hits and introduced the world to critically acclaimed and best selling artists such as The Four Tops, Michael Jackson, The Jackson 5, Marvin Gaye, The Isley Brothers, Gladys Knight & The Pips, Martha Reeves and The Vandellas, Smokey Robinson and The Miracles, The Supremes, The Temptations, Mary Wells, and Stevie Wonder. In 1959, Berry Gordy, the founder of Motown, purchased a house and lived upstairs after converting an attached photography studio into a well-engineered recording studio, "Studio A," where nearly all of Motown's hits were recorded for a decade. In 1985, Esther Gordy Edwards, Berry Gordy's sister, began rehabilitating the space to its Motown-era condition and acquiring artifacts. Today, the beautifully restored space features thousands of historic photos, stage outfits, records, posters, gold records, original sheet music, and artifacts, including Michael Jackson's black fedora and studded glove. The museum offers regularly scheduled one-hour tours that take visitors through the large interpretative display area, the original echo chamber, the uniform wardrobe room, Berry Gordy's second-floor flat, the perfectly preserved control room, and the fabled "Studio A." A highlight of the tour experience is the brief Motown dance lesson, held in "Studio A." The professional docents are friendly and outgoing and have seemingly unparalleled knowledge of the label's history and culture. Stars such as Reeves or Wonder occasionally drop in to greet fans, particularly on weekends. Don't forget to "Shop Around" at the well-stocked gift shop. *2648 W. Grand Blvd., www.motownmuseum.org, (313) 875-2264.*

The RED - The first and only children's art museum in Detroit, on its first floor, The RED showcases a permanent collection of art created by local youth, as well as rotating exhibitions. In the back, visitors will find an inviting creative playspace geared towards littler ones, with books and toys to encourage building and making. Both young and old alike can visit the studio spaces upstairs to work on arts and crafts projects, utilizing the onsite supplies. The RED was founded in 2018 by longtime Detroiter and artist Yvette Rock, who is well known for engaging Detroit neighborhoods with the arts, through her traveling arts mobile, an artists collective, and her previous project, Live Coal Gallery. Check The RED's website for hours, workshops, and events. The museum is free, but donations are welcome. *80 Clairmount Ave., www.theredmuseum.org, (313) 472-5427.*

Red Door - Once a steel foundry, this industrial building in the North End now houses a gallery, makerspace, and digital communications studio. Founded in 2000, owner Roger Robinson's private collection of mid-century American art, including vintage advertisements and prints, are shown alongside artwork by Detroit-based artists like Robert Sestok, Benny Andrews, and Kevin Joy. Natural light seeps in through the skylights and brighten the cavernous gallery, which features an enormous brick fireplace. The quirky mélange of artwork on display is rotated out quarterly. The gallery also hosts an artist in residence program. Enter through the red door in the parking lot. *7500 Oakland Ave., (248) 632-6156.*

Russell Industrial Center - The brainchild of Greek immigrant entrepreneur and controversial figure Dennis Kefallinos, the Russell Industrial Center is a massive arts incubator space housed in a sprawling, 2.2-million-square-foot former chassis manufacturing complex originally designed by Albert Kahn in 1915. Since being reimagined as an inexpensive home base for artists and craftspeople in 2003—so far, 650,000 square feet of the complex have been renovated and leased—the facility has become the headquarters, workshop, studio, or office of 300 creative small businesses, from architects to glassblowers, candle makers to artistic welders. Compartmentalized into hundreds of smaller, private units, two of our favorite tenants with public hours are **Cave Gallery**, a contemporary art gallery that showcases emerging and established artists and **Michigan Hot Glass Workshop**, a mammoth 4,000-square-foot glass blowing facility and gallery that offers classes for all skill levels. In addition to studio space, Russell Industrial also hosts a number of concerts throughout the year for fans of all genres, from hip hop to EDM. Don't miss the unmistakable mechanical lion mural, which greets passing motorists on the I-75 expressway. Though the doors are often unlocked, because the building itself does not hold regular public hours, unless you are attending a pre-scheduled event, so be sure to make contact with the party you intend to visit prior to your trip. *1600 Clay St., www.ricdetroit.org, (313) 872-4000.*

Submerge Records - A Detroit techno distributor, Submerge Records has offered an archive exhibit and retail outlet in New Center since 2003. In accordance with the culture and legacy of the music, the facility is discreet: its building bares no signs signaling that it's there, and it doesn't hold regular open hours. However, the minimal planning required to arrange a visit to Submerge and its store Somewhere in Detroit is well worth it. The archive, Exhibit 3000, is situated in a mellow, sleek lobby framed with glass display cases that highlight the technological, social, artistic, and apocryphal aspects of Detroit techno. Artifacts on display include the sequencer used by Kevin Saunderson to make the track "Big Fun," a 1920s-era lathe used to press numerous unique and landmark Detroit releases, gold and platinum record awards from the UK, and original album artwork. The archive, though small, is greatly enhanced by tours of the exhibit that give context, anecdotes, and personal perspective to the role Submerge played in the music, as well as the larger techno scene itself. The store, set bunker-style in the basement, features thousands of signatures from the visitors who've come from all over the world, and sells Underground Resistance clothing and relevant 12-inch and 7-inch records. Tours and visits must be arranged by e-mail *(support@submerge.com)* in advance, except during the annual Movement open house. *3000 E. Grand Blvd., www.submerge.com.*

Tangent Gallery & Hastings Street Ballroom - This gallery and performance venue, built in a former paper plant, has been offering performers the chance to rent unique and adaptive space for more than a decade. The gallery is whitewashed with an elevated stage at the front and has a full sound system, while the ballroom is curtained in black with a full stage at its front and has a full liquor license available at either for events. Notable performers at the space have included John Sinclair, Kevin Saunderson, and Thornetta Davis. Check the website for upcoming shows, concerts, and happenings, or for more information about hosting your own. *715 E. Milwaukee St., www.tangentgallery.com, (313) 873-2955.*

ENTERTAINMENT & RECREATION

Fisher Theatre - One of Detroit's oldest theater venues, the Fisher is the city's home for touring Broadway productions. Located in the lavish Fisher Building (see separate entry), the Fisher Theatre originally featured an ornate Aztec-themed interior replete with live macaws, a goldfish pond, and banana trees. After a several-decade stint as primarily a movie and vaudeville house, it was completely remodeled in 1961 and transformed into a simple, yet still elegant, midcentury modern design with marble, walnut, and Indian rosewood paneling, and crystal and bronze details. It also has superior acoustics and 2,100 seats, all with good sightlines. Broadway greats from Mary Martin to Bernadette Peters and Lynn Redgrave have graced the Fisher's stage, and it has hosted the world premieres of *Hello Dolly* and *Fiddler on the Roof*, among others. Check the website to see the schedule for upcoming shows and to buy tickets. *3011 W. Grand Blvd., www.broadwayindetroit.com, (313) 872-1000.*

Jam Handy Building - A two-time Olympic bronze medalist in aquatic sports (1904 and 1924), Henry Jamison "Jam" Handy was also a successful commercial filmmaker who dominated the field of short-format film production through the late-1960s. His production company produced countless instructional videos and advertisements for major clients such as Lucky Strike and Chevrolet. While hundreds of Jam Handy films can be found on YouTube, the essential view is Detroit: City on the Move, a film produced in 1966. Though the production company has long-since vanished and the building is somewhat rundown, renovations are ongoing and the facility is selectively open to the public. What was once the company's main film studio, complete with 40-foot ceilings, exposed-brick walls, cat walks, and large loading bays, is now used intermittently for special events and is the home of monthly community microgranting dinners called Detroit Soup (see listing in Events). *2900 E. Grand Blvd., Detroit Soup: www.detroitsoup.com.*

Marble Bar - Behind an understated exterior, tucked away on a New Center block brimming with uncut grass, you'll find this casual hotspot that moonlights as one of Detroit's best independent venues. Inside, you'll find not only the namesake marble, but also elegant sconces and chandeliers, mid-century furniture, wood accents, and a cozy mezzanine-level lounge—it's almost hard to imagine this was once a leather-daddy dive bar. Now a popular place to catch live music, the bar hosts local talent, as well as independent national touring acts (think Timmy's Organism and Parquet Courts), and specializes in indie and garage rock, with the occasional hip-hip or techno act. The bar is also a favorite place to dance the night away, and hosts epic DJ nights, including the wildly popular Motor City Soul Club. Despite soaring ceilings, the venue boasts a superb sound system and intimate feel. The stage sits at crowd level, which makes the audience is part of the experience—but even with a packed house, the bar never feels cramped, thanks in to an expansive covered patio out back. If stories are more your jam, look for The Moth story series the first Thursday of the month. *1501 Holden St., (313) 338-3674.*

New Center Park - A tranquil, well-manicured pocket park and outdoor venue in a scenic, urban setting, New Center Park is surrounded by some of Detroit's most majestic architecture. Though it's open daily as an escape from the office blues, under the night sky, with the surrounding buildings illuminated, the popular park offers a rich summer calendar (June-September) of free programming. Classic crowd-pleasing movies are screened in an outdoor movie theater on Wednesday evenings; live jazz and blues acts take the stage on Thursdays; and local bands take it up a notch on Saturdays. With a luscious, rolling hill well-positioned for optimal viewing of the stage and screen, grab one of the provided red folding chairs or bring a blanket and hunker down on the lawn. As part of the attraction, in the attached contemporary conservatory cafe that opens to the park, visitors can grab sandwiches, burgers, and booze to augment the show-going experience. *2990 W. Grand Blvd., www.newcenterpark.com, (313) 784-9475.*

The Schvitz Health Club - Perhaps the most discussed and until recent years, least experienced gem of old Detroit, the Schvitz was built in the 1930s as a classic Russian bathhouse and was a notorious Purple Gang hangout back when that was a terrifying phrase. Until 2017, it was a gathering place for men—and couples, on select infamous nights—to gather, catch up, and sweat. Today, the Schvitz has cleaned up its act and welcomes both men and women to its gorgeous historic saunas, with separate bathing times for each (as well as coed sessions—bathing suit required). Join old-timers and newcomers alike in the Himalayan salt sauna (a fan favorite) or the banya, where you may opt for a *platza*—a massage with a "broom" made of oak leaves dipped in warm water. After you sweat it out, further decompress with one of many typical spa services, like a manicure or pedicure, and then hit the Schvitz's restaurant to refuel. (And don't forget to BYOB— they have a refrigerator to keep it cool for you!) On certain nights, you'll find special events, such as Sound Bath, where bathers are treated to the soothing sounds of local DJs as they relax. $30 to enter on most nights; check the website for male, female, and co-ed times. *8295 Oakland Ave., www.schvitzdetroit.com, (313) 724-8489.*

SITES

★ **Boston-Edison** - Once one of Detroit's most prestigious addresses, Boston-Edison is home to some of the city's most stately and breathtaking turn-of-the-century residential architecture. Comprised of 900 residences on 36 blocks, the neighborhood is bounded by Boston Boulevard to the north, Woodward Avenue to the east, Edison Avenue to the south, and Linwood Street to the west. Developer Edward Voigt, who began acquiring land for the neighborhood in 1884, established building restrictions and a stately boulevard and street pattern to assure and encourage the construction of the city's most palatial homes by its most elite citizens, the first of whom arrived in 1905. Largely constructed by 1925, the archetype of American individuality is evident in the eclecticism of classical design present in the neighborhood, with masterful examples of English Revival, Roman Revival, Greek Revival, French Provincial, Colonial Revival, Italian Renaissance, Prairie, and Vernacular. All of the homes in the neighborhood are impressively large, built of brick, stone, or stucco, and set back at least 30 feet from the front lot line, creating a stately appearance augmented by elaborate exterior details, extensive landscaping, slate or tile roofs, and leaded-glass windows. Though the neighborhood has transitioned from a residential capital of world commerce to a middle-class enclave, because of the dedication of committed residents, much of the original character and quality of the neighborhood is preserved to this day, and self-guided tours, whether by foot or on two or four wheels, still capture the magic of a time when Detroit was the world's foremost industrial power and the captains of industry lived in this neighborhood. Visitors to the area should be sure to also explore **Arden Park**, a 92-home historic district across Woodward, just east of Boston-Edison, on East Boston and Arden Park streets, between Woodward Avenue and Oakland Street. With a similar history and similar stature of residents, the neighborhood was developed at the same time as Boston-Edison, but was begun later. While nearly every house in the neighborhood is a sight to behold, notable highlights include:

- **Berry Gordy Jr. Mansion:** Founder of Motown Records. *918 W. Boston Blvd.*

- Five (of the seven) Fisher Brother Mansions, of automotive fame:

  - **Charles T. Fisher Mansion.** *670 W. Boston Blvd.*

  - **Alfred J. Fisher Mansion.** *1556 W. Chicago Blvd.*

  - **Edward F. Fisher Mansion.** *892 W. Boston Blvd.*

  - **Frederick J. Fisher House.** *54 Arden Park Blvd.* (Located in Arden Park)

  - **William A. Fisher Mansion.** *111 Edison Ave.*

- **Henry Ford Mansion:** Ford's residence from 1907 to 1915, until the construction of the Fairlane Estate in Dearborn. *140 Edison Ave.*

- **J.L. Hudson Mansion:** Founder of Hudson's Department Store, now Macy's. *121 E. Boston Blvd.* (Located in Arden Park)

- **Joe Louis Home:** The modest home of the American icon and Heavyweight Champion of the World. *1683 Edison Ave.*

- **John Dodge Mansion:** Along with brother Horace, founder of the Dodge brand of automobiles, now a part of Chrysler, *75-91 E. Boston Blvd.* (Located in Arden Park)

- **Sebastian S. Kresge Mansion:** Founder of S.S. Kresge stores, now Kmart. *70 W. Boston Blvd.*

- **Walter Briggs Mansion:** Auto baron and owner of Detroit Tigers. *700 W. Boston Blvd.*

- **Walter P. Reuther Home:** Early UAW labor leader. *2292 Longfellow St.*

Cadillac Place - Listed as a National Historic Landmark, the building now known as Cadillac Place was designed by Albert Kahn in 1919 to be the world headquarters for General Motors—the largest company in the U.S. for more than 70 years. When it was completed in 1923, it was the second largest office building in the world. Kahn designed the Neo-Classical building made of limestone, granite, marble, and steel, with four parallel 15-story wings to allow sunlight and ventilation to each of the hundreds of offices housed in the building. The exterior of the building features a crown of exquisite two-story Corinthian columns and a colonnade of ionic columns around the base, which hint at the ornate interior, the most noteworthy feature of which is the lobby arcade with its vaulted ceilings made of Italian marble. Although since converted into a cafeteria, the lower level once housed two swimming pools for use by executives. The building is connected to its neighbor across Grand Boulevard—The Fisher Building—by an underground pedestrian tunnel. After General Motors moved its headquarters to the Renaissance Center in 2001, the building underwent one of the largest historic renovation projects in United States history and was renamed Cadillac Place, in tribute to Detroit's founder. It now houses offices for many major state officials, including several Michigan Supreme Court Justices, and the former executive suite now serves as the Detroit office for Michigan's governor and attorney general. If Cadillac Place looks familiar, you may recognize it from the Michael Moore film Roger & Me, in which it was featured prominently. *3044 West Grand Blvd.*

Cathedral of the Most Blessed Sacrament - The elegant Gothic Revival seat of Detroit's archbishop, this cruciform cathedral boasts striking architecture and magnificent sculptures, and stained glass to match. Though built between 1913 and 1915, the church's elaborate ornaments were finished more gradually, with many installed after Pope Pius XI's 1938 designation of the facility as a cathedral. Beneath the cathedral's massive rose window, the main archway is lined with intricate relief carvings and flanked by a pair of traditional pinnacled Gothic bell towers soaring 135 feet in the air. Most Blessed Sacrament's symmetrical facade features sweeping architectural traceries, buttress facings, and most notably, beautiful statuary by legendary sculptor Corrado Parducci. In addition to the fine ornamentation, the design's clean lines showcase the fine natural grain of the Ohio sandstone and Indiana limestone of the interior and exterior. Inside, the sanctuary is brightly lit by the church's 22 stained-glass windows and dominated by the formal presbytery. The church is best visited in the afternoon, when the setting sun makes the stained glass glow, flooding the nave with colored light. *9844 Woodward Ave., www.archdioceseofdetroit.org, (313) 865-6300.*

Clairmount and 12th: 1967 Riots Site - The northwestern corner of Clairmount Street and Rosa Parks Boulevard, now home to Gordon Park, played an integral role in the city's history as the point of origin for the 1967 riots. In the early morning hours of July 23, 1967, Detroit police officers raided an after-hours party at a blind pig celebrating the return of two Vietnam veterans. Crowd anger over the raid escalated into widespread clashes, resulting in five days of looting, police brutality, and mob violence that saw 43 people killed, 467 injured, 7,231 arrested, and 2,509 buildings burned or looted. Nearly 13,000 U.S. Army and National Guard troops were deployed to quell the rioting, while prominent citizens like Detroit Tiger Willie Horton and Congressman John Conyers made direct appeals to crowds to stop the violence. Ultimately, nearly a quarter of the city was physically affected by the violence and destruction, but its impact as an evocative symbol of contemporary racial discrimination and conflict was felt around the country and still resonates in the city today. While surveying the aftermath, then-Mayor Jerome Cavanagh said, "Today we stand amidst the ashes of our hopes." Although most frequently described as riots, today, some now refer to the grim event as a rebellion, uprising, or civil disturbance to reflect a more nuanced view of the circumstances and context leading up to the violence. Many commentators now agree with the findings of President Lyndon B. Johnson's Kerner Commission: that racial tensions over police brutality, economic discrimination, and dissatisfaction with housing and educational options were the catalysts for the violence.

The events of the summer of 1967 have been cited as both political protest highlighting grievances in Detroit's black community and as an accelerant to the city's pre-existing population and economic decline. In 2017, on the 50th anniversary of these events, the city placed a historical marker at the park and installed upgraded playground equipment and renovated facilities alongside the site's original sculpture by artist Jack Ward, which was installed in 1975. Today, the quiet Gordon Park offers visitors a poignant place to sit and reflect on the ongoing social inequity and racial tension that continue to plague our region. *Clairmount St. and Rosa Parks Blvd.*

Fisher Body 21 - At one time, the Milwaukee Junction district was a major hub of Detroit industry, and Fisher Body Plant 21 was its epicenter. Built in 1919 by Detroit architect Albert Kahn—as famous for his many ornate commercial and residential structures as for his industrial designs. Kahn's work revolutionized factory design with walls of windows to let in light and reinforced concrete to withstand the vibrations and weight of heavy machinery. Founded in 1908, Detroit's Fisher Body Company set the industry standard for auto bodies and supplied for Cadillac, Ford, Studebaker, and Hudson, among others. As the company expanded rapidly, it grew to more than 40 plants in the Midwest, including this six-story factory, located just down the street from Henry Ford's original workshop. After 75 years of operation, the plant was finally abandoned in 1994. Now the domain of scrappers, explorers, and artists, graffiti lines the interior and exterior, and eerie stalactites cling to the ceiling over the winding abandoned track that once moved automobile bodies through the assembly line. *700 Piquette St.*

★**Fisher Building -** Dubbed Detroit's largest art object, the 441-foot cascading Art Deco tower of the Fisher Building has been dropping jaws since its completion in 1928. Originally intended to be a complex of three buildings—a 60-story behemoth flanked by two 30-story skyscrapers—only the first of the lesser towers was completed before the onset of the Great Depression, and the grand plans were simplified. The wealthy Fisher brothers of Fisher Body fame viewed the project as a gift to the city of Detroit and gave virtuoso architect Albert Kahn free reign to build "the most beautiful building in the world" to be their company headquarters and, along with the General Motors Headquarters (now Cadillac Place, see separate entry), to establish New Center as a center for shopping and entertainment. Beyond the artful exterior, the highlight of the masterpiece is the opulent interior exemplified by the stunning and ornate three-story lobby, which features forty varieties of marble and hand-painted barrel-vaulted ceilings which were described upon the building's unveiling as "a mass of gorgeous color, shimmering like the plumage of exotic birds." In addition to being a world-class architectural attraction, the Fisher Building is a world of shops, theater, and art. See the separate entries for the building's other rich offerings, including the Fisher Theater and the building's many retail offerings. *3011 W. Grand Blvd.*

The Lee Plaza - A seemingly out-of-place 15-story skyscraper in an otherwise low-density neighborhood, the Lee Plaza went from being a towering symbol of Detroit's wealth to a sad symbol of the city's decline. Built by real-estate magnate Ralph T. Lee in anticipation of future growth into the area, the Lee Plaza opened in 1929 as a "residential hotel," complete with luxuriously furnished rooms, concierge service, room and maid service, a shopping center, and an upscale grocery. The architectural flourishes and sculptures by Corrado Parducci were extravagant but fitting for its high-class tenants. Unfortunately, due initially to the Great Depression, the city's development and growth never caught up with the hotel, which stood as a lone sentinel on West Grand Boulevard. Since closing in 1997, the building has been ravaged by scrappers, including the notable thefts of its copper roof and 50 terra cotta lion heads from its facade. Now a windowless relic, the ghostly ruin is a popular site for photographers and stands as a reminder of the city's architectural legacy. *2240 W. Grand Blvd.*

Michigan Urban Farming Initiative - Abbreviated as MUFI, the Michigan Urban Farming Initiative is a multi-acre urban agriculture project, founded in 2011 by University of Michigan grads Tyson Gersh and Darin McLeskey. It sprouted in Detroit's North End as a unique mixture of volunteer urban revitalization, experimental eco-farming, and art. Gersh has remained with MUFI as its president and is virtually one with the project. He can often be found pruning plants or tilling mulch, and is always on hand to discuss the initiative. MUFI's campus is impressive: The farm is comprised of rows upon rows of micro-cultivated produce, including peppers, leafy greens, exotic gourds, and staples, like cucumbers. Across Brush is a muraled, three-story building, which is in development, a Child's Sensory Garden, which winds along a shade grove of apple, peach, and cherry trees, and an industrial-scale hoop house. MUFI is a non-profit organization, and almost all materials and labor are donated. Community members volunteer to tend to the crops, and the organization gives away its produce (free of charge) to members of the community every Saturday. *7432 Brush St., www.miufi.org, (313) 444-6834.*

Pallister Street - Beginning in 1978, General Motors began a development called New Center Commons, just north of what was then the location of its world headquarters in New Center. Designed to simultaneously attract General Motors employees to the neighborhood, while revitalizing beleaguered residential areas, the complex project entailed rehabilitations, new construction, traffic rerouting, and street closures. The most beautiful phase of the development project remains the brick-paved, pedestrian-only block of Pallister, between Second Avenue and Third Avenue. With a park-like setting created by the trees and antique-style lamps that line the brick street, a stroll down Pallister more closely resembles a period film set of old Detroit than the active residential street that it is. Though it's small and difficult to find because of road closures, the photogenic turn-of-the-century homes and picturesque brick street are worth the trip. *Pallister St. from Second Ave. to Third Ave.*

Sacred Heart Major Seminary - This awe-inspiring, sprawling red brick complex was completed in 1926 in the English Tudor Gothic style, and is a Catholic seminary affiliated with the Archdiocese of Detroit, offering both vocational divinity programs and an Institute for Ministry, geared toward laity. The entire structure was constructed at one time—rather than in sections—prompting claims that the resulting stability would ensure the structure would stand 300 years. It is bedecked with Tudor flourishes throughout, such as small paned windows and steeply gabled roofs. However, the focal point of the exterior is the imposing square bell tower topped by four intricately detailed spires. In recent decades, one of the most distinct attractions at Sacred Heart has been the shrine on the southwest corner of Linwood and Chicago featuring a statue of a black Jesus, painted such during the '67 riots, perhaps as a rejoinder to the violence. Regardless of its inspiration, Sacred Heart has subsequently maintained the statue and its challenge to prevailing racial assumptions. The interior of Sacred Heart offers an artisanal wooden reredos (a decorative altarpiece) of the apostles and is home to the largest collection of Pewabic tile in the world, with gorgeous inlays in both chapels and the school facility. *2701 Chicago Blvd., www.shms.edu, (313) 883-8500.*

United Sound Systems - Though less renowned than its big brother up the street, Hitsville U.S.A. (see separate entry), this humble recording studio has had nearly as great an impact, serving as the production house for some of the most influential recordings in music history. Opened by Jimmy Siracuse in 1933, the facility was Detroit's first major recording studio. With Siracuse's son Joe in the engineer's booth, United Sound Systems recorded cuts for stars living in Detroit at the time, including Miles Davis, Charlie Parker, and John Lee Hooker, who recorded his seminal song "Boogie Chillen'" in Studio A. In 1958, a young Berry Gordy bought studio time at United Sound Systems to produce "Come to Me" by Marv Johnson. After recording the record, Gordy was inspired to open his own studio nearby, which would become Motown Records, and mimicked many of the facility's design features. After Don Davis purchased United Sound Systems in 1971, the studio's musical palette expanded. Though soul masters like Aretha Franklin and Marvin Gaye continued to record at the facility, acts such as Isaac Hayes, Funkadelic, the Rolling Stones, the MC5, and Underground Resistance grew the breadth of the studio's output. Though it has been boarded up for nearly a decade, the historic sign from the Don Davis era is still in place and stands as a beacon reminding passersby of the building's legacy and contribution to music history. *5840 Second Ave.*

POINTS OF INTEREST

Aretha Franklin Home - The Queen of Soul lived in this amazing home in historic Boston-Edison, surrounded by a canopy of trees. *649 E. Boston Blvd.*

Best Deals Market - Now operating as a liquor store, this building's history as a former Purple Gang headquarters can still be seen in the metal letters affixed to the facade, which spell out the name of the gang's number-making chief, "Charlie the Pencilman." *Oakland Ave. and Clay St.*

Buffalo Bill Train Crash Site - On July 20, 1900, the train carrying the Buffalo Bill Wild West Show infamously crashed here, killing one and injuring nine. *E. Grand Blvd. and Russell St.*

Bust of MLK - This gorgeous three-foot-tall aluminum bust acts as the centerpiece of a small pocket park at the intersection of Rosa Parks and West Grand Boulevard. *7334 Rosa Parks Blvd.*

Charles Brady King Auto - Three months before Henry Ford built his first automobile, Charles Brady King built a gas-powered automobile on this, the former site of Lauer's Machine Shop. Ford, on his bicycle, was reported to have been following King's horseless carriage as it became the first of its kind on the streets of Detroit. *618 Antoine St.*

Clairmount Folk Art - Flanking Clairmount Street, these engaging works of folkart draw the eye of passersby. On the south side of the street are towering steel sculptures, while the north side is occupied by eerie and colorful abstract figures. *136 Clairmount Ave.*

Collingwood Manor Massacre Site - Now a parking lot, on September 6, 1931, three Chicago mobsters were gunned down in the Collingwood Manor Apartments, which once stood on this site. The shooting led to a trial that would send important members of the notorious Purple Gang to prison, ultimately leading to the downfall of the powerful crime syndicate. *1740 Collingwood Ave.*

David Alan Grier Home - This lovely brick home was the childhood abode of actor and comedian David Alan Grier, perhaps best known for his work on the hit '90s comedy show *In Living Color.* *2200 W Boston Blvd.*

The Detroit Portrait Series - These 16 large portraits fill empty second- and third-story windows along Grand River. They were created by artist Nicole Macdonald to elevate homegrown activists and leaders such as Rosa Parks, John Conyers, Walter Reuther, Maryann Mahaffey, Helen Thomas, and Grace Lee Boggs. *5729 W. Grand River Ave.*

D-Town Records - This reserved, historic three-story home was the home base of Mike Hank's soul imprint D-Town Records, which pressed a bevy of now legendary singles between 1963 and 1966. Essential listen: "Detroit, Michigan" by Ronnie Love. *3040 E. Grand Blvd.*

Food Field Garden - This urban farm, located on the former site of Peck Elementary, is committed to growing all of its produce organically and can be found at many of the farmer's markets around the city. *1600 Lawrence St.*

Fourth Street - This single block is the last remnant of what was once a thoroughfare of homes demolished for M-10 and I-94. Today, this shared history and small area has fostered a vibrant, tight-knit community. *Fourth St. and Holden St.*

George Peppard Home - Actor George Peppard, best known for starring opposite Audrey Hepburn in *Breakfast At Tiffany's* and as the cigar chomping leader of TV's *A-Team*, was born and raised in this stately brick home. *99 Burlingame St.*

Golden World Records - Before being bought out by Motown in 1966, like its sister label, Ric-Tic, in 1968, Ed Wingate ran his soul and R&B label, alongside Joanne Bratton, from his home on the western edge of Boston-Edison. *2307 Edison St.*

James Lipton Home - James Lipton, of *Inside the Actors Studio*, grew up at this home in the North End neighborhood. While living here, he worked as an usher at the now shuttered Cass Theater, and was a copy boy at the *Detroit Times*, a now-defunct daily newspaper. *280 Hague St.*

Metropolitan United Methodist Church - Completed in 1926, this elaborate English Gothic church was constructed with ochre granite from Massachusetts, and features a traditional cruciform and, especially off of Chandler Street, beautiful traditional detailing. The interior boasts large murals depicting the history of Protestantism and Methodism, as well as Michigan's second largest organ. *8000 Woodward Ave.*

Motown Records Original Site - Before moving into the iconic location on West Grand Boulevard, this was where Berry Gordy officially started Tamla Records, a forerunner to Motown Records, in 1959. *1719 Gladstone St.*

New Bethel Baptist Church - Once known as the Oriole Theater, this Lasalle Gardens building became the home for Rev. C.L. Franklin's New Bethel Baptist Church in 1963. The church is fondly remembered for its activism during the civil rights era, but is best known as the launching pad for Rev. Franklin's daughter, Aretha Franklin, who got her start singing at the services here. *8430 Linwood St.*

Oakland Avenue Urban Farm - The work of noted neighborhood institution Jerry Hebron, this expansive urban farm features an enormous hoop house, several art installations, and numerous garden beds. *9227 Goodwin St.*

Oakland Sugar House - Now a vacant lot, the bar that once occupied this site was the home base for the infamous Purple Gang, organized criminals who ruled much of the city's illegal alcohol trade during Prohibition. *8606 Oakland St.*

Olympia Stadium Site - Designed by C. Howard Crane, the Detroit Olympia, also known as The Old Red Barn, was the home arena for the Detroit Red Wings from 1927 to 1979. It also hosted a number of other athletic events, as well as concerts, including performances by The Beatles and Elvis Presley. The building was demolished in 1987. *5920 Grand River Ave.*

Reinvented Detroit Flag Mural - This clever muralist's reinterpretation of the City of Detroit flag includes Old English Ds, urban gardens, a Cadillac, and greater racial diversity, incorporated into the traditional design. *918 Custer St.*

Rise Up Tiger Mural - Australian artist David "MEGGS" Hooke splashed this enormous mural onto the side of a vacant building in 2015. A tiger leaps kinetically through a field of bright colors, contrasting sharply with its industrial surroundings. *6314 Russell St.*

Rosa Parks Virginia Park Home - Rosa Parks lived at this address from 1964-1988, just a few blocks south of Wildemere Street, where her husband had work as a barber. *3201 Virginia Park St.*

Rosa Parks Wildemere Home - In 1988, at the age of 75, Rosa Parks moved into this modest home just west of Boston Edison. She stayed here until 1994, when she was attacked by a burglar, after which she moved into the Riverfront Towers where she spent the remainder of her life. *9336 Wildemere St.*

Silverbolt - Molded from automobile bumpers, this John Kearney horse sculpture stands proudly in front of the Children's Museum, which is currently not open to the public. *6134 Second Ave.*

Smokey Robinson Home - The Motown favorite grew up in this house just a few doors down from Diana Ross and around the corner from Aretha Franklin. *581 Belmont St.*

The Illuminated Mural - It's hard to miss this massive nine-story mural, designed by Katie Craig, which looks like a beautiful melting rainbow. The installation uses paint splatters to convey a sense of movement and action. *2937 E. Grand Blvd.*

Ty Cobb Home - The all-time Detroit Tigers great—famous as much for his surly demeanor as he is for his astounding skill on the baseball diamond—lived in this relatively modest home. *800 Atkinson St.*

Walter P. Reuther Home - The famed UAW president lived in this well-kept home on the city's west side until his death in a plane crash in 1970. *3240 W. Philadelphia St.*

Westbound Records - This modest residence was once home to the funk and soul label most famous for records by Funkadelic. *5603 Sixteenth St.*

White Boy Rick Film Site - Scenes from the 2018 film *White Boy Rick* were filmed at this brown behemoth of a building. *6115 W. Grand River Ave.*

CHAPTER 7
EAST RIVERFRONT

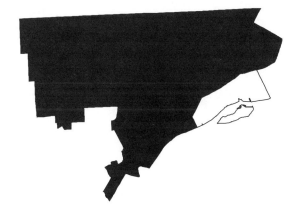

Running along the north shore of the Detroit River, the East Riverfront is among the most photographed districts in the city, and is popular among locals and visitors alike for its delicious eateries, scenic vistas, historic neighborhoods, memorable cultural amenities, emerging shopping and entertainment districts, and its incredible parks, including the lauded island park, Belle Isle. The East Riverfront, as we define it, is bounded by the Detroit River, I-375, Eastern Market, Mack Avenue, and Alter Road.

As one of the city's oldest areas, the East Riverfront is steeped in local history. This portion of Detroit was once home to most of the city's ribbon farms—long, narrow farms that typically measured 250 feet by one to three miles, to maximize river access. Beginning in 1707, Detroit's founder, Antoine de La Mothe Cadillac, granted 34 farmers much of the land in what is now the city's city east side. Many of these earliest families are remembered in Detroit's street names, such as Witherell, Livernois, Riopelle, St. Aubin, Chene, Beaubien, Moran, and De Quindre. As the city developed, the area blossomed as a stately residential corridor along Jefferson Avenue, with industrial land along the river and Beaufait Street, and block upon block of more modest single-family homes. In the early 20th Century, the western end of the area became known as Black Bottom—named for the rich soil—and grew to be a renowned, vibrant African-American neighborhood in the pre-war era of housing discrimination. In the post-war era, much of this history and vibrancy was lost in the wake of numerous urban renewal projects, such as freeway development, major factory and public housing construction, and widespread demolition.

Annexed into a growing Detroit between 1832 and 1917, and primarily built out between 1880 and 1929, the East Riverfront is distinctive both for its role in the city's history and for its diverse physical design. This 11-square-mile area is home to 32,000 people, and encompasses a host of neighborhoods, including Elmwood Park, Gold Coast, Indian Village, Island View, Jefferson Chalmers, Joseph Berry Subdivision, Lafayette Park, Marina District, McDougall-Hunt, and West Village. Although each neighborhood is distinct, with a unique history and architecture, they collectively showcase the diversity of forms in architecture and urban design during the city's peak development years, including grand apartment complexes, scores of cape cod, craftsman, foursquare, and tudor homes, stately mansions, and once-grand pre-war commercial thoroughfares.

In recent years, the East Riverfront has played host to an array of residential and commercial development, especially along the waterfront and around West Village. These developments have made the East Riverfront area an increasing center for dining and drinking in the city, and have led it to be one of a few areas of the city believed to be growing in population.

The East Riverfront is also a treasure trove of parks and greenspaces. With this embarrassment of riches, visitors are never more than a short bike ride from a park or greenway. The RiverWalk runs east/west along the waterfront, connecting downtown and Belle Isle. The Dequindre Cut greenway runs north/south, connecting the RiverWalk to Eastern Market. Heading east, the area is home to Belle Isle, an island park dense with sculptures, beaches, piers, and cultural amenities. Further east, visitors will find a necklace of beautiful riverside parks dotting the waterfront, including the verdant Maheras-Gentry Park. In recent years, protected bike lanes have landed on East Jefferson Ave., connecting all of these amenities even more seamlessly.

No visit to the city is too short for visit to the East Riverfront. The area is a destination for its fine architecture, emerging entertainment district, and recreational and cultural assets. Although many areas in this chapter make for a fine visit, five stand out. For those looking to admire historic architecture, the picturesque group of neighborhoods collectively called The Villages—Berry Subdivision, East Village, Gold Coast, Island View, West Village, and especially Indian Village—offer some of the city's finest architecture, with hundreds of opulent mansions set back from lush lawns and stunning tree-lined streets, alongside the diverse retail district in West Village. Visitors looking to experience modern architecture should head for Lafayette Park's impressive array of Ludwig Mies van der Rohe-designed townhomes, shops, and apartment towers set in a verdant park-like campus. Followers of art shouldn't miss the controversial and essential outdoor multi-block Heidelberg Project and the storied, historic Pewabic Pottery. For culinary adventurers, the area offers an irresistible mix of off-the-beaten-path stalwarts and innovative chef-driven newcomers. For all visitors, the area's parks, including Detroit's island playground, Belle Isle, offer some of the city's finest cultural experiences, athletics facilities, public art, and recreation space.

BARS & RESTAURANTS

Andrews on the Corner - Opened in 1918 by Gus Andrews—and still owned by his grandson Tom—this charming old-school sports bar and grill maintains much of its original character, complete with its beautiful woodwork, retro detailing, and tin ceiling. Prepare your taste buds for a dance with all-fresh Eastern Market meat and a menu a cut above regular bar food—including the ever-popular club and au jus sandwiches. In addition to its extensive food options, Andrews has more than 25 beers on draft and an impressive liquor selection. Although the plethora of TVs and a free shuttle to the stadiums make this an excellent sports bar, Andrews also offers "Drinking With Doggies" night on Tuesdays—a chance to bring your pooch along for some hooch—and live music on Thursdays and Saturdays. *201 Joseph Campau St., www.andrewsonthecorner.com, (313) 259-8325.*

ASHE Supple Co. Atwater Cafe - Located in Rivertown, the city's industrially scenic historic warehouse district, this raw, contemporary cafe is the smaller satellite location of the Downtown roastery and coffee shop. See separate ASHE Supply Co. Flagship Cafe entry for more details. *225 Joseph Campau Ave., www.ashesupplyco.com.*

Atwater Brewery Tap House - Tucked away in the city's historic Rivertown Warehouse District, Atwater launched as a brewpub more than 20 years ago, and has expanded its Detroit tap room into a spacious and comfortable spot to sample some of the best microbrews the region has to offer. With more than a dozen options on tap, the bartenders are passionate about their beers, and they tend to let the drinks speak for themselves. Enjoy an Atwater favorite like the Dirty Blonde (a refreshing, lightly sweet wheat ale) or a Vanilla Java Porter (a luscious copper-hued, English-style porter), or savor one of many creative options like Pumpkin Spice Latte Ale and festive Christmas Ale. In classic pub style, you can pair your drinks with soft, oven-baked pretzels, tasty personal pizzas, or generous sandwich options to soak up the booze. Best of all, you can watch the brewery in action from behind the tap room's glass windows. In warmer months, Atwater features one of the city's best rooftop decks—breeze from the riverfront included. *237 Joseph Campau St., www.atwaterbeer.com, (313) 877-9205.*

Bai Mai Thai - A rarity in the city's east, a place for Thai snack or feast. A place with tall booths, full of workers and youths. An outside inspired by master Mies, great to see if you please. Walls with carvings cut real tight, very tall windows give you light. The fountain makes for nice venue, a charming place to read a menu. Options aplenty of noodles and rice, or chicken and beef with plenty of spice. The pad khing tames you pang, second best item is gaeng dang. Someone attentive will be your server, to bring your meal with a fervor. Knowing guests get food to go, eat in park to see plants grow. Full bar offers range of booze, beer, wine, cocktails if you choose. *1541 E. Lafayette St., www.baimaithai.com, (313) 567-8424.*

Bayview Yacht Club - A nearly century-old institution devoted to freshwater sailing in Michigan, the Bayview Yacht Club occupies five acres along Detroit's riverfront, with a marina of more than 100 slips that accommodate yachts as large as 70 feet. Since 1925, the club has run the renowned Port Huron to Mackinac Race, a competitive midsummer regatta that attracts hundreds of majestic sailboats, and is noted as one of the longest freshwater races in the world. In addition, the club holds a private, local racing series, and offers sailing lessons for those still gaining their sea legs. Inside the clubhouse, members and their guests can dine in understated elegance at the riverfront restaurant, which serves classic American cuisine, while the bar offers a condensed menu to pair with its touted cocktails, including the legendary Hummer (think boozy milkshake), which was invented at the club. *100 Clairpointe St., www.byc.com, (313) 822-1853.*

Belle Isle Pizza - From airy, flaky Neapolitan rounds to crisp, buttery Detroit-style squares, owners Leor Barak and Dave Essig have built a piping-hot reputation since opening in 2015. The simple grab-and-go space boasts a contemporary atmosphere, with a reclaimed wood counter, chalkboard signage, bright red trim, and expansive windows facing the restaurant's namesake island. Though the delicate, charcoal-speckled crust is delightful, the highlight of this pie is the signature BIPizza sauce. The generous lather of this hearty, tangy, and sweet sauce will leave you feeling that other uses for tomatoes are a pity. In addition to classic options, the menu offers a strong list of inventive, toothsome pies named for the city's neighborhoods, such as the Corktown, with Sy Ginsberg corned beef, Swiss cheese, sauerkraut and Thousand Island dressing, alongside a solid stable of sandwiches, salads, and desserts. Customize your pie with this dough temple's expansive list of tasty toppings (think fontina, fried eggs, and golden pickles). Delivery available, including to nearby Belle Isle. *7869 E. Jefferson Ave., www.belleislepizza.com, (313) 331-1222.*

Bread Basket Deli - Don't judge this book by its cover. Behind a sleepy facade, utilitarian waiting area, and bulletproof glass, the Bread Basket Deli offers a bevy of traditional delicatessen staples, including pastrami, peppered beef, corned beef, turkey pastrami, and potato knishes, alongside dishes with a distinctly Detroit flavor, such as pastrami sliders and Detroit-style sweet potato pie, which incorporates bacon as a key ingredient. The food is of unparalleled freshness. Many of the ingredients, including the corned beef, pickles, and bread and rolls, are locally made and delivered daily. Don't be deceived by the affordable prices—portion control is a foreign concept to this meat palace. The small waiting area is carryout only. Along with the west side location, located at 15603 Grand River Ave., this is one of two Detroit locations in this small, regional chain. *3242 E. Jefferson Ave., www.breadbasketdelis.com, (313) 865-3354.*

★ **Bucharest Grill Rivertown -** A fast, cheap, and outrageously delicious destination in the tradition of Romanian street food (an amalgamation of Middle Eastern and German cuisine) with a healthy dose of greasy American bar fare thrown in for good measure, Bucharest serves shawarmas, hummus, sausage, sliders, meat-on-a-stick, curly fries, and pretty much anything else that goes well with pickles, cabbage, or garlic. Billed as "Detroit's best sandwich wraps," the claim is justified! Popular favorites include their signature Bucharest, a delightful garlicky, marinated chicken wrap; the Vegetarian Shawarma, lovingly known as the "french fry sandwich" (it's as good as it sounds); The Detroiter—a knockwurst coney that's worth every penny, and traditional Romanian food like their stuffed pepper. While the popular restaurant now has four locations, with branches in New Center, Corktown, and the Avenue of Fashion, this 80-seat behemoth—the main attraction in an otherwise non-descript shopping center—is their largest. Take advantage of quick carryout, order delivery to your door, or dine-in in the packed but warm and inviting wood-filled space. Open late! *2684 E. Jefferson Ave., www.bucharestgrill.com, (313) 965-3111.*

The Clique - Though it's attached to a drive-up motel, don't miss out. This old-school greasy spoon serves up some of the best diner-style breakfast in town (and serves it until 3pm). The Clique turns out all the staples with working-class panache: The hash browns are buttery; the grits are mild and perfectly textured; the cinnamon rolls are split and cooked on the flattop; the French toast is fluffy; and the bacon is perfectly thin. The joint draws an eclectic, colorful mix of patrons and has been popular with celebrities visiting Detroit, including Stevie Wonder and Aretha Franklin, who have autographed placemats and napkins that adorn the walls. As an added perk, the restaurant is strategically located near the RiverWalk, so you can scenically walk off your indulgences. *1326 E. Jefferson Ave., (313) 259-0922.*

The Commons - Reinventing what a community space could and should be, The Commons is an immaculately designed coffee shop— and laundromat and neighborhood gathering space. Intended to simultaneously attract visitors and neighbors, the project was conceived by the non-profit MACC Development organization, and designed by notable local architect Kaija Wuollet. Housed in an historic corner storefront, the inviting, sun-filled space features a contemporary interplay of wood and tile treatments, and is a perfect stop for a mid-morning (or afternoon or evening) boost. The coffee shop offers a full complement of espresso and coffee drinks, as well as locally made baked goods. For locals, the space also offers the full-service laundromat and meeting hall, which round out the balanced model for this innovative development. Look for the black and white photo depicting this very same stretch of Mack as it once was, but don't be saddened by the decline, be inspired by this catalytic development. *7900 Mack Ave., www.thecommonsdetroit.com, (313) 447-5060.*

Craft Work - The perfect mix of warmth and unpretentious elegance, this neighborhood bar and restaurant is a popular destination on one of West Village's most bustling blocks. Split between a serene sit-down dining room and a stunning, historic wood-filled bar space in the Parkstone Apartments, we recommend opting for the the latter, which resembles a well-appointed library, with antique bookshelves, a beautiful wood bar, and period-appropriate lighting. The perfect place to meet friends or make friends, come for happy hour at the long, communal high tops, or sit down for a romantic dinner, where Chef Aaron Solley offers cuisine rooted in the Mediterranean and French traditions. Though the menu is seasonal, look for standouts like pork shoulder and lamb and couscous, or elevated classics like fish and chips, fried chicken, and the Le Big Mack Ave. burger. Also don't miss Solley's raw bar, which features ceviche, oysters, and fresh sushi. Behind the bar, look for several craft drafts, an impressive selection of wine, and classic cocktails that are prepared with excellence, precision, and haste—and frequently inspire "I'll have another" as a refrain. *8047 Agnes St., www.craftworkdetroit.com, (313) 469-0976.*

★ **Detroit Vegan Soul East** - After tempting Detroiters with pop-ups for years, vegetarians, vegans, and even omnivores celebrated when this outrageously delicious vegan destination (known as DVS for short) opened on the charming Agnes commercial strip in 2014. The sun-filled dining room, painted in bright, calming, earthy hues, makes the space inherently welcoming. DVS offers a bountiful, locally sourced, organic, vegan menu that manages to be healthful, without compromising on flavor, inventiveness, or variety. While we love the Soul Platter, BBQ Tofu, and almost every one of their sandwiches, the "Catfish" Tofu Sandwich, an addictive cornmeal-battered delight, is one of the best vegetarian sandwiches in the city! In addition to lunch and dinner offerings throughout the week, DVS offers up brunch all day Sunday, with a tasty tofu scramble, a vegan "homestyle breakfast" and a slew of other breakfast offerings. Don't miss out on their selection of vegan and gluten free baked goods, too! If you find yourself on the west side, check out their western outpost, Detroit Vegan Soul West (see separate entry). *8029 Agnes St., www.detroitvegansoul.com, (313) 649-2759.*

Elbow Lounge - Popular with longtime area residents, this vintage neighborhood watering hole is the kind of place where everyone is called baby, thumping 1980s R&B hangs in the air, barbeque is for sale by the plate, and on the wild dance floor, seniors send the holy spirit packing. Inside this former house, the well-loved interior and its mismatched ceiling tiles give the space a sense of charm and comfort. At first blush, the dizzying array of disco balls, party streamers, foil stars, and general dive detritus can feel like Marie Kondo's nightmare, but after a few trips to the bar, you'll see the light. The well-worn wood bar plays host to the usual dive fare of domestic and imported bottles and mainstream spirits, though at Elbow, they're served with a friendly sense of frivolity that is much rarer. *7310 Mack Ave., (313) 878-2061.*

Gingerberry - Like its name, Gingerberry is a little bit spicy and a little bit sweet—but all delicious. This made-to-order, takeout-only spot on the east side is owned by a mother-daughter team who serve up comfort food with character. With a selection of salads—try the salmon Caesar with homemade dressing—and sandwiches, you can grab a healthy lunch to take with you to Belle Isle. Or stop by at dinnertime for one of Gingerberry's classic (and filling!) entrees, like catfish, lamb chops, or the "Big Boy"—steak, shrimp and lobster tail in one amazing dish. Those with a sweet tooth can't go wrong with the restaurant's gorgeous, powdered sugar and strawberry-topped red velvet waffle served with chicken wings. If you've got enough room after that, top it off with sinfully good fried Oreos. You won't be disappointed. *12626 E. Jefferson Ave., (313) 473-8229.*

Le Petit Dejeuner - Borrowing from French and Southern breakfast traditions, owner Tina Motley has created an ace breakfast experience that is flavorful, approachable, and eminently likeable. Inside this 1899 brick beauty, the interior feels clean and contemporary but not avant garde, with imitation-stone accents, cinnamon-colored walls, and angled dropped ceilings set among vestigial historical features. The menu is elevated but accessible. With attentive preparation, Motley conquers both the familiar—crepes, sweet potato pancakes, buttermilk waffles, obscenely flaky croissants, and pillowy omelettes—and the more inventive—house sun-dried tomato chicken sausage, creamed corn pancakes, and carrot-cake pancakes in convincing fashion. All dishes are served family style and with several sides, creating a unique breakfast tapas experience. With a BYOB-friendly beverage policy and live Caribbean jazz on Saturdays, you won't be alone in your quest for this breakfast treasure on weekends. Reservations are highly recommended. *6470 E Jefferson Ave., (313) 725-0257.*

★**Marrow -** Through the inspired marriage of traditional craft and culinary ingenuity, Chef Sara Welch's fine-restaurant/butcher-shop concept has earned every bit of its critical acclaim. The restaurant's two connected halves—the cocktail bar and butcher counter on one side and the restaurant on the other—share a refined, if unpretentious, aesthetic punctuated by exposed brick, vintage meat ads, and industrial pendant lights. The whole-animal retail counter focuses on locally sourced organic pork, beef, and chicken, alongside options such as housemade sausage, meatballs, deli cuts, dry-aged steaks, duck rillette, and rabbit mortadella. At the restaurant, the exquisite rotating menu reads like a protein-centered tour de force, highlighted by offal yakitori, tallow tempura delicata, marrow croquettes, pig skin popcorn, corned pork tongue with carrot mochi, and crispy duck quarter with kabocha mash. The drink list is every bit its equal. This multipage affair offers an extensive selection of fine wines alongside a more curated draft craft beer roster and house cocktail selection. *8044 Kercheval Ave., www.marrowdetroit.com, (313) 652-0200.*

Marshall's Bar - Just north of the Fox Creek neighborhood lies this blue-collar watering hole that celebrates the area and its customers. Owned by Ted Kapuscinski, a starting pitcher for the Tigers' farm system in the 1940s and 1950s, Marshall's is a low-key watering hole with cheap drinks, zero fuss, and enough personal touches to give it plenty of character. So, tip back an Old Milwaukee, grab a grey faux-leather stool, and abseil into incandescence. The rear of the bar opens onto Fox Creek, and on warm nights patrons can sit by the water and soak in this rustic sliver of the city. Marshall's is partisan to showing Detroit sports but pinch hits with old movies in the off season. *14716 E. Jefferson Ave., (313) 821-0610.*

My Dad's Bar - Someone raised the kids right. The brother and sister team that runs My Dad's Bar—Frank and Lola Gegovic—have given the joint a level of character uncommon for low-key watering holes. With a skillfully thrifted decor that surreally emulates the best of 1950s basement bars, the upscale dive is appropriately named. Seat yourself at the multicolored bar stools, refashioned hardwood card tables, or on the outdoor patio to soak in the class of carefully chosen, stylishly retro decor, such as decommissioned typewriters, a shapely mannequin lamp, vintage bar accessories, and framed photos of the fathers amongst us. Cheap wells, domestics, and local imports are among the offerings, along with board games and, yes, TV. Don't forget to bring some quarters for the well-curated jukebox. *14911 Kercheval St., (313) 831 3237.*

Norma G's - After a successful run as a food truck, Chef and owner Lester Gouvia opened the doors to this brick and mortar location in 2018. Named for his beloved mother, Norma G's is a warm and welcoming east side spot that dishes up Caribbean specialties, including beef patties, jerk chicken sliders, and curry. The lovely, modern interior is surrounded by floor-to-ceiling windows that fill the spacious restaurant with light, and make it a rewarding east side respite. Menu highlights include the house mac and cheese, curry goat, cod fish balls, frozen custard desserts, and doubles, a classic (and yummy) Trinidadian street food that pairs flatbread with curried chickpeas. Vegans and vegetarians will find a bevy of other tasty options, too. If you're looking to wet your whistle, enjoy a sorrel drink, specialty cocktails, and local brews on tap. In the summer months, the roll-up doors open up to the cozy, landscaped patio where the jerk chicken is grilled. *14628 East Jefferson Ave., www.normagscuisine.com, (313) 290-2938.*

Rattlesnake Club - This elegant riverfront restaurant is a popular destination among the city's movers and shakers, thanks to sweeping views of the river and the city's skyline, a lavish yet chic interior, and renowned upscale American cuisine. The au courant dining room features beautiful table settings and a fine collection of two- and three-dimensional art. The seasonal menus feature certified prime Angus beef and offer an emphasis on organic and sustainable ingredients. The "upscale dude food" menu includes an irreproachable apple-cider-cured duck breast, dunkel-braised beef short ribs, and sizzling, tender porterhouses that could feed a small family. The staff and managers are warm and professional, with the knowledge to suggest wine pairings and experience to make informed recommendations. The wine list is thorough and interesting, with fine offerings from Traverse City to Bordeaux. *300 River Place Dr., www.rattlesnakeclub.com, (313) 567-4400.*

★The Red Hook - After relocating to Detroit from Red Hook, Brooklyn, owners Sandi Bache Heaselgrave and Andy Heaselgrave brought their coffee prowess to West Village in 2014. One of Detroit's most beloved coffee shops, this charming cafe is the sister store to the equally popular Ferndale location. The space features cozy banquettes and enormous windows that fill the cafe with sunshine and highlight the minimal, wood-rich interior, which is punctuated by colorful murals, including a stunning pheasant by local artist Ouizi. The shop offers a full slate of expertly crafted coffee and espresso drinks, as perfect to look at as they are on your lips. However, almost as much of a draw as their coffee is their tempting selection of house-made pastries and baked goods, because honestly, what pairs better with caffeine than sugar? The shop offers exceptional scones and delectable cookies, brownies, and even toaster pastries, but you would be especially remiss to leave without trying a slice of the vegan chocolate salted-caramel cake. *8025 Agnes St., www.theredhookcoffee.com, (313) 458-8761.*

★Rose's Fine Food - This east side staple, serving both breakfast and lunch, takes the classic diner and aims to perfect it. Instead of focusing on the trendy or exotic, Rose's Fine Food revels in creating the most delicious versions of everyday fare, sourcing much of the menu from local farms. Sit down at one of the handful of tables or, even better, at the long countertop, and soak in the local chatter as you dig into the artfully prepared comfort food. The humble egg sandwich is elevated here by the house-made bread and aioli, perfectly paired with a slice of sharp Michigan cheddar and crunchy greens. The stack of pancakes, made from organic stone-ground flour, is finished with local syrup and cultured butter. Depending on the season, you may also find a lamb burger topped with caramelized onions, pulled chicken in a yogurt dressing, or a chickpea curry ladled over heirloom rice. Be sure to save room for something from the bakery case—an ever-changing selection of house-made donuts, cinnamon rolls, and cakes. *10551 E. Jefferson Ave., www.rosesfinefood.com, (313) 822-2729.*

Sindbads - Named for one of the greatest (mythical) sailors to ever wander the high seas, Sindbads has been a staple on the Detroit waterfront since 1948. With a retro, nautical ambiance, the classic eatery offers floor-to-ceiling windows that afford guests beautiful, sweeping views of the Detroit River. In the spacious, scenic dining room, patrons can choose from a wide selection of classic sandwiches and "treasures from the land and sea." House specialties include thick Angus steaks, a "man-size" chicken sandwich called the Land Lubber, and, of course, selections from the comprehensive seafood offerings—of which we suggest The Mariner, a triple threat of fresh white fish, scallops, and frog legs. While Sindbads is a decidedly Surf & Turf establishment, it happily accommodates vegetarian guests off-menu. The restaurant also features a large wooden bar, which is usually packed with regulars discussing pressing issues. While most guests come by land, if you're looking for a more scenic route, Sindbads has a private marina with 86 boat slips—and offers economical overnight rates. *100 St. Clair St., www.sindbadsdetroit.com, (313) 822-7817.*

★**Sister Pie -** Think of the long lines as the spinach of your visit—you've got to get through them before you can get to dessert. Launched in 2012 by jaunty owner Lisa Ludwinski, Sister Pie is the city's breadquarters for savory hand pies, scones, cookies, breakfast sandwiches, breakfast porridges, coffee and, of course, sumptuous pies—whole or by the slice. The interior is a bright, light-filled space anchored by an open kitchen and a contemporary geometric counter, with antique bakery cases, Edison-bulb pendant lights, and plentiful succulents. Making use of available Michigan produce, the seasonal pies reward adventurous diners with their contemporary spins on traditional recipes, such as Grapefruit Black Pepper Meringue, Apple Sage Gouda, Brandy Pecan, and Ginger Peach Biscuit. All of the pies make use of the shop's signature flaky, flavorful, buttery crust, freshly handmade with French butter. The pies aren't alone as confection perfection, however: Leaving without a Buckwheat Chocolate Chip Cookie or Leek and Cauliflower Scone is almost criminally negligent. *8066 Kercheval Ave., www.sisterpie.com, (313) 447-5550.*

Southern Fires - Located on the first floor of a former warehouse, Southern Fires has become a classic upscale soul food destination on the east side. The menu is a modified prix fixe—all entrees, such as succulent marinated chicken, fish, or ribs, are served with two sides (the dulcet sweet potatoes are delicious) and buttery, moist cornbread. Dine-in in the sprawling, warm, open dining room at tables with tall wooden benches or grab your meal to go. Check out the panoramic street scene mural reminiscent of the iconic painting *The Sugar Shack* (you might know it from the cover of Marvin Gaye's album "I Want You") in the back of the dining room. *575 Bellevue St., www.southernfiresrestaurant.com, (313) 393-4930.*

Steve's Soul Food and The Key Club - In a beautifully restored industrial brick building, near the Detroit River, you'll find Steve's Soul Food and The Key Club. Steve's buffet stretches the length of the building and offers all the standard soul food fare from catfish to mac and cheese, and all varieties of pie. Guests can take carryout, or they can dine-in on the main floor with airy lofted ceilings and tall booths or open tables surrounding large flat-screen televisions. Venture up to the third floor of the Key Club for a great view of the Detroit River and downtown—there's no cover charge if you stop by during the day. At night, The Key Club often hosts special events from concert after-parties to birthday celebrations. Check the bulletin board for upcoming Key Club events, or call. *1440 Franklin St., (313) 393-0018.*

They Say - So, what exactly are they saying? Good things. If the curious name doesn't attract your attention to this jazz club and restaurant, the exposed brick, wood trim, and Art Deco bar will. Nestled in a spacious and handsome historic former warehouse building in the resurgent Rivertown Warehouse District, They Say brings live jazz and blues talent to its first-floor lounge five nights a week—and occasionally on afternoons, as well. Out of its impressively small open kitchen, the joint turns out a solid but compact menu of standards, many of which involve a Cajun twist. Of its offerings, favorites are the Buffalo wings, thick-crust pizza, and steak, which are backed up by a cornucopia of other options. Though it is sometimes overtaken by a club atmosphere—and cover—during less inclement months, the scenic outdoor patio on the second floor offers unmatched views of the Renaissance Center and a soothing breeze off the river. Check the restaurant's Facebook page for upcoming events. *267 Joseph Campau St., (313) 446-4682.*

The Villages Bier & Weingarten - Previously known as the Tashmoo Biergarten, this seasonal neighborhood hangout at the intersection of Agnes and Van Dyke attracts Detroiters of all stripes. Order a beer or glass of wine at the shipping-container bar and gather at one of many large picnic tables adorned with festive lights, imbibing al fresco from Memorial Day through the end of October. Though beer is the order of the day, the space is family-friendly, offering occasional bonfires on chillier days and a bocce court for some good-natured competition. Guests are invited to bring their own food—though you can't go wrong with a meal from YumVillage, an outstanding Afro-Carribean food truck that's often parked next door. *1416 Van Dyke St., www.bwgdetroit.com.*

Ye Olde Tap Room - With more than 280 draft and bottled beers from six continents, including many hard-to-find Belgian and German varieties, this storied tavern is a bona fide brewski-lover's fantasy. Once a gambling hall and a house of ill-repute, the place became a blind pig in 1922 during Prohibition and has been in continuous operation as a bar ever since. Inside, the dark, cozy beer hall has wood tables and a fireplace that hint at its past and make it a popular east side destination. For the hungry set, tasty, well-paired cheese and sausage are available, as are complimentary peanuts that will help keep you thirsty. For entertainment, the bar frequently hosts live music and offers darts to keep patrons active and help them work off some of their caloric intake. Don't miss the annual Repeal Day party in May, which always packs the house. *14915 Charlevoix St., (313) 824-1030.*

SHOPPING & SERVICES

★ **Detroit Denim** - Tucked away in a brightly lit brick loft in the historic Rivertown Warehouse District, this shop is a testament to the quality and potential of traditional American manufacturing. Founder Eric Yelsma was told it wasn't possible to produce entirely USA-made jeans and denim products, with American-made materials, but this shop proved the doubters wrong. The shop space is beautiful, industrial, raw, and impeccably designed, with exposed steel trusses, antique fixtures, and thoughtful displays of the housemade wares. While you browse the racks and shelves of perfectly crafted denim goods, including jeans, aprons, and totes, admire the manufacturing process through the glass-walled divider. Before you commit, know your material: Most denim in the shop is either raw (untreated, to gradually wear to the owner's shape) or selvedge (a tighter, denser weave that is more rugged). The jeans, which cost about $200, come in a range of styles for both men and women, and include an impressive lifetime repair warranty! The shop also stocks a slew of other housemade accessories, including leather bags, wallets, and refashioned vintage denim jackets! *2987 Franklin St., www.detroitdenim.com, (313) 626-9216.*

★ **Pewabic Pottery** - Founded in 1903 by ceramic artist Mary Chase Perry Stratton and her partner, Horace James Caulkins, as part of the Arts and Crafts movement, Pewabic Pottery is a renowned National Historic Landmark. Known for its distinctive iridescent glazes, hundreds of Detroit's most prestigious buildings and homes contain Pewabic tiles, and installations of them can be found across the country from the Shedd Aquarium in Chicago to the Nebraska State Capitol. Stratton was an important figure in the arts scene in Detroit in the early 20th century, serving as a trustee of what is now the Detroit Institute of Arts and founding the University of Michigan ceramics department. Now run by a nonprofit, Pewabic maintains an active fabrication studio creating commissioned large-scale installations as well as its traditional tiles, dishes, ornaments, and gifts. Shop for these smaller wares, as well as work by talented local ceramic artists, in its wonderful on-site shop, or check out its wide array of fantastic class and workshop offerings for a chance to hone your pottery skills in a historic, intimate setting. When you visit, be sure to take a self-guided tour of the production facility to see ceramic artists at work creating pieces in much the same way that Stratton did more than 100 years ago. *10125 E. Jefferson Ave., www.pewabic.org, (313) 626-2000.*

★ **POST** - Set in a sprawling and long-shuttered post office, POST is the brainchild of Clare Fox and Wayne Maki. With collaborative studio spaces for their own endeavor, **Mutual Adoration**—a company that creates reclaimed-wood furniture and home goods—as well as a handful of other rotating small companies, like popular designer-manufacturer **Tait Design Co.** (renowned for their beautiful gliders and yoyos), the public component of the space is the beautiful shop. Located in the former lobby of the building, POST highlights the goods created onsite, as well as complementary work from other makers. The gorgeous custom fixtures created by Mutual Adoration set off the shop's wares and make it an unexpected and delightful shopping experience. A real highlight of the shop is their robust calendar of diverse and enticing art and craft workshops taught by a roster of local artists. See their website for details and to register. *14500 Kercheval St., www.post-detroit.com, (313) 939-2172.*

Three Thirteen - Owner Clement "Fame" Brown wants to make an impact on Detroit streetwear fashion. This dream is apparent at his store, Three Thirteen, which is named for the city's area code. Inside, Brown highlights his own house line of Detroit-themed apparel, as well as popular local brands, like Detroit vs. Everybody, Detroit Hustles Harder, Filthie Rich, and others, making the store a family gathering of Detroit labels and imprints. Brown has been a clothing designer his whole life, and the Three Thirteen logo, a mix of hash marks and Roman numerals representing the area code, accents Detroit streetwear with a novel expression of the city's identity. Dubbed "Detroit's Brand Name," the line features hoodies, knit caps, T-shirts, and branded catwalk-worthy, house-designed jeans. Coupled with the apparel from other Detroit brands, the store is a one-stop shop for Renaissance City and streetwear enthusiasts. The brick-and-mortar store lets the clothing be the focus, but visitors shouldn't miss the large-scale mural by street artist Sintex. *2642 E. Jefferson Ave., www.threethirteenstore.com, (313) 818-0050.*

Wheelhouse Detroit - Scenically located on the Detroit RiverWalk (see separate entry), Wheelhouse is a small, but exceedingly well-curated, contemporary bike shop that serves as the home base for RiverWalk bicycle traffic. Enter through the raised glass garage door to find a well-stocked selection of essential accessories and new bicycles, with a range of options available for both beginners and two-wheeled veterans. If you don't see something that's quite the right fit, the staff is known to happily, and speedily, assist in special ordering any part. To keep you moving, the shop also offers an exceptional repair service, boasting some of the city's most experienced and amicable bike mechanics. However, despite these offerings, the Wheelhouse is most loved for its bike rental and tour services. Make your selection from the 11 bike rental options—from road bike to cruiser, BMX, or tandem—and cruise the streets of Detroit right—on two wheels! On weekends and some weekdays, the Wheelhouse runs a variety of bike tours, including architecture, public art, automotive heritage, and local dining. Open seasonally. Check the website for hours and tour offerings. *1340 E. Atwater St., www.wheelhousedetroit.com, (313) 656-2453.*

CULTURAL ATTRACTIONS

★**Anna Scripps Whitcomb Conservatory -** This historic conservatory was designed by Albert Kahn in 1904 (modeled after Thomas Jefferson's Monticello) and features an 85-foot central dome. Sitting on a scenic 13-acre parcel of Belle Isle featuring a formal perennial garden, a rose garden, and a serene lily pond, the conservatory itself is packed with beautiful native and exotic plants of all kinds, including large palms, a cactus room, a fernery, the largest municipal collection of orchids in the country (including rare orchids saved from Britain during World War II and transported to Detroit). It is a long Detroit tradition to visit the conservatory on Christmas and Easter to see the special seasonal displays. Strolling the meandering path is a meditative experience and especially restorative in the winter months. Free admission. *876 Picnic Way, www.belleisleconservancy. org, (313) 852-4064.*

Bahamas Biennale - With its tongue-in-cheek name (a wink to artist Maurizio Cattelan's Caribbean Biennale), Sean Thomas Blott opened Bahamas Biennale's in 2014. The second location for the gallery, which is based in Blott's native Wisconsin, the Detroit location is housed in an enormous industrial space that was once a broom factory, and is more than 100 years old. Bahamas Biennale maintains a focus on contemporary art with an experimental angle, and offers compelling solo and group exhibitions of artists from Detroit, New York, and beyond. Some shows are by appointment only so please visit Bahamas Biennale's website for an exhibition schedule, or to contact the gallery. *3106 Bellevue St., www.bahamasbiennale.com, (262) 441-9257.*

★ **Belle Isle Aquarium** - Designed by Albert Kahn, the 10,000-square-foot Belle Isle Aquarium opened in 1904. The grand entrance opens into a large gallery with tank-lined walls and an incredible arched ceiling covered in shimmering green glass tile to mimic the feeling of being underwater. Though the facility was closed to the public in 2005, it was maintained by volunteers and reopened by the Friends of Belle Isle on the aquarium's 108th birthday in 2012. While volunteers are still working to restore and repopulate some of the aquarium's tanks, most have been reactivated and are teeming with aquatic life, including turtles, eels, and a wide variety of salt and freshwater fish. Because the aquarium is run completely by volunteers, it is currently regularly open only Friday to Sunday. Admission is free, but donations are welcome. *3833 Insulruhe Ave., www.belleisleconservancy.org.*

Belle Isle Nature Zoo - Opened in 2005 to replace the larger Safariland, the Belle Isle Nature Zoo is a lively interpretive center dedicated to showcasing Michigan's native flora and fauna. The updated facility is always abuzz with the sounds of enthusiastic children enjoying the zoo's many educational programs and installations, including the native deer enclosure, lecture auditorium, turtle exhibit, indoor beehive, reptile and amphibian areas, spider display, and crafts area. The friendly and knowledgeable staff brings these offerings to life, particularly for the youngest Detroiters. The zoo complex is also home to a protected six-acre forested wetland, an impressive trail network, and a large bird watching and observation area. The well-maintained bathrooms are open 362 days a year, making it a popular place to discover nature when nature calls for many island visitors. *176 Lakeside Dr., www.detroitzoo.org, (313) 852-4056, Ext. 3023.*

Boggs Center - Since 1995, the James and Grace Lee Boggs Center to Nurture Community Leadership has operated as a nonprofit organization in the Boggs' former home, located just north of Belle Isle. In this green, grassy neighborhood full of old-growth oaks and colorful houses, new ideas and networks for transformative leadership blossom. Named for the couple, who settled in Detroit in the 1940s and dedicated their lives to organizing in labor unions and the civil rights movement, the Boggs Center organizes conferences and international publications, such as Reimagining Work and The Next American Revolution. Despite the passing of Grace Lee Boggs in 2015, the center continues to actively nurture leadership to foster a more fair and just world. By appointment only, visitors are encouraged to call ahead to schedule a visit for what will likely be a transformative experience. *3061 Field St., www.boggscenter.org, (313) 923-0797.*

Department of Natural Resources Outdoor Adventure Center - Bringing Michigan's great outdoors indoors, this kid-centric stationary trip up north offers all the trappings of Michigan's countryside. Housed in the beautifully rehabilitated Globe Trading Company building, the contemporary space is centered around an indoor waterfall, and includes a climbable 40-foot man-made tree, indoor archery range, 3,000-gallon freshwater aquarium, and vivid simulators for off-road vehicles, canoes, kayaks, snowmobiles, and fishing boats for children and the adults lucky enough to take them. Collectively, the center's exhibits engage every sense, from interactive pelt displays, an airplane visitors can sit in, and a treetop suspension bridge allowing visitors to smell their way through an old-growth forest. Don't leave without bagging a few virtual critters at the realistic fishing and squirrel hunting simulators. *1801 Atwater St., www.michigan.gov/oac, (844) 622-6367.*

Dossin Great Lakes Museum - A must-see for any historian, maritime enthusiast, or imaginative child, the Dossin Great Lakes Museum is located on the south side of Belle Isle and is home to several notable exhibits, including the first speedboat to reach 100 miles per hour (Miss Pepsi), the opulent smoking lounge from the steamship City of Detroit III (yes, the whole lounge was installed here!), and intriguing rotating exhibits pertaining to the Great Lakes. Most exciting for the young or young-at-heart is the pilot house of the William Clay Ford, mounted atop the museum and facing the river— allowing any visitor to "captain" a Great Lakes freighter. An additional fun feature of the Dossin—and one that can be enjoyed from the comfort of your own home—is the Dossin Great Lakes Museum Detroit River Watch webcam, which you can maneuver remotely to spy on passing freighters, boats, and rowers. Be sure to check out the cannons on the way in—they were captured from the British during the Battle of Lake Erie in the War of 1812. Hours vary seasonally, but winter brings spectacular views of an ice-filled river. *100 Strand Dr., www.detroithistorical.org, (313) 852-4051.*

★ **The Heidelberg Project -** A labor of love and an act of resistance, the Heidelberg Project is Detroit's best-known outdoor art installation, and one of its most controversial. When Tyree Guyton and his grandfather Sam Mackey started painting polka dots on abandoned houses and attaching stuffed animals to trees in 1986, it was a defiant gesture meant, in part, to draw attention to their crumbling east side neighborhood. Heidelberg continued to grow, ultimately transforming two full city blocks into a constantly evolving, imaginative wonderland of found objects and outsider art that is as angry and challenging as it is colorful and inspiring. While the installations are popular with many, they remain contentious: Some elements of the project were demolished by order of two separate mayoral administrations, and a rash of arsons in 2013 destroyed multiple Heidelberg structures, including the famous Clock House. Undaunted, Guyton continued to grow and rebuild the project, work that is ongoing. To this day, the Heidelberg is an internationally acclaimed destination (visited by more than 275,000 people a year), a nonprofit organization, and an art education center. Visitors may partake in a self-guided tour, or can opt for a free docent-led tour (many of which are led by Guyton himself). Heidelberg is a must-see. *3600 Heidelberg St., www.heidelberg.org, (313) 974-6894.*

ISKCON Temple of Detroit at the Fisher Mansion - Built in 1927, the Fisher Mansion was a monument to auto-body magnate Lawrence Fisher. The 22,000-square-foot Spanish Mission-style estate boasts a music room with Japanese ceilings, a dining room with pillars from a 15th-century German castle, a covered boat slip that once held Fisher's 104-foot yacht, and, according to rumor, hidden Prohibition-era wine cellars. That era's gilded grandeur has vanished. But with every death comes a new beginning, as Bhaktivedanta Swami Prabhupada—founder of the Hare Krishna movement—might say. The mansion was donated to the Krishnas in 1975 by Alfred Brush Ford (great-grandson of Henry Ford) and Elisabeth Reuther (daughter of union leader Walter P. Reuther) and now serves as a temple and cultural center, which are headquartered in the former ballroom. Outdoors, the four acres of landscaped grounds are still beautifully maintained and are home to altars of sacred icons, three fountains, a waterfall, and peacocks that grace the facility with their presence. The center offers free prasadam feasts after public worship and lecture on Sunday evenings. Visitors are asked to remove their shoes. *383 Lenox St., www.iskcondetroit.com, (313) 824-6000.*

The Seafoam Palace - Founded by a group of artists, the Seafoam Palace describes itself as an organization that "celebrates the absurd while fostering curiosity, exploration, and new perspectives of the marvelous." They create otherworldly experiences with their cabinet-of-curiosities sensibility intertwined with local history, and offer an eclectic array of programming from film screenings to workshops, and from a creepy still life drawing salon to staging phantom island sightings in the Detroit River. Most recently, the organization staged an exhibition of surreal moving digital paintings in the windows of the David Whitney Building Downtown (see separate entry). They plan to open their exhibition space for regular hours in the near future, but in the meantime, check their website to learn about their latest exhibitions, events, and workshops. *6460 Kercheval Ave., www.seafoampalace.org.*

Whitdel Arts - A contemporary art gallery on Detroit's east side, Whitdel Arts was originally founded in Southwest Detroit in 2010. In their current space, located on the ground floor of the Letts Industrial Inc. building, the organization mounts thoughtfully curated solo and group exhibitions approximately every two months. They show local and international artists, both emerging and established, in a range of media. In addition to opening receptions for shows, as well as talks and workshops, the venue is available for event rentals. A registered 501c3 non-profit organization, the gallery is entirely volunteer-run by a small and passionate group of artists and creatively minded individuals. Check their website or social media for a calendar of events. *1111 Bellevue St., Ste. 110, www.whitdelarts.com.*

ENTERTAINMENT & RECREATION

Aretha Franklin Park - Formerly **Chene Park**, but renamed to honor Detroit's Queen of Soul in 2018, this amphitheater is perched at the water's edge, with stunning views of downtown Detroit and Canada. The venue offers a capacity of 6,100, in the form of both lawn and outdoor theater seating. With its enormous, defining, white tent structure that resembles a ship's sails, the amphitheater hosts an annual summer concert series featuring an exciting music menu of jazz, hip hop, R&B, and soul. Though sometimes the outdoor acoustics are known to be a little imbalanced, it has established itself as a scenic gem of the summer entertainment season, and a popular date spot for an evening of music, food, and drinks while watching the sunset on the river. *2600 Atwater St., www.cheneparkdetroit.com, (313) 393-7128.*

★**Belle Isle -** Discover some of the city's most popular cultural amenities, cycling routes, scenic natural landscapes, public art, outdoor athletic venues, historic architecture, and picnic spots on

Belle Isle. The city's second largest park, and the nation's largest public island park, Belle Isle spans 982 acres and includes the region's most diverse collection of programmed amenities, many of which have been delighting Detroiters for generations. The park, which measures six miles around, is home to a host of natural features, including four lakes—Takoma, Muskoday, Blue Heron Lagoon, and Okonoka—the latter of which recently underwent a $5 million restoration effort to connect it to the Detroit River and improve water quality and fishing opportunities. The island also boasts a dense woodland, making it a popular destination for ducks and migrating birds—including warblers, geese, and birds of prey—and the birders who love them. Belle Isle is in the nation's busiest inland waterway, the Detroit River, making for picturesque views of Detroit, Windsor, and the frequent Canadian-side freighter traffic. On windy days, lucky visitors will pick up the sweet smell of corn from the nearby Canadian Club distillery.

Deemed Île aux Cochons—"Hog Island"—by the 18th-century French settlers who kept their pigs on the island to eliminate a rattlesnake infestation and to protect their livestock from mainland coyotes, the island first entered private hands in 1769, when George McDougall traded Ottawa and Ojibwa residents eight barrels of rum, three rolls of tobacco, six pounds of vermilion, and a wampum belt for the island. Belle Isle changed hands twice before being renamed in honor of Governor Lewis Cass' daughter Isabelle "Belle" Cass, or French statesman Charles Louis Auguste Fouquet, duc de Belle-Isle—depending on whom you ask. In 1879, the City of Detroit purchased the island for $200,000, with plans to create one of the nation's premier parks. Toward this end, the city enlisted renowned landscape architect Frederick Law Olmsted—who designed New York City's Central Park—to design the park in 1883. Since the Olmsted plan, the park has been the beneficiary of numerous incidental projects, which, together, create a vibrant patchwork of art, woodlands, and recreational destinations. In 2013, the city of Detroit entered into a 30-year agreement allowing the park to be operated by the Michigan Department of Natural Resources in return for improvements to the park's facilities and environmental management—and a planned six-mile paved trail which will serve as the terminus of the state-spanning Iron Belle Trail, stretching from Ironwood in the north to Belle Isle in the south. Although the island is home to a constellation of sites and recreational and cultural opportunities, including a band shell, model yacht basin, giant floral clock, Coast Guard station, and numerous picnic shelters, a number of attractions stand out. *Entry to the park is via the MacArthur Bridge on E. Jefferson Avenue at E. Grand Boulevard. Visitors may walk or bike onto the island for free, but there is an $11/car or $5/motorcycle fee for Michigan residents (valid for a year at all Michigan State Parks), or $9/car day pass for non-Michigan residents. www.belleisleconservancy.org.*

- **Anna Scripps Whitcomb Conservatory** - See separate entry in this chapter.

- **Athletic Field & Field House** - Built in 1898, the Field House was designed as a bicycle rental facility by local architect Edward A. Schilling and anchors the 36-acre Athletic Field. The Athletic Field includes nine baseball diamonds, 10 lighted tennis courts, a running track, the World Cup Soccer Field, handball courts, racquetball courts, and basketball courts. *Loiter Way and Vista Drive.*

- **Belle Isle Aquarium** - See separate entry in this chapter.

- **Belle Isle Beach** - Open from Memorial Day through Labor Day, the public beach is a well-maintained, half-mile sandy beach, fronting a large, buoyed swimming area. *Riverbank Road at Oakway Trail.*

- **Belle Isle Boat House** - Built in 1902, this large Spanish Colonial Revival-style structure was the first concrete structure in the United States and was once the opulent center of boating and rowing on the Great Lakes before falling into disrepair. Today, restorations are ongoing, and the facility—with its seahorse stair balusters and rich old-growth woodwork—is available to rent for weddings and other events. The Detroit Boat Club Crew also calls the facility home and sponsors competitive and recreational rowing classes and competitions at the club. *E. Picnic Way, www.belleisleboathouse.com, (248-821-1128).*

- **Belle Isle Casino** - Named not for gambling, but for its intended resemblance to an Italian villa, this elegant 1908 design features a yellow-brick facade, four corner towers, a two-story arcaded veranda, and a terra cotta tile roof. Originally used as a park management and visitor dining facility, today the casino is used for public and private events and is available for year-round rental. *Casino Avenue and The Strand, (313) 821-9844.*

- **Belle Isle Nature Zoo** - See separate entry in this chapter.

- **The Belle Isle Practice Center** - See separate entry in this chapter.

- **Borreal Wetlands Forest** - The island's 200-acre woodlands are one of the last remaining remnants of the region's original old growth forests, which once covered Southeast Michigan. Visitors will find diverse species including bur oak, pin oak, hawthorn, silver maple, shagbark hickory, and pumpkin ash. The island's woodlands are home to miles of trails and paths for walking, running, birding, and mountain biking. *East side of the island, along Woodside Drive, Central Avenue, and Oakway Road.*

- **Detroit Yacht Club** - See separate entry in this chapter.

- **Dossin Great Lakes Museum** - See separate entry in this chapter.

- **Fishing Piers and Bulkheads** - Although fishing is permitted on all of the shores, canals, and lakes—except for the protected Blue Heron Lagoon—anglers are most commonly found on the island's two piers and two bulkheads. While the Detroit River is home to game fish like walleye and sturgeon, the piers are best for panfish, including yellow perch, white bass, bluegill, rock bass, and smallmouth bass. *Located along Riverbank Road and The Strand.*

- **Flynn Pavilion** - Designed by Eliel Saarinen and opened in 1949, this beautiful, modernist structure on the bank of Lake Takoma allows visitors to rent charming two-seater, swan-shaped paddle boats and kayaks to explore the inland waterways. The structure is available for private rentals during the offseason. *Loiter Way and Picnic Way, (313) 821-9844.*

- **Giant Slide** - Take a ride in a potato sack down this blazing fast, four-story metal slide. The supervised facility is lighted and open during only the summer. *Central Avenue and Inselruhe Avenue.*

- **Hipster Beach** - Though it is unsanctioned and, according to authorities, unsafe, the sandy inlet unofficially known as Hipster Beach is a popular semi-private outdoor bathing oasis of choice for Bohemians of all types and anyone in the know. To get there, drive or bike to the east end of Belle Isle. When The Strand turns north, park in the dirt lot on the right side of the road, by the swings. Follow the path around the William Livingstone Memorial Lighthouse, and continue across the cement footbridge. Follow the path until you spot the mythical place on a narrow canal: Hipster Beach. The whole hike is just more than a mile. Please be cautioned that the area is not a sanctioned beach. There is no lifeguard on duty, so swim safely. and bathers are subject to potential police reprimand.

- **Ice Tree -** What began as the "Ice Fountain," a Washington Boulevard tradition in the 1910s, the Ice Tree is a 30-foot-tall seasonal ice sculpture built from ice-covered Christmas trees. *Riverbank Road at Inselruhe Avenue.*

- **James Scott Memorial Fountain -** A monument to millionaire gambler and Detroit playboy prankster James Scott, the Scott Fountain and associated bronze sculpture were built amid great controversy, as many residents were hesitant to accept Scott's funds to memorialize such a rascal. Designed by architect Cass Gilbert, who designed the U.S. Supreme Court Building, this lavish, white marble fountain was completed in 1925 and is adorned with lions, dolphins, and even the head of Neptune, Roman god of the sea. *Casino Avenue and The Strand.*

- **Kids Kingdom Playscape -** This expansive, impressive half-acre playground features brightly colored play equipment for children 12 and younger, including swings, tunnels, slides, climbing surfaces, climbable animal sculptures, and a large space capsule-themed merry-go-round. *Central Avenue and Inselruhe Avenue.*

- **MacArthur Bridge -** Among the nation's first cantilevered arch bridges, the General Douglas MacArthur Bridge was built in 1923, after its predecessor burned following a construction accident. The bridge's 19 spans run 2,356 feet. Shortly after being named for MacArthur in 1942, the Belle Isle side of the bridge played host to the beginning of a three-day race riot when a now disproven rumor suggested a white man had thrown an African-American woman and her baby from the bridge in 1943. The riot, which stemmed from a simmering controversy surrounding the construction of the Sojourner Truth Homes and housing discrimination facing African-American war material-workers, caused 600 injuries, 34 deaths, and more than 1,200 arrests. For its aesthetics and history, the bridge is a national historic landmark. *E. Grand Boulevard and E. Jefferson Avenue.*

- **Nancy Brown Peace Carillon -** Unveiled in 1940, this bell tower was built with public donations from 60,000 loyal readers of Detroit News columnist Annie Louise Brown, who used the nom de plume Nancy Brown. At the behest of the tower's pen-namesake, the 85-foot Neo-Gothic bell tower is dedicated to world peace. The automated, computer-controlled 49-bell carillon chimes every half hour. *Muse Road and Picnic Way.*

- **Playground on Oakway Road** - Built in 2016, this beautiful nature-themed playground is ADA-compliant and designed to have wide accessibility. With its zipline swings, rocking boat, winding pathways, merry-go-round, and variety of slides (including one that's enclosed and two stories tall!) this playground is a hit with kids of all ages and abilities. *On the corner of Lakeside Dr. and Oakway Rd, between the Belle Isle Nature Zoo and Lake Muskoday.*

- **Statuary** - In addition to the opulent James Scott Memorial Fountain (see above), Belle Isle is home to beautiful statuary spread across the island. Most impressive among these, perhaps, is the Levi L. Barbour Memorial Fountain, a breathtaking black granite and bronze 1936 installation by famed sculpture Marshall Fredericks. The fountain, Fredericks's first public work, centers on a wheeling bronze gazelle surrounded by black granite depictions of a grouse, a hawk, an otter, and a rabbit. Other notable works on the island include Allen Newman's bronze Spanish-American War Monument (1932), Samuel Cashwan's bronze James J. Brady Memorial (1927), Herman Martzen's bronze Johann Friedrich von Schiller sculpture (1907), Raefello Romanelli's bronze bust of Dante Alighieri (1927), and Richard Bennett's stainless steel Atom Gazelle (1991).

- **Sunset Point** - Although every part of the island offers uniquely stunning views, Sunset Point (first pavilion after you enter the island) provides—you guessed it—breathtaking views of the city skyline during sundown. *At the end of Sunset Dr.*

- **William Livingstone Memorial Lighthouse** - The nation's only marble lighthouse, this 1929 Art Deco structure memorializes Great Lakes shipping safety advocate William Livingstone. Designed by Albert Kahn, the fluted 80-foot tall white Georgia marble structure features a brilliant, bronze 11,500-candlepower lantern that can be seen for up to 15 miles. This area is also a great spot for an off-the-beaten-path picnic or a quiet morning stroll, as it's one of the most remote destinations on the island. *Located on the far east end of the park, off of Lakeside Drive.*

The Belle Isle Practice Center - Putter have a little patina? Open March through Thanksgiving, the Belle Isle Practice Center is perhaps Michigan's finest golf practice center and a destination for Detroiters and college and high school teams from throughout the region and state looking to improve their game. Located on a scenic portion of the east end of Belle Isle, the practice center offers a 30-bay, full-length driving range—including grass tees—three putting greens, four chipping greens, three sand traps, a full acre grass fairway, and a short, albeit challenging, five-hole course. The grounds and facilities are beautifully maintained, and the professional staff is friendly, knowledgeable, and happy to share pointers. The clubhouse offers complimentary club rental, and offers a variety of new and used equipment at reasonable prices. See you on the links! *175 Lakeside Dr., www.thebelleislepracticecenter.com, (313) 821-5218.*

★**Dequindre Cut** - A former Grand Trunk Railroad line converted into an inspiring east side recreation path in 2009, the Dequindre Cut runs a happy 1.65-miles from Mack Avenue (just north of Eastern Market) to Atwater Street, connecting with the RiverWalk (to the east and west, see separate entry) from there. The wildly popular, scenic, and handsomely landscaped 20-foot-wide path has designated space for pedestrians and cyclists, and it is home to some of Detroit's most accessible and vibrant street art, including large-scale sanctioned murals by more than a dozen local artists. Located 25-feet below grade, the Dequindre Cut manages to feel at once enclosed and airy, public, and intimate. It's great on its own for a leisurely stroll, or as a handy connector on a longer excursion. The Cut is well-lit and always busy with joggers, walkers, and cyclists, and features many places for a rest along the way. However, once you've worked up a sweat, you could always stop by the **Dequindre Cut Freight Yard** (located near the Wilkins Street entrance), a seasonal bar, pop-up shopping area, and gathering place on the Cut built out of repurposed shipping containers for libations and good conversation. *Between Mack and Atwater, parallel to St. Aubin. Entrance ramps at Mack, Wilkins, Gratiot, Lafayette, Woodbridge, and Atwater. www.detroitriverfront.org/dequindre.*

Detroit City Fieldhouse - Fans and players of the beautiful game will have plenty to cheer about at this ice rink-turned-soccer arena. The 75,000-square-foot facility includes two soccer pitches and a bar and grill overlooking the fields. On the fields, spectators will find a mixture of tot league games, young adult co-ed, semi-professional, lacrosse, and bubble soccer—a variety of games whose chief commonality is how fun they are to watch. Upstairs, the **Detroit City Clubhouse** offers a polished sports bar experience with a central hardwood bar, maroon leather chairs, soccer memorabilia, reclaimed-wood tables, several TVs, and glass walls overlooking the fields. The menu offers many dishes whose charms are hard to resist: Irish Nachos built on a bed of potato chips, a variety of English/UP-style pasties, and Srodek's kielbasa on brioche. Wash it all down with a curated collection of drafts and cocktails, or an impressive array of bottled beers. Behind the bar, the **Detroit City Futbol Club Store** offers plenty of gear emblazoned with the team's slogans and logos. *3401 E Lafayette St., www.detcityfc.com/fieldhouse, (313) 265-3630.*

★ **Detroit RiverWalk -** With the first phase completed in 2007, and dynamic expansions since, this celebrated three-and-a-half mile dedicated walkway and bicycle path that connects a host of waterfront attractions, and has become a wildly popular, vibrant destination in its own right. The scenic walk connects a series of parks, plazas, and pavilions with a brick-paved path dotted with public art, ornamental gardens, recreational opportunities, and educational installations along the way. Except for a couple of short detours, the RiverWalk is a continuous path that stretches from the foot of Rosa Parks Boulevard in Corktown to Mt. Elliott Park, near Belle Isle. From the path, visitors will enjoy unique, up-close views of Detroit landmarks such as Joe Louis Arena, Hart Plaza, the Renaissance Center, and Aretha Franklin Park, as well as a relaxing and enjoyable walk or bicycle ride along the picturesque Detroit River. **Cullen Plaza** is the focal point of the span, located roughly in the middle of the Riverwalk, and it includes a pavilion housing a cafe, Wheelhouse Detroit (see separate entry), and restroom facilities. A playground and the Cullen Carousel—with seats that resemble native (and imagined) wildlife—offer fun for children. The plaza features gardens, fountains, a granite inlay map of the Detroit River, and an ornate glass depiction of the St. Lawrence Seaway. The carousel and cafe hours vary seasonally. West from Cullen Plaza, visitors will find the heart of Downtown, with spectacular views of the city's core, as well as a small splash pad in front of the Renaissance Center, with access to and from Hart Plaza. The western terminus of the RiverWalk is **Ralph C. Wilson, Jr. Centennial Park**, for which more elaborate amenities are planned and under development. East from Cullen Plaza, visitors will find the educational **Milliken State**

Park Wetlands, with short, self-guided nature walks; the southern entrance to the Dequindre Cut bicycle and walking path (see separate entry); and the Aretha Franklin Park amphitheater. The Eastern terminus of the Riverwalk is **Mt. Elliott Park**, where children and their families will find a second pavilion and a fanciful splash pad that resembles a sunken schooner, with water cannons. Though the RiverWalk can be accessed by bicycle or on foot almost anywhere along the span, including from the Dequindre Cut, parking is available at Cullen Plaza for four-wheeled visitors, and it is a great place to start. Cullen Plaza: *1340 Atwater St., www.detroitriverfront.org, (313) 877-8057.*

Detroit Yacht Club - Founded in 1868, the nearly 100,000-square-foot DYC is the largest yacht club in the United States and one of the grandest, most storied clubs in Detroit. Located on a private island adjacent to Belle Isle, the current facility, which was designed by architect George D. Mason, was designed in the Mediterranean style and completed in 1922. The historic clubhouse and grounds feature a 380-slip marina, two swimming pools, athletic courts, casual and formal dining rooms, ballrooms, and exercise facilities. The club offers a packed schedule of family-friendly activities, including sailing lessons and races, summer camp, and special events, the highlight of which is the annual Venetian Night. Since 1921, the club has been a title sponsor of the annual hydroplane races, a tradition it began with the encouragement of legendary racer and club member Commodore Gar Wood. Though only members and guests are allowed into the club on most days, select rooms are available for public event rental. Discounted memberships are available for young people. *1 Riverbank Dr., www.dyc.com, (313) 824-1200.*

East Side Parks - Don't tell anyone, but tucked along the Detroit River on the city's east side lies one of the area's greatest secrets: a string of 12 quiet, scenic, and pastoral parks with unparalleled views of the river. The 12 massive parks—Henderson, Owen, Alfred Brush Ford, Mariner, Chene, Peter Maheras-Bronson Gentry, Mt. Elliott, Orleans Atwater, Riverfront-Lakewood, Gabriel Richard, Stockton, and Memorial Annex—total more than 210 acres. Although a few of them offer lovely amenities—such as the five baseball diamonds at Peter Maheras-Bronson Gentry, the amphitheater at Chene, or the playground equipment at Stockton, these east side parks are largely unprogrammed and intentionally left as lush, green space. While the parks' general simplicity allows visitors to enjoy the serenity of nature, many visitors make use of the river access and open expanses to go fishing, fly kites, take romantic picnics, bird watch, launch model rockets, play lawn games, and watch the passing freighters. Although all of the parks are worth a visit, three offer truly unique features: Stockton is next to the Manoogian Mansion, Peter Maheras-Bronson Gentry includes a large island, and Mariner is home to an operating lighthouse. While a secret to many residents, area geese are no stranger to these parks and often leave behind tokens of their appreciation, so plan on wearing shoes. *The parks are along or south E. Jefferson Avenue, between E. Grand Boulevard, and Alter Road.*

The Goatyard / Boatyard / Detroit Sail Club - With about 25 boat slips, The Goatyard—or Boatyard—is not the biggest marina in town, but it certainly has the most character. The yard occupies the property of an old brick factory and is situated on a musty canal near Detroit Edison's Conner Creek Power Plant, with the city's only private tugboat bar and a weathered dock that floats barely two inches above the water next to a sunken schooner. It's home to the city's most unique sailboats, including the first fiberglass-hull, "unsinkable" Crescent sloop, which was designed in Detroit by engineer Dick Hill in 1953. The yard is littered with a host of industrial relics, including a derelict brick-making machine, several trucks, a pair of school buses (one of which serves as an office), rusty bikes, abandoned motorcycles, and of course, tons of boats. Goatyard members are known to the rest of the Metro Detroit sailing community as the Pirates of Lake St. Clair. If you want to become a pirate, or just want to have a good time sailing with the laid-back manager Stephen Hume and his partner Susan McDonald in the Detroit Sail Club, reserve your slips early in winter because they're hard to come by. *10 St. Jean St.*

The Players Club - With an exterior designed in the Florentine Renaissance style, and an interior that is somewhere between Art Deco and medieval castle, the 90-year-old Players Club is a pint-sized architectural treat maintained by caretakers who have remained faithful to the club's historic legacy and the traditional Shakespearean method as an all-male amateur theatrical organization. Amid breathtaking narrative Art Deco murals and stunning classical architectural flourishes, guests sit at private tables as they enjoy three one-act theatrical productions called "frolics." *3321 E. Jefferson Ave., www.playersdetroit.org, (313) 259-3385.*

William G. Milliken State Park and Harbor - Serving as a link to Chene Park, the Dequindre Cut, and Rivard Plaza, Milliken State Park is situated on the Detroit River, just east of downtown. The 31-acre park has restored wetlands, which mimic the original botanical shore life and attract migratory birds, making it a restful oasis for city dwellers. This beautifully designed park provides welcome facilities for fishing, picnicking, walking, bicycling, and boating, as well as a 52-slip harbor marked by a lighthouse at the entrance. *1900 Atwater St., (313) 396-0217.*

SITES

Detroit's Last Lustron Home - Designed by Carl Strandlund in 1947, Lustron homes were all-steel modernist prefabricated homes clad in porcelain-enameled steel that rose to prominence during the postwar housing shortage. Stemming from the same impetus and ideology as Buckminster Fuller's Dymaxion House, the comparatively traditional Lustron homes featured built-in furniture, integrated appliances, and enameled steel walls, ceilings, drawers, doors, and floors. Strandlund marketed the homes as offering a "new and richer experience for the entire family," where "Mother has far more hours." The company went bankrupt in 1950, after building only 2,500 homes nationwide. Only a fraction of these remain unaltered. The last unaltered Lustron home in the city, 654 Ashland St., is an unparalleled example of a two-bedroom Model 02 Westchester Lustron home complete with the original maize yellow enamel. An architectural gem of the Jefferson Chalmers community, the home features massive red street numbers, making it easy to find. This home is serial #00708. Because the home is privately owned and occupied, please be respectful and only check it out from the street. *654 Ashland St.*

Elmwood Cemetery - With acres of sculptural grave markers and ornate mausoleums, rolling hills, defiant spires, stone angels, towering old trees, benches designed by Robert Moses for the 1932 World's Fair, and centuries of Detroit history at every turn, Elmwood is the oldest nondenominational cemetery in Michigan, and it's a sight to behold. A park-like urban oasis established in 1846, Elmwood is the final resting place of numerous notable figures in the city's long history, including 29 former mayors of Detroit, as well as state and U.S. senators and representatives, Michigan governors, a postmaster

general, presidential cabinet members, and soldiers and officers of
every American war since the Revolution, including 205 Civil War
veterans. Its 86 acres were sumptuously landscaped by influential
American landscape architect Frederick Law Olmstead, making it
one of Detroit's most remarkably scenic and serene outdoor spaces,
representative of Detroit's natural topography prior to development.
Even the tranquil creek in the valley has a story to tell: In 1763, British
soldiers attempting to ambush Chief Pontiac's camp were surprised
to find the Indians expecting them. Legend has it that the creek ran
red from the carnage and was known thereafter as Bloody Run. This
resplendent, contemplative setting is ideal for a leisurely stroll, bike
ride, or historical exploration. Expect to see many graves bearing
names that are familiar now as Detroit streets. Notable burials include:

- **Bernhard Stroh (1822–1882):** German immigrant who founded
  Stroh Brewery Company, maker of Stroh's beer. *Section Q.*

- **Coleman A. Young (1918–1997):** World War II Tuskegee
  Airman and Detroit's first black mayor; served five terms. Equally
  revered and reviled, the powerful, polarizing Young presided over
  a period of social and economic change in the city. *Hazel Dell.*

- **Fred "Sonic" Smith (1949–1994):** Guitarist for the MC5, and
  husband of singer Patti Smith. *Section V.*

- **Hiram Walker (1816–1899):** Distiller, founder of the Hiram
  Walker & Sons Distillery Company in Windsor, Ontario, makers
  of Canadian Club whiskey. *Section A2.*

- **Lewis Cass (1782–1866):** Michigan territorial governor,
  ambassador to France, secretary of war under President Andrew
  Jackson, secretary of state under President James Buchanan, and
  Democratic nominee for President in 1848. *Section A, Lot 25.*

- **William Woodbridge (1780–1861):** Secretary of the Michigan
  Territory and, after statehood, Michigan's second governor and
  a U.S. senator from Michigan. Namesake of the Woodbridge
  neighborhood. *Section A, Lot 13.*

- **Zachariah Chandler (1813–1879):** Mayor of Detroit, four-term
  U.S. senator, secretary of the interior under President Ulysses S.
  Grant, and nearly a candidate for president. *Section B, Lot 49.*

In the cemetery's southeast corner is Beth El, a small lot purchased
from Elmwood in 1850 that's the oldest Jewish graveyard in the
state. Across the eastern fence is Detroit's oldest extant cemetery,

Mt. Elliott Cemetery, founded for the city's Catholics in 1841. Families of blended religious heritage would sometimes buy plots along the fence line and bury their Protestants on one side, Catholics on the other. *1200 Elmwood Ave., www.elmwoodhistoriccemetery.org, (313) 567-3454.*

Harbor Island Canal Area - Yes, there's island housing in Detroit. Along Alter Street, south of Jefferson Avenue, are some of the most unique backyards in the city—lush backyards with hoists, finger docks, greenery, and watercraft jutting into Fox Creek and the many narrow man-made canals and small bridges that form the neighborhood, making the area popular with adventurous Jet Skiers and kayakers seeking one of the city's most unique aquatic navigation opportunities. While only small watercraft can explore the creek and canals, landlubbers and seafarers alike can explore the extended Creekside area. Mariner Park, an island formed by Fox Creek, two canals, and the mouth of the Detroit River, is a kempt, treed, and lush green park that features river's-edge fishing spots (with dedicated rod-holders) and Windmill Point Lighthouse. Across the river, visitors can spy Peche Island, a partier's haven, and can watch the heavy traffic of sail and motor boats, freighters, and kayaks during the day. Close to the west, also an island, but one that is reachable via bridge, is Riverfront-Lakewood Park, an under-maintained park that is delightfully rambunctious with nature, including pheasants, cattails, and thick, tall grass. Who needs Venice?

- **Fox Creek:** *Along Alter Road, south of E. Jefferson Avenue.*

- **Harbor Island:** *Lakewood Street south, right on Harbor Island Drive.*

- **Klenk Street:** *Alter Road south, right on Klenk Street.*

- **Mariner and Riverfront-Lakewood Parks:** *Alter Road south continues to Riverside Drive west.*

★**Indian Village -** One of Detroit's most exquisite historic neighborhoods, Indian Village contains 352 stately homes and mansions—some as large as 12,000 square feet—designed by some of the city's most esteemed architects. Bounded by Mack Avenue to the north, Burns Street to the east, Jefferson Avenue to the south, and Seminole Street to the west. The land was originally occupied by the Rivard and St. Aubin ribbon farms (narrow farms running perpendicularly out from the river) but became a state fairground and then horseracing track before being purchased by developer

James Owen in the 1880s. Owen playfully dubbed the development Indian Village after the streets, Iroquois and Seminole, which were named for popular local thoroughbred racehorses—not directly after Native American tribes, as one might infer. Between 1895 and 1929, the area, which was then a relatively remote, rural oasis, became a bedroom community for Detroit's captains of industry. Set back from the street, with carriage houses larger than many middle-class homes, the impressive homesteads were designed by such names as Louis Kamper, C. Howard Crane, Albert Kahn, George D. Mason, and Smith, Hinchman & Grylls. Outfitted with intricate ornamentation and flourishes, leaded and stained glass, sculpture, and other exterior details, prominent architectural styles in the neighborhood include Georgian, Federal, Colonial Revival, Arts and Crafts, Romanesque, and Tudor Revival. Because of the dedication of committed residents, much of the original character of the charming tree-lined neighborhood is preserved to this day, and self-guided tours, whether by foot or on two or four wheels are essential for fans of historic homes and architecture. A tradition since 1958, the best time to see Indian Village is during its home and garden tour the first Saturday of June. Though smaller, there are also lovely homes in adjoining historic **West Village** to the west, from Seyburn Street to Parker Street, between Kercheval Street and Jefferson Avenue. While nearly every structure in the regal Indian Village neighborhood is magnificent, notable highlights include:

- **Arthur and Clara Buhl House:** Gothic Tudor Mansion. *1116 Iroquois St.*

- **James Hamilton House:** Tudor Revival Home. *8325 E. Jefferson Ave.*

- **Bingley Fales House:** A Neo-Georgian. At 15,000 square feet, it is the largest home in Indian Village. *1771 Seminole St.*

- **Louis Kamper House:** Neo-Renaissance Home of the renowned architect. *2150 Iroquois St.*

- **Henry Leland House:** Tudor Revival home of the founder of Lincoln and Cadillac Motors. *1052 Seminole St.*

- **Edsel and Eleanor Ford Honeymoon House:** Home of Henry Ford's son from 1917 to 1921, and birthplace of Henry Ford II. *2171 Iroquois St.*

- **Mary S. Smith House:** A palatial Neo-Renaissance mansion. *8445 E. Jefferson Ave.*

- **Frederick K. Stearns House:** An impressive Tudor Revival. *8109 E. Jefferson Ave.*

- **Detroit Waldorf School:** Designed by Albert Kahn, originally the Liggett School, now a private school in the Steiner tradition. *2555 Burns St.*

- **Jefferson Avenue Presbyterian Church:** Stately Gothic Revival church designed by Wirt Rowland in 1926. *8625 E. Jefferson Ave.*

Joseph Berry Subdivision - Largely built between 1898 and 1929, Berry Sub, as it's known locally, is part of the Villages neighborhoods, and its 90 homes—heavy on Tudors and Colonials—are tucked away east of Indian Village, on four streets, between Jefferson Avenue and the Detroit River. The neighborhood boasts a dynamic, diverse mix of residents, including Kid Rock and the mayor (who resides in the Manoogian Mansion, the official mayoral residence at the east end of Dwight Street) and some of the city's most recognized leaders in local politics and business. Of special architectural note are the seven homes on Dwight Street along the Detroit River, which include the Manoogian (see separate entry), as well as lumberman Joseph Weber's colony. The colony was comprised of the westernmost five homes, all built in 1920, as the family's private compound. Although all the homes are owned independently today, the pipes that heated all five from a central heating plant still run through their basements. Berry Sub residents enjoy the quiet, country-like setting on the river, and relish in a rich variety of wildlife, including pheasants, red foxes, opossum, raccoons, rabbits, waterfowl, and even the occasional turtle or bird of prey. *E. Jefferson Ave. at Fiske Rd.*

★**Lafayette Park -** Completed between 1958 and 1965, Lafayette Park is a seminal work by renowned architect Ludwig Mies van der Rohe and a masterpiece of the International Style. Spanning 78 verdant acres, the beautiful campus is home to 186 one- and two-story townhomes, four high-rise apartment buildings, a covered pedestrian shopping mall, and a school, making the complex the largest collection of Mies van der Rohe structures in the world. The townhomes, especially, are distinctive for their clean lines, simple aesthetic, minimal presence, structural order, perfect proportions, and tinted glass-and-aluminum-clad exterior, all of which embody the intrinsic design elements characteristic of Mies van der Rohe.

The development includes thoughtful details, such as parking lots that are recessed below the sightline of the nearby dwellings, pathways to school that aren't interrupted by streets, and a spare but breathtaking 19-acre park that offers inspiring views of the surrounding masterpiece of modernity. *The complex is located north of Lafayette Ave., between Rivard St. and Orleans St.*

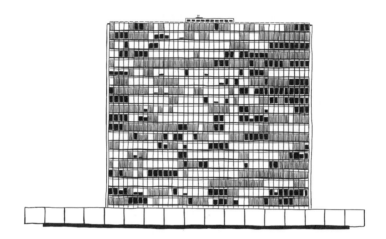

Liberty Motor Car Company Headquarters - Detroit is the only metropolitan area in the world with two full-size replicas of Philadelphia's iconic Independence Hall. Though Henry Ford commissioned such a structure for Greenfield Village (see separate entry) in 1929, he was not the first auto baron to do so. In 1919, the now defunct Liberty Motor Car Company was a fledgling automobile brand looking to expand. With founder Percy Owens—a man with East Coast ties—at the helm, the company selected this site for its new factory and stately Liberty Hall-copping headquarters. Though the company sold 21,000 cars in 1921, because of supplier competition with the big four (Ford, GM, Packard, and Hudson) the company went defunct by 1923—leaving this curious replication as its legacy. Though the building was used by Thyssen-Krupp until 2007, it is now vacant. *Located on a private, guarded drive at 2909 Connor St.*

Ossian H. Sweet House - In 1925, Ossian Sweet—a prominent African-American physician—purchased a one-and-one-half story brick bungalow in an all-white neighborhood. When word spread, segregationist white neighbors took arms, and Sweet, fearful for his life, invited a number of family and friends to spend the night. On the night of September 9, 1925, an angry mob of 500 neighbors encircled the house and pelted the home with stones, while shouting death threats and slurs. A single shot rang out from the house, killing one member of the mob. Police immediately arrested the family and charged them with murder. At the behest of the NAACP, legendary attorney Clarence Darrow—fresh off the renowned Scopes Monkey Trial—served as defense counsel before presiding Judge Frank Murphy. Despite facing an all-white jury, Darrow successfully argued self-defense and, after an impassioned seven-hour closing statement, the Sweets were acquitted. The landmark case played a pivotal role in the subsequent overturn of racial redlining laws and was the inspiration for author Kevin Boyle's award-winning book *Arc of Justice*. The home is an occupied private residence, so visitors should be respectful of the owner's privacy. *2905 Garland St.*

Water Works Park & Hurlbut Memorial Gate - Once one of the city's most popular attractions, when the 110-acre site was selected for the city's principal water pumping station in the 1870s—as it remains today—it was also designed to serve as a park. Though it featured a lagoon, tennis courts, a baseball diamond, an 8-foot-tall mechanical floral clock, playground equipment, and 12 pear trees said to have been planted by the city's French settlers, the highlight of the park was the opulent 185-foot-tall minaret-style stand-pipe tower that not only maintained water pressure but doubled as a breathtaking observation deck for tourists. While the tower, which was demolished in 1945, and other amenities have been lost to time, the ornate **Hurlbut Memorial Gate** remains. More an opulent monument to Beaux Arts architecture than a gateway, the intricate stone gate was restored in 2007, stands 50 feet high and 132 feet wide, and has a dual stairway leading to a terrace 12 feet above the ground. Though entrance is no longer permitted, visitors to the Brede-Mueller masterpiece, which fronts the street, can also spy the classical, historic High Lift Building pumping station, which is still in operation today, behind the wrought iron fence, in the distance. Please note that the horse troughs on the gate are no longer operational, so seek water for your steed elsewhere. *Located at the intersection of Cadillac Blvd. and Jefferson Ave.*

POINTS OF INTEREST

Bicycling Scene From White Boy Rick - The memorable bicycling scene from the film *White Boy Rick* was filmed at this intersection. *Korte Ave. and Alter Rd.*

Carhartt Ghost Sign - The iconic Detroit brand name is unmistakable from the street, as the ghostly vintage ad promises well made overalls—and overall durability and staying power. *14111 Kercheval Ave.*

Charles Trowbridge House - Sitting quietly on the southern side of busy East Jefferson Avenue, this Victorian home is the oldest building in the city, built as a private residence in 1826. The building is now home to a handful of small businesses. *1380 E. Jefferson Ave.*

Christ Church of Detroit - The oldest Protestant church in Michigan, this Episcopalian English Gothic Revival church was completed in 1863. The stunning light-stone church features ornate stained-glass windows and a five-story bell tower topped by an ornamental spire. *960 E. Jefferson Ave.*

Cow Head - Built in 1959, this curious piece of commercial statuary—a gigantic bull head—sits atop a shuttered neighborhood dairy. You may have caught a glimpse of it in the movie *8 Mile*. *13099 Mack Ave.*

Earthworks Urban Farm - Founded in 1997 as a small garden, this now sizable farm grows fresh produce that goes directly into the meals served at the attached Capuchin Soup Kitchen and serves as a learning and advocacy center to help all people get access to fresh food. *1264 Meldrum St.*

Father Bernard "Solanus" Casey Grave - Father Casey (1870–1957), the first U.S.-born man to be named "venerable" by the Vatican (the second step of four along the Catholic path to sainthood), and later beatified (the third step) is buried here in Saint Bonaventure Monastery. Miraculous cures have been attributed to Father Casey and account for the pilgrimages some people make to this resting place. *1740 Mt. Elliott St.*

Father Gabriel Richard Sculpture - This bold granite sculpture depicting one of Detroit's most important historical figures was commissioned by the Works Progress Administration in the late 1930s and executed by sculptor Leonard Jungwirth. *7478 E. Jefferson Ave.*

Feedom Freedom Garden - This community garden beautifies its neighborhood and acts as a platform for the social justice mission of its founders, Myrtle Thompson Curtis and Wayne Curtis. *876 Manistique St.*

Hantz Woodlands - Thousands of young hardwood trees, mostly maple and oak, have been planted in this patchwork 140-acre urban forest, in an effort to transform formerly vacant lots in this east side neighborhood into a green oasis. *9100 Louis Ave.*

Indian Village Centennial Garden - Maintained by the Indian Village Men's and Women's Garden Clubs, this beautifully landscaped ornamental garden features wrought-iron gates, a gazebo, and manicured lawns. *2568 Seminole St.*

Indian Village Tennis Club - Established in 1912, this members-only tennis club's three clay courts fit neatly in this neighborhood of stately homes. With a $5 guest pass, visitors can swing racquets with higher-income brackets. *1502 Parker Ave.*

Jack White Home - Jack White once owned this 5,200 sq. ft. mansion, designed by noted Detroit architect C. Howard Crane. The idyllic grounds were the surprising setting for The White Stripes' 2005 album, *Get Behind Me Satan*, which was largely recorded on the home's grand staircase. *1731 Seminole St.*

Kid Rock Home - This 6,000 square foot colonial-style mansion, just a few doors down from the Mayor's residence, is the Detroit home of Romeo-born musician Robert James Ritchie, AKA Kid Rock. *9090 Dwight St.*

Manoogian Mansion - Located in the historic Berry Subdivision, this 1928 Mediterranean Revival Style mansion serves as the official residence of the city's mayor. *9240 Dwight Dr.*

Martha Reeves Home - This two-story building was home to the young singer as she was moving up the ranks at Motown Records. *2409 Townsend St.*

Moses W. Field House - Now sandwiched in an early 20th century city block, this 1860s brick and stone home is one of only two known remaining farm houses in the city, built when the area around it was countryside. *2541 Field St.*

Nicole Curtis Home - This 3,000 square foot Tudor was bought and rehabbed by HGTV "star" Nicole Curtis in 2014. The home remains her Detroit residence. *571 E. Grand Blvd.*

Ouizi Floral Mural - This colorful floral mural, by Detroit artist Ouizi, covers the entire length of the Parkstone Garage building, brightening this West Village block. *1111 Parker St.*

Row of Sears Kit Houses - Built circa 1915, these homes represent an incredibly rare assemblage of intact early Sears kit homes. Two of the homes are the "Arlington" model. *605-635 Chalmers St.*

Site D-23 - These two concrete cylinders, rising conspicuously up out of the grass at Alfred Brush Ford Park, are ghostly reminders of the paranoia of the Cold War Era. These columns once housed radar equipment for the Nike Missile Defense System, designed to target foreign aircraft and shoot them down from a missile site on Belle Isle. *100 Lenox St.*

Sonny Bono Home - The non-Cher half of Sonny and Cher spent his first year of life in this cozy east side home. *5380 Holcomb St.*

Summer in the City Jefferson East Mural - Painted by the group in 2005, this lively installation is a meta-mural, featuring a colorful collage of other favorite Summer in the City murals, including ionic columns and contrasting geometric shapes, alongside the Woodbridge giraffe. *14367 E. Jefferson Ave.*

Swoon Mural - This intricate mural, created by renowned street artist Swoon, celebrates the people and places of the Jefferson Chalmers neighborhood. *14600 E. Jefferson Ave.*

Yondotega - A brick wall keeps prying eyes out of this exclusive and incredibly secretive club, which has offered its 150 members fine food and the company of other "true gentlemen" since 1891. They've been located at this location since 1959, after the first headquarters was demolished to make room for the Chrysler Freeway. *1450 E. Jefferson Ave.*

Ze Mound - When the nearby marina was dredged, this enormous, grassy hill was the inadvertent byproduct. Today, it serves as a spectacular place to have a picnic or watch the International Freedom Festival fireworks display, and plays host to an annual Bastille Day celebration. *1687 Atwater St.*

CHAPTER 8
UPPER EAST SIDE

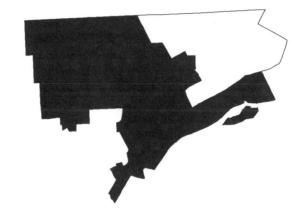

As the second-largest chapter in this book by area and population, the Upper East Side as defined by this guide covers nearly a quarter of the city, and consequently offers visitors perhaps the most diverse range of experiences. The area, roughly bounded by Mack Avenue, Hamtramck, Highland Park, Woodward Avenue, 8 Mile Road, and the city limits, encompasses a host of neighborhoods steeped in history that often showcase resident pride and energy. These neighborhoods—including Conant Gardens, East English Village, Gratiot Woods, Greenbriar, Grixdale, Krainz Woods, LaSalle College Park, Mohican Regent, MorningSide, Nortown, Pulaski, Regent Park, Von Steuben, and Yorkshire Woods—typically feature wide, tree-lined streets with homes ranging from starter bungalows and red-brick Tudors to stately historic homes. The Upper East Side is among the newest areas in the city, having been annexed into Detroit between 1915-1926 and constructed beginning in the late 1920s through the post-war period.

As in most areas of the city, population decline and abandonment have taken a toll on many parts of the Upper East Side, although the impacts may be more apparent here than elsewhere. Many of the area's once prim and charming neighborhoods have developed a patina of decline, punctuated by vacant homes and vacant land. In many neighborhoods, blocks have lost half or more of their homes. These challenges have at once sparked an unparalleled evolution in the traditional urban fabric and showcased the resolve of dedicated residents. In many neighborhoods beset by encroaching vacancy, residents have responded with a host of gardens, community spaces, beautiful murals, and community-led redevelopment projects. These remarkable efforts make the Upper East Side a destination for visitors looking to admire the city's burgeoning population of urban farms and gardens.

The Upper East Side is home to a majority of the city's industrial land. This proximity to industrial work has made it popular with generations of industrial workers and as a result, this area has been home to many waves of new immigrants from other countries, other states, and other parts of the city. The collective neighborhoods have been home to large numbers of Germans, Flemish, Romanians, Italians, Poles, Czechs, African Americans, and more recently, Chaldean and Hmong residents. Although the area is now predominantly African-American—aside from a burgeoning Bengali population northeast of Hamtramck— many former residents have left their

mark in the form of active ethnic businesses that continue to operate alongside the many African-American-owned businesses.

Like the neighborhood's ongoing residential evolution, many of the Upper East Side's commercial corridors have a few missing teeth. However, these thoroughfares, namely East Warren Avenue, East McNichols Road, Gratiot Avenue, Mack Avenue, John R Street, Woodward Avenue, Conner Street, and Harper Avenue, offer a range of destinations including an array of antique stores, outstanding Detroit-style barbeque, and other legendary Detroit dining institutions.

Those in Detroit for a limited time and eager to visit the Upper East Side should be sure to not miss a few essential highlights. One of the city's largest urban farms, RecoveryPark, offers an engaging opportunity to see large-scale agriculture up close. The Detroit side of the Popps Packing campus and Power House Productions together form a one-of-a-kind bootstrap art district, with engaging murals, sculptures, and arts events scattered around the area north of Hamtramck. The antique store district along Mack Avenue, between Three Mile Drive and Woodhall Street, offers the opportunity to explore several shops at once, each with a unique speciality. Finally, the old-school dining options available on the Upper East Side are without match—the old-timey German beer hall, the Dakota Inn Rathskeller; the Belgian mussel and feather bowling haven, Cadieux Cafe; the city's most famous Detroit-style pizza joint, Buddy's; and the city's finest live blues bar, the Raven Lounge, all call this area home. Because so many of these destinations are often far apart, some frequent visitors to the city suggest leaving the Upper East Side for repeat or longer visits.

Like any major city, Detroit has some neighborhoods that are best visited during the day or in groups. Although many neighborhoods within this chapter are very safe and vibrant, some areas may be unsafe late at night, and we recommend exercising a bit of caution and practicing the same safety rules you would when visiting parts of any urban center. Many of these businesses offer secure parking.

BARS & RESTAURANTS

8 Mile Pancake House - Since this pancake joint offers an expansive menu of lunch favorites and breakfast options, including a selection of more than 25 kinds of omelets, 8 Mile does much more than just pancakes well. That said, the namesake dishes at this diner are fluffy, Frisbee-size delights, available with a variety of mix-ins, such as pecans, fruit, or chocolate chips, and they are priced affordably to accommodate any carbo-loader. Visitors dine at the counter on well-used faux leather stools, or at similarly well-loved booths, in a warmly colored and mellow-lit dining room. Closed by 4pm. Wi-Fi available. *12930 E. 8 Mile Rd., (313) 839-7030.*

Asian Corned Beef Deli - As a self-proclaimed "Asian-Jewish" restaurant, Asian Corned Beef is a New York-style dive deli serving a unique take on deli fare, including its home-cured pastrami and corned beef, home-roasted turkey, and hand-brined pickles. While the deli offers a host of delicious—and more typical—deli options, it is most renowned for its delectable corned beef and pastrami egg rolls, and kimchi-laden Asian wraps. Offering only a single table, visitors should plan on carryout. Vegetarians might look elsewhere. *2847 E. 7 Mile Rd., (313) 893-1650.*

Avalon Bakehouse Outlet - This friendly down-to-business cafe offers a selection of basics and pantry items, as well as still-tasty day-olds and seconds from the wildly popular Avalon International Breads. See separate entry for for more information about this iconic Detroit business. *4731 Bellevue St., (313) 308-0150.*

Bogart'z Cafe - This neighborhood bar and grille, dedicated to the man who believed "a hot dog at the game beats roast beef at the Ritz," stays true to form: Bogart'z offers an upscale take on bar fare in an ideal game-watching environment. Especially popular with neighboring Grosse Pointers, Bogart'z is a large, charming space dominated by Humphrey Bogart-related decor, a number of TVs, church-pew booths, and an impressive array of contemporary woodwork. Although known for its mouth-watering Buffalo burger, Bogart'z is no one-hit wonder. The less well-known Cajun burger, salmon tacos, and crab cake sliders all put on Oscar-worthy performances and are rightly revered by regulars. The carefully curated beer list and solid liquor choices offer ample reasons to raise a glass. *17441 Mack Ave., www.bogartzcafe.com, (313) 885-3995.*

★ **Buddy's Rendezvous Pizzeria** - Opened in 1936 as a neighborhood bar, Buddy's began serving its now-famous, deep-dish square pizza in 1946. It's the originator of what has come to be known as Detroit-style pizza—a deep-dish square pie with Sicilian roots featuring a deliciously greasy, chewy, and crispy crust with the sauce on the top and toppings under the cheese to prevent scorching. True to its Detroit origins, the square-shaped pizza is the result of being baked, not in a pizza pan, but in an automotive parts tray. Buddy's is now a small Metro Detroit chain, but this is the original (and, in our opinion, best) location. It's got an unpretentious 1950s vibe and charming decor including a pizza-themed homage to Diego Rivera's *Detroit Industry* Murals in the entryway. While it serves a full menu of burgers, sandwiches, soups, salads, and more that are reportedly delicious, we've never been able to resist just ordering one of its many award-winning pies. Enjoy your pizza with a pitcher or boomba of beer and be sure to step out back for a game of bocce ball after dinner. *17125 Conant St., www.buddyspizza.com, (313) 892-9001.*

★ **Cadieux Cafe** - A destination bar on the east side for delectable Belgian cuisine and heady Trappist ales, Cadieux has been serving lovers of Flanders and Wallonia for more than 50 years. The comfy, mellow dining room is decorated with portraits of famous Belgians and is the perfect place to enjoy steamed mussels, Belgian pommes frites with mayonnaise, its notable Belgian beer soup, or Sunday rabbit dinner. In addition to live sets from local bands, the cafe features feather bowling, a game similar to bocce ball but with flattened wooden balls rolled down earthen lanes toward a feather at the other end. Open to the public all nights except Tuesday or Thursday, when League experts go to work. *4300 Cadieux Rd., www.cadieuxcafe.com, (313) 882-8560.*

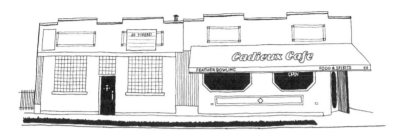

★**Capers** - A destination steakhouse for the carnivore on a budget, Capers puts menu first and dispenses with unnecessary fussiness. Hidden behind an unassuming facade on Gratiot's northeast stretch, the mellow, wood-paneled dining room is usually packed to the gills with chummy, convivial regulars. Serving priced-by-the ounce steaks, Capers may offer the best cuts of meat for the value in the city. Patrons looking to prioritize their drinks over their eats can perch on the wooden stools at the bar while they sip on the gargantuan, bargain-priced 32-ounce beers. Customers may park in the private lot for free and are buzzed in. Although the beef comes a la carte, combo meals and hearty portions of sides are available at an affordable price. Dress code is casual and calling ahead is recommended. *14726 Gratiot Ave., (313) 527-2100.*

Carmen's Community Market - Never mind that you order through bulletproof glass, wait among racks of batteries, gum, and trail mix, and that the kitchen is a corner store closet behind a Trojan Magnum display: The food is incredible. Though Carmen and Lonnie Montgomery opened this store/sandwich shop in 2016, the joint feels like it has history: The 1923 brick building is a delightfully cluttered warren of candy-apple-red string lights, throwback ads for Pepsi and rolling papers, and charming hand-painted signs selling food and baked goods. From the kitchen, Carmen prepares a limited, albeit outstanding, menu of foil-wrapped BBQ and sandwiches, as well as salty-umami oxtail soup, deluxe succulent smoke-glazed ribs, rich and savory hamburgers, smoked ham hocks, and traditional soul sides like cake-sweet cornbread. All of the meat is shipped fresh from Eastern Market, ground, and smoked each day. As a corner store, there's also plenty of options to wash things down. *2145 Dearing St., (313) 854-4032.*

Cleopatra Mediterranean Grill - Since hanging the shingle in 2012, owner Sam Tobia's quaint neighborhood Middle Eastern spot has been pleasing east side palates with some of the city's finest, fit-for-a-pharaoh Mediterranean fare. The low-key restaurant is pleasantly clad in Egyptian mementos and ancient-Egypt-themed artwork. This unassuming ambience contributes to the restaurant's accessible atmosphere. The offerings are highly navigable for ghallaba greenhorns—the menu has vivid descriptions of every dish, and while all the dishes are flavorful, the spices are not overwhelming. The menu is large and varied, featuring outstanding takes on saji, shawarma, crushed lentil soup, koshary and mujadara. Cleopatra emphasizes quality over quantity, and while the portions are ample, they are not particularly shareable. After your bicuspids discover the heavenly shawarma, however, you won't want to share. Great vegetarian options. *19027 Mack Ave., www.cleopatragrill.com, (313) 640-9000.*

★**The Dakota Inn Rathskeller -** Celebrating Detroit's rich German heritage since 1933, this charming, authentic, historic rathskeller, replete with dirndl-clad servers, dishes up delicious, hearty German food and beers (more than 20!). The original owner, Karl Kurz, worked at the Highland Park Ford Plant and toiled away during nights and weekends to transform a dilapidated Chinese laundry into this traditional German-style rathskeller in the architectural style of his native Wiekersheim, Germany. The original establishment consisted of a tiny three-stool bar, but over three generations, his family has greatly expanded on the original building and tradition. Currently run by the grandson of Kurz, the cozy, dark-wood-paneled interior is decorated with German beer steins, trophy animal mounts from family hunting trips, and hand-painted German scenes. Many nights feature live bands, and most conclude in a rousing sing-along to the traditional Schnitzelbank drinking song depicted in a lively mural in the dining room. Once a year, Dakota Inn pitches its yellow-and-white-striped tent for an authentic German biergarten, complete with German bands and polka contests, and September and October bring Oktoberfest, an especially celebratory time featuring oompah bands, chicken hats, joyous sing-alongs, and, of course, plenty of beer.

Vegetarians will enjoy the vegetarisch plate. The Dakota Inn also has a downstairs banquet room available for private parties for up to 50 people, and it offers off-site German catering. Open for only lunch Wednesday-Friday and dinner Thursday-Saturday. Check the website for frequent special events. *17324 John R. St., www.dakota-inn.com, (313) 867-9722.*

Dan & Vi's Pizza Deli - Whether it's the lower east side terroir, the seasoned ovens, or 50 years of practice, this eminent east side staple has been heralded for its buttery, pleasantly crisp crust since opening in 1963. Situated on a quiet stretch of Chene Street, this venerable institution is housed in a converted home clad in colorful murals. Inside, this combination grab-and-go pizza shop and liquor store, visitors will find a Spartan, old-timey interior, dominated by the large, open kitchen in the rear of the space. Though worth a trip for the pizza alone, the deli's calling card is its signature "deli slice," a delectable mashup of pizza and an Italian sub: A tall stack of salami, ham, cheese, shredded lettuce, diced tomato, onions, and Italian dressing sandwiched between two hearty slabs of that perfect pizza crust, seasoned with butter and Parmesan, and cut into triangles. Owners Marian and Bill Skinner don't operate a one-trick pony, however—the menu has a strong supporting cast, too, boasting a range of submarines, salads, divine fried chicken, and cheesecake. *5951 Chene St., (313) 924-6077.*

Detroit Blues Cafe - It's no secret that some of the best music in the world was made in Detroit—and that this city knows how to get down. Places like the Detroit Blues Cafe serve as a welcome reminder that the scene is still very much alive. With live music and DJs all week, come prepared, with your dancing shoes on. On the weekends, you'll likely have to pay a cover—but trust us, the bands are well worth it. If your hustle works up an appetite, flag down a friendly server and order soul-warming soul food like fried chicken, shrimp and grits, or pork chops, with a host of classic sides including yams and mac and cheese. Once you've licked your plate clean, grab another drink and rejoin the fun out on the dance floor. *14493 Gratiot Ave., www.detroitbluescafedetroit.com, (313) 466-3400.*

Dish - There is an awfully large amount of high-quality food coming out of the tiny kitchen at Dish, a lunch-and-dinner takeout counter on the east side. With a menu shaped by a professional chef and described by customers as "gourmet," Dish offers an array of new American cuisine, including thoughtfully prepared sandwiches, salads, soups, quesadillas, pasta dishes, and a rotating selection of specials (potato-encrusted salmon is a popular option), with an emphasis on locally sourced ingredients. Wait times are minimal. *18441 Mack Ave., www.dishdetroit.biz, (313) 886-2444.*

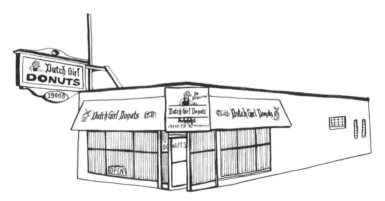

★**Dutch Girl Donuts -** A magnet for Detroiters for more than 50 years, Dutch Girl is Detroit's place for doughnuts. This independent corner shop is a beloved local favorite, featuring quaint vintage blue and white awnings and signage with illustrated emblems of its namesake lass. Inside are a few spots for customers to indulge in delectable, handmade fried dough delights in flavors like blueberry, raisin, and chocolate cake, as well as traditional favorites like glazed or jelly. Open

24/6 (closed Sundays). We highly recommend their cake doughnuts. *19000 Woodward Ave., (313) 368-3020.*

East Bar - In a town where you can't swing an empty Stroh's without hitting a neighborhood dive bar, few stand out. The East Bar stands out. With boatloads of sailing bric-a-brac, a knotty pine interior, over-the-bar aquarium and exposed beams, this charming spot has an unassuming atmosphere reminiscent of bars in northern Michigan. Despite the fire-sale prices on its impressive beer list, this friendly dive is more than a gymnasium for practicing Milwaukee curls. The pool table, occasional live music, dog-friendly policy, dartboard, and jovial staff make this spot a destination for a laid-back good time. Owner Clyde's small kitchen also offers a limited but delicious menu of bar fare. *15045 Mack Ave., (313) 885-6630.*

Flic of the Wrist Eatery - If by "flic of the wrist," Chef Chimere means "use wrist to frantically shovel food into mouth after first bite," the name is apt. On its quiet stretch of Seven Mile, Flic of the Wrist stands out with its brightly stylized food murals, and a large only slightly hubristic painted guarantee "best food on the east side." Inside the no-top lobby, the family-run effect is on full display: Odds are the clerk behind the plexiglass is a few years shy of a learner's permit, and the cooks all eat at the same Thanksgiving table. Fear not, however, kitchen skills run in the family. From the large grill, look for a number of pleasant, well-prepared options, including lobster, shrimp, turkey chops, whole wings, and chicken. Pair these with something from the stable of soul staples, including macaroni and cheese, greens, baked beans, corn, and potato salad. The decadent lamb chops and tasty, southern-style yams are not to be missed. Carry out or dine in… your car. *14901 E. Seven Mile Rd., (313) 290-5956.*

Food Exchange - Put your cardiologist on standby. Walk past the dining room walls covered with photoshopped images of President Obama and Muhammad Ali dining here, step up to the bulletproof glass, place your order, and prepare for your dieters' penance. With its irresistible mix of blue-collar comforts, owner Big Bruce's menu is a divine, meaty, and thoughtful take on traditional diner fare. The signature sandwich, the Big Baby, is to die for—fortunately so, since it might be lethal—and boasts a half pound of freshly ground chuck shoulder and a half pound of corned beef, along with three slices of cheese and all the traditional fixings. A favorite of rapper Danny Brown, the burger pattie is prepared magnificently, with a distinct umami flavor and a kick of pepper—a standout in a city of fine burger options. The expansive menu also boasts a normal-sized hamburger for under a buck, a "Fajizzle" steak dinner, a "Fachizzle" chicken dinner, and remarkable breakfast options, including salmon croquettes served over rice. *8451 Harper Ave., www.foodexchangerestaurant.com, (313) 579-5616.*

Georgia Cafe - The heir to the classic east side joint Geneva's, both in location and spirit, Georgia's has duly taken on the mission of serving eastsiders stick-to-the-ribs food at a price anyone can afford. This shotgun-style sliders-and-more counter is a cozy, charming place to get a quick breakfast or lunch. The restaurant features a plain white laminate interior, and customers eat sitting on short, comfy, chrome stools with the scent of grilled onions wafting over from the grill. Grab a bag of hot, fresh sliders (five for $4.50) with minimal wait. *17179 Harper Ave., (313) 882-8262.*

Golden Gate Cafe - Golden Gate Cafe's welcoming, colorful exterior is a contrast to the surrounding neighborhood, which is largely vacant. Part healing center, part vegetarian cafe, and part Bohemian meeting place, Golden Gate is a surprising oasis of friendly conversation, delicious food, and a warm atmosphere. Dine inside at the counter or at a warm booth nearby, or eat in the serene sculpture garden outside replete with wandering chickens and a fountain. They also offer non-traditional chiropractic services combining natural chiropractic practice with cranial sacral work, shiatsu, applied kinesiology, and nutritional counseling. *18700 Woodward Ave., www.innatedetroit.com, (313) 366-2247.*

Hashbrown Cafe - Less than a mile down the road from the Conant Gardens Historic District lies this mom-and-pop business, a brunch and soul food cafe famous for fried catfish, salmon croquettes, and hand-cut hash browns. From morning to night, the menu selections are cooked to order, so visitors often take one of the purple, red, or yellow seats at the diner counter and watch the cooks chopping up fresh ingredients through the window to the kitchen. In typical diner fashion, the cafe features spacious booths lined along the front window, where families can dine and watch the Conant Street traffic. *19458 Conant St., (313) 366-0433.*

Hec's Bar - According to state liquor records—and the faded old-timey awning outside—Hec's has been in operation since 1933. According to poorly kept rumors, it was actually opened much earlier—originally as a prohibition-era blind pig. Passed down through three generations, this family-owned watering hole is now operated by Hec's grandson, himself now an elder statesman. The man behind the bar, the grill, and the rumors, he dispenses his gruff wisdom one Stroh's at a time. Find a seat somewhere in the baby-blue bar and watch the backslapping old timers show their skill at corner pocket and embellishment, or catch the game on TV—any game, as long as it's Tigers baseball. Even though Hec's is a one-man operation, the surprisingly complete grill menu includes all the diner classics, as well as gizzards and "boneless, meatless chickens" (hard-boiled eggs to the rest of us). A surreal low-frills gem of a classic working-man's dive from another time, Hec's is worth pulling over for—just look for the snazzy neon cocktail glass in the window. Check out the stuffed marlin above the bar. *20005 Van Dyke Ave., (313) 893-1016.*

Holy Moly Donut Shop - If you're not prone to more profane exclamations, you'll be saying the shop's name after the first bite. This contemporary, upscale postage stamp of a shop is a bright space dominated by a Yellow Submarine-esque donut and ice cream mural on one side, and a wall of TV menus and bakery cases on the other. Look for 32 varieties of donuts—including devil's food cake, birthday cake, and blueberry—each cooked fresh throughout the day to cakey, fluffy, airy perfection. Add a glaze, or one of a slew of toppings— including candied bacon, chopped Andes mints, and Cap'n Crunch. With 5,568 ways to order, between the donuts and toppings, it's impossible to find a favorite without shopping in the muumuu aisle afterwards, but the apple crisp donut with strawberry frosting and Pop-Tart chunks is a good place to start. Bagels, coffees, breakfast sandwiches, and ice cream are also available. *201 8 Mile Rd., (313) 826-0132.*

★**Ivanhoe Cafe / Polish Yacht Club -** Run by Polish pub keeper Patti Galen, this cheerful, old-school Polish restaurant and neighborhood watering hole has been delighting eastsiders for generations. Open since 1909, the century-old Ivanhoe Cafe is in its original brick building, replete with a tin ceiling, hand-carved bar, walls decked with antique photos and newspaper clippings, and fresh flowers, candles, and vintage lamps on tables in the cozy dining rooms. In addition to the full bar, the restaurant offers a delectable Polish menu, including stuffed cabbage, kielbasa, homemade coleslaw, pan-fried perch, pierogi, and hearty potato pancakes, along with variety of classic bar-fare sandwiches, including the renowned Polish Reuben—kielbasa, sauerkraut, and cheese. The landlocked cafe plays host to the Polish Yacht Club, a good-natured social club and charitable organization with a tongue-in-cheek alias. Founded in 1961, the club's landlubber "commodore" and members often sport sailor's attire and love sharing stories and good cheer with guests. *5249 Joseph Campau St., www.ivanhoecafe-pyc.com, (313) 925-5335*

Joe Ann's Bar B-Q - Pull over at the bright yellow mural of a pig wearing sunglasses and a chef hat, grilling one of his barnyard friends. Second-generation owner Joe Ann Proctor continues a family legacy over the charcoal grill built by her father in 1951. This lifetime of meaty practice has brought meaty perfection. Proctor's delicious recipes are distinctive for their Carolina influence—thin, vinegary sauce envelopes dishes with a subtle sweetness. The impressive battery of bone-in barbecue bonafides includes pork and beef ribs, rib tips, chicken, pork chops, pig feet, pork shoulder, wings, shrimp, catfish, and tilapia. The side and dessert menu includes all of the usual suspects, though the fresh cut french fries, green beans with turkey, and egg custard pie should not be missed. Although the modest cinnamon-hued dining room offers several booths, most customers take their styrofoam clamshell of barbeque bounty to go. *3139 Jerome St., www.joeannsbbq.com, (313) 366-3775.*

Krakus Restaurant and Bar - Though this restaurant is located just outside of Hamtramck, the little brick building maintains all of the Polish flair found there. Krakus is a family-run place with homey '70s decor, authentic homemade food, a full bar featuring Polish beers and vodka, and plenty of polka music. Some locals even prefer the food at Krakus to the Hamtramck heavy hitters Polish Village Cafe and Polonia (see separate entries). The portions are large and a great value—the Ukrainian borscht, dill pickle soup, homemade pierogi, and potato pancakes are divine—at this low-key spot for regulars and neighborhood folks who want to pop in for delicious carryout. On Saturday nights, Krakus is the place to party, with a live polka band playing until 2am, with secure parking. *12900 Joseph Campau St., (313) 368-4848.*

La Cina - Slide into a cozy booth, and prepare for culinary Mexcellence. This Tex-Mex joint has a decidedly vintage basement bar ambiance, complete with small booths divided by black chili pepper fabric valances, walls clad in mirrors and Pueblo murals, and an aquarium keeping watch over the bar. The food is equally classic. Expect tasty botanas (a Detroit speciality), mesquite grilled fish tacos, flautas, wet burritos, quesadillas, and enchiladas, all served with a distinctly Tex-Mex flair. Each of the fork-tender tortillas is buttressed by generous dollops of rice and beans, and covered with enough melted cheese and shredded lettuce to sink a ship. The standout items, however, are the fajitas. Each order is served with a sizzle, deft seasoning, and the tender sear that comes from deliberate, patient preparation. Behind the bar, look for a full selection of liquor and beer. *17201 Mack Ave., www.lacinarestaurant.com, (313) 881-8226.*

La Dolce Vita - The sweet life renews itself at this Italian restaurant hugging the edge of Palmer Park. Temporarily exit contemporary America in favor of lambent old-world elegance and understated class. La Dolce Vita serves traditional and modern Italian/continental fare, including a popular lasagna béchamel, decadent escargot, homemade gnocchi, and flavorful seafood, all with an emphasis on freshness and distinct flavor profiles. Among the desserts is a world-renowned tiramisu (OK, perhaps just city-renowned, but you could have fooled us). The entrance is off Parkhurst, through the restaurant's utopian garden patio, which is available for al fresco dining and occasional live music in the summer. Despite its popularity, the restaurant retains an allure of seclusion, making it suitable for a romantic meal or a peaceful brunch. *17546 Woodward Ave., www.ldvrestaurant.net, (313) 865-0331.*

Lost River - Demarcated by a subtle old-school pink neon sign, this delightfully kitschy Tiki-oriented watering hole—the east side's answer to Southwest's Mutiny Bar (see separate entry)—splashed on the scene in 2018. Inside, the bar features a gorgeous bar-spanning mural by talented florally inspired painter Ouizi, a genre-appropriate 1940s back bar, and tasteful decor to help transport you to a mythologized Polynesian wonderland. Going way beyond just your usual Tiki-tumblers, Lost River reserves specific goblets for each libation, running the gamut from a ceramic coconut, to a fez-wearing elephant, and a drink-sized bathtub (replete with chrome hardware.) The bar offers all of the Tiki drink essentials, including the Painkiller and the Zombie, as well as some fun twists on cocktail classics, including the Negroni Sbagliato (a champagne Negroni) and a Tiki Old Fashioned (a playful rum old fashioned), and a daily slushy drink special. Our favorite of their offerings is their well-balanced Mai Tai, which honors the 1944 original, and is a perfect way to soak in the ambiance of this fun and friendly destination bar. *15421 Mack Ave., www.lostrivertiki.com, (313) 720-0673.*

Louie's Ham and Corned Beef - An east side favorite for more than 40 years, Louie's Ham and Corned Beef is a charming yet unassuming gem with a healthy dose of both hominess and pluck. The restaurant is simple and straightforward with formica booths, porcine-related art, and a vintage open kitchen. In a city known for its high corned beef standards, Louie's stands out for its tender, fresh, and flavorful corned beef. Although the entire menu—including the all-day breakfast items—will not disappoint, the renowned stacked ham sandwich and Louie's Combo—stacked pastrami and corned beef on grilled rye—are the belles of the ball. *16661 Harper Ave., (313) 881-4250.*

Marcus Hamburgers Restaurant - Opened in 1929, this unassuming dive diner is best known for its acclaimed Marcus burger—a harmonica-shaped burger served in a hot dog bun with onions. With the ever-present gang of bantering regulars at the distinctive horseshoe counter providing free entertainment, visitors can enjoy Marcus burgers or one of the many slobber-worthy Polish options, such as the handmade pierogi or chicken dumpling soup. With recipes honed over several generations, Macedonian-immigrant owners Mike and Louie Lozanovski never disappoint. A great place for a sighting of Detroit's finest. *6349 E. McNichols Rd., (313) 891-6170.*

Nunn's Barbeque - Barbecue is a hot topic in Detroit, and while people are passionate about their opinions, this is definitely the kind of city where there is room for more than one kind of 'cue. Nunn's is carryout-only and offers barbecue in the Southern soul food tradition: meaty fall-off-the-bone ribs cooked in a massive smoker and slathered in Nunn's own seasoning blend and spicy-sweet sauce, hand-battered jumbo shrimp, garlicky greens, decadent yams, pig feet, and homemade banana pudding and peach cobbler. There's nothing fancy about this sparkling-clean BBQ joint, but it takes its food seriously, and serious barbecue fans need to do themselves a favor and check this place out—it's "the meat that can't be beat!" *19196 Conant St., (313) 893-7210.*

Rabaut's Cafe - In a moment of urban planning serendipity, the sole building on a small wedge-shaped block of Detroit is a top-notch lunch cafe. Meet the Rabauts, husband and wife Chris and Colleen, who have owned and operated this delightful, warm sandwich shop for more than twenty-five years. The cafe offers polished versions of traditional fare, as well as artisan sandwiches (think a grilled turkey reuben and a piled-high veggie delight on grilled rye) and sides, which make the place a perfect mid-day lunch spot. The artful and cozy dining room is decorated with family artwork, fresh flowers, pottery, and colored-glass lampshades, all of which accent and highlight the couple's amicable bonhomie. Customers looking for a small-town diner experience in a big city will be delighted by Rabaut's. Closed on weekends. Lunch only. *18536 E. Warren Ave., www.rabautscafe.com, (313) 886-3370.*

★**Raven Lounge -** Open since the 1950s, this unassuming east side club is the oldest continuously operating rhythm and blues bar in Michigan. According to legend, if Motown stars of the day weren't playing the stage, they were sitting in the audience. While much of the surrounding neighborhood has rejoined the earth, the near-legendary venue is still rocking strong and remains a destination. Look for a packed house of welcoming regulars and first-timers every Thursday, Friday, and Saturday with $5 soul, funk, and rhythm and blues shows. Though music is the highlight at the Raven, the bar offers a sizeable selection of beers and call liquors, and the kitchen rounds out the experience with a full menu of soul favorites. If you come to the Raven once, you'll come twice. And, as the owner of the club, Tommy Stephens, will let you know, if you return to the Raven, "you're family." *5145 Chene St., www.theravenloungeandrestaurant.com, (313) 924-7133.*

Royal Barbecue Pizza - Look for the building that's an amalgamation of Spanish Revival and strip mall Chi-Chi's, and you will have found this unexpected gem of a barbecue, pizza, chicken, burger, and deli joint. With late-night drive through and delivery, and comfortable, modern booth seating for dine-in customers, the eatery offers a wide-variety of heavy-duty greasy spoon takes on American classics, one of the house specialties being a BLT made with a pound (!) of bacon. Get ready for the royal treatment. *5844 Mount Elliott St., www.royalbar-b-q.com, (313) 923-2222.*

The Sandwich Shop - Since opening in 2012, these maestros of meat have been winning—and perhaps clogging—the hearts of eastsiders with their brilliant and delicious sandwiches. While the exterior of the recently rehabbed space is adorned with murals of anthropomorphized sandwiches merrily chasing one another, the interior is far more plain and unassuming, dominated by a handful of tables and a large wall of bulletproof glass. Thankfully, this glass is not sandwich proof. Although The Sandwich Shop has a fairly diverse menu—including jumbo shrimp, catfish, stuffed potatoes, and fried okra—the focus is on its 12 equally delicious signature sandwiches and burgers. Among these, the Texan—a half-pound of ground beef stuffed with corned beef and Swiss cheese—and the Renaissance— a half-pound of corned beef with Swiss, coleslaw, and Russian dressing—are the most exceptional. In every case, the meat is fresh, well-seasoned, and cooked perfectly. Vegetarians should wait in the car. *19153 Van Dyke Ave., (313) 826-1437.*

The Stone House Bar - Billed as "Michigan's oldest continuously operating bar," the Stone House has been voted Michigan's best biker bar for three years running and has the history to back it up: The Purple Gang ran a brothel out of this 1860s farmhouse during Prohibition, complete with a tunnel dug under Woodward Avenue (then a dirt road) to smuggle in the hooch. It was a carnie haven during the life of the recently shuttered State Fairgrounds. These days, you can expect a mix of bikers, neighborhood eccentrics, and Detroit lifers. Its defining feature is the two-story front porch, where you can grab a bird's-eye view of the surrounding environs on a lazy summer afternoon. In addition, there's a horseshoe pit outside, but don't step up to the plate unless you're bringing your A-game: The regulars are pros. The bar frequently hosts fowling (a combination of football and bowling) and holds live rock and blues shows most Saturday nights. *19803 Ralston St., (313) 891-3333.*

Taylor Made Burgers - A casual, no-frills takeout joint on a busy stretch of East Seven Mile Road, Taylor Made Burgers serves up unexpectedly tasty, made-to-order greasy goodness. Survey the poster-sized photos of the offerings that cover the lobby to make your selection. On an extensive menu that features wings, chicken, corned beef, ribs, fish, and various styles of sandwiches, its the namesake burgers that stand out. These aren't the dinky sliders you find at other Detroit hamburger castles, but big juicy patties served as singles, doubles, or triples on sesame buns or onion rolls, and priced to sell: The signature Taylor Burger is an ungodly whole pound of beef for just $9! Taylor Made is an ideal place to grab food before or after a late-night session at the nearby Two Way Inn (see separate entry), but it's worth calling ahead to place your order, as the wait can be long. Cash only. *4844 E. Seven Mile Rd., (313) 891-5858.*

Trolleys - Historically a sleepy neighborhood sports bar, Trolleys is undergoing a gradual transition toward becoming a Filipino restaurant. This transformation makes for a fascinating aesthetic and cultural juxtaposition and makes the place a destination for delicious Filipino fare. Aside from the usual sports bar options, Trolleys offers lumpia—a type of beef eggrolls, adobo—chicken cooked in vinegar, fried rice—and tom kha soup, alongside a host of other Filipino offerings. Besides the varied decor and Filipino food, the joint is also home to an Internet jukebox, a pool table, and cheap, stiff drinks. By far the best place to have pancit noodles and a Budweiser while watching the game. *17315 Mack Ave., (313) 886-1060.*

Two Way Inn - Although called Two Way Inn, its name stems from the fact that it has two ways out—when your old lady comes looking for you through the front door, you can dash out the back. If these walls could talk, you could expect a lot of winking wisdom from the venerable Two Way Inn. Originally opened in 1876, it's Detroit's oldest existing bar, and it looks the part, with an interior of ancient wooden floors, antique kegs, and long-abandoned farm tools decorating the walls. These days, the bar draws a steady crowd of Hamtramck boosters, who make the short trek every first Friday for a neighborhood hootenanny. Be careful with that bell above the bar though—give it a ring, and you might find yourself buying a round for the bar. *17897 Mt. Elliott St., (313) 891-4925.*

Vegginini's Paradise Cafe - A literal mom-and-pop family operation, the talented Heaven (Mom), works her magic on the grill while personable Ishmael (Pop) works his on the crowd. This leaves their entrepreneurial boys to take care of the other details—from bussing, to taking orders, to running the juice press. The corner might look a little rough from the wrong angle, but this hidden gem, an affordable, all-vegan east side destination, is absolutely worth the trek. Billed as Michigan's most diverse vegan menu, the claim is probably true—as is the fact that the food is outrageously good. Although the offerings lean towards Southern and soul food, look for flirtations with Italian, Indian, Central American, and other fare. An absolute highlight on the menu is their "chickless" fried "chicken"—a juicy, flavorful delight with crispy breading—that comes in many permutations, the grand dame being spicy barbecue. However, patrons also shouldn't miss their pastellias, similar to empanadas, their flavorful, house-made black bean burger, their satisfying ginger lemon tea, and—as one might expect—their extensive menu of paninis. Delivery available. *15439 Mack Ave., www.veggininiscafe.com, (313) 332-0447.*

Vergote's - This affordably priced "you buy, we fry" joint on the east side is a cut above other spots of its kind and the oldest in Detroit— around since 1939 and still family-owned and operated. A large selection of fresh fish—filleted or whole—is visible in dozens of feet of display cases, along with an assortment of chicken cuts, frozen selections, breading, seasoning, and sauces. "You buy, we fry" is just what it sounds like—fresh or frozen is available for in-house frying, grilling, Cajun prep, or uncooked. There is also a carryout menu of dinner specials available and house-made soups—gumbo, étouffée, and chowder. *16523 Harper Ave., (313) 882-9030.*

SHOPPING & SERVICES

Archer Record Pressing - One of the last record-pressing plants in the world (Midtown's Third Man Records is another, see separate entry), this third-generation family business has been working hard for Detroit music since 1965. Because record production equipment has been manufactured only intermittently since the mid-1980s, Archer family members employ specialized repair skills and knowledge of the finicky equipment to keep the plant's five presses running. From Motown artists, to rock 'n' roll, to hip-hop, to techno and other electronic music, Archer has helped create the music that has put Detroit on the map. With record pressing plants closing as owners retire without anyone left to take the torch, we're glad that business is up at Archer, due in large part to the major Detroit techno artists who rely on vinyl, such as Kevin Saunderson, Juan Atkins, Derrick May, and Theo Parrish releasing internationally acclaimed records pressed locally. Archer is a favorite among local groups large and small who want to put out LPs the old- fashioned way. *7401 E. Davison St., www.archerrecordpressing.com, (313) 365-9545.*

Arts & Scraps - A crafter's paradise, this nonprofit recycles 28 tons of reusable industrial material a year, sorting it into hundreds of affordable and useful creative materials, including cans, frames, sewing notions, cardboard, fabrics, tickets, canisters, yarn—you name it. Be sure to check out the craft kits it assembles from donated materials ($2 each, with discounts for multiples). Arts & Scraps gives back to the community to help people think, create, and learn through its many programs, providing recycled scraps for minimal cost to 3,300 organizations and classrooms annually, reaching 275,000 people of all ages and abilities each year, and it can even bring programs and materials to those who can't get to the facility, with the ScrapMobile bus. Arts & Scraps is open only Tuesdays, Thursdays, and Saturdays for shopping, but check the website for information on workshops, birthday parties, field trips, volunteer opportunities, and more. *16135 Harper Ave., www.artsandscraps.org, (313) 640-4411.*

Better Made Potato Chip Factory & Store - Distinguished by the bonnet-clad Miss Better Made who graces every bag, Better Made potato chips have been a Detroit institution since 1930. Located on a once-busy stretch of Gratiot Avenue, the factory, which sources Michigan potatoes for eight in-season months, processes 60 million pounds of potatoes every year through an automated system of lifts, conveyors, washers, peelers, slicers, fryers, and packaging machines. While it no longer offers factory tours, the factory store is the only place to buy the classic thin, crispy chips fresh, straight off the line. In addition to all of the standard varieties—and they do have all the standard varieties—the factory store sells dozens of harder to find snack foods, such as chocolate covered potato chips, potato sticks, a variety of popcorns, and the famously elusive Rainbow Chips—made from potatoes with a higher sugar content, which gives them color marks and a slightly sweet taste. *10148 Gratiot Ave., www.bmchips.com, (313) 925-4774.*

Bike Tech - Whether you're looking to hit the beach, the trails, the ramps, or the streets, or just looking to ride off your February thighs, the knowledgeable and friendly mechanics at Bike Tech can help you whip your whip into shape or find you the perfect new ride. Owner Brian Pikielek's large shop carries an almost-unparalleled selection of restored vintage bicycles alongside their impressive selection of new bicycles—namely, Raleigh, Diamondback, and Fuji models—and a diverse parts selection. Though the shop is unique for its knowledge of classic road bikes, the experienced staff works on everything from penny-farthings to pursuit bikes. Ideal for the cost-conscious cyclist. *18401 E. Warren Ave., www.biketech.us, (313) 884-2453.*

Energy 4 Life Health Food Store - Energy 4 Life is a veritable apothecary of alternative remedies and supplements. Customers walking into the store will enjoy a bouquet of herbs, loose teas, nettles, and seeds emanating from the oversized glass jars along the sidewall and available by the ounce. Aside from teas and supplements, the store also sells cleanses and hygiene products, and services such as infrared saunas and herbal body wraps. The setting for Energy 4 Life is far from boilerplate new age—instead, a simple black tin ceiling, white walls, worn furniture, and durable wood cabinetry, underscore the emphasis of the devotion dedicated to craft, rather than image. *16135 Mack Ave., www.energy4lifehealth.com, (313) 640-5790.*

Hats Galore & More - As the store's slogan goes, "Hats Galore! Hats Galore! We're your favorite fine hat store!" It's a statement that's hard to deny, once you discover the old-school charms of this classic, east-side staple. The family-owned shop offers a timeless selection of caps with staying power: Brands like Stetson and Kangol, apple hats, fashionable bowlers, fascinators, and feathered fedoras for days. Customers—men, women and children—will receive an uncommonly warm welcome, expert service, and serious style. From the hand-painted exterior mural of—you guessed it—hats, to the rows and rows of styles and colors, the shop is brimming with character and charm. Legendary customers have included the likes of Luciano Pavarotti, who bought a cream-colored El Dorado for his wedding day, in 2003. While the details are dear, the prices are not, and you can find everything from everyday caps to church hats in a great range of prices, starting around $25—the perfect way to start your millinery collection! *10061 Gratiot Ave., (313) 579-1761.*

Lucki's Gourmet Cheesecakes - The brainchild of Lucki Word, Lucki's Gourmet Cheesecakes specializes in exceptionally soft, delicate cheesecakes, in more than 50 flavors. Covering all the bases, the establishment deliciously slings all the standards, like strawberry and Oreo, but also takes daring forays into new territory, with less-traditional varieties, such as junk food and salmon and sausage. In addition to her cheesecakes, Lucki whips up homemade cobblers, ice cream, and cakes of the cheeseless persuasion, including a number of sugar-free varieties. To tempt your sweet tooth and help you make a selection, the staff offers up plentiful free samples of Lucki's tasty treats. If you're feeling as creative as the staff, you can even design your own dessert and order custom cakes. *7111 W. McNichols Rd., and 5063 Trumbull Ave, Suite 2, www.luckischeesecakes.com, (313) 272-3190.*

Mike's Antiques - On his piece of the east side, Mike might be considered the neighborhood "pops." He gives advice to the younger visitors, offers them deals on bikes and secondhand household items, and discusses his ideas about politics and the world today. Customers won't find a specialized selection of antiques, but Mike's Antiques carries more secondhand items that people in the neighborhood are looking for. Come for the conversation, for the advice on antiquing (and life), and for the chance to dig around through stacks of books, lamps, paintings, furniture pieces, and a few racks of vintage clothing. *11109 Morang Dr., (313) 881-9500.*

On the Rise Bakery - This arm of the Capuchin Soup Kitchen is much more than a bakery. On the Rise is part of the ROPE (Reaching Our Potential Everyday) program established in 2006 to develop life skills for former prisoners and addicts and to prevent recidivism or relapse by providing a stable work environment as well as regular income while they reintegrate into society. On the Rise serves a wide selection of yummy, homemade sweets and baked goods, including cakes, breads, cookies, rolls, and other treats, with a special flair for fruit pies. Located in a brick building, the retail counter for the social enterprise is warm and welcoming and exudes the positivity inherent in the organization's work. *8900 Gratiot Ave., www.cskdetroit.org/bakery, (313) 922-8510.*

Park Antiques - The largest shop along Antique Row, this large, friendly, and eclectic neighborhood antique shop is known for its relatively modest prices and impressive selection of picture frames, bookends, and equestrian-themed gewgaws. Given the eclectic array of products from the mid-19th through mid-20th centuries, it is hard to leave empty-handed. Visitors are free to wander the narrow trails between packed shelves of curiosities and vintage goods among the store's four large rooms. *16311 Mack Ave., (313) 884-7652.*

Shantinique Music - Operating on the east side's Harper Avenue for more than 40 years, Shantinique Music is a relic of an era when the far reaches of the city's commercial corridors were bustling, and teeming with independent businesses. Originally only a music purveyor, as the neighborhood changed, and trends came and went, the shop adapted and filled voids by adding to its offerings. Today, in addition to carrying a wide selection of hip-hop, R&B, and soul music on compact disc and vinyl, the storied shop carries movies, concert tickets, and men's and women's apparel. Look for footwear and urban gear, as well as an epic selection of Detroit team-branded caps, jerseys, and T-shirts, making Shantinique a go-to shop for anyone looking to rep the city. A legendary music store in some circles, the shop has been patronized by hip-hop royalty, from Biggie Smalls to TI, as well as local R&B noteworthies like Kem. Lottery fans will be relieved to know that Shantinique also sells tickets. *8933 Harper Ave., (313) 923-3040.*

CULTURAL ATTRACTIONS

555 Arts - Founded in 2002, 555 Arts has occupied spaces in several locations around Detroit, most notably, a former police precinct in Southwest. Now in their new home, the Banner Tobacco building (designed by Louis Kamper), the organization offers a gallery and event space, as well as affordable artist studios, including a working foundry for casting iron, bronze, and aluminum sculpture. While these amenities are located on the first floor and in the basement of the space, the organization plans to renovate and activate the other floors over time, in phases. The adjacent house on Mitchell Street serves as a residence for visiting artists, and across the street, visitors can admire sculptures and installations at the 555 Art Park. Check their website and social media for the latest workshops and events. *2941 E. Warren Ave., www.555arts.org, (888) 495-2787.*

Parade Company Tours - Take a peek backstage and see the Parade Company studio at work. The Parade Company—the beloved nonprofit that hosts the nationally televised America's Thanksgiving Parade, the Target Fireworks, and the Turkey Trot fun run—allows visitors to see behind the scenes as the staff prepares for the next Thanksgiving parade and to explore its extensive 110,000-square-foot warehouse. The exceedingly friendly and knowledgeable tour guides introduce visitors to the artists who develop costumes and floats and show visitors 60 spectacular floats, more than 3,000 costumes, and the world's largest collection of papier-mâché heads. While a guaranteed hit among younger visitors, adults will enjoy seeing these marvels up close and seeing how they're built. *9500 Mt. Elliott St., www.theparade.org, (313) 923-7400.*

ENTERTAINMENT & RECREATION

Balduck Park - The area coloquially known as Balduck Park is actually two separate well-maintained parks on either side of Chandler Park Drive on the city's far east side. One is a campus with an open field with baseball diamonds (including backstops), soccer and peewee football fields, outdoor basketball courts, a small fieldhouse, and Balduck's most-loved feature, which sees use typically only a few weeks a year: a sledding hill—perfect for youths or irrepressible grownups on snowy days. Across Chandler Park Drive is a much smaller field surrounded by a small urban forest that is great for barbecuing and summer gatherings. In recent years, Friends of the Alger Theatre has offered free feature movies on the hill every summer, including live music, cartoons, and refreshments. *Chandler Park Dr. between Radnor St. and Canyon St., www.algertheater.org, (313) 343-9087.*

Bel Air 10 Theater - In a town with only two first-run movie theaters, the 10-screen Bel Air is a relative mammoth. Tucked off 8 Mile Road in the Bel Air Center Plaza shopping center, the theater boasts many contemporary updates, including digital projection, Dolby Digital 7.1 Surround Sound, and 3D projection capability. In addition to a healthy selection of first-run titles, which favors action and horror films, the theater also offers live projections of Detroit Lions football games. Pricing is generally a bargain: Matinees are $5, regular adult pricing is $7, and sports broadcasts are free with a concession purchase. *10100 E. 8 Mile Rd., www.belair10theater.com, (313) 438-3494.*

Chandler Park Golf Course - Located in the northern half of Detroit's verdant Chandler Park, the Chandler Park Golf Course has been delighting generations of golfers since opening in 1929. The subtle slopes and gentle terrain on this Williams, Gill & Associates-designed course make it easy on the dogs and on the scorecard. This merciful, par-71 course measures 5,832 yards from the blue tees and features wide, sweeping tree-lined fairways and forgiving greens, making it popular among those new to the game—and those who play like it. Aggressive golfers should be wary of the sand and grass traps flanking many of the fairways, which favor those with a solid irons game. The greens and fairways are watered, so the course stays green into the summer. The course was truncated when I-94 was built, so the front nine is shorter than the back. If you're playing only nine and want more of a challenge, play the back nine. The course is home to a putting and chipping area for pregame warm-ups, as well as a beautiful, full-service pro shop. *12801 Chandler Park Dr., www.chandlerparkgolfcourse.com, (313) 331-7755.*

Detroit Rugby Football Club - Detroit Rugby has a legacy that is more than 40 years old and more than 1,500 players proud. A men's team originally dubbed the Cobras (for its players, who engineered the Ford sports car) began playing competitive national rugby on the fields of Belle Isle in 1968 and moved its practice and home field to northeast Detroit in 1979. DRFC has three teams, including a Division II men's team, a Division I women's team that won national championships in 2003 and 2004, and an over-35 Detroit Old Guys Select (D.O.G.S.) that plays under modified rules. The verdantly gritty Farwell Field hosts three pitches, which are cleared of tall grass for clean, proper play. Spectating at spring and fall matches is welcome, though seating is BYO. Alcohol prohibited. *Farwell Field: 4400 E. 8 Mile Rd., www.detroitrugby.org.*

Dorais Velodrome - Initialized during the '67 riots and completed (perhaps apocryphally) the day Neil Armstrong set foot on the moon, the Dorais Velodrome is a certain anomaly for the Motor City. This 250-meter oval-shaped concrete bicycle racing track with 45-degree banks and a green median featuring sunflower plants has endured a generation of neglect and abuse to persist in its present state. The track has been tagged with spray paint and is scarred with cracks and patches up to 4 inches in height, so road riding is somewhat dicey, but attentive riders will find the track navigable. The velodrome is set in the well-maintained Dorais Park at the foot of Derby Hill but sees little casual use. *Mound Rd. and E. Outer Drive, www.thunderdrome.com.*

Family Aquatic Center at Chandler Park - Based in the southern half of beautiful Chandler Park, the Family Aquatic Center is a destination for those looking for un-watered-down aquatic fun. The updated, 22,000-square-foot facility accommodates up to 2,023 patrons and offers a range of activities, including two massive water slides that allow 15-mile-per-hour tube or body sliding, a 570,000-gallon wave pool with nine-foot crests, and a toddler area with more than 100 spray fountains and other water rides. If you forget your trunks or need a snack, visit the well-stocked Tiki Hut, which offers swim gear and other accessories, or the concession canteen that serves up summer grub. Visitors must be 48 inches tall to ride the slide. Open Memorial Day through Labor Day. Call ahead for prices and relevant weather information, or to inquire about event rental. *12660 Chandler Park Dr., (313) 822-7665.*

Harpos Concert Theatre - This independent cinema-cum-rock-hall, which books its own shows, is known in the area as the optimal venue to see thrash, metal, hardcore, speed, industrial, and modern crossover acts. Built during an era when economic depression was waiting for world war to spark the country into action, Harpos has endured over the years to become a destination metal hall. Originally the Harper Theatre, this movie house built in the Art Moderne style mutated into a discotheque in the 1970s, giving it its (seldom-deployed) light-up dance floor. The end of the decade saw Harpos reinvented as a rock venue, featuring bands like Bachman-Turner Overdrive and Blue Öyster Cult, even introducing U2 to the Motor City concert scene. Eventually, Harpos transitioned to a venue fully devoted to metal and hardcore, attracting major acts such as Motörhead, Anthrax, The Misfits, Slayer, and GWAR to perform from its prominent 10-foot stage deep into the cavernous remnants of an ornate ballroom. Action is fueled by affordable alcohol. *14238 Harper Ave., www.harposconcerttheatre.com, (313) 824-1700.*

★**John's Carpet House -** Every Sunday in the summer between 2pm and sundown, music fans in the know can catch live (amplified) music from some of Detroit's finest blues musicians in the fields of the near east side. The event started as a regular jam session in the garage of John Estes, who insulated the walls with carpet to muffle the sound, inspiring the nickname of the ad hoc venue. Though Estes passed away long ago and his house and garage no longer occupy the site, the honored tradition of a free public Sunday jam session continues today. Visitors are welcome to bring their own brown-bagged food (or beverages) but can also enjoy tasty fried chicken and other downhome vittles from the food trucks and stands that set up shop near the action. If you feel like dancing, you're in luck—just make sure you bring your best moves because the regulars put on a show. Though there's no admission fee, guests are encouraged to "put a ducat in the bucket" to give the musicians a little something for their time and to make sure the grass gets mowed and the Porta-Johns get emptied. *St. Aubin Street at Frederick Street.*

Renaissance Bowling Center - With an exterior decorated in bright red triangular stalactites and a neon-fringed sign, this community bowling area is impossible to overlook. Inside Renaissance are 50 new lanes outfitted with modern scoring computers and screens, as well as an updated bar and a kitchen for rollers to refuel. Renaissance prides itself on being the only bowling alley in Michigan owned by a black woman and emphasizes providing a venue for local residents to meet and socialize. Group deals, event rental, and opportunities for fund-raisers are all available. Closed Monday. Call for daytime hours. *19600 Woodward Ave., (313) 368-5123.*

SITES

Georgia Street Community Collective - GSCC is a campus of vegetable gardens, fruit orchards, animal pens, a small park, a library and computer lab, and a community center. At the collective, food and resources are shared among residents, including myriad vegetables, fruits, duck and chicken eggs, and goat's milk. The campus encompasses numerous lots on a quiet east side intersection, used and supported by the neighborhood. GSCC is the result of the efforts of local resident Mark "Cub" Covington, who began reclaiming the area in 2007 by clearing vacant lots of trash, and then planting gardens to create litter-resistant space. Cub hosts an array of public events, including a street fair, movie nights, Easter egg hunts, and holiday dinners. The collective attracted international interest when London's Observer wrote about it in 2010—which led British trance label Anjunabeats to pay for landscaping work and park resources. GSCC is a destination for those looking to visit one of the city's most renowned urban farms and visitors looking to make a difference. The organization is constantly seeking partners and donations of any kind—tools, school supplies, dry goods, financial support, and volunteer teachers to further their admirable mission. Although Cub welcomes visitors to admire and explore the garden at any time, it is best to visit during one of his public events. *8902 Vinton St., www.georgiastreetcc.com, (313) 452-0684.*

Packard Motor Car Company - You have to see it to believe it— even then you might not trust your eyes. At 3.5 million square feet of abandoned steel and concrete extending over 40 acres of property, the Packard Plant is either an urban explorer's dream or a city planner's nightmare. Both have fretted over the fate of the Detroit's largest symbol of bygone prosperity. Completed in 1911 and designed by Albert Kahn, the state-of-the-art plant assembled luxury vehicles until the Packard Motor Company merged with Studebaker and halted production in 1958. There have been several demolition attempts, but because of the intimidating cost and scale of the endeavor, none has come to fruition. Artists, some internationally renowned, have used the plant as their ephemeral canvas, most notably Banksy's "I Remember When All This Was Trees" and Scott Hocking's "Garden of the Gods." In 2017, new owner Fernando Palazuelo kicked off a 15-year, $300 million renovation effort, beginning with the revitalization of the original administration building and opening the site to official tours. A brewery is expected, along with other mixed-use development to follow. Tours are offered on Saturdays and Sundays, and must be booked on the website in advance. *1540 E. Grand Blvd., www.packardplantproject.com.*

Power House Productions - Acclaimed local artists and husband-and-wife-team Mitch Cope and Gina Reichart founded their expansive Power House project 2008. The endeavor, which now encompasses several blocks, began with the **Power House**—an abandoned home they bought for a widely reported song, and used to investigate off-grid power and public art with neighborhood participation. The Power House is run on solar and wind power, and Cope and Reichert hope to turn the system into a replicable model. Since the house's launch, and vast media exposure, the project has grown and expanded into a constellation of other homes and sites in the neighborhood as they've taken on new projects, helped others buy homes, and worked with their neighbors and dozens of local and international artists. Now a nonprofit called Power House Productions, the organization utilizes the space and neighborhood as a laboratory for methods, explorations, off-grid energy solutions, public art initiatives, and as a center for fostering community and collaboration. While the Power House is located at 12650 Moran Street, the surrounding neighborhood is dotted with eye-catching public art, as well as other substantial connected projects. **The Squash House** is a formerly abandoned house turned sculptural indoor sports facility and greenhouse located at 13133 Klinger Street. **The Sound House** is an experimental sound studio at 13181 Moran Street. A popular, collaborative skate park, **The Ride It Sculpture Park** is located at the corner of East Davison Street and Klinger Street, and is almost always active. *www.powerhouseproductions.org, (313) 576-6941.*

St. Albertus Church - Though it closed and was desanctified in 1990, St. Albertus has been painstakingly maintained and remains one of the city's most historic and most visually striking religious monuments. Completed in 1885, it was the first church in the city to be constructed with steam heating and electric lighting, and it is the oldest standing Polish church building in the city. Though stately, the red brick exterior with its central oxidized copper steeple belies the stunning and opulent interior in which the sweeping turquoise vaulted ceiling soars 40 feet above the sanctuary. Illuminated by the rainbow of hues that emanate from the numerous narrative stained glass windows, the nave—with capacity for 2,500 parishioners—terminates at the stunning altar, which features intricate reliefs, sculptures, and painted details. While the parish is no longer active, the church is actively maintained by the Polish American Historic Site Association, which loosely operates the facility as a Polish heritage site and a center for Polish history and culture. In addition to monthly Roman Catholic masses, the association offers tours and hosts special events, including a fall Harvest Dinner. Call to make a reservation. *4231 St. Aubin St., www.stalbertusdetroit.org, (313) 831-9727.*

Sweetest Heart of Mary - Completed in 1893, this magnificent Gothic Revival church was once the nation's largest Polish Catholic church and among the area's most beautiful. Begun by a splinter congregation from the older St. Albertus Church (see separate entry), Sweetest Heart of Mary grew to be a largely Polish parish, peaking at 4,000 families. The red brick cruciform structure features a gabled roof, an elegant entranceway with oak bas-relief doors in arched doorways, twin buttressed 217-foot spires, and three bells named for Saints Mary, Joseph, and Barbara. The structure's most stunning architectural feature, however, may be the original, monumental stained glass windows lining the sanctuary. Depicting several saints, Jesus, and Mary with vivid colors, the windows won numerous awards at Chicago's famed Columbian Exposition World's Fair. The nave is perhaps more elegant than the facade. The exquisite sanctuary features groined vaulting clad in gold tapestry, marble pillars with intricate Corinthian capitals, religious murals, and an intricate red oak Vatican II altar. Visitors should attend mass, schedule a tour, or visit the annual pierogi festival to admire the interior. *4440 Russell St., www.sweetestheart.org, (313) 831-6659.*

Ulysses S. Grant Home - Following his service in the Mexican-American War—long before he was a dominant Union leader in the Civil War or elected president of the United States, Ulysses S. Grant was assigned to a post in Detroit and lived in this home. Though this Greek Revival house was originally located on Fort Street, just outside of Fort Wayne, it was bought by the Michigan Mutual Liability Company in the 1950s and moved to the State Fairgrounds to preserve its historical legacy. Naturally, it was during his time in Detroit that then-Lieutenant Grant developed the "taste for good times" that would eventually lead to him being decommissioned in 1854—until his career was redeemed by a desperate Lincoln. *Though the home is not currently open to the public, it is visible from State Fair St., just east of the foot of Ralston St.*

POINTS OF INTEREST

1943 Uprising Memorial - This somber monument memorializes a little-known chapter of the 1943 racial uprising in Detroit. Built in 1946, these stone benches and tablet recognize Dr. Joseph De Horatiis, who crossed police lines to aid victims, only to be claimed by the violence. The sculpture sits in the traffic island encircled by *E. Warren Ave., E. Grand Blvd., and Gratiot Ave.*

Bangladesh: Coming to America Mural - This enormous, bright mural, by New York's Marka27, celebrates the large and growing Bangladeshi-American community, the third-largest in the nation, in Hamtramck and throughout Metro Detroit. *3105 Carpenter Ave.*

Birdie Records - This abandoned storefront, just across the street from the blistering glow of "The Gold Mine," was once home to the 1980s label that produced a mix of soul, funk, and disco from artists such as Ronnie Hudson, Salvatore, and The Exportations. *6352 Gratiot Ave.*

Blessed Hands Hair and Nail Salon Sign - This salon has finally figured out a way to merge the Detroit skyline with Egyptian pyramids, disembodied hands, and an incredibly muscular pharaoh who is emerging from the Detroit River. *19111 Helen Ave.*

Burnside Farm - Artist Kate Daughdrill bought this home for $600 in 2011 and has transformed it, and the surrounding land, into an incredible hub for everything from dinner gatherings in the garden and musical performances to ceremonial rituals inspired by the diverse cultures of the neighborhood. *3333 Burnside St.*

C.C.C. Club - It was here in 2006 that rapper Proof, mentor to Eminem and member of the hip-hop group D12, was tragically shot and killed during a fight over a game of pool. *15304 E. 8 Mile Rd.*

Coleman A. Young International Airport - Though it no longer offers commercial flights, Coleman A. Young International Airport (formerly City Airport), FAA code DET, was the city's main airport until 1947. Today, it fields primarily private planes. *11499 Conner St.*

Farnsworth Neighborhood - This small, dynamic, collaborative, tight-knit, neighborhood is home to the **Farnsworth Community Garden**, **Rising Pheasant Farms**, and several other family farms and pocket gardens, as well as a couple of community arts organizations and endeavors such as **The Yes Farm**. *Farnsworth St. and Moran St.*

Faygo Factory - A favorite since 1907, Detroit's popular Faygo soda pop has been manufactured and headquartered here since 1935. *3579 Gratiot Ave.*

Federal Reserve Bank - The only branch office of the Federal Reserve Bank of Chicago was founded in Detroit in 1927, in their historic building at 160 West Fort Street. The office moved into this new, modern complex near Eastern Market in 2004. *1600 E. Warren Ave.*

GM Poletown Plant - Once home to the active Poletown community—and its 4,200 residents—the neighborhood was contentiously erased through eminent domain to make way for this plant in 1981. The protests, some of which turned violent, resulted in Supreme Court rulings that restricted municipal takings throughout the country. *Harper Ave. and Mt. Elliott St.*

John DeLorean Home - This cozy home on the northeast side of the city was where the man famous for designing the car immortalized in the *Back to the Future* films spent most of his childhood. *17199 Marx St.*

Laid in Detroit - Playing off the phrase "Made in Detroit," this small plot on the east side of the city is host to a fabulous duck farm and acts as a great resource for anyone looking for help raising poultry of all kinds. *4121 Neff Ave.*

Lakewood Sears Kit House - Built in 1922, this Craftsman-style Kilbourne model home from Sears, Roebuck, and Co. was sold for $2,554, including everything but the "cement, brick, and plaster." *3895 Lakewood St.*

Lost River Film Site - Scenes for Ryan Gosling's film *Lost River* were filmed on the premises of this vacant warehouse. *17472 Van Dyke Ave.*

Malcolm X Home - Born in Omaha, Nebraska, and spending much of his life on the road, Malcolm X spent some important time living here with Nation of Islam member Robert Davenport and his wife, Dorothy. *18827 Keystone St.*

Marshall Mathers Home Site - Hip-hop superstar Marshall Mathers (better known as Eminem) lived in the house that once occupied this lot as a teenager in the late 1980s and early 1990s. Though now demolished, the home was featured on the cover of his albums "The Marshall Mathers LP" and "The Marshall Mathers LP 2." *19946 Dresden Ave.*

Midland Steel Strike - In 1936, 1,200 day-shift steelworkers sat down and halted production for eight days at this location, performing the first sit-down strike in the city's history. *6660 Mt. Elliott St.*

Mohawk Rock & Rye Ghost Sign - This ancient advertisement for the once-popular beverage was uncovered when the adjacent structure was demolished, revealing this ghostly vintage mural. *15311 E. Warren Ave.*

Nurturing our Seeds Farm - Operating in nine formerly vacant lots on the city's east side, this farm's fantastic organic produce and medicinal herbs can regularly be found in Shed Two in Eastern Market. *7733 Helen St.*

Pingree Farms - This impressive urban farm and hoophouse complex spans several city blocks and is an example of farming and gardening as vacant-land reclamation. *Corner of Omira St. and E. Grixdale St.*

RecoveryPark Farm - This urban farm, operated by the RecoveryPark non-profit organization, aims to grow fresh produce for the best restaurants in southeast Michigan, by utilizing vacant land on the city's east side and employing people who traditionally have had a difficult time finding work. *5470 Chene St.*

Sippie Wallace Grave - Buried in Trinity Cemetery, Sippie Wallace was one of the great blues singers of her time—with a career stretching across much of the 20th century and featuring collaborations with Louis Armstrong, B.B. King, Johnny Dodds, and Clarence Williams. *5210 Mt. Elliott St.*

Sylhet Farms - Owned by the Detroit Hope Center, a nonprofit organization, this farm sits in the heart of Banglatown. Its name, in fact, comes from a region in Bangladesh from which many of the nearby residents have emigrated. *2930 Meade Ave.*

Theatre Bizarre - From 2000 to 2009, this was the site of an elaborate, unlicensed Halloween spectacle highlighted by enormous hand-built sets. Shut down by the city in 2010, the artists have moved the party to the Masonic Temple (see event listing), but the sets remain behind. *967 W. State Fair Rd.*

Tom Selleck Home - This east-side home was where the young actor gained his appreciation for the Detroit Tigers and, presumably, beautiful mustaches. *10530 Lakepointe St.*

CHAPTER 9
AVENUE OF
FASHION AREA

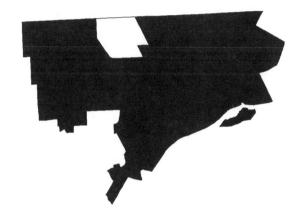

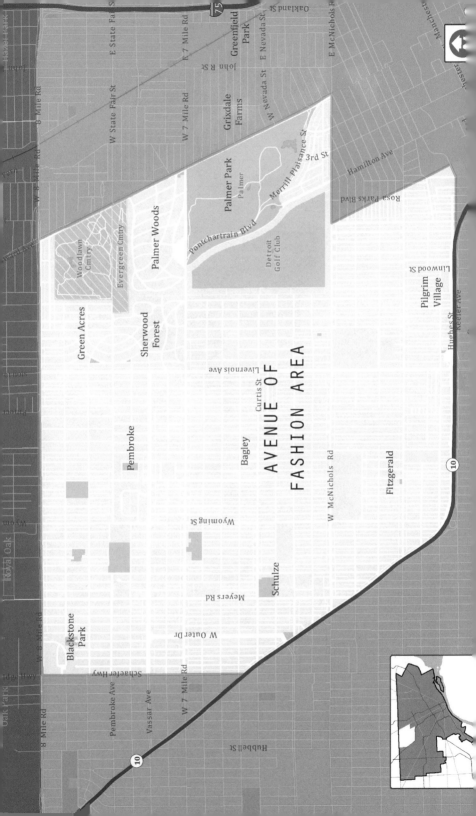

Unlike perhaps any other part of the city, Detroit's northern gateway offers a lens into its opulent past and contemporary revitalization. Annexed by the city between 1916 and 1925, the neighborhood began development as Detroit was reaching its industrial pinnacle and financial high-water mark, and has the architecture to prove it. Spanning 11 square miles, the area is home to nearly 60,000 people, and is a destination for breathtaking historic architecture, heavenly comfort food, and distinctive art and apparel retailers. This area, bounded by 8 Mile Road, the Lodge Freeway, the city of Highland Park, and Woodward Avenue—the region we call Avenue of Fashion Area—is a compact district, dense with attractions and a microcosm of the city, showcasing some of its greatest assets, opportunities, and challenges.

This constellation of historic neighborhoods is bisected by Livernois Avenue, a defining part of the area's identity and its primary commercial corridor. Running from McNichols Road to 8 Mile Road, this resurgent boulevard is a historic tree-lined thoroughfare, dotted with cafes, galleries, and apparel outfitters. In the 1950s, this two-mile stretch earned the moniker Avenue of Fashion as a luxury destination known for high-end attire and accessories retailers, showrooms, and wholesalers. As its fortunes waned in the 1960s, the corridor developed a new reputation as a destination for jazz music and a center of African-American life and culture. As these challenges continued into the 1970s, this area and the adjoining Palmer Park community became a regional hub for the LGBTQ community in the city. Today, these varied legacies remain, even as the corridor becomes more commercially diverse, with a growing roster of clothiers, boutiques, salons, restaurants, and professional services calling the area home.

The area east of Livernois—home to neighborhoods such as Green Acres, Sherwood Forest, Palmer Woods, Palmer Park, and the University District—offers the city's largest contiguous swath of still-opulent, intact, historic neighborhoods. These largely interwar homes often boast leaded glass windows, intricate masonry, and elaborate architectural flourishes. With the classical University of Detroit Mercy campus, the Detroit Golf Club, Woodlawn Cemetery, and the expansive Palmer Park as additional anchors, this area offers almost limitless opportunities for scenic walks that are especially picturesque with fall colors.

Still grand, though more modest by comparison, the resurgent western portion of the neighborhood represents a more paradigmatic cross section of the city. This area, home to the Bagley, Fitzgerald, Marygrove, Blackstone Park, Oak Grove, and Schulze neighborhoods, as well as the grand Marygrove College campus, offers a more varied physical form. Many blocks include a dense patchwork of interwar brick Tudors, Garrisons, and Dutch Revival homes on idyllic tree-lined streets, while other areas are known for postwar bungalows with a more suburban character. Some areas have fared quite well in the generations since their construction, while others have faced immense social, economic, and physical challenges as their populations became part of the Detroit diaspora. In the face of this transitional nature, many residents have beautified their communities with murals, gardens, and three-dimensional public art, making these neighborhoods an engaging destination to visit.

As the number of businesses on the Avenue of Fashion has grown, the geographic core of this chapter has become more walkable. The diverse shops, restaurants and adjoining architecturally lavish neighborhoods make for a varied, engaging place to visit on foot. Destinations west of Livernois are often dispersed geographically and best visited by car. Although many neighborhoods within this multifarious chapter are safe and vibrant, some areas may be unsafe late at night, and we recommend exercising a bit of caution and practicing the same safety rules you would when visiting similar areas of any urban center.

BARS & RESTAURANTS

Bucharest Grill Avenue of Fashion - The northern satellite of this justifiably wildly popular Romanian/Middle Eastern/American mashup restaurant, offering carryout and some high-top seating. See separate Bucharest Grill Rivertown entry for more details. *19492 Livernois Ave., www.bucharestgrill.com, (313) 965-3111.*

Caribbean Citchen - Famous in northwest Detroit for its tender curry goat, jerk chicken, oxtails, and alliteration, Caribbean Citchen serves excellent food in the Jamaican tradition. In addition to its tasty entrees, be sure to try some of the succulent sides. Be forewarned that you'll have plenty extra for lunch tomorrow! Carryout orders comprise a majority of its business, along with catering for any occasion, but should you find yourself in the mood for the Jamaican-themed ambiance, the Citchen offers a small dining area with courteous service. Friday features escovitch snapper or kingfish, but the place sells out fast enough to warrant calling ahead. *10500 W. McNichols Rd., (313) 345-3746.*

★ **Chef Greg's Soul "N" the Wall** - With his entrees of grilled meat, historic sandwiches, and soul food served with sides of down-to-earth wisdom, Chef Greg Beard fills both the belly and the soul. Thanks to a large mural of Chef Greg and the artist Allee Willis presiding over a dance party, this otherwise modest structure stands out. Inside, Beard has leveraged his role as Four Top Obie Benson's nephew to document many celebrity visits with glossies that adorn the walls of the unassuming two-table pumpkin-orange dining room. Behind the plexiglass, Chef Greg oversees a masterful soul food menu in the meat-and-three, or in this case two, style. Prepared beautifully, order-by-order, chicken wings, meatloaf, ribs, oxtails, and turkey chops, among others, appear alongside greens, mashed potatoes, black eyed peas, and other soul standards. The most unique item, however, may be the best. The Boogaloo Wonderland sandwich is a Detroit classic reborn, boasting a pile of lean pork mixed with a secret sauce, grilled onions, and cheese, spread on a loafer-sized loaf of french bread. Wars have been fought over lesser dishes. *10009 Curtis St., (313) 861-0331.*

Detroit Sip - It figures that a former upholstery shop would give rise to one of the city's most comfortable coffee shops. Owner Jevona Watson opened the shop in 2017 to give area neighbors a freshly-ground antidote to the daily grind on this once-vacant stretch of McNichols. The spacious shop has an easygoing, everyman atmosphere, and simple gallery aesthetic, with a mix of cafe tables and barcaloungers amid local art installations. A dedication to art is easily apparent, from the frequent performances, gallery displays, hand-painted inspirational quotes on tables, and elaborate drawings on the chalkboard menu. Between said drawings, the menu boasts an impressive roster of hot and iced coffee and espresso options, all made with beans from local favorites Germack and Ashe Supply Co. Detroit-made sweets from Dutch Girl Donuts, A-Team Cheesecakes, Brooklynn's Brownies with Love, and other treats are also on offer for when caffeine alone won't do it. *7420 W McNichols Rd., www.detroitsip.com, (313) 635-5130.*

Detroit Vintage - If you love coffee as much as you love books, you'll love Detroit Vintage. Packed with personality, this character-rich hideaway, which is two-thirds cafe, and one-third used book and antique store, is a calm refuge from the hubbub, high speeds, and vice-related trappings that have enveloped the rest of 8-Mile. Enter, and be greeted by warmth, friendliness, classical music, and wafting incense as you soak in the atmosphere. From the antique sleds, skis, skates, lamps, and flowing fabric suspended from the exposed joists, to the teetering displays of antique homegoods and used books, this loving wonderland is a feast for the eyes. Take in the surroundings and browse the hardgoods and books as you enjoy a selection from the full menu of teas, coffees, and espresso drinks, as well as decadent baked goods, including coffee cakes, and sweets. Look for knitting meetups on first and third Sundays, as well as occasional low-key music performances and readings. Open only on weekends. *10335 W. 8 Mile Rd., (313) 341-4810.*

Faustina's Creole & Soulfood - The son of former Detroit Mayor Coleman Young's personal chef, Chef Anthony Faustina has carried on a family tradition of fine cajun, creole, and deep-South cooking since opening in 2010. The interior is a modest, simple space punctuated by a handful of tables, several awards, and sweeping views of the open kitchen—which, like the Constitution, the Hope Diamond, and other national treasures, is wrapped in bulletproof glass, but still manages to exude an inviting, friendly, neighborly feel. Faustina's menu is a tour de force of Delta cooking. The jambalaya is striking, with bold, deep flavors from the aromatic roux and spices, piled high with shrimp, crawfish, and spicy beef sausage. The alligator bites and chicken wings are both battered delicately, and seasoned and salted in a way that highlights the flavor and texture of the meat. Other highlights on the menu include the fried okra, caramel cake, lobster mac and cheese, jerk chicken, and seafood gumbo, which should also not be missed. *16155 Wyoming Ave., www.faustinasdetroit.weebly.com, (313) 397-8010.*

Good Cakes and Bakes - With organic ingredients and a wide array of vegan options, this bakery is sure to satisfy that sweet tooth craving for everyone. Pastry chef and co-owner April Anderson is a master baker who creates some of the finest desserts and baked goods in the city. The bright colors and decor are welcoming, and feel like stepping into the board game Candyland. Between the cupcakes (the red velvet and chocolate salted caramel cupcakes are favorites), cookies, cheesecakes, banana pudding, and cake slices (try the tasty 7-Up pound cake), it can be difficult to choose just one treat. So, feel free to indulge. We won't judge. Coffee, breakfast pastries, and soups are also on the menu. *19363 Livernois Ave., www.goodcakesandbakes.com, (313) 468-9915*

Gregg's Pizza & Bar-B-Que - This distinctive hand-tossed pizza and barbecued chicken has been the talk of the neighborhood for more than a generation. Gregg's specializes in perfectly cooked thin crust pizza loaded with toppings—which includes the de rigueur options and more fresh and obscure options, like shrimp and Italian-style broccoli—which make for a healthier pie with flavors evocative of summertime. Although the diverse menu runs the gamut of the popular options, the chicken parmesan pizza, steak and cheese pizza, and supplí Italian rice balls stand out. The unassuming, Spartan interior is all business, with a small waiting area, from which customers can witness their carryout pies being spun in the air and wings dumped in the fryer. With meals that can feed a family for less than the cost of a movie ticket, this place offers an affordable option for hungry Detroiters. *17160 Livernois Ave., (313) 341-2400.*

★ **Kuzzo's Chicken & Waffles** - Prepare to stuff your bowel with fowl. Executive Chef Laditra Jackson has assembled a rare bird: a menu of contemporary provisions with a Southern slant, boasting impeccable options for breakfast, lunch, and dinner. The restaurant's bright red walls, exposed brick accents, polished concrete floors, canning jar pendant lamps, and work by local artists give the space a distinctly handsome atmosphere. The signature dish, chicken and waffles, is the definition of perfection: the juicy, tender chicken is fried to a delightful golden-brown with a crunchy crust, while the waffles draw a superb balance of light, airy, and crispy. We recommend starting with the namesake dish, but the shrimp po boy, Kuzzo's Kobb salad, red velvet cake, and fried green tomatoes also won't disappoint. Expect to be treated like family by the affable staff—kuzzo is a slang term of endearment for friends, after all. *19345 Livernois Ave., www.kuzzoschickenandwaffles.com, (313) 861-0229.*

Locker Room Lounge - Welcome to the Locker Room, your new favorite neighborhood dive. Meet Phyllis, the convivial, attentive hostess behind the bar for more than thirty years. She'll treat you like family, even if you're unfamiliar. Opened as a sports bar in 1985, this watering hole ditched the TVs long ago, and evolved into a music-oriented gathering place where the only thing louder than the classic R&B jams is the friendly conversation between patrons. The bar's welcoming regulars range from landscapers to lawyers, as well as soul legends like Bettye LaVette and members of the Spinners. The interior is well used, but lovingly maintained, with a sinuous bar, a bold red and black color scheme, and a patron-level "stage" that comes alive every Sunday night for a weekly jam session where Dennis Coffey and other Motown greats are rumored to join the fray occasionally. *18290 Livernois Ave., (313) 864-1220.*

Lou's Deli - Corned beef connoisseurs will meet their match at Lou's Deli, a carryout sandwich shop that boasts more than 10 "good-for-the-beli" creations centered around that salty-sweet deli meat. Beefheads might find it hard to look at corned beef again after tackling the intimidating Big Louie—a full pound of juicy corned beef nestled on an onion roll. For customers who aren't looking to break the bank or bust any buttons on their pants, Lou's Deli also serves up more than 20 sandwiches and subs with heart-healthy deli meats, salads, and fried sides. Expect four-inch tall sandwiches no matter the meat, so plan on sitting and enjoying these hot specials. *8220 W. McNichols Rd., www.lousdeli.net, (313) 861-1321.*

Louisiana Creole Gumbo North - The newer and bigger, but less character-filled, northwest Detroit outpost of this popular and delicious cajun joint. See separate Louisiana Creole Gumbo entry for more details. *13505 W. Seven Mile Rd., www.detroitgumbo.com, (313) 397-4052.*

Menjo's Complex - In the 1970s, beautiful art deco architecture, friendly building management, and open-minded residents drew gay Detroiters to the Palmer Park neighborhood, which was once known as "Michigan's gayest square mile." The area contained multiple gay bars, two bookstores, and a restaurant—and although many of the businesses are gone, the scene is still thriving. One of the iconic original clubs, Menjo's, also remains, and it plays bangers—disco, hip-hop, and top 40—until the wee hours in a space that feels at once contemporary and classic. It's a place to discover new music, a new flirtation, a new love—and a place to discover yourself. Adjacent space **Olympus Theater** serves as an even larger venue for bands and special events. Committed to preserving LGBTQ history, a mini museum inside Menjo's pays homage to bygone Detroit's gay bars like Diamond Jim's Saloon—a gay Western club that featured line dancing. The museum also contains Menjo's first disco ball, from 1976, beneath which Madonna is rumored to have grooved. Allies and friends are welcome at Menjo's, and should be sure to stop by for the monthly Macho City, Detroit's best glittery disco dance party, as well as the complex's sex-positive shop. *928/950 W. McNichols Rd., www.newmenjoscomplex.com, (313) 863-3934.*

Motor City Soul Food - Behind the simple yellow awning lies this carryout restaurant, a favorite of the Travel Channel's Bizarre Foods America. Motor City Soul Food serves up a genuine soul food buffet, featuring classic candied yams and ham hocks, perch, and meatloaf sandwiches. Hot, fresh, and ready to go, each dish is refreshed quickly as lines of loyal customers push politely through the buffet line and point through the plate glass at each item ready for their carryout boxes. *12700 W. 7 Mile Rd., (313) 863-7685.*

Mr. & Mrs. Benson Bakery - The tagline on the door says it all: "Home of the Sweets, Treats, and Eats." With its whimsical, multicolor displays of candies, cupcakes, and ice cream, and peach and lavender walls, the bright, airy interior of this dessert bakery and ice cream shop is at once contemporary and nostalgic. The deserving focal point of the room is the colorful cupcake display. The large bakery case is overflowing with sumptuous caramel, Oreo, red velvet, strawberry, and chocolate cupcakes, delicately covered with indulgent frosting, as well as cookies, candies, and fresh fruit. Farther down, the Ashby's Sterling Ice Cream cooler offers decadent flavors like Nana's Banana Puddin', O-o-oreo, and Superman by the scoop. Custom cakes and numerous local and imported candies available. *19126 Livernois Ave., (313) 307-8877.*

Narrow Way Cafe - Skip the carryout: Lingering limits the risk that caffeine-deficiency induced obliviousness costs you the opportunity of appreciating the beauty of the striking, beautifully-designed space. The coffee shop's sleek interior, with its tufted leather seating, stark tile walls, contemporary pendant lighting and embellishments, is at once bright and inviting, lively and mellow. The most pleasant part of the cafe, though, is in the cup. Michigan-based Zingerman's Coffee, with its signature refined, aromatic flavors, roasts the beans behind Narrow Way's coffee and espresso-based offerings. In the bakery case, look for an extensive array of heavenly, locally sourced options, including bagels, samosas, croissants, banana bread, and bostock. The spinach brioche, with an airiness that teeters on buoyancy, should not be missed. At select times, the cafe offers a fuller menu of inventive salads and sandwiches, such as soba noodle salads, and butternut squash vegetarian sandwiches. Fast and free Wi-Fi, and printer available. *19331 Livernois Ave., www.thenarrowwaycafe.com, (313) 397-7727.*

Noni's Sherwood Grille - The large, devoted brunch and lunch crowds are on to something. With its perimeter of cozy booths, fashionable pendant lights, African paintings, and massive windows, the clean, comfortable, and contemporary interior reflects the menu. This modern family restaurant plays a strong American diner/deli fare game, offering an extensive menu of breakfast, soup, salad, and sandwich classics alongside a curated stable of Italian, Greek, breakfast, barbeque, and Mexican options. The Greek omelette, steak fajita, Reuben, Philly steak pita, and fried smelt are popular options, though the exceptionally fresh Caesar salad and big man breakfast— three eggs, ham, bacon, sausage, toast, and hashbrowns—are the highlights. Among smart, sit-down options, Noni's stands out for being open 24 hours and serving breakfast all day. Carry-out available. *19700 Livernois Ave., www.nonissherwood.com, (313) 342-6000.*

Pasta Bowl - If the smell of cheesy pasta doesn't draw you inside, the bright, modern lobby of this Italian soul pasta paragon will. The inside has a modern, open feel uncommon among Detroit takeout joints, thanks in part to sweeping windows, chalkboard menus, fire engine red walls, and open kitchen views. Owner Museya Glenn's menu puts a comfort food spin on an inspired variety of dishes, including traditional pasta options such as bolognese, cajun crab, drunken noodles, chicken alfredo, and shrimp scampi, alongside more imaginative options, such as pizza lasagna, marsala stroganoff, and bacon cheeseburger mac and cheese. Thanks to lead-handed portions of butter and cheese, most dishes are decadently rich and enticing, though the Valaise Amare—marinated grilled shrimp with spinach alfredo sauce atop angel hair—is a highlight. Save room for the outstanding Superman cheesecake. *17301 W. McNichols Rd., www.thepastabowldetroit.com, 313-272-BOWL.*

Uptown BBQ - Follow the bright blue arrow dotted with light bulbs to Uptown BBQ, a carryout haven for fans of Detroit's own surf and turf: the rib and shrimp dinner. The most notable feature of this simple, unassuming building might be the wonderful aromatic siren's song of fresh barbecue that hangs in the air inside and out. The welcoming staff—perhaps the city's friendliest service behind bulletproof glass—are famous for making some of the city's most tantalizing ribs, with delicate seasoning, tender texture, and smoky flavor. Thanks to its renowned barbecue sauce—with a perfect balance of sweet, salty, and smoky flavor—most of the entrees are solid, including the catfish, turkey wings, perch, chickens, pork chops, and beef ribs. On the long list of sides, the collard greens, candied yams, and mac and cheese are the tastiest triumvirate. *15700 Livernois Ave., www.uptownbbq.zoomshare.com, (313) 861-7590.*

SHOPPING & SERVICES

Art In Motion - Open since 2013, owner Kay Willingham's striking ceramic studio is a bright and airy destination for unique, handmade pottery. Drawing on her training at Pewabic Pottery (see separate entry), Willingham curates an impressive gallery of handmade ceramics, jewelry, textiles, and artwork by local artists. Art in Motion also offers private studios, ceramics workshops, and independent classes in the extensive on-site ceramic studio. Sharing the retail space is **Love Travel Imports**, owner Yvette Jenkins' thoughtful boutique for natural-material apparel and decor from around the globe. Jenkins curates a selection of fair trade goods from Africa, Asia, South America, and the Caribbean, with imported commercial pieces alongside handmade work made of materials like Ghanaian reeds, Guatemalan wool, or Nepalese felt. The colorful caftans, dervish jackets, handbags, decorative fans, and baskets make it hard to leave empty handed. *19452 Livernois Ave. Art in Motion: www.artinmotiondet.com, (313) 980-1265; Love Travels Imports: www.lovetravelsimports.com, (313) 623-5800.*

Avenue of Fashion Clothiers - Located on Livernois Avenue, between Seven and Eight Mile Roads, the aptly named Avenue of Fashion is a beloved and historically significant regional shopping destination that acquired the nickname during its 1950s heyday. Though the area has seen some ups and downs, it is re-emerging today as a destination for stylish Detroiters, creative designers, and the next generation of independent fashion in Detroit. Amidst a slew of other commercial amenities, the Avenue of Fashion again offers a concentration of old-school and new-school apparel retailers, comprised of both mainstays and new arrivals. While there are others, some highlights include:

- **Blo Basics Clothing Boutique** - An offshoot of the local Blo Beauty Lounge, this trendy store offers streamlined dresses, tops, bodysuits, jumpsuits, and of one-of-a-kind looks for one-of-a-kind women. *19450 Livernois Ave., www.shopblobasics.com, (313) 307-7216.*

- **C.Grantston Bullard Design Studio** - The eponymous showroom for C. Grantston Bullard's imagination—and original designs—this sleek, contemporary shop specializes in exotic furs, finely crafted leather goods, jewelled eyewear, and designer quality dresses for the luxury minded. *19132 Livernois Ave., www.grantston.com, (313) 367-2057.*

- **DCreated Boutique** - See separate entry.

- **Flagship Boutique** - Calling all sneakerheads: This boutique offers coordinated casual wear with serious style, including T-shirts, hoodies, and track sets from District 81 Clothing. *19456 Livernois Ave., (313) 397-3029.*

- **Prisca's African Fashion For Less** - Prisca's is the local leader in traditional African clothing, including sarong sets, colorful dresses, and accessories. *19110 Livernois Ave., 313-341-2695.*

- **The Shoe Box** - A men's shoe store offering stylish dress shoes, wingtips, loafers and boots, in classic styles for the modern man. *19186 Livernois Ave., 313-855-6028.*

- **Simply Casual** - See separate entry.

- **Teaser's Boutique** - As the name suggests, this shop features barely there, racy fashions for the truly adventurous woman. *19355 Livernois Ave., (313) 341-3131.*

- **Times Square Men's Custom Clothing** - This timeless custom suit shop for men and boys offers onsite tailoring, accessories, and more. *19330 Livernois Avenue., (313) 342-9005.*

Bosco Fish Market - Bad day fishing? Head to Bosco. Open since 1951, this longtime seafood market offers a host of fresh fish and shellfish that are delivered daily. The impressive inventory includes standards like perch, catfish, orange roughy, cod, tilapia, salmon, red snapper, lake trout, shrimp, crab, and oysters, alongside less-common options like whiting, blue gill, smelt, and croaker. For the more successful anglers, Bosco also offers fish cleaning for your daily haul. Aside from fresh seafood, Bosco also offers a you-buy-we-fry service and a limited menu of yummy carryout options like hush puppies, onion rings, and chicken nuggets. The vintage signage, friendly service, and convenient location make it a pleasure to visit. *16227 Livernois Ave., www.boscofishandseafood.com, (313) 863-8675.*

DCreated Boutique - The fashionable destination for kids on the Avenue of Fashion, DCreated offers hand-sewn organic baby clothing handcrafted in Detroit. From floral linen rompers, to coordinating vests, to patterned bell bottoms and bloomers, owner Brianna Williams creates most of the shop's vintage-inspired inventory in the studio tucked in the back of the shop. The bright and compact storefront displays her wares on simple, charming displays, including clothes racks made from tree branches. In addition to their house-made designs, the selection is supplemented with complementary handmade goods from other makers. While unisex and boys' clothing as well as a larger range of sizes are often available, darling outfits for little girls from babies to toddlers take the center stage here. Don't see what you're looking for on their racks? Brianna can create custom pieces for your child starting at around $60 in six to eight weeks. *19480 Livernois Ave., www.dcreatedboutique.com, (313) 246-1800.*

Detroit Fiber Works - Open since 2013, Detroit Fiber Works was one of the first art galleries to open on the Avenue of Fashion as part of the modern resurgence in the area, helping to establish a growing collection of art spaces along Livernois. Established by two artists, Mandisa Smith and Leslie "Najma" Wilson, the gallery features a rotating selection of artwork, and also acts as a boutique and learning space, offering workshops for all ages, with a focus on fiber art techniques, such as eco-dyeing (dyeing using natural, organic materials), felting, and fabric painting. The boutique features locally handmade art and goods including jewelry, body butter, and gorgeous one-of-a-kind clothing, such as scarves and dresses. If you see a yarn bomb around the neighborhood, it likely originated here. Don't miss Detroit Fiber Works' colorful permanent installation on the green space in the traffic median in front of the gallery. Every second Saturday of the month, the gallery hosts an event, such as an artist talk or opening. *19359 Livernois Ave., www.detroitfiberworks.com, (313) 610-5111.*

Detroit Store Fixture Company - A mecca for those looking to hang their shingle since 1898, the Detroit Store Fixture Company offers a cornucopia of cornucopias, baskets, mannequins, display cases, slatwall panels, bins, racks, shelving, signage, and other store fixtures and supplies. The store's simple yet well-merchandised interior demonstrates the company's expertise in store displays and design. The vast inventory is spread across two showrooms and includes both new and used fixtures, assuring customers of finding just the right left-hand mannequin at a price within their budget. *7545 W. 8 Mile Rd., www.detroitstorefixture.com, (313) 341-3255.*

Jo's Gallery - Started by the late Jo Griffin, an avid art collector who was a fixture in the Detroit arts scene, Jo's Gallery is one of the oldest family-owned businesses on the Avenue of Fashion. Daughter Garnette Archer continues her mother's work of presenting artwork by African-American artists from Detroit and beyond. Styles range from traditional to contemporary, with works available as prints, lithographs, limited editions, and originals. Highlighted artists include LaShun Beal, Judy Bowman, Adwoa Muwzea, and William Tolliver. The shop also features a selection of locally made jewelry and gifts, as well as artifacts and objects from Africa, including one-of-a-kind furniture pieces and stunning, intricate masks. As an added bonus, the gallery also offers custom framing. If Jo's is a gallery and shop with framing, nearby **Eric's I've Been Framed** is a frame specialist with a gallery, and is another lovely option in the area if you're in the market for framing or decor. Eric's offers a vast library of more than 3,000 frames and custom mats to choose from, in addition to a more focused selection of art prints. *Jo's Gallery: 19376 Livernois Ave., (313) 864-1401; Eric's I've Been Framed: 16527 Livernois Ave., www.ericsivebeenframed.com, (313) 861-9263.*

Kingpin Airbrushing Academy - Home to Kingpin Kustomz, Liquidman Bodyart, and Cori "Tha Guru King" Tattoo, this studio is most famed for its virtuosic airbrushing, for which it caters to customers across the nation, from Beyonce to Drake. Buzz at the door, and resident artist Felle will usher you into his showroom, which is dominated by a hyper-realistic airbrushed ocean scene that stretches from floor to ceiling. In the showroom, they offer a wide selection of pre-painted masterworks, from tromp l'oeil motorcycle helmets to decked-out kicks. Additionally, Kingpin artists will customize anything, from T-shirts to SUVs to concert backdrops. Don't be afraid to inquire about Celebies—dolls realistically custom painted to resemble celebrities, complete with embedded MP3 speech and song. *20094 Livernois Ave., (313) 415-6308.*

People's North - A smaller, satellite location of the legendary destination for soul and funk records. See People's Records (separate entry) more details. *20140 Livernois Ave., www.peoplesdetroit.com (313) 831-0864.*

Professional Racquet Services - Since 1984, Professional Racquet Services has kept Detroit's squash, tennis, badminton, and racquetball players serving in style. Here you'll find every piece of equipment you'll need, from racquets to Rec Specs. Step back 30 years in time into the neighboring discount showroom to browse through dead stock tennis attire: a rainbow of tennis skirts, Wilson polos, and multicolored windbreakers. Looking for a place to play? Just ask the friendly and quirky owner, who hand-strings racquets behind the sales counter—he knows every court within city limits. *19444 Livernois Ave., www.prsracquets.com, (313) 863-1880.*

Simply Casual - Since 1997, Simply Casual has been a destination on the historic Avenue of Fashion. Despite its name, shopping here is far from a casual experience and the store keeps its customers well-dressed in a range of urban to dressy to business-casual styles. Shop for everything from basic, everyday clothing to high-end designer goods in its clean, contemporary setting featuring a former dry cleaners' conveyor that allows a two-level display of up to 1,800 garments, or sit in the red velvet chairs and play a game of chess while you wait for a friend in the fitting room. Designer selections range from Betsey Johnson to Seven for All Mankind to Sean Jean, but generous sale prices and attentive salespeople make it easy for anyone to find the perfect outfit. *19400 Livernois Ave., www.simplycasual.org, (313) 864-7979.*

CULTURAL ATTRACTIONS

Ant T Bettie OK Puppets Museum - If Sesame Street comes with a take-away point—besides the "letter of the day"—it's that children love to learn from puppets. Although she wasn't inspired by Elmo but by her own interest in arts and crafts, retired Detroit Public Schools teacher Ms. Bettie created her own papier-mâché puppets as teaching aids. Throughout her career, Ms. Bettie brought elementary school lessons to life using her depictions of Native American leaders, larger-than-life models of ants, and hand puppets. Today, she decorates her home as a gallery and museum with collections of local artists and her own paintings. Portraits of Bettie's mother and influential civil rights leaders, Matisse-esque still-life paintings, and miniature dolls and puppets hang on display in her living and dining rooms. However, Ms. Bettie keeps her prized puppet collection in her basement, perched atop the felt black curtains of her homemade puppet theater. Ms. Bettie still dreams of owning a gallery space in Northwest, but for now she requests that visitors please call ahead to schedule a visit to her home art collection. *(313) 861-7426.*

ENTERTAINMENT & RECREATION

★ **Baker's Keyboard Lounge -** What started in 1933 as a small sandwich shop in the middle of farmland has turned into one of the most iconic and revered jazz venues in the country. The world's oldest continuously running jazz club, Baker's intimate stage has been graced by the likes of John Coltrane, Sarah Vaughan, Nat "King" Cole, Dave Brubeck, Cab Calloway, Miles Davis, and Ella Fitzgerald. Its intimate Art Deco interior features a distinctive curved, piano-shaped bar painted with a keyboard motif and tilted mirrors installed so the audience can watch the pianist's hands playing the gorgeous Steinway piano, which was handpicked by Art Tatum in the 1950s. Steaming crisp fried chicken, creamy mac and cheese, and the city's best collard greens come rolling out of the kitchen to the dim and cozy dining room that is centered around the stage. Enjoy a stiff drink, snuggle up in a booth, and experience one of the greatest cultural assets Detroit has to offer. *20510 Livernois Ave., www.theofficialbakerskeyboardlounge.com, (313) 345-6300.*

Detroit Golf Club - Tucked between historic Palmer Woods, the University of Detroit, and the stately University District homes on Fairway Drive is this prestigious, private club. Established in 1899, the club is home to two verdant 18-hole courses—the par-72 North Course and the par-68 South Course—designed by famed course designer Donald Ross. Measured from the black tees, the North Course spans 6,837 yards and is a formidable challenge for players of any golf handicap. The tall trees, narrow fairways, and plentiful sand traps force golfers to play with the entire bag. The South Course, in contrast, is a short 5,967 yards, and favors those with local knowledge. Defined by its tight landing areas, steep ridges, and poor sightlines, this course—and especially the sixth hole—is built for golfers with long irons. Hang out on the green or at the 19th hole long enough and you're sure to spot famous Detroit movers and shakers or sports stars, such as the mayor of Detroit (who always has a complimentary membership), former Tigers manager Jim Leyland, or retired NFL halfback Jerome Bettis. The impressive Albert Kahn-designed clubhouse was added to the club in 1916. The club is available for weddings and other elegant functions. *17911 Hamilton Rd., www.detroitgolfclub.org, (313) 345-4400.*

Palmer Park - Located along Woodward between McNichols Road and 7 Mile Road, Palmer Park is a verdant, beautiful, green city gem. The sprawling park, designed by Frederick Law Olmsted and Charles Eliot at the turn of the 19th century, spans 296 acres of lush lawns, woodlands, recreational amenities, and a lake. The park's many trees make it beautiful year-round, punctuated with lush gardens, changing fall colors, and serene snowfall. The park is home to more than 13 miles of hiking and biking trails, the Detroit Mounted Police station, a scenic lake, 16 tennis courts, an 18-hole golf course, a historic log cabin, and numerous picnic pavilions and playscapes. The log cabin was built in 1885 for the park's namesake, Senator Thomas W. Palmer and his wife, Mary, and remains as a charming reminder of the city's history and earliest architecture. In recent years, a local community group called the People for Palmer Park has begun implementing physical improvements to the park—such as a new 800-tree apple orchard and restored handball courts—and hosting fun community events such as bike rides, fund-raisers, free yoga classes, and tennis leagues. *910 Merrill Plaisance St., www.peopleforpalmerpark.org, (313) 757-2751.*

University of Detroit Mercy Titans Men's Basketball at Calihan Hall - Though more of a potential March Madness Cinderella than a perennial powerhouse, that doesn't stop the UDM Titans from putting on a great show at home. Since the arena known as Calihan was opened in 1952, the squad has won more than 70% of its home games and held the current best home winning streak of 39 games from 2001–2002. Notable team alumni include Dave DeBusschere, Bad Boy John Long, and iconic former coach and broadcaster Dick Vitale, for whom the court was named in 2011. Calihan Hall is a great intimate venue for college basketball. The gymnasium holds 8,300, and the steep, tight seating arrangement ensures good sightlines and an energetic crowd. *4001 W. McNichols Rd., www.detroittitans.com, (313) 973-1305.*

SITES

The Birwood Wall - Detroit's Berlin Wall, the Birwood Wall, is a relic and symbol of the city's historic and ongoing racial strife and segregation. At the time of the wall's construction in 1940, the neighborhood to the west, Blackstone Park, was predominantly African-American and consequently a victim of federal mortgage redlining. To circumvent federal restrictions, the developer of the nascent all-white middle-class neighborhood to the east, Eight Mile Wyoming, constructed this six-foot-tall concrete slab wall, that spans more than a half mile, to enable potential purchasers to get mortgages and to protect housing values. Today, the wall has been reimagined as an artistic canvas popular among area muralists and graffiti artists. *The Birwood Wall is located between Mendota Street and Birwood Street, running south from 8 Mile Rd.*

Dorothy S. Turkel House - Though he was born in 1867, Chicago native Frank Lloyd Wright is known as arguably the most important and innovative architect of the 20th century. While Wright—who is famous for his prefabricated concrete designs, flat roofs, use of natural light, and integration with nature—designed 30 buildings in Michigan, the Turkel House is the only structure the pioneering architect designed in Detroit. Dorothy S. Turkel commissioned the home in 1955 after she read Wright's book *The Natural House*. The L-shaped, 4,300-square-foot home, which cost $525,000 in today's dollars, is designed in the architect's Usonian Automatic style, which entailed precast reinforced concrete blocks designed to expedite and streamline construction. Though the home is intriguing from the street, with its immaculately manicured gardens, 400 windows, two-story all-glass living room, and a second-story terrace with a bank of custom doors, it is most breathtaking from the inside, as it has recently been lovingly restored and features original built-in hardwood furniture and hundreds of intricate interior pre-cast concrete details. The home is privately owned and occupied, so please be respectful and only admire it from afar. *2760 W. 7 Mile Rd.*

Palmer Woods - One of the premier historic neighborhoods in Detroit, Palmer Woods' 188 acres were originally part of a donation by Thomas Palmer, Detroit land developer, Michigan senator, and ambassador to Spain. The neighborhood was designed by renowned landscape architect and William Le Baron Jenney disciple Ossian Cole Simonds, who implemented the area's trapezoidal property lines to force architects to create distinctive designs, as each parcel had a one-of-a-kind shape. The area is known for its beautiful, winding elm-lined streets, manicured lawns, and recessed large brick and stone houses in a variety of classical architectural styles. The neighborhood's 298 homes showcase a range of designs, featuring examples of the Colonial Revival, Tudor Revival, Arts and Crafts, Neo-Georgian, Mediterranean, and Modern architectural styles. Although some homes were built later, the neighborhood was largely built between 1917 and 1929, by renowned architects such as Albert Kahn, C. Howard Crane, Maginnis & Walsh, and Richard H. Marr, with later additions by Minoru Yamasaki and Frank Lloyd Wright. The neighborhood offers a scenic and charming destination for a bike ride or walk. Though Palmer Woods offers the grandest homes in northern Detroit, those looking to admire historic homes nearby are encouraged to explore **Sherwood Forest** to the west and **University District**, **Green Acres**, and **Palmer Park** to the south. Palmer Woods is bounded by Strathcona Dr. to the north, Woodward Ave. to the east, W. Seven Mile Rd. to the south, and Strathcona Dr. to the west. Although nearly all of the homes in Palmer Woods are architectural treasures, highlights include:

- **Bishop Gallagher Residence:** Detroit's largest home, at 40,000 square feet. *1880 Wellesley Dr.*

- Two (of the seven) Fisher brother mansions, of automotive fame:

  - **Alfred Fisher Mansion:** *1771 Balmoral Dr.*

- **William Fisher Mansion:** The city's second largest home, at 35,000 square feet. *1791 Wellesley Dr.*
- **Dorothy S. Turkel House:** Frank Lloyd Wright design. See separate entry. *2760 W. 7 Mile Rd.*
- **Brooks Barron Home:** An understated home by Minoru Yamasaki. *19631 Argyle Crescent.*

Marygrove College and University of Detroit Mercy Campus Architecture - Two historic urban educational institutions, Marygrove College and the University of Detroit Mercy are an oasis of architectural integrity and pastoral beauty in a sea of neighborhoods and busy boulevards. Originally established in 1905 as a Catholic women's college in Monroe, Michigan, **Marygrove College** moved its campus to the once rural and heavily forested area of McNichols and Wyoming in 1927. Oscar D. Bohlen was selected as the architect to design the Liberal Arts Building and the adjoining Madame Cadillac Hall, which to this day remain the focal points of the campus. Designed in the Tudor Gothic style, the Bedford stone buildings bring a classic collegiate appearance to the grounds. The campus is flanked by a gorgeous Indiana Oolitic limestone gate that sets the campus' aesthetic tone for visitors. Due east of the school lies the **University of Detroit Mercy**, which has roots dating back to 1877. A private Catholic university in the Jesuit and Mercy traditions, the school is the largest Roman Catholic university in Michigan. Though less consistently architecturally splendid than its sister to the west, UDM's sprawling, lush campus has many highlights. The campus is anchored by the World War I Memorial Tower, which is a functioning clock tower that was built in 1926 and still regulates the school day. The campus is also dotted by an impressive array of early 20th-century Spanish Baroque architecture, demonstrated in the School of Architecture Building, Chemistry Building, and Lansing-Reilly Hall. Though both campuses are guarded and private, they are accommodating to respectful visitors and photographers—and maybe picnickers. *Marygrove College is located at 8425 McNichols Rd., UDM is located at 4001 W. McNichols Rd.*

Woodlawn Cemetery - Established in 1895, Woodlawn was once a place where barons of industry were laid to rest in temple-like mausoleums far away from the city. It has since been surrounded by the city and has become the cemetery of choice for Motown greats (Stevie Wonder and Diana Ross, long may they live, have both reserved Woodlawn plots). Wooded with giant pine and oak trees, Woodlawn is best explored on foot or by bicycle, and it's exceptionally pretty in the fall. Its collection of family mausoleums is one of the largest in the country and gives the cemetery the character of a small, silent city. *19975 Woodward Ave., www.woodlawncemeterydetroit.com, (313) 368-0010.*

Notable burials:

- **Alex Manoogian (1901–1996)**: Armenian-American entrepreneur, founder of the Masco Corporation, and donor of the Manoogian Mansion, now Detroit's mayoral residence.

- **Aretha Franklin (1942–2018)**: Detroit's Queen of Soul. With hits like "Respect," "Think," and "(You Make Me Feel Like) A Natural Woman," she lives on as a giant of American music and culture. *Main Mausoleum.*

- **David Ruffin (1941–1991)**: Lead singer of the Temptations. *Section 3, Lot 243.*

- **Edsel B. Ford (1893–1943)**: Son of Henry Ford and president of Ford Motor Company from 1919 until his death. *Section 10.*

- **Hazen S. Pingree (1840–1901)**: Mayor of Detroit, governor of Michigan, and "idol of the people."

- **James Couzens (1872–1936)**: Vice president and general manager of Ford Motor Company, U.S. senator, and mayor of Detroit.

- **James Jamerson (1939–1983)**: Bassist for Motown studio band the Funk Brothers. *Section 37, Lot 265.*

- **J.L. Hudson (1846–1912)**: Founder of Hudson's department store. *Section 10.*

- **John (1864–1920)** and **Horace (1868–1920) Dodge**: Founders of Dodge Bros. Motor Company. Their Sphinx-guarded mausoleum is one of Woodlawn's most famous. *Section 10, Lot 5.*

- **Levi Stubbs (1936–2008)**: Lead singer of the Four Tops. *Section 3, Lot 325 (directly behind the office).*

- **Michael Jackson (1958–2009)**: Not actually buried at Woodlawn, but you can visit a memorial to him, where gifts that were left at the Motown Museum after his death were symbolically buried.

- **Rosa Parks (1913–2005)**: Activist and "first lady" of civil rights, buried in the Rosa Parks Freedom Chapel.

POINTS OF INTEREST

Charles Mcgee Sculpture - This 24-foot-tall sculpture, which features a vibrant blue steel base and striking figures in white, was designed by renowned local artist Charles McGee. *Wyoming Rd. and McNichols Ave.*

David Ruffin Home - This historic University District house belonged to Temptations singer David Ruffin from 1970-1982, when he lost the property to foreclosure while in prison for tax evasion. *17385 Parkside St.*

Eddie Kendricks Home - Temptations singer and solo star Eddie Kendricks bought this two-story yellow brick home in the summer of 1966, just as "Ain't Too Proud to Beg" ascended the charts. *16531 Baylis St.*

First Concrete Mile - In 1909, this mile-long stretch of Woodward Avenue between McNichols Road and 7 Mile Road acted as a test case for the durability of concrete as a road surface. The success of the project changed the way roads were built around the world. *17763 Woodward Ave.*

Francis Ford Coppola Home - Although he spent most of his childhood growing up in Queens, New York, this was the birthplace of the famed director. *17540 Kentucky St.*

George C. Scott Home - This lovely brick home in Palmer Woods was the childhood residence of the actor most famous for his leading role in *Patton*. *18981 Pennington Dr.*

Gilda Radner Home - The famous comedian, a member of the original *Saturday Night Live* cast, spent large parts of her childhood in this solid brick home in Palmer Woods. *17330 Wildemere Ave.*

Gladys Knight Home - The Motown singer lived in this gorgeous brick home just south of McNichols Road. 16860 La Salle Blvd.

Houdini Death Site / Old Grace Hospital - Demolished in 1979, this hospital was where famed magician Harry Houdini died of a ruptured appendix and peritonitis on Halloween in 1926. *3990 John R.*

Jackie Wilson Home - The singer, known as "Mr. Excitement" and famous for the songs "Higher and Higher" and "Lonely Teardrops," lived in this lovely brick home with his wife. 16522 La Salle Blvd.

Martha Reeves Home - Martha Reeves lived in this elegant brick home in the late '60s and early '70s, when she and the Vandellas were churning out hits such as "Dancing in the Street" and "Heat Wave." Fellow Motown star Gladys Knight lived only a few blocks away. *16170 La Salle St.*

Marvin Gaye Home - Marvin Gaye spent the late '60s and early '70s in this sleek mid-century ranch. His seminal 1971 hit, "What's Going On," was conceived here, on a gold grand piano in the home's sunken living room. *3067 W. Outer Dr.*

Marvin Gaye Home - The singer and his wife, Anna—sister of Motown founder Berry Gordy—lived in this charming brick home on the city's west side in the late 1960s. *19315 Appoline St.*

Otis Williams Home - The Temptations singer lived in this modest two-story home from 1966-1973. *19734 Appoline St.*

Philip Levine Home - This pleasant brick house is where the U.S. poet laureate and Wayne State University graduate first began to write poetry seriously. *19360 Santa Rosa Dr.*

Reynolds Metals Building - The former regional headquarters for Reynolds Aluminum, this Minoru Yamasaki masterpiece is technically in neighboring Southfield, but is visible from Eight Mile Road. Implementing ingenious (and unusual) uses for aluminum, the building's geometry and lace-like sheath make it a true mid-century stunner. *16200 Northland Dr., Southfield.*

Robert Wagner Home - This was residence number one for the actor perhaps best known for playing "Number 2" in the Austin Powers films. *17410 Fairway Dr.*

Ruby Cleaners - This bright blue and white dry cleaner was once owned by Earl Ruby, whose older brother, Jack, infamously murdered Lee Harvey Oswald in 1963. *18135 Livernois Ave.*

Sidra Records - Now a garage, during the 1960s, this building was home to the mysterious Sidra label, which cut a slew of incredible soul singles that went largely unnoticed at the time. According to rumor, off-duty Motown session musicians and Cass Technical High School music students made up the backing bands for the instrumentally rich recordings. Check out the instrumental "Sidra's Theme," credited to Ronnie and Robyn. *18292 Wyoming St.*

Stevie Wonder Home - The singer moved into this home with his family with the help of Motown founder Berry Gordy, who wanted his stars living in desirable neighborhoods. *18074 Greenlawn St.*

Tom's Tavern - Affectionately dubbed the "Slanty Shanty," this unusual, charmingly ramshackle one-story bungalow bar was a beloved watering hole from 1928 until its closure in 2017. *10093 W. 7 Mile Rd.*

Vernors Ghost Sign - The iconic yellow and green of Detroit's favorite ginger ale, Vernors, still appear vibrant on this decades-old painted advertisement. This "ghost sign" was preserved from the elements by an adjacent building, the demolition of which exposed the ancient advertising. *7421 McNichols Rd.*

Walter Reuther Home - Legendary UAW President Walter Reuther lived in this modest ranch home with his wife and two daughters. An assassin attempted, and failed, to kill Reuther here in 1948, firing a shotgun through the kitchen window located at the rear of the house. *20101 Appoline St.*

CHAPTER 10
FAR WEST SIDE

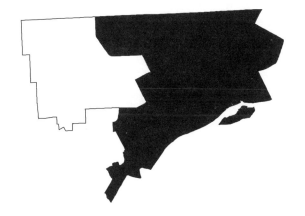

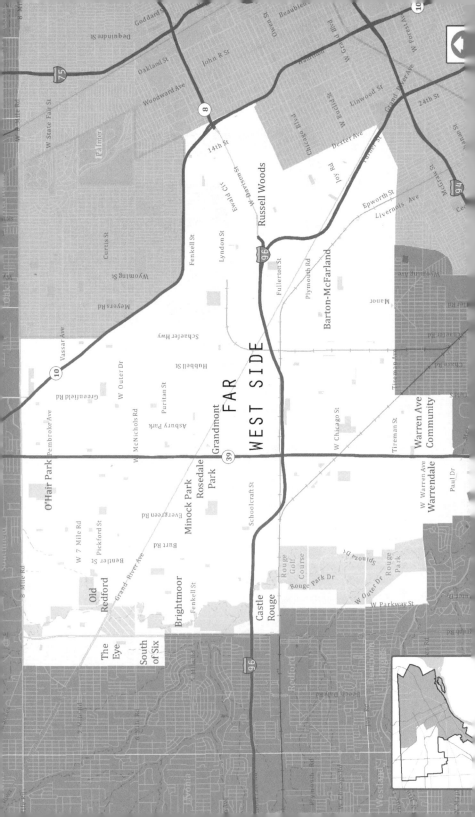

The Far West Side has a reputation as one of the city's hidden havens for vintage blue-collar bars and restaurants, charming off-the-beaten-path cultural amenities, and many delightful confectioneries and bakeries. As we've defined it, the Far West Side is this guide's largest chapter by area, measuring 49 square miles, and bounded by Schaefer, M-10, and Dexter Avenue on the east, and the city limits to the north, west, and south.

Annexed into the city between 1824 and 1926, and largely built between 1915 and 1964, the area is among the newest in the city, and it developed during the rise of the city's bedroom-community suburbs. Like contemporary suburbs, the area was developed subdivision by subdivision by large developers, causing each neighborhood to be distinct from the next, even to this day. The area showcases a spectrum of neighborhood types, from beautiful, dense Depression-era neighborhoods, to workers' cottages, to pre-war duplexes, to post-war tract housing. This large 49-square-mile area is home to many neighborhoods, including Aviation Subdivision, Berg Lahser, Brightmoor, Castle Rouge, Eliza Howell, The Eye, Five Points, Franklin Park, Grandmont, Grandmont #1, Herman Gardens, Minock Park, North Rosedale Park, Old Redford, Rosedale Park, Warren Avenue Community, and Warrendale. Because of their distinct development patterns and social histories, each neighborhood has its own character and draw. Among these, several stand out: Grandmont Rosedale (see separate entry in this chapter), a collection of five beautiful, vibrant 1920s neighborhoods; Brightmoor, a once dense neighborhood of small wood frame homes for Appalachian immigrants that is now largely vacant and home to many community gardens; Old Redford, a quaint neighborhood, home to a resurgent commercial corridor centered around the gorgeous Redford Theatre; and Warrendale, a tight-knit community welcoming a new Arab-American population that is bringing a host of Middle Eastern eateries and shops to the area.

The Far West Side offers a bevy of amenities and destinations that make it an attractive, fascinating, and lively destination. A treasure for visitors with a nostalgic eye, the area is home to a host of charming 1940s- and 1950s-era businesses, such as chip shops, slider joints, penny candy stores, and roller rinks. For those looking to admire the city's greenscapes, the Far West Side offers beautifully manicured lawns and gardens in Grandmont Rosedale, hundreds of urban gardens in Brightmoor, and the city's largest park—the heavily forested Rouge Park. For the traveling sweet tooth, the area has an almost unparalleled concentration of bakeries, cake shops, and donut shops. The Far West Side's artistic and cultural amenities run the gamut, from a small community theater to a Civil War center to a spectacular 1920s movie house.

BARS & RESTAURANTS

Akbar's Restaurant - Akbar's wears its basic food premises on its sleeve: Food should be homemade, fresh, affordable, and pork-free. This independent diner proudly advertises its support for the Detroit-born belief system of the Nation of Islam, whose most visible adherent is former Detroiter Malcolm X. Akbar's has a casual dining room of bright red wooden booths, low-key incandescent lighting, and artwork and portraiture commemorating the history and development of the civil rights movement. By no means, however, is creed a barrier to the agnostically hungry—Akbar's maintains a base of regulars with friendly service, quality ingredients, and excellent value. A breakfast special including eggs, beef sausage, potatoes, toast, and grits checks in at under $4. Open early and seven days a week. *12943 Fenkell St., (313) 491-9398.*

Always Brewing Detroit - This caffeinated escape evokes an artist's studio with its local-art-adorned walls, charmingly mismatched furniture, and chalkboard signage. The sweeping front windows— and their friend, copper-tone tin ceiling—give this coffee shop a light-filled, warm glow, and provide a constant street theater at least as interesting as most cable channels. In this theater, however, the concessions take center stage. Owner Cody Williams brews with beans from a rotating cast of single-origin roasts from local favorites Chazzano Coffee Roasters and Great Lakes Coffee Roasting Co. With handcrafted syrups and locally sourced dairy, Williams offers an outstanding slate of coffee, espresso drinks, teas, and a topgallant chai latte. If your molars get itchy, look for a diverse, distinctive selection of cafe bites, such as lava cakes, vegan blueberry muffins, butternut squash quiche, pozole, garlic herb jerk chicken wraps, and an especially tasty breakfast sandwich. *19180 West Grand River Ave., www.alwaysbrewingdetroit.com, (313) 473-7167.*

Auntie Betty's Café - Delicious take-out comfort food is Auntie Betty's specialty. Place your order at the carryout counter and take a seat on the comfy multicolored vinyl chairs overlooking Grand River while you wait. Auntie Betty serves her food fresh and hot, so it's the perfect temperature by the time you make it home. From rib tips to chicken by the piece to fried okra to mac 'n' cheese, Betty has the soul food selection covered. If you have any questions about the menu, Auntie Betty herself will be happy to recommend a dish to fit your tastes. Don't miss the $4.99 lunch specials. Open late. *19601 Grand River Ave., (313) 537-6050.*

Bob's Pizza Palace - A Detroit staple since 1966, Bob's Pizza Palace is a pizzeria in the most classic sense: dough is made fresh daily; sauce is made from scratch using Bob's own secret recipe; mozzarella cheese is browned and bubbly; and the pepperoni is small and crispy, all curled up at the edges. This is a neighborhood family place that is as much a part of the community as the people in it. Order the classic hand-tossed round or the Detroit-style square with some hand-battered fried shrimp, wing dings, or ribs. *20510 W. 7 Mile Rd., (313) 538-2742.*

Cafe Gigi - Open since 1973, Cafe Gigi—known by locals as Gigi's—is a gay club renowned for its amazing cabaret shows featuring go-go boys and drag queens. Inside, patrons enter through a narrow hallway before finding the barely lit performance space and a stage packed with characters out of a John Waters movie. Around them are elevated tables and seating, pool tables, and a long bar with cheap, strong pours. Upstairs from the venue is the dance club, which is especially lively on show nights. Mondays and Fridays are often the best nights to enjoy a show and the karaoke on Sundays is exceptional. Obviously, most patrons are men, but Gigi's welcomes everyone. Keep your eyes peeled for local queen of queens Cindy Elmwood. *16920 W. Warren Ave., (313) 584-6525.*

Cardoni's Bar and Grill - More bar than grill, this far west side staple is a laid-back neighborhood watering hole. Built into an old house, Cardoni's has a comfortable, man-cave atmosphere punctuated by an array of old photographs, sports memorabilia, and beer ephemera, and it offers a great casual venue to watch the game, shoot pool, or play darts while enjoying a limited menu of tasty pub fare—including burgers, patty melts, steak, chicken fingers, and shrimp. The full bar has a wide array of middle-shelf liquors as well as domestic and imported bottles. The staff, like the crowd, is friendly and cheerful. Check out their billiards and darts leagues. *6615 Greenfield Rd., (313) 584-1993.*

Chick's Bar - Chick's was opened in Warrendale in the 1950s by a World War II veteran who earned the nickname "Chick" during his military days, and it has remained the quintessential neighborhood dive bar with ambience. A regular spot for neighborhood folks, as well as for visitors, the crowd here is relaxed and friendly, and the drinks are cheap and plentiful, with draft specials starting at less than $2. The food menu runs the gamut of traditional bar fare, and the bar's legendary fish fries on Fridays are worth the trip—just look for the vintage yellow sign! *18550 W. Warren Ave., (313) 441-6055.*

Connie & Barbara Soul Food - The retro White Tower facade, well-loved paneling, vintage mismatched chairs and tables, and shining metal grill top smothered with hash browns and pancakes intimate the fact that Connie and Barbara haven't strayed from their winning formula for generations. Although a little rough around the edges, this otherwise charming neighborhood breakfast spot is packed with regulars and longtime fans of the restaurant's delicious collision of soul food and breakfast, such as catfish and grits, and salmon croquettes and pancakes. From the house hot sauce to a secret Kool-Aid recipe, most everything here is homemade, and the servers have a knack for remembering every visitor's name. Bring a few quarters to feed the R&B-packed jukebox. Breakfast and lunch only. *13101 W. McNichols Rd., (313) 862-5240.*

Crab House - This family-operated shellfish and barbecue restaurant offers affordable surf and turf for carryout or dining in. The main room features a Plexiglas-encased cashier's counter and a few periwinkle booths with small personal TVs, so you can catch your shows while you dine. If the front booths are full, never fear: Just walk toward the back of the room, follow the hallway next door, and you'll find the newly expanded main dining room. Try the barbecue chicken or ribs—rich and smoky in flavor, with a mildly sweet sauce glazed on top—or the popular garlic shrimp, crab leg clusters, turkey neck, or pasta. If you're feeling saucy, try the giant Dump Truck special that includes every seafood item you can imagine. *19721 W. 7 Mile Rd., (313) 535-1400.*

Deangelo's Soul Food, Deli & More - To a jazz soundtrack, this diner-style greasy spoon serves up outstanding soul food to the Old Redford neighborhood. The decor is simple and cozy, but that's because the focus is on the vittles. Slide into one of the old-timey white booths or order to go—you can go a la carte or select an entree, two sides, and a corn muffin. We especially recommend the expertly seasoned fried catfish, the crispy butterfly shrimp, and the collards and green beans which both pack some heat. Though the house specialty is soul-satisfying Southern food, they also sling a strong selection of soups, salads, sandwiches, and other deli delights. *17425 Telegraph Rd., (313) 535-7157.*

Detroit Vegan Soul West - This full-service Rosedale Park outpost of the fabulous, insanely delicious, all-vegan east side soul food destination offers dine-in or carryout. See separate Detroit Vegan Soul East entry for more details. *19614 Grand River Ave., www.detroitvegansoul.com, (313) 766-5728.*

Eleos Coffee House - This welcoming coffee shop is the only place like it nearby—in fact it's one of only a handful of operating businesses of any kind for blocks. Since opening in 2016, the neighborhood has embraced this local hangout, but the cafe is a gem for anyone who wants a getaway work or study spot with maximum friendliness and minimum price. Eleos is technically a nonprofit Christian ministry, designed to create a community space and promote Christian ideals through progress, if not ecumenicism. However, it's immediately apparent that being a nonprofit has never meant subpar quality for customers. First-timers should try the zippy espresso, a house-brewed chai latte, a signature dessert latte, or an aromatic Mexican hot chocolate. Hungry first-timers might pick between a panini-pressed Dorito-loaded grilled cheese, or the decadent Nutella Fitzgerald, both of which are just three bucks. While décor isn't the draw, Eleos still checks plenty of those boxes: The barista counter is located in a warm vivant room, while the accompanying lounge is a relaxing, cozy, and subdued alternative. Closes at 2pm. *12041 Dexter Ave., www.eleoscoffee.com, (313) 307-7137.*

Elias Donuts - More than 30 years ago, the space where Elias Donuts is now was a Dunkin' Donuts. A lot of that old-school DD charm is still present—from the fuchsia facade and awning to the stainless steel and pink formica counters and stools—but this sweet independent doughnut shop is so much more. Every morning at 5am, Elias fries the shop's fresh, delicious, cakey doughnuts—and if you're lucky, you can watch them being made while you order. From traditional flavors like sour cream and chocolate to the more imaginative red velvet, cherry chip, or Froot Loop-encrusted, it's fortunate that when you order a dozen, you get three more free, so you can try them all! If a bag of delicious doughnuts isn't your bag, they also serve other, more savory fare, from bagel sandwiches to burgers to fried fish dinners. Visit on Paczki Day to get your fix. Open 24/7. *19231 Grand River Ave., (313) 535-0070.*

Elmer's Hamburgers - With an exterior that is the definition of classic White Tower architecture, Elmer's has been serving up its unique take on sliders for more than 50 years. Though the immediate neighborhood surrounding the burger palace has seen better days, faithfuls still line up for the joint's sliders, which are well done yet extra juicy, with a massive, balanced flavor, and laid out over a bed of sautéed onions and pickles. Don't let the Plexiglas separating patrons from the cashier temper your curiosity; at $1.25 each, Elmer's trademark burgers—which are larger than normal sliders—are worth the trip. Open 24 hours. *8515 W. Chicago St., (313) 933-7766.*

Great Lakes Sports Bar - If cocktail selection and contemporary design are your yardsticks, welcome to the best sports bar in Detroit. Great Lakes Sports Bar's eclectic appearance and unusual drink selection offer something for everyone. The sleek industrial bar and Edison pendants lend a sense of downtown cool, while the silken drapery and corner sofas evoke a contemporary nightclub, and the pallet-clad walls and Boblo boat mural add a bit of bootstrap DIY flair. Of course, the projector, half dozen televisions, and preponderance of Lions fans remind you that this is, in fact, a sports bar. The curated food menu emphasizes ballgame fare, with burgers, chicken wings, french fries, deep fried oreos, and cheese sticks. Behind the rectangular center bar, look for a limited selection of craft drafts, domestic bottles, and an an impressive cocktail selection drawing on a spirit list tall enough to ride a roller coaster. *17602 W. Seven Mile Rd., (313) 693-4762.*

The Hayloft Saloon - One of the city's most popular gay bars, especially for men, the Hayloft is a friendly, well-loved destination dive with a vaguely country-western theme. Founded in 1980, the bar features a variety of seating—including the long bar, the intimate high-tops, and a comfortable lounge area—but regulars often congregate around the pool table, which sees lots of action, including league and tournament play. Look for Karaoke on Tuesdays, as well as frequent barbecues and parties in the massive yard when weather permits, as well as themed events, including leather and bear nights. The bar shares ownership with **Adams Apple Bar** nearby, which is similarly popular, but features a more polished aesthetic. *Adams Apple: 18931 W. Warren Ave., (313) 240-8482; The Hayloft: 8070 Greenfield Rd., (313) 581-8913.*

Jamaica Jamaica Restaurant & Bakery - Don't let its size fool you. This small diner in Northwest Detroit serves some of the best Jamaican and Caribbean grub around. So good, it's named twice, the service is as warm and friendly as the climate from the restaurant's namesake. While the ambience is lacking, the authentic, incredibly delicious food more than makes up for it. Try the acclaimed tender curry goat, jerk chicken, oxtail, jerk burger, reggae-fried chicken, or chicken curry, along with some of the yummy sides like sweet fried doughy dumplings, roti, plantains, patties, or perfect rice and beans. Wash it all down with one of Jamaica Jamaica's spectacular house-made juices and sodas—try the Irish moss, mango, ginger beer, or punch black—and while you're at it, have a slice of homemade cake. If you need the food to come to you, they cater to boot. *17550 W. 7 Mile Rd., (313) 534-3226.*

Jamaican Pot - In need of a tropical getaway? Your next island escape may be as close as this cozy carryout spot nestled in a strip mall on Eight Mile. Featuring Caribbean staples like oxtail stew, curry goat, and fried plantains, the Jamaican Pot offers delectable options for omnivores and vegetarians alike—and even halal meat. Expect generous portions and even heartier amounts of flavor and spice, all of which you can wash down with a refreshing Jamaican ginger beer. Don't miss the Brown Stew Chicken, a transportative medley spiced with scallion, garlic, thyme, and a secret blend of house spices. While the bamboo wallpaper flanking the Jamaican Pot's order window may not immediately remind you of warmer climes, rest assured that a large order of the jerk chicken certainly will. *14615 8 Mile Rd., www.thejamaicanpot.com, (313) 659-6033.*

John's Grill - Hurry if you want to get to John's Grill, because they're probably closing up for the day soon; service at this modest time-travel diner ends at two o'clock. John's has been serving breakfast and lunch on Detroit's west side since 1971, and it has been a nuptial venture for four decades of that time: Marsha, John's wife, handles the service counter, while John mans the grill in a traditional white cook's cap. The food is simple, good, old-school, and affordable: The burgers are hand-patted, and use only fresh beef, and John's massive, flavorful omelets are legendary around the neighborhood. The interior is a testament to the budgetary philosophy of "austerity," but it exudes a vintage charm that, coupled with the food, makes the place worth a visit, even if everything comes in to-go containers. John's is a reliable dine-in or carry-out spot, and has its share of loyal customers, but first timers in a rush should call ahead, as sometimes food is made at the "just finishing that up" pace. Cash only. *10534 W. Chicago Ave., (313) 933-5733.*

Just A Bit Eclectic - The first time you enter this tea shop, you might feel like Dorothy opening the door to color for the first time. Indeed, the space is more than just a bit eclectic, and can be transportive to first-timers. A guest to Darlene Alston's nonprofit tea shop will feel ensconced and welcome in her small, warm, diversely decorated Druidian kitchen where tea is a spiritual drink to be savored contemplatively. The flourishes in the shop include twin lamps with rose-colored shades that drape down like mounted jellyfish; a flawless vintage Garland stove; busts, mannequins, and wireframe dress forms; decorative sprays of faux flowers; and a doily trail on the shop's ceiling. Alston also provides a separate sitting room in the back for dedicated lounging, where guests can put on one of the store's vinyl records and curl up on a peacock loveseat. The nonprofit component of the shop is called **A Place to Begin** and it provides service industry experience to youths. It also hosts a book club, knitting group, and other small social gatherings, as well as an operational herb garden. Open Thursday-Saturday. *19015 W. McNichols St., www.justabiteclectic.com, (313) 533-5692.*

Kabob Arbeel Restaurant - Though you won't find luxury or quaintness at this hole-in-the-wall eatery named for a citadel in Iraq's Kurdistan region, the place cranks out authentic, delicious renditions of authentic Iraqi food for cheap carryout or dine-in. The $3 sandwiches are served in fresh, fluffy Iraqi samoon bread (more like an envelope than a wrap), and the menu offers customers full dinners of likely familiars: shawarma, falafel, beef or chicken tikka, as well as tilapia or quail. Association football (read soccer) fans will likely enjoy catching a game on Arbeel's flat screen if they show up at the right time. *6551 Greenfield Rd., (313) 582-9209.*

★ **Maty's African Restaurant** - With its bright yellow walls, bazin batik tablecloths, and colorful Senegalese wall hangings, you can judge this book by its cover: Owners Amady and Maty Gueye are preparing food that is homemade, authentic, unpretentious, and vibrant—just like the atmosphere. From the open kitchen, look for piquant, traditional Senegalese food, with its distinct marriages of French, Vietnamese, Arabic, and Caribbean influences. Begin with a fataya (a Senegalese take on empanadas, exploding with rich flavor) or nems (spring rolls that might rival the finest in Hanoi). Next, order the whole chicken yassa. Though the entire entree section makes a writer want to review it several more times, the whole chicken yassa, with its meticulous preparation—including rounds of seasoning, broiling, frying, and grilling, and a vivid garnish of caramelized onions, mustard, and peppers—is a must-order. While the adult beverage list is drier than the Sahara, housemade baobab smoothies, sorrel and ginger juices, as well as soda and water, are available. *21611 Grand River Ave., (313) 472-5885.*

Motor City Java House - Owner Alicia Marion collaborated with the local nonprofit Motor City Blight Busters to remodel a vacant space to realize her dream of opening a coffee shop where neighbors can sip hot beverages, nibble on fresh baked goods and salads, and discuss their vision for the community. With a copper-painted tin ceiling and cheery yellow and green walls, Motor City Java House is a quiet, friendly place, furnished with comfy couches, spacious tables, and free Wi-Fi. Visit Saturdays for an afternoon yoga class or an open mic night, or drop in any old time to order espresso drinks from the rich granite coffee counter, surrounded by serene photography and local artwork. Closed Sunday and Monday. *17336 Lahser Rd., (313) 766-7578.*

Omega Coney Island #3 - Though the exterior is reminiscent of a Denny's, the large seating area with green calico booths, wood paneling, vintage photos of Detroit landmarks, and a bakery showcase full of pies seems more reminiscent of a modern neighborhood diner. The parking lot is large, but finding a spot can be difficult when the breakfast crowd rolls in. Although the menu offers a delicious mix of lunch and breakfast options, including omelets, home fries, classic Greek pitas, soups, coney dogs, and burgers, its specialty items—including Daryl's Grill and the South of the Border Fries—are outstanding. Despite being located on one of the city's busiest thoroughfares, the down-home atmosphere and affable staff give the restaurant a small-town feel. *22501 W. 8 Mile Rd., (313) 533-6000.*

Panini Grill & Juice Bar - Hungry Detroiters rejoice! From her modest counter inside the Coinless Laundromat, Lynda Laurencin has elevated the lowly panini into gourmet fare. Easily the city's best (and only?) laundromat restaurant, the Panini Grill uses all fresh ingredients and innovative flavors to produce some of the city's finest sandwiches and smoothies. Although the delicious, gobbler-laden Jive Turkey is the best-seller, the shop is unique for the wide variety of carnivore-approved vegetarian offerings, such as the Corny Beef—an incredible vegetarian TVP corned beef panini—and the Ribless—an outstanding faux-beef riblet panini. Although delivery is available, the nearby launderers make for good people-watching. *1281 Oakman Blvd., www.paninigrilljuicebar.com, (313) 334-4001.*

River Bistro - This intimate, three-table, weekend brunch spot assumes a casual, Pinterest-friendly vibe of vibrant murals, chalkboard specials, live edge tables, and designer stools, while the menu is more subdued. Taking inspiration from Caribbean, African, and Low Country cuisines, Chef Max Hardy's highly curated menu is a multicultural masterpiece of innovative takes on brunch staples. The shrimp and smoked cheddar grits, fluffy sweet potato waffle and honey-fried chicken, and shrimp Caribbean omelette with sausage gravy are thoughtful, balanced, and delicious. However, it's the steak and eggs that are not to be missed, even if only as an Anthony Bourdain-style side dish—expect cilantro fried eggs, herb hollandaise, delicate laced potatoes, and a ribeye grilled to juicy pink perfection that is large enough to make a rottweiler ask for a doggie bag. While doing battle with your meal, rehydrate with raspberry lemonade, mango lemonade, various fountain drinks, or bring your own adult beverage. *18456 Grand River Ave., www.riverbistrodetroit.com, (313) 953-2225.*

Rono's Family Dining - Though the exterior may look a little institutional, don't be fooled: Rono's is the place for really, really good Caribbean Cuisine. Opened more than 30 years ago by Mama Rono, the restaurant, which emphasizes flavor over decor, has become a destination for island specialties, such as oxtail, meat patties, curry goat and turkey, ackee and saltfish, and—of course—jerk chicken, authentically smoked on a wood-chip-burning grill. Any dish is best chased with a bottle of the exceptional house-made ginger beer and followed up with a desert, like the vegan-friendly Jamaican Coconut Drops: diced coconut drizzled in brown sugar and ginger and hardened into a perfect, crunchy clump! *14001 W. McNichols Rd., (313) 862-1295.*

★ **Scotty Simpson's Fish and Chips** - Founded by James "Scotty" Simpson in 1950, this spot has been an authentic English-style fish-and-chips staple and Brightmoor community anchor since its postwar opening. The simple, vintage yellow-brick exterior features beautiful murals and antique signage, and it complements the charming interior's classic patterned carpet, '50s-era wood-lined walls, taxidermy fish mounts, and Happy Days-esque wood tables and chairs. Affable owner Harry Barber and his four friendly staff members have more than 150 collective years of experience at the restaurant and create a laid-back and welcoming atmosphere. Known for its light, crispy, and bubbly batter, the menu is dedicated to all things golden-fried, including its renowned fish and chips, as well as delicious smelt, shrimp, perch, and frog legs. For landlubbers who prefer the bounty of the shore, Scotty's offers scrumptious grilled cheese, hamburgers, and steak. Wash your meal down with an old school ginger beer or orange soda. Scotty's gladly takes call-ahead orders, but beware, Barber says, because "once I get them in the door, they're hooked!" *22200 Fenkell Rd., www.scottysfishandchips.com, (313) 533-0950.*

Sonny's Hamburgers - A beautiful example of 1950s White Tower architecture on a quiet strip in Detroit's Brightmoor neighborhood, Sonny's serves some of the city's most delicious and traditional sliders. As an onion-lover's mecca, Sonny's is not first-date material: the burgers are made of fresh beef from Eastern Market—with onions ground in—cooked on a bed of onions, and served with a healthy dollop of onions. While revered for its sliders, Sonny's also offers delicious shoestring fries, homemade chili, wing dings, and a traditional diner breakfast menu. Although offering carryout, visitors should plan on sitting down to enjoy the original 1950s architecture and decor and the constant stream of entertaining regulars. *20001 Schoolcraft Rd., (313) 535-2278.*

Southern Smokehouse - An award-winning barbecue and soul food joint on Detroit's west side, Southern Smokehouse is noted for its smoke-saturated brisket, signature ribs, moist chicken, fried pork chops, and deep, sweet barbecue sauce. Beyond its distinct recipes for sundry meal options, the Smokehouse shines at preparation: cornbread and other sides are made fresh, with attention to flavor and quality, and make every customer's call-ahead meal more complete. Do call ahead, as orders are carry-out or delivery only, and the low-frills, fire engine red waiting area is strictly reserved for standing, but the Motown music and smoke-scented ambience should be enough food for the senses to tide you over until your meal is ready. Please note that guests are expected to not sneak any bites of their food in the parking lot for two very important reasons: One, Southern Smokehouse has signs saying that it's against the law to do so; two, nobody ever breaks the law. *14340 W. McNichols St., www.southernsmokehouse.com, (313) 397-4050.*

Sweet Potato Sensations - Perched across the street from the Redford Theatre, Sweet Potato Sensations is a cozy pastry and ice cream shop that welcomes customers with the enticing aroma of its fresh pies and friendly staff. Inspired by her husband's love of sweet potatoes, owner Cassandra Thomas sought to create a business centered around this tasty, hearty, and nutritious tuber. With the vintage pumpkin-colored vinyl chairs, orange floor tiles, buttery pecan walls, eclectic antiques in various shades of tangerine, and every sweet potato dessert you could imagine—from ice cream to cookies and cheesecakes—this business warms its customers inside and out with sweet potato goodness. *17337 Lahser Rd., www.sweetpotatosensations.com, (313) 532-7996.*

Teenie's Deli - A few bites through your corned beef, and you're likely to begin considering the contortions necessary to lick your styrofoam clamshell clean. Open since 1977, the deli is a family operation led by patriarch Johnnie "Corned Beef King" Christopher. The modest dining room seemingly sports the original wood paneling, venerable booth upholstery, and Carter-era drop ceiling, but maintains a spirit that the city's French ancestors might have called "élan." In addition to an old school hip hop soundtrack and meaty aromas, the open kitchen creates highly flavorful, delicate, almost rubescent corned beef. Christopher offers standard breakfast and lunch deli fare, including club sandwiches, Maurice salads, patty melts, French toast, grits, and Dinty Moore sandwiches that are sapid and affordable. The ironically named Teenie offers three tiers of corned beef, pastrami, turkey, roast beef, Swiss cheese, coleslaw, and Russian dressing among four slices of bread, and the sandwich is a culinary highlight, but not for the figuratively, or literally, faint of heart. *18244 W. 7 Mile Rd., (313) 533-7744.*

Tijuana's Mexican Kitchen - For more than 25 years, this restaurant has been serving up Jalisco Mexico specials, including enchiladas, dried peppers, homemade flour tortillas, and salsas. Originally a carryout-only kitchen, Tijuana's is now a dine-in restaurant, complete with a full bar serving Mexican draft beers, house sangria, and hand-squeezed lime margaritas. Aside from the bar, the restaurant features bright orange and yellow walls, warm, glowing stained-glass light fixtures, and Western High School-themed artwork—an homage to the owner's alma mater and Southwest Detroit roots. *18950 Ford Rd., (313) 383-9100.*

SHOPPING & SERVICES

Cakes By Claudette, "The Cake Lady" - Prepare yourself to say several Hail Marys after finishing your cake. Selling her manna by the cake or the slice, Claudette draws customers from far and wide for her incredibly delectable caramel cake. Not a one-hit wonder, she also offers carrot, red velvet, lemon pound, yellow chocolate, double chocolate, coconut pineapple, and German chocolate cakes, all of which are outstanding and trend toward sweet and moist. In addition to selling her relatively inexpensive cakes from her unassuming store, Claudette also dispenses complimentary advice with each purchase, such as, "Cake is cheaper than therapy." *19210 W. McNichols Rd., (313) 537-4782.*

Detroit Police Auctions - Looking for the perfect gift for that special someone? Nothing says love quite like medical scales, exotic animal care equipment, or gently used Sawzalls. Held the first Saturday of every month, the live Detroit Police Seized Goods Auctions at The

Auction Block offer Detroiters an opportunity for an unusual cultural experience and a chance to score bargains with stories. Although the items vary widely and depend on the season's enforcement priorities among Detroit's finest, savvy shoppers can score antique cameras, power tools, DVDs, watches, knives, sports cards, coin collections, video equipment, and furniture at prices that are a steal—both figuratively and perhaps literally. Detailed auction lists—featuring pictures—are posted online several days ahead of each auction. All bids start at $5. *12660 Greenfield Rd., www.theauctionblock.com, (313) 659-3376.*

G&R Bike Shop - Offering great deals and bikes to match, this bright yellow shop has been a beacon of hope for Detroiters with two-wheeled trouble for more than 30 years. Although the shop sells many of the season's newest models, G&R is more renowned for its expert repair services and its wide selection of parts and accessories, especially those suited for early model rides. From behind the long counter, the attentive staff helps customers navigate the shop's large inventory and give tips on the finer points of bike maintenance. The veteran staff offers expert, honest repair services for all types, from commuter to cruiser. Pick up one of the complimentary maintenance primers or Detroit maps on your way out. *21706 Grand River Ave., (313) 531-1146.*

Leddy's Wholesale Candy - Hidden behind a sleepy façade, Leddy's Wholesale Candy has been among the city's largest candy stores since it opened in 1926. Leddy's is a candy coliseum; the original hardwood floors, vintage decorations, and historic fixtures are obscured by the overwhelming candy selection. The shop seems to stock every candy ever sold. Saltwater taffy, rock candy, penny candy, candy jewelry, candy cigarettes and exotic candy from around the world—as well as all of the usual suspects—are piled in neat rows from floor to ceiling. Despite being a wholesaler, Leddy's is open to the public, and sells smaller, consumer quantities of most products. Don't spoil your dinner. *15928 Grand River Ave., (313) 272-2218.*

Lewis Trade Center - For 15 years, the Lewis Trade Center has been the perfect place to score treasures you didn't know you needed. With narrow winding "aisles" beset on all sides by 12-foot piles of finds—from lawn ornaments to VHS tapes to mod vases to lawn mowers—this classic, massive, neighborhood junk shop will keep the curious interested and the interested curious. Don't be afraid to ask for assistance. The proud staff will help you navigate the disorderly array—or will help remove obstacles from your path. *4500 Oakman Blvd., (313) 834-2023.*

Metro Music - For more than 60 years, Metro Music has been a go-to for fledgling musicians on the west side. Specializing in economical rock instruments such as guitars, basses, drum kits, and related equipment, Metro isn't the place for a virtuoso, but it's well-suited for beginners. While the shop is a little rough around the edges, showing signs of wear, it has remained dedicated to providing neophytes places to pick up new instruments, as well as learn them. Mark Lamonte, the son of the original owner, holds a B.M.E. from Eastern Michigan University and teaches lessons in almost every instrument from woodwinds to strings to percussion for only $5 per half hour—economical enough to let people keep practicing. *8647 Southfield Fwy., (313) 258-1918.*

New World Antique Gallery - Perched on a quiet block of Grand River Avenue, New World Antique Gallery has been serving northwest Detroit for more than 20 years. Despite the elegant name, the shop is more of a no-nonsense rummage sale—you are more likely to find an old lawn Santa or bucket of vintage doorknobs than ancient pottery. Although the fascinating and sometimes bizarre products are loosely organized into large piles with categories such as "metal" and "outdoors," the friendly owner will expertly guide you. Plan on spending a while here—the gallery is built for browsing. Haggle-friendly. *12101 Grand River Ave., (313) 834-7008.*

Pages - This small but bright independent bookstore in Detroit's Grandmont Rosedale neighborhood features one of the city's best-curated selection of books for readers of all stripes. Whether you're looking for literary fiction, biographies, local-interest topics, or children's literature, Pages is bound (pun definitely intended!) to have a title that will pique your interest. Not sure what your next beach read should be? The knowledgeable and helpful staff at Pages is known for their recommendations; and if, by chance, the shop happens not to stock a certain title you've got in mind—never fear—they'll order it for you. Stop in for one of the store's frequent literary readings and events featuring local and national authors, and keep your eyes peeled for Pip, the bookshop's resident cat. *19560 Grand River Ave., www.pagesbkshop.com, (313) 473-7342.*

Pinky's Shuga Shack - This charming stop-in bakery on the West Side has a menu of sugary treats that mirrors its setting: cute, sweet, and homemade. Pinky's is made up in the favorite color of its owner to resemble a pink 1950s bakery counter, where you can take a seat at the chrome stools or at one of the two small tables with matching-colored dishes. The real attraction, however, isn't the ambience—it's the confections. Pinky's serves up homemade cupcakes, brownies, pies (regular or fried), cobblers, cakes, muffins, and cookies, emphasizing quality ingredients (only butter, no oils), and has quickly caught on as a neighborhood favorite for in-and-out treats or special orders. Closed Mondays and Tuesdays; Wi-Fi available. *18929 Schoolcraft Rd., www.pinkysshugashack.com, (313) 837-2253.*

Shrine of the Black Madonna Cultural Center and Bookstore - Founded in 1970 as a nonprofit educational and cultural institution, the shrine is equal parts museum, art gallery, bookstore, and gift shop. The cultural center is affiliated with the Shrine of the Black Madonna Church, which was founded in Detroit by civil rights activist the Reverend Albert B. Cleage Jr. in 1953. Visit to browse through the largest African-American owned bookstore in the nation, chat with the helpful staff about the variety of African art pieces, or purchase African clothing and handcrafted jewelry. Visitors can walk through the museum and gallery on their own, but they should call ahead to schedule a guided tour. *13535 Livernois Ave.., www.shrinebookstore.com, (313) 491-0777.*

Sisters Cakery - This charming Warrendale classic has been family-owned since the 1950s. The maroon vitrolite tiles still jazz up the facade, just as they did on opening day, and the vintage blade sign and retro awning still beckon to customers. Inherited by the sisters, the children of the original owners and the namesakes of the business, this shop continues to whip up some of the finest baked goods in the area, offering a wide selection of sweets, from cookies to baklava. However, the house specialty is its moist, yummy cakes, which can be skillfully custom-decorated. *15730 W. Warren Ave. (313) 846-4777.*

Strictly Sportswear - Detroit's first hip-hop apparel store, Strictly opened in Highland Park in 1984 but moved to this location in 1989. Take a peek at the photos taped to the counter, of owner Kathy Hamlin with LL Cool J, Jay-Z, Eminem, and the many other stars who have visited the shop. Kathy knows the history of the neighborhood, as well as the hip-hop artists and fashion labels that got their start there. Visitors who aren't into hip-hop history can strictly shop the vast selection of men's sportswear: Pelle Pelle jeans, hoodies, Adidas track jackets, 59 Fifty flat-brimmed hats, sport coats, sneakers, boots, and dress shoes, and even colorful Coogi sweaters that your grandpa would be proud to wear. A small selection of women's jeans can be found here, but for a fuller selection, just down the road is **Strictly Women's**, a hip-hop apparel store for women owned by the same family. *17644 W. 7 Mile Rd., (313) 534-5110.*

Teresa's Place - Once visitors pass through the first entryway full of signage asking customers to "keep it classy" and to abide by the two-drink minimum, Teresa's Place transforms into a dimly lit, but surprisingly sleek neighborhood hangout that lies somewhere between dive bar and upscale lounge. The interior features exposed brick walls, a flaming copper fireplace, tall, intimate booth seating, and a full bar serviced by a white-collared bartender who jokes with the regulars perched along the leather cushioned stools. Patrons are mature, polite older folks who are far from shy, so come ready to swap stories over strong drinks! Aside from good conversation, customers can enjoy tasty bar food specials like wings and burgers, while dining in or taking out. *14000 W. McNichols Rd., (313) 862-2831.*

CULTURAL ATTRACTIONS

Artist Village - Resident artist Chazz Miller owns and operates Artist Village, a community arts space and studio that houses Miller's nonprofit, Detroit Art City. Visit once a month for the Creative Juices open mic nights or drop by one afternoon to tour the artist studio, admire the murals, and explore the urban gardens. Detroit Art City also accepts volunteers to help revitalize the Old Redford area through mural painting, urban gardening, and lot cleanup projects. Call ahead to inquire about the event schedule or to plan a volunteer opportunity. Parking available next door, at the corner of Lahser Road and Orchard Street. *17336 Lahser Rd., (313) 544-0848.*

Buffalo Soldiers Heritage Center - Opened in 2007, the Buffalo Soldiers Heritage Center educates area youths on the historical significance of the Buffalo Soldiers and exposes children to horses by teaching horseback riding. The beautiful and bucolic center, housed in a former mounted police station within Rouge Park, is home to a large barn, several large, fenced horseback-riding paddocks, and a display area featuring a number of Buffalo Soldier artifacts. The president and resident re-enactor, James H. Mills, prides himself on the center's youth-orientated programming, including re-enactments, educational lessons, and riding sessions on the center's nine horses. Horse and pony rides are available for youths ages four and older. The facility is open year-round, except for when it's raining. If you visit, bring carrots and red apple treats for your equestrian hosts! *21800 Joy Rd., (313) 270-2939.*

Curtis Museum at the House of Beauty Hair Mall - Although featuring information on a range of figures that punctuate contemporary black history—including Nelson Mandela, Ed Bradley, Dr. Martin Luther King Jr., and General Colin Powell—this small, albeit fascinating, storefront museum and local curiosity lives to celebrate the life and work of longtime Detroiter Dr. Austin Wingate Curtis, Jr., chief lab assistant to famed peanut researcher George Washington Carver. Located inside of the affiliated House of Beauty Hair Mall since its founding in 2000, the eccentric space winds through a series of brightly lit rooms that document different aspects of Curtis's life. The museum has an impressive array of scattered artifacts, ephemera, and art that chronicle the life of its namesake, including handmade figures in the doctor's likeness, photos of Curtis with Carver, and correspondence between the two men. Museum co-founder Mary Jones, who leads many of the tours, has a passion for sharing her knowledge and enthusiasm for the legacy of Dr. Curtis and this interesting chapter in black history. Visitors should call ahead to make an appointment, as hours vary from those posted. *14034 W. McNichols Rd., (313) 341-1512.*

Detroit Repertory Theatre / Millan Theatre Company - This cultural gem lies off the beaten path, just outside of Highland Park. The Detroit Repertory Theatre produces four major productions and approximately 180 performances each year with a strong focus on diverse casting and community involvement. Backed by expansive sets, intricate costumes, and stimulating performances, the Detroit Repertory Theatre is a must for theatre lovers and novices alike. The small, charming space features a full bar and 184 seats, creating an intimate theatrical environment and atmosphere. *13103 Woodrow Wilson St., www.detroitreptheatre.com, (313) 868-1347.*

Norwest Gallery of Art - One of the newest galleries to open in the Grandmont Rosedale neighborhood, Norwest Gallery of Art is dedicated to contemporary art with a curatorial focus on African and African-American art. Director and chief curator Asia Hamilton sees art as "a visual representation of what the soul yearns to express," and is committed to connecting the audience with high-caliber artists practicing in a wide range of media, from photography to abstract painting. The space is not only for exhibitions, but serves as a gathering space for events such as talks, live music, film screenings, workshops, and pop-ups for local businesses. See their website or social media for current programming. *19556 Grand River Ave., www.norwestgallery.com, (313) 293-7344.*

Plantation House - A retired line worker, 83-year-old Jother Woods grew up in a sharecropping family in rural Horseshoe Lake, Louisiana. As a young man, he moved to Detroit to seek his fortune, but he never relinquished his lifelong fantasy of one day owning one of the palatial Southern plantation homes he admired as a boy. Over the past three decades, Woods realized his dream and hand-built his own country estate—at 1:30 scale. Built slowly, evolving and growing piece by piece, the folk-art masterwork is now 52 feet long and six feet wide. Tinkering in the basement of his lower flat, Woods painstakingly constructed the artwork with tens of thousands of discarded found objects. All to scale, a highway roars past a private drive, which winds through well-manicured gardens, over a lake, past the 16-room gated mansion and private pool, before giving way to a farm, silos, and horse barn. Filled with surprises at every turn, every minute detail, every flower, tree, road, vehicle, and structure is made from someone else's trash, beautifully reimagined here as another man's tranquil dream world. Though the project is too big for Woods to keep in one piece, he displays it, in sections, throughout his home and proudly grants tours of the grounds of his plantation to visitors lucky enough to see it. Mr. Woods requests that visitors make arrangements to see the work through the G.R. N'Namdi Gallery in Midtown. *(313) 831-8700.*

ENTERTAINMENT & RECREATION

Doll's Go Kart Track - With the elephant-size speaker pumping bumping disco jams, Doll's is hard to miss, which is a good thing for go kart fans, because the next closest facility is almost a half hour drive away and would most assuredly offer less attitude. Especially on weekends, Doll's pulls in a steady rotation of aspiring racers, and boasts five laps around the tire-lined oval track for a mere $3. Though they don't offer the latest in video entertainment, video game fans will be relieved to know that Doll's does offer a small arcade, so bring quarters. Doll's is open seven days a week. Come on now, go, kart! *4455 Oakman Blvd., (248) 508-3747.*

Northland Roller Rink - Serving the west side of the city for more than 60 years, Northland is Michigan's largest roller rink and is absolutely packed almost every night of the week with skaters of all ages and abilities. The beautiful rink is well-maintained, and the inside has been upgraded over the years. Call ahead or check out the rink's website for its many scheduled nights targeted toward different age groups and musical tastes, including adult skates, dance skating events, laser tag, and classes. Great for private parties (there is a "party room" off to the side—call ahead to reserve it), admission is affordable, the sound system is superior, and there is a snack bar with typical pizza and hot dog fare. Although it offers full rental services, check out Northland's well-stocked skate shop if you're in the market for some new skates or gear of your own. *22311 W. 8 Mile Rd., www.northlandrink.com, (313) 535-1443.*

North Rosedale Park Community House & The Park Players - Opened in 1939, this charming community-owned venue is surrounded by a beautiful six-acre park and located in the heart of the city's historic North Rosedale Park neighborhood. While the community house is a cozy and beautiful space used for community gatherings and private parties much of the year, it comes alive several times a year for Park Players performances. Since its founding in the early 1950s, the Park Players have become renowned for their lively, thought-provoking theatrical productions of comedies, musicals, and dramas including *Joseph and the Amazing Technicolor Dreamcoat*, *Much Ado About Nothing*, and *One Flew Over the Cuckoo's Nest*. The cabaret-style seating and occasional delicious dinner theater performances offer an intimate visitor experience not to be missed. *18445 Scarsdale St., www.northrosedalepark.org, (313) 835-1103.*

★**Redford Theatre -** A Detroit treasure that was once billed as "America's Most Unique Suburban Playhouse," the Redford Theatre is a stunning Japanese-themed movie house that first opened its doors in 1928. With 1,661 seats spread over the first floor and balcony, the theater has been lovingly restored by the Motor City Theater Organ Society, which has been working on the restoration since 1977. Centered around the theater's original Barton organ, the ornate show space is dotted with intricate painted details and fixtures, and it features a night sky with illuminated stars above the audience and a stage and screen flanked by a two-story Japanese village. Volunteer-run, the theater screens classic films accented by live organ performances, intermissions with live entertainment, and old-timey cartoon preludes. As if the theater's offerings didn't sell themselves, shows are generally just $5, and the concessions are comparably economical. *17360 Lahser Rd., www.redfordtheatre.com, (313) 537-2560.*

Rouge Park - The largest park within the city of Detroit, Rouge Park is a bucolic, serenely forested space that features small programmed areas offering diverse recreational opportunities. Named for the industrial waterway that snakes through it for two miles, Rouge Park was purchased and developed by the city in the 1920s. The park spans more than 1,184 acres—making it nearly 40% larger than Central Park in New York City. In the face of limited parks spending by the City of Detroit, the Friends of Rouge Park has begun maintaining the space and offering occasional programming since its founding in 2002. Rouge Park features a number of attractions that make it a unique leisure opportunity, including an 18-hole golf course, 14 regulation baseball diamonds, 11 tennis courts, the Brennan pools, more than 200 picnic tables, a driving range, an archery range, playgrounds, eight miles of hiking and mountain-bike trails, a model-airplane field, a sledding hill, and, in 2012, the largest urban farm in Michigan. Among these amenities, a few stand out:

- **Rouge Park Driving Range** is a full-service driving range adjacent to the Rouge Park Golf Course clubhouse. The range offers yardage flags, target greens, and both turf and natural grass tees, allowing golfers to practice with irons, woods, and drivers.

- Opened in 1923, the **Rouge Park Golf Course** is an 18-hole, par-72, public course stretching 6,325 yards from the black tees. Built on hilly, sloping terrain, the golf course's circuitous fairways and numerous water traps and sandy bunkers make it unforgiving for those with rusty drivers. The extremely challenging 11th hole still haunts some golfers.

- **Brennan Pools** is the park's aquatic area. The facility includes a comfortable, paved pool deck, two Olympic-size pools, and a smaller diving pool with a diving tower. The pools hosted the trials for the U.S. Olympic Swimming Team in 1948, 1956, and 1960.

- The **Buffalo Soldiers Heritage Center** is an active horse farm and interpretive center dedicated to the Buffalo Soldiers. See separate entry for more details.

- **D-Town Farm**, the largest urban farm in Michigan, is the work of the local nonprofit Detroit Black Community Food Security Network and encompasses seven acres of Rouge Park. The farm offers many, many, organic vegetable plots, mushroom beds, hoop houses, and a compost pile.

Beyond its rich infrastructure, Rouge Park offers hundreds of acres of dense woodlands and scenic prairies, both of which are home to a rich diversity of urban wildlife—including, most notably, raccoons, deer, pheasants, an array of birds, and seasonal butterflies, which flock to the park's fields of milkweed. In the fall months, the park becomes a picturesque landscape as the many trees change color. *Rouge Park runs along W. Outer Drive, between W. Warren Avenue, and Schoolcraft Street, www.rougepark.org.*

SITES

American Concrete Institute Building - Designed by Minoru Yamasaki, a master of modernity, the oft-overlooked American Concrete Institute Building is an underappreciated miniature modern masterpiece. Built in 1959 to house offices for the ACI, a technical and educational society dedicated to all aspects of concrete structures, the one-story building is quintessential Yamasaki, with an airy, sun-laden interior, "floating" pre-cast concrete elements, and triangular flourishes that meld modern minimalism and Japanese traditionalism. ACI sold the property in 1996. After changing hands a couple of times since then, it is now in use by EcoWorks, an environmental advocacy non-profit. *22470 W. 7 Mile Rd.*

The Blue Bird Inn - Though it appears insignificant from the outside and has been shuttered for nearly 20 years, the Blue Bird Inn was opened in the 1930s in a small enclave on the city's west side and has a prominent place in the annals of jazz history. A popular club throughout the modern era—attracting acts such as Charlie Parker, John Coltrane, and Yusef Lateef—it is most notable for being the venue that is said to have saved the career of a young Miles Davis. As a promising horn player in New York, by the early 1950s, Davis had developed an uncontrollable heroin habit that threatened his future as a musician. He came to Detroit in 1953—where the drugs were said to be weaker than those on the East Coast—to kick his habit and was recruited as a resident player at the Blue Bird. According to legend, Davis beat his addiction there and returned to New York five months later to continue his ascent into stardom. Because of the club's contribution to jazz music, there are at least two pieces that identify the humble landmark: Thad Jones' "5021" and Tommy Flannigan's "Beyond the Bluebird." *5021 Tireman St.*

The Grande Ballroom - Though it's been shuttered for more than 40 years and functioned as a music venue for only six, the Grande Ballroom has firmly secured its status as a pantheon of Detroit rock 'n' roll history. Built in 1928, the music palace was designed by Charles N. Agree, and was used as a dance hall venue through its early life. This changed when local schoolteacher Russ Gibb took over the building in 1966. With house bands the Stooges and the MC5—whose breakout live album *Kick Out the Jams* was recorded at the venue in 1968— playing weekly, the ballroom became a revolving door for future Hall of Fame talent. Among hundreds of others, the Velvet Underground, Led Zeppelin, Pink Floyd, Chuck Berry, Howlin' Wolf, John Lee Hooker, Cream, John Coltrane, the Who, and Sun Ra graced the stage. Though the building is long abandoned and has fallen into extreme disrepair, the walls still ooze history. If you listen carefully, you can still hear Rob Tyner urging us to "Kick out the Jams." *8952 Grand River Ave.*

Grandmont Rosedale - North Rosedale Park, Rosedale Park, Grandmont, Grandmont #1, and Minock Park, the five neighborhoods collectively known as Grandmont Rosedale, form a dense, contiguous historic district defined by its incredible density of architectural beauty and charming oak- and maple-lined streets. Primarily built during the 1920s, the area features custom-built homes in an array of architectural styles, including Prairie, French Renaissance, Tudor Revival, Cape Cod, International, Colonial, and Arts and Crafts. Although the homes in Grandmont Rosedale are more modest than those in some other notable historic districts, such as Indian Village, Palmer Woods, and Boston Edison, the area is unique for its scale. The neighborhood includes more than 5,000 homes and spans 2.5 square miles, and consequently is home to the state's largest national historic district. The solid, gracious homes were built with unique, custom architectural features and details, with fireplaces, Pewabic tile, and high-end construction materials. Today, the area is a vibrant, diverse community with beautiful parks and landscaped boulevards, making it one of Detroit's neighborhood gems. Although the entire neighborhood has beautiful homes, the area's grandest streets are Bretton Drive, Glastonbury Avenue, and Warwick Street. *Grandmont Rosedale is bounded by Evergreen Ave., McNichols Rd., Southfield Fwy., Grand River Ave., and Asbury Park St., and Schoolcraft Rd., www.grandmontrosedale.com.*

POINTS OF INTEREST

Archdale Kit House - Built in 1925, this unusual stucco home was purchased as a kit house from Sears, Roebuck, and Co., before being assembled on site. *15775 Archdale St.*

Beaverland Farms - This two acre farm, located in the Brightmoor neighborhood, utilizes eco-friendly farming practices in an effort to help revitalize land that has been harmed through industrialization. Their produce can be purchased directly from the farmers, but is most often found on menus at restaurants throughout the city. *15078 Beaverland St.*

Chris Webber Home - This small brick house was the childhood home of Chris Webber, a five-time NBA All-Star and, perhaps most infamously, a key member of the University of Michigan's Fab Five team. *16725 Biltmore St.*

Dee Gee Records - Formed on this residential block in 1951 by Dizzy Gillespie and Dave Usher, the label put out a number of notable records by Gillespie himself and was bought up by New Jersey's Savoy Records in 1953. *4015 Leslie St.*

Diana Ross Home - After a childhood spent in the Brewster Projects, the singer purchased this modest brick home located on the same street as fellow Supremes Florence Ballard and Mary Wilson. *3762 W. Buena Vista St.*

Ebenezer AME Church - This incredible, ornately constructed English Gothic giant was constructed in 1928 and now functions as an African Methodist Episcopal parish. The sprawling stone sanctuary and building are punctuated by the large square tower at the center. *5151 W. Chicago St.*

Edwin Starr Home - Most famous for the 1970 hit, "War," this singer lived in this modest home with his wife, Annette, in the late 1960s. *20511 Ardmore St.*

Florence Ballard Home - Motown mogul Berry Gordy helped Florence Ballard, a member of the Supremes, purchase this pretty brick home in 1965. Ballard lived here until 1974, when, facing hard times, she was forced to move back into the Brewster Projects, the place where the Supremes were formed. *3767 Buena Vista St.*

Ford Family Burial Plot - Now located across the street from a derelict gas station and a moderate-income housing development, the small St. Martha's Episcopal Church Cemetery is the final resting place of one of the world's most powerful and wealthy luminaries, Henry Ford, the pioneering industrialist and founder of Ford Motor Company. His wife, Clara, as well as many other members of the Ford family, join Henry in eternal slumber nearby. *15801 Joy Rd.*

Grass Menagerie - Hidden away in this esoteric private backyard, passersby will find a veritable statuary zoo that would make Noah smile, featuring almost two dozen disparate sculpted jungle, desert, and barnyard animals. *6268 Artesian St.*

Grave of the Lone Ranger - The famous voice of the WXYZ radio show The Lone Ranger, Earle W. Graser, is buried in Grand Lawn Cemetery. Hi-Yo Silver! *23501 Grand River Ave.*

Growing Together Sculpture - Artist Larry Halbert carved this 15-ton marble statue, which features three conjoined figures, representing the hope and growth of the local community. The statue was placed in Rouge Park in 2010. *11320 Spinoza Dr.*

Jalen Rose Home - Former home to University of Michigan Fab Five star, career NBA guard and ESPN sports analyst, Jalen Rose, which he still owns to this day. *16231 Appoline St.*

James Smith Farm House - The inconspicuous vinyl siding on this residence hides the fact that the home dates from sometime between

1830 and 1850 and is one of two remaining log cabins in the city. *2015 Clements St.*

Jerome Bettis Home - This now-abandoned building was home to the famous Pittsburgh Steelers running back for much of his childhood before he was "The Bus." *10384 Aurora St.*

Jerry Bruckheimer Home - The director, who put "Beverly Hills Cop" character Axel Foley in a Mumford High School shirt, grew up in this modest home on the city's northwest side. *19784 Ardmore St.*

Jimmy Hoffa Home - Jimmy Hoffa, who would ascend to the role of Teamsters President in 1957, purchased this small northwest Detroit home in 1939 for $6,800. *16154 Robson St.*

Magic City Records - This spot once housed the recording studios and office for the label, perhaps most famous for its releases by teen funk outfit Mad Dog and the Pups in the late 1960s and early 1970s. *8912 Grand River Ave.*

Mary Wilson Home - The Motown star, who was a founding member of the Supremes, purchased this home in 1965, while wrapping up recording sessions for "I Hear A Symphony." *4099 West Buena Vista St.*

New Light Baptist Church - Completed in 1929, the sandstone facade of this classical-revival church is dominated by the massive Romanesque columns. The yellow sandstone structure with its bronze entryways almost seems to glow on sunny mornings. *5240 W. Chicago St.*

North Rosedale Park Tree Nursery and Outdoor Classroom - Nestled inside of a primarily residential neighborhood, this nursery has transformed an abandoned lot into a gathering place for the community. *16857 Stahelin Ave.*

Orsel and Minnie McGhee House - This unassuming home became the epicenter of a battle over discrimination, when the McGhee family attempted to become the first black homeowners in an all-white neighborhood. They won their case in front of the Supreme Court, which ended legal housing segregation in America, with the help of a promising young lawyer named Thurgood Marshall. *4626 Seebaldt St.*

Philip Levine House - Philip Levine, whose poetry referencing working-class Detroit earned him the title of Poet Laureate of the United States for 2011-2012, was born in this house in 1928. *3779 Clements St.*

Queen of Soul Mural - This mural, which depicts the visage of Detroit's Queen of Soul, honors her legacy and impact. *11926 Livernois Ave.*

Ray Parker Jr. Home - "Who you gonna call? Ghostbusters!" Musician Ray Parker Jr. moved into this home in 1963, at the age of nine. Bustin' made him feel good. *3780 Virginia Park St.*

Ric-Tic Records - Joanne Bratton and Ed Wingate ran their soul music label on this quiet residential street, recording singers like J.J. Barnes and Edwin Starr, before being bought by their big competitor at Motown Records. *4039 W. Buena Vista St.*

Son House's Grave - Famous for the songs "Death Letter" and "John the Revelator," legendary Mississippi bluesman Eddie James "Son House," Jr. played with Robert Johnson and idolized by Muddy Waters and Jack White. His gravestone reads, "Go away, Blues; go away and leave poor me alone." *18507 Lahser Rd.*

Ted Nugent Home - "The Motor City Madman" spent his early childhood in this small home on the city's west side. *23251 Florence Ave.*

This Old House Fullerton Home - PBS mainstay *This Old House* covered the full rehab of this 1939 home during the show's 38th season in 2017. *4055 Fullerton Ave.*

This Old House Keeler Home - Kevin O'Connor, Tom Silva, and Richard Trethewey, the stars of *This Old House*, helped put this house back together in 2016. The project aired during the show's 38th season in 2017. *17540 Keeler St.*

Tiny House Community - This quaint micro-neighborhood of tiny houses, each one ranging from 250-400 square feet, is the brainchild of local non-profit Cass Community Social Services. The charming and colorful homes and offered to low-income residents as a creative way to make home ownership more affordable. *564 Elmhurst St.*

Tom Skerritt Home - The mustachioed *Alien* and *Top Gun* actor (he was Viper!) grew up in this modest home on Detroit's northwest side. *12003 Cheyenne St.*

World War II Memorial - In the median of Outer Drive in Brightmoor stands a small but proud monument to honnor the sacrifices of soldiers who served in World War II. *Outer Drive and Lahser Rd.*

Wrigley's Ghost Sign - Bold lettering graces this brick wall, an antique plea for shoppers to patronize long-gone Wrigley's Super Market. This ghost sign was revealed when the neighboring building was demolished. *16910 Schaefer Hwy.*

CHAPTER 11
HAMTRAMCK &
HIGHLAND PARK

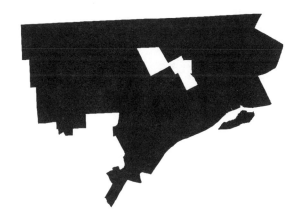

Nestled within Detroit, and surrounded by the city on all sides, are two tiny individual municipalities with distinct histories and cultures—Hamtramck (pronounced Ham-tram-ick) and Highland Park. Because of their small size (2.08 and 2.97 square miles, respectively) and their proximity to and location completely within Detroit, their stories are intrinsically linked to the city. In many ways they feel less like separate cities and more like neighborhoods within Detroit. Although very different, the two cities, together, offer visitors a wide range of opportunities to admire the unique character of the region's past, present, and future.

HAMTRAMCK

Named for Colonel Jean Francis Hamtramck—the revolutionary war hero who seized Detroit from British control—Hamtramck is an ethnic enclave with a reputation for diverse international grocers and restaurants, vintage dive bars, popular events, and a storied rock and roll heritage. Although the city has followed its larger neighbor through an ongoing social and physical evolution, the city's distinct waves of Polish, African-American, Yugoslav, Yemeni, Bangladeshi, and Arab residents have continually renewed the city and buoyed its municipal trajectory. Although many of these immigrants have moved to other communities—often only to be replaced by counterparts from other countries—the city's diverse current and past residents have left lasting imprints on the commercial landscape of this cheerful urban hamlet.

Founded in 1798, Hamtramck was a largely agrarian village until the dawn of the industrial revolution, a period marked by remarkable, record-setting growth. In 1910, the Dodge brothers built their Dodge Main plant to build parts for Ford, and ultimately, built Hamtramck. Between 1910 and 1920, the city grew from 3,559 to 48,615, a rate of 1,266%—the nation's fastest growth at the time. The Dodge brothers were far more culturally tolerant than other contemporary magnates, creating one of the most diverse plants and cities at the time. This tolerance and resultant diversity helped lead Dodge Main to become the first plant organized by the UAW, and it was the site of the union's first sit-down strike, in 1937. The city's population peaked in 1930, at 56,268, and has gradually declined since, in the wake of plant downsizing and suburban development. Today, 21,752 residents call Hamtramck home.

Despite population loss, Hamtramck remains the densest city in the state, among the most diverse and vibrant, and an exciting place to visit. Generations of the city's increasingly diverse residents have hung their shingles, creating a bustling commercial center, full of neighborhood-scale shops, grocers, restaurants, bars, and cultural and recreational amenities—many of which preserve the flavors of proprietors' home countries. In addition, the city has a rich musical heritage and thriving music scene. The city inherited a host of corner dive bars from previous generations of autoworkers, and today Hamtramck, home to the most bars per capita of any city in the U.S., boasts scores of small live music venues as these bars have added stages. The city—the birthplace of Mitch Ryder of "Devil in a Blue Dress" fame—is engulfed each year by the Hamtramck Music Festival, a multi-venue celebration of local music—and many of the region's favorite rock bands. Once a year, on Fat Tuesday, Hamtramck becomes the center of the region, as thousands of metro Detroiters descend on the city to take part in Paczki Day, the Polish tradition of eating donut-like paczki before Lent.

Hamtramck's primary commercial corridors form a hashmark, with two main north/south arterial streets—Joseph Campau Avenue and Conant Street—intersecting with three east/west thoroughfares—Holbrook Street, Caniff Street, and Carpenter Avenue—at half-mile increments. This dense, walkable grid, alongside the sights of colorful dress shops, the smells of classic bakeries, and sounds of pervasive live music, make a leisurely visit to Hamtramck a highlight of any visit to the Motor City.

HIGHLAND PARK

As a small factory town enclave within Detroit, Highland Park has paralleled its larger neighbor through periods of meteoric growth and tumultuous decline. Despite navigating many chapters of challenging history and bearing the resultant scars from population decline, plant closures, and vacant homes, Highland Park has soldiered on.

The city draws its name from a large ridge once located at Woodward Avenue and Highland Street. In 1818, the feature's natural beauty and strategic location piqued the interest of famed Judge Augustus Woodward, who platted a new community, Woodwardville in 1825. Although the plan was never built, his early work facilitated piecemeal development and eventually led residents to incorporate the area as the Village of Highland Park in 1889. Taking advantage of the low property taxes in this small farming community, Henry Ford purchased 160 acres in 1907 to build what would become the Highland Park Ford Plant, which ignited a population explosion. Aspiring auto workers immigrated in droves, building block after block of Arts and Crafts homes. Between 1900 and 1920, the population increased by 10,815%, from 427 to 46,499. In order to protect its burgeoning tax base, the area incorporated as a city in 1918, to withstand Detroit's annexation attempts. In 1925, the Chrysler Corporation was founded in the city, and Highland Park would remain the site of its world headquarters until the mid-1990s. After Henry Ford moved automotive production to River Rouge in 1927, the city began a sustained population loss. After peaking in 1930 with nearly 53,000 residents, the city's population has continuously declined since, to 10,900 today.

Despite this difficult past, visitors to Highland Park today will find numerous historic automotive heritage sites, a handful of working class restaurants and shops that remain from the automotive heyday, and a variety of social enterprises. From the historic Ford factory and the original Chrysler headquarters site, to the nation's first freeway and a neighborhood diner once popular with hungry Ford workers, the city is littered with automotive history. With innovative redevelopment examples like a non-profit solar street light initiative and a community-oriented boutique art gallery, this city-within-a-city has a nascent, empowered future.

Two areas in Highland Park, the Medbury's-Grove Lawn Subdivision and Highland Heights-Stevens' Subdivision historic districts showcase the city's regionally unique concentration of Craftsman homes. These character-rich remnants of the early 20th Century Arts and Crafts movement are distinctive for their broad rooflines, sweeping porches with stout pillars, and colorful palettes. Built from 1910 to 1920 during the movement's peak, these homes are thought to represent the largest collection of the style in the state. The Medbury's-Grove Lawn Subdivision is in northwest Highland Park, along Eason Street, Moss Street, and Puritan Street, between Woodward Avenue and Hamilton Avenue. Highland Heights-Stevens' Subdivision is in the opposite corner, bounded by Farrand Park Street, Massachusetts Street, Woodward Avenue, and Oakland Avenue.

Some neighborhoods within Highland Park may be unsafe, especially at night. We recommend visitors remain aware of their surroundings and employ common sense safety rules, including avoiding travelling distances on foot.

BARS & RESTAURANTS

(revolver) - An upscale eatery for chef's table meals and pop-ups, (revolver) is a nook of haute cuisine in Hamtramck. The restaurant presents a new chef every weekend, and offers communal seating, prepaid seatings, and a (likely) resplendent multi-course *prix-fixe* menu. Depending on the chef and night, diners will encounter a range of cuisines, flavors, ideas, and themes, but one thing's for sure: The food will be delicious, the atmosphere will be convivial, and the evening will be an experience. Nothing on the menu is static, but (revolver) distinguishes itself with ambience, curatorial panache, and small touches, like a commitment to locally sourced ingredients. The dining room is minimal, cozy, and warm, and promotes conversation—guests dine at long, wooden communal tables. Past chefs have included local stars Brad Greenhill of Takoi and Kate Williams of Lady of the House. (revolver) is reservation only but allows BYOB. Explore upcoming offerings on the restaurant's website. *9737 Joseph Campau Ave., Hamtramck, www.revolverhamtramck.com, (313) 757-3093.*

Aladdin Sweets & Cafe - Interested in enjoying delicious and authentic Bengali and Indian cuisine? Expect to hear Bengali drifting through the air of this neighborhood spot. Since 1998, Aladdin has offered its own delicious (and very inexpensive) takes on all of your favorites: masala, paneer, samosas, naan—especially the naan!—and more. If you can't decide what to order, they offer a bountiful buffet for only $8.50. Grab some carryout, and take a peek at the selection of decadent desserts in the case at the carryout counter. Take a seat with the locals in the cramped, worn booths in the original location, or dine-in at their "formal" dining room next door. In the summer months, an adjoining patio offers lovely, expanded outdoor seating. *11945 Conant St., Hamtramck, www.aladdinsweet.com, (313) 891-8050.*

Ali Baba Shish Kabob - You've heard of Ali Baba and the forty thieves, but have you heard of Ali Baba and the tasty menu? A traditional Middle Eastern restaurant in the heart of Hamtramck, this neighborhood spot offers an expansive and comprehensive menu, with a heavy (and delicious) Iraqi influence. In addition to flavorful beef and chicken kabobs, don't miss the crisp falafel, the hot Iraqi Samoon bread (free for dine-in customers), and the copious salads, many of which come with an exceptional house dressing, which is slightly sweet with a borderline spicy finish. Grab carryout, or dine in in the hospitable and homey dining room, with pictures that highlight great scenes of the region, from "Middle East Desert" to Babylon. In addition to a full food menu, you can find a selection of freshly pressed juices and smoothies. *3124 Caniff St., Hamtramck, (313) 265-3701.*

Amar Pizza - Within a nondescript storefront without much decor, owner Khurshed Ahmed's Bangladeshi pizzeria offers some of Detroit's most unorthodox pies. Although the pizza has strong fundamentals—fluffy and crunchy crust, flavorful seasonings, a nice cheese-to-sauce balance—the real distinguishing characteristic is the variety of toppings: ghost peppers, naga sauce, cilantro, tandoori chicken, crab, dried shrimp, and eggplant represent only a fraction of the available options. While all the pies are solid, the tandoori pizza and dry fish pizza are exceptional. Lovers of unusual pizza will also enjoy the nearby **Al Qamar Pizza** (10240 Conant Street), which offers fine halal pies alongside a stable of tasty subs and sandwiches. *12195 Joseph Campau St., Hamtramck, www.amarpizza.biz, (313) 366-0980.*

Amicci's Pizza - Detroit's entrant in the international super-greasy-yet-super-delicious pizza competition, Amicci's is an unassuming neighborhood joint offering all the staples—ribs, wings, grinders, shrimp, burgers, and pizza. This Hamtramck location—like the Southwest Detroit Amicci's Pizza (3849 W. Vernor Hwy.) across town—serves up its tasty, distinctively cheesy and affordable pies until the cows come home. Although Amicci's offers all the usual toppings, it's renowned for its inventive and delicious specialty pizzas, like the Chicken Thai Pie, Pesto Delight, and The Greek. *9841 Joseph Campau St., Hamtramck, www.amiccispizza.com, (313) 875-1992.*

Atomic Cafe - This is a gallery (not a cafe) with a name that's a nod to the 1982 cult classic documentary of the same title. With artist and proprietor Luke MacGilvray at the helm, this isn't your typical white cube, but a creative gallery and salon that aims to show outsider artists who typically don't exhibit their work. In between shows, the 4,300 square feet are used as studio space, evident by the splotches of paint on the concrete floor. The Atomic Cafe holds four annual exhibitions from April to November, which coincide with programming like film screenings and live performances. The annual "Small Wonders" show of tiny works of art and films takes place every July. Exhibitions are short lived so check their Facebook page for the latest information on shows and events. *10326 Joseph Campau Ave., Hamtramck, (248) 568-0488.*

Baker Streetcar Bar - Named for the old streetcar line that once ferried workers from Joseph Campau Street to the Ford plant in Dearborn, this friendly, shotgun-style dive bar in downtown Hamtramck isn't much on eye candy but is heavy on charm, comfort, personality, and cheap beer ($1.50 High Life drafts and bottled Tyskie). The counter is bookended by TVs and overlooked by a carved Polish Eagle in the middle. There's not much of a kitchen, but there are periodic steak nights on Fridays and live music on a regular basis. The bar is marked only by a small red-and-blue neon sign in the window, so don't miss it. *9817 Joseph Campau St., Hamtramck, (313) 873-8296.*

Bonoful Sweets and Cafe - Since opening in 2011, owners Abu Bokkor, Nazmul Islam, and Mohammed Malik have developed a restaurant and menu worthy of the name Bonoful, which means "bouquet of flowers" in Bengali. The interior of the restaurant is a stark departure from the bright neon lights of the strip-mall exterior. The cozy contemporary space features intimate booths, chandeliers, and high-back leather chairs, offering a dignified environment in which to enjoy your food. Bonoful offers a composite menu of Bengali, Indian, and Pakistani dishes at excellent prices, including a daily lunch buffet. Goat meat, chicken, tandoori, and biryani dishes are the keystones, complemented by several varieties of homemade bread. Bonoful also offers a fine selection of ambrosiac desserts, including gulab jamun (fried milk and flour balls served chilled, drenched in sugar syrup) and ras malai (a sweet dairy/paneer concoction) as well as figs and lassi. Bonoful isn't decorated as a fine dining establishment, but the highlights are food, selection, and service. *12085 Conant Ave., Hamtramck, www.bonofulsweetsandcafe.com, (313) 368-8800.*

Boostan Cafe - A couple of rules to obey regarding Boostan Cafe: First, go to Boostan Cafe; second, do not *not* go to Boostan Cafe. This quirky, friendly micro-cafe is situated on the southwest corner of Conant and Holbrook. Though small, it is most definitely mighty—and the fresh-squeezed mango juice alone is worth the trip. With a lightning fast kitchen that is ready to please (extra garlic, stat!), the unpretentious setting gives way to an encyclopedic menu: a vast and delightful hodge-podge of American, Yemeni, and other Middle Eastern dishes—think falafel, but also burgers and fries, but also breakfast sandwiches—all of which hit the spot. Just how extensive is the menu at Boostan? The only thing a completist would find missing is blank space. Don't miss the chicken shawarma, the unusual lamb chili, and the buttery lentil soup. Did we mentioned you should try that mango juice? Delivery and carryout available. *3470 Holbrook Ave., Hamtramck, www.boostancafehamtramck.com, (313) 456-8100.*

★ **Bumbo's -** A diminutive red, neon "BAR" sign is all that lights the way to Bumbo's in Hamtramck, and it doesn't get much brighter inside, at this dark, hip, historic dive. The storied space was constructed in 1928, and was once home to Hank's Lounge, the longest running family-owned bar in Hamtramck. Current owners Tia and Brian "Bumbo" Krawczyk opted to keep nearly all of the original fixtures and details in this stunning space, including the tin ceiling, the gorgeous wooden bar, period light fixtures, and even the cooler—though they did their best to patch up what they're pretty sure were bullet holes (maybe the Purple Gang was here?). Bumbo's also hits all the right dive bar notes with its uber-dim, cozy vibes, snug patio, popular pool table, and a drink menu that boasts cheap beer and cocktails for less than $10. Don't let the reasonably priced drinks fool you though; they are delicious. Look for some of Hamtramck's best pierogi (that's saying something!) on Wednesdays. Yes, there are potato, charred scallion, ginger, sesame, and wasabi-hoisin pierogi, and you need to try them! *3001 Holbrook Ave., Hamtramck, www.bumbosbar.com, (313) 285-8239.*

Burk's Igloo - A seriously one-of-a-kind destination for summertime treats, you can spot Burk's by the nearly 20-foot-tall ice cream cone it flaunts from its sidewalk spot in Hamtramck. Offering all the delights you'd expect from a classic roadside ice cream stand, customers can enjoy soft-serve flavors, dipped cones, sundaes, floats, blizzard-type creations, and fried foods galore. After ordering at the walk-up window, plant yourself at one of the nearby picnic tables for some grade-A people watching. Burk's ascribes to a seasonal schedule, so it's generally open spring to fall. *10300 Conant St., Hamtramck, (313) 872-6830.*

Café 1923 - Built in 1923 by Polish immigrants as a corner store and owned by four generations of the same family, this building has been lovingly restored into a beautiful community coffee shop. Enjoy a cup of joe, a tasty treat, comfortable chairs, tons of outlets, and Wi-Fi without the corporate coffeehouse atmosphere. A favorite among locals, this charming spot is the perfect place to dig into a book, a conversation, or some serious work. The gracious front room features an original tin ceiling, counter, and wood floors, and if you're in need of some inspiration, the rear reading room is packed with floor-to-ceiling oak shelves of kitsch and books. Look for frequent exhibits and events from Hamtramck art collective, HATCH. *2287 Holbrook St., Hamtramck, www.cafe1923.com, (313) 319-8766.*

California Burgerz - What do you most associate with California? Hollywood? Surf culture? Burgerz? This idiosyncratically named Hamtramck burger joint hopes it's the latter. Whether or not Burgerz from California are a thing, one thing *is* for sure, the burgers at this hot spot are delicious, juicy, and loosen-the-belt satisfying. Each decadent patty is made with fresh halal beef and served loaded— and one, two, or three patties high—on buttery brioche or a pretzel bun. Of course, a good bun can make a great burger, but California Burgerz typically does the bun's work for it. The restaurant also makes fries from fresh potatoes daily and boasts five varieties of creamy milkshakes, including cappuccino and banana. The atmosphere at

California Burgerz is clean, commercial, retro 50s—think Chuck Berry, checkerboard flooring, and bright colors, but without the ashtrays or vigorous anti-communism. Open until 11pm. *12045 Conant Ave., Hamtramck, www.californiaburgerz.com, (313) 703-8000.*

Dos Locos Tacos - Hamtramck has a new counter for hungry late-night debauchers who are *un poco borracho*. Opened in 2018, Dos Locos Tacos offers lip-smacking (and halal) variations on traditional taco truck fare, including tacos, quesadillas, and burritos, with an emphasis on vegetarian options. To round out the menu, the late-night counter offers baskets of freshly fried tortilla chips, homemade pico de gallo, and delightful Co-Op hot sauces, which are available for retail purchase or for splashing on your chorizo. Dos Locos is legacy decorated, compliments of the former Campau Tower, and has inherited the timeless vinyl stools with chrome plating, white vitrolite paneling, shotgun-style eating, and the customary open micro-kitchen. Open until 4am on weekends. *10337 Joseph Campau Ave., Hamtramck, www.doslocostacos.com, (313) 872-6838.*

Family Donut Shop - As the name suggests, this wood-paneled corner shop on Conant favors the sweet side of the menu, with a cornucopia of tasty, economical cake doughnuts and pączki. However, the neighborhood secret is that the Family Donut Shop is a great place to grab a burek, a delicious, generously portioned Bosnian flake pastry stuffed with meat or feta, served cold or hot, though we suggest the latter. Those looking to sit while they indulge can belly up to the L-shaped vinyl counter and eat under the watchful eye of a framed photograph of Princess Diana. The shop is welcoming and friendly, and gets busy early—weekday hours start at 5:30am. Smoothies, soft serve, and hand-dipped ice cream are also available. *11300 Conant St., Hamtramck, (313) 368-9214.*

Fat Salmon Sushi - Hamtramck has many charms: a ridiculous number of bars per capita, a bustling streetscape, and authentic eccentricities. Its best virtue, though, might be its status as a melting pot, with a vibrant mix of cultures, peoples, and cuisines. Fat Salmon Sushi is a welcome addition to the mélange of excellent restaurants in this tiny city-within-a-city, featuring (no surprise), an epic selection of hand-rolled sushi at incredibly reasonable prices. With friendly servers, raw and hip yet unpretentious decor, and K-pop music on heavy rotation, the space is welcoming and warm. On the menu, you can be as adventurous as you choose: Sample a Fat Salmon specialty roll like the Jos Campau, with spicy tuna and "special sauce," nibble on sashimi so fresh you can almost taste the ocean, warm your belly—and your soul—with a generous bowl of ramen, or try a Korean barbecue combo plate. Even vegetarians will rejoice: Fat Salmon has plenty of meatless munchies, too, including tasty tempura. *11411 Joseph Campau Ave., Hamtramck, (313) 305-4347.*

Ghost Light - Sometimes, you can make the wheel just a little bit rounder. In a city famous for dive bars, this relative newcomer has shaken up the local formula with an attention to cleanliness, an inspired bar program, and diverse performances on stage. Make no mistake, the bar checks a lot of traditional dive boxes: a formica bar with more sharpie scribbles than a detention desk, a hodgepodge of secondhand chairs, and domestic cans cheaper than gas station hot dogs, to name a few. To wet your whistle, the bar offers all the dive staples as well as craft beers from the likes of Founders on tap, and the type of liquor selection that includes multiple amaros. The staff—many of whom are expats from beloved former watering hole **St. CeCe's**—also oversee a limited food menu, including succulent burgers and seasoned waffle fries. On the postage stamp stage, look for a diverse mix of musical acts, as well as avant garde theater, improv, poetry, karaoke, and trivia. Drink up to ensure a visit to the the moon-themed lunar loo. *2314 Caniff St., Hamtramck, (313) 402-4418.*

Hadramaut - Named for a thin sliver along the southern Arabian peninsula known as the Hadramaut, which is the native home of the Hadhrami and now a part of Yemen, Hadramaut serves an uncommon—and uncommonly delicious—variation of Middle Eastern cuisine. The expansive menu features dozens of favorites, including falafel, kabob, and shawarma, but the true prizes are the regional specialities, including the bright and wildly flavorful vegetable or meat gallaba sandwiches, the fried samboosa (similar to thin samosas), the bean-based fasoolia, the soup-like saltah, or the breakfast shakshooka stew. Though the restaurant is clean and tidy (and white-glove-test approved) too much thought has been put into the tastebud-tickling menu to deck out the interior—which is understated and leans on digitally rendered windows opening to ancient Hadrami city-scapes—but this will be fine by you, once you sample the vittles yourself. *3535 Caniff St., Hamtramck; (313) 368-8878.*

Halal Desi Pizza - This place is not your typical demure mom-and-pop Indian, Italian, Chinese, American, and Mexican sandwich and pizza shop. Alongside his more conventional dishes, jolly owner Kazi Miah serves a number of spectacular and unique fusion dishes, including the renowned chicken tikka pizza, malai kebab pizza, chili cheese samosas, and the customizable Hamtramck Sandwich. With only eight always-packed seats, visitors should plan on carryout or free delivery. *2200 Caniff St., Hamtramck, (313) 365-0111.*

Hamtramck Coney Island - Unlike the typical Detroit coney island, Hamtramck Coney Island is known for its locally made sausage and traditional dogs served Polish-style with green peppers, onions, and mustard—just like the hot dog in the restaurant logo. This family-owned business can still do the traditional Detroit coney, as well as other tasty greasy fixtures, like omelets and hash browns that come fast and cheap. You won't find any Greek items on the menu, as is common in Greek-owned coneys, but you will find pierogi. The charming wood paneling, mural of a polish landscape, and counter seating right by the cook's grill make for a cozy breakfast or lunch spot. *9741 Joseph Campau St., Hamtramck, (313) 873-4569.*

High Dive - Part cocktail bar, part dive, part art installation, this natty nitery defies easy definition. The austere, jet black facade of this mold-breaking project by noted L.A. muralist Shark Toof is punctuated by a solitary, illuminated red fiberglass shark head and the word "cocktails." Illuminated by dimmed crystal chandeliers and red spotlights, the interior is equally dark, but maintains an approachable atmosphere. Inside, the mismatched wooden bar has a charming folkart quality, everything from big band to grindcore plays over the soundsystem, church pew booths ring the space, salvaged stained glass hangs on the walls, and the faux-coco restrooms sport fixtures painted gold. On the diverse drink menu, the affable bartenders turn Faygo, smoked orange peels, Jolly Ranchers, and a deep liquor library into ten winning concoctions. Don't leave without trying the wildly popular Shark Punch. *11474 Joseph Campau Ave., Hamtramck, (313) 334-5517.*

Kelly's Bar - A lively dive open since 1984, Kelly's is renowned among fans of blues and booze. Set in an old house on a quiet block of Holbrook, the bar is a blithe, dark space full of character, with Christmas-tree lights over the bar, simple wood paneling, and old school breweriana. Although Kelly's offers all the de rigueur mid-shelf liquor and beer options, many guests opt for the Carter administration-era prices on select domestics during the nightly beer deals. The bar's small kitchen offers a small but tasty menu of bar fare, such as coneys, burgers, and fries, but is renowned for the weekly food specials, including the popular Friday night fish fry.

Although delightful every night, the bar comes alive on Wednesdays, Fridays, and Saturdays, when some of the area's finest local blues bands take the stage. *2403 Holbrook St., Hamtramck, (313) 872-0387.*

Nandi's Knowledge Cafe - "Knowledge" is too limited a word for what you'll find at Nandi's. In addition to a cafe set in a used bookstore, Nandi's also has a boutique art gallery one store north. Both are heavily oriented toward illuminating issues in the black community with their selection of literature and artwork, respectively. Whether dining or reading, the bookstore is a comfortable, casual place to browse and relax at a mixture of used tables spruced up with live plants, and lit by glass lamps hung beneath a tin ceiling. The reasonably priced, satisfying cuisine leans toward vegetarian Southern, with wings and burgers also available. Street-side dining is offered. The gallery is decked floor to ceiling with diverse, eye-catching work from local artists, as well as authentic African masks and carvings, aromatically intoned with incense, and decorated with live greenery, which is available for sale. The gallery regularly hosts lectures and open mic poetry nights. Except for events, both the cafe and gallery close early. *12522 Woodward Ave., Highland Park, www.nandiscafe.com, (313) 865-1288.*

New Dodge Lounge - Standing behind the unassuming brown and red neon sign on Hamtramck's main drag is the New Dodge Lounge, perhaps Metro Detroit's most under-appreciated rock and roll bar. Inside, you'll find lofted ceilings with exposed rafters and a balcony that once doubled as a brothel. The well-equipped stage (well, by dive bar standards, at least) is home to local rock, punk, and metal bands on the weekends. The crowd is a mix of townies and tattooed rockers, but the handcrafted bar, wood floors, and tasteful light fixtures give this bar a touch of class that's all-too-absent from most rock 'n' roll havens. Be sure not to miss the New Dodge during Blowout each winter, when the bar regularly hosts a not-to-be missed lineup. Also, see that bright red short bus out front (the one with an "I love roadhead" bumper sticker)? Once Lions season starts, that sucker will ferry you to and from the game for free, with a free post-game buffet. Very nice, New Dodge. *8850 Joseph Campau St., Hamtramck, www.newdodgelounge.com, (313) 874-5963.*

The Nosh Pit - After building a massive cult following and racking up awards with their inventive lime green all-vegan food truck, the Nosh Pit crew roared onto Yemens Street in Hamtramck in 2018. Enter through the reserved don't-blink-or-you'll-miss-it brick facade to find the warm, inviting, and homey interior centered around family-style communal tables, and an open prep kitchen. The menu builds off of the popular truck incarnation—with a focus on uncommonly good grilled vegan sandwiches—but goes way beyond, with an exceptional vegan mac and cheese, delicious potato beet latkes, wholesome salads, and dozens of other options. Among the mains, our favorites are The Larry (a vegan reuben with corned beets), The Redmond (a housemade vegan meatball finger-licker) and The Kaz (a veggie burger topped with apples). While the brick-and-mortar restaurant is open for dinner Thursday-to-Saturday, look out for the food truck, which makes frequent appearances throughout the region and can be tracked down on their website. *2995 Yemans St., Hamtramck, www.noshpitdetroit.com, (248) 417-9894.*

Oloman Cafe - The exterior of Oloman Cafe is understated and easy to miss, but to do so would be a shame. Inside this coffee shop, named for a bygone Sarajevo cafe of the same name, patrons will find an urbane, beautifully designed space with an artistic edge. A dramatic, floor-to-ceiling black, red, and white mural anchors the space, which features a long geometric counter, a tin ceiling, and complementary natural textures. Serving roasts from Michigan-based White Pines and Baobab Fare, the cafe offers excellent coffees, espresso drinks, and tea lattes, and also offers locally made pastries and baked goods. Patrons can enjoy the cafe seating inside or, in warmer months, venture to the canopied patio that turns the Hamtramck alleyway behind the space absolutely oasitic. Aside from a place to confer, work, or read a book over coffee, Oloman doubles as a local hobnobbery for arts and culture patrons: Owner Zlatan Sadikovic has a photography studio in the space, the café is often decorated with rotating exhibits from local artists, and the cafe works with Detroit organization **Cinema Lamont** to offer world cinema screenings in the space next door. *10215 Joseph Campau Ave, Hamtramck, (313) 800-5089.*

Outer Limits Lounge - Rock and roll takes center stage at this colorful, gritty dive on the Hamtramck/Detroit border. Owned by local music royalty John Szymanski (Hentchmen, Paybacks, and SSM) and Kelly Jean Caldwell (Wiccans and Saturday Looks Good to Me), this longtime local venue was reborn in 2017 with a renewed reputation as a go-to live music destination. The curated stage draws mid-size and up-and-coming rock acts from across the region, and sometimes country, most nights each week. The engaging interior looks the part, with an L-shaped 70s bar along one wall and a small stage on the other, and all manner of vintage kitsch gracing the walls, from liberated street signs, sci-fi puzzles, and cowboy-boot Christmas lights, to oversized portraits of Richard Nixon and Jimmy Carter, and Pee Wee Herman dolls. Behind the bar, domestic bottles reign supreme, though a limited two-tap rotation of craft drafts and a typical selection of spirits are available. No food is available aside from bagged chips, though the bar frequently hosts pop-up vendors. Smokers rejoice: One of the city's finest dive patios is out back. *5507 Caniff St., Hamtramck, www.outerlimitslounge.com, (313) 826-0456.*

Painted Lady Lounge - A dive bar's dive bar, this is a charmingly grungy Hamtramck joint. Look for the bubblegum pink and mint green facade and enter through the side door to the right of the main front door (that's for bands only). Inside, you'll find an ornate curved wooden bar and a tin ceiling mixed with a punk rock dive bar aesthetic, including a Pabst Blue Ribbon mirror. The Painted Lady is home to live music every weekend—usually of the punk or rockabilly variety. Take a seat at one of the handful of tables and catch a band, or if you're so inclined, hit the well-loved dance floor. Check the venue's Facebook page for nightly specials and events. *2930 Jacob St., Hamtramck, (313) 874-2991.*

Palma Restaurant - Located in an adaptively reused bright yellow duplex, Palma is a casual destination for Bosnian food. The unassuming interior is simple yet beautiful, featuring illustrations of Bosnia, an array of plants, and the unmistakable smells of the mother country emanating from the small kitchen. The pleasant staff is happy to help rookies navigate the menu, which is mostly in Bosnian. Among the constellation of delicious fare, the cevapi (a grilled kebab dish), pileca snicla (chicken schnitzel), and teleca corba (veal noodle soup), stand out. While the menu is solidly Bosnian, fans of Croatian, German, and Mediterranean cuisine will find a handful of nice options. *3028 Caniff St., Hamtramck, (313) 875-2722.*

Polish Sea League - In the classic tradition of Hamtramck houses turned storefront bars, this modest neighborhood watering hole has fully embraced the low-profile, simple, no-sign approach to exterior decoration. Pull over when you see the gaggle of young barflies sucking down Parliaments out front. With its lattice ceiling, old oaken bar, darts and billiard room, jukebox, bright atmosphere, and surprisingly clean bathrooms, the Polish Sea League is a cut above the traditional Hamtramck dive. While the bar is technically a private club, guests are always welcome. Whether you're looking to cool your heels or make bad decisions, the quiet vibe and jovial crowd will accommodate. The bartenders are knowledgeable enough to put the expansive liquor selection—including Hamtramck-favorite Jezynowka—to use, or help you navigate the strong selection of local, imported, and domestic drafts and bottles. The annual Opening Day and St. Pat-ski Day parties are not to be missed. *2601 Edwin St., Hamtramck, (313) 872-8772.*

★ **Polish Village Cafe** - Originally established as a basement biergarten in 1925, Polish Village has been an integral part of Hamtramck culture for almost 100 years. The interior, which features Old World accents and an elaborate antique wood and stained-glass bar, has retained every ounce of its aesthetic charm and character. But it's got more than looks. The food here is as authentic as it is reasonably priced: Dinners are less than $10, and most come with vegetables, mashed potatoes, sauerkraut, and a soup or salad. Those craving comfort food would be advised to try the pierogi, crepes, dill pickle soup, or potato pancakes; those with more adventurous tastes might venture to try the duck blood soup or fried chicken livers. Can't decide what to get? Try the Polski Talerz, a Polish sampler plate that includes stuffed cabbage, pierogi, kielbasa, and sauerkraut. Of course, be sure to sample the wide selection of Polish beers and liquors. *2990 Yemans St., Hamtramck, www.thepolishvillagecafe.com, (313) 874-5726.*

Polonia - Just down the street from Polish Village Cafe lies another of Hamtramck's classic Polish haunts. Beyond the red awning and vintage signage, Polonia is kitschy and comfortable. Sit at a booth or a table under the murals depicting Polish country life and lavish displays of traditional handicraft, and order up some of the exceptional, hearty Old World fare. Of course, there are classics like golabki (stuffed cabbage), dill pickle soup, and the "polish trio" of killer kielbasa, potato pancakes, and your choice of pierogi. But, if you're feeling more adventurous, try the "city chicken" for some Hamtramck flair. Naturally, a meal is best washed down with a bottle of Okocim, Żywiec, or a shot of bison grass vodka. For herbivores, Polonia is the best bet in town for Polish food. The place is very accommodating with substitutions on the "trio," and, unlike some other spots, boasts veg-friendly dill pickle soup and potato pierogi made with fake bacon. *2934 Yemans St., Hamtramck, www.polonia-restaurant.net, (313) 873-8432.*

Remas - A former coney turned sleek, modernized Yemeni hot spot, Remas opened its doors in 2018, taking on the fierce Hamtramck Yemeni restaurant scene—and this gem was more than up to the task. Though this sit-down destination offers exceptional versions of Mediterranean classics, including shawarma, hummus, and falafel, the true magic of Remas lies in the Yemeni specialities. Guests will find a breadth of enticing traditional recipes, which are as fresh, delicious, and flavorful as they are new to the American pallet. First timers should try a vegetarian *saltah* or lamb *fahsah*, which are savory stews, served boiling-hot in stone pots; *haneeth*, a succulent, well-spiced smoked lamb dish; or *fasoolia*, a smashed kidney bean pancake that is technically a breakfast dish, but delicious any time. Any selection can be rounded out with an order of Yemeni bread, which is somewhere between naan and pita, and a must-try. If you like spice, make sure to ask for a side of *sawhawik*, which will satisfy your craving. Remas is known for uncommonly attentive service, but if you need additional help, just press the in-booth call button! *11444 Joseph Campau Ave., Hamtramck, www.remasrestaurant.com, (313) 707-0920.*

Royal Kabob - Located next door to sister business Al-Haramain International Foods, this Mediterranean gem is a shawarma- and falafel-lover's dream. Despite the plain—albeit well-kept—interior, Royal Kabob serves up Middle Eastern food that stacks up to the best in the region (and in Metro Detroit, that's saying something!). Mainly featuring Lebanese food, it dishes up incredible, heaping versions of all the favorites: tabbouleh, hummus, kibbee, fattoush, almond rice salad, lentil soup, mujadara, fluffy warm pita, and—yes—kebabs. Their meat dishes—from lamb to beef to chicken to quail—are perfectly cooked and seasoned and, of course, there are vegetarian options aplenty. It's cheap. It's fast. And the delectable garlic sauce alone is worth a visit. *3236 Caniff St., Hamtramck, www.hroyalkabob.com, (313) 872-9454.*

Sheeba Restaurant - A Yemeni restaurant that lacks the industrial edge of its surroundings, Sheeba is nearly all kitchen, with a half-dozen well-worn booths and two flat-screen TVs broadcasting the latest Middle Eastern news. The menu can be a bit difficult to decipher, and communicating in English with the servers can be a little tricky. But with a bit of patience and some hand signals, you'll be fine. The food shines as the main attraction, with a fan favorite being the hearth-baked tandoor bread that resembles a larger, chewier, and tastier version of the familiar pita. Order this with rice, house-made hummus, and a meat or bean dish, and you'll be glad you came! The Seltah and Fattah stews are popular, but everything is flavorful, filling, and mouthwateringly delicious. Portions are large and good for sharing. *8752 Joseph Campau St., Hamtramck, (313) 874-0299.*

Small's Bar - "They're playing THERE?!" This Hamtramck rock venue has attained a near-mythic status for booking rock bands that could easily sell out much larger venues. The club is an intimate, dark room with killer sound; the bar is a gothic dive (note: not goth) with stained glass and one of the city's best jukeboxes. Keep an eye on the listings to get a chance to tug at the pants of your favorite punk rock legend, and start training now for Pączki Day in February, when Small's brings back its signature pączki bomb: a polish custard doughnut injected with locally produced Hard Candy vodka. Who says you can't have your cake and drink it, too? *10339 Conant St., Hamtramck, www.smallsbardetroit.com, (313) 873-1117.*

Suzy's Bar - Tucked on a little side street just off Joseph Campau Street is Suzy's Bar, a little bar with a lot of old school rock 'n' roll soul. Buzz to enter at the heavy metal door, and step into a jukebox-spinning, well drink-spouting, Polish party. The walls are decorated with multicolored Christmas lights, 1950s antique trinkets, and Hamtramck T-shirts sporting slogans like: "It's not a party until the kielbasa comes out!" The drinks are cheap, the outdoor smoking patio is cozy, and the bathrooms are cleaner and more cluttered with kitschy antiques than your grandma's sewing room. *2942 Evaline St., Hamtramck, (313) 872-9016.*

Trixie's Bar - With a sculpted, portly, mustachioed mascot holding court over Carpenter Street from the bar's pitched roof, Trixie's is hard to miss. Inside, patrons will find a lively bar that takes its laid-back aesthetic cues from Grandma's rec room—if Grandma was into the local rock scene and liked accenting with string lights. A Detroit-band incubator, the bar turns it up to 11 on weekends, with bands playing the postage-stamp-sized stage most Fridays and Saturdays, and karaoke on the Lord's day. The bar offers a wide range of canned and bottled beer, including classic craft options, and an impressive (for a dive bar) selection of imports, including German Leffe and Polish Okocim and Tyskie. On warmer nights, guests can sprawl out in the massive, fenced-in side yard. For fans of banging the skins, wooden drumsticks are curiously also available for purchase. Check their Facebook page for event listings. *2656 Carpenter Ave., Hamtramck, (313) 316-5376.*

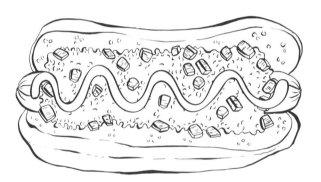

Victor Red Hots - Coney dog fanatics who crave the classic diner atmosphere—good manners, good cooks, oldies music, and all—will love Victor Red Hots. The scent of fresh-cooked vinegar fries wafts through this old-style coney diner, complete with red counter stool seating, antique cola signs on the walls, quaint booths, and friendly servers decked out in white aprons and paper cooks' caps. Victor Red Hots serves all the traditional diner fare, with one other special menu item: beer! Hurry in for breakfast or lunch, because this pleasant blast from the past closes around 4:00 pm. *12 Victor St., Highland Park, (313) 868-0766.*

Whiskey in the Jar - It's small and dark. The coolers are covered with stickers from long-defunct bands. And its mascot is a stuffed "ratalope" (like a jackalope, but a rat with horns). Ask for a PBR, and they'll want to know whether you want a can, tallboy, or draft. If that doesn't sound like your quintessential neighborhood bar, you must not be from around these parts. Whiskey in the Jar's cheap drinks and affable staff have made this one of the top locals bars for drinkers in both Hamtramck and Detroit. Sit on a barstool, and you'll rub elbows with everyone from the neighborhood drunk to political campaign organizers relaxing after a long day of pounding the pavement. It's hard to explain the easy camaraderie of a true, free-flowing neighborhood joint, but this one has it. You rarely leave without making a new friend, hearing a piece of gossip, and maybe drinking a bit more than you intended. Added points: It's possibly the only bar in town that keeps its bottle of Jezy (Hamtramck's ubiquitous Polish blackberry brandy) on ice, should you be looking for a chilled nip of the syrupy booze. *2741 Yemans St., Hamtramck, (313) 873-4154.*

Yemen Cafe - If you've never tried Yemeni cuisine but want to explore some of Detroit's lesser-known culinary delights, stepping into Yemen Cafe is akin to being transported through a portal to a local dive on the outskirts of Sana'a. The interior and seating are hardly glamorous, and one can easily see into the back kitchen. But the smells coming from within are as enticing as they are exotic, and they make up for any aesthetic deficiencies. Salta, the national dish of Yemen, is brown meat stew spiced with a healthy amount of fenugreek and served in a boiling clay pot. Vegetarian alternatives include fasolia—a white bean stew cooked with eggs and spices—or foul, mashed fava beans with garlic, tomatoes, and onions. Dipping the naan-like bread and sharing over the boiling pots is the custom in Yemen, so don't expect any plates or cutlery unless your request them. *8735 Joseph Campau St., Hamtramck, (313) 871-4349.*

ZamZam Restaurant - The Bangladeshi community of Hamtramck has a jewel in ZamZam. With a unique two-for-the-price-of-one setup, the eatery offers guests a down-and-divey carryout-oriented dining room (favored by Bangladeshi locals) adjoined to a full-service dining room that's easier on the eyes and more date-night friendly (favored by everyone else). The menu features a compendium of succulently prepared and vibrantly flavored Bangladeshi cuisine (which is similar to Indian) including a wide range of halal meat, fish, and vegetarian dishes served with a choice of fragrant naan or basmati rice and chutneys. Favorite dishes are the lamb and tandoori chicken biryani, though the kormas are also excellent. *11917 Conant St., Hamtramck, www.zamzamcafe.com, (313) 893-9902.*

SHOPPING & SERVICES

Al-Haramain International Foods - A destination for its abundant, high-quality, fresh, inexpensive, and hard-to-find Middle Eastern and Eastern European groceries, Al-Haramain is a delightful cultural experience. In addition to staples, pantry basics, fresh produce basics, and socially minded essentials like organic foods, cage-free eggs, and hormone-free milk, the popular store is a destination for a panoply of olives, bulk grains and nuts, unusual spices, exotic cheeses, halal meat, uncommon fruits and vegetables like taro root and cactus pears, fresh breads and cookies from beloved **New Yasmeen Bakery** in Dearborn, and a vast selection of European chocolates and candy bars. As an added bonus, Al-Haramain is open until midnight or 1am every day of the week! The company operates its original, more compact location on Caniff Street, as well as its massive new location on Joseph Campau Avenue. *3306 Caniff St., Hamtramck, (313) 870-9748; 9329 Joseph Campau Ave., Hamtramck, (313) 875-8920.*

Better Life Bags - This custom baggage shop is the serendipitous result of Rebecca Smith making a diaper bag during her pregnancy. From there, she started getting requests for more custom bags, leading to an Etsy shop, and eventually to a small brick-and-mortar operation. For Better Life, process is as important as product: The foundation of the store's offerings are its custom bags, which customers help design and receive in about two weeks. Adding a socially driven layer, the goods are manufactured by women who previously faced barriers of opportunity, brought into the company to learn valuable skills and earn a living wage. The baggage is well made and contemporary, with soft burnt sienna leather and eye-catching fabric patterns, and comes in a variety of styles, including shoulder bags, backpacks, purses, handbags, laptop bags, and of course, diaper bags. While the storefront is more workroom than showroom, it is a boutique space where guests can sit on a chaise, take in the rich smell of leather, and browse the Better Life line and some other fair trade goods. Guests are encouraged to make an appointment or order online, as regular retail hours are limited to Saturdays. *9411 Joseph Campau St., Hamtramck, www.betterlifebags.com.*

★**Bon Bon Bon -** Since opening in 2014, Alexandra Clark's inventive chocolatier has become a wildly popular local currency of affection, and a perennial favorite of national and regional food writers. In the charming, brightly-muraled storefront, customers are greeted by bon-vivial staff and sweeping views of the adjoining production kitchen where creative artisans prepare the revered two-bite-sized chocolates. These artisans create glittering combinations of surprisingly bon-gruent flavors through the inspired applications of approachable ingredients, such as birthday cake, earl grey tea, balsamic vinegar, and pulverized potato chips. The seasonal selection of bon-fectionary treats rotates, though often includes creme brulee, black truffle, bour-bon bon-bon, cider and donuts, cocoa-cacao, Boston cooler, and Mexican hot chocolate. If available, don't miss the bite-sized rendition of Detroit's famous bumpy cake—chocolate cake cream and buttercream piped into a dark chocolate shell—or take a nostalgic bite of their s'mores—graham cracker, milk chocolate ganache, and bruleed marshmallow inside of a milk chocolate shell. Be sure to build your own box of chocolates to take home; they'll cut you a custom cardboard box to fit exactly as many chocolates as you want. *11360 Joseph Campau Ave., Hamtramck, www.bonbonbon.com, (313) 236-5581.*

Book Suey - Housed in an elegant historic corner bank building, turned Chinese restaurant, turned community nexus dubbed **Bank Suey**, the cleverly monikered Book Suey is a delightful, compact, cooperatively run independent book store. With a mix of new and used books, the curated but diverse selection boasts especially strong arrays of graphic novels and non-fiction titles, with a dedicated Detroit-focused section. Staffed by volunteers and owner-members, the shop offers uncommonly enthusiastic and passionate service, and always surprises with new finds. With the bookstore currently only open on Wednesdays and Saturdays, look for a roster of community-oriented events in the Bank Suey space throughout the rest of the week, including pop-up restaurants, lectures, musical performances, political debates, art openings, film screenings, alcoholics anonymous meetings—and just about everything in between. *10345 Joseph Campau Ave., Hamtramck. Book Suey: www.booksuey.com, (313) 398-2017; Bank Suey: www.banksuey.com, (313) 402-4402.*

Bozek's Meat and Groceries - Located just a block away from Joseph Campau Street, the highlight of this midsize market is the big walk-in meat cooler featuring cuts from small to massive at affordable prices. Bozek's also features a large selection of Central and Eastern European-imported and prepared foods, including a broad selection of pierogi, smoked meats, fresh produce, imported candies and chocolates, and a great variety of European soft drinks and juices.

Check out the yummy pay-by-the-pound hot-food bar at the back of the market. *3317 Caniff St., Hamtramck, www.bozekmarkets.com, (313) 369-0600.*

Detroit Threads - Since 1997, Mike Smith has kept Hamtramck pulsing with the sounds of Detroit electronic music. Racks of vintage shoes, clothing, and Detroit-themed apparel (designed by Smith and other local designers) line the perimeter. One of the main attractions of the shop, however, is the vast selection of used and new house, electro, techno, ambient, IDM, drum and bass, synth pop, dubstep, soul, rock, and blues music on vinyl and CD. During the Detroit Electronic Music Festival, internationally renowned artists are known to stop in to visit Smith, pick up some records and shirts, and even spin for a few hours. *10238 Joseph Campau St., Hamtramck, www.detroitthreadsstore.com, (313) 872-1777.*

Dunwell Dry Goods - Detroit skaters have a haven at Dunwell. Located in a bright, beautifully contemporary space in Hamtramck, this shop sells house-machined maple skateboards alongside an array of assertively decked-out boards from local vendors (Anti-Hero, Alien Workshop, and others). The shop offers skaters competitively priced boards and a range of skate-friendly clothing, as well as custom screen-printing services. Dunwell's most noticeable feature is a four-foot-tall, 16-foot-long skate ramp available for use at no charge, backdropped by an epically sized Old Glory. Just don't try to visit in the morning—the shop opens at 2pm most days. *10229 Joseph Campau St., Hamtramck, (313) 818-3715.*

Euro Mini Mart - Owner Hane Dreshaj's appealing Albanian market offers an incredible selection in a tiny shop. Euro Mini Mart squeezes in a bakery and deli counter, fresh produce selection, European pastas and packaged goods, and traditional corner-store fare. The main floor is stocked with Eastern and Western European sparkling juices, American sodas, and shelves of classic dry goods, imported candies, and canned sauces. Head toward the back into the walk-in cooler, which is stocked with imported beer, wine, and fresh produce. For fresh bread, burek, and baklava, homemade yogurt and sausages, and a decent selection of deli meats, cut through the main floor and head to the deli counter. Try one of the tasty, freshly made sandwiches. *11415 Joseph Campau St., Hamtramck, (313) 365-1371.*

Holbrook Market - This midsize neighborhood Mediterranean market offers all the grocery store staples, but with a great selection of halal products and prepared specialties. Take home delicious salad garnishes from the olive bar, buy a bulk package of hummus with fresh flatbreads, and be sure to try a container of the homemade garlic sauce. In addition to a wide selection of fresh produce, Holbrook Market sells Sharifa Halal packaged lunch meats and boasts a butcher counter that displays such specialties as whole skinned lamb and goat. The newly remodeled space features tile floors and bright red signage, which help shoppers navigate around tightly packed grocery shelves. *3201 Holbrook St., Hamtramck, (313) 972-8001.*

Lo & Behold! Records & Books - This charming, pleasantly cluttered shop is the perfect place to spend an afternoon sifting through plastic milk crates filled with LPs, tables of chapbooks, quirky secondhand reads, vintage clothing bargains, and affordably priced antique finds. LP fans growing their collections will appreciate the build-your-own crate options and four-for-a-dollar record deals. The comfortable secondhand vibe thrives in this eclectic space, where knowledgeable owner Richie Wohlfeil often hosts in-store events featuring live music or movie screenings. A musician himself, he may occasionally close up shop for tour dates or gigs, so be sure to check hours on the shop's Facebook page. *10022 Joseph Campau St., Hamtramck, www.lo-behold.net, (313) 759-0075.*

Mom and Pop Toy Shop - This resale toy shop, the lifelong dream of owner Quentin Howell, offers affordably priced vintage and pre-loved toys. Howell's inventory comes from his personal collection, which he amassed over four decades and stashed away in two storage units until opening the store. Browsers of all generations will get pangs of nostalgia for treasures from bygone eras throughout the 20th and 21st centuries, including store specialities like action figures, model cars, board games, and dolls of all kinds. Items, while not new, are rarely "used"; most toys fall in the good-to-mint range, and Mom and Pop allows curious shoppers to take most toys and figurines out of their box in a nod to toy stores of yore. Of particular interest to collectors and tykes alike are the store's narrative, thematic wall displays of toys and collectibles, which juxtapose different Batman figures through the years, pit wrestling figurines against each other in a toy wrestling ring, or put Barbie in her dream house with her dream furniture. *9528 Joseph Campau Ave., Hamtramck, (313) 888-9934.*

Never Ending Yard Sale - Beyond-colorful owner Pete Jackson has single-handedly developed a peculiar magnum opus, a nameless curiosity that is equal parts outsider art installation, aberrant antiques rummage shop, and one-man oral history library. The exhibition is housed in Mr. Jackson's ancestral Sears kit home as well as several adjoining lots and a nearby derelict storefront, all clad in found-art decorations. While the indoors is home to tintypes, Civil War powder horns, and Ottoman sidearms, the outdoors is the local go-to for 1970s nativity scenes, gently used paint buckets, and colorful garden sculptures. The yards are punctuated by Mr. Jackson's art installations, including a life-size crucifix made of insulation, and a monument to the Ten Commandments fashioned from wainscoting. Even for those not in the market for depression-era lamps, 48-star American flags, tires, or post-industrial urban detritus, the gregarious host's stories of growing up in Louisiana, service life, and watching Highland Park change are more than worth a visit. The shop keeps irregular hours, though it's generally open late morning to late afternoon, spring through fall. *277 W. Grand St., Highland Park.*

New Martha Washington Bakery - Though it became "new" about 65 years ago, New Martha Washington has been faithfully serving Hamtramck residents since 1925. With immense Old World, small-town appeal, this compact storefront bakery offers customers a full range of classic indulgences and Polish favorites—such as angel wings, kolaczki (a flaky folded pastry with filling), cakes by the slice or whole, and pączki—which bring lines around the block on Fat Tuesday. Though a 1997 tornado destroyed many of the historic elements of this storied establishment, the charming original display cases and a counter scale remain. Visitors shouldn't leave without a peek in the back to see the room-size oven. Domestic shipping is available. *10335 Joseph Campau St., Hamtramck, (313) 872-1988.*

★**New Palace Bakery -** With its delightful old-timey front window display, this inviting bakery is an institution that has held court in downtown Hamtramck for more than a century. Inside the diet danger zone, patrons can choose from delectable Polish favorites, such as kruschiki, airy fruit kolaczki, sugary angel wings, poppy seed or almond coffee cake, marbled and braided breads, and a cast of other traditional bakery favorites. For pączki lovers, New Palace's "secret" is that pączki are available year-round, including traditional fillings, as well as less common options, such as rosehip or the

New Palace's combination of custard, blueberry, and strawberry (patriotically known as the United). All treats are served in a casual counter setting. *9833 Joseph Campau St., Hamtramck, (313) 875-1334.*

★ **Polish Art Center** - Founded in 1958 by Polish immigrants, Hamtramck's Polish Art Center is one of the country's premier emporiums of Polish cultural and traditional goods. Spread over two storefronts, it carries every traditional Polish ware you can think of and quite a few that you probably can't! The welcoming, colorful shop is absolutely jam-packed with Polish treasures including amber and crystal, decorative Boleslawiec Polish Stoneware, Polish food delicacies, Pajaki Paper Chandeliers, Wycinanki Paper Cuts, and a vast array of books, DVDs, and novelties. Family-owned, the proprietors are deeply involved in the community and extremely knowledgeable, welcoming, and helpful. Check the Facebook page to learn about book signings, workshops, and other events. *9539 Joseph Campau St., Hamtramck, www.polartcenter.com, (313) 874-2242.*

Rat Queen Vintage and 3-Ring Traveling Apothecary - The laboratory experiment of owners Joanna Komajda and Monique Given brought to life, Rat Queen Vintage and 3-Ring Traveling Apothecary are two concepts fused into a single store, each featuring distinct collections of urban style and discussion pieces. Komajda's **Rat Queen Vintage** consists of unusual, wryly fashionable women's and men's apparel, jewelry, housewares, and ephemera inspired by the burlesque and the tragic, typified by the casket-cum-display chest (which is potentially available for rent). Her personally curated collection spans more than eight decades, where the taste is oddity with a healthy dose of camp. The **3-Ring Traveling Apothecary** further drives home the bourgeois moribund. Given's wares include antique jewelry, mounted butterfly artwork, assorted taxidermy of real and hypothetical creatures, and the Apothecary's own line of handmade, artisanal lotions, bath salts, and candles. There are some genuine cringe-thrill pieces like a set of old dental instruments, a glass case with a partial jaw, and some ethically superseded medical literature. Candles and apothecary goods can also be made to order, including candles for a customer's container and scent preferences. There's also decorative lepidoptery (and other creative insect display-making) for hire. *10031 Joseph Campau Ave., Hamtramck, (256) 652-4105.*

Record Graveyard - Contrary to what the store's name may suggest, vinyl is alive and well at Record Graveyard. Selling LPs, 45s, and even

78 RPM records, the store carries a wide range of music. The shop's 1920s minimalist facade, vintage aesthetic, and original tin ceiling contribute to the store's old-fashioned atmosphere. It's best known for its outstanding jazz collection, although it also carries blues, gospel, and soul. It also has enough obscure rock and punk to keep the leather-jacket-clad set happy. Owner Jeff Garbus is always buying used records, so the store's inventory changes daily. *2610 Carpenter St., Hamtramck, (313) 870-9647.*

Srodek's Campau Quality Sausage Co. - A "modern" classic—by historic Hamtramck standards, at least—Srodek's has been one of the city's premier specialty food stores since 1981. This family-owned Polish market is best known as a local destination for its fully stocked deli counter and incredible house-smoked meats, from bacon to kielbasa to hunter's sticks to everything in-between. Offering locally baked (often Polish) breads and sweets—including delectable cakes and tortes—Eastern European beers and wines, and a healthy selection of specialty canned and dry goods, Srodek's also sells more than 30 varieties of house-made pierogi—from potato to fruit—that will dissuade you from ever settling for Mrs. T's again. Visitors with more adventurous palates should ask to try the spicy head cheese and jellied pig's feet, two dishes featured in an episode of the Travel Channel's "Bizarre Foods America." *9601 Joseph Campau St., Hamtramck, www.srodek.com, (313) 871-8080.*

Tekla Vintage - You might have heard of the owner of Tekla Vintage—it's Karen Majewski, Mayor of Hamtramck! A passion-rendered, civic-minded business, Majewski opened her shop in part to see another storefront activated. The store occupies a space that, in a past life, was Cody's, a women's hat store during Hamtramck's retail golden age. Some of that history and elegance is reflected in Tekla today. The storefront is large, the displays are generous, and the design is grand, with chic wooden mannequins, drop chandeliers, and a display case of vintage necklaces laid on anonymous velvet necks. The store's selection is enormous, with a diverse selection of women's clothes, some with space-age colors and designs; revival flapperware; rafts of Hawaiian shirts; traditional European folk dresses; an impressive selection of women's hats; and an impressive selection of glamorous jewelry. Tekla is primarily for women, but there's a solid selection of menswear, particularly for shoppers with a taste for ample lapels. *9600 Joseph Campau St., Hamtramck, www.teklavintage.com, (313) 638-2768.*

Victor Bakery - Long known for preparing delicious baked goods from various ethnic traditions, Victor Bakery carries everything from southern-style caramel cakes, to Armenian flatbreads, Italian bread loaves, rolls, sugar cookies, and pastries. With an old-timey sign and hand-painted windows distinguishing it from the silent, formerly industrial neighborhood around it, this "dessert oasis" lies just down the street from Victor Red Hots. Coney dog fans who saved room for a cup of coffee to-go and a delicious fresh-baked cake should take advantage of Victor Bakery's perfectly portioned to-go slices. *36 Victor St., Highland Park, (313) 869-5322.*

Wheelhouse Detroit Hamtramck - A bigger sister store to the popular riverfront location (see separate entry), Wheelhouse opened this spacious location along Joseph Campau Avenue in 2016, simultaneously creating a destination neighborhood bike shop and a new anchor for Hamtramck's developing downtown. The shop is intended to stimulate and encourage interest in urban cycling and it succeeds. The floor-to-ceiling plate glass windows stream light into the shop and make it a welcoming, friendly space that draws browsers in to inspect the inventory of new and used bicycles. New bike brands include locally made Detroit Bikes (see separate entry) and Brooklyn Bicycle Company, while used rides include vintage models ranging from Schwinn to Trek to Cannondale, depending on the local resale market. Wheelhouse also provides full-service repairs, from flat fixes to complete overhauls, and retails gear and equipment, to make sure you're riding in safety and style. Take a moment to admire Wheelhouse's neon logo within a bike wheel in the window, a clever play on Detroit's spoke-based street grid. *9401 Joseph Campau Ave., Hamtramck, www.wheelhousedetroit.com, (313) 871-2811.*

Woodward Throwbacks - Located in the wonderous, sprawling former Al Deeby Dodge dealership building, Woodward Throwbacks is an innovative reclaimed lumber company that offers well-designed wood furniture and objects made with materials salvaged from across the city. The beautifully designed showroom, with an eye-catching mural and a vintage truck, features displays that highlight the line of production goods, as well as the scope of their custom work. The company's house line includes a range of gifts, home goods, and decor, including their popular Michigan-themed beer flights and mounted bottle openers. Custom work has included tabletops made from bowling lanes, enormous commercial cabinetry, dressers, tables, and reclaimed doors. Each piece comes with a custodial history, including the location from which the materials were salvaged, and a catalog of work performed. Woodward Throwbacks also offers restored vintage furniture uncovered during their material collection process. The building itself is something of a marvel: Each floor is connected by an old car ramp resembling an enormous cement slide, and there is also access to the sprawling roof, with views of church spires and city life, where the store hosts occasional cookouts and yoga classes. *11500 Joseph Campau Ave., Hamtramck, www.woodwardthrowbacks.com, (989) 860-4095.*

CULTURAL ATTRACTIONS

333 Midland and the Annex Gallery - Located in a formerly industrial stretch of Highland Park, this artists' studio space and gallery was founded by sculptor Robert Onnes, who purchased and renovated a vacant former stamping plant constructed in the 1930s. Open since 2014, this vibrant complex offers creative working spaces for artists who practice in media ranging from sculpture to painting, as well as a gallery space for showing their work. **The Annex Gallery** is housed in an adjacent building and provides 2,200 square feet of exhibition space spread over two levels. Check their calendar of events to see current and upcoming exhibits and programming. Please note, the studio building is open to the public by invitation only. *333 Midland St., Highland Park, www.333midland.com, (313) 649-3243.*

Hamtramck Historical Museum - Hamtramck's history isn't simply "pierogi," or "pierogi, then shawarma." The city has a rich and winding heritage as a distinct community within Detroit, and the Hamtramck Historical Museum narrates this story. The museum—stewarded by author and lifelong Hamtramckan Greg Kowalski—is a living project that celebrates the 20th and 21st centuries in the city-within-the-city. The museum was founded in 1997, became a storefront in 2013, and in 2018, wowed museumgoers with an enormous, multipanel Hamtramck mural by local artist Dennis Orlowski on the museum walls. Throughout that time, the storefront institution has added to its collection of memorabilia, anachronistic fixtures and appliances, local literature, and previously unpublished rumor, making the museum an incredible depository for basic vital stats (i.e. death records), nostalgia for the boom times of the city, and a de-scandalized chronicle of Hamtramck saloon keepers, before, during, and after Prohibition. However, the museum's finest resource is arguably Kowalski himself.

An enthralling one-man archive, visitors who are interested in the saga of Hamtramck should ask him to be their wise, witty, and knowledgeable guide. Open Saturday and Sunday only. Donations encouraged but not mandatory. *9525 Joseph Campau Ave., Hamtramck, www.hamtramckhistory.org, (313) 893-5027.*

Popps Packing - A former meat-packing plant turned cookie factory, Popps Packing has been transformed into a residence/studio/gallery/performance space by artists and husband-and-wife team Graem Whyte and Faina Lerman. The yard to the north of the former plant serves as a space for events and installations, which have included an eight-foot hole filled with fog and light, painted animals, and a "light henge" erected for an expressionistic pinewood derby. The space hosts a broad range of thoughtful, high-quality, and fun exhibitions, artist talks, concerts, performances, and happenings. While some events are held in the Popps Packing building itself, others are held across Carpenter Street at the affiliated **Popps Emporium**, which is a gallery, artist residency space, and community resource center. Check the website for upcoming events and artist residency opportunities. *12138 St. Aubin St., Hamtramck, www.poppspacking.org, (313) 283-5501.*

Public Pool - Public Pool - Public Pool is a gritty, inviting, and exciting cooperative art space in a Hamtramck storefront that presents the work of a wide range of (mostly) local artists. The single, Spartan room seems endlessly repurposable, hosting installations, performance pieces, concerts, talks, dance parties, and visual art shows, including the Good Tyme Writers Buffet—a regular reading event that includes a potluck, a DJ, and plenty of beverages. The work, by some of Detroit's most original and compelling artists, is consistently impressive, and receptions are well-attended, relaxed, not-to-be-missed affairs. While you're there, pick up a copy of Stupor, founding member Steve Hughes's hilarious, heartbreaking zine of hard-luck stories, each issue illustrated by a different artist. Gallery hours are 1pm-6pm on select Saturdays or by appointment. Check the website for upcoming events. *3309 Caniff St., Hamtramck, www.apublicpool.com, (313) 587-9572.*

Ukrainian American Archives & Museum of Detroit - Founded in 1958 as a separate establishment on Woodward Avenue, the Ukrainian American Museum merged with the personal collection of Hamtramck resident and Ukrainian-American Roman Dacko, who collected artwork, documents, and literature from the Ukrainian community. When Dacko passed away, he donated his home to the community as a museum and library. Today, the main floor features rotating exhibits, including mannequin displays of embroidery-laden traditional clothing and Ukrainian folk art. The second floor houses archives of Ukrainian newspapers, organized by year in charming floral shoeboxes and neatly shelved on wire racks. *9630 Joseph Campau St., Hamtramck, www.ukrainianmuseumdetroit.org, (313) 366-9764.*

ENTERTAINMENT & RECREATION

★ **Detroit City FC -** Get ready for celebratory smoke bombs, brilliant chants, dedicated fans, intense rivalries, a jean-short cannon (catch the shorts and win free refreshments), and riveting soccer. With a name honoring the city's French heritage, **Le Rouge** is Detroit's beloved National Premier Soccer League soccer team. On game days, **Keyworth Stadium**—where games are held—has a friendly, electric atmosphere that brings out the hooligan in all of us. By mid-match, you'll know all the chants, including our favorite, "Allez Allez! Allez Allo! Detroit City, we love you so!" Although all the games are fun to watch, the vuvuzelas are a little louder, and the flags wave a little faster during games against Midwest Division arch rivals FC Buffalo and AFC Cleveland. Tickets are always available at the door. Come hungry—the concessions are top notch. *3201 Roosevelt St., Hamtramck, www.detcityfc.com.*

★ **Fowling Warehouse -** In an enormous old warehouse on the south side of Hamtramck sits the epicenter of a sports mash-up the likes of which can be found almost nowhere else. Walk inside and you'll find throngs of people chucking footballs, dodging bowling pins bouncing wildly toward them, and bellying up to the bar to order from a beer list with more than 100 choices. Fowling, a game that asks your team to knock over your opponents' bowling pins with a football before they wipe out yours, is the main attraction at this hugely popular venue. Patrons can either pay for open bowling and challenge anyone out on the court or, if they call in advance, can reserve their own private lane. The huge industrial space features a fantastically well-stocked bar, a stage for musicians, and a mystery vending machine that spits out random cans of beer. Although there's no food available on-site, you can a have a pizza from elsewhere delivered right to you as you attempt to knock over those last few pesky pins. And, for the record, it rhymes with bowling. *3901 Christopher St., Hamtramck, www.fowlingwarehouse.com, (313) 264-1288.*

Planet Ant Theatre - Without the stark mural and marquee, it would be easy to overlook the otherwise understated converted row house that is home to the Planet Ant Theatre. But this neighborhood staple is one of the best places in the city to see some serious comedic acting talent, while staying light on the wallet. It's most renowned for its $5 Monday night improv show, which is the longest running in Metro Detroit. On weekends, the cozy 40-seat venue runs a seasonal series of full-scale productions that are both intimate and entertaining, but never pretentious. Come an hour early for a chance to share a beer and grill out with the cast members. *2357 Caniff St., Hamtramck, www.planetant.com, (313) 365-4948.*

Sanctuary - A recent arrival to Hamtramck, the opening of this venue marks the culmination of a multi-year series of DIY shows at a former church on the east side (hence the name). The new home, formerly Paycheck's Lounge, is modern, down-to-earth, and personable, but with a subterranean atmosphere in the shotgun-style space. The venue has a polished floor, exposed brick, unfinished hardwood, corrugated stainless steel paneling, and some cute touches, like custom Dick and Jane colored neon, repurposed pew wood, and a Ms. Pac-Man arcade game, for between sets. Performance is close at Sanctuary: The stage is right above the floor which allows for eye-to-eye engagement, creating a raised pit that can radiate energy through a crowd. The venue leans towards metal and punk, but has a zero-borders policy; any acts that are good, are good, and welcome, regardless of genre. The venue is open on event nights only, so visitors should check the schedule and should consider bringing a set of ear plugs—not because Sanctuary is unduly loud, but because unlike some places, the music fills the whole space. *2932 Caniff St., Hamtramck, www.sanctuarydetroit.com, (313) 462-4117.*

SITES

★ **Hamtramck Disneyland -** The magnum opus of a former General Motors line worker, Hamtramck Disneyland is a curious mechanical folk art carnival that explodes out of the backyard of the late Dmytro Szylak, a Ukraine native, who passed away in 2015. Szylak began his masterpiece as a "minor" post-retirement hobby in 1992. While, initially, the project began as a touch of ornamentation atop his garage, the vision and scope grew, and the "hobby" expanded with it: first over and through the artist's 30-foot-wide backyard, then atop the adjoining neighbor's garage, and then two stories into the air. Today, constructed out of brightly colored metal and wood—and hundreds of toys and artifacts that embody kitsch and Americana— the curious and transfixing structure towers over the sea of workers' housing around it. From rocket ships to the Statue of Liberty to plastic horses to wind-activated contraptions to photos of American icons, the endearing spectacle is a splendid sight not to be missed. Fortunately, after Szylak's passing, a group of local artists banded together to purchase and preserve the property to ensure that this beloved work is enjoyed by visitors for years to come. *Located in the alley that runs from Carpenter St. to Commor St., between Sobieski St. and Klinger St., Hamtramck.*

Highland Park Ford Plant - This unassuming 1910 Albert Kahn-designed complex is significant not for its aesthetics or design, but rather for the technology developed within its walls: the assembly line. Ford Motor Company's former Highland Park Plant is a six-story, three-million-square-foot utilitarian campus built of reinforced concrete and brick, with spare architectural details and monitored, flat, and saw-tooth roofs. The quilt-like brick façade and patchwork of roofs hint at the fact that the factory was gradually built over time to accommodate Ford's rapidly evolving contemporary assembly approaches. Between 1910 and 1922, Ford continually demolished, built, expanded, and altered parts of the campus as the company developed new methods for mass production. In 1913, the plant employed 60,000 workers and became the first automobile factory in the world to implement the now ubiquitous assembly line. The plant became an unmitigated success and was able to produce a million automobiles a year. Within 10 years, production time for a Model T fell from 728 minutes to 93 minutes, and the cost decreased from $850 to $260. Ultimately, however, the plant was a victim of its own invention. By the early 1920s, the technology developed at the facility favored an even larger factory, and so, Ford began developing the massive River Rouge Complex. In 1927, the final assembly line was moved to River Rouge, and the Highland Park factory was used for tractor assembly for many years. Now it is used only for storage. Although none of the original 1910 structures stand—they were supplanted by the adjacent strip mall—the remaining 1915 portions of the plant stand as a monument to Henry Ford's crowning achievement. *91 Manchester Ave., Highland Park.*

POINTS OF INTEREST

Davison Freeway - This stretch of road was the first urban depressed freeway in the country, built to keep heavy traffic off of regular commercial streets. *Davison Fwy. and Woodward Ave., Highland Park.*

Detroit Beautification Project Murals:

- **"The Death of Street Art" Mural** - Cartoonish representations of famous street artists carry a casket labeled "Street Art," in this striking piece by Sever. *Joseph Campau St. and Goodson St., Hamtramck.*

- **American Flag Mural** - This amazing mural, by New Zealand artist Askew, reconfigures the American flag as a whirlpool of symbols, bubbling up toward the sky. *8584 Joseph Campau St. Hamtramck.*

- **Jumble Mural** - This swirling jumble of shapes, painted by Reyes, has a companion piece on the side of the Brooklyn Street Local in Corktown. *2238 Holbrook St., Hamtramck.*

- **Owl Mural** - This gorgeous, flowing mystical creature was painted onto the wall above a dentist's office by Triston Eaton. *11451 Joseph Campau St., Hamtramck.*

- **Welcome to Hamtramck Mural** - This smiling figure, painted by Revok and German artist Flying Fortress, welcomes visitors and residents alike to the city within our city. *8327 Joseph Campau St., Hamtramck.*

Detroit City Futbol Club Mural - Artist Kyle Danley, aka Wetiko, painted this large, dynamic mural near Keyworth Stadium in 2018 to honor the Detroit City Football Club. Note that the "ball" being saved by the goalie is modeled after the bronze sphere held by the iconic Spirit of Detroit statue. *8820 Joseph Campau Ave., Hamtramck.*

Elijah Muhammad Home - From 1923 to 1935, the early leader of the Nation of Islam and mentor to Malcolm X, Louis Farrakhan, and Muhammad Ali, lived in this home, where he started his family while he built the movement. *3059 Yemans St., Hamtramck.*

Ford Model T Mural - This folksy mural depicting an early 20th-century Ford factory was painted in 2011, and commemorates the company's first Model T assembly plant, located only a few blocks away. *Southeast corner of Gerald St. and Woodward Ave., Highland Park.*

Hamtown Farms - Although the more common vegetables found growing in gardens around the city can be found here, this massive farm sets itself apart by cultivating more obscure produce, including hazelnuts, rutabagas, and pawpaws. *9100 Lumpkin St., Hamtramck.*

Hamtramck Stadium - One of only five remaining Negro League Stadiums, this site was once home to both the Detroit Stars and the Detroit Wolves. Although it's currently unused, preservationists and community members are working to redevelop the historic site for use as a neighborhood sports facility. *3201 Dan St., Hamtramck.*

Harry Morgan Home - Actor Harry Morgan, of Dragnet and M*A*S*H fame, was born in this modest two-story home. *198 Rhode Island St., Highland Park.*

Kowalski House from Gran Torino - You might want to stay off the lawn of this Highland Park home that was featured in the Clint Eastwood film Gran Torino. *268 Rhode Island St., Highland Park.*

Kowalski Sausage Sign - An iconic symbol of Hamtramck for years, this oversize neon sausage looms over Holbrook and looks especially great at night. *2270 Holbrook St., Hamtramck.*

Ohana Gardens - This farm, founded by Keith and Diane Hoye, grows organic produce, with an emphasis on providing real, unprocessed nourishment to the community. *32 Church St., Highland Park.*

Pope Park - Created in 1982, a life-size stone statue of Pope John Paul II with wide, welcoming arms, stands 15 feet above this pocket park dedicated in his honor. *Joseph Campau St. and Belmont St., Hamtramck.*

Tiny Acres Garden - This garden, which is almost an acre, has been producing organic fruits and vegetables since 2011, and has paired up with local elementary schools to help teach kids about the environment and the foods they eat every day. *2373 Grayling St., Hamtramck.*

Woodward Tribute Sculpture - With sister installations on Woodward in Ferndale and Pontiac, this 30-foot-tall, solar-powered glass and concrete illuminated sculpture tells the story of Henry Ford and his $5 work day. *Woodward Ave. and Gerald St., Highland Park.*

Yemeni Triptych Mural - This 80-foot-wide mural, by Chilean artist Dasic Fernández, celebrates Yemeni immigrants, and employs the artist's' signature vivid and expressive style. *8752 Joseph Campau Ave., Hamtramck.*

CHAPTER 12
SUBURBS

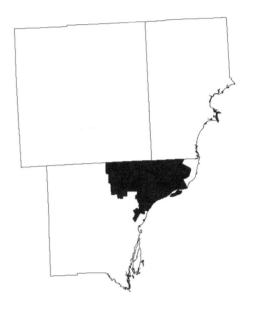

Centered around Detroit, the tri-county Metro Detroit region is the 14th most populous metropolitan area in the country, home to 133 municipalities and more than 3.8 million people spread across nearly 2,000 square miles. The area is relatively dense, as the majority the region's residents live just outside the city.

The suburban region's history and geography are inextricably intertwined. As a general pattern, the city's inner-ring suburbs nearest the city were built first, while more outlying areas farther from the city were developed more recently. With a short drive, visitors can see a century of urban design evolution. While Detroit's innermost suburbs, such as Dearborn and Grosse Pointe Park, were developed along with the city and are rich with historical features, most suburban homes were built during and after the postwar period. Older suburbs often feature the sweeping tree-lined streets and dense blocks of charming brick homes common in the city. In contrast, newer municipalities at the periphery of the tri-county area are defined by winding, auto-centric blocks with spacious lawns and recently constructed vinyl-sided homes in new subdivisions.

The area's older, inner-ring suburbs, especially, are home to well-known cultural enclaves. While suburban Detroit is largely Caucasian, some areas are far more diverse, including Dearborn's Arab-American population, Oak Park's Jewish population, Southfield and Inkster's African-American population, and Canton's Asian population.

Like the city that anchors them, the outlying suburban areas collectively offer a diverse culture, a rich automotive tradition, and an engaging history. Many of these areas, including Dearborn, Grosse Pointe, and Wyandotte, in Wayne County; as well as Pontiac, Ferndale, Royal Oak, and Birmingham in Oakland County; and St. Clair Shores, Warren, Mount Clemens, and Sterling Heights in Macomb County, are home to a host of popular destinations, including bars, restaurants, and cultural attractions that showcase the work, flavors and histories of area residents.

While *Belle Isle to 8 Mile* is intentionally focused on the city of Detroit, there are some institutions and sites in the outlying communities that are so extraordinary or unique as to make them a compelling part of a visit to the city. Know that there are many exceptional dining, drinking, and shopping options in the suburbs that were simply beyond the scope of this guide, and we encourage you to explore them if you are visiting the institutions below or other places in Metro Detroit.

BARS & RESTAURANTS

★ **West Warren Enclave** - Heading west on Warren Avenue, from Detroit into Dearborn, is like magically stepping into another, far-away world. As you drive, you'll notice the enormous Shatila Bakery, then suddenly Arabic signs begin to accompany English ones on everything from supermarkets to restaurants to gas stations. Dearborn is home to a vibrant, culturally rich Middle Eastern diaspora, with one of the largest and most concentrated populations of Arab and Chaldean people outside of the Middle East. The city's diverse community largely includes residents of Lebanese, Syrian, Iraqi, Yemeni, and Palestinian descent. This rich milieu manifests itself as a dynamic and inspiring multi-cultural destination comprised of small businesses. In particular, West Warren Avenue is known for the restaurants and bakeries that line the thoroughfare. Often open well into the evening, these hotspots feature generous Midwest-meets-Middle East portions, wildly delicious food, friendly crowds, and plenty of options to please omnivores and vegetarians, alike. Among the almost limitless options, a few favorites include:

- **Al Ameer** - One of Dearborn's original Middle Eastern restaurants, with beautiful decor that pays homage to the restaurant's Lebanese roots, Al Ameer offers exceptional versions of all the classics, from shawarma to kafta to shish kebab in multiple meat choices. That is, if you have room for entrees after chowing down on a basket of their pillowy homemade pita fresh from the oven, and the city's best mujadara. Al Ameer won the James Beard America's Classics award in 2016, and the quality for which they were recognized is evident in every bite. *12710 W. Warren Ave., Dearborn, www.alameerrestaurant.com, (313) 582-8185.*

- **Al Chabab** - Before the Syrian civil war, Aleppo had garnered a reputation for its food culture, owing to its uniquely rich soils and ability to grow crops in all four seasons. Already an accomplished chef in Syria, Chamo Barakat fled the country in 2006 with his family and opened Al Chabab, bringing his recipes and love of Aleppian cuisine with him. Sample many regional dishes, like muhammara hummus-like dish made of peppers, nuts, olive oil, and spices) or cherry kebabs (lamb in a cherry-pomegranate sauce). *12930 W. Warren Ave., Dearborn, (313) 582-2927.*

- **Cedarland** - This colorful and brightly adorned restaurant is consistently rated at the top for Middle Eastern cuisine, offering halal options for every taste, with friendly staff and portions large enough for tomorrow's lunch, not to mention the unusual and charming setting in a vintage diner—Swiss Alps skiing mural included. The lentil soup (free with every order) receives especially high praise. Drive-through available! *13007 W. Warren Ave., Dearborn, (313) 582-4849.*

- **Hamido** - With a coney island-like exterior, this casual fan-favorite features inexpensive and fresh Lebanese fare in a no-frills, family-friendly environment. You can't go wrong with a Hamido's Special Plate for Two (that could likely feed four!) featuring meat and chicken shawarma, shish kebab, shish tawook, kafta, hummus, rice, and a salad. *13251 W. Warren Ave., Dearborn, (313) 582-0660.*

- **Shatila Bakery** - Step up to what seems like endless glass cases of delicate baklava (in various shapes, sizes, and fillings), knafeh (dough filled with sweet cream or cheese), cookies, and ice cream, and see why Shatila is every kid's—and let's be honest, adult's—dream. Best of all, this bakery and creamery features ice cream flavors not commonly found in western cuisine, like rose water and mango, as well as a full-size indoor palm tree under which you can enjoy your treat. Visit during Ramadan and you'll encounter a festive atmosphere, with families gathering and dining well into the night. Oh, and try the pistachio ice cream. Trust us. *14300 W. Warren Ave., Dearborn, www.shatila.com, (313) 582-1952.*

CULTURAL ATTRACTIONS

Arab American National Museum - The first—and only—museum in the United States dedicated to the Arab-American experience, the Arab American National Museum brings together stories, artifacts, and exhibits to illustrate the rich history and culture of the Arab people. The only affiliate of the Smithsonian Institution in Michigan, the gargantuan museum, which is architecturally stunning—especially on the inside—is contemporary in its presentation, favoring interactive, multimedia, kid-friendly exhibits that focus their attention on a rich tapestry of stories as much as they do artifacts. Coloring these narratives, the permanent collection includes a fascinating array of art, artifacts, documents, personal papers, and photographs to help visitors relate. In addition to regular and special exhibits, the museum contains a vast resource library through which visitors can browse, and it hosts a rich calendar of programming, including film screenings, lectures, festivals, classes, readings, and concerts. Check the website for more information. *13624 Michigan Ave., Dearborn, www.arabamericanmuseum.org, (313) 582-2266.*

Cranbrook Art Museum and Institute of Science - The campus of the Cranbrook Educational Community comprises 319 walkable, verdant acres in Bloomfield Hills and features stately academic and public buildings designed in the Arts and Crafts style by renowned architects Albert Kahn and Eliel Saarinen. Cranbrook—home to a top-10 fine arts graduate program and an esteemed K-12 academy—has a great deal to offer visitors. In addition to a wealth of public art—such as the renowned *Orpheus Fountain* by Swedish sculptor Carl Milles—the campus is home to two major cultural attractions, the Cranbrook Art Museum and the Cranbrook Institute of Science. The Cranbrook Art Museum, designed by Saarinen and opened in 1942, is devoted to exhibitions of contemporary art, architecture, and design for Cranbrook students to engage with and for the community to enjoy. The museum provides an intimate, yet spacious environment for visitors, and the grounds boast sculptures made by Milles, including several fountains throughout the campus. The museum offers regular guided tours of its new wing—including the permanent collection—as well as tours of the Art Deco Saarinen House. Reservations are recommended. The Cranbrook Institute of Science took residence in its current home, also designed by Saarinen, in 1938, and welcomes more than 200,000 visitors each year to its natural history exhibits and programs. The institute features the Acheson Planetarium, as well as an observatory, the Bat Zone (featuring live bats with wingspans of up to six feet), and the Erb Family Science Garden which includes a life study of Michigan plants over different seasons. The institute also offers a variety of family and youth programs. *39221 Woodward Ave., Bloomfield Hills, www.cranbrook.edu, (248) 645-3320.*

★**Detroit Zoo -** Each year, the Detroit Zoo hosts more than 1.5 million visitors to its sprawling, 125-acre campus in Royal Oak, just two miles north of Detroit. One of the great zoos of North America, the zoo is owned by the city but operated by a nonprofit zoological society. Built in 1928, the zoo was the first in the U.S. to use barless exhibits

widely. Featuring 2,000 animals of 230 species, here are some of our favorites of the zoo's award-winning exhibits:

- North America's largest polar bear exhibit, **The Arctic Ring of Life**, is a four-acre facility featuring an opportunity to walk through a 70-foot-long clear underwater tunnel amidst swimming polar bears and seals.

- The dreamlike tropical indoor **Butterfly Garden** features hundreds of Central and South American species, and the adjacent free-flight aviary is housed in a stately sanctuary with Pewabic-tile peacocks at its entrances.

- **Amphibiville** is two acres of wetlands and a pond featuring diverse frogs, toads, and other amphibians. It was called a "Disneyland for toads" by the Wall Street Journal.

- The zoo is also home to a four-acre ape exhibit featuring a naturalistic habitat filled with gorillas and chimpanzees.

- In 2016, the zoo opened its award-winning **Polk Penguin Conservation Center**, where visitors can explore the 33,000-square-foot home to more than 75 of these mesmerizing birds. Be sure to spend some time in the underwater viewing area, where you can watch penguins swim, eat, and play up close.

Other attractions include a variety of diverse outdoor habitats, a carousel with 33 hand-carved, hand-painted wooden figures, a small passenger train for intra-zoo transport (for a few bucks extra, kids can even ride with the engineer), movie theaters, a 75,000-gallon fountain with two sculptures of bronze bears, the expansive exhibit of kangaroos and wallabies, an opportunity to feed giraffes, many picnic areas, and a spate of regular and seasonal special events, for families and adults alike. *8450 W. 10 Mile Rd., Royal Oak, www.detroitzoo.org, (248) 541-5717.*

Other attractions include a variety of diverse outdoor habitats, a carousel with 33 hand-carved, hand-painted wooden figures, a small passenger train for intra-zoo transport (for a few bucks extra, kids can even ride with the engineer), movie theaters, a 75,000-gallon fountain with two sculptures of bronze bears, the expansive exhibit of kangaroos and wallabies, an opportunity to feed giraffes, the Penguinarium, many picnic areas, and a spate of regular and seasonal special events, for families and adults alike. *8450 W. 10 Mile Rd., Royal Oak, www.detroitzoo.org, (248) 541-5717.*

Edsel and Eleanor Ford House - Born from a trip Edsel and Eleanor Ford took with architect Albert Kahn to England, the design of the resulting mansion closely resembles the vernacular architecture of the Cotswold region. Opened in 1929, the Kahn-designed exterior is a masterpiece, including sandstone walls, a slate roof and thick patches of ivy. Kahn's interior was even more elegant and reminiscent of the English countryside, punctuated by a bevy of 14th-century stained-glass window medallions, 16th-century oak-carved linenfold relief paneling, and stone chimneys. The home holds countless treasures of design, furnishings, pieces of Ford family history, and works of art. In addition to the home, visitors will enjoy touring the stunning Jens Jensen-designed grounds on Gaukler Point and the many outbuildings, including the two-third scale Tudor playhouse built for the Ford children. Spanning 87 acres, Jensen's beautifully manicured gardens and meadows use lush flowers, wildlife habitat and fruit to engage all five senses, and make use of his traditional "long view" aesthetic, making them, alone, worth the trip. Visitors can tour the home hourly throughout the week, year-round. *1100 Lake Shore Rd., Grosse Pointe Shores, www.fordhouse.org, (313) 884-4222.*

★ **The Henry Ford -** The largest indoor-outdoor museum complex in the country, The Henry Ford is an astonishing, sprawling, must-see history attraction named for its founder, who sought to reserve sites and buildings of historical significance—illustrating and celebrating America's past for future generations. Originally opened as the Edison Institute, the institution was dedicated by President Herbert Hoover to Ford's longtime friend Thomas Edison on October 21, 1929—the 50th anniversary of Edison's first successful incandescent light bulb—with several hundred luminaries in attendance, including Marie Curie, George Eastman, John D. Rockefeller, Will Rogers, and Orville Wright. What began as Henry Ford's personal collection of historic objects has become a world-class multifaceted institution crammed with fascinating artifacts, recording and celebrating Americana and history. The complex is made up of three main attractions, detailed below. Check the website for their many fantastic events, including the unforgettable Hallowe'en at Greenfield Village featuring seemingly endless paths of carved jack-o-lanterns, and the annual holiday lighting ceremony. *20900 Oakwood Blvd., Dearborn, www.thehenryford.org, (800) 835-5237.*

- **Henry Ford Museum of American Innovation -** From the legendary Rosa Parks bus to the chair where Abraham Lincoln

was seated that fateful night in the theater to the only remaining prototype of Buckminster Fuller's Dymaxion House to Edison's last breath sealed in a tube to George Washington's camp bed to the 1961 Lincoln Continental in which President John F. Kennedy was assassinated to an Oscar Mayer Wienermobile to a gargantuan, 600-ton steam locomotive, the mind-blowing attractions bring American history and innovation alive. The Henry Ford Museum of American Innovation is a national mecca for history lovers—or the place to go to become one. In addition to the amazing exhibits and attractions, the museum features an exceptional IMAX theater with a full program of screenings. Check the website for further information.

- **Greenfield Village** - Step back in time and explore Greenfield Village's 80 acres of the sights and sounds of American history. With almost 100 authentic, historic structures punctuated by Model Ts, 19th-century baseball games, delicious historic dining options, a 19th-century steam engine, an antique carousel, authentic artisans at work (namely blacksmiths, glassblowers, tinsmiths, and potters), a working farm, and hundreds of historical re-enactors partaking in authentic daily tasks like cooking, farming, and sewing, visiting the village is an immersive exploration of the buildings, stories, and people of our country's history. Some of our favorite attractions in the village include the Wright brothers' bicycle shop from Ohio, Harvey Firestone's family farm, the Illinois courthouse where Lincoln practiced law, Henry Ford's prototype garage where he built the Ford Quadricycle, Noah Webster's Connecticut home where he wrote the first American dictionary, Henry Ford's birthplace, Luther Burbank's office, William Holmes McGuffey's birthplace, and a replica of Edison's Menlo Park laboratory complex from New Jersey. In addition to these relics of American innovation, be sure to visit the Hermitage Slave Quarters, two 1850 brick buildings that were formerly the dwellings of African-American families who were enslaved on the 400-acre Hermitage Plantation in Georgia—compelling and poignant reminders of this painful period in our nation's history.

- **Ford Rouge Factory Tour** - After his first plants in Detroit and Highland Park, Henry Ford created the River Rouge Complex, which at one time was the largest industrial complex in the world, producing almost everything necessary to build a Model A

Ford car, from steel to tires to glass. Visit the factory on a self-guided tour and, from an elevated walkway, watch Ford F-150 pickups being made. Additional attractions include multi-sensory 360-degree theatre experiences, historic manufacturing footage, the largest living roof in the world, and a gallery of five historic vehicles made at the factory. Public tours begin at The Henry Ford's main campus with buses departing for this off-site factory tour every 20 minutes, from 9:20am–3pm. Buses return regularly from the visitor center at the factory, with the last bus returning to The Henry Ford at 5pm.

The Holocaust Memorial Center Zekelman Family Campus - This important institution was the first museum in the United States dedicated to the Holocaust, and as such, many of the excellent exhibits were used as models for the United States Holocaust Memorial Museum in Washington, D.C. Recently expanded, the Holocaust Memorial Center is an extremely moving, impressive, and essential experience. The cutting-edge, thoughtful exhibits tell the story, not only of the incredible evil, but of great courage and strength in the face of it. Often, Holocaust survivors are on the premises to give personal, heart-wrenching testimony about their experiences. Notwithstanding the brutal history and images of the period, the presentations are moving and an eloquent testimony to the power of the human spirit. A must-see experience. There is no admission fee, but donations are accepted. *28123 Orchard Lake Rd., Farmington Hills, www.holocaustcenter.org, (248) 553-2400.*

Islamic Center of America - Beautifully housed in modern Islamic architecture within an intricately ornamented, imposing central temple with a 150-foot gilded dome, flanked by two 10-story minarets, the center is an unmistakable embassy for Islam in America. Built at its present location in 2005 to serve Dearborn's vast Muslim population after more than three decades in Highland Park, the center is foremost a Shia mosque—and it is the largest mosque in North America. It is also an institute for promoting cultural and religious awareness, including emphasis on resources for students of Arabic. After the Sept. 11, 2001, attacks, the need for greater dialogue and diplomacy about Islam among Americans has sometimes thrust the center into an unfortunate spotlight as a representative scapegoat for Islamic strife. In 2011, however, a group composed of different religious believers locked arms in solidarity outside the center in rejection of a protest by controversial Florida pastor Terry Jones,

showing their support for tolerance rather than divisiveness. E-mail admin@icofa.com to schedule a tour. *19500 Ford Rd., Dearborn, www.icofa.com, (313) 593-0000.*

Marvin's Marvelous Mechanical Museum - Part arcade, part museum, the late Marvin Yagoda's mechanical repository is a 5,500-square-foot fantasyland packed from floor to ceiling with hundreds of curious and fascinating coin-operated games, animatronic dummies, rides, and other quarter-hungry sights and oddities from throughout the last century. An experience for children and adults alike, the museum is listed in the World Almanac's top 100 most unusual museums in the U.S. Complete with ticket prizes and a concession stand, the collection boasts vintage machines, such as gypsy fortune tellers, "ancient" torture chambers, and mechanical bands, pinball from every decade, and video arcade classics from your childhood. Some of Marvin's collection is extremely rare, some was built specifically for the museum, but everything is playable, so come prepared with a roll of quarters and a couple of hours to spend. *31005 Orchard Lake Rd., Farmington Hills, www.marvin3m.com, (248) 626-5020.*

Selfridge Military Air Museum - Housed in a former hangar, Selfridge Military Air Museum is a museum and air park dedicated to the history and memory of its historic namesake airbase and to the numerous units stationed there over the past century. In addition to a host of informative interpretative displays, the museum is home to 31 antique aircraft and helicopters and an array of military vehicles and missiles. The knowledgeable docents show visitors through the extensive collections of military artifacts and ephemera, scale aircraft models, photographs, cut-away aircraft equipment and engines, an authentic F-16 cockpit, a hands-on air-traffic control system, a hands-on replica link trainer display, and a small gift shop. Don't leave without admiring the World War I airplane. *27333 C St., Selfridge ANG Base, Harrison Twp., (586) 307-5035.*

Yankee Air Museum - Founded in 1981 and based in historic Willow Run Airport, the Yankee Air Museum is an independent nonprofit aviation museum dedicated to celebrating the rich aviation history and tradition of Southeast Michigan. The museum's volunteers and docents have a passion for sharing their unparalleled combat aviation knowledge. In addition to an impressive array of static interpretive displays, the museum's impressive collection of airworthy WWII-era aircraft includes a Douglas C-47, a B-17G Flying Fortress, and a B-25D

Mitchell. Visitors looking for a truly unique hands-on experience in an historical aircraft can book a short flight on the museum's B-17G or B-25D. *47884 D St., Belleville, www.yankeeairmuseum.org, (734) 483-4030.*

ENTERTAINMENT & RECREATION

★ **Ford-Wyoming Drive-In Theater** - America's largest drive-in, and a Detroit treasure, the Ford-Wyoming offers a nightly two-movies-for-the price-of-one deal. Showing largely first-run Hollywood blockbusters interspersed with vintage cartoon concession advertisements between pictures, the theater features an original, Art Deco main screen and four ancillary outdoor theaters. Veteran visitors sometimes bring lawn chairs for a laid-back silver-screen experience and are rumored to occasionally bring their own refreshing beverages. For families, several of the theater areas feature swing sets and other playground equipment in front of the screens for that between-film stretch. Though the theater runs year-round—heaters are complimentary—movies are shown only after dark. *10400 Ford Rd. Dearborn, www.fordwyomingdrivein.com, (313) 846-6910.*

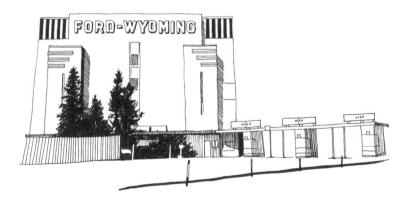

Yates Cider Mill - An essential autumn tradition for Detroiters, an afternoon spent sipping hot spiced cider while soaking in the fall colors at one of our region's many cider mills makes the bittersweet end of summer a bit more palatable. One of our favorites, Yates Cider Mill in Rochester Hills has been operating since 1863 and is situated on 1,200 picturesque park-like acres along the Clinton

River. The bucolic campus is home to a range of activities beyond the namesake cider mill, including an ice cream shop, a fudge shop, a pony ride pavilion, a petting zoo, a half mile scenic river walk, portrait artists, pumpkin paintings, and stalls selling fall delicacies, like apple cider, apple cider doughnuts, and caramel apples. Since the mill uses seasonal apples, the cider changes as the apple harvest evolves with the season—from Paula reds in August to honeycrisps in the late fall. This unparalleled freshness creates some of the region's finest cider—the perfect complement to the delicious apple-cider doughnuts. Aside from the obvious family attractions, the beautiful landscape and river walk make Yates a destination for nature lovers, and the 118-year-old water turbine and cider press make it popular among history buffs, too. Although the mill is open spring through fall, many attractions are open only in September and October. For those looking for a similar experience a little closer to Detroit, try another favorite, the **Franklin Cider Mill** (7450 Franklin Rd., Bloomfield Hills), which is renowned for its cinnamon-spice donuts. *1990 E. Avon Rd., Rochester Hills, www.yatescidermill.com, (248) 651-8300.*

CHAPTER 13
TOP DESTINATIONS
& EVENTS

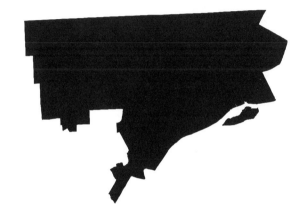

TOP DESTINATIONS

In this section, we've collected some of our favorite destinations in each of the listed categories. While Detroit offers a bounty of attractions beyond these locales, these selections are a great place to start when planning a visit to the city.

ARCHITECTURE

- Boston-Edison, 331.
- Daniel Burnham Architecture, 100.
- Fisher Building, 335.
- Guardian Building, 102.
- Indian Village, 380.
- Lafayette Park, 382.
- Michigan Central Station, 253.
- Penobscot Building, 106.
- Renaissance Center, 107.
- Yamasaki Architecture on the WSU Campus, 191.

ART

- African Bead Museum, 319.
- Detroit Institute of Arts, 169.
- The Heidelberg Project, 366.
- Library Street Collective, 85.
- Murals in the Market, 225, 550.
- Museum of Contemporary Art Detroit, 175.
- N'Namdi Center for Contemporary Art, 173.
- Pewabic Pottery, 360.
- Simone DeSousa Gallery, 176.
- Wasserman Projects, 224.

BEER SPOTS

- 8° Plato, 121.
- Atwater Brewery Tap House, 349.
- Batch Brewing Company, 233.
- Brew Detroit, 234.
- Cøllect, 206.
- Founders Brewing Co., 130.
- HopCat, 134.
- Jolly Pumpkin, 136.
- Motor City Brewing Works, 139.
- Slows Bar B Q, 244.

BREAKFAST SPOTS

- Brooklyn Street Local, 234.
- Detroit Institute of Bagels, 235.
- Dime Store, 46.
- Folk, 236.
- Honest John's, 134.
- Parks & Rec Diner, 61.
- River Bistro, 462.
- Rose's Fine Food, 356.
- Russell Street Deli, 210.
- Sister Pie, 357.

BURGERS & SLIDERS

- The Bronx Bar, 124.
- Carmen's Community Market, 395.
- Cutter's Bar & Grill, 206.
- Green Dot Stables, 237.
- Grey Ghost, 132.
- Lovers Only, 57.
- Marcus Hamburgers Restaurant, 404.
- Mercury Burger & Bar, 240.
- Motz's Hamburgers, 281.
- Roast, 66.

CHEAP EATS

- Bucharest Grill Rivertown, 351.
- The Clique, 351.
- Duly's Place Coney Island, 269.
- Evie's Tamales & Family Restaurant, 271.
- Lafayette Coney Island, 55 / American Coney Island, 32.
- Motz's Burgers, 281.
- Pupusaría y Restaurante Salvedoreño, 284.
- Royal Kabob, 500.
- Taqueria El Rey, 287, 288.
- Telway Hamburgers, 289.

COCKTAIL BARS

- Bad Luck Bar, 36.
- Candy Bar, 39.
- Castalia (In Sfumato), 126, 162.
- The Keep, 53.
- Lost River, 403.
- Kiesling, 315.
- Mutiny Bar, 281.
- The Skip, 69.
- Standby, 69.
- The Sugar House, 244.

COFFEE SHOPS

- ASHE Supply Co. Flagship Cafe, 35.
- Astro Coffee, 232.
- Bikes & Coffee, 123.
- Fourteen East, 131.
- Germack Coffee and Tea Shop, 208.
- Great Lakes Coffee, 132.
- Narrow Way Cafe, 433.
- New Order Coffee, 139.
- Oloman Cafe, 497.
- The Red Hook, 356.

DIVE BARS

- Abick's Bar, 262.
- Bumbo's, 491.
- Donovan's Pub, 268.
- Ghost Light, 494.
- My Dad's Bar, 355.
- Nancy Whiskey, 242.
- The Old Miami, 139.
- Outer Limits Lounge, 497.
- Temple Bar, 147.
- Two Way Inn, 407.

FAMILY ACTIVITIES

- Belle Isle, 368.
- Department of Natural Resources Outdoor Adventure Center, 365.
- Detroit Historical Museum (including the Streets of Old Detroit and the Glancy Trains), 167.
- Detroit Institute of Arts, 169.
- Detroit People Mover, 106.
- Detroit Zoo, 525.
- Dequindre Cut / Detroit RiverWalk (including the Mt. Elliott Park Splash Pad), 374.
- Family Aquatic Center at Chandler Park, 415.
- The Henry Ford, 527.
- Michigan Science Center, 174.

FAMILY-FRIENDLY RESTAURANTS

- Avalon Downtown Cafe and Bakery, 35.
- Batch Brewing Company, 233.
- Buddy's Rendezvous Pizzeria, 394.
- Detroit Institute of Bagels, 235.

- Kuzzo's Chicken & Waffles, 431.
- Selden Standard, 144.
- Seva Detroit, 144.
- Slows Bar B Q, 244.
- Taqueria Mi Pueblo, 288.
- Traffic Jam & Snug, 149.

LOCAL MUSIC

- Baker's Keyboard Lounge, 440.
- Bert's Marketplace, 205.
- Cliff Bell's, 87.
- Deluxx Fluxx, 89.
- El Club, 298.
- John's Carpet House, 415.
- Majestic Theatre, 184 / Magic Stick, 183.
- Marble Bar, 330.
- Museum of Contemporary Art Detroit, 175.
- PJ's Lager House, 243.
- Raven Lounge, 405.
- Third Man Records Cass Corridor, 164.
- Trinosophes, 224.
- The UFO Factory, 246.
- Willis Showbar, 185.

NICE NIGHT OUT

- Gold Cash Gold, 236.
- Grey Ghost, 132.
- Lady of the House, 238.
- Marrow, 354.
- Prime + Proper, 63.
- SavannahBlue, 67.
- Selden Standard, 144.
- SheWolf Pastificio & Bar, 145.
- Takoi, 245.
- Wright & Company, 74.

OUTDOOR DRINKS

- Dequindre Cut Freight Yard, 374.
- El Barzon, 269.
- El Club, 298.
- Motor City Brewing Works, 139.
- Motor City Wine, 241.
- The Old Miami, 139.
- Ottava Via, 242.
- The Pump Room (at Red Dunn Kitchen), 243.
- Selden Standard, 144.
- The Villages Bier & Weingarten, 359.

PIZZA

- Amar Pizza, 489.
- Belle Isle Pizza, 350.
- Buddy's Rendezvous Pizzeria, 394.
- El Club, 298.
- La Noria Bistro, 275.
- Motor City Brewing Works, 139.
- Pie-Sci, 141.
- PizzaPlex, 283.
- Pop + Offworld, 62.
- Supino Pizzeria, 212.

RESTAURANT INSTITUTIONS

- Amore da Roma, 204.
- Baker's Keyboard Lounge, 440.
- Buddy's Rendezvous Pizzeria, 394.
- Caucus Club, 40.
- Cliff Bell's, 87.
- The Dakota Inn Rathskeller, 396.
- Lafayette Coney Island, 55 / American Coney Island, 32.
- London Chop House, 56.
- Mexican Village Restaurant, 280.
- Sindbads, 357.

SOUL FOOD & BBQ

- Chef Greg's Soul "N" the Wall, 429.
- Detroit Vegan Soul East, 353.
- Joe Ann's Bar B-Q, 402.
- Nunn's Barbeque, 404.
- Parks Old Style Bar-B-Q, 317.
- Slows Bar B Q, 244.
- SavannahBlue, 67.
- Southern Smokehouse, 464.
- Uptown BBQ, 434.
- Vicki's Barbecue & Shrimp, 290.

VEGETARIAN & VEGAN OPTIONS

- Chili Mustard and Onions, 127.
- Detroit Vegan Soul East, 353 / Detroit Vegan Soul West, 457.
- Laika Dog (in The UFO Factory), 246.
- Norma G's, 355.
- Nosh Pit, 47.
- Pie-Sci, 141.
- Russell Street Deli, 210.
- Selden Standard, 144.
- Seva Detroit, 144.
- Vegginini's Paradise Cafe, 407.

MONTHLY EVENTS

Critical Mass - A festive monthly ad hoc peloton composed of hundreds of bicyclers, Critical Mass snakes around the city to promote cyclist rights and awareness. Riders meet at the corner of Trumbull Avenue and Warren Avenue on the last Friday of each month starting at 6:30pm.

Detroit SOUP - At these monthly micro-funding dinners, that appear throughout the city, guests enjoy community dialogue and delicious homemade food while hearing pitches from four creative, benevolent, urban-agricultural, or social entrepreneurship projects. For $5, or $10 for the city-wide variation, guests get soup and a vote, and the most popular project receives the admission proceeds. *www.detroitsoup.com.*

Slow Roll - What began as a small neighborhood bike ride is now a full-fledged phenomenon on wheels. Slow Roll is a weekly casual ride held throughout the summer that attracts many thousands of cyclists from all walks of life who share a common passion for bikes, camaraderie, and a good time. Each route gives cyclists a unique view of the city and is accompanied by a police escort. *www.slowroll.bike.*

ANNUAL EVENTS

JANUARY

Meridian Winter Blast - One weekend near the end of January each year, Campus Martius welcomes tens of thousands of visitors to enjoy live outdoor music, ice skating, marshmallow roasting, ice carving, sledding, and pavilions for food and drink in a collective effort to enliven winter. *www.winterblast.com.*

North American International Auto Show - This century-old event, usually hosted each January in Cobo Hall, brings 750,000 visitors to downtown Detroit to inspect hundreds of new car models, custom designs, and prototypes from manufacturers worldwide. A ritzy charity night kicks off the event before it opens to general enthusiasts. *www.naias.com.*

FEBRUARY

Cold Hearted - An annual winter carnival held around Valentine's Day in southwest Detroit's Clark Park, Cold Hearted features outdoor ice skating, food trucks, warm beverages, toasty bonfires, marshmallow roasting, and more.

Detroit Restaurant Week - An annual 10-day dining affair each February, Detroit Restaurant Week features reduced-price, prix-fixe tasting menus at more than a dozen high-end eateries throughout the city's core. The event invites new and familiar diners to explore the city's fine dining options. *www.detroitrestaurantweek.com.*

Hair Wars - A hair stylists' showcase that blends a fashion runway with live performance, Hair Wars features 250–300 outlandish, inspired, and gravity-defying hair designs by local stylists. Though it originated in Detroit in 1986, the spectacle has become a national phenomenon, touring cities including L.A., San Diego, Chicago, Las Vegas, and Miami—but it returns to Detroit every spring. *www.hairwarsustour.com.*

Pączki Day - Every year, Hamtramck rings in the Lenten season with two days of gluttony and good times, centered around music, drinks, and the incredibly tasty pączki—a donut-like filled Polish pastry. Though the best way to celebrate Fat Tuesday is with a booze-filled pączki in downtown Hamtramck, people throughout the region celebrate their real or imagined Polish heritage with a few thousand calories of jam- or custard-filled pączki.

Shiver on the River - Friends of the Detroit River, a nonprofit dedicated to educating the public about the importance of the beloved strait, throw their annual Shiver on the River winter fete on Belle Isle each February. At various locations across the island, look for ice rescue demonstrations, marshmallow roasting, an ecological fair, kid-friendly entertainment, refreshments, and much more. *www.detroitriver.org.*

MARCH

Detroit Greek Independence Day Parade - Each spring, in the heart of Greektown, marchers in authentic Greek costumes, Greek-American boosters, and lovers of Greek culture and history assemble to commemorate the 1821 uprising by Greece to overthrow the

Ottoman occupation—and the impact of Greek culture on the world. The parade runs a half mile eastbound on Monroe on a Sunday at the end of March. *www.greekparades.com.*

Hamtramck Music Festival - With hundreds of local rock bands playing in dozens of intimate dive-bar venues, this Hamtramck festival is dubbed "the largest local music festival of its kind," and is held the first weekend of March. *www.hamtramckmusicfest.com.*

La Marche du Nain Rouge - Based on the French-Detroit legend, the Marche du Nain Rouge is an annual all-day Mardi Gras-style costume parade that attracts thousands to the Cass Corridor to banish the impish red dwarf said to have cursed Detroit since 1701. *www.marchedunainrouge.com.*

St. Patrick's Day Parade - Corktown's annual St. Patrick's Day parade brings tens of thousands of spectators to the neighborhood as Irish-American organizations, bagpipe brigades, horseman, and others parade down Michigan avenue. The parade typically falls before the holiday, and is preceded by the Corktown Race, a three-decade-old 5K that draws more than 8,000 runners. *www.detroitstpatricksparade.com, www.corktownrace.com.*

APRIL

Free Press Film Festival - Each year, the Free Press Film Festival showcases documentaries, many of which are about Detroit, the state of Michigan, or the Great Lakes, at theaters throughout the city and nearby suburbs. Films touch on the people, history, culture, and environment that make the region unique, and are often accompanied by talks with filmmakers, critics, and academics. *www.freepfilmfestival.com.*

Opening Day - More than 100,000 Tigers fans fill downtown each year for this unofficial holiday to celebrate the Tigers' inaugural game with drinks, food, tailgating, and parties. Fans pack bars, fill parks, and swarm the stadium in anticipation of the game, and the raucous post-game parties.

MAY

Cinco de Mayo - Revelers flock to Mexicantown each May to celebrate Mexican-American food, music, and culture. A parade celebrating Mexicans and Mexican-Americans runs along Vernor Highway starting noon on Sunday of the holiday, and restaurants are packed to the gills all weekend with patrons enjoying margaritas and authentic Mexican cuisine, or just people-watching.

Flower Day - Eastern Market's Saturday crowds are no match for Flower Day. Each May, hundreds of thousands of people flock to the historic outdoor market to choose from 15 acres of plants along Russell Street, soaking up the beginning of summer and a dense array of colors and aromas. *www.detroiteasternmarket.com.*

Movement: Detroit's Electronic Music Festival - Every year, on Memorial Day weekend, tens of thousands of electronic music fans from all over the world descend on Hart Plaza for a three-day celebration of the musical genre Detroit defined. The festival offers scores of performers from many subgenres spread across multiple stages and has featured iconic Detroit-area techno artists like Carl Craig, Kevin Saunderson, Derrick May, and Richie Hawtin, as well as acts like Afrika Bambaataa and The Dirtbombs. *www.movement.us.*

Touch-A-Truck - Among the Detroit Riverfront's many family-friendly events, Touch-A-Truck, is an annual opportunity for children to get up close and personal with many of their favorite large vehicles—for free. Kids can get behind the wheel of a bus, semi-truck, tractor, and other vehicles—and meet the people who operate them for a living.

Trip Metal Fest - A twisted and beguiling avant-garde and noise music festival, Trip Metal Fest normally runs the same weekend as Movement, and is hosted at El Club.

JUNE

Allied Media Conference - An annual conference for independent media activists, the Allied Media Conference employs Wayne State University's campus as its hub and offers informative seminars, meetings, lectures, and roundtables on alternative or grassroots media approaches to the thousands of annual attendees. *www.alliedmedia.org/amc.*

Chevrolet Detroit Belle Isle Grand Prix - On Belle Isle, fans of professional series racing gather to watch widely varied performance racing events over the island's 2.3-mile course. The first day of racing is free to visitors, with a range of reasonable ticket packages for different seating options available thereafter. The racing event attracts 100,000 people annually over the weekend-long event. *www.detroitgp.com.*

Corktown Neighborhood Tour - This annual afternoon strolling tour of the distinct homes and gardens in Detroit's historic Corktown neighborhood takes place each June. The tour provides both architectural and design notes as well as relevant historical background. *www.historiccorktown.org.*

The Detroit Windsor International Film Festival - Usually held at the campus of Wayne State University, the Detroit Windsor International Film Festival is a festival of short films emphasizing regional filmmakers in different cinematic styles. The festival includes the Challenge event, where filmmakers have 48 hours to script, shoot, and edit a film. *www.dwiff.org.*

Ford Fireworks - Timed to coincide with both the American and Canadian Independence Day celebrations, the Ford Fireworks, also known as the **International Freedom Festival**, are a five-decade tradition that boasts more than 10,000 pyrotechnic effects. The spectacular display draws more than a million people downtown to watch. Hart Plaza, Belle Isle, and the RiverWalk are the hottest spots for viewing the action, with a small flotilla of personal boats taking in the view from offshore. *www.theparade.org.*

Indian Village Home & Garden Tour - The historic Indian Village neighborhood hosts a highly anticipated annual summer walking tour of its beautiful and noteworthy mansions and gardens. Participants spend an afternoon viewing different architectural styles and interesting design features, and have the option of lunching at a neighborhood church. *www.historicindianvillage.org.*

Motor City Pride - A weekend-long festival and parade in Detroit's Hart Plaza, Motor City Pride celebrates members of the Michigan LGBTQ community with exhibits, live entertainment, community affirmations, and food and drink. The event is more than a quarter century old and draws tens of thousands of attendees. *www.motorcitypride.org.*

Palmer Park Art Fair - Featuring a juried art contest, the Palmer Park Art Fair is set on the beautiful grounds of Palmer Park and showcases local artists showing off their best painting, sculpture, photography, and more. Watch live art demonstrations, grab some grub from the food trucks, and enjoy the view. *www.palmerparkartfair.com.*

River Days - A family-friendly weekend festival designed to show off Detroit's riverfront, River Days boasts carnival rides, live music (local bands with classic rock headliners), sand sculptures, outdoor activities, tall ships, and programming that celebrates the city's cultural and historical legacies. A nominal admission fee applies. *www.riverdays.com.*

Shimmer on the River - Today, the Detroit RiverWalk is one of the city's greatest assets—and much of that is thanks to the Detroit Riverfront Conservancy, which hosts its annual fundraiser Shimmer on the River each June. Serving also as the official kickoff to the River Days festival, this event offers donors a delicious strolling dinner, open bar, and unlimited access to carnival rides. *www.detroitriverfront.org.*

Techstars Startup Week Detroit - A free five-day event, Startup Week features seminars, classes, pitch competitions, and other components geared towards encouraging entrepreneurship in Detroit. *www.detroitstartupweek.com*

JULY

Arab and Chaldean Festival - Billed as the largest Arab and Chaldean festival in North America, this free weekend-long event draws thousands every year to Hart Plaza to celebrate Middle Eastern culture, food, and people. This unique event is open to anyone interested in learning more about the history, music, art, and fashion of Arab and Chaldean people, or simply munching on mouth-watering regional cuisine. *www.arabandchaldeanfestival.com.*

Concert of Colors - Detroit's free summer world music concert series, the Concert of Colors grew rapidly from a single outdoor show at Chene Park to a nearly week-long celebration attracting more than 80,000 people. Well-known performers are drawn from Africa, Asia, the Middle East, and the Americas. *www.concertofcolors.com.*

Crash - These aren't your high school marching bands. Every year, nearly a dozen street bands from across the country convene on

Detroit for a weekend to "crash" bars and other locations with their colorful, fun, and energetic music and costumes. Be ready to dance your butt off. *www.crashdetroit.org.*

Detroit Art Week - There's no better time than a beautiful July day to explore Detroit's many artistic offerings, from galleries, to museums, to studios—not to mention afterparties. Over three days, Detroit Art Week invites visitors to attend an array of art-related openings, talks, and performances taking place throughout the city. *www.detroitartweek.org.*

The Detroit Kite Festival - Celebrating the art of kites, this one-day outdoor festival is free and features kite making and flying, professional demonstrations, live music, vendors, and food trucks. You've never seen this many kites in the air before. *www.detroitkitefestival.org.*

Hotter Than July - Since 1996, Palmer Park has hosted the Hotter Than July Festival, a celebration of black LGBT people and culture. This welcoming festival draws thousands of participants each year to its events, which include live entertainment and food and drink. *www.lgbtdetroit.org.*

Mo Pop Festival - Like a cooler Bonnaroo, this popular festival features indie, hip hop, rock, and more, highlighting established artists and up-and-comers alike. Music-lovers can purchase single-day tickets or whole-weekend passes to see acts like Solange, Foster the People, St. Vincent, and Bon Iver, and others. *www.mopopfestival.com.*

AUGUST

African World Festival - The African World Festival is a free public street fair offering traditional music, dance performances, a parade of nations, more than 100 different artists, crafts merchants, and vendors of authentic African cuisine. An estimated 300,000 people attend the annual weekend festival, which is sponsored by and held near The Charles H. Wright Museum of African American History. *www.thewright.org.*

Annual Tour of Detroit Gardens and Farms - For more than two decades, this yearly tour has offered an up-close-and-personal look at some of the farms—and farmers—leading the way in Detroit's thriving gardening and farming scene. The tour, sponsored by Keep Growing Detroit and the Detroit Office of Sustainability,

allows you to meet the people who are making their neighborhoods healthier, greener, and more connected. You can opt for either a bike or bus tour; both end with live music and locally grown eats. *www.detroitagriculture.net.*

APBA Gold Cup Hydroplane Races - These annual races on the Detroit river feature performance racing boats topping out at speeds close to 200 mph. The cup has been awarded since 1904 and draws tens of thousands of spectators to watch the adrenalized speedboats fly around the course from on-shore seating. *www.detroitboatraces.com.*

Belle Isle Art Fair - Highlighting more than 100 artists and makers, this event is located near Scott Fountain on Belle Isle and also features live music and food trucks. *www.belleisleartfair.com.*

Copa Detroit - The Detroit City Futbol League—a municipal soccer league composed of dozens of amateur, co-ed neighborhood-based teams—crowns its champion through this hardscrabble day-long bracketed tournament held at Historic Fort Wayne. *www.detcityfc.com/dcfl.*

Detroit Caribbean Cultural Festival - This annual summer festival celebrating Caribbean culture, cuisine, music, and artwork is three-day family friendly event held in New Center Park each August. Admission is free and open to all. *www.myccco.org.*

Fash Bash - An annual fundraiser fashion show for the DIA, Fash Bash celebrates Detroit art and fashion, including a cocktail reception, runway show, and an afterglow party to wind down the evening. Held at the DIA, Fash Bash attracts a "who's who" crowd and invites guests to show off their own fashion sensibilities. *www.dia.org.*

Jazz on the Ave - A Summer tradition on the Avenue of Fashion, Jazz on the Ave takes place the first Saturday of August. The festival features three stages of music, contests, kid-friendly, activities, and more.

Noise Camp - Since 1994, experimental, noise, and other music acts have performed at this kitschy, nomadic grown-up summer camp party—crafts tent, staff nurses, and bonfire included. *www.timestereo.com.*

Old Redford Sidewalk Festival - In the Old Redford neighborhood, you'll find this vibrant performing and visual arts festival, where the action takes place on sidewalks, alleys, parking lots, and in the roofless warehouses of nearby Artist Village. The all-ages Sidewalk Festival features local food vendors, music, and live painting. *www.sidewalkdetroit.com.*

Ribs R&B Jazz Festival - A three-day outdoor live soul, R & B, and contemporary jazz showcase, this festival attracts tens of thousands of fans and is held in Hart Plaza. In addition to classic tunes, the festival features a (delicious) rib cook-off competition that draws barbecue talent from around country. *www.ribsrnbjazzfest.com.*

Sweetest Heart of Mary Pierogi Festival - A weekend-long pierogi festival to celebrate Polish cultural heritage takes place at the historic Sweetest Heart of Mary Church north of Eastern Market. In addition to Polish dinners for sale, there are Polka masses, live music, traditional Polish dance performances, and activities for children. *www.sweetestheart.org.*

SEPTEMBER

Dally in the Alley - Since its christening more than three decades ago, the Dally has been a growing all-day music and art festival in the Cass Corridor. Local bands, independent craftspeople, and food and drink vendors attract thousands of attendees annually on the first Saturday after Labor Day. *www.dallyinthealley.com.*

Detroit International Jazz Festival - This annual Labor Day weekend festival in downtown Detroit is one of the most visible free jazz concerts in America, having hosted iconic jazz performers like Sonny Rollins, Dave Brubeck, Pat Metheny, and Wynton Marsalis, as well as local jazz legends like Curtis Fuller and Marcus Belgrave. Hundreds of thousands of concertgoers trek to Detroit over the course of several days for a diverse array of jazz. Food and drinks available. *www.detroitjazzfest.com.*

Detroit Month of Design - This annual festival hosted by Design Core Detroit celebrates the city's designation as a UNESCO City of Design by gathering artists and designers (and those interested in both), from the emerging to the well-established, to share their latest work and ideas. Events take place across the city, and feature a diverse array of artists representing the fields of architecture, visual design, urban design, web design, and many more. *www.designcore.org.*

Eastern Market After Dark - As part of the Detroit Month of Design every September, Eastern Market comes alive at night with open

houses at dozens of galleries, and activities, demonstrations, food, and parties filling the historic sheds.

Hamtramck Labor Day Festival - Hamtramck responded to the closing of Dodge Main in 1980 by throwing a festival around which the city could rally. The three-day festival was so successful that it endured and expanded in the decades since, growing to include live music, street canoe races, kielbasa eating contests, a carnival, an art fair, and plenty of food and drink. *www.hamtownfest.com.*

Light up Livernois - In conjunction with the Detroit Month of Design, Light Up Livernois is an epic open-house for businesses along the Livernois Avenue corridor. The event features musical performances, design installations, a fashion show, and other special activities.

Murals in the Market - A two-week international mural festival celebrating street art, Murals in the Market features live painting, panel discussions, artist dinners, meet and greet opportunities, site-specific installations, block parties, and nighttime events as part of Eastern Market After Dark. Watch as artists create Eastern Market's newest artworks. *www.muralsinthemarket.com.*

North Rosedale Park Home and Garden Tour - Each fall, the Rosedale Park neighborhood hosts an annual day-long tour for visitors of the architecturally diverse homes and gardens in its community. Attendees have the option of purchasing a buffet lunch with an advance ticket. *www.northrosedalehometour.org.*

Renegade Detroit - The Detroit branch of the massively popular DIY craft fair, Renegade Detroit features hip artists and makers, DJ sets, workshops, food trucks, and booze. *www.renegadecraft.com/city/detroit*

TEDxDetroit - An independently organized offshoot of the national TED (technology, entertainment, design) Conference, TEDxDetroit showcases live speakers and talks, with group discussions, for a dynamic and engaging experience. *www.tedxdetroit.com*

Tour De Troit - A gargantuan one-day organized ride for bicyclists that snakes through the city, Tour De Troit draws thousands of riders of all ages for either a 25- or 62-mile route at a modest pace on a closed course enforced by police escorts. The after party in Roosevelt Park features a festival atmosphere and ample food and drink. *www.tour-de-troit.org.*

OCTOBER

Detroit Fall Beer Festival - Autumn in Detroit is rung in each year in Eastern Market by thousands of beer lovers who sample from hundreds of available brews made by Michigan craft breweries. Drinks—and live music—are included with admission, but purchase your tickets in advance as the event sells out early. *www.mbgmash.org.*

Detroit Marathon - Each fall, tens of thousands of runners lace up for the Detroit marathon, which features a route that crosses the Ambassador Bridge and the tunnel to Canada, making it both an international event and the only marathon with an underwater mile. Team marathons, half marathons, and 5K races are also offered. *www.freepmarathon.com.*

Dlectricity - Inaugurated in 2012, this two-night spectacle captivates Midtown with dozens of free public light art exhibits that run the gamut from entertaining to thought provoking, including projected films that interact with their architectural backdrops, kinetic animation, and curious light displays. Event runs semi-annually. *www.dlectricity.com.*

Open Streets Detroit - A sprawling day of fun, Open Streets closes large portions of Michigan Avenue and West Vernor Highway to vehicular traffic. In the place of cars, expect to see thousands of people walking, running, bicycling, rollerblading, skateboarding, and playing in the streets. Along the route, look for programming including art, games, demonstrations, music, theater, oddities, and more. *www.openstreetsdet.org.*

Theatre Bizarre and Associated Events - Detroit's carnival of darkness, running from dusk 'til dawn two weekends every October, Theatre Bizarre boasts hundreds of creatively macabre performers including musicians, burlesque dancers, ghouls, sideshow acts, and performance artists throughout seven floors of the Masonic Temple. Advanced tickets and costumes are required to attend this unparalleled, interactive spectacle. *www.theatrebizarre.com.*

DETROIT
EVENTS

NOVEMBER

America's Thanksgiving Day Parade - Bringing cheer and
Thanksgiving revelry to Detroit since 1924, America's Thanksgiving
Day Parade attracts more than 1,000,000 spectators who line the
route down Woodward Avenue to see hundreds of floats, balloons,
marching bands, and other favorites. The 10,000 seats available in
the grandstand make for in-demand tickets each year.
www.theparade.org.

Dia de Los Muertos - A multi-day celebration in honor of Day of
the Dead on All Saints' Day, Dia de Los Muertos festivities, which are
centralized in Southwest Detroit, include a Run of the Dead race,
packed bars, and incredible street food.

Tree Lighting - Nothing says "the holidays" quite like a massive
Christmas tree—or ice skating. Luckily, there are both at Detroit's
annual tree-lighting ceremony, when the city officially illuminates
a 60-foot Norwegian spruce in the middle of Campus Martius Park.
More than 40,000 people attend this free event each year, which also
marks the opening of the park's popular ice skating rink.

Turkey Trot - As a token of healthfulness to offset some of
Thanksgiving's indulgence, the Turkey Trot ushers in the holiday
season with a set of short (timed) 10K, 5K, and one-mile fun runs
in the morning before the parade. Participants—numbering in the
tens of thousands—are known to wear holiday-themed costumes,
and cheering crowds at "cheer stations" along the downtown routes
provide encouragement for runners. *www.theparade.org.*

DECEMBER

Corktown Aglow - Starting at noon and going into the evening,
businesses and organizations throughout the Corktown
neighborhood open their doors and offer plenty of holiday cheer
and family friendly activities such as a tree-lighting, marshmallow
roasting, and a visit with Santa. Stop by to shop, dine, or get in the
holiday spirit.

Detroit Urban Craft Fair - Held annually at the labyrinthine Masonic
Temple, the DUCF is a three-day DIY craft fair featuring 100+ crafters
and artists that represent some of the region's best maker talent.
Fair entrance is $1. *www.detroiturbancraftfair.com.*

Motor City NYE Drop - Sometimes referred to as the "D Drop," Motor City NYE Drop is the city's annual New Year's Eve celebration. Located in Beacon Park, the event features music, refreshments, entertainment, and—of course—a theatrical D-drop countdown. *www.motorcitynye.com.*

Noel Night - This celebration of Detroit's cultural center draws tens of thousands of visitors each year to venerable institutions such as the DIA, the Scarab Club, the Detroit Historical Museum, and the Main Library, as well as dozens of smaller venues, each of which hosts appropriately themed events. Look for live music, readings, food and drink, Santa sightings, and horse-drawn carriage rides throughout the neighborhood. *www.noelnight.org.*

Santarchy - Santarchy is a national movement of December pub crawls for citizens costumed in Santa garb. Detroit's Santarchy busses more than a thousand appropriately cheered revelers to bars in Detroit from pick-up points throughout the Metro area. *www.detroitsantarchy.net.*

INDEX

INDEX

INDEX

INDEX

INDEX

INDEX

INDEX

INDEX

INDEX